SB

Mazda 323 & Protegé Automotive Repair Manual

by Louis LeDoux
and John H Haynes
Member of the Guild of Motoring Writers

Models covered:

Mazda 323 and Protegé models
1990 through 1997

Does not include information on 4WD models

(11A1 - 61015)

ABCDE
FGHIJ
KLMNO
PQR

Haynes

AUTOMOTIVE PARTS & ACCESSORIES ASSOCIATION MEMBER

Haynes Publishing Group
Sparkford Nr Yeovil
Somerset BA22 7JJ England

Haynes North America, Inc
861 Lawrence Drive
Newbury Park
California 91320 USA

Acknowledgements

We are grateful for the help and cooperation of the Mazda Motor Corporation for their assistance with technical information, certain illustrations and vehicle photos. The technical writer who contributed to this project is Jay Storer.

A book in the Haynes Automotive Repair Manual Series

Printed in the U.S.A.

ISBN 1 56392 251 7

Library of Congress Catalog Card Number 97-71411

97-320

Contents

Haynes mechanic, author and photographer with 1992 Mazda Protegé

About this manual

Its purpose

The purpose of this manual is to help you get the best value from your vehicle. It can do so in several ways. It can help you decide what work must be done, even if you choose to have it done by a dealer service department or a repair shop; it provides information and procedures for routine maintenance and servicing; and it offers diagnostic and repair procedures to follow when trouble occurs.

We hope you use the manual to tackle the work yourself. For many simpler jobs, doing it yourself may be quicker than arranging an appointment to get the vehicle into a shop and making the trips to leave it and pick it up. More importantly, a lot of money can be saved by avoiding the expense the shop must pass on to you to cover its labor and overhead costs. An added benefit is the sense of satisfaction and accomplishment that you feel after doing the job yourself.

Using the manual

The manual is divided into Chapters. Each Chapter is divided into numbered Sections, which are headed in bold type between horizontal lines. Each Section consists of consecutively numbered paragraphs.

At the beginning of each numbered Section you will be referred to any illustrations which apply to the procedures in that Section. The reference numbers used in illustration captions pinpoint the pertinent Section and the Step within that Section. That is, illustration 3.2 means the illustration refers to Section 3 and Step (or paragraph) 2 within that Section.

Procedures, once described in the text, are not normally repeated. When it's necessary to refer to another Chapter, the reference will be given as Chapter and Section number. Cross references given without use of the word "Chapter" apply to Sections and/or paragraphs in the same Chapter. For example, "see Section 8" means in the same Chapter.

References to the left or right side of the vehicle assume you are sitting in the driver's seat, facing forward.

Even though we have prepared this manual with extreme care, neither the publisher nor the author can accept responsibility for any errors in, or omissions from, the information given.

NOTE

A **Note** provides information necessary to properly complete a procedure or information which will make the procedure easier to understand.

CAUTION

A **Caution** provides a special procedure or special steps which must be taken while completing the procedure where the Caution is found. Not heeding a Caution can result in damage to the assembly being worked on.

WARNING

A **Warning** provides a special procedure or special steps which must be taken while completing the procedure where the Warning is found. Not heeding a Warning can result in personal injury.

Introduction to the Mazda 323 and Protegé

Mazda 323 and Protegé models are available in hatchback, two- and four-door sedan body styles.

The transversely mounted inline four-cylinder engines used in these models are equipped with electronic fuel injection.

The engine drives the front wheels through either a five-speed manual or a four-speed automatic transaxle via independent driveaxles.

Independent suspension, featuring coil spring/strut damper units, is used on the front wheels, while independent suspension using shock absorbers and coil springs or coil spring/strut dampers is used at the rear. The rack and pinion steering unit is mounted behind the engine with power-assist available as an option.

The brakes are disc at the front and drums or disc at the rear, with power assist standard. An Anti-lock Brake System (ABS) became available on later models.

Vehicle identification numbers

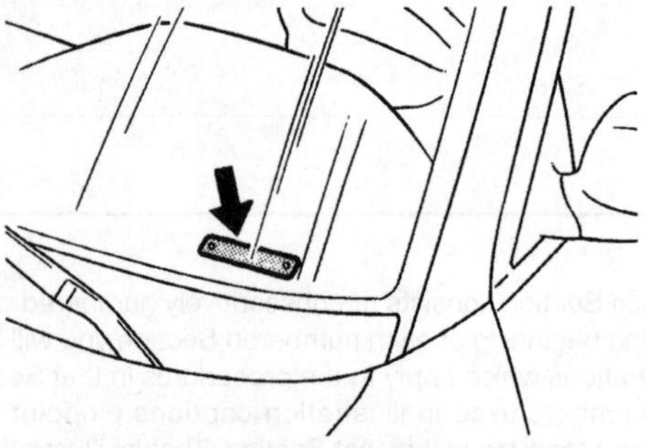

The Vehicle Identification Number (VIN) is stamped into a metal plate fastened to the dashboard on the driver's side - it is visible through the windshield

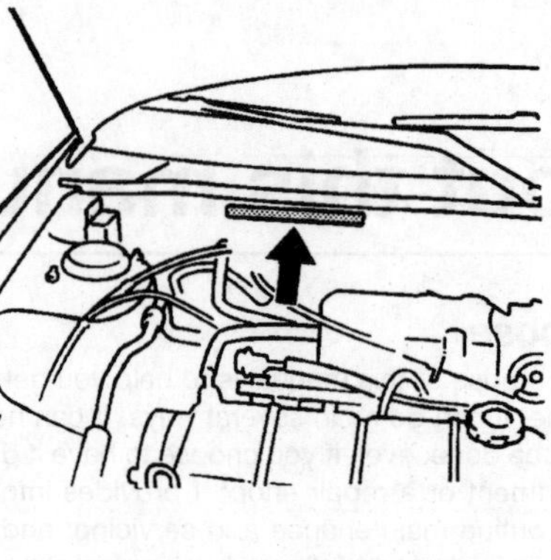

The chassis number is stamped into the firewall

Modifications are a continuing and unpublicized process in vehicle manufacturing. Since spare parts manuals and lists are compiled on a numerical basis, the individual vehicle numbers are essential to correctly identify the component required.

Vehicle Identification Number (VIN)

This very important identification number is located on a plate attached to the dashboard inside the windshield on the driver's side of the vehicle **(see illustration)**. The VIN also appears on the Vehicle Certificate of Title and Registration. It contains information such as where and when the vehicle was manufactured, the model year and the body style.

Chassis number

The chassis number is a repetition of the VIN number stamped on the firewall in the engine compartment **(see illustration)**.

Vehicle Safety Certification label

The Vehicle Safety Certification label is attached to the driver's side door end or post **(see illustration)**. The label contains the name of the manufacturer, the month and year of production, the Gross Vehicle Weight Rating (GVWR), the Gross Axle Weight Rating (GAWR) and the certification statement.

Engine identification number

The engine identification number can be found stamped on a pad on either the right rear or left rear of the cylinder block **(see illustration)**.

Transaxle identification number

The transaxle identification information can be found on a bar code label located on the transaxle bellhousing.

Vehicle Emissions Control Information (VECI) label

The emissions control information label is found under the hood, normally on the bottom side of the hood. This label contains information on the emissions control equipment installed on the vehicle, as well as tune-up specifications (see Chapter 6).

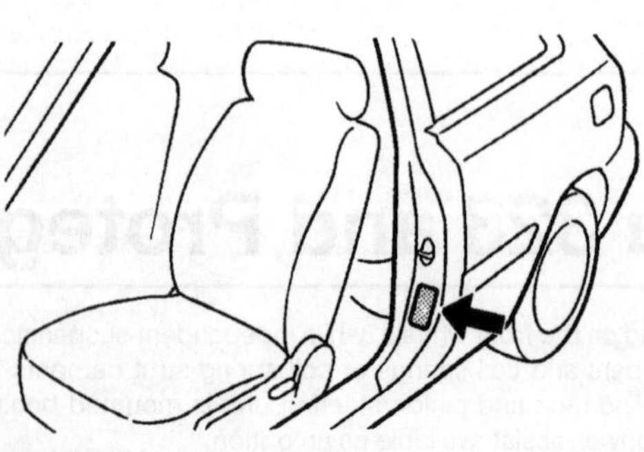

The Vehicle Safety Certification label is affixed to the drivers door pillar

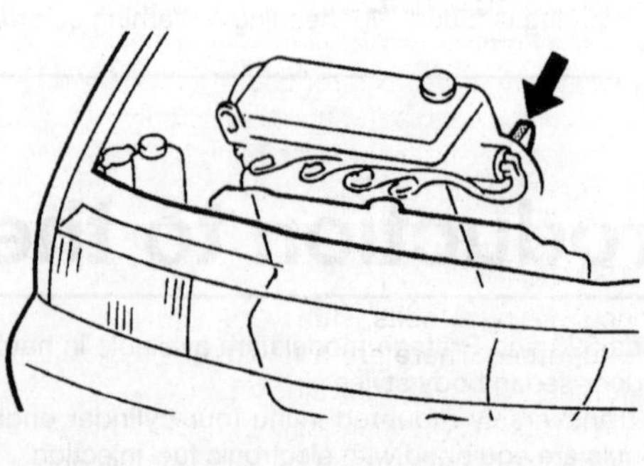

The engine identification number is stamped on a pad at the rear of the engine block

Buying parts

Replacement parts are available from many sources, which generally fall into one of two categories - authorized dealer parts departments and independent retail auto parts stores. Our advice concerning these parts is as follows:

Retail auto parts stores: Good auto parts stores will stock frequently needed components which wear out relatively fast, such as clutch components, exhaust systems, brake parts, tune-up parts, etc. These stores often supply new or reconditioned parts on an exchange basis, which can save a considerable amount of money. Discount auto parts stores are often very good places to buy materials and parts needed for general vehicle maintenance such as oil, grease, filters, spark plugs, belts, touch-up paint, bulbs, etc. They also usually sell tools and general accessories, have convenient hours, charge lower prices and can often be found not far from home.

Authorized dealer parts department: This is the best source for parts which are unique to the vehicle and not generally available elsewhere (such as major engine parts, transmission parts, trim pieces, etc.).

Warranty information: If the vehicle is still covered under warranty, be sure that any replacement parts purchased - regardless of the source - do not invalidate the warranty!

To be sure of obtaining the correct parts, have engine and chassis numbers available and, if possible, take the old parts along for positive identification.

Maintenance techniques, tools and working facilities

Maintenance techniques

There are a number of techniques involved in maintenance and repair that will be referred to throughout this manual. Application of these techniques will enable the home mechanic to be more efficient, better organized and capable of performing the various tasks properly, which will ensure that the repair job is thorough and complete.

Fasteners

Fasteners are nuts, bolts, studs and screws used to hold two or more parts together. There are a few things to keep in mind when working with fasteners. Almost all of them use a locking device of some type, either a lockwasher, locknut, locking tab or thread adhesive. All threaded fasteners should be clean and straight, with undamaged threads and undamaged corners on the hex head where the wrench fits. Develop the habit of replacing all damaged nuts and bolts with new ones. Special locknuts with nylon or fiber inserts can only be used once. If they are removed, they lose their locking ability and must be replaced with new ones.

Rusted nuts and bolts should be treated with a penetrating fluid to ease removal and prevent breakage. Some mechanics use turpentine in a spout-type oil can, which works quite well. After applying the rust penetrant, let it work for a few minutes before trying to loosen the nut or bolt. Badly rusted fasteners may have to be chiseled or sawed off or removed with a special nut breaker, available at tool stores.

If a bolt or stud breaks off in an assembly, it can be drilled and removed with a special tool commonly available for this purpose. Most automotive machine shops can perform this task, as well as other repair procedures, such as the repair of threaded holes that have been stripped out.

Flat washers and lockwashers, when removed from an assembly, should always be replaced exactly as removed. Replace any damaged washers with new ones. Never use a lockwasher on any soft metal surface (such as aluminum), thin sheet metal or plastic.

Fastener sizes

For a number of reasons, automobile manufacturers are making wider and wider use of metric fasteners. Therefore, it is important to be able to tell the difference between standard (sometimes called U.S. or SAE) and metric hardware, since they cannot be interchanged.

All bolts, whether standard or metric, are sized according to diameter, thread pitch and length. For example, a standard 1/2 - 13 x 1 bolt is 1/2 inch in diameter, has 13 threads per inch and is 1 inch long. An M12 - 1.75 x 25 metric bolt is 12 mm in diameter, has a thread pitch of 1.75 mm (the distance between threads) and is 25 mm long. The two bolts are nearly identical, and easily confused, but they are not interchangeable.

In addition to the differences in diameter, thread pitch and length, metric and standard bolts can also be distinguished by examining the bolt heads. To begin with, the distance across the flats on a standard bolt head is measured in inches, while the same dimension on a metric bolt is sized in millimeters (the same is true for nuts). As a result, a standard wrench should not be used on a metric bolt and a metric wrench should not be used on a standard bolt. Also, most standard bolts have slashes radiating out from the center of the head to denote the grade or strength of the bolt, which is an indication of the amount of torque that can be applied to it. The greater the number of slashes, the greater the strength of the bolt. Grades 0 through 5 are commonly used on automobiles. Metric bolts have a property class (grade) number, rather than a slash, molded into their heads to indicate bolt strength. In this case, the higher the number, the stronger the bolt. Property class numbers 8.8, 9.8 and 10.9 are commonly used on automobiles.

Strength markings can also be used to distinguish standard hex nuts from metric hex nuts. Many standard nuts have dots stamped into one side, while metric nuts are marked with a number. The greater the number of dots, or the higher the number, the greater the strength of the nut.

Metric studs are also marked on their ends according to property class (grade). Larger studs are numbered (the same as metric bolts), while smaller studs carry a geometric code to denote grade.

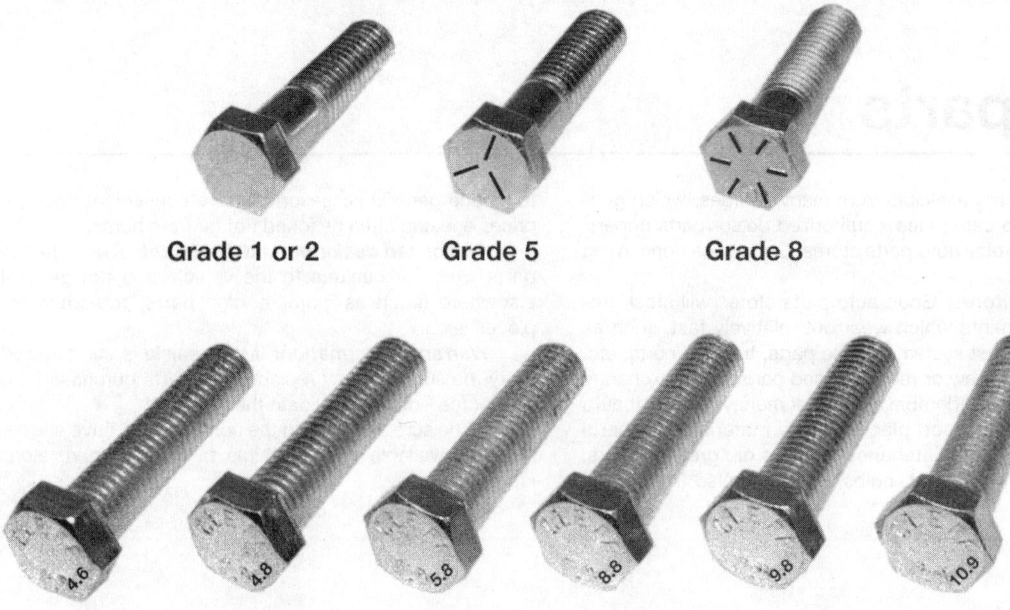

Bolt strength marking (standard/SAE/USS; bottom - metric)

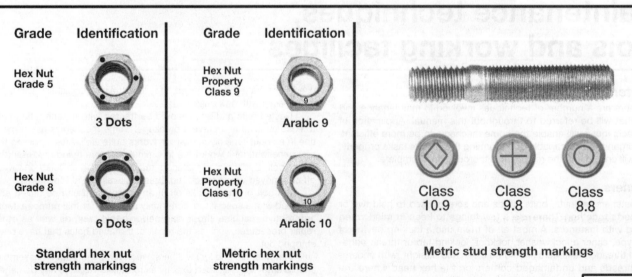

Grade | **Identification**

Hex Nut Grade 5

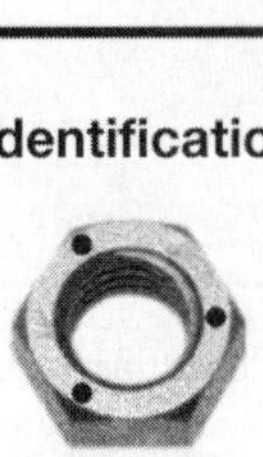

3 Dots

Hex Nut Grade 8

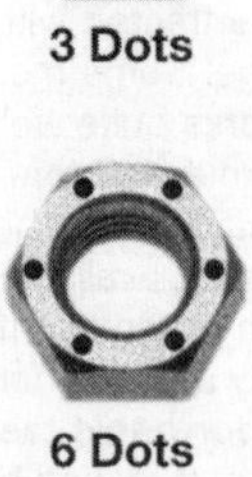

6 Dots

Standard hex nut strength markings

Grade | **Identification**

Hex Nut Property Class 9

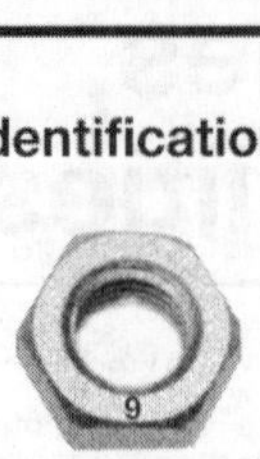

Arabic 9

Hex Nut Property Class 10

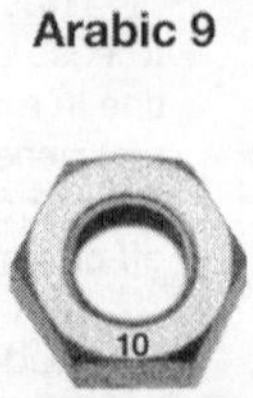

Arabic 10

Metric hex nut strength markings

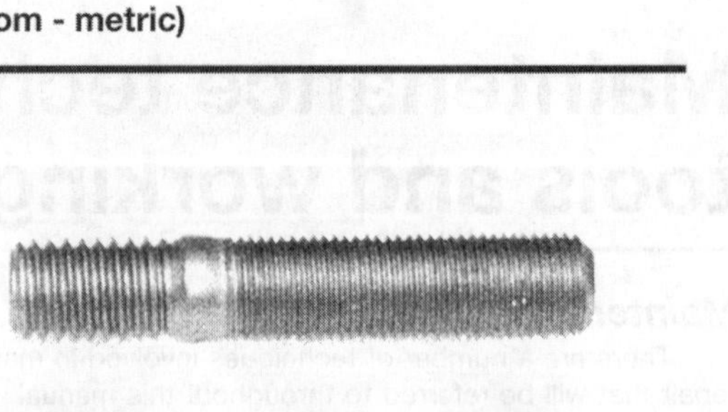

Class 10.9 | Class 9.8 | Class 8.8

Metric stud strength markings

00-1 HAYNES

It should be noted that many fasteners, especially Grades 0 through 2, have no distinguishing marks on them. When such is the case, the only way to determine whether it is standard or metric is to measure the thread pitch or compare it to a known fastener of the same size.

Standard fasteners are often referred to as SAE, as opposed to metric. However, it should be noted that SAE technically refers to a non-metric fine thread fastener only. Coarse thread non-metric fasteners are referred to as USS sizes.

Since fasteners of the same size (both standard and metric) may have different strength ratings, be sure to reinstall any bolts, studs or nuts removed from your vehicle in their original locations. Also, when replacing a fastener with a new one, make sure that the new one has a strength rating equal to or greater than the original.

Tightening sequences and procedures

Most threaded fasteners should be tightened to a specific torque value (torque is the twisting force applied to a threaded component such as a nut or bolt). Overtightening the fastener can weaken it and cause it to break, while undertightening can cause it to eventually come loose. Bolts, screws and studs, depending on the material they are made of and their thread diameters, have specific torque values, many of which are noted in the Specifications at the beginning of each Chapter. Be sure to follow the torque recommendations closely. For fasteners not assigned a specific torque, a general torque value chart is presented here as a guide. These torque values are for dry (unlubricated) fasteners threaded into steel or cast iron (not aluminum). As was previously mentioned, the size and grade of a fastener determine the amount of torque that can safely be applied to it. The figures listed

Metric thread sizes	Ft-lbs	Nm
M-6	6 to 9	9 to 12
M-8	14 to 21	19 to 28
M-10	28 to 40	38 to 54
M-12	50 to 71	68 to 96
M-14	80 to 140	109 to 154
Pipe thread sizes		
1/8	5 to 8	7 to 10
1/4	12 to 18	17 to 24
3/8	22 to 33	30 to 44
1/2	25 to 35	34 to 47
U.S. thread sizes		
1/4 - 20	6 to 9	9 to 12
5/16 - 18	12 to 18	17 to 24
5/16 - 24	14 to 20	19 to 27
3/8 - 16	22 to 32	30 to 43
3/8 - 24	27 to 38	37 to 51
7/16 - 14	40 to 55	55 to 74
7/16 - 20	40 to 60	55 to 81
1/2 - 13	55 to 80	75 to 108

Standard (SAE and USS) bolt dimensions/grade marks

G *Grade marks (bolt strength)*
L *Length (in inches)*
T *Thread pitch (number of threads per inch)*
D *Nominal diameter (in inches)*

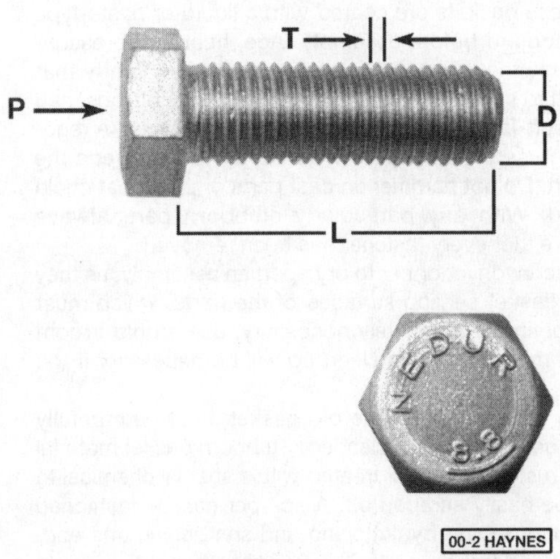

Metric bolt dimensions/grade marks

P *Property class (bolt strength)*
L *Length (in millimeters)*
T *Thread pitch (distance between threads in millimeters)*
D *Diameter*

here are approximate for Grade 2 and Grade 3 fasteners. Higher grades can tolerate higher torque values.

Fasteners laid out in a pattern, such as cylinder head bolts, oil pan bolts, differential cover bolts, etc., must be loosened or tightened in sequence to avoid warping the component. This sequence will normally be shown in the appropriate Chapter. If a specific pattern is not given, the following procedures can be used to prevent warping.

Initially, the bolts or nuts should be assembled finger-tight only. Next, they should be tightened one full turn each, in a criss-cross or diagonal pattern. After each one has been tightened one full turn, return to the first one and tighten them all one-half turn, following the same pattern. Finally, tighten each of them one-quarter turn at a time until each fastener has been tightened to the proper torque. To loosen and remove the fasteners, the procedure would be reversed.

Component disassembly

Component disassembly should be done with care and purpose to help ensure that the parts go back together properly. Always keep track of the sequence in which parts are removed. Make note of special characteristics or marks on parts that can be installed more than one way, such as a grooved thrust washer on a shaft. It is a good idea to lay the disassembled parts out on a clean surface in the order that they were removed. It may also be helpful to make sketches or take instant photos of components before removal.

When removing fasteners from a component, keep track of their locations. Sometimes threading a bolt back in a part, or putting the washers and nut back on a stud, can prevent mix-ups later. If nuts and bolts cannot be returned to their original locations, they should be kept in a compartmented box or a series of small boxes. A cupcake or muffin tin is ideal for this purpose, since each cavity can hold the bolts and nuts from a particular area (i.e. oil pan bolts, valve cover bolts, engine mount bolts, etc.). A pan of this type is especially helpful when working on assemblies with very small parts, such as the carburetor, alternator, valve train or interior dash and trim pieces. The cavities can be marked with paint or tape to identify the contents.

Whenever wiring looms, harnesses or connectors are separated, it is a good idea to identify the two halves with numbered pieces of masking tape so they can be easily reconnected.

Gasket sealing surfaces

Throughout any vehicle, gaskets are used to seal the mating surfaces between two parts and keep lubricants, fluids, vacuum or pressure contained in an assembly.

Many times these gaskets are coated with a liquid or paste-type gasket sealing compound before assembly. Age, heat and pressure can sometimes cause the two parts to stick together so tightly that they are very difficult to separate. Often, the assembly can be loosened by striking it with a soft-face hammer near the mating surfaces. A regular hammer can be used if a block of wood is placed between the hammer and the part. Do not hammer on cast parts or parts that could be easily damaged. With any particularly stubborn part, always recheck to make sure that every fastener has been removed.

Avoid using a screwdriver or bar to pry apart an assembly, as they can easily mar the gasket sealing surfaces of the parts, which must remain smooth. If prying is absolutely necessary, use an old broom handle, but keep in mind that extra clean up will be necessary if the wood splinters.

After the parts are separated, the old gasket must be carefully scraped off and the gasket surfaces cleaned. Stubborn gasket material can be soaked with rust penetrant or treated with a special chemical to soften it so it can be easily scraped off. A scraper can be fashioned from a piece of copper tubing by flattening and sharpening one end. Copper is recommended because it is usually softer than the surfaces to be scraped, which reduces the chance of gouging the part. Some gaskets can be removed with a wire brush, but regardless of the method used, the mating surfaces must be left clean and smooth. If for some reason the gasket surface is gouged, then a gasket sealer thick enough to fill scratches will have to be used during reassembly of the components. For most applications, a non-drying (or semi-drying) gasket sealer should be used.

Hose removal tips

Warning: *If the vehicle is equipped with air conditioning, do not disconnect any of the A/C hoses without first having the system depressurized by a dealer service department or a service station.*

Hose removal precautions closely parallel gasket removal precautions. Avoid scratching or gouging the surface that the hose mates against or the connection may leak. This is especially true for radiator hoses. Because of various chemical reactions, the rubber in hoses can bond itself to the metal spigot that the hose fits over. To remove a hose, first loosen the hose clamps that secure it to the spigot. Then, with slip-joint pliers, grab the hose at the clamp and rotate it around the spigot. Work it back and forth until it is completely free, then pull it off. Silicone or other lubricants will ease removal if they can be applied between the hose and the outside of the spigot. Apply the same lubricant to the inside of the hose and the outside of the spigot to simplify installation.

As a last resort (and if the hose is to be replaced with a new one anyway), the rubber can be slit with a knife and the hose peeled from the spigot. If this must be done, be careful that the metal connection is not damaged.

If a hose clamp is broken or damaged, do not reuse it. Wire-type clamps usually weaken with age, so it is a good idea to replace them with screw-type clamps whenever a hose is removed.

Tools

A selection of good tools is a basic requirement for anyone who plans to maintain and repair his or her own vehicle. For the owner who has few tools, the initial investment might seem high, but when compared to the spiraling costs of professional auto maintenance and repair, it is a wise one.

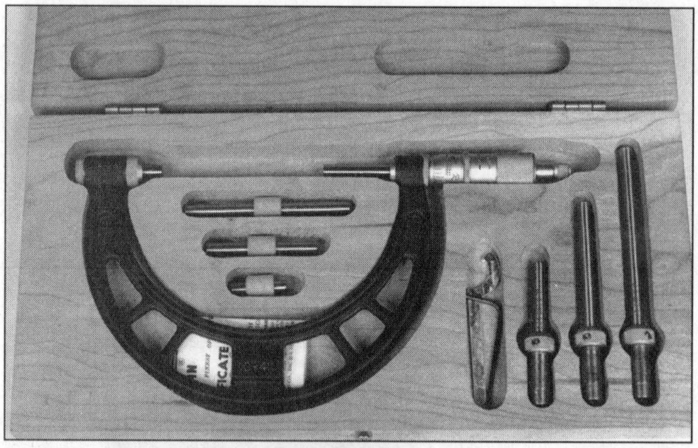

Micrometer set

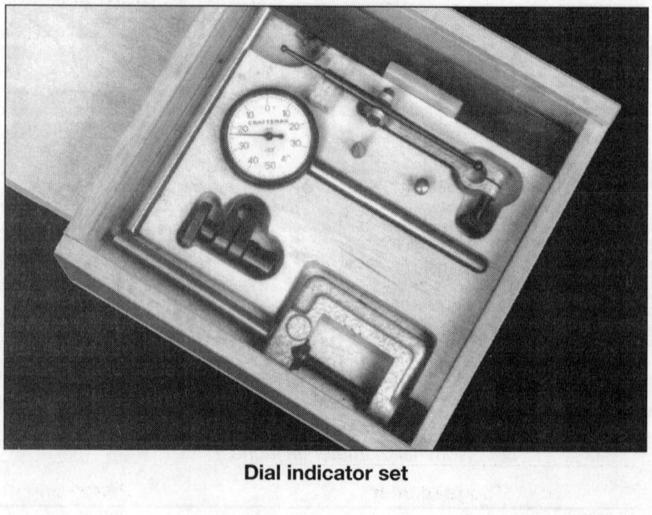

Dial indicator set

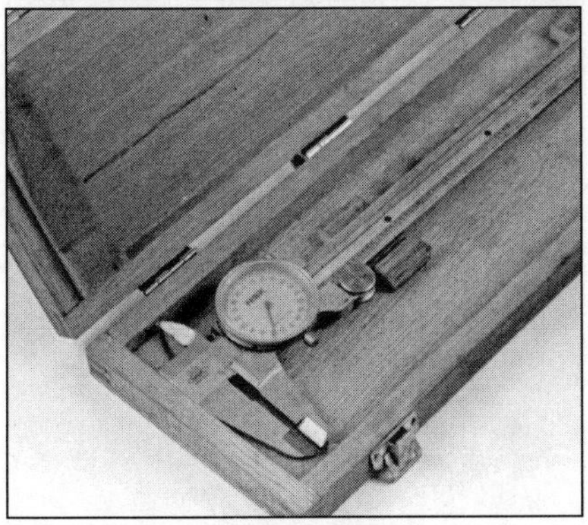
Dial caliper

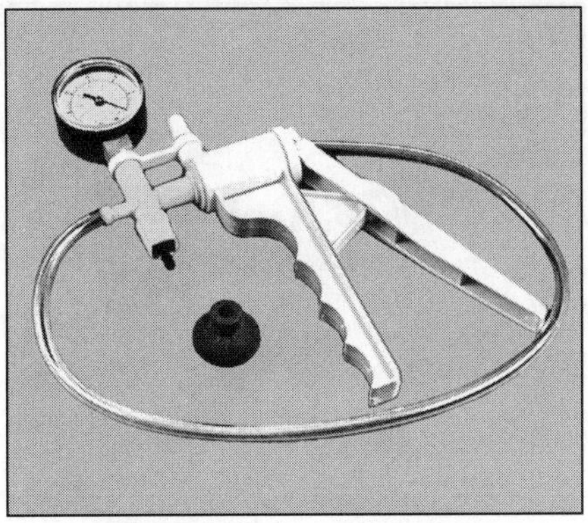
Hand-operated vacuum pump

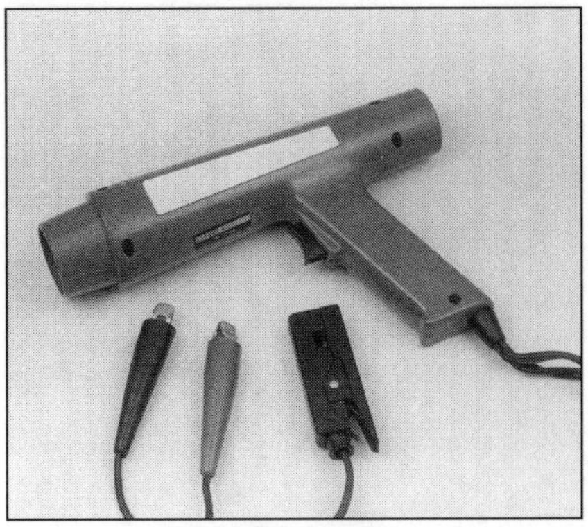
Timing light

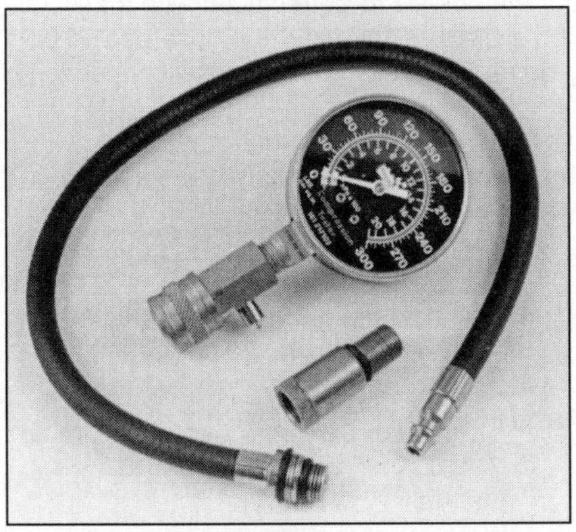
Compression gauge with spark plug hole adapter

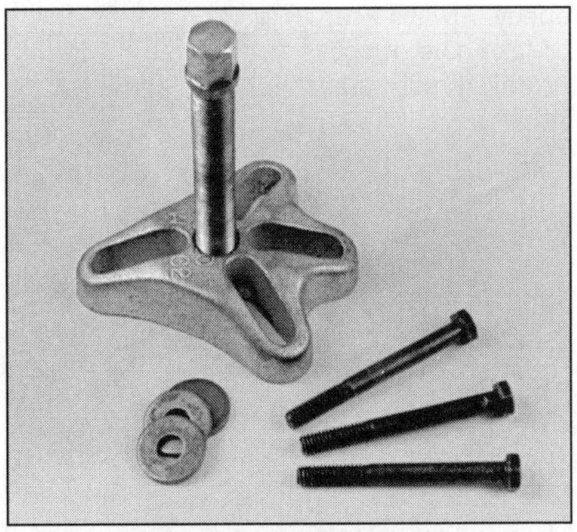
Damper/steering wheel puller

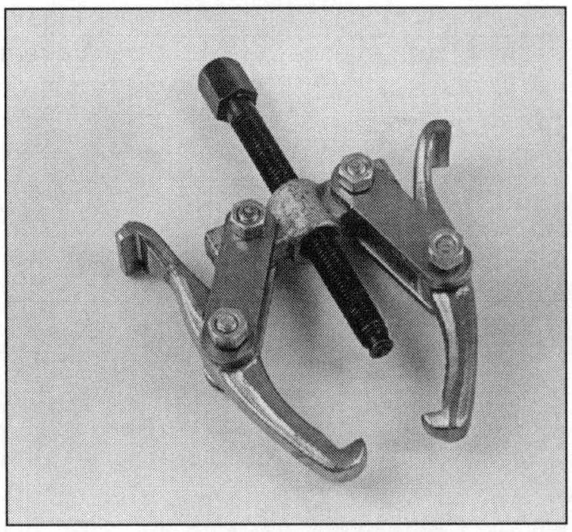
General purpose puller

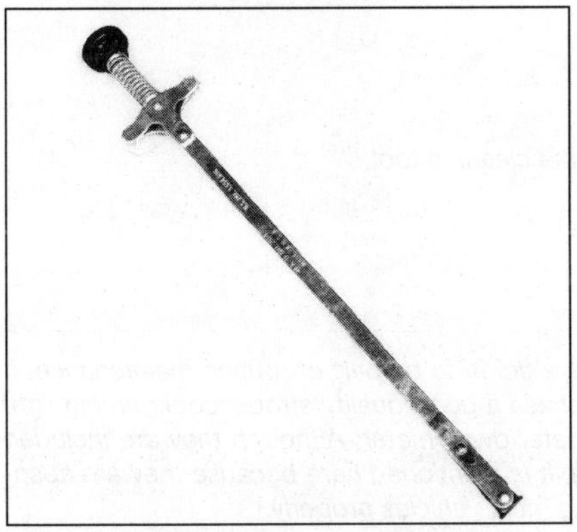
Hydraulic lifter removal tool

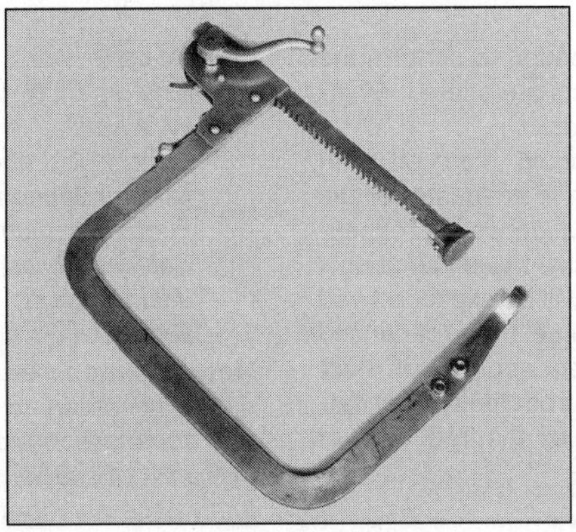
Valve spring compressor

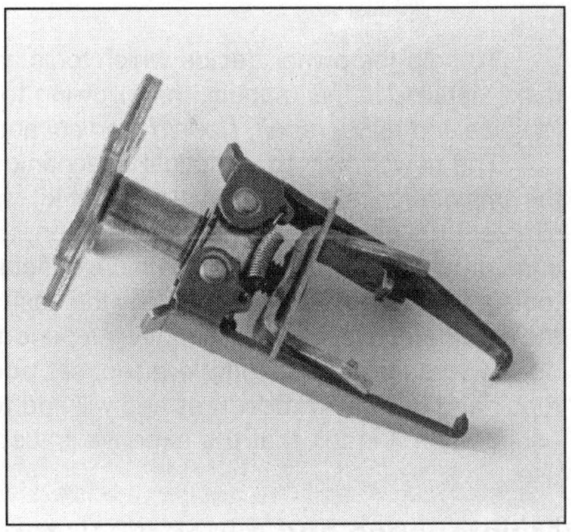
Valve spring compressor

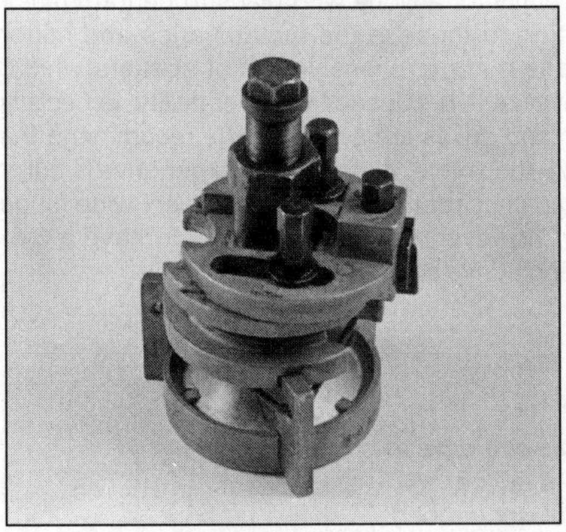
Ridge reamer

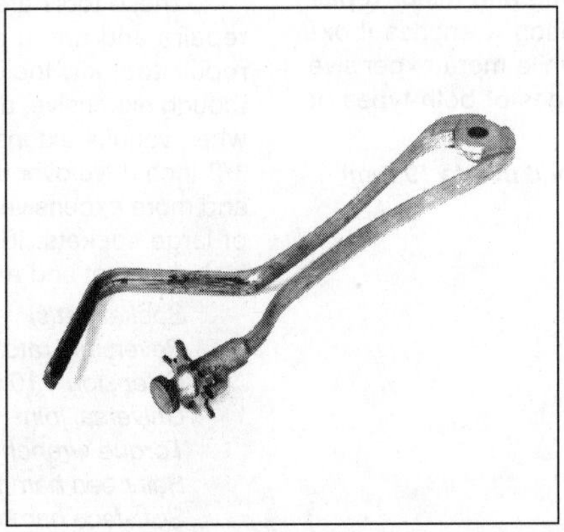
Piston ring groove cleaning tool

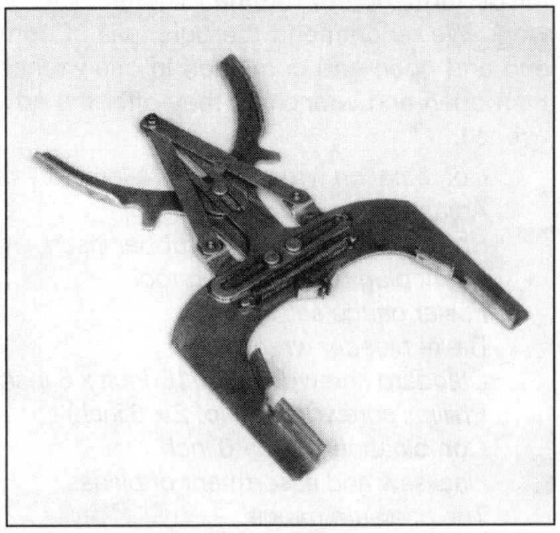
Ring removal/installation tool

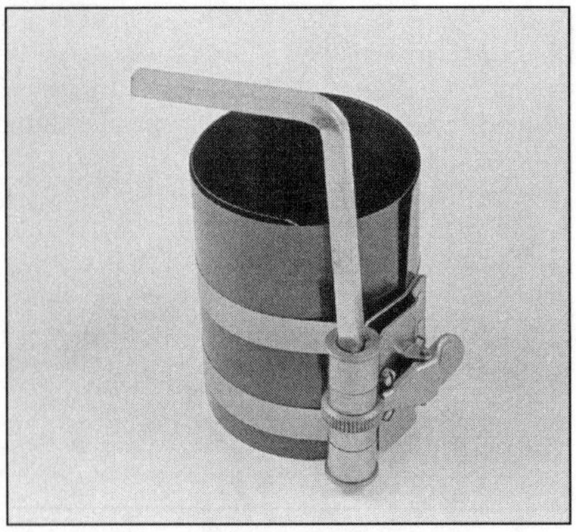

Ring compressor

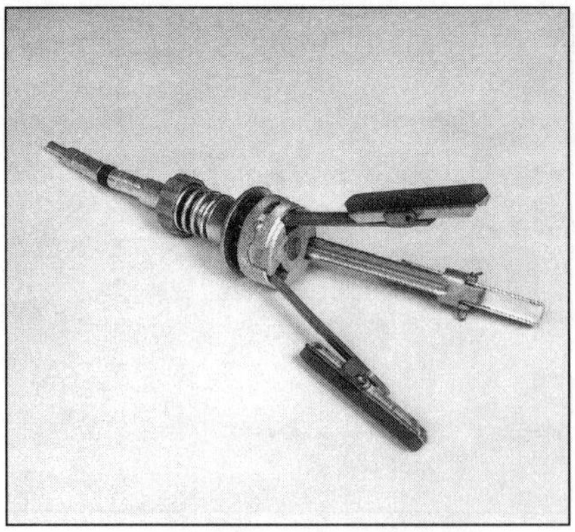

Cylinder hone

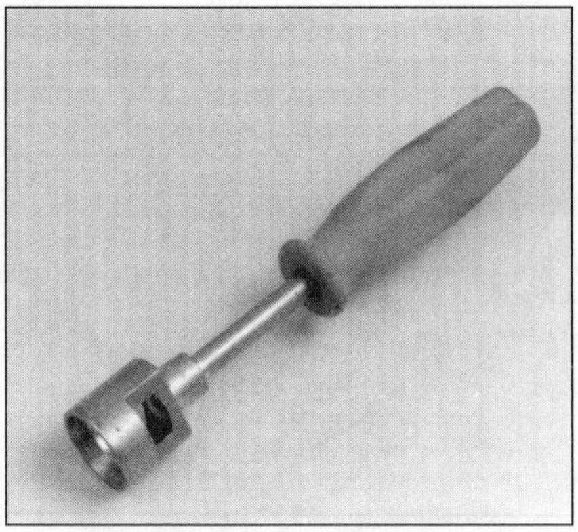

Brake hold-down spring tool

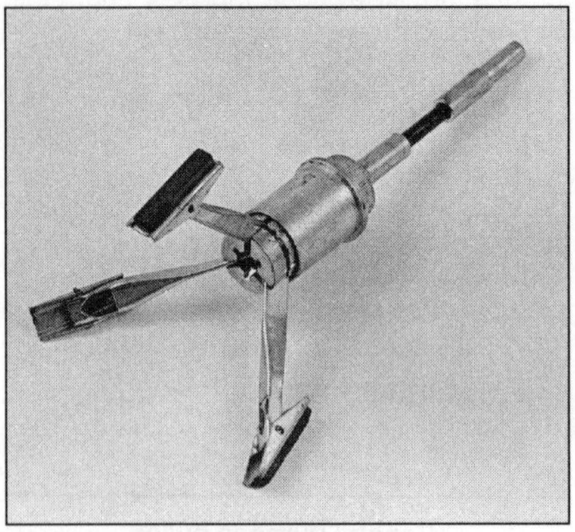

Brake cylinder hone

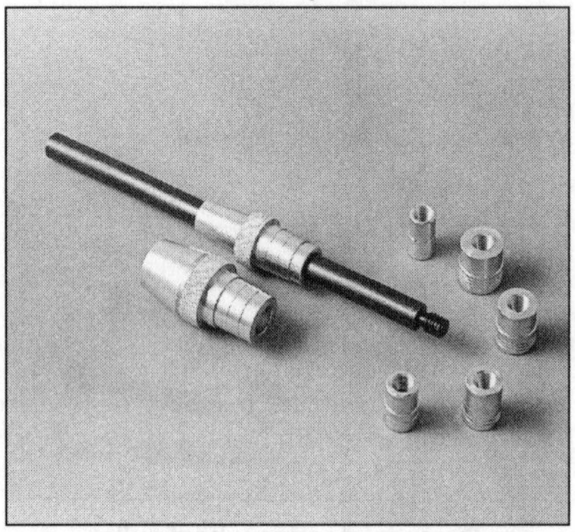

Clutch plate alignment tool

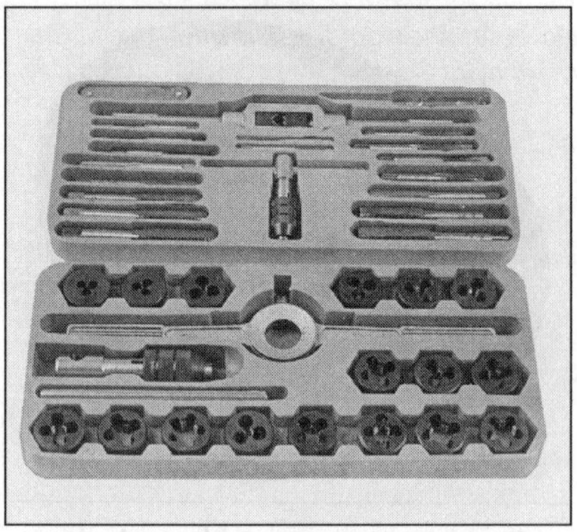

Tap and die set

To help the owner decide which tools are needed to perform the tasks detailed in this manual, the following tool lists are offered: *Maintenance and minor repair, Repair/overhaul* and *Special.*

The newcomer to practical mechanics should start off with the *maintenance and minor repair* tool kit, which is adequate for the simpler jobs performed on a vehicle. Then, as confidence and experience grow, the owner can tackle more difficult tasks, buying additional tools as they are needed. Eventually the basic kit will be expanded into the *repair and overhaul* tool set. Over a period of time, the experienced do-it-yourselfer will assemble a tool set complete enough for most repair and overhaul procedures and will add tools from the special category when it is felt that the expense is justified by the frequency of use.

Maintenance and minor repair tool kit

The tools in this list should be considered the minimum required for performance of routine maintenance, servicing and minor repair work. We recommend the purchase of combination wrenches (box-end and open-end combined in one wrench). While more expensive than open end wrenches, they offer the advantages of both types of wrench.

Combination wrench set (1/4-inch to 1 inch or 6 mm to 19 mm)
Adjustable wrench, 8 inch
Spark plug wrench with rubber insert
Spark plug gap adjusting tool
Feeler gauge set
Brake bleeder wrench
Standard screwdriver (5/16-inch x 6 inch)
Phillips screwdriver (No. 2 x 6 inch)
Combination pliers - 6 inch
Hacksaw and assortment of blades
Tire pressure gauge
Grease gun
Oil can
Fine emery cloth
Wire brush
Battery post and cable cleaning tool
Oil filter wrench
Funnel (medium size)
Safety goggles
Jackstands (2)
Drain pan

Note: *If basic tune-ups are going to be part of routine maintenance, it will be necessary to purchase a good quality stroboscopic timing light and combination tachometer/dwell meter. Although they are included in the list of special tools, it is mentioned here because they are absolutely necessary for tuning most vehicles properly.*

Repair and overhaul tool set

These tools are essential for anyone who plans to perform major repairs and are in addition to those in the maintenance and minor repair tool kit. Included is a comprehensive set of sockets which, though expensive, are invaluable because of their versatility, especially when various extensions and drives are available. We recommend the 1/2-inch drive over the 3/8-inch drive. Although the larger drive is bulky and more expensive, it has the capacity of accepting a very wide range of large sockets. Ideally, however, the mechanic should have a 3/8-inch drive set and a 1/2-inch drive set.

Socket set(s)
Reversible ratchet
Extension - 10 inch
Universal joint
Torque wrench (same size drive as sockets)
Ball peen hammer - 8 ounce
Soft-face hammer (plastic/rubber)
Standard screwdriver (1/4-inch x 6 inch)

Standard screwdriver (stubby - 5/16-inch)
Phillips screwdriver (No. 3 x 8 inch)
Phillips screwdriver (stubby - No. 2)
Pliers - vise grip
Pliers - lineman's
Pliers - needle nose
Pliers - snap-ring (internal and external)
Cold chisel - 1/2-inch
Scribe
Scraper (made from flattened copper tubing)
Centerpunch
Pin punches (1/16, 1/8, 3/16-inch)
Steel rule/straightedge - 12 inch
Allen wrench set (1/8 to 3/8-inch or 4 mm to 10 mm)
A selection of files
Wire brush (large)
Jackstands (second set)
Jack (scissor or hydraulic type)

Note: *Another tool which is often useful is an electric drill with a chuck capacity of 3/8-inch and a set of good quality drill bits.*

Special tools

The tools in this list include those which are not used regularly, are expensive to buy, or which need to be used in accordance with their manufacturer's instructions. Unless these tools will be used frequently, it is not very economical to purchase many of them. A consideration would be to split the cost and use between yourself and a friend or friends. In addition, most of these tools can be obtained from a tool rental shop on a temporary basis.

This list primarily contains only those tools and instruments widely available to the public, and not those special tools produced by the vehicle manufacturer for distribution to dealer service departments. Occasionally, references to the manufacturer's special tools are included in the text of this manual. Generally, an alternative method of doing the job without the special tool is offered. However, sometimes there is no alternative to their use. Where this is the case, and the tool cannot be purchased or borrowed, the work should be turned over to the dealer service department or an automotive repair shop.

Valve spring compressor
Piston ring groove cleaning tool
Piston ring compressor
Piston ring installation tool
Cylinder compression gauge
Cylinder ridge reamer
Cylinder surfacing hone
Cylinder bore gauge
Micrometers and/or dial calipers
Hydraulic lifter removal tool
Balljoint separator
Universal-type puller
Impact screwdriver
Dial indicator set
Stroboscopic timing light (inductive pick-up)
Hand operated vacuum/pressure pump
Tachometer/dwell meter
Universal electrical multimeter
Cable hoist
Brake spring removal and installation tools
Floor jack

Buying tools

For the do-it-yourselfer who is just starting to get involved in vehicle maintenance and repair, there are a number of options available when purchasing tools. If maintenance and minor repair is the extent of the work to be done, the purchase of individual tools is satisfactory. If, on the other hand, extensive work is planned, it would be a good idea to purchase a modest tool set from one of the large retail chain stores. A set can usually be bought at a substantial savings over the individual tool prices, and they often come with a tool box. As additional tools are needed, add-on sets, individual tools and a larger tool box can be purchased to expand the tool selection. Building a tool set gradually allows the cost of the tools to be spread over a longer period of time and gives the mechanic the freedom to choose only those tools that will actually be used.

Tool stores will often be the only source of some of the special tools that are needed, but regardless of where tools are bought, try to avoid cheap ones, especially when buying screwdrivers and sockets, because they won't last very long. The expense involved in replacing cheap tools will eventually be greater than the initial cost of quality tools.

Care and maintenance of tools

Good tools are expensive, so it makes sense to treat them with respect. Keep them clean and in usable condition and store them properly when not in use. Always wipe off any dirt, grease or metal chips before putting them away. Never leave tools lying around in the work area. Upon completion of a job, always check closely under the hood for tools that may have been left there so they won't get lost during a test drive.

Some tools, such as screwdrivers, pliers, wrenches and sockets, can be hung on a panel mounted on the garage or workshop wall, while others should be kept in a tool box or tray. Measuring instruments, gauges, meters, etc. must be carefully stored where they cannot be damaged by weather or impact from other tools.

When tools are used with care and stored properly, they will last a very long time. Even with the best of care, though, tools will wear out if used frequently. When a tool is damaged or worn out, replace it. Subsequent jobs will be safer and more enjoyable if you do.

How to repair damaged threads

Sometimes, the internal threads of a nut or bolt hole can become stripped, usually from overtightening. Stripping threads is an all-too-common occurrence, especially when working with aluminum parts, because aluminum is so soft that it easily strips out.

Usually, external or internal threads are only partially stripped. After they've been cleaned up with a tap or die, they'll still work. Sometimes, however, threads are badly damaged. When this happens, you've got three choices:

1) *Drill and tap the hole to the next suitable oversize and install a larger diameter bolt, screw or stud.*
2) *Drill and tap the hole to accept a threaded plug, then drill and tap the plug to the original screw size. You can also buy a plug already threaded to the original size. Then you simply drill a hole to the specified size, then run the threaded plug into the hole with a bolt and jam nut. Once the plug is fully seated, remove the jam nut and bolt.*
3) *The third method uses a patented thread repair kit like Heli-Coil or Slimsert. These easy-to-use kits are designed to repair damaged threads in straight-through holes and blind holes. Both are available as kits which can handle a variety of sizes and thread patterns. Drill the hole, then tap it with the special included tap. Install the Heli-Coil and the hole is back to its original diameter and thread pitch.*

Regardless of which method you use, be sure to proceed calmly and carefully. A little impatience or carelessness during one of these relatively simple procedures can ruin your whole day's work and cost you a bundle if you wreck an expensive part.

Working facilities

Not to be overlooked when discussing tools is the workshop. If anything more than routine maintenance is to be carried out, some sort of suitable work area is essential.

It is understood, and appreciated, that many home mechanics do not have a good workshop or garage available, and end up removing an engine or doing major repairs outside. It is recommended, however, that the overhaul or repair be completed under the cover of a roof.

A clean, flat workbench or table of comfortable working height is an absolute necessity. The workbench should be equipped with a vise that has a jaw opening of at least four inches.

As mentioned previously, some clean, dry storage space is also required for tools, as well as the lubricants, fluids, cleaning solvents, etc. which soon become necessary.

Sometimes waste oil and fluids, drained from the engine or cooling system during normal maintenance or repairs, present a disposal problem. To avoid pouring them on the ground or into a sewage system, pour the used fluids into large containers, seal them with caps and take them to an authorized disposal site or recycling center. Plastic jugs, such as old antifreeze containers, are ideal for this purpose.

Always keep a supply of old newspapers and clean rags available. Old towels are excellent for mopping up spills. Many mechanics use rolls of paper towels for most work because they are readily available and disposable. To help keep the area under the vehicle clean, a large cardboard box can be cut open and flattened to protect the garage or shop floor.

Whenever working over a painted surface, such as when leaning over a fender to service something under the hood, always cover it with an old blanket or bedspread to protect the finish. Vinyl covered pads, made especially for this purpose, are available at auto parts stores.

Booster battery (jump) starting

Observe these precautions when using a booster battery to start a vehicle:

a) *Before connecting the booster battery, make sure the ignition switch is in the Off position.*
b) *Turn off the lights, heater and other electrical loads.*
c) *Your eyes should be shielded. Safety goggles are a good idea.*
d) *Make sure the booster battery is the same voltage as the dead one in the vehicle.*
e) *The two vehicles MUST NOT TOUCH each other!*
f) *Make sure the transaxle is in Neutral (manual) or Park (automatic).*
g) *If the booster battery is not a maintenance-free type, remove the vent caps and lay a cloth over the vent holes.*

Connect the red jumper cable to the positive (+) terminals of each battery **(see illustration)**.

Connect one end of the black jumper cable to the negative (-) terminal of the booster battery. The other end of this cable should be connected to a good ground on the vehicle to be started, such as a bolt or bracket on the body.

Start the engine using the booster battery, then, with the engine running at idle speed, disconnect the jumper cables in the reverse order of connection.

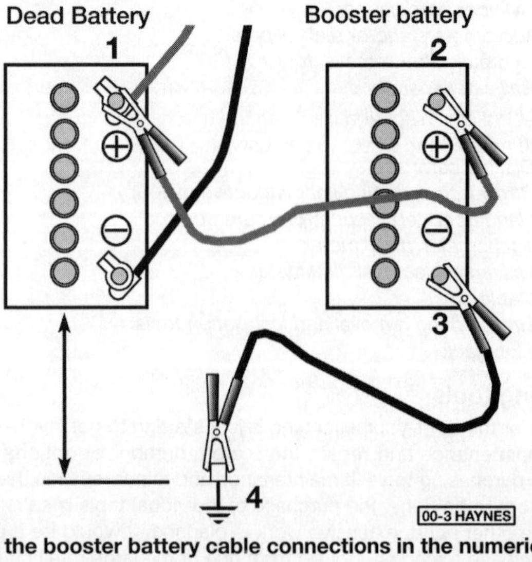

Make the booster battery cable connections in the numerical order shown (note that the negative cable of the booster battery is NOT attached to the negative terminal of the dead battery)

Jacking and towing

Jacking

Warning: *The jack supplied with the vehicle should only be used for changing a tire or placing jackstands under the frame. Never work under the vehicle or start the engine while this jack is being used as the only means of support.*

The vehicle should be on level ground. Place the shift lever in Park, if you have an automatic, or Reverse if you have a manual transaxle. Block the wheel diagonally opposite the wheel being changed. Set the parking brake.

Remove the spare tire and jack from stowage. Remove the wheel cover and trim ring (if so equipped) with the tapered end of the lug nut wrench by inserting and twisting the handle and then prying against the back of the wheel cover. Loosen the wheel lug nuts about 1/4-to-1/2 turn each.

Place the scissors-type jack under the side of the vehicle and adjust the jack height until it fits in the notch in the vertical rocker panel flange nearest the wheel to be changed. There is a front and rear jacking point on each side of the vehicle **(see illustration)**.

Turn the jack handle clockwise until the tire clears the ground. Remove the lug nuts and pull the wheel off. Replace it with the spare.

Install the lug nuts with the beveled edges facing in. Tighten them snugly. Don't attempt to tighten them completely until the vehicle is lowered or it could slip off the jack. Turn the jack handle counterclockwise to lower the vehicle. Remove the jack and tighten the lug nuts in a diagonal pattern.

Install the cover (and trim ring, if used) and be sure it's snapped into place all the way around.

Stow the tire, jack and wrench. Unblock the wheels.

Towing

As a general rule, the vehicle should be towed from the front with the front (drive) wheels off the ground. If the vehicle must be towed from the rear, place the front wheels on a towing dolly. **Caution:** *Never tow a front wheel drive vehicle from the rear with the front wheels on the ground.*

Equipment specifically designed for towing should be used. It should be attached to the main structural members of the vehicle, not the bumpers or brackets. Do not use the tie-down hook loops at the front or the rear of the vehicle for towing. These hooks loops are designed for securing the vehicle during transport, if used for towing, damage to the front or rear bumper may occur.

The ignition key must be in the ACC position, since the steering lock mechanism isn't strong enough to hold the front wheels straight while towing. Pace the shift lever in neutral and release the parking brake.

Safety is a major consideration when towing and all applicable state and local laws must be obeyed. A safety chain system must be used at all times.

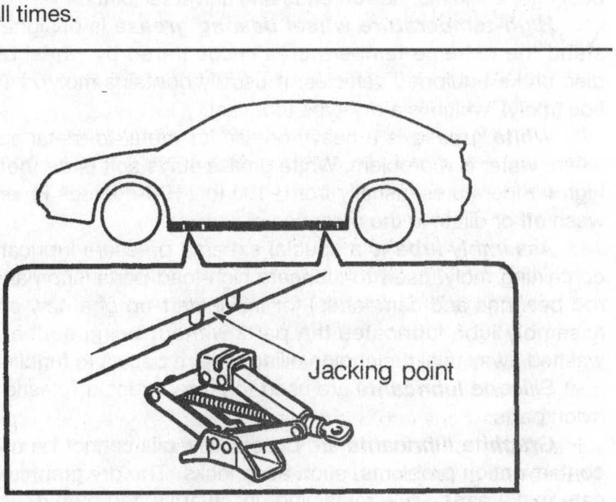

The jack fits under the rocker panel (there are two jacking points on each side of the vehicle, indicated by a notch in the rocker panel flange)

Automotive chemicals and lubricants

A number of automotive chemicals and lubricants are available for use during vehicle maintenance and repair. They include a wide variety of products ranging from cleaning solvents and degreasers to lubricants and protective sprays for rubber, plastic and vinyl.

Cleaners

Carburetor cleaner and choke cleaner is a strong solvent for gum, varnish and carbon. Most carburetor cleaners leave a dry-type lubricant film which will not harden or gum up. Because of this film it is not recommended for use on electrical components.

Brake system cleaner is used to remove grease and brake fluid from the brake system, where clean surfaces are absolutely necessary. It leaves no residue and often eliminates brake squeal caused by contaminants.

Electrical cleaner removes oxidation, corrosion and carbon deposits from electrical contacts, restoring full current flow. It can also be used to clean spark plugs, carburetor jets, voltage regulators and other parts where an oil-free surface is desired.

Demoisturants remove water and moisture from electrical components such as alternators, voltage regulators, electrical connectors and fuse blocks. They are non-conductive, non-corrosive and non-flammable.

Degreasers are heavy-duty solvents used to remove grease from the outside of the engine and from chassis components. They can be sprayed or brushed on and, depending on the type, are rinsed off either with water or solvent.

Lubricants

Motor oil is the lubricant formulated for use in engines. It normally contains a wide variety of additives to prevent corrosion and reduce foaming and wear. Motor oil comes in various weights (viscosity ratings) from 5 to 80. The recommended weight of the oil depends on the season, temperature and the demands on the engine. Light oil is used in cold climates and under light load conditions. Heavy oil is used in hot climates and where high loads are encountered. Multi-viscosity oils are designed to have characteristics of both light and heavy oils and are available in a number of weights from 5W-20 to 20W-50.

Gear oil is designed to be used in differentials, manual transmissions and other areas where high-temperature lubrication is required.

Chassis and wheel bearing grease is a heavy grease used where increased loads and friction are encountered, such as for wheel bearings, balljoints, tie-rod ends and universal joints.

High-temperature wheel bearing grease is designed to withstand the extreme temperatures encountered by wheel bearings in disc brake equipped vehicles. It usually contains molybdenum disulfide (moly), which is a dry-type lubricant.

White grease is a heavy grease for metal-to-metal applications where water is a problem. White grease stays soft under both low and high temperatures (usually from -100 to +190-degrees F), and will not wash off or dilute in the presence of water.

Assembly lube is a special extreme pressure lubricant, usually containing moly, used to lubricate high-load parts (such as main and rod bearings and cam lobes) for initial start-up of a new engine. The assembly lube lubricates the parts without being squeezed out or washed away until the engine oiling system begins to function.

Silicone lubricants are used to protect rubber, plastic, vinyl and nylon parts.

Graphite lubricants are used where oils cannot be used due to contamination problems, such as in locks. The dry graphite will lubricate metal parts while remaining uncontaminated by dirt, water, oil or acids. It is electrically conductive and will not foul electrical contacts in locks such as the ignition switch.

Moly penetrants loosen and lubricate frozen, rusted and corroded fasteners and prevent future rusting or freezing.

Heat-sink grease is a special electrically non-conductive grease that is used for mounting electronic ignition modules where it is essential that heat is transferred away from the module.

Sealants

RTV sealant is one of the most widely used gasket compounds. Made from silicone, RTV is air curing, it seals, bonds, waterproofs, fills surface irregularities, remains flexible, doesn't shrink, is relatively easy to remove, and is used as a supplementary sealer with almost all low and medium temperature gaskets.

Anaerobic sealant is much like RTV in that it can be used either to seal gaskets or to form gaskets by itself. It remains flexible, is solvent resistant and fills surface imperfections. The difference between an anaerobic sealant and an RTV-type sealant is in the curing. RTV cures when exposed to air, while an anaerobic sealant cures only in the absence of air. This means that an anaerobic sealant cures only after the assembly of parts, sealing them together.

Thread and pipe sealant is used for sealing hydraulic and pneumatic fittings and vacuum lines. It is usually made from a Teflon compound, and comes in a spray, a paint-on liquid and as a wrap-around tape.

Chemicals

Anti-seize compound prevents seizing, galling, cold welding, rust and corrosion in fasteners. High-temperature ant-seize, usually made with copper and graphite lubricants, is used for exhaust system and exhaust manifold bolts.

Anaerobic locking compounds are used to keep fasteners from vibrating or working loose and cure only after installation, in the absence of air. Medium strength locking compound is used for small nuts, bolts and screws that may be removed later. High-strength locking compound is for large nuts, bolts and studs which aren't removed on a regular basis.

Oil additives range from viscosity index improvers to chemical treatments that claim to reduce internal engine friction. It should be noted that most oil manufacturers caution against using additives with their oils.

Gas additives perform several functions, depending on their chemical makeup. They usually contain solvents that help dissolve gum and varnish that build up on carburetor, fuel injection and intake parts. They also serve to break down carbon deposits that form on the inside surfaces of the combustion chambers. Some additives contain upper cylinder lubricants for valves and piston rings, and others contain chemicals to remove condensation from the gas tank.

Miscellaneous

Brake fluid is specially formulated hydraulic fluid that can withstand the heat and pressure encountered in brake systems. Care must be taken so this fluid does not come in contact with painted surfaces or plastics. An opened container should always be resealed to prevent contamination by water or dirt.

Weatherstrip adhesive is used to bond weatherstripping around doors, windows and trunk lids. It is sometimes used to attach trim pieces.

Undercoating is a petroleum-based, tar-like substance that is designed to protect metal surfaces on the underside of the vehicle from corrosion. It also acts as a sound-deadening agent by insulating the bottom of the vehicle.

Waxes and polishes are used to help protect painted and plated surfaces from the weather. Different types of paint may require the use of different types of wax and polish. Some polishes utilize a chemical or abrasive cleaner to help remove the top layer of oxidized (dull) paint on older vehicles. In recent years many non-wax polishes that contain a wide variety of chemicals such as polymers and silicones have been introduced. These non-wax polishes are usually easier to apply and last longer than conventional waxes and polishes.

Conversion factors

Length (distance)					
Inches (in)	X 25.4	= Millimetres (mm)	X 0.0394	= Inches (in)
Feet (ft)	X 0.305	= Metres (m)	X 3.281	= Feet (ft)
Miles	X 1.609	= Kilometres (km)	X 0.621	= Miles
Volume (capacity)				
Cubic inches (cu in; in^3)	X 16.387	= Cubic centimetres (cc; cm^3)	X 0.061	= Cubic inches (cu in; in^3)
Imperial pints (Imp pt)	X 0.568	= Litres (l)	X 1.76	= Imperial pints (Imp pt)
Imperial quarts (Imp qt)	X 1.137	= Litres (l)	X 0.88	= Imperial quarts (Imp qt)
Imperial quarts (Imp qt)	X 1.201	= US quarts (US qt)	X 0.833	= Imperial quarts (Imp qt)
US quarts (US qt)	X 0.946	= Litres (l)	X 1.057	= US quarts (US qt)
Imperial gallons (Imp gal)	X 4.546	= Litres (l)	X 0.22	= Imperial gallons (Imp gal)
Imperial gallons (Imp gal)	X 1.201	= US gallons (US gal)	X 0.833	= Imperial gallons (Imp gal)
US gallons (US gal)	X 3.785	= Litres (l)	X 0.264	= US gallons (US gal)
Mass (weight)				
Ounces (oz)	X 28.35	= Grams (g)	X 0.035	= Ounces (oz)
Pounds (lb)	X 0.454	= Kilograms (kg)	X 2.205	= Pounds (lb)
Force				
Ounces-force (ozf; oz)	X 0.278	= Newtons (N)	X 3.6	= Ounces-force (ozf; oz)
Pounds-force (lbf; lb)	X 4.448	= Newtons (N)	X 0.225	= Pounds-force (lbf; lb)
Newtons (N)	X 0.1	= Kilograms-force (kgf; kg)	X 9.81	= Newtons (N)
Pressure				
Pounds-force per square inch (psi; lbf/in^2; lb/in^2)	X 0.070	= Kilograms-force per square centimetre (kgf/cm^2; kg/cm^2)	X 14.223	= Pounds-force per square inch (psi; lbf/in^2; lb/in^2)
Pounds-force per square inch (psi; lbf/in^2; lb/in^2)	X 0.068	= Atmospheres (atm)	X 14.696	= Pounds-force per square inch (psi; lbf/in^2; lb/in^2)
Pounds-force per square inch (psi; lbf/in^2; lb/in^2)	X 0.069	= Bars	X 14.5	= Pounds-force per square inch (psi; lbf/in^2; lb/in^2)
Pounds-force per square inch (psi; lbf/in^2; lb/in^2)	X 6.895	= Kilopascals (kPa)	X 0.145	= Pounds-force per square inch (psi; lbf/in^2; lb/in^2)
Kilopascals (kPa)	X 0.01	= Kilograms-force per square centimetre (kgf/cm^2; kg/cm^2)	X 98.1	= Kilopascals (kPa)
Torque (moment of force)				
Pounds-force inches (lbf in; lb in)	X 1.152	= Kilograms-force centimetre (kgf cm; kg cm)	X 0.868	= Pounds-force inches (lbf in; lb in)
Pounds-force inches (lbf in; lb in)	X 0.113	= Newton metres (Nm)	X 8.85	= Pounds-force inches (lbf in; lb in)
Pounds-force inches (lbf in; lb in)	X 0.083	= Pounds-force feet (lbf ft; lb ft)	X 12	= Pounds-force inches (lbf in; lb in)
Pounds-force feet (lbf ft; lb ft)	X 0.138	= Kilograms-force metres (kgf m; kg m)	X 7.233	= Pounds-force feet (lbf ft; lb ft)
Pounds-force feet (lbf ft; lb ft)	X 1.356	= Newton metres (Nm)	X 0.738	= Pounds-force feet (lbf ft; lb ft)
Newton metres (Nm)	X 0.102	= Kilograms-force metres (kgf m; kg m)	X 9.804	= Newton metres (Nm)
Power				
Horsepower (hp)	X 745.7	= Watts (W)	X 0.0013	= Horsepower (hp)
Velocity (speed)				
Miles per hour (miles/hr; mph)	X 1.609	= Kilometres per hour (km/hr; kph)	X 0.621	= Miles per hour (miles/hr; mph)
Fuel consumption*				
Miles per gallon, Imperial (mpg)	X 0.354	= Kilometres per litre (km/l)	X 2.825	= Miles per gallon, Imperial (mpg)
Miles per gallon, US (mpg)	X 0.425	= Kilometres per litre (km/l)	X 2.352	= Miles per gallon, US (mpg)

Temperature

Degrees Fahrenheit = (°C x 1.8) + 32

Degrees Celsius (Degrees Centigrade; °C) = (°F - 32) x 0.56

****It is common practice to convert from miles per gallon (mpg) to litres/100 kilometres (l/100km), where mpg (Imperial) x l/100 km = 282 and mpg (US) x l/100 km = 235***

Safety first!

Regardless of how enthusiastic you may be about getting on with the job at hand, take the time to ensure that your safety is not jeopardized. A moment's lack of attention can result in an accident, as can failure to observe certain simple safety precautions. The possibility of an accident will always exist, and the following points should not be considered a comprehensive list of all dangers. Rather, they are intended to make you aware of the risks and to encourage a safety conscious approach to all work you carry out on your vehicle.

Essential DOs and DON'Ts

DON'T rely on a jack when working under the vehicle. Always use approved jackstands to support the weight of the vehicle and place them under the recommended lift or support points.

DON'T attempt to loosen extremely tight fasteners (i.e. wheel lug nuts) while the vehicle is on a jack - it may fall.

DON'T start the engine without first making sure that the transmission is in Neutral (or Park where applicable) and the parking brake is set.

DON'T remove the radiator cap from a hot cooling system - let it cool or cover it with a cloth and release the pressure gradually.

DON'T attempt to drain the engine oil until you are sure it has cooled to the point that it will not burn you.

DON'T touch any part of the engine or exhaust system until it has cooled sufficiently to avoid burns.

DON'T siphon toxic liquids such as gasoline, antifreeze and brake fluid by mouth, or allow them to remain on your skin.

DON'T inhale brake lining dust - it is potentially hazardous (see *Asbestos* below).

DON'T allow spilled oil or grease to remain on the floor - wipe it up before someone slips on it.

DON'T use loose fitting wrenches or other tools which may slip and cause injury.

DON'T push on wrenches when loosening or tightening nuts or bolts. Always try to pull the wrench toward you. If the situation calls for pushing the wrench away, push with an open hand to avoid scraped knuckles if the wrench should slip.

DON'T attempt to lift a heavy component alone - get someone to help you.

DON'T rush or take unsafe shortcuts to finish a job.

DON'T allow children or animals in or around the vehicle while you are working on it.

DO wear eye protection when using power tools such as a drill, sander, bench grinder, etc. and when working under a vehicle.

DO keep loose clothing and long hair well out of the way of moving parts.

DO make sure that any hoist used has a safe working load rating adequate for the job.

DO get someone to check on you periodically when working alone on a vehicle.

DO carry out work in a logical sequence and make sure that everything is correctly assembled and tightened.

DO keep chemicals and fluids tightly capped and out of the reach of children and pets.

DO remember that your vehicle's safety affects that of yourself and others. If in doubt on any point, get professional advice.

Asbestos

Certain friction, insulating, sealing, and other products - such as brake linings, brake bands, clutch linings, torque converters, gaskets, etc. - may contain asbestos. Extreme care must be taken to avoid inhalation of dust from such products, since it is hazardous to health. If in doubt, assume that they do contain asbestos.

Fire

Remember at all times that gasoline is highly flammable. Never smoke or have any kind of open flame around when working on a vehicle. But the risk does not end there. A spark caused by an electrical short circuit, by two metal surfaces contacting each other, or even by static electricity built up in your body under certain conditions, can ignite gasoline vapors, which in a confined space are highly explosive. Do not, under any circumstances, use gasoline for cleaning parts. Use an approved safety solvent.

Always disconnect the battery ground (-) cable at the battery before working on any part of the fuel system or electrical system. Never risk spilling fuel on a hot engine or exhaust component. It is strongly recommended that a fire extinguisher suitable for use on fuel and electrical fires be kept handy in the garage or workshop at all times. Never try to extinguish a fuel or electrical fire with water.

Fumes

Certain fumes are highly toxic and can quickly cause unconsciousness and even death if inhaled to any extent. Gasoline vapor falls into this category, as do the vapors from some cleaning solvents. Any draining or pouring of such volatile fluids should be done in a well ventilated area.

When using cleaning fluids and solvents, read the instructions on the container carefully. Never use materials from unmarked containers.

Never run the engine in an enclosed space, such as a garage. Exhaust fumes contain carbon monoxide, which is extremely poisonous. If you need to run the engine, always do so in the open air, or at least have the rear of the vehicle outside the work area.

If you are fortunate enough to have the use of an inspection pit, never drain or pour gasoline and never run the engine while the vehicle is over the pit. The fumes, being heavier than air, will concentrate in the pit with possibly lethal results.

The battery

Never create a spark or allow a bare light bulb near a battery. They normally give off a certain amount of hydrogen gas, which is highly explosive.

Always disconnect the battery ground (-) cable at the battery before working on the fuel or electrical systems.

If possible, loosen the filler caps or cover when charging the battery from an external source (this does not apply to sealed or maintenance-free batteries). Do not charge at an excessive rate or the battery may burst.

Take care when adding water to a non maintenance-free battery and when carrying a battery. The electrolyte, even when diluted, is very corrosive and should not be allowed to contact clothing or skin.

Always wear eye protection when cleaning the battery to prevent the caustic deposits from entering your eyes.

Household current

When using an electric power tool, inspection light, etc., which operates on household current, always make sure that the tool is correctly connected to its plug and that, where necessary, it is properly grounded. Do not use such items in damp conditions and, again, do not create a spark or apply excessive heat in the vicinity of fuel or fuel vapor.

Secondary ignition system voltage

A severe electric shock can result from touching certain parts of the ignition system (such as the spark plug wires) when the engine is running or being cranked, particularly if components are damp or the insulation is defective. In the case of an electronic ignition system, the secondary system voltage is much higher and could prove fatal.

Troubleshooting

Contents

This section provides an easy reference guide to the more common problems which may occur during the operation of your vehicle. These problems and their possible causes are grouped under headings denoting various components or systems, such as Engine, Cooling system, etc. They also refer you to the chapter and/or section which deals with the problem.

Remember that successful troubleshooting is not a mysterious black art practiced only by professional mechanics. It is simply the result of the right knowledge combined with an intelligent, systematic approach to the problem. Always work by a process of elimination, starting with the simplest solution and working through to the most complex - and never overlook the obvious. Anyone can run the gas tank dry or leave the lights on overnight, so don't assume that you are exempt from such oversights.

Finally, always establish a clear idea of why a problem has occurred and take steps to ensure that it doesn't happen again. If the electrical system fails because of a poor connection, check the other connections in the system to make sure that they don't fail as well. If a particular fuse continues to blow, find out why - don't just replace one fuse after another. Remember, failure of a small component can often be indicative of potential failure or incorrect functioning of a more important component or system.

Engine

1 Engine will not rotate when attempting to start

1 Battery terminal connections loose or corroded (Chapter 1).
2 Battery discharged or faulty (Chapter 1).
3 Automatic transaxle not completely engaged in Park (Chapter 7) or clutch pedal not completely depressed (Chapter 8).
4 Broken, loose or disconnected wiring in the starting circuit (Chapters 5 and 12).
5 Starter motor pinion jammed in flywheel ring gear (Chapter 5).
6 Starter solenoid faulty (Chapter 5).
7 Starter motor faulty (Chapter 5).
8 Ignition switch faulty (Chapter 12).
9 Starter pinion or flywheel teeth worn or broken (Chapter 5).
10 Defective fusible link (see Chapter 12).

2 Engine rotates but will not start

1 Fuel tank empty.
2 Battery discharged (engine rotates slowly) (Chapter 5).
3 Battery terminal connections loose or corroded (Chapter 1).
4 Leaking fuel injector(s), faulty fuel pump, pressure regulator, etc. (Chapter 4).
5 Broken or stripped timing belt Chapter 2).
6 Ignition components damp or damaged (Chapter 5).
7 Worn, faulty or incorrectly gapped spark plugs (Chapter 1).
8 Broken, loose or disconnected wiring in the starting circuit (Chapter 5).
9 Broken, loose or disconnected wires at the ignition coils or faulty coils (Chapter 5).
10 Defective crankshaft sensor or PCM (see Chapter 6).

3 Engine hard to start when cold

1 Battery discharged or low (Chapter 1).
2 Malfunctioning fuel system (Chapter 4).
3 Faulty coolant temperature sensor or intake air temperature sensor (Chapter 6).
4 Fuel injector(s) leaking (Chapter 4).
5 Faulty ignition system (Chapter 5).

4 Engine hard to start when hot

1 Air filter clogged (Chapter 1).
2 Fuel not reaching the fuel injection system (Chapter 4).
3 Corroded battery connections, especially ground (Chapter 1).
4 Faulty coolant temperature sensor or intake air temperature sensor (Chapter 6).

5 Starter motor noisy or excessively rough in engagement

1 Pinion or flywheel gear teeth worn or broken (Chapter 5).
2 Starter motor mounting bolts loose or missing (Chapter 5).

6 Engine starts but stops immediately

1 Loose or faulty electrical connections at ignition coil (Chapter 5).
2 Insufficient fuel reaching the fuel injector(s) (Chapters 4).
3 Vacuum leak at the gasket between the intake manifold/plenum and throttle body (Chapter 4).
4 Fault in the engine control system (Chapter 6).
5 Intake air leaks, broken vacuum lines (see Chapter 4)

7 Oil puddle under engine

1 Oil pan gasket and/or oil pan drain bolt washer leaking (Chapter 2).
2 Oil pressure sending unit leaking (Chapter 2).
3 Valve covers leaking (Chapter 2).
4 Engine oil seals leaking (Chapter 2).

8 Engine lopes while idling or idles erratically

1 Vacuum leakage (Chapters 2 and 4).
2 Leaking EGR valve (Chapter 6).
3 Air filter clogged (Chapter 1).
4 Fuel pump not delivering sufficient fuel to the fuel injection system (Chapter 4).
5 Leaking head gasket (Chapter 2).
6 Timing belt and/or pulleys worn (Chapter 2).
7 Camshaft lobes worn (Chapter 2).

9 Engine misses at idle speed

1 Spark plugs worn or not gapped properly (Chapter 1).
2 Faulty spark plug wires (Chapter 1).
3 Vacuum leaks (Chapters 2 and 4).
4 Faulty ignition coil(s) (Chapter 5).
5 Uneven or low compression (Chapter 2).
6 Faulty fuel injector(s) (Chapter 4).

10 Engine misses throughout driving speed range

1 Fuel filter clogged and/or impurities in the fuel system (Chapter 1).
2 Low fuel output at the fuel injector(s) (Chapter 4).
3 Faulty or incorrectly gapped spark plugs (Chapter 1).
4 Leaking spark plug wires (Chapters 1 or 5).
5 Faulty emission system components (Chapter 6).
6 Low or uneven cylinder compression pressures (Chapter 2).
7 Burned valves (Chapter 2).

8 Weak or faulty ignition system (Chapter 5).
9 Vacuum leak in fuel injection system, throttle body, intake manifold or vacuum hoses (Chapter 4).

11 Engine stumbles on acceleration

1 Spark plugs fouled (Chapter 1).
2 Problem with fuel injection system (Chapter 4).
3 Fuel filter clogged (Chapters 1 and 4).
4 Fault in the engine control system (Chapter 6).
5 Intake manifold air leak (Chapters 2 and 4).
6 EGR system malfunction (Chapter 6).

12 Engine surges while holding accelerator steady

1 Intake air leak (Chapter 4).
2 Fuel pump or fuel pressure regulator faulty (Chapter 4).
3 Problem with fuel injection system (Chapter 4).
4 Problem with the emissions control system (Chapter 6).

13 Engine stalls

1 Idle speed incorrect (Chapter 1).
2 Fuel filter clogged and/or water and impurities in the fuel system (Chapters 1 and 4).
3 Ignition components damp or damaged (Chapter 5).
4 Faulty emissions system components (Chapter 6).
5 Faulty or incorrectly gapped spark plugs (Chapter 1).
6 Faulty spark plug wires (Chapter 1).
7 Vacuum leak in the fuel injection system, intake manifold or vacuum hoses (Chapters 2 and 4).

14 Engine lacks power

1 Worn camshaft lobes (Chapter 2).
2 Burned valves or incorrect valve timing (Chapter 2).
3 Faulty spark plug wires or faulty coil (Chapters 1 and 5).
4 Faulty or incorrectly gapped spark plugs (Chapter 1).
5 Problem with the fuel injection system (Chapter 4).
6 Plugged air filter (Chapter 1).
7 Brakes binding (Chapter 9).
8 Automatic transaxle fluid level incorrect (Chapter 1).
9 Clutch slipping (Chapter 8).
10 Fuel filter clogged and/or impurities in the fuel system (Chapters 1 and 4).
11 Emission control system not functioning properly (Chapter 6).
12 Low or uneven cylinder compression pressures (Chapter 2).
13 Restricted exhaust system (Chapters 4).

15 Engine backfires

1 Emission control system not functioning properly (Chapter 6).
2 Faulty spark plug wires or coil(s) (Chapter 5).
3 Problem with the fuel injection system (Chapter 4).
4 Vacuum leak at fuel injector(s), intake manifold or vacuum hoses (Chapters 2 and 4).
5 Burned valves or incorrect valve timing (Chapter 2).

16 Pinging or knocking engine sounds during acceleration or uphill

1 Incorrect grade of fuel.
2 Problem with the engine control system (Chapter 6).
3 Fuel injection system faulty (Chapter 4).
4 Improper or damaged spark plugs or wires (Chapter 1).
5 EGR valve not functioning (Chapter 6).
6 Vacuum leak (Chapters 2 and 4).

17 Engine runs with oil pressure light on

1 Low oil level (Chapter 1).
2 Idle rpm below specification (Chapter 1).
3 Short in wiring circuit (Chapter 12).
4 Faulty oil pressure sender (Chapter 2).
5 Worn engine bearings and/or oil pump (Chapter 2).

18 Engine diesels (continues to run) after switching off

1 Idle speed too high (Chapter 1).
2 Excessive engine operating temperature (Chapter 3).
3 Excessive carbon deposits on valves and pistons (see Chapter 2).

Engine electrical system

19 Battery will not hold a charge

1 Alternator drivebelt defective or not adjusted properly (Chapter 1).
2 Battery electrolyte level low (Chapter 1).
3 Battery terminals loose or corroded (Chapter 1).
4 Alternator not charging properly (Chapter 5).
5 Loose, broken or faulty wiring in the charging circuit (Chapter 5).
6 Short in vehicle wiring (Chapter 12).
7 Internally defective battery (Chapters 1 and 5).

20 Alternator light fails to go out

1 Faulty alternator or charging circuit (Chapter 5).
2 Alternator drivebelt defective or out of adjustment (Chapter 1).
3 Alternator voltage regulator inoperative (Chapter 5).

21 Alternator light fails to come on when key is turned on

1 Warning light bulb defective (Chapter 12).
2 Fault in the printed circuit, dash wiring or bulb holder (Chapter 12).

Fuel system

22 Excessive fuel consumption

1 Dirty or clogged air filter element (Chapter 1).
2 Emissions system not functioning properly (Chapter 6).
3 Fuel injection system not functioning properly (Chapter 4).
4 Low tire pressure or incorrect tire size (Chapter 1).

23 Fuel leakage and/or fuel odor

1 Leaking fuel feed or return line (Chapters 1 and 4).
2 Tank overfilled.
3 Evaporative canister filter clogged (Chapters 1 and 6).
4 Problem with fuel injection system (Chapter 4).

Cooling system

24 Overheating

1 Insufficient coolant in system (Chapter 1).
2 Water pump defective (Chapter 3).
3 Radiator core blocked or grille restricted (Chapter 3).
4 Thermostat faulty (Chapter 3).
5 Electric coolant fan inoperative or blades broken (Chapter 3).
6 Radiator cap not maintaining proper pressure (Chapter 3).

25 Overcooling

1 Faulty thermostat (Chapter 3).
2 Inaccurate temperature gauge sending unit (Chapter 3).

26 External coolant leakage

1 Deteriorated/damaged hoses; loose clamps (Chapters 1 and 3).
2 Water pump defective (Chapter 3).
3 Leakage from radiator core or coolant reservoir bottle (Chapter 3).
4 Engine drain or water jacket core plugs leaking (Chapter 2).

27 Internal coolant leakage

1 Leaking cylinder head gasket (Chapter 2).
2 Cracked cylinder bore or cylinder head (Chapter 2).

28 Coolant loss

1 Too much coolant in system (Chapter 1).
2 Coolant boiling away because of overheating (Chapter 3).
3 Internal or external leakage (Chapter 3).
4 Faulty pressure cap (Chapter 3).

29 Poor coolant circulation

1 Inoperative water pump (Chapter 3).
2 Restriction in cooling system (Chapters 1 and 3).
3 Thermostat sticking (Chapter 3).

Clutch

30 Pedal travels to floor - no pressure or very little resistance

1 Master cylinder or release cylinder faulty (Chapter 8).
2 Fluid line, hose or connection leaking (Chapter 8).
3 No fluid in reservoir (Chapter 8).
4 Broken release bearing or fork (Chapter 8).

31 Unable to select gears

1 Faulty transaxle (Chapter 7).
2 Faulty clutch disc or pressure plate (Chapter 8).
3 Faulty release lever or release bearing (Chapter 8).
4 Faulty shift lever assembly or rods (Chapter 8).

32 Clutch slips (engine speed increases with no increase in vehicle speed)

1 Clutch plate worn (Chapter 8).
2 Clutch plate is oil soaked by leaking rear main seal (Chapter 8).
3 Clutch plate not seated (Chapter 8).
4 Warped pressure plate or flywheel (Chapter 8).
5 Weak diaphragm springs (Chapter 8).
6 Clutch plate overheated. Allow to cool.

33 Grabbing (chattering) as clutch is engaged

1 Oil on clutch plate lining, burned or glazed facings (Chapter 8).
2 Worn or loose engine or transaxle mounts (Chapters 2 and 7).
3 Worn splines on clutch plate hub (Chapter 8).
4 Warped pressure plate or flywheel (Chapter 8).
5 Burned or smeared resin on flywheel or pressure plate (Chapter 8).

34 Transaxle rattling (clicking)

1 Release fork loose (Chapter 8).
2 Low engine idle speed (Chapter 1).

35 Noise in clutch area

Faulty bearing (Chapter 8).

36 Clutch pedal stays on floor

1 Broken release bearing or fork (Chapter 8).
2 Clutch master cylinder piston binding in bore (Chapter 8).

37 High pedal effort

1 Master cylinder piston binding in bore (Chapter 8).
2 Pressure plate faulty (Chapter 8).

Manual transaxle

38 Knocking noise at low speeds

1 Worn driveaxle constant velocity (CV) joints (Chapter 8).
2 Worn side gear shaft counterbore in differential case (Chapter 7A).*

39 Noise most pronounced when turning

Differential gear noise (Chapter 7A).*

40 Clunk on acceleration or deceleration

1 Loose engine or transaxle mounts (Chapters 2 and 7A).
2 Worn differential pinion shaft in case.*
3 Worn side gear shaft counterbore in differential case (Chapter 7A).*
4 Worn or damaged driveaxle inboard CV joints (Chapter 8).

41 Clicking noise in turns

Worn or damaged outboard CV joint (Chapter 8).

42 Vibration

1 Rough wheel bearing (Chapters 1 and 10).
2 Damaged driveaxle (Chapter 8).
3 Out of round tires (Chapter 1).
4 Tire out of balance (Chapters 1 and 10).
5 Worn CV joint (Chapter 8).

43 Noisy in neutral with engine running

1 Damaged input gear bearing (Chapter 7A).*
2 Damaged clutch release bearing (Chapter 8).

44 Noisy in one particular gear

1 Damaged or worn constant mesh gears (Chapter 7A).*
2 Damaged or worn synchronizers (Chapter 7A).*
3 Bent reverse fork (Chapter 7A).*
4 Damaged fourth speed gear or output gear (Chapter 7A).*
5 Worn or damaged reverse idler gear or idler bushing (Chapter 7A).*

45 Noisy in all gears

1 Insufficient lubricant (Chapter 7A).
2 Damaged or worn bearings (Chapter 7A).*
3 Worn or damaged input gear shaft and/or output gear shaft (Chapter 7A).*

46 Slips out of gear

1 Worn or improperly adjusted linkage (Chapter 7A).
2 Transaxle loose on engine (Chapter 7A).
3 Shift linkage does not work freely, binds (Chapter 7A).
4 Input gear bearing retainer broken or loose (Chapter 7A).*
5 Foreign material between clutch cover and engine housing (Chapter 7A).
6 Worn shift fork (Chapter 7A).*

47 Leaks lubricant

1 Driveshaft seals worn (Chapter 7A).
2 Excessive amount of lubricant in transaxle (Chapters 1 and 7A).
3 Loose or broken input gear shaft bearing retainer (Chapter 7A).*
4 Input gear bearing retainer O-ring and/or lip seal damaged (Chapter 7A).*
5 Vehicle speed sensor O-ring leaking (Chapter 7A).

48 Hard to shift

Shift linkage loose or worn (Chapter 7A).

** Although the corrective action necessary to remedy the symptoms described is beyond the scope of this manual, the above information should be helpful in isolating the cause of the condition so that the owner can communicate clearly with a professional mechanic.*

Automatic transaxle

Note: *Due to the complexity of the automatic transaxle, it is difficult for the home mechanic to properly diagnose and service this component. For problems other than the following, the vehicle should be taken to a dealer or transaxle shop.*

49 Fluid leakage

1 Automatic transaxle fluid is a deep red color. Fluid leaks should not be confused with engine oil, which can easily be blown onto the transaxle by air flow.
2 To pinpoint a leak, first remove all built-up dirt and grime from the transaxle housing with degreasing agents and/or steam cleaning. Then drive the vehicle at low speeds so air flow will not blow the leak far from its source. Raise the vehicle and determine where the leak is coming from. Common areas of leakage are:

a) Pan (Chapters 1 and 7)
b) Dipstick tube (Chapters 1 and 7)
c) Transaxle oil lines (Chapter 7)
d) Speed sensor (Chapter 7)
e) Driveaxle oil seals (Chapter 7).

50 Transaxle fluid brown or has a burned smell

Transaxle fluid overheated (Chapter 1).

51 General shift mechanism problems

1 Chapter 7, Part B, deals with checking and adjusting the shift linkage on automatic transaxles. Common problems which may be attributed to poorly adjusted linkage are:

a) Engine starting in gears other than Park or Neutral.
b) Indicator on shifter pointing to a gear other than the one actually being used.
c) Vehicle moves when in Park.

2 Refer to Chapter 7B for the shift linkage adjustment procedure.

52 Transaxle will not downshift with accelerator pedal pressed to the floor

The transaxle is electronically controlled. This type of problem - which is caused by a malfunction in the control unit, a sensor or solenoid, or the circuit itself - is beyond the scope of this book. Take the vehicle to a dealer service department or a competent automatic transmission shop.

53 Engine will start in gears other than Park or Neutral

Neutral start switch out of adjustment or malfunctioning (Chapter 7B).

54 Transaxle slips, shifts roughly, is noisy or has no drive in forward or reverse gears

There are many probable causes for the above problems, but the home mechanic should be concerned with only one possibility - fluid level. Before taking the vehicle to a repair shop, check the level and condition of the fluid as described in Chapter 1. Correct the fluid level as necessary or change the fluid and filter if needed. If the problem persists, have a professional diagnose the cause.

Driveaxles

55 Clicking noise in turns

Worn or damaged outboard CV joint (Chapter 8).

56 Shudder or vibration during acceleration

1 Excessive toe-in (Chapter 10).
2 Incorrect spring heights (Chapter 10).
3 Worn or damaged inboard or outboard CV joints (Chapter 8).
4 Sticking inboard CV joint assembly (Chapter 8).

57 Vibration at highway speeds

1 Out of balance front wheels and/or tires (Chapters 1 and 10).
2 Out of round front tires (Chapters 1 and 10).
3 Worn CV joint(s) (Chapter 8).

Brakes

Note: *Before assuming that a brake problem exists, make sure that:*
- a) *The tires are in good condition and properly inflated (Chapter 1).*
- b) *The front end alignment is correct (Chapter 10).*
- c) *The vehicle is not loaded with weight in an unequal manner.*

58 Vehicle pulls to one side during braking

1 Incorrect tire pressures (Chapter 1).
2 Front end out of alignment (have the front end aligned).
3 Front, or rear, tire sizes not matched to one another.
4 Restricted brake lines or hoses (Chapter 9).
5 Malfunctioning drum brake or caliper assembly (Chapter 9).
6 Loose suspension parts (Chapter 10).
7 Loose calipers (Chapter 9).
8 Excessive wear of brake shoe or pad material or disc/drum on one side.

59 Noise (high-pitched squeal when the brakes are applied)

Front and/or rear disc brake pads worn out. The noise comes from the wear sensor rubbing against the disc (does not apply to all vehicles). Replace pads with new ones immediately (Chapter 9).

60 Brake roughness or chatter (pedal pulsates)

1 Excessive lateral runout (Chapter 9).
2 Uneven pad wear (Chapter 9).
3 Defective disc (Chapter 9).

61 Excessive brake pedal effort required to stop vehicle

1 Malfunctioning power brake booster (Chapter 9).
2 Partial system failure (Chapter 9).
3 Excessively worn pads or shoes (Chapter 9).
4 Piston in caliper or wheel cylinder stuck or sluggish (Chapter 9).
5 Brake pads or shoes contaminated with oil or grease (Chapter 9).
6 Brake disc grooved and/or glazed (Chapter 1).
7 New pads or shoes installed and not yet seated. It will take a while for the new material to seat against the disc or drum.

62 Excessive brake pedal travel

1 Partial brake system failure (Chapter 9).
2 Insufficient fluid in master cylinder (Chapters 1 and 9).
3 Air trapped in system (Chapters 1 and 9).

63 Dragging brakes

1 Incorrect adjustment of brake light switch (Chapter 9).
2 Master cylinder pistons not returning correctly (Chapter 9).
3 Restricted brakes lines or hoses (Chapters 1 and 9).
4 Incorrect parking brake adjustment (Chapter 9).

64 Grabbing or uneven braking action

1 Malfunction of proportioning valve (Chapter 9).
2 Malfunction of power brake booster unit (Chapter 9).
3 Binding brake pedal mechanism (Chapter 9).

65 Brake pedal feels spongy when depressed

1 Air in hydraulic lines (Chapter 9).
2 Master cylinder mounting bolts loose (Chapter 9).
3 Master cylinder defective (Chapter 9).

66 Brake pedal travels to the floor with little resistance

1 Little or no fluid in the master cylinder reservoir caused by leaking caliper piston(s) (Chapter 9).
2 Loose, damaged or disconnected brake lines (Chapter 9).

67 Parking brake does not hold

Parking brake linkage improperly adjusted (Chapters 1 and 9).

Suspension and steering systems

Note: *Before attempting to diagnose the suspension and steering systems, perform the following preliminary checks:*
- a) *Tires for wrong pressure and uneven wear.*
- b) *Steering universal joints from the column to the rack and pinion for loose connectors or wear.*
- c) *Front and rear suspension and the rack and pinion assembly for loose or damaged parts.*
- d) *Out-of-round or out-of-balance tires, bent rims and loose and/or rough wheel bearings.*

68 Vehicle pulls to one side

1 Mismatched or uneven tires (Chapter 10).
2 Broken or sagging springs (Chapter 10).
3 Wheel alignment out-of-specifications (Chapter 10).
4 Front brake dragging (Chapter 9).

69 Abnormal or excessive tire wear

1 Wheel alignment out-of-specifications (Chapter 10).

2 Sagging or broken springs (Chapter 10).
3 Tire out-of-balance (Chapter 10).
4 Worn strut damper (Chapter 10).
5 Overloaded vehicle.
6 Tires not rotated regularly.

70 Wheel makes a thumping noise

1 Blister or bump on tire (Chapter 10).
2 Improper strut damper action (Chapter 10).

71 Shimmy, shake or vibration

1 Tire or wheel out-of-balance or out-of-round (Chapter 10).
2 Loose or worn wheel bearings (Chapters 1, 8 and 10).
3 Worn tie-rod ends (Chapter 10).
4 Worn lower balljoints (Chapters 1 and 10).
5 Excessive wheel runout (Chapter 10).
6 Blister or bump on tire (Chapter 10).

72 Hard steering

1 Lack of lubrication at balljoints, tie-rod ends and rack and pinion assembly (Chapter 10).
2 Front wheel alignment out-of-specifications (Chapter 10).
3 Low tire pressure(s) (Chapters 1 and 10).

73 Poor returnability of steering to center

1 Lack of lubrication at balljoints and tie-rod ends (Chapter 10).
2 Binding in balljoints (Chapter 10).
3 Binding in steering column (Chapter 10).
4 Lack of lubricant in steering gear assembly (Chapter 10).
5 Front wheel alignment out-of-specifications (Chapter 10).

74 Abnormal noise at the front end

1 Lack of lubrication at balljoints and tie-rod ends (Chapters 1 and 10).
2 Damaged strut mounting (Chapter 10).
3 Worn control arm bushings or tie-rod ends (Chapter 10).
4 Loose stabilizer bar (Chapter 10).
5 Loose wheel nuts (Chapters 1 and 10).
6 Loose suspension bolts (Chapter 10)

75 Wander or poor steering stability

1 Mismatched or uneven tires (Chapter 10).
2 Lack of lubrication at balljoints and tie-rod ends (Chapters 1 and 10).
3 Worn strut assemblies (Chapter 10).
4 Loose stabilizer bar (Chapter 10).
5 Broken or sagging springs (Chapter 10).
6 Wheels out of alignment (Chapter 10).

76 Erratic steering when braking

1 Wheel bearings worn (Chapter 10).
2 Broken or sagging springs (Chapter 10).
3 Leaking wheel cylinder or caliper (Chapter 10).
4 Warped rotors or drums (Chapter 10).

77 Excessive pitching and/or rolling around corners or during braking

1 Loose stabilizer bar (Chapter 10).
2 Worn strut dampers or mountings (Chapter 10).
3 Broken or sagging springs (Chapter 10).
4 Overloaded vehicle.

78 Suspension bottoms

1 Overloaded vehicle.
2 Worn strut dampers (Chapter 10).
3 Incorrect, broken or sagging springs (Chapter 10).

79 Cupped tires

1 Front wheel or rear wheel alignment out-of-specifications (Chapter 10).
2 Worn strut dampers (Chapter 10).
3 Wheel bearings worn (Chapter 10).
4 Excessive tire or wheel runout (Chapter 10).
5 Worn balljoints (Chapter 10).

80 Excessive tire wear on outside edge

1 Inflation pressures incorrect (Chapter 1).
2 Excessive speed in turns.
3 Front end alignment incorrect (excessive toe-in). Have professionally aligned.
4 Suspension arm bent or twisted (Chapter 10).

81 Excessive tire wear on inside edge

1 Inflation pressures incorrect (Chapter 1).
2 Front end alignment incorrect (toe-out). Have professionally aligned.
3 Loose or damaged steering components (Chapter 10).

82 Tire tread worn in one place

1 Tires out-of-balance.
2 Damaged or buckled wheel. Inspect and replace if necessary.
3 Defective tire (Chapter 1).

83 Excessive play or looseness in steering system

1 Wheel bearing(s) worn (Chapter 10).
2 Tie-rod end loose (Chapter 10).
3 Steering gear loose (Chapter 10).
4 Worn or loose steering intermediate shaft (Chapter 10).

84 Rattling or clicking noise in steering gear

1 Steering gear loose (Chapter 10).
2 Steering gear defective.

Notes

Chapter 1
Tune-up and routine maintenance

Contents

Specifications

Recommended lubricants and fluids

Note: *Listed here are manufacturer recommendations at the time this manual was written. Manufacturers occasionally upgrade their fluid and lubricant specifications, so check with your local auto parts store for current recommendations.*

Engine oil	
Type	API Service SG or SH Energy Conserving II (ECII)
Viscosity	See accompanying chart
Fuel	Unleaded gasoline, 87 octane or higher
Automatic transaxle fluid	DEXRON II automatic transmission fluid
Manual transaxle lubricant	
1.5L DOHC, 1.6L and 1.8L SOHC engines	API GL-5, SAE 75W-90 gear oil
1.8L DOHC engine	API GL-5, SAE 75W-80 gear oil
Brake/clutch fluid	DOT 3 brake fluid
Power steering fluid	DEXRON II automatic transmission fluid

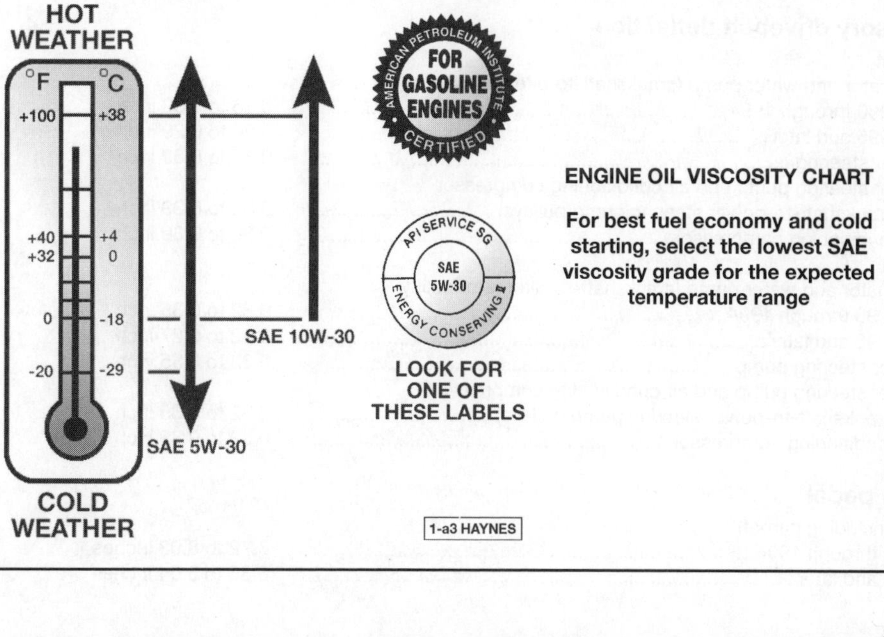

Capacities*

Engine oil (including filter)	
1.5L engine	3.4 quarts
1.6L engine	3.6 quarts
1.8L engine	4.2 quarts
Engine coolant	
1990 through 1994	
Manual transaxle	5.3 quarts
Automatic transaxle	6.3 quarts
1995 and later	6.3 quarts
Transaxle lubricant	
Manual	
1.6L and 1.8L SOHC engines	2.83 quarts
1.8L DOHC engine	3.55 quarts
Automatic	
1990 and 1991	6.1 quarts
1992 through 1994	6.7 quarts
1995 and later	5.7 quarts

**All capacities approximate. Add as necessary to bring up to appropriate level.*

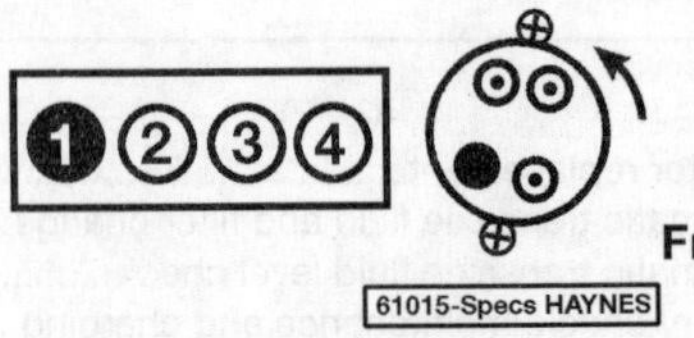

Cylinder location and distributor rotation

The blackened terminal shown on the distributor cap indicates the Number One spark plug wire position

Ignition system

Spark plug type	
1990 through 1991	
1.6L engine	NGK BPR5ES11, BPR6ES11 or equivalents
1.8L engine	NGK BKR5E11, BKR6E11 or equivalents
1992	NGK BKR5E11, BKR6E11 or equivalents
1993 through 1994	
California	NGK BKR5E11, BKR6E11 or equivalents
Federal and Canada	NGK BPR5ES11, BPR6ES11 or equivalents
1995 and later	NGK BKR5E11 or equivalent
Spark plug gap	0.040 to 0.043 inch
Spark plug wire resistance	400 ohms per inch
Engine firing order	1-3-4-2

Valve clearance (engine cold)

1.5L DOHC engine	
Intake valve	0.010 to 0.012 inch
Exhaust valve	0.010 to 0.012 inch
1997 1.8L DOHC engine	
Intake valve	0.008 to 0.009 inch
Exhaust valve	0.012 to 0.013 inch

Cooling system

Thermostat	
Starts to open	183- to 193-degrees F
Fully open	212-degrees F

Accessory drivebelt deflection

Used belt	
Alternator and water pump (crankshaft-to-alternator pulley)	
1990 through 1994	0.36 to 0.39 inch
1995 and later	0.24 to 0.29 inch
Power steering	0.36 to 0.39 inch
Power steering pump and air conditioning compressor (crankshaft-to-power steering pump pulleys)	0.36 to 0.39 inch
Air conditioning compressor	0.36 to 0.39 inch
New belt	
Alternator and water pump (crankshaft-to-alternator pulley)	
1990 through 1994	0.32 to 0.35 inch
1995 and later	0.22 to 0.27 inch
Power steering pump	0.32 to 0.35 inch
Power steering pump and air conditioning compressor (crankshaft-to-power steering pump pulleys)	0.32 to 0.35 inch
Air conditioning compressor	0.32 to 0.35 inch

Clutch pedal

Height (including carpet)	
1990 through 1994	7.72 to 8.03 inches
1995 and later	8.35 to 8.54 inches

Freeplay	
1990 through 1991	0.22 to 0.69 inch
1992 through 1994	0.197 to 0.512 inch
1995 and later	0.03 to 0.13 inch
Disengagement height (minimum - including carpet)	
1990 through 1994	1.61 inches
1995 and later	2.3 inches

Brakes

Front disc brake pad lining thickness (minimum)	
1990 through 1994	0.08 inch
1995 and later	0.04 inch
Rear disc brake pad lining thickness (minimum)	0.04 inch
Drum brake shoe lining thickness (minimum)	0.04 inch
Parking brake adjustment	5 to 7 clicks

Suspension and steering

Steering wheel freeplay limit	1.18 inches
Balljoint allowable movement	0 inch

Torque specifications

	Ft-lbs (unless otherwise indicated)
Engine oil drain plug	22 to 30
Spark plugs	
1990 through 1994	168 in-lbs
1995 and later	132 to 192 in-lbs
Automatic transaxle	
Drain plug	29 to 39
Oil pan bolts	74 to 95 in-lbs
Oil strainer/filter bolts	70 to 95 in-lbs
Manual transaxle	
Speedometer driven gear retaining bolt	70 to 104 in-lbs
Level and fill plug (1995 and later models)	29 to 43
Drain plug	29 to 39
Wheel lug nuts	
1990 through 1994	65 to 87
1995 and later	66 to 94

1

Typical engine compartment components

1 *Engine oil dipstick*
2 *Power steering fluid reservoir*
3 *Brake fluid reservoir*
4 *Main fuse/relay block*
5 *Battery*
6 *Air cleaner assembly*
7 *Coolant reservoir*
8 *Automatic transaxle dipstick*
9 *Distributor*
10 *PCV valve*
11 *Radiator cap*
12 *Spark plug*
13 *Oil filler cap*
14 *Drivebelts*
15 *Windshield washer fluid reservoir*

Typical engine compartment underside components

1. *Driveaxle boot*
2. *Automatic transaxle drain plug*
3. *Exhaust system catalytic converter*
4. *Engine oil drain plug*
5. *Front suspension strut unit*
6. *Radiator drain fitting*
7. *Front disc brake caliper*

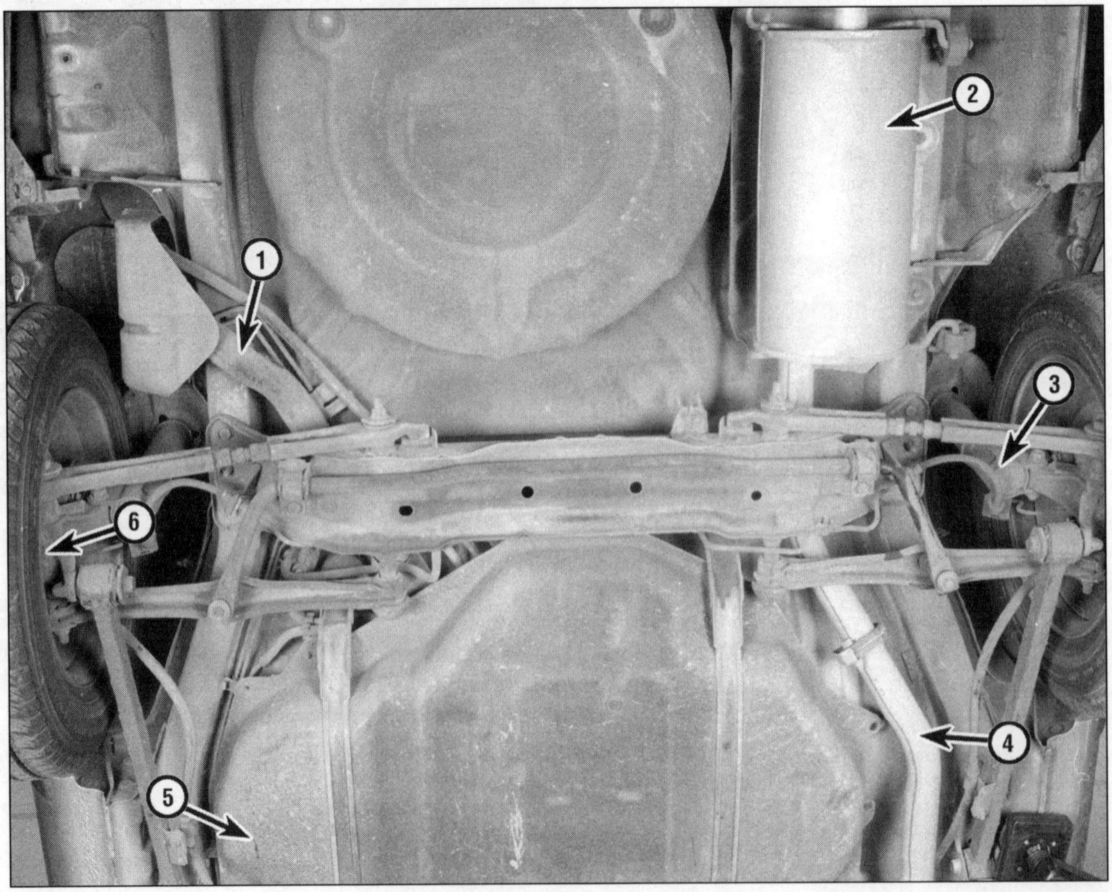

Typical rear underside components

1. *Gas tank filler pipe*
2. *Muffler*
3. *Suspension strut*
4. *Exhaust pipe*
5. *Gas tank*
6. *Rear brake assembly*

1 Mazda 323 and Protegé Maintenance schedule

The maintenance intervals in this manual are provided with the assumption that you, not the dealer, will be doing the work. These are the minimum maintenance intervals recommended by the factory for vehicles that are driven daily. If you wish to keep your vehicle in peak condition at all times, you may wish to perform some of these procedures even more often. Because frequent maintenance enhances the efficiency, performance and resale value of your car, we encourage you to do so. If you drive in dusty areas, tow a trailer, idle or drive at low speeds for extended periods or drive for short distances (less than four miles) in below freezing temperatures, shorter intervals are also recommended.

When your vehicle is new, it should be serviced by a factory authorized dealer service department to protect the factory warranty. In many cases, the initial maintenance check is done at no cost to the owner.

Every 250 miles or weekly, whichever comes first

Check the engine oil level (Section 4)
Check the engine coolant level (Section 4)
Check the windshield washer fluid level (Section 4)
Check the brake/clutch fluid level (Section 4)
Check the tires and tire pressures (Section 5)

Every 3000 miles or 3 months, whichever comes first

All items listed above plus:

Change the engine oil and oil filter (Section 6)
Rotate the tires (Section 7)

Every 7500 miles or 6 months, whichever comes first

Check the power steering fluid level (Section 8)
Check the automatic transaxle fluid level (Section 9)
Inspect and replace if necessary the windshield wiper blades (Section 10)
Check the clutch pedal for proper height and freeplay (Section 11)
Check and service the battery (Section 12)
Check and adjust if necessary the engine drivebelts (Section 13)
Inspect and replace if necessary all underhood hoses (Section 14)
Check the cooling system (Section 15)

Every 15,000 miles or 12 months, whichever comes first

All items listed above plus:

Inspect the brake system (Section 16)*
Replace the air filter (Section 17)
Check the manual transaxle lubricant level (Section 18)
Inspect the steering and suspension components (Section 19)*
Check the driveaxle boots (Section 20)

Every 30,000 miles or 24 months, whichever comes first

All items listed above plus:

Inspect the fuel system (Section 21)
Replace the spark plugs (Section 22)
Inspect and replace if necessary the spark plug wires, distributor cap and rotor (Section 23)
Service the cooling system (drain, flush and refill) (Section 24)
Inspect the fuel evaporative emissions control system (Section 25)
Inspect the exhaust system (Section 26)
Change the automatic transaxle fluid (Section 27)**
Change the manual transaxle lubricant (Section 28)**
Check and replace if necessary the PCV valve (Section 29)

Every 60,000 miles or 48 months, whichever comes first

Replace the fuel filter (Section 30)
Replace the timing belt (Chapter 2A)
Check and adjust valve clearance (1.5L DOHC engine only) (Section 31)

**This item is affected by "severe" operating conditions as described below. If your vehicle is operated under "severe" conditions, perform all maintenance indicated with an asterisk (*) at 3000 mile/3 month intervals. Severe conditions are indicated if you mainly operate your vehicle under one or more of the following conditions:*

Operating in dusty areas
Towing a trailer
Idling for extended periods and/or low speed operation
Operating when outside temperatures remain below freezing and when most trips are less than four miles

***If operated under one or more of the following conditions, change the manual or automatic transaxle fluid and differential lubricant every 15,000 miles:*

In heavy city traffic where the outside temperature regularly reaches 90-degrees F (32-degrees C) or higher
In hilly or mountainous terrain
Frequent trailer pulling

1

4.2 The engine oil dipstick location (arrow)

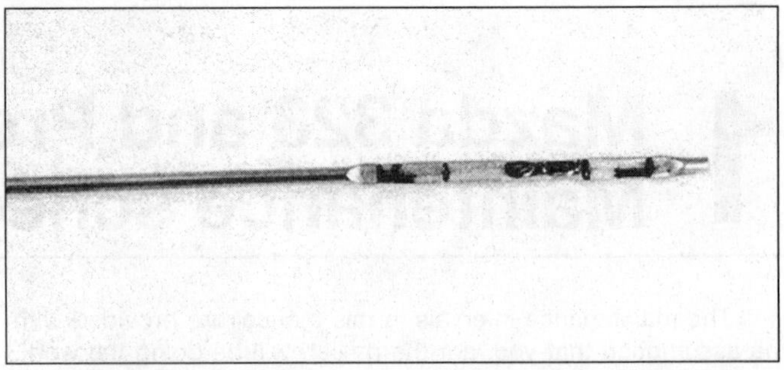
4.4 The oil level should be at or near the F mark - if it isn't, add enough oil to bring the level to near the F mark (it takes slightly less than 14 ounces to raise the level from the L to the F mark)

2 Introduction to routine maintenance

This Chapter is designed to help the home mechanic maintain the Mazda 323 or Protegé for peak performance, economy, safety and long life.

Included is a master maintenance schedule, followed by sections dealing specifically with each item on the schedule. Visual checks, adjustments, component replacement and other helpful items are included. Refer to the **accompanying illustrations** of the engine compartment and the underside of the vehicle for the location of various components.

Servicing your 323 or Protegé in accordance with the mileage/time maintenance schedule and the following Sections will provide it with a planned maintenance program that should result in a long and reliable service life. This is a comprehensive plan, so maintaining some items but not others at the specified service intervals will not produce the same results.

As you service your 323 or Protegé, you will discover that many of the procedures can - and should - be grouped together because of the nature of the particular procedure you're performing or because of the close proximity of two otherwise unrelated components to one another.

For example, if the vehicle is raised for any reason, you should inspect the exhaust, suspension, steering and fuel systems while you're under the vehicle. When you're rotating the tires, it makes good sense to check the brakes and wheel bearings since the wheels are already removed.

Finally, let's suppose you have to borrow or rent a torque wrench. Even if you only need to tighten the spark plugs, you might as well check the torque of as many critical fasteners as time allows.

The first step of this maintenance program is to prepare yourself before the actual work begins. Read through all Sections pertinent to the procedures you're planning to do, then make a list of and gather together all the parts and tools you will need to do the job. If it looks as if you might run into problems during a particular segment of some procedure, seek advice from your local parts man or dealer service department.

3 Tune-up - general information

The term tune-up is used in this manual to represent a combination of individual operations rather than one specific procedure.

If, from the time the vehicle is new, the routine maintenance schedule is followed closely and frequent checks are made of fluid levels and high wear items, as suggested throughout this manual, the engine will be kept in relatively good running condition and the need for additional work will be minimized.

More likely than not, however, there will be times when the engine is running poorly due to lack of regular maintenance. This is even more likely if a used vehicle, which has not received regular and frequent maintenance checks, is purchased. In such cases, an engine tune-up will be needed outside of the regular routine maintenance intervals.

The first step in any tune-up or engine diagnosis to help correct a poor running engine would be a cylinder compression check. A check of the engine compression (Chapter 2, Part B) will give valuable information regarding the overall performance of many internal components and should be used as a basis for tune-up and repair procedures. If, for instance, a compression check indicates serious internal engine wear, a conventional tune-up will not help the running condition of the engine and would be a waste of time and money.

The following series of operations are those most often needed to bring a generally poor running engine back into a proper state of tune.

Minor tune-up

Clean, inspect and test the battery (Section 12)
Check all engine related fluids (Section 4)
Check and adjust the drivebelts (Section 13)
Replace the spark plugs (Section 22)
Inspect the distributor cap and rotor (Section 23)
Inspect the spark plug and coil wires (Section 23)
Check all underhood hoses (Section 14)
Check the cooling system (Section 15)
Check the air filter (Section 17)

Major tune-up

All items listed under Minor tune-up, plus . . .

Check the ignition system (Section 23)
Check the charging system (Chapter 5)
Check the fuel system (Section 21)
Replace the air filter (Section 17)
Replace the distributor cap and rotor (Section 23)
Replace the spark plug wires (Section 23)

4 Fluid level checks (every 250 miles or weekly)

1 Fluids are an essential part of the lubrication, cooling, brake, clutch and other systems. Because these fluids gradually become depleted and/or contaminated during normal operation of the vehicle, they must be periodically replenished. See *Recommended lubricants and fluids and Capacities* at the beginning of this Chapter before adding fluid to any of the following components. **Note:** *The vehicle must be on level ground before fluid levels can be checked.*

Engine oil

Refer to illustrations 4.2, 4.4 and 4.6

2 The engine oil level is checked with a dipstick located on the right side of the engine compartment at the front of the engine **(see illustration)**. The dipstick extends through a metal tube from which it pro-

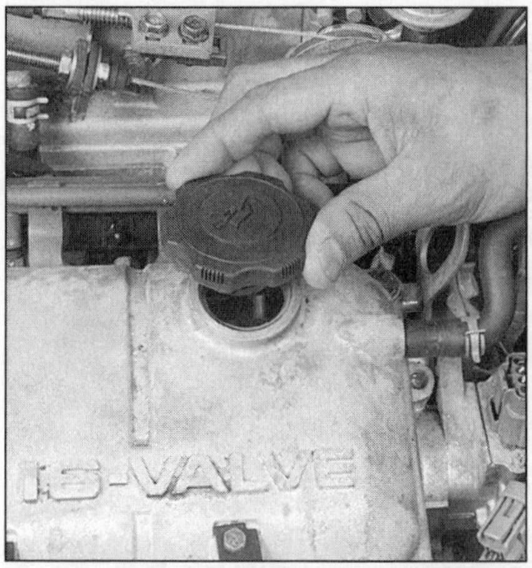

4.6 **The threaded oil filler cap is located on the valve cover - always make sure the area around the opening is clean before unscrewing the cap to prevent dirt from contaminating the engine**

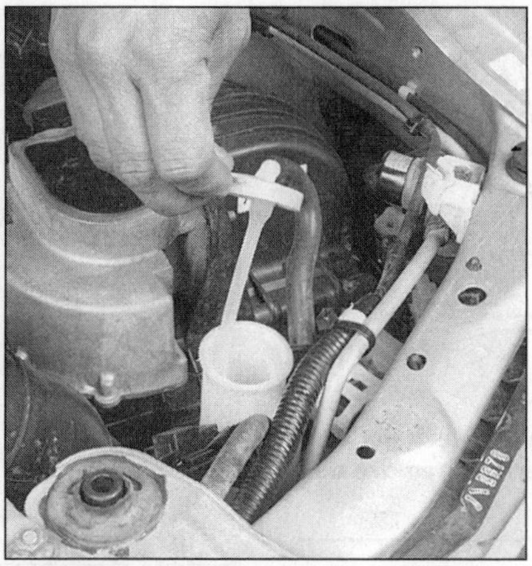

4.9 **The coolant reservoir is located in the left front corner of the engine compartment - make sure the level is between the F and L marks on the dipstick attached to the reservoir cap**

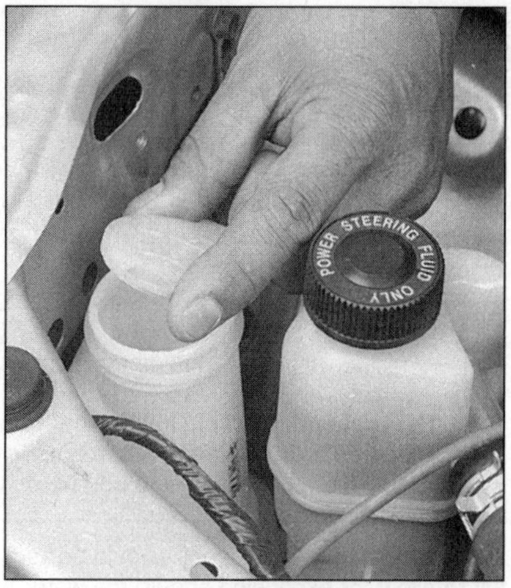

4.14 **The windshield washer fluid reservoir tank is located on the right front corner of the engine compartment**

trudes down into the engine oil pan.

3 The oil level should be checked before the vehicle has been driven, or about 15 minutes after the engine has been shut off. If the oil is checked immediately after driving the vehicle, some of the oil will remain in the upper engine components, producing an inaccurate reading on the dipstick.

4 Pull the dipstick from the tube and wipe all the oil from the end with a clean rag or paper towel. Insert the clean dipstick all the way back into its metal tube and pull it out again. Observe the oil at the end of the dipstick. At its highest point, the level should be between the L (Low) and F (Full) marks **(see illustration)**.

5 It takes slightly less than 14 ounces of oil to raise the level from the L mark to the F mark on the dipstick. Do not allow the level to drop below the L mark or oil starvation may cause engine damage. Conversely, overfilling the engine (adding oil above the F mark) may cause oil fouled spark plugs, oil leaks or oil seal failures.

6 Remove the threaded cap from the valve cover to add oil **(see illustration)**. Use a funnel to prevent spills. After adding the oil, install the filler cap hand tight. Start the engine and look carefully for any small leaks around the oil filter or drain plug. Stop the engine and check the oil level again after it has had sufficient time to drain from the upper block and cylinder head galleys.

7 Checking the oil level is an important preventive maintenance step. A continually dropping oil level indicates oil leakage through damaged seals, from loose connections, or past worn rings or valve guides. If the oil looks milky in color or has water droplets in it, a cylinder head gasket may be blown. The engine should be checked immediately. The condition of the oil should also be checked. Each time you check the oil level, slide your thumb and index finger up the dipstick before wiping off the oil. If you see small dirt or metal particles clinging to the dipstick, the oil should be changed (Section 6).

Engine coolant

Refer to illustration 4.9

Warning: *Do not allow antifreeze to come in contact with your skin or painted surfaces of the vehicle. Flush contaminated areas immediately with plenty of water. Don't store new coolant or leave old coolant lying around where it's accessible to children or pets - they're attracted by its sweet smell and may drink it. Ingestion of even a small amount of coolant can be fatal! Wipe up garage floor and drip pan spills immediately. Keep antifreeze containers covered and repair cooling system leaks as soon as they're noticed.*

8 All vehicles covered by this manual are equipped with a pressurized coolant recovery system. A white coolant reservoir located in the left front corner of the engine compartment is connected by a hose to the base of the coolant filler cap. If the coolant heats up during engine operation, coolant can escape through a pressurized filler cap, then through a connecting hose into the reservoir. As the engine cools, the coolant is automatically drawn back into the cooling system to maintain the correct level.

9 The coolant level should be checked before the vehicle has been driven when the engine is cool. It must be between the F (Full) and L (Low) marks on dipstick attached to the reservoir cap **(see illustration)**. Use only ethylene-glycol type coolant and soft (demineralized) water in the mixture ratio recommended by your owner's manual. Do not use supplemental inhibitor additives. If only a small amount of coolant is required to bring the system up to the proper level, water can be used. However, repeated additions of water will dilute the recommended antifreeze and water solution. In order to maintain the proper ratio of antifreeze and water, it is advisable to top up the coolant level with the correct mixture. Refer to your owner's manual for the recommended ratio.

10 If the coolant level drops within a short time after replenishment, there may be a leak in the system. Inspect the radiator, hoses, engine coolant filler cap, drain plugs, air bleeder plugs and water pump. If no leak is evident, have the radiator cap pressure tested by your dealer.

Warning: *Never remove the radiator cap or the coolant recovery reservoir cap when the engine is running or has just been shut down, because the cooling system is hot. Escaping steam and scalding liquid could cause serious injury.*

11 If it is necessary to open the radiator cap, wait until the system has cooled completely, then wrap a thick cloth around the cap and turn it to the first stop. If any steam escapes, wait until the system has cooled further, then remove the cap.

12 When checking the coolant level, always note its condition. It should be relatively clear. If it is brown or rust colored, the system should be drained, flushed and refilled. Even if the coolant appears to be normal, the corrosion inhibitors wear out with use, so it must be replaced at the specified intervals.

13 Do not allow antifreeze to come in contact with your skin or painted surfaces of the vehicle. Flush contacted areas immediately with plenty of water.

Windshield/window washer fluid

Refer to illustration 4.14

14 Fluid for the windshield washer system is stored in a plastic reservoir which is located in the right front corner of the engine compartment **(see illustration)**. Fluid for the rear hatchback window washer system is stored in a plastic reservoir located in the right rear corner of the cargo space. In milder climates, plain water can be used to top up

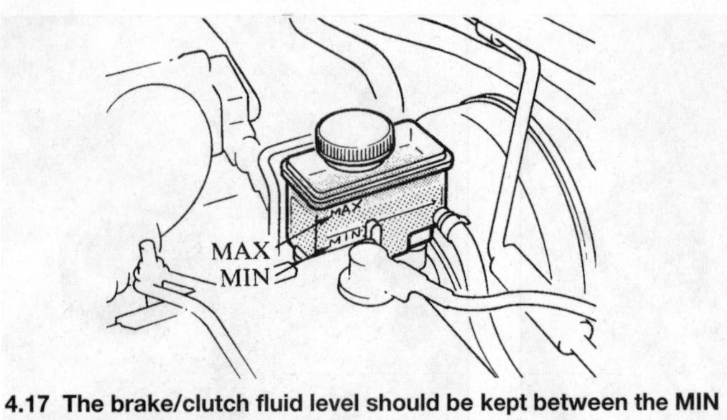
MAX
MIN
MAX
MIN

4.17 The brake/clutch fluid level should be kept between the MIN and MAX marks on the translucent plastic reservoir - remove the cap to add fluid

the reservoir, but the reservoir should be kept no more than two-thirds full to allow for expansion should the water freeze. In colder climates, the use of a specially designed windshield washer fluid, available at your dealer and any auto parts store, will help lower the freezing point of the fluid. Mix the solution with water in accordance with the manufacturer's directions on the container. Do not use regular antifreeze. It will damage the vehicle's paint.

Battery electrolyte

15 On models not equipped with a sealed battery, unscrew the filler/vent cap and check the electrolyte level. It must be between the upper and lower levels. If the level is low, add distilled water. Install and securely retighten the cap. **Caution:** *Overfilling the cells may cause electrolyte to spill over during periods of heavy charging, causing corrosion or damage.*

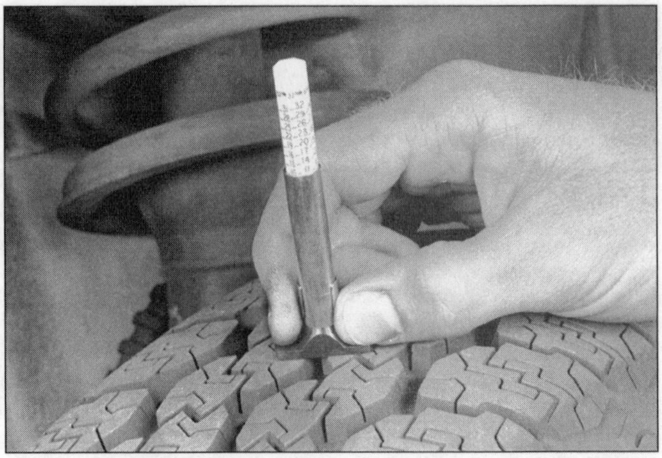

5.2 A tire tread depth indicator should be used to monitor tire wear - they are available at auto parts stores and service stations and cost very little

Brake/clutch fluid

Refer to illustration 4.17

16 A common reservoir is used for the brake and clutch hydraulic systems. The reservoir is mounted in front of the brake power booster unit in the engine compartment.

17 To check the fluid level of the brake/clutch reservoir, simply look at the MAX (Maximum) and MIN (Minimum) marks on the reservoir **(see illustration)**. The level should be at or near the MAX fill line on the reservoir.

18 If the level is low, wipe the top of the reservoir cap with a clean

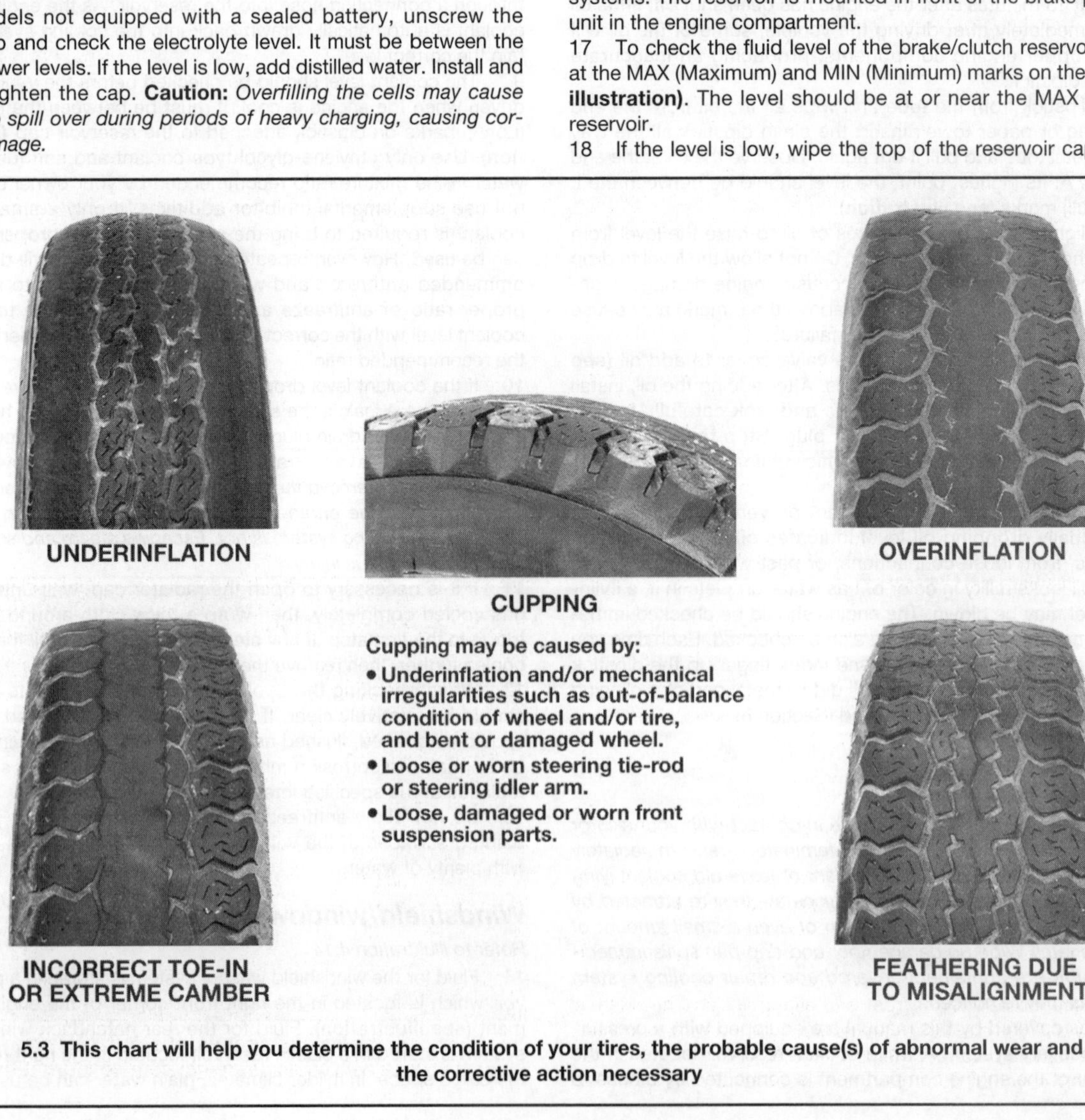
UNDERINFLATION
OVERINFLATION
CUPPING
Cupping may be caused by:
• Underinflation and/or mechanical irregularities such as out-of-balance condition of wheel and/or tire, and bent or damaged wheel.
• Loose or worn steering tie-rod or steering idler arm.
• Loose, damaged or worn front suspension parts.
INCORRECT TOE-IN OR EXTREME CAMBER
FEATHERING DUE TO MISALIGNMENT

5.3 This chart will help you determine the condition of your tires, the probable cause(s) of abnormal wear and the corrective action necessary

5.4a If a tire loses air on a steady basis, check the valve core first to make sure it's snug (special inexpensive wrenches are commonly available at auto parts stores)

rag to prevent contamination of the brake and clutch systems before lifting the cap.

19 Add only the specified brake fluid to the brake/clutch reservoir (refer to *Recommended lubricants and fluids* at the front of this Chapter or to your owner's manual). Mixing different types of brake fluid can damage the system. Fill the brake master cylinder reservoir only to the MAX level. **Warning:** *Use caution when filling the reservoir- brake fluid can harm your eyes and damage painted surfaces. Do not use brake fluid that has been opened for more than one year (even if the cap has been on) or has been left open. Brake fluid absorbs moisture from the air. Excess moisture can cause a dangerous loss of braking.*

20 While the reservoir cap is removed, inspect the fluid for contamination. If deposits, dirt particles or water droplets are present, the system should be drained and refilled (see Chapter 8 for clutch fluid replacement and Chapter 9 for brake fluid replacement).

21 After filling the reservoir to the proper level, make sure the cap is properly seated to prevent fluid leakage and/or system pressure loss.

22 The brake/clutch fluid in the master cylinder will drop slightly as the brake pads at each wheel wear down during normal operation. If the fluid requires repeated replenishing to keep it at the proper level, this is an indication of leakage in the brake or clutch hydraulic systems, which should be corrected immediately. Check all brake lines and connections, along with the wheel cylinders and booster (see Section 16). Check all clutch fluid lines and connections, along with the clutch master cylinder (see Chapter 8).

23 If, upon checking the master cylinder fluid level, you discover the reservoir empty or nearly empty, the brake and clutch system must be diagnosed immediately (see Chapters 8 and 9).

5 Tire and tire pressure checks (every 250 miles or weekly)

Refer to illustrations 5.2, 5.3, 5.4a, 5.4b and 5.8

1 Periodic inspection of the tires may spare you from the inconvenience of being stranded with a flat tire. It can also provide you with vital information regarding possible problems in the steering and suspension systems before major damage occurs.

2 Normal tread wear can be monitored with a simple, inexpensive device known as a tread depth indicator **(see illustration)**. When the tread depth reaches the specified minimum, replace the tire(s).

3 Note any abnormal tread wear **(see illustration)**. Tread pattern irregularities such as cupping, flat spots and more wear on one side than the other are indications of front end alignment and/or balance problems. If any of these conditions are noted, take the vehicle to a tire shop or service station to correct the problem.

4 Look closely for cuts, punctures and embedded nails or tacks.

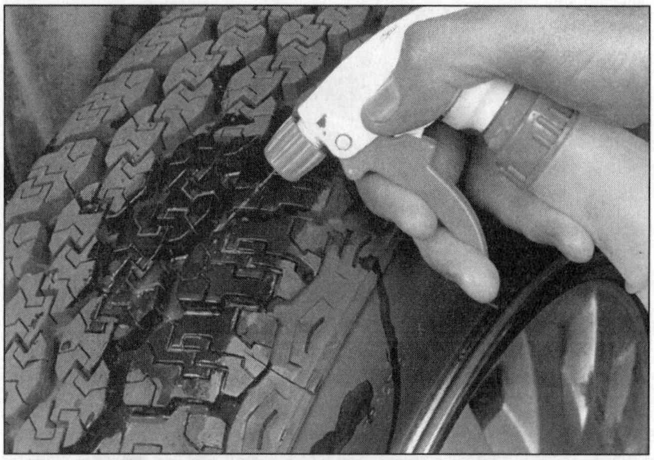

5.4b If the valve core is tight, raise the corner of the vehicle with the low tire and spray a soapy water solution onto the tread as the tire is turned slowly - slow leaks will cause small bubbles to appear

Sometimes a tire will hold its air pressure for a short time or leak down very slowly even after a nail has embedded itself into the tread. If a slow leak persists, check the valve stem core to make sure it is tight **(see illustration)**. Examine the tread for an object that may have embedded itself into the tire or for a "plug" that may have begun to leak (radial tire punctures are repaired with a plug that is installed in a puncture). If a puncture is suspected, it can be easily verified by spraying a solution of soapy water onto the puncture area **(see illustration)**. The soapy solution will bubble if there is a leak. Unless the puncture is inordinately large, a tire shop or gas station can usually repair the punctured tire.

5 Carefully inspect the inner sidewall of each tire for evidence of brake fluid leakage. If you see any, inspect the brakes immediately.

6 Correct tire air pressure adds miles to the lifespan of the tires, improves mileage and enhances overall ride quality. Tire pressure cannot be accurately estimated by looking at a tire, particularly if it is a radial. A tire pressure gauge is therefore essential. Keep an accurate gauge in the glovebox. The pressure gauges fitted to the nozzles of air hoses at gas stations are often inaccurate.

7 Always check tire pressure when the tires are cold. "Cold," in this case, means the vehicle has not been driven over a mile in the three hours preceding a tire pressure check. A pressure rise of four to eight pounds is not uncommon once the tires are warm.

8 Unscrew the valve cap protruding from the wheel or hubcap and push the gauge firmly onto the valve **(see illustration)**. Note the read-

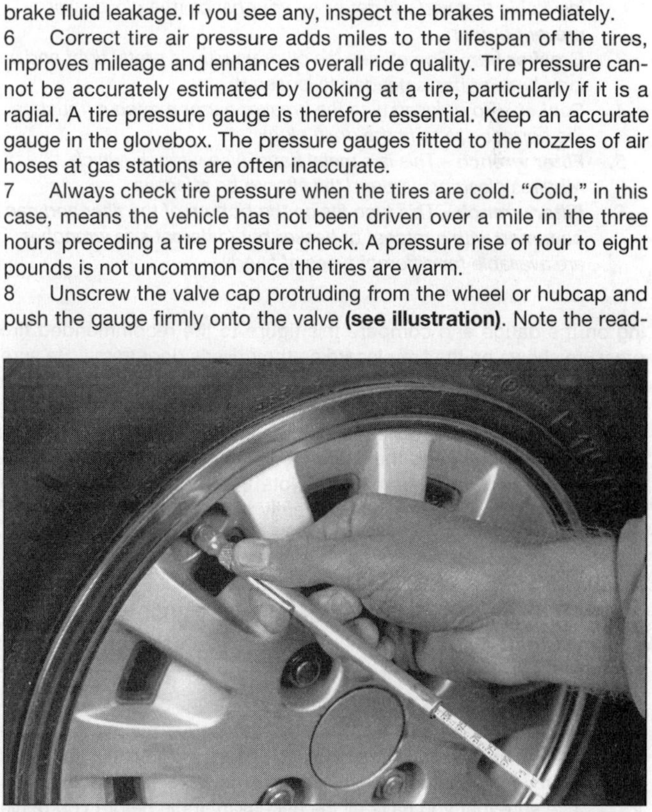

5.8 To extend the life of your tires, check the air pressure at least once a week with an accurate gauge (don't forget the spare!)

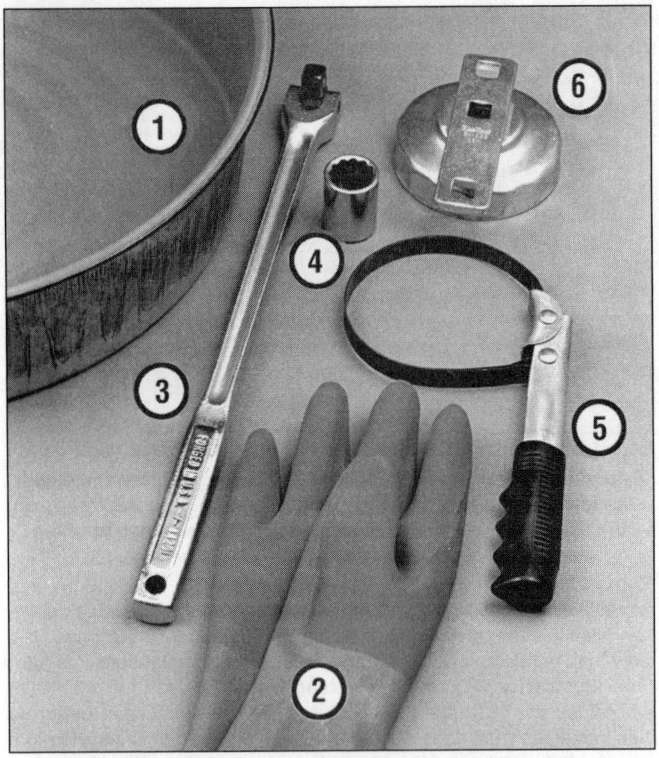

6.2 These tools are required when changing the engine oil and filter

1. ***Drain pan*** *- It should be fairly shallow in depth, but wide in order to prevent spills*
2. ***Rubber gloves*** *- When removing the drain plug and filter, it is inevitable that you will get oil on your hands (the gloves will prevent burns)*
3. ***Breaker bar*** *- Sometimes the oil drain plug is pretty tight and a long breaker bar is needed to loosen it*
4. ***Socket*** *– To be used with the breaker bar or a ratchet (must be the correct size to fit the drain plug)*
5. ***Filter wrench*** *- This is a metal band-type wrench, which requires clearance around the filter to be effective*
6. ***Filter wrench*** *- This type fits on the bottom of the filter and can be turned with a ratchet or beaker bar (different size wrenches are available for different types of filters)*

ing on the gauge and compare this figure to the recommended tire pressure shown on the tire placard on the driver's door frame. Be sure to reinstall the valve cap to keep dirt and moisture out of the valve stem mechanism. Check all four tires and, if necessary, add enough air to bring them up to the recommended pressure levels.

9 Don't forget to keep the spare tire inflated to the specified pressure (consult your owner's manual). Note that the air pressure specified for the compact spare is significantly higher than the pressure of the regular tires.

6 Engine oil and oil filter change (every 3000 miles or 3 months)

Refer to illustrations 6.2, 6.7, 6.12 and 6.14

1 Frequent oil changes are the best preventive maintenance the home mechanic can give the engine, because aging oil becomes diluted and contaminated, which leads to premature engine wear.

2 Make sure that you have all the necessary tools before you begin this procedure **(see illustration)**. You should also have plenty of rags or newspapers handy for mopping up any spills.

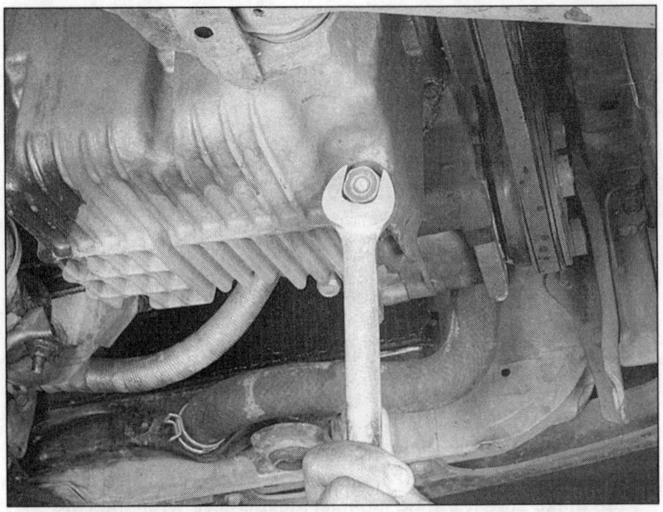

6.7 Use a proper size box-end wrench or socket to remove the oil drain plug and avoid rounding it off

3 Access to the underside of the vehicle is greatly improved if the vehicle can be lifted on a hoist, driven onto ramps or supported by jackstands. **Warning:** *Do not work under a vehicle which is supported only by a bumper, hydraulic or scissors-type jack.*

4 If this is your first oil change, get under the vehicle and familiarize yourself with the location of the oil drain plug. The engine and exhaust components will be warm during the actual work, so try to anticipate any potential problems before the engine and accessories are hot.

5 Park the vehicle on a level spot. Start the engine and allow it to reach its normal operating temperature (the needle on the temperature gauge should be at least above the bottom mark). Warm oil and sludge will flow out more easily. Turn off the engine when it's warmed up. Remove the filler cap in the valve cover.

6 Raise the vehicle and support it on jackstands. **Warning:** *To avoid personal injury, never get beneath the vehicle when it is supported by only by a jack. The jack provided with your vehicle is designed solely for raising the vehicle to remove and replace the wheels. Always use jackstands to support the vehicle when it becomes necessary to place your body underneath the vehicle.*

7 Being careful not to touch the hot exhaust components, place the drain pan under the drain plug in the bottom of the pan and remove the plug **(see illustration)**. You may want to wear gloves while unscrewing the plug the final few turns if the engine is really hot.

8 Allow the old oil to drain into the pan. It may be necessary to move the pan farther under the engine as the oil flow slows to a trickle. Inspect the old oil for the presence of metal shavings and chips.

9 After all the oil has drained, wipe off the drain plug with a clean rag. Even minute metal particles clinging to the plug would immediately contaminate the new oil.

10 Clean the area around the drain plug opening, reinstall the plug and tighten it securely, but do not strip the threads.

11 Move the drain pan into position under the oil filter.

12 Loosen the oil filter **(see illustration)** by turning it counterclockwise with the filter wrench. Any standard filter wrench should work. Once the filter is loose, use your hands to unscrew it from the block. Just as the filter is detached from the block, immediately tilt the open end up to prevent the oil inside the filter from spilling out. **Warning:** *The engine exhaust components may still be hot, so be careful.*

13 With a clean rag, wipe off the mounting surface on the block. If a residue of old oil is allowed to remain, it will smoke when the block is heated up. It will also prevent the new filter from seating properly. Also make sure that the none of the old gasket remains stuck to the mounting surface. It can be removed with a scraper if necessary.

14 Compare the old filter with the new one to make sure they are the same type. Smear some engine oil on the rubber gasket of the new filter and screw it into place **(see illustration)**. Because overtightening

6.12 The oil filter is usually on very tight, so you'll need a special wrench for removal - DO NOT use the wrench to tighten the new filter

6.14 Lubricate the oil filter gasket with clean engine oil before installing the filter on the engine

the filter will damage the gasket, do not use a filter wrench to tighten the filter. Tighten it by hand until the gasket contacts the seating surface. Then seat the filter by giving it an additional 3/4-turn.

15 Remove all tools, rags, etc. from under the vehicle, being careful not to spill the oil in the drain pan, then lower the vehicle.

16 Add new oil to the engine through the oil filler cap in the valve cover. Use a spout or funnel to prevent oil from spilling onto the top of the engine. Pour three quarts of fresh oil (four quarts in the 1.8L engine) into the engine. Wait a few minutes to allow the oil to drain into the pan, then check the level on the oil dipstick (see Section 4 if necessary). If the oil level is at or near the F mark, install the filler cap hand tight, start the engine and allow the new oil to circulate.

17 Allow the engine to run for about a minute. While the engine is running, look under the vehicle and check for leaks at the oil pan drain plug and around the oil filter. If either is leaking, stop the engine and tighten the plug or filter slightly.

18 Wait a few minutes to allow the oil to trickle down into the pan, then recheck the level on the dipstick and, if necessary, add enough oil to bring the level to the F mark.

19 During the first few trips after an oil change, make it a point to check frequently for leaks and proper oil level.

20 The old oil drained from the engine cannot be reused in its present state and should be discarded. Check with your local refuse disposal company, disposal facility or environmental agency to see if they will accept the oil for recycling. Don't pour used oil into drains or onto the ground. After the oil has cooled, it can be drained into a suitable container (capped plastic jugs, topped bottles, milk cartons, etc.) for transport to one of these disposal sites.

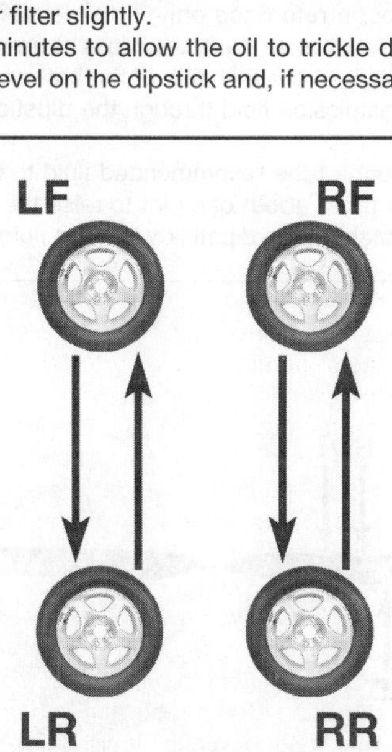

7.2 The recommended tire rotation pattern for these vehicles

7 Tire rotation (every 3000 miles or 3 months)

Refer to illustration 7.2

1 The tires should be rotated at the specified intervals and whenever uneven wear is noticed. Since the vehicle will be raised and the tires removed anyway, check the brakes (see Section 16) at this time.

2 Radial tires must be rotated in a specific pattern **(see illustration)**.

3 Refer to the information in *Jacking and towing* at the front of this manual for the proper procedures to follow when raising the vehicle and changing a tire. If the brakes are to be checked, do not apply the parking brake as stated. Make sure the tires are blocked to prevent the vehicle from rolling.

4 Preferably, the entire vehicle should be raised at the same time. This can be done on a hoist or by jacking up each corner and then lowering the vehicle onto jackstands placed under the frame rails. Always use four jackstands and make sure the vehicle is firmly supported.

5 After rotation, check and adjust the tire pressures as necessary and be sure to check the lug nut tightness.

6 For further information on the wheels and tires, refer to Chapter 10.

8 Power steering fluid level check (every 7500 miles or 6 months)

Refer to illustrations 8.2 and 8.4

1 Unlike manual steering, the power steering system relies on fluid which may, over a period of time, require replenishing.

2 The fluid reservoir for the power steering pump is located in the right front corner of the engine compartment, next to the windshield

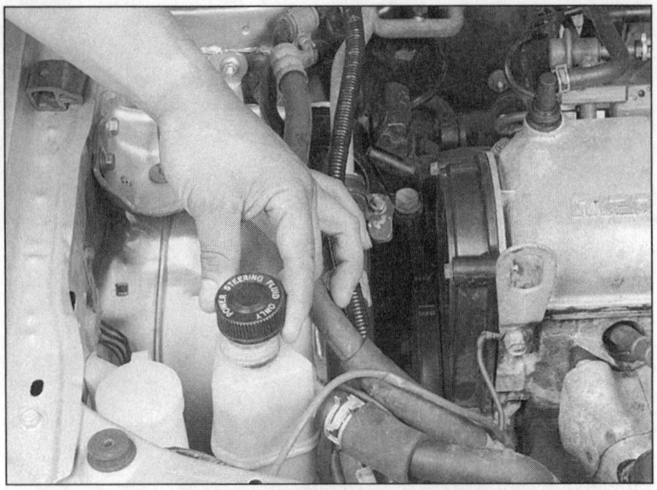

8.2 The power steering fluid reservoir is located in the right rear corner of the engine compartment

washer fluid reservoir **(see illustration)**.

3 For the check, the front wheels should be pointed straight ahead and the engine should be off.

4 To check the fluid level, simply look at the F (Full) and L (Low) lines on the reservoir **(see illustration)**. The fluid level should be between the F and L lines.

5 If additional fluid is required, pour the specified type directly into the reservoir, using a funnel to prevent spills. Fill the reservoir to the F line.

6 If the reservoir requires frequent fluid additions, all power steering hoses, hose connections, the power steering pump and the rack and pinion assembly should be carefully checked for leaks.

9 Automatic transaxle fluid level check (every 7500 miles or 6 months)

Refer to illustrations 9.4a and 9.4b

1 The level of the automatic transaxle fluid should be carefully maintained. Low fluid level can lead to slipping or loss of drive, while overfilling can cause foaming, loss of fluid and transaxle damage.

2 The transaxle fluid level should only be checked when the transaxle is hot (at its normal operating temperature). If the vehicle has just been driven over 10 miles (15 miles in a frigid climate), and the fluid

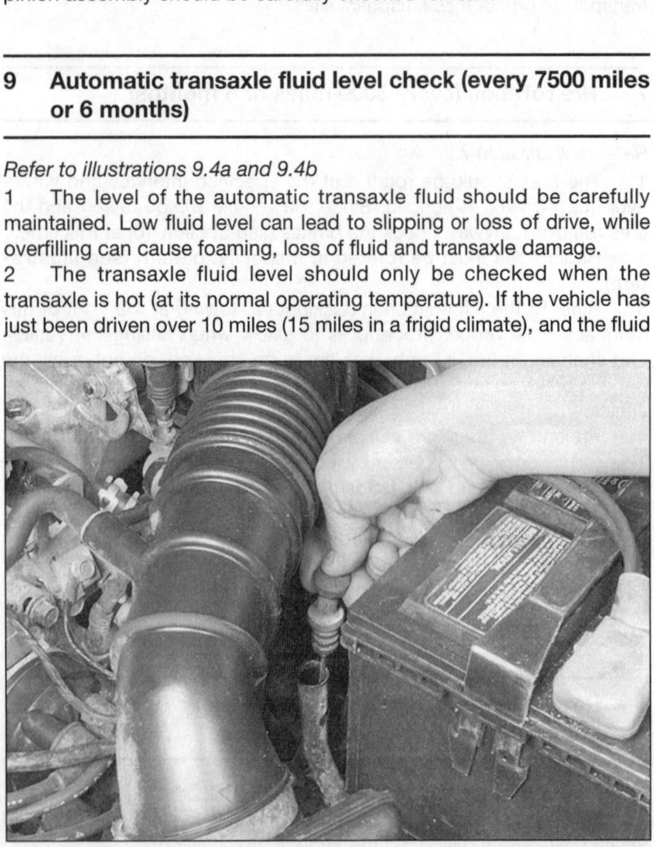

9.4a The automatic transaxle dipstick (arrow) is located in a tube which extends upward from the transaxle near the battery

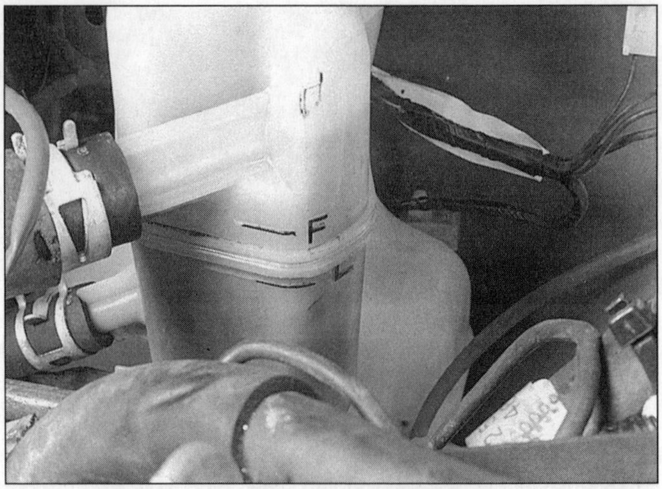

8.4 The power steering fluid level is checked by looking at the F and L lines on the reservoir and can be checked hot or cold

temperature is about 150-degrees F (65-degrees C), the transaxle is hot. **Caution:** *If the vehicle has just been driven for a long time at high speed or in city traffic in hot weather, or if it has been pulling a trailer, an accurate fluid level reading cannot be obtained. Allow the fluid to cool down for about 30 minutes.*

3 If the vehicle has not just been driven, park the vehicle on level ground, set the parking brake and start the engine. While the engine is idling, depress the brake pedal and move the selector lever through all the gear ranges, beginning and ending in Park.

4 With the engine still idling, remove the dipstick from its tube **(see illustration)**. Check the level of the fluid on the dipstick **(see illustration)** and note its condition.

5 Wipe the fluid from the dipstick with a clean rag and reinsert it back into the filler tube until the cap seats.

6 Pull the dipstick out again and note the fluid level. If the transaxle is cold, the level should be in the 20-degree C range on the dipstick. If it is hot, the fluid level should be in the 65-degree C range. Use the cold scale as a rough reference only; if the level is low on the cold scale, recheck the level when the transaxle is at normal operating temperature. If the level is at the low side of the hot range, add the specified automatic transmission fluid through the dipstick tube with a funnel.

7 Add just enough of the recommended fluid to fill the transaxle to the proper level. It takes about one pint to raise the level from the low notch to the full notch on the dipstick when the fluid is hot, so add the

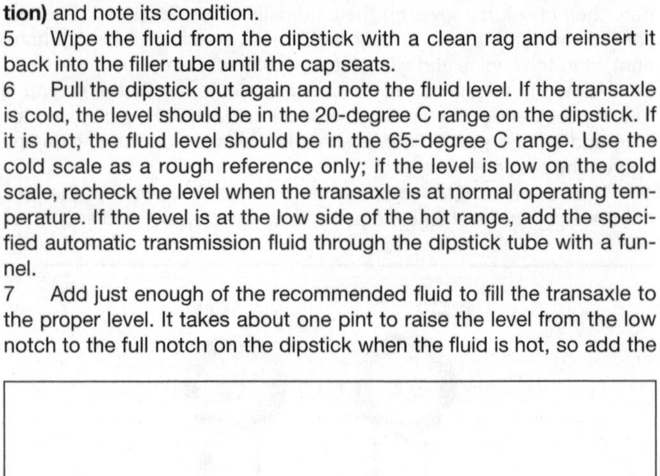

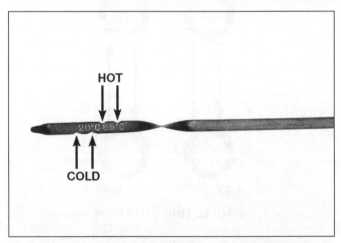

9.4b If the automatic transaxle fluid is cold, the level should be between the two lower notches; if it's at operating temperature, the level should be between the two upper notches

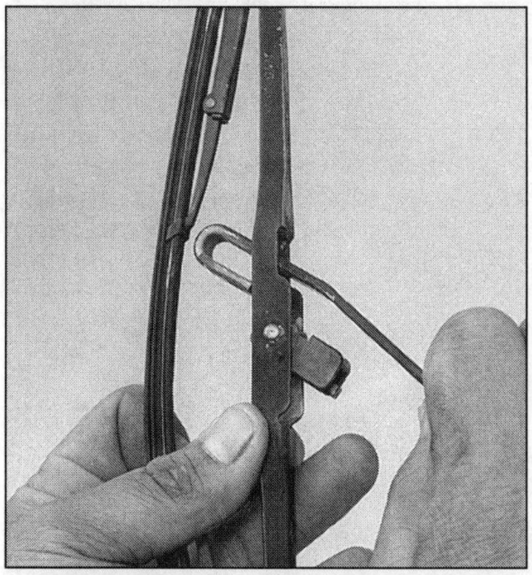

10.5 Push on the release lever and slide the wiper assembly down out of the hook in the end of the wiper arm

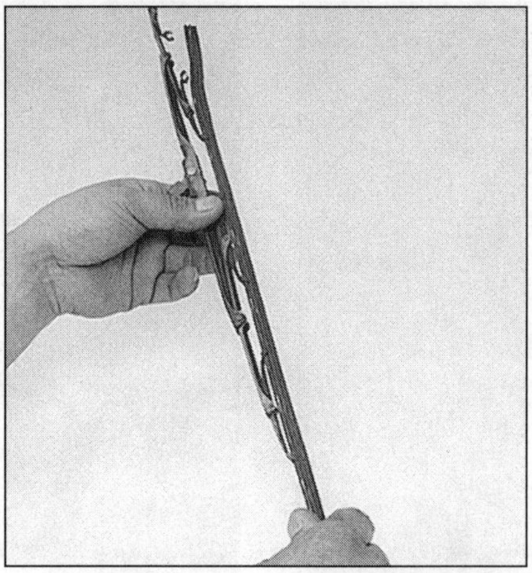

10.6 After detaching the end of the element, slide it out of the end of the frame

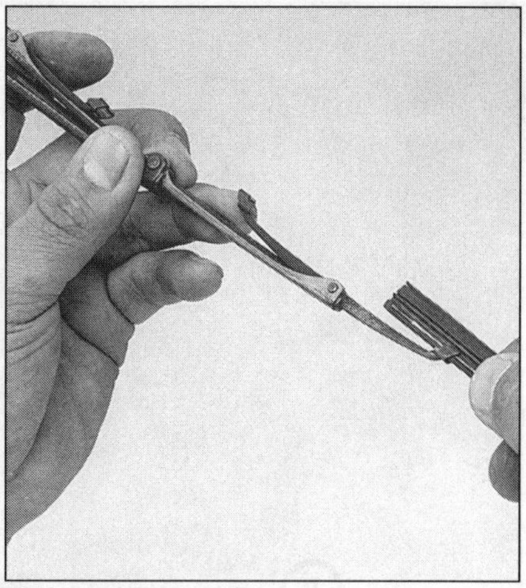

10.7 Insert the end of the element with the protrusions in first

fluid a little at a time and keep checking the level until it is correct.

8 The condition of the fluid should also be checked along with the level. If the fluid at the end of the dipstick is black or a dark reddish brown color, or if it emits a burned smell, the fluid should be changed (see Section 27). If you are in doubt about the condition of the fluid, purchase some new fluid and compare the two for color and smell.

10 Windshield wiper blade inspection and replacement (every 7500 miles or 6 months)

Refer to illustrations 10.5, 10.6 and 10.7

1 The windshield wiper and blade assembly should be inspected periodically for damage, loose components and cracked or worn blade elements.

2 Road film can build up on the wiper blades and affect their efficiency, so they should be washed regularly with a mild detergent solution.

3 The action of the wiping mechanism can loosen bolts, nuts and fasteners, so they should be checked and tightened, as necessary, at the same time the wiper blades are checked.

4 If the wiper blade elements are cracked, worn or warped, or no longer clean adequately, they should be replaced with new ones.

5 Remove the wiper blade assembly from the arm by pushing on the release lever, then sliding the assembly down and out of the hook in the end of the arm **(see illustration)**.

6 Detach the blade insert element and pull it out of the right end of the wiper frame **(see illustration)**.

7 Insert the new element end with the small protrusions into the right side of the wiper frame **(see illustration)**. Slide the element fully into place, then seat the protrusions in the end of the frames to secure it.

11 Clutch pedal height and freeplay - check and adjustment (every 7500 miles or 6 months)

Refer to illustration 11.1

1 To check the clutch pedal height, measure the horizontal distance from the center of the clutch pedal surface to the carpet or pad on the firewall **(see illustration)**. The height should be within the limits listed in this Chapter's Specifications. If it isn't, it must be adjusted.

2 To adjust the clutch pedal height, disconnect the clutch switch electrical connector.

3 Loosen the switch locknut **(see illustration 11.1)**.

4 Turn the clutch switch until the pedal height is correct.

5 Tighten the locknut and recheck the pedal height to verify it is correct. **Note:** *Whenever the pedal height is adjusted it will most likely be necessary to adjust the freeplay because increasing or decreasing pedal height will cause a similar change in pedal freeplay.*

6 Check the clutch pedal freeplay by lightly pushing the clutch pedal down and, with a small steel ruler, measure the distance that it moves freely before the clutch resistance is felt **(see illustration 11.1)**. The freeplay should be within the limits listed in this Chapter's Specifications. If it isn't, it must be adjusted.

7 To adjust the clutch pedal freeplay, loosen the locknut on the pedal end of the clutch pushrod **(see illustration 11.1)**.

8 Turn the pushrod until pedal freeplay is correct.

9 Tighten the locknut and recheck the pedal freeplay to verify it is correct.

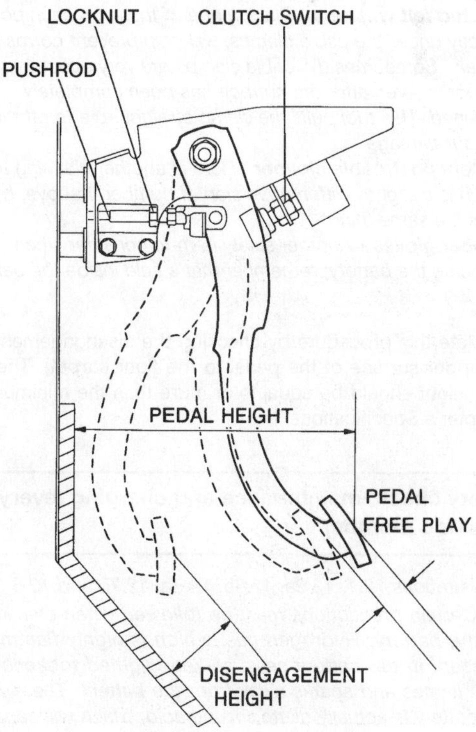

11.1 Clutch pedal adjustment details

1

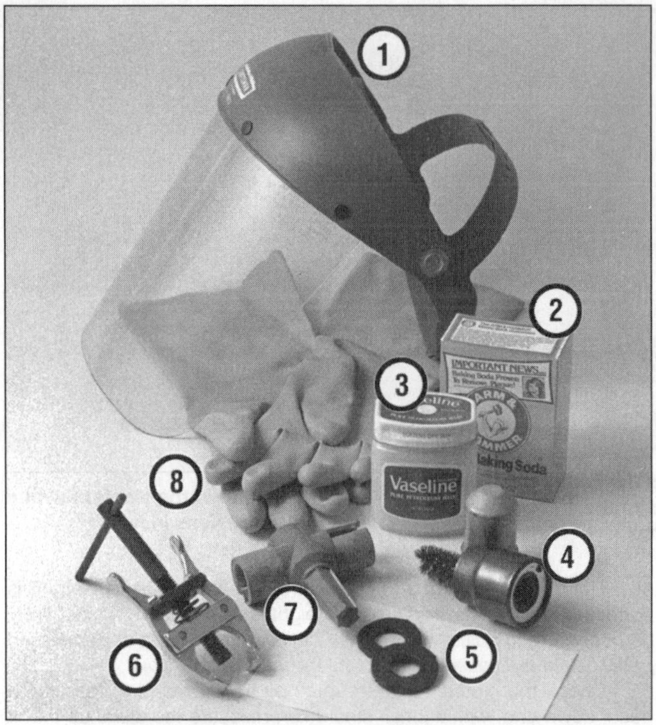

12.1 Tools and materials required for battery maintenance

1 ***Face shield/safety goggles*** *- When removing corrosion with a brush, the acidic particles can easily fly up into your eyes*
2 ***Baking soda*** *- A solution of baking soda and water can be used to neutralize corrosion*
3 ***Petroleum jelly*** *- A layer of this on the battery posts will help prevent corrosion*
4 ***Battery post/cable cleaner*** *- This wire brush cleaning tool will remove all traces of corrosion from the battery posts and cable clamps*
5 ***Treated felt washers*** *- Placing one of these on each post, directly under the cable clamps, will help prevent corrosion*
6 ***Puller*** *- Sometimes the cable clamps are very difficult to pull off the posts, even after the nut/bolt has been completely loosened. This tool pulls the clamp straight up and off the post without damage*
7 ***Battery post/cable cleaner*** *- Here is another cleaning tool which is a slightly different version of number 4 above, but it does the same thing*
8 ***Rubber gloves*** *- Another safety item to consider when servicing the battery; remember that's acid inside the battery*

10 Complete this procedure by checking the disengagement height (from the upper surface of the pedal to the floor carpet). The disengagement height should be equal to or more than the minimum listed in this Chapter's Specifications.

12 Battery check, maintenance and charging (every 7500 miles or 6 months)

Refer to illustrations 12.1, 12.6a, 12.6b, 12.7a, 12.7b and 12.8

Warning: *Certain precautions must be followed when checking and servicing the battery. Hydrogen gas, which is highly flammable, is always present in the battery cells, so keep lighted tobacco and all other open flames and sparks away from the battery. The electrolyte inside the battery is actually dilute sulfuric acid, which will cause injury if splashed on your skin or in your eyes. It will also ruin clothes and painted surfaces. When removing the battery cables, always detach the negative cable first and hook it up last!*

12.6a Battery terminal corrosion usually appears as light, fluffy powder

12.6b Removing a cable from the battery post with a wrench - sometimes a pair of special battery pliers are required for this procedure if corrosion has caused deterioration of the nut hex (always remove the ground (-) cable first and hook it up last!)

1 A routine preventive maintenance program for the battery in your vehicle is the only way to ensure quick and reliable starts. But before performing any battery maintenance, make sure that you have the proper equipment necessary to work safely around the battery **(see illustration).**

2 There are also several precautions that should be taken whenever battery maintenance is performed. Before servicing the battery, always turn the engine and all accessories off and disconnect the cable from the negative terminal of the battery.

3 The battery produces hydrogen gas, which is both flammable and explosive. Never create a spark, smoke or light a match around the battery. Always charge the battery in a ventilated area.

4 Electrolyte contains poisonous and corrosive sulfuric acid. Do not allow it to get in your eyes, on your skin on your clothes. Never ingest it. Wear protective safety glasses when working near the battery. Keep children away from the battery.

5 Note the external condition of the battery. If the positive terminal and cable clamp on your vehicle's battery is equipped with a rubber protector, make sure that it's not torn or damaged. It should completely cover the terminal. Look for any corroded or loose connections, cracks in the case or cover or loose hold-down clamps. Also check the entire length of each cable for cracks and frayed conductors.

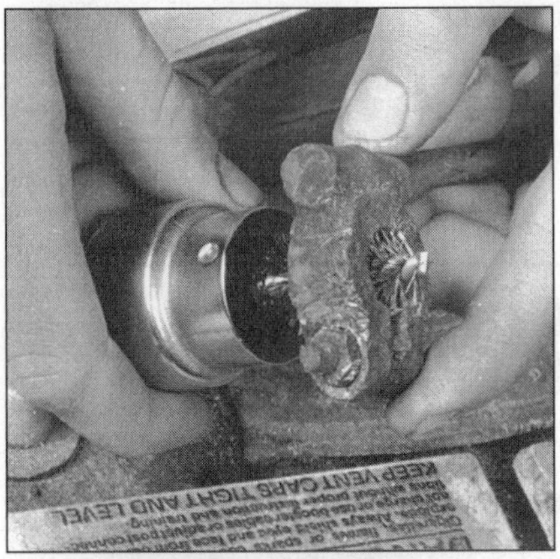

12.7a When cleaning the cable clamps, all corrosion must be removed (the inside of the clamp is tapered to match the taper on the post, so don't remove too much material)

12.7b Regardless of the type of tool used to clean the battery posts, a clean, shiny surface should be the result

12.8 Make sure the battery clamp nut and bolt (arrow) are tight

6 If corrosion, which looks like white, fluffy deposits **(see illustration)** is evident, particularly around the terminals, the battery should be removed for cleaning. Loosen the cable clamp bolts with a wrench, being careful to remove the ground cable first, and slide them off the terminals **(see illustration)**. Then disconnect the hold-down clamp bolt and nut, remove the clamp and lift the battery from the engine compartment.

7 Clean the cable clamps thoroughly with a battery brush or a terminal cleaner and a solution of warm water and baking soda **(see illustration)**. Wash the terminals and the top of the battery case with the same solution but make sure that the solution doesn't get into the battery. When cleaning the cables, terminals and battery top, wear safety goggles and rubber gloves to prevent any solution from coming in contact with your eyes or hands. Wear old clothes too - even diluted, sulfuric acid splashed onto clothes will burn holes in them. If the terminals have been extensively corroded, clean them up with a terminal cleaner **(see illustration)**. Thoroughly wash all cleaned areas with plain water.

8 Make sure that the battery tray is in good condition and the hold-down nut and bolt are tight **(see illustration)**. If the battery is removed from the tray, make sure no parts remain in the bottom of the tray when the battery is reinstalled. When reinstalling the hold-down clamp bolt or nut, do not overtighten it.

9 Information on removing and installing the battery can be found in Chapter 5. Information on jump starting can be found at the front of this manual. For more detailed battery checking procedures, refer to the *Haynes Automotive Electrical Manual*.

Cleaning

10 Corrosion on the hold-down components, battery case and surrounding areas can be removed with a solution of water and baking soda. Thoroughly rinse all cleaned areas with plain water.

11 Any metal parts of the vehicle damaged by corrosion should be covered with a zinc-based primer, then painted.

Charging

Warning: *When batteries are being charged, hydrogen gas, which is very explosive and flammable, is produced. Do not smoke or allow open flames near a charging or a recently charged battery. Wear eye protection when near the battery during charging. Also, make sure the charger is unplugged before connecting or disconnecting the battery from the charger.*

12 Slow-rate charging is the best way to restore a battery that's discharged to the point where it will not start the engine. It's also a good way to maintain the battery charge in a vehicle that's only driven a few miles between starts. Maintaining the battery charge is particularly important in the winter when the battery must work harder to start the engine and electrical accessories that drain the battery are in greater use.

13 It's best to use a one or two-amp battery charger (sometimes called a "trickle" charger). They are the safest and put the least strain on the battery. They are also the least expensive. For a faster charge, you can use a higher amperage charger, but don't use one rated more than 1/10th the amp/hour rating of the battery. Rapid boost charges that claim to restore the power of the battery in one to two hours are hardest on the battery and can damage batteries not in good condition. This type of charging should only be used in emergency situations.

14 The average time necessary to charge a battery should be listed in the instructions that come with the charger. As a general rule, a trickle charger will charge a battery in 12 to 16 hours.

13 Drivebelt check, adjustment and replacement (every 7500 miles or 6 months)

Refer to illustrations 13.1, 13.3a, 13.3b, 13.4, 13.5 and 13.6

Check

1 The alternator/water pump and power steering pump/air conditioning compressor drivebelts, are located at the front of the engine **(see illustration)**. Because of their composition and the high stresses

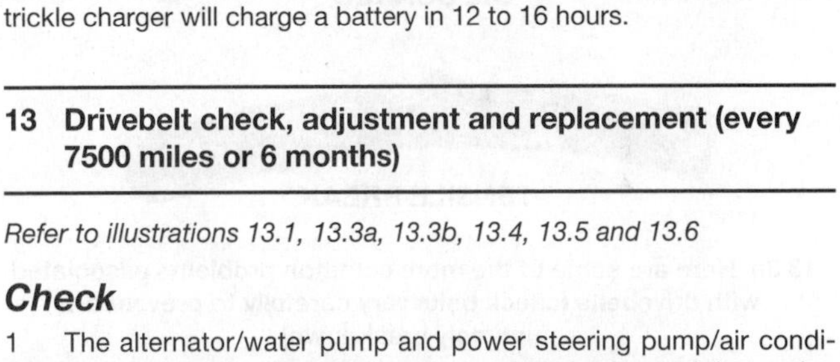

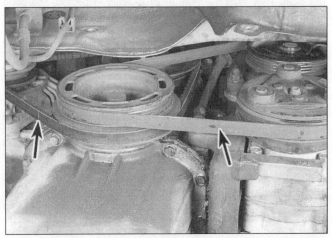

13.1 Drivebelts (arrows) stretch and deteriorate as they age and must be carefully inspected

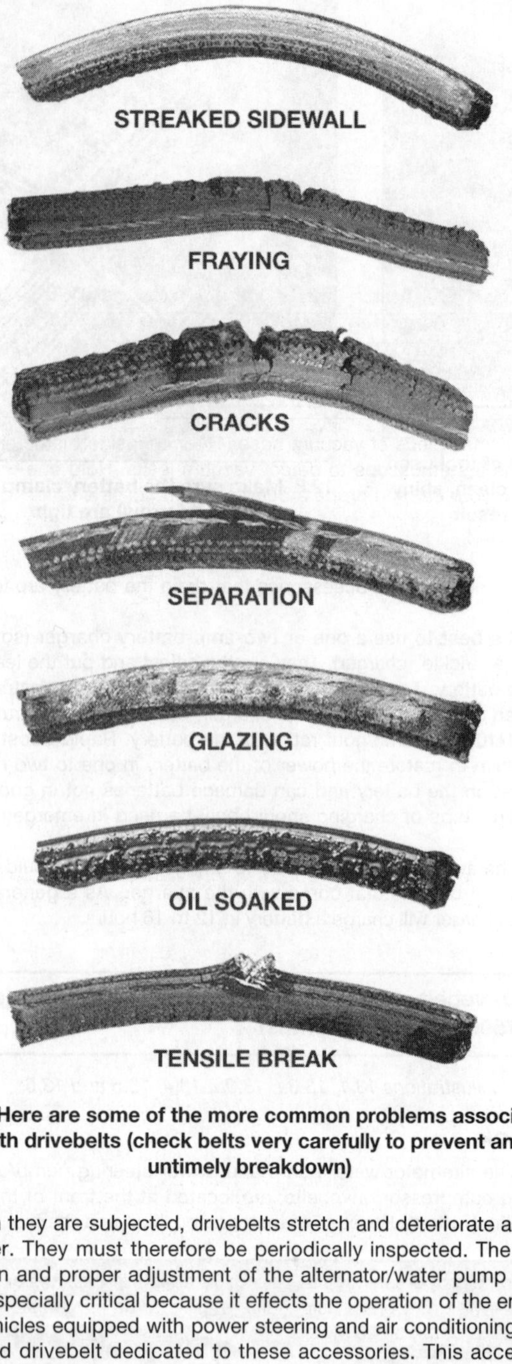

13.3a Here are some of the more common problems associated with drivebelts (check belts very carefully to prevent an untimely breakdown)

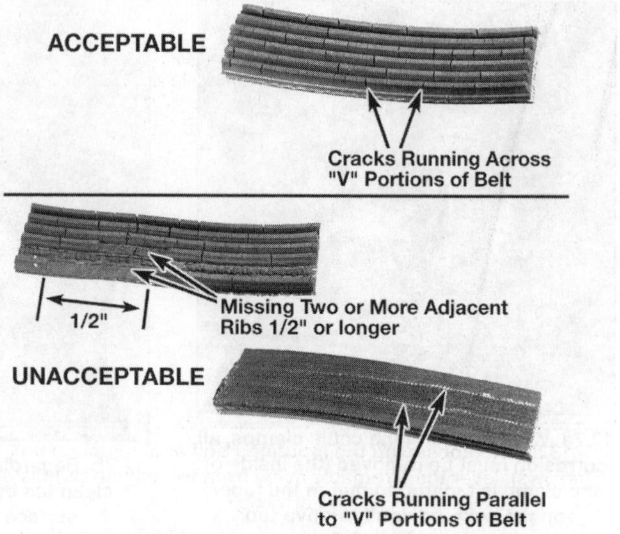

13.3b Small cracks in the underside of a V-ribbed belt are acceptable - lengthwise cracks, or missing pieces that cause the belt to make noise, are cause for replacement

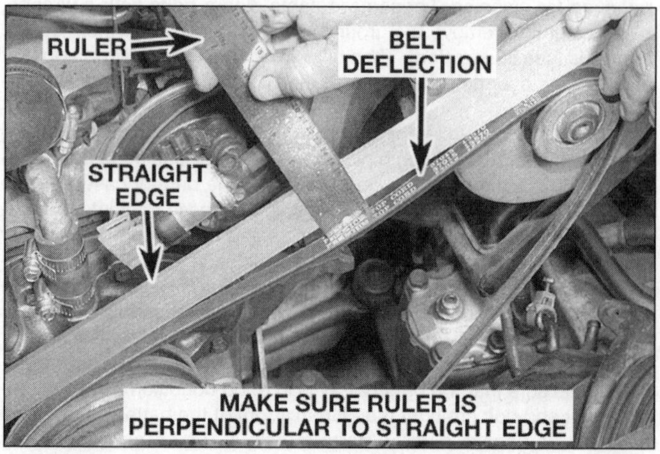

13.4 Measuring drivebelt deflection with a straightedge and ruler

to which they are subjected, drivebelts stretch and deteriorate as they get older. They must therefore be periodically inspected. The good condition and proper adjustment of the alternator/water pump drivebelt is especially critical because it effects the operation of the engine.

2 Vehicles equipped with power steering and air conditioning have a second drivebelt dedicated to these accessories. This accessory drivebelt is mounted outboard of the alternator/water pump drivebelt on the crankshaft pulley.

3 With the engine off, open the hood and locate the drivebelts. With a flashlight visually check the belts. Look for cracking, fraying, separation, tears and glazing, which gives the belt a shiny appearance **(see illustrations)**. Both sides of the belt should be inspected, which means you will have to twist the belt to check the underside. Use your fingers to feel the belt where you can't see it. If any of the above conditions are evident, replace the belt (go to Step 8).

4 To check the tension of each belt in accordance with factory specifications, apply moderate pressure (22 pounds) midway between the specified pulleys. Measure the deflection **(see illustration)** and compare your measurement to the specified drivebelt deflection for either a used or new belt. **Note:** *A "used" belt is defined as any belt which has been operated more than five minutes on the engine; a "new" belt is one that has been used for less than five minutes.*

Adjustment

5 If the alternator/water pump belt must be adjusted, loosen the alternator mounting bolt located under the alternator. Loosen the adjusting bolt on the top of the alternator and lever the alternator away from the engine to tension the belt **(see illustration)**. Tighten the mounting and adjusting bolt. Measure the belt deflection in accordance with the above method. Repeat this step until the drivebelt is properly adjusted.

6 Adjust the power steering pump belt by loosening the bolt and the locknut that secure the pump to the engine and the adjusting locknut under the pump. Adjust the belt tension by turning the adjusting bolt **(see illustration)**. Tighten the adjusting locknut and the pump bolt and nut. Measure the belt deflection in accordance with the above method. Repeat this step until the drivebelt is properly adjusted.

7 Vehicles that do not have power steering but are equipped with air conditioning have an idler pulley installed above the compressor. Loosen the idler pulley locknut and turn the adjusting bolt to tension the drivebelt. Tighten the locknut. Measure the belt deflection in accordance with the above method. Repeat this step until the drivebelt is properly adjusted.

Replacement

8 To replace a belt, follow the above procedures to loosen the drivebelt enough to slip the belt off the crankshaft pulley and remove it.

13.5 After loosening the mounting bolt and adjusting bolt (arrows), lever the alternator away from the engine to tension the drivebelt

If you are replacing the alternator/water pump belt, you will have to remove the power steering and/or air conditioning belt first because of the way they are arranged on the crankshaft pulley. Because of this and because belts tend to wear out more or less together, it is a good idea to replace both belts at the same time. Mark each belt and its appropriate pulley groove so the replacement belts can be installed in their proper positions.

9 Take the old belts to the parts store in order to make a direct comparison for length, width and design.

10 After replacing the drivebelt, make sure that it fits properly. When installing a multi-ribbed belt, make sure that it is centered - it must not overlap either edge of the pulley.

11 Adjust the drivebelt(s) in accordance with the procedure outlined above.

14 Underhood hose check and replacement (every 7500 miles or 6 months)

Caution: *Replacement of air conditioning hoses must be left to a dealer service department or air conditioning shop that has the equipment to depressurize the system safely. Never remove air conditioning components or hoses until the system has been depressurized.*

General

1 High temperatures in the engine compartment can cause the deterioration of the rubber and plastic hoses used for engine, accessory and emission systems operation. Periodic inspection should be made for cracks, loose clamps, material hardening and leaks.

2 Information specific to the cooling system hoses can be found in Section 15.

3 Some, but not all, hoses are secured to the fittings with clamps. Where clamps are used, check to be sure they haven't lost their tension, allowing the hose to leak. If clamps aren't used, make sure the hose has not expanded and/or hardened where it slips over the fitting, allowing it to leak.

Vacuum hoses

4 It's quite common for vacuum hoses, especially those in the emissions system, to be color coded or identified by colored stripes molded into them. Various systems require hoses with different wall thickness, collapse resistance and temperature resistance. When replacing hoses, be sure the new ones are made of the same material.

5 Often the only effective way to check a hose is to remove it completely from the vehicle. If more than one hose is removed, be sure to label the hoses and fittings to ensure correct installation.

6 When checking vacuum hoses, be sure to include any plastic T-fittings in the check. Inspect the fittings for cracks and the hose where it fits over the fitting for distortion, which could cause leakage.

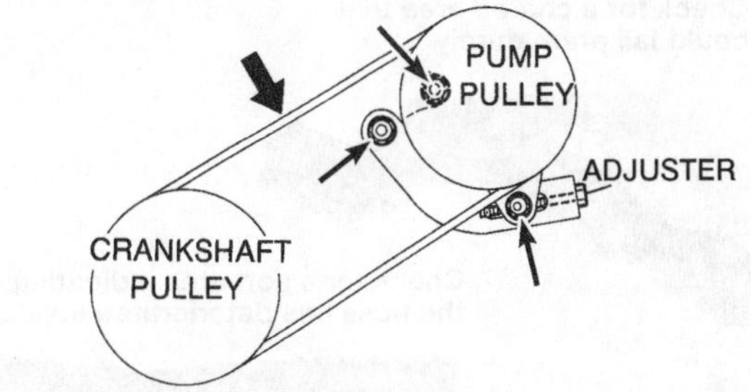

13.6 After loosening the bolt and two locknuts (arrows) that secure the pump, turn the adjusting bolt to tension the drivebelt (vehicles with air conditioning that do not have power steering have an adjustable idler pulley to tension the drivebelt)

7 A small piece of vacuum hose (1/4-inch inside diameter) can be used as a stethoscope to detect vacuum leaks. Hold one end of the hose to your ear and probe around vacuum hoses and fittings, listening for the "hissing" sound characteristic of a vacuum leak. **Warning:** *When probing with the vacuum hose stethoscope, be very careful not to come into contact with moving engine components such as the drivebelts, cooling fan, etc.*

Fuel hose

Warning: *There are certain precautions which must be taken when inspecting or servicing fuel system components. Work in a well ventilated area and do not allow open flames (cigarettes, appliance pilot lights, etc.) or bare light bulbs near the work area. Mop up any spills immediately and do not store fuel soaked rags where they could ignite.*

8 Check all rubber fuel lines for deterioration and chafing. Check especially for cracks in areas where the hose bends and just before fittings, such as where a hose attaches to the fuel filter.

9 High quality fuel line, specifically designed for fuel injection systems, must be used for fuel line replacement. **Warning:** *Never use anything other than the proper fuel line for fuel line replacement.*

10 Spring-type clamps are commonly used on fuel lines. These clamps often lose their tension over a period of time, and can be "sprung" during removal. Replace all spring-type clamps with screw clamps whenever a hose is replaced.

Metal lines

11 Sections of metal line are often used for fuel line between the fuel pump and fuel injection unit. Check carefully to be sure the line has not been bent or crimped and that cracks have not started in the line.

12 If a section of metal fuel line must be replaced, only seamless steel tubing should be used, since copper and aluminum tubing don't have the strength necessary to withstand normal engine vibration.

13 Check the metal brake lines where they enter the master cylinder and brake proportioning unit (if used) for cracks in the lines or loose fittings. Any sign of brake fluid leakage calls for an immediate thorough inspection of the brake system.

15 Cooling system check (every 7500 miles or 6 months)

Refer to illustration 15.4

1 Many major engine failures can be attributed to a faulty cooling system. If the vehicle is equipped with an automatic transaxle, the cooling system also cools the transaxle fluid and thus plays an important role in prolonging transaxle life.

2 The cooling system should be checked with the engine cold. Do this before the vehicle is driven for the day or after the engine has been shut off for at least three hours.

3 Remove the radiator cap by turning it to the left until it reaches a stop. If you hear a hissing sound (indicating there is still pressure in the system), wait until it stops. Now press down on the cap with the palm of your hand and continue turning to the left until the cap can be removed. Thoroughly clean the cap, inside and out, with clean water.

1

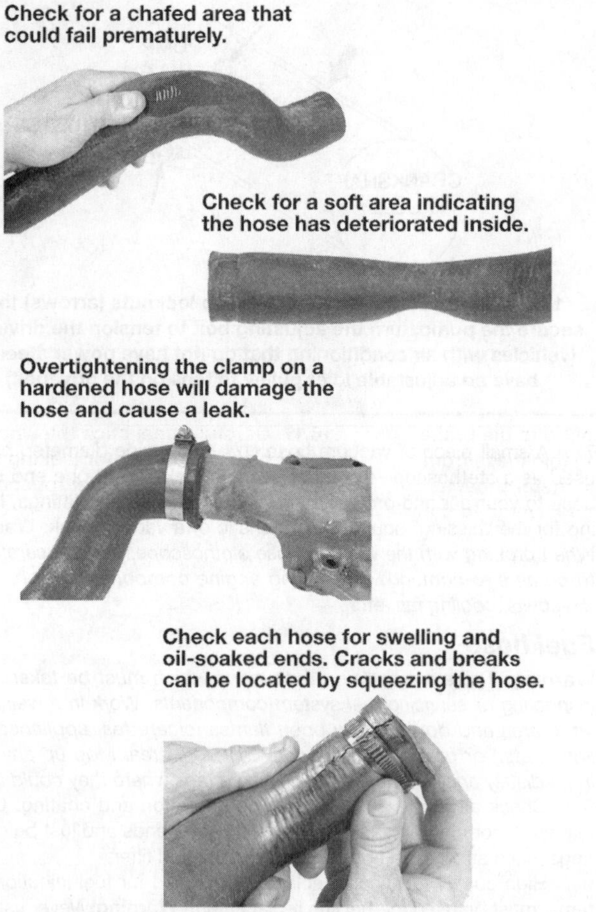
Check for a chafed area that could fail prematurely.
Check for a soft area indicating the hose has deteriorated inside.
Overtightening the clamp on a hardened hose will damage the hose and cause a leak.
Check each hose for swelling and oil-soaked ends. Cracks and breaks can be located by squeezing the hose.

15.4 Hoses, like drivebelts, have a habit of failing at the worst possible time - to prevent the inconvenience of a blown radiator or heater hose, inspect them carefully as shown here

Also clean the filler neck on the radiator. All traces of corrosion should be removed. The coolant inside the radiator should be relatively transparent. If it's rust colored, the system should be drained and refilled (see Section 24). If the coolant level isn't up to the top, add additional antifreeze/coolant mixture (see Section 4).

4 Carefully check the large upper and lower radiator hoses along with the smaller diameter heater hoses which run from the engine to the firewall. Inspect each hose along its entire length, replacing any hose which is cracked, swollen or shows signs of deterioration. Cracks may become more apparent if the hose is squeezed **(see illustration)**. Regardless of condition, it's a good idea to replace hoses with new ones every two years.

5 Make sure that all hose connections are tight. A leak in the cooling system will usually show up as white or rust colored deposits on the areas adjoining the leak. If wire-type clamps are used at the ends of the hoses, it may be a good idea to replace them with more secure screw-type clamps.

6 Use compressed air or a soft brush to remove bugs, leaves, etc. from the front of the radiator or air conditioning condenser. Be careful not to damage the delicate cooling fins or cut yourself on them.

7 Every other inspection, or at the first indication of cooling system problems, have the cap and system pressure tested. If you don't have a pressure tester, most gas stations and repair shops will do this for a minimal charge.

16 Brake check (every 15,000 miles or 12 months)

Note: *For detailed photographs of the brake system, refer to Chapter 9.*

1 In addition to the specified intervals, the brakes should be inspected every time the wheels are removed or whenever a defect is suspected. Any of the following symptoms could indicate a potential brake system defect: The vehicle pulls to one side when the brake pedal is depressed; the brakes make squealing or dragging noises when applied; brake travel is excessive; the pedal pulsates; brake fluid leaks, usually onto the inside of the tire or wheel.

2 The disc brake pads have built-in wear indicators which should make a high-pitched squealing or scraping noise when they are worn to the replacement point. When you hear this noise, replace the pads immediately or expensive damage to the discs can result.

3 Loosen the wheel lug nuts.

4 Raise the vehicle and place it securely on jackstands.

5 Remove the wheels (see *Jacking and towing* at the front of this book, or your owner's manual, if necessary).

Disc brakes

Refer to illustration 16.6

6 There are two pads - an outer and an inner - in each caliper. The pads are visible by looking at the top of the caliper **(see illustration)**.

7 Check the pad thickness by measuring the pad lining. If the lining material is less than the thickness listed in this Chapter's Specifications, replace the pads. **Note:** *Keep in mind that the lining material is riveted or bonded to a metal backing plate and the metal portion is not included in this measurement.*

8 If it is difficult to determine the exact thickness of the remaining pad material by the above method, or if you are at all concerned about the condition of the pads, remove the caliper(s), then remove the pads from the calipers for further inspection (see Chapter 9).

9 Once the pads are removed from the calipers, clean them with brake cleaner and re-measure them with a small steel pocket ruler or a vernier caliper.

10 Measure the disc thickness with a micrometer to make sure that it still has service life remaining. If any disc is thinner than the specified minimum thickness, replace it (see Chapter 9). Even if the disc has service life remaining, check its condition. Look for scoring, gouging and burned spots. If these conditions exist, remove the disc and have it resurfaced (see Chapter 9).

11 Before installing the wheels, check all brake lines and hoses for damage, wear, deformation, cracks, corrosion, leakage, bends and twists, particularly in the vicinity of the rubber hoses at the calipers. Check the clamps for tightness and the connections for leakage. Make sure that all hoses and lines are clear of sharp edges, moving parts and the exhaust system. If any of the above conditions are noted, repair, reroute or replace the lines and/or fittings as necessary (see Chapter 9).

Rear drum brakes

Refer to illustrations 16.15 and 16.17

12 To check the brake shoe lining thickness without removing the brake drums, remove the rubber plug from the backing plate and use a flashlight to inspect the linings. For a more thorough brake inspection, follow the procedure below.

13 Refer to Chapter 9 and remove the rear brake drums.

14 **Warning:** *Brake dust produced by lining wear and deposited on brake components contains asbestos, which is hazardous to your health. DO NOT blow it out with compressed air and DO NOT inhale it! DO NOT use gasoline or solvents to remove the dust. Brake system cleaner should be used to flush the dust into a drain pan. After the brake components are wiped clean with a damp rag, dispose of the contaminated rag(s) and solvent in a covered and labeled container. Try to use non-asbestos replacement parts whenever possible.*

15 Note the thickness of the lining material on the rear brake shoes **(see illustration)** and look for signs of contamination by brake fluid and grease. If the lining material is within 1/16-inch of the recessed rivets or metal shoes, replace the brake shoes with new ones. The shoes should also be replaced if they are cracked, glazed (shiny lining surfaces) or contaminated with brake fluid or grease. See Chapter 9 for the replacement procedure.

16 Check the shoe return and hold-down springs and the adjusting mechanism to make sure they're installed correctly and in good condi-

16.6 **Place a steel ruler across the brake pads to determine the thickness of remaining pad material for both inner and outer pads**

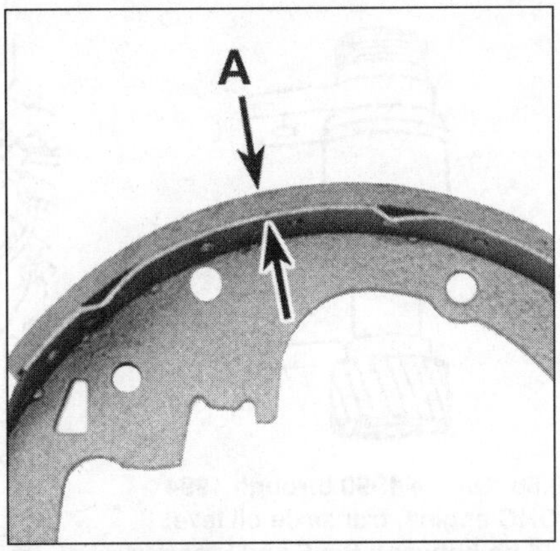

16.15 **If the lining is bonded to the brake shoe, measure the lining thickness from the outer surface to the metal shoe, as shown here; if the lining is riveted to the shoe, measure from the lining outer surface to the rivet head**

16.17 **Carefully peel back the wheel cylinder boot and check for leaking fluid indicating that the cylinder must be replaced or rebuilt**

tion. Deteriorated or distorted springs, if not replaced, could allow the linings to drag and wear prematurely.

17 Check the wheel cylinders for leakage by carefully peeling back the rubber boots **(see illustration)**. If brake fluid is noted behind the boots, the wheel cylinders must be replaced (see Chapter 9).

18 Check the drums for cracks, score marks, deep scratches and hard spots, which will appear as small discolored areas. If imperfections cannot be removed with emery cloth, the drums must be resurfaced by an automotive machine shop (see Chapter 9 for more detailed information).

19 Refer to Chapter 9 and install the brake drums.

20 Install the wheels and lug nuts.

21 Remove the jackstands and lower the vehicle.

22 Tighten the wheel lug nuts to the torque listed in this Chapter's Specifications.

Brake booster check

23 Sit in the driver's seat and perform the following sequence of tests.

24 With the engine stopped, depress the brake pedal several times - the travel distance should not change.

25 With the brake fully depressed, start the engine - the pedal should move down a little when the engine starts.

26 Depress the brake, stop the engine and hold the pedal in for about 30 seconds - the pedal should neither sink nor rise.

27 Restart the engine, run it for about a minute and turn it off. Then firmly depress the brake several times - the pedal travel should decrease with each application.

28 If your brakes do not operate as described above when the preceding tests are performed, the brake booster is either in need of repair or has failed. Refer to Chapter 9 for the removal procedure.

Parking brake

29 Slowly pull up on the parking brake and count the number of clicks you hear until the handle is up as far as it will go. The adjustment is correct if you hear the specified number of clicks. If you hear more or fewer clicks, it's time to adjust the parking brake (refer to Chapter 9).

30 An alternative method of checking the parking brake is to park the vehicle on a steep hill with the parking brake set and the transaxle in Neutral. If the parking brake cannot prevent the vehicle from rolling, it is in need of adjustment (see Chapter 9).

17 Air filter replacement (every 15,000 miles or 12 months)

Refer to illustrations 17.2a and 17.2b

1 The air filter is located inside a housing in the left front corner of the engine compartment.

2 To remove the air filter, loosen the intake air duct band and remove the duct/hose **(see illustration)**. Remove the five bolts attaching the air cleaner cover the box, then lift the cover up and remove the air filter element **(see illustration)**.

17.2a **Remove the air intake duct and the cover bolts**

17.2b **Remove the cover and lift the element out**

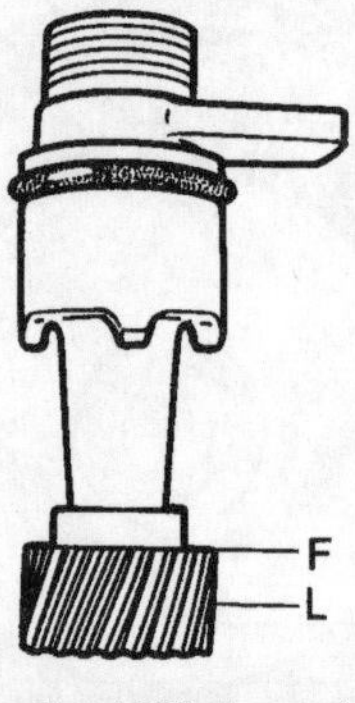

18.6a On the 1990 through 1994 SOHC engines, transaxle oil level should be between the F and L points

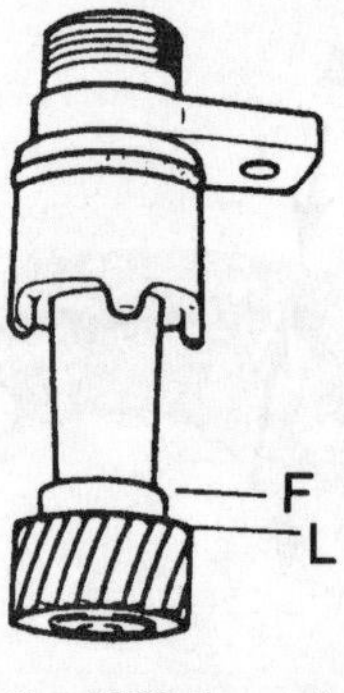

18.6b On the 1990 through 1994 DOHC engine, transaxle oil level should be between the F and L points

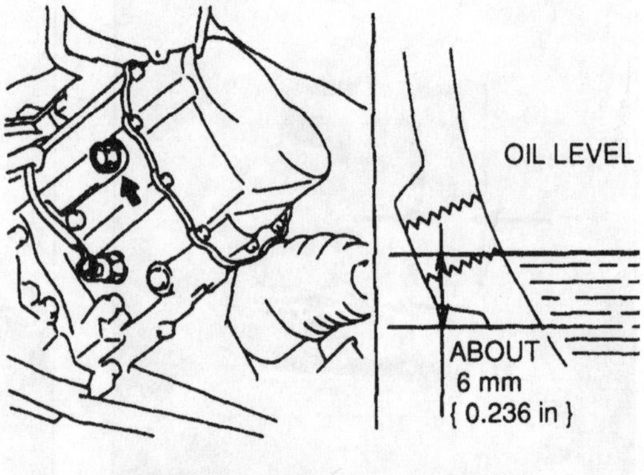

18.7 Oil level and fill plug - 1995 and later models

3 Inspect the outer surface of the filter element. If it is dirty, replace it. If it is only moderately dusty, it can be reused by blowing it clean from the back to the front surface with compressed air. Because it is a pleated paper type filter, it cannot be washed or oiled. If it cannot be cleaned satisfactorily with compressed air, discard and replace it. While the cover is off, be careful not to drop anything down into the housing. **Caution:** *Never drive the vehicle with the air cleaner removed. Excessive engine wear could result and backfiring could even cause a fire under the hood.*

4 Wipe out the inside of the air cleaner housing with a damp cloth.

5 Place the new filter into the air cleaner housing, making sure it seats properly.

6 Installation of the cover is the reverse of removal.

18 Manual transaxle lubricant level check (every 15,000 miles or 12 months)

Refer to illustrations 18.6a, 18.6b and 18.7

1 On 1990 through 1994 models the oil level is checked by removing the speedometer cable and driven gear from the transaxle in the engine compartment. The speedometer cable and driven gear are located at the left rear of the engine compartment on the top of the transaxle.

2 Park the vehicle on level ground and set the parking brake firmly. Turn the engine off.

3 Disconnect the speedometer cable by turning the knurled nut securing it to the driven gear assembly.

19.7 To check a balljoint for wear, raise the vehicle and support it on jackstands, place a 7-inch thick block of wood under the tire, block the wheel with chocks and lower the jack until there is about half a load on the coil spring - then move the lower arm up and down with a prybar to make sure there is no play in the balljoint (if there is, replace it)

4 Remove the hex head bolt securing the driven gear assembly to the transaxle and slowly pull the driven gear assembly from the transaxle.

5 Wipe the driven gear clean and reinsert the assembly in the transaxle.

6 Pull it out again. The oil level should be between L (Low) and F (Full) **(see illustrations)**.

7 On 1995 and later models the oil level is checked by removing the oil level and fill plug **(see illustration)**.

8 If the oil level is low, add oil until it is at the proper level. **Warning:** *Do not overfill.*

9 On 1990 through 1994 models, inspect the O-ring seal on the driven gear. Replace it if it appears damaged, flattened or age hardened. Re-install the driven gear in the transaxle and tighten the retaining bolt to the torque listed in this Chapter's Specifications. The reinstall the speedometer cable.

10 On 1995 and later models install the oil level and fill plug. Tighten the plug to the torque listed in this Chapter's Specifications.

11 Drive the vehicle a short distance, then check carefully for leaks.

19 Steering and suspension check (every 15,000 miles or 12 months)

Refer to illustrations 19.7 and 19.8

Note: *For detailed illustrations of the steering and suspension components, refer to Chapter 10.*

With the wheels on the ground

1 With the vehicle stopped and the front wheels pointed straight ahead, rock the steering wheel gently back and forth. If freeplay is excessive , a front wheel bearing, main shaft yoke, intermediate shaft yoke, lower arm balljoint or steering system joint is worn or the steering gear is out of adjustment or broken. Refer to Chapter 10 for the appropriate repair procedure.

2 Other symptoms, such as excessive vehicle body movement over rough roads, swaying (leaning) around corners and binding as the steering wheel is turned, may indicate faulty steering and/or suspension components.

3 Check the shock absorbers by pushing down and releasing the vehicle several times at each corner. If the vehicle does not come back to a level position within one or two bounces, the shocks/struts are worn and must be replaced. When bouncing the vehicle up and down, listen for squeaks and noises from the suspension components. Additional information on suspension components can be found in Chapter 10.

Under the vehicle

4 Raise the vehicle with a floor jack and support it securely on jackstands. See *Jacking and towing* at the front of this manual for the proper jacking points.

19.8 Push on the balljoint boot to check for damage

20.2 Flex the driveaxle boots by hand to check for cracks and/or leaking grease

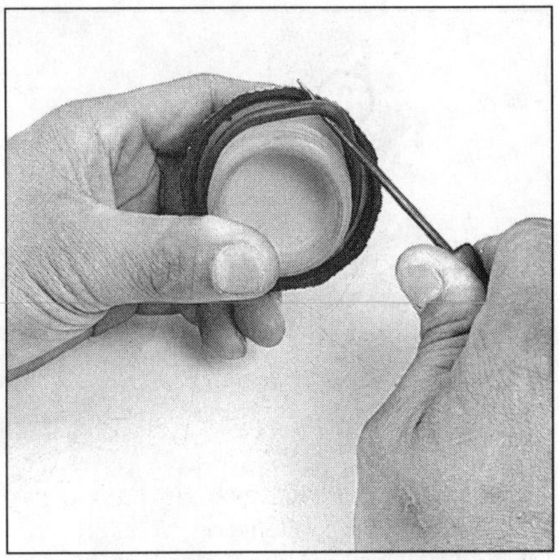

21.2 Use a small screwdriver to carefully pry out the old gasket - take care not to damage the cap

5 Check the tires for irregular wear patterns and proper inflation. See Section 5 in this Chapter for information regarding tire wear and Chapter 10 for the wheel bearing replacement procedures.

6 Inspect the universal joint between the steering shaft and the steering gear housing. Check the steering gear housing for grease leakage or oozing. Make sure that the dust seals and boots are not damaged and that the boot clamps are not loose. Check the steering linkage for looseness or damage. Check the tie-rod ends for excessive play. Look for loose bolts, broken or disconnected parts and deteriorated rubber bushings on all suspension and steering components. While an assistant turns the steering wheel from side to side, check the steering components for free movement, chafing and binding. If the steering components do not seem to be reacting with the movement of the steering wheel, try to determine where the slack is located.

7 Check the balljoints for wear by placing a 7-inch thick wooden block under each tire. Lower the jack until there is about half a load on the coil spring. Make sure that the front wheels are in a straight forward position and block the wheel with chocks. Move each lower arm up and down with a pry bar **(see illustration)** to ensure that its balljoint has no play. If any balljoint does have play, replace it. See Chapter 10 for the front balljoint replacement procedure.

8 Inspect the balljoint boots for damage and leaking grease **(see illustration)**. Replace the balljoints with new ones if they are damaged (see Chapter 10).

20 Driveaxle boot check (every 15,000 miles or 12 months)

Refer to illustration 20.2

1 The driveaxle boots are very important because they prevent dirt, water and foreign material from entering and damaging the constant velocity (CV) joints. Oil and grease can cause the boot material to deteriorate prematurely, so it's a good idea to wash the boots with soap and water. Because it constantly pivots back and forth following the steering action of the front hub, the outer CV boot wears out sooner and should be inspected regularly.

2 Inspect the boots for tears and cracks as well as loose clamps **(see illustration)**. If there is any evidence of cracks or leaking lubricant, they must be replaced as described in Chapter 8.

21 Fuel system check (every 30,000 miles or 24 months)

Refer to illustrations 21.2 and 21.5

Warning: *Certain precautions should be observed when inspecting or servicing the fuel system components. Work in a well ventilated area and do not allow open flames (cigarettes, appliance pilot lights, etc.) near the work area. Mop up spills immediately and do not store fuel soaked rags where they could ignite. It is a good idea to keep a dry chemical (Class B) fire extinguisher near the work area any time the fuel system is being serviced.*

1 If you smell gasoline while driving or after the vehicle has been sitting in the sun, inspect the fuel system immediately.

2 Remove the gas filler cap and inspect if for damage and corrosion. The gasket should have an unbroken sealing imprint. If the gasket is damaged or corroded, remove it and install a new one **(see illustration)**.

3 Inspect the fuel feed and return lines for cracks. Make sure that the threaded flare-nut type connectors which secure the metal fuel lines to the fuel injection system are tight.

4 Since some components of the fuel system - the fuel tank and part of the fuel feed and return lines, for example - are underneath the vehicle, they can be inspected more easily with the vehicle raised on a hoist. If that's not possible, raise the vehicle and support it securely on jackstands.

5 With the vehicle raised and safely supported, inspect the gas tank and filler neck for punctures, cracks and other damage. The hose connecting the filler neck to the tank is particularly critical. Sometimes this hose will leak because of loose clamps or deteriorated rubber **(see illustration)**. These are problems a home mechanic can usually rectify.

Warning: *Do not, under any circumstances, try to repair a fuel tank (except rubber components). A welding torch or any open flame can easily cause fuel vapors inside the tank to explode.*

6 Carefully check all rubber hoses and metal lines leading away from the fuel tank. Check for loose connections, deteriorated hoses, crimped lines and other damage. Carefully inspect the lines from the tank to the fuel injection system. Repair or replace damaged sections as necessary (see Chapter 4).

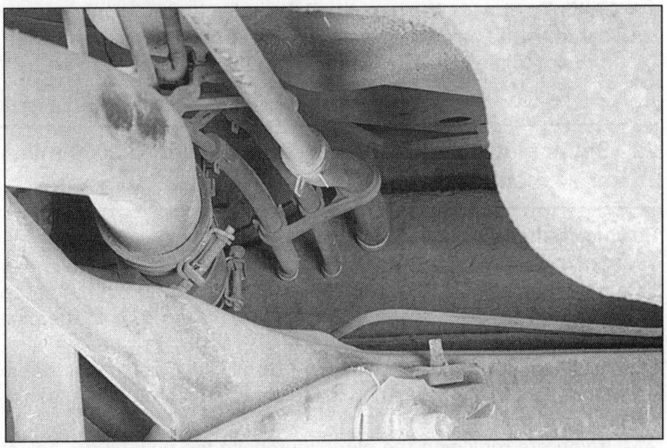

21.5 Inspect the filler/tank connecting hose for cracks and make sure the clamps are tight

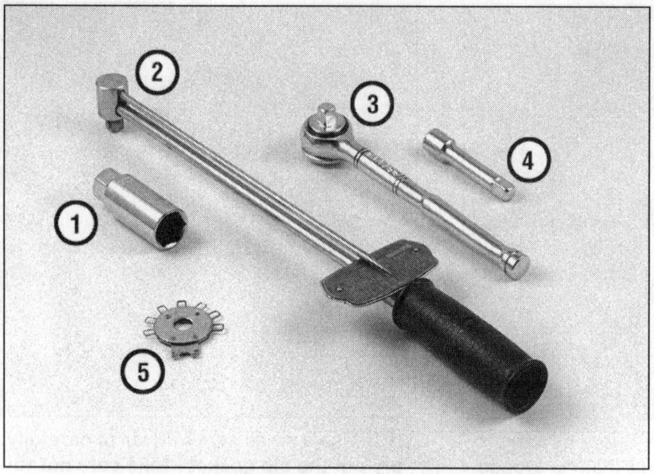

22.1 Tools required for changing spark plugs

1. ***Spark plug socket** - This will have special padding inside to protect the spark plug porcelain insulator*
2. ***Torque wrench** - Although not mandatory, use of this tool is the best way to ensure that the plugs are tightened properly*
3. ***Ratchet** - Standard hand tool to fit the plug socket*
4. ***Extension** - Depending on model and accessories, you may need special extensions and universal joints to reach one or more of the plugs*
5. ***Spark plug gap gauge** - This gauge for checking the gap comes in a variety of styles. Make sure the gap for your engine is included*

22.4a Spark plug manufacturers recommend using a wire-type gauge when checking the gap - if the wire does not slide between the electrodes with a slight drag, adjustment is required

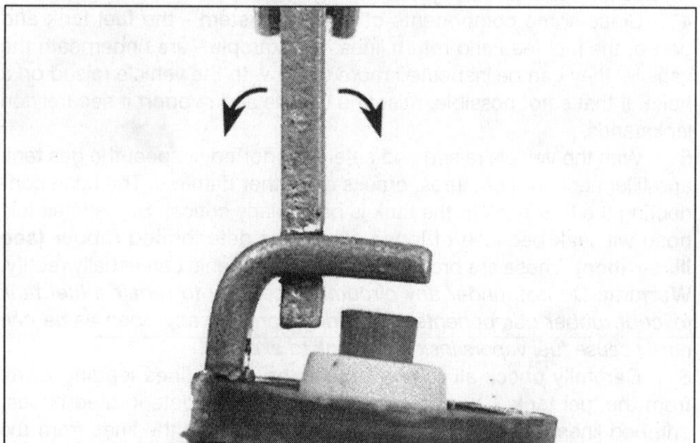

22.4b To change the gap, bend the side electrode only, as indicated by the arrows, and be very careful not to crack or chip the porcelain insulator surrounding the center electrode

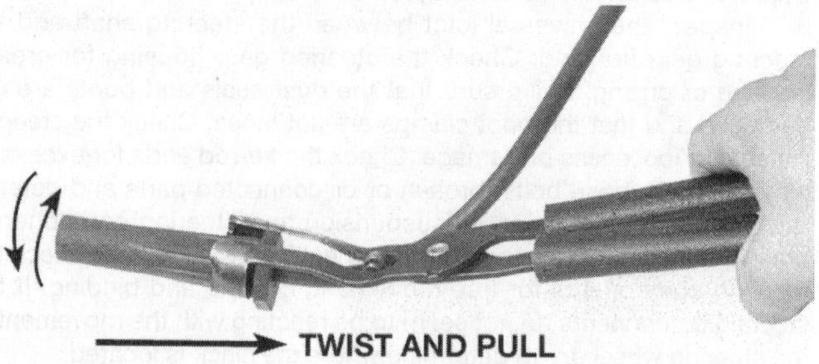

22.6 When removing the spark plug wires, pull only on the boot and use a twisting/pulling motion

22 Spark plug check and replacement (every 30,000 miles or 24 months)

Refer to illustrations 22.1, 22.4a and 22.4b

1 Spark plug replacement requires a spark plug socket which fits onto a ratchet wrench. This socket is lined with a rubber grommet to protect the porcelain insulator of the spark plug and to hold the plug while you insert it into the spark plug hole. You will also need a wire-type feeler gauge to check and adjust the spark plug gap and a torque wrench to tighten the new plugs to the specified torque **(see illustration)**.

2 If you are replacing the plugs, purchase the new plugs, adjust them to the proper gap and then replace each plug one at a time. **Note:** *When buying new spark plugs, it's essential that you obtain the correct plugs for your specific vehicle. This information can be found in the Specifications Section at the beginning of this Chapter, on the Vehicle Emissions Control Information (VECI) label located on the underside of the hood or in the owner's manual. If these sources specify different plugs, purchase the spark plug type specified on the VECI label because that information is provided specifically for your engine.*

3 Inspect each of the new plugs for defects. If there are any signs of cracks in the porcelain insulator of a plug, don't use it.

4 Check the electrode gaps of the new plugs. Check the gap by inserting the wire gauge of the proper thickness between the electrodes at the tip of the plug **(see illustration)**. The gap between the electrodes should be identical to that listed in this Chapter's Specifications or on the VECI label. If the gap is incorrect, use the notched adjuster on the feeler gauge body to bend the curved side electrode slightly **(see illustration)**.

5 If the side electrode is not exactly over the center electrode, use the notched adjuster to align them. **Caution:** *If the gap of a new plug must be adjusted, bend only the base of the ground electrode – do not touch the tip.*

Removal

Refer to illustrations 22.6 and 22.8

6 To prevent the possibility of mixing up spark plug wires, work on one spark plug at a time. Remove the wire and boot from one spark plug. Grasp the boot - not the cable - as shown, give it a half twisting motion and pull straight up **(see illustration)**.

7 If compressed air is available, blow any dirt or foreign material away from the spark plug area before proceeding (a common bicycle pump will also work).

8 Remove the spark plug **(see illustration)**.

22.8 Use a spark plug socket with a long extension to unscrew the spark plug

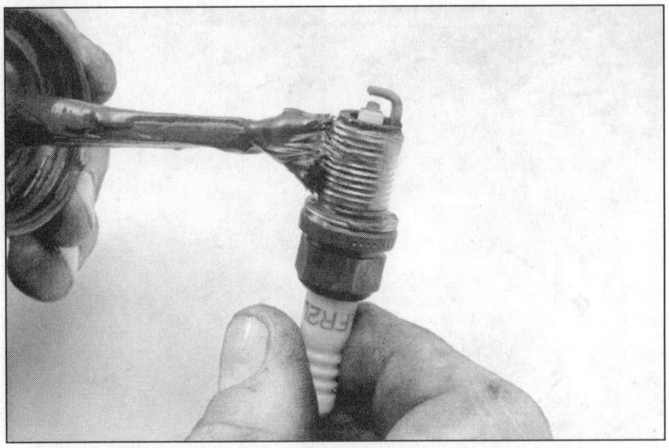

22.10a Apply a thin coat of anti-seize compound to the spark plug threads

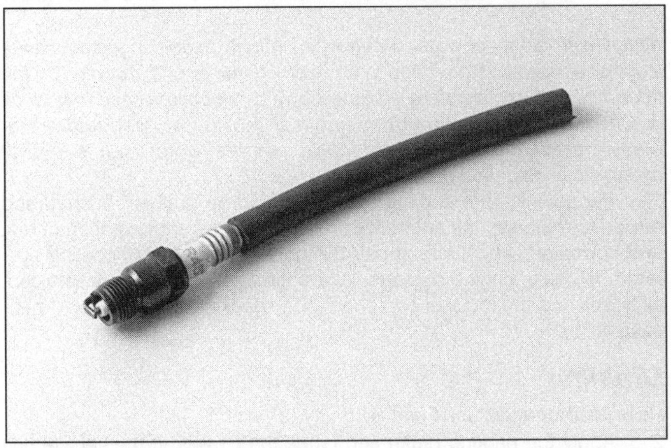

22.10b A length of 3/8-inch ID rubber hose will save time and prevent damaged threads when installing the spark plugs

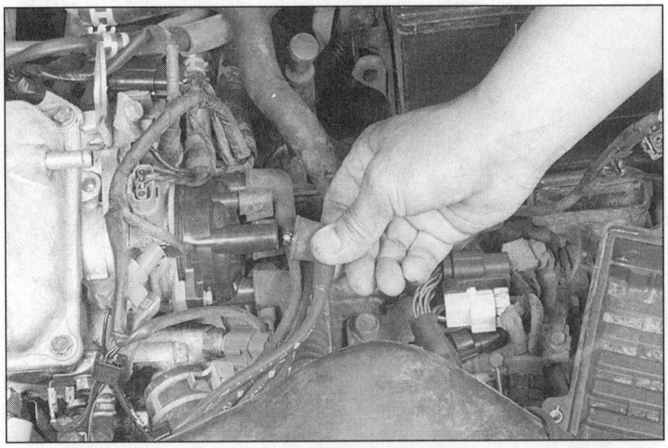

23.8 Pull only on the boot when removing ignition wires from the distributor

9 Whether you are replacing the plugs at this time or intend to reuse the old plugs, compare each old spark plug with the chart on the inside back cover of this manual to determine the overall running condition of the engine.

Installation

Refer to illustrations 22.10a and 22.10b

10 Prior to installation, it's a good idea to coat the spark plug threads with anti-seize compound **(see illustration)**. Also, it's often difficult to insert spark plugs into their holes without cross-threading them. To avoid this possibility, fit a short piece of 3/8-inch ID rubber hose over the end of the spark plug **(see illustration)**. The flexible hose acts as a universal joint to help align the plug with the plug hole. Should the plug begin to cross-thread, the hose will slip on the spark plug, preventing thread damage. Tighten the plug to the torque listed in this Chapter's Specifications.

11 Attach the plug wire to the new spark plug, again using a twisting motion on the boot until it is firmly seated on the end of the spark plug.

12 Follow the above procedure for the remaining spark plugs, replacing them one at a time to prevent mixing up the spark plug wires.

23 Spark plug wire, distributor cap and rotor check and replacement (every 30,000 miles or 24 months)

Refer to illustrations 23.8, 23.11a, 23.11b, 23.12 and 23.13

1 The spark plug wires should be checked whenever new spark plugs are installed.

2 Begin this procedure by making a visual check of the spark plug wires while the engine is running. In a darkened garage (make sure there is ventilation) start the engine and observe each plug wire. Be careful not to come into contact with any moving engine parts. If there is a break in the wire, you will see arcing or a small spark at the damaged area. If arcing is noticed, make a note to obtain new wires, then allow the engine to cool and check the distributor cap and rotor.

3 The spark plug wires should be inspected one at a time to prevent mixing up the order, which is essential for proper engine operation. Each original plug wire should be numbered to help identify its location. If the number is illegible, a piece of tape can be marked with the correct number and wrapped around the plug wire.

4 Disconnect the plug wire from the spark plug. A removal tool can be used for this purpose or you can grasp the rubber boot, twist the boot half a turn and pull the boot free. Do not pull on the wire itself.

5 Check inside the boot for corrosion, which will look like a white crusty powder.

6 Push the wire and boot back onto the end of the spark plug. It should fit tightly onto the end of the plug. If it doesn't, remove the wire and use pliers to carefully crimp the metal connector inside the wire boot until the fit is snug.

7 Using a clean rag, wipe the entire length of the wire to remove built-up dirt and grease. Once the wire is clean, check for burns, cracks and other damage. Do not bend the wire sharply, because the conductor might break.

8 Disconnect the wire from the distributor cap. Again, pull only on the boot **(see illustration)**. Check for corrosion and a tight fit. Replace the wire in the distributor cap.

9 Inspect the remaining spark plug wires, making sure that each

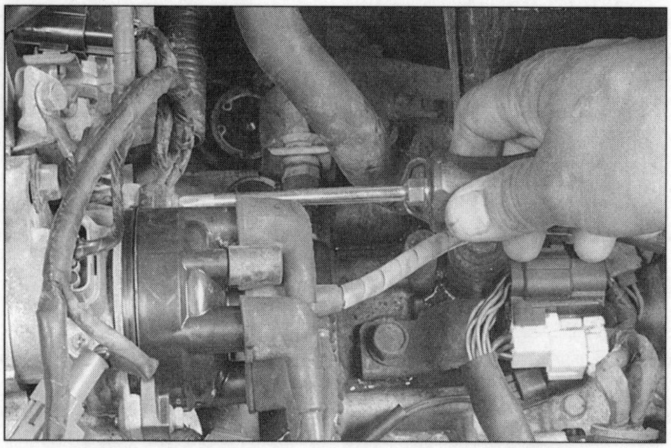

23.11a Remove the two screws (arrows) and detach the distributor cap

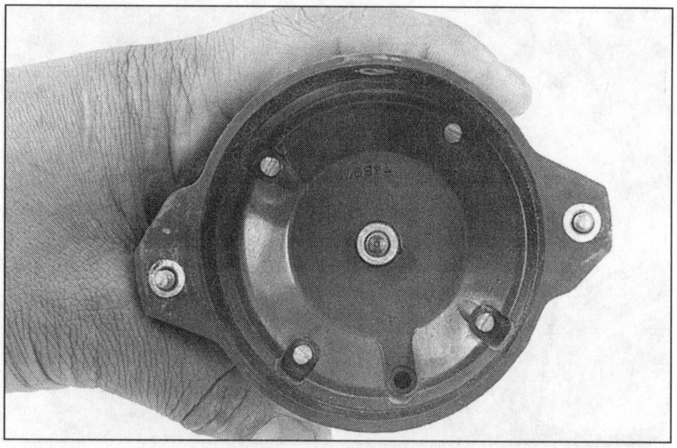

23.11b Inspect the distributor cap for carbon tracks, charred or eroded terminals and other damage (if in doubt about its condition, install a new one)

23.12 Check the rotor for damage, wear and corrosion (if in doubt about its condition, buy a new one)

one is securely fastened at the distributor and spark plug when the check is complete.

10 If new spark plug wires are required, purchase a set for your specific engine model. Pre-cut wire sets with the boots already installed are available. Remove and replace the wires one at a time to avoid mix-ups in the firing order.

11 Detach the distributor cap by removing the two retaining screws **(see illustration)**. Look inside it for cracks, carbon tracks and worn, burned or loose contacts **(see illustration)**.

12 Pull the rotor off the distributor shaft and examine it for cracks and carbon tracks **(see illustration)**. Replace the cap and rotor if any damage or defects are noted.

13 It is common practice to install a new cap and rotor whenever new spark plug wires are installed, but if you wish to continue using the old cap, check the resistance between the spark plug wires and the cap first **(see illustration)**. If the indicated resistance is more than the maximum value listed in this Chapter's Specifications, replace the cap and/or wires.

14 When installing a new cap, remove the wires from the old cap one at a time and attach them to the new cap in the exact same location – do not simultaneously remove all the wires from the old cap or firing order mix-ups may occur.

24 Cooling system servicing (draining, flushing and refilling) (every 30,000 miles or 24 months)

Warning: *Do not allow engine coolant (antifreeze) to come in contact with your skin or painted surfaces of the vehicle. Rinse off spills immediately with plenty of water. Antifreeze is highly toxic if ingested. Never leave antifreeze laying around in an open container or in puddles on the floor; children and pets are attracted by it's sweet smell and may drink it. Check with local authorities about disposing of used antifreeze. Many communities have collection centers which will see that antifreeze is disposed of safely.*

1 Periodically, the cooling system should be drained, flushed and refilled to replenish the antifreeze mixture and prevent formation of rust and corrosion, which can impair the performance of the cooling system and cause engine damage. When the cooling system is serviced, all hoses and the radiator cap should be checked and replaced if necessary.

Draining

Refer to illustrations 24.4 and 24.5

2 Apply the parking brake and block the wheels. If the vehicle has just been driven, wait several hours to allow the engine to cool down before beginning this procedure.

3 Once the engine is completely cool, remove the radiator cap.

4 Move a large container under the radiator drain to catch the coolant. Attach a 3/8-inch inner diameter hose to the drain fitting to direct the coolant into the container (some models are already equipped with a hose), then open the drain fitting (a pair of pliers may be required to turn it) **(see illustration)**.

5 After the coolant stops flowing out of the radiator, move the container under the engine block drain plug **(see illustration)**. Loosen the plug and allow the coolant in the block to drain.

6 While the coolant is draining, check the condition of the radiator hoses, heater hoses and clamps (refer to Section 14 if necessary).

7 Replace any damaged clamps or hoses (see Chapter 3).

Flushing

8 Once the system is completely drained, flush the radiator with fresh water from a garden hose until water runs clear at the drain. The flushing action of the water will remove sediments from the radiator but will not remove rust and scale from the engine and cooling tube surfaces.

9 These deposits can be removed by the chemical action of a cleaner. Follow the procedure outlined in the manufacturer's instructions. If the radiator is severely corroded, damaged or leaking, it should be removed (see Chapter 3) and taken to a radiator repair shop.

10 Remove the overflow hose from the coolant recovery reservoir. Drain the reservoir and flush it with clean water, then reconnect the hose.

Refilling

11 Close and tighten the radiator drain. Install and tighten the block drain plug.

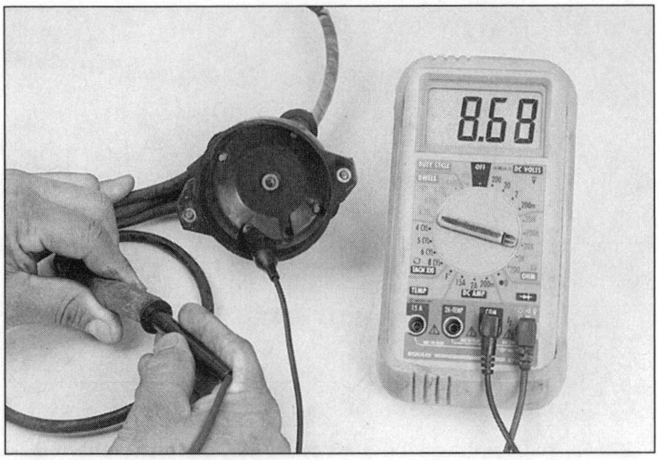

23.13 Measure the resistance value of the distributor cap and the spark plug wires - if it exceeds the specified maximum value, replace either the cap, or the wires, or both

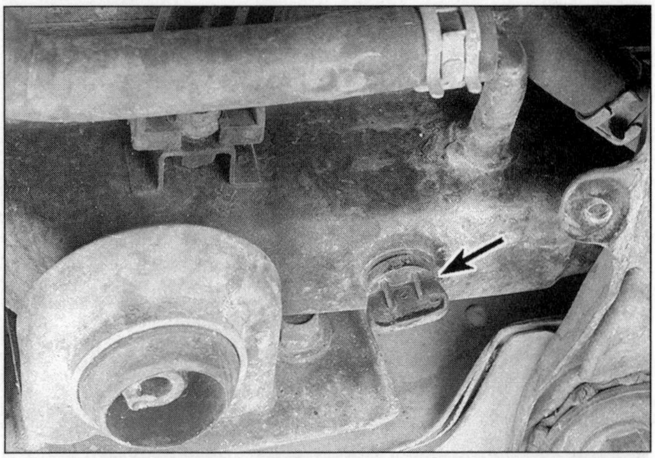

24.4 On most models you will have to remove a cover for access to the radiator drain fitting located at the bottom of the radiator - before opening the valve, push a short section of 3/8-inch ID hose onto the plastic fitting to prevent the coolant from splashing

12 Place the heater temperature control in the maximum heat position.
13 Slowly add new coolant (a 50/50 mixture of water and antifreeze) to the radiator until it's full. Add coolant to the reservoir up to the lower mark.
14 Leave the radiator cap off and run the engine in a well-ventilated area until the thermostat opens (coolant will begin flowing through the radiator and the upper radiator hose will become hot).
15 Turn the engine off and let it cool. Add more coolant mixture to bring the level back up to the lip on the radiator filler neck.
16 Squeeze the upper radiator hose to expel air, then add more coolant mixture if necessary. Replace the radiator cap.
17 Start the engine, allow it to reach normal operating temperature and check for leaks.

25 Evaporative emissions control system check (every 30,000 miles or 24 months)

Refer to illustration 25.2

1 The function of the evaporative emissions control system is to draw fuel vapors from the gas tank and fuel system, store them in a charcoal canister and then burn them during normal engine operation.
2 The most common symptom of a fault in the evaporative emissions system is a strong fuel odor in the engine compartment. If a fuel odor is detected, inspect the charcoal canister, located at the front of the engine compartment. Check the canister and all hoses for damage and deterioration **(see illustration).**
3 The evaporative emissions control system is explained in more detail in Chapter 6.

26 Exhaust system check (every 30,000 miles or 24 months)

Refer to illustration 26.4

1 With the engine cold (at least three hours after the vehicle has been driven), check the complete exhaust system from its starting point at the engine to the end of the tailpipe. This should be done on a hoist where unrestricted access is available.
2 Check the pipes and connections for evidence of leaks, severe corrosion or damage. Make sure that all brackets and hangers are in good condition and tight.
3 At the same time, inspect the underside of the body for holes, corrosion, open seams, etc. which may allow exhaust gases to enter the passenger compartment. Seal all body openings with silicone or body putty.
4 Rattles and other noises can often be traced to the exhaust sys-

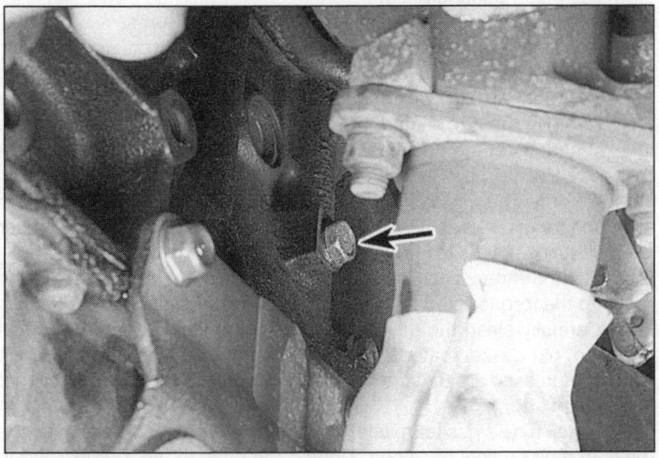

24.5 After draining the radiator, be sure to fully drain the cooling system by removing the block drain plug (arrow) located on the side of the engine block

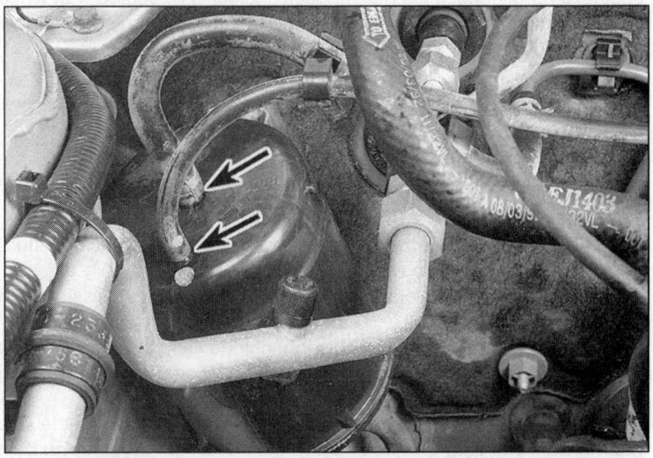

25.2 Check the evaporative emissions control canister for damage and the hose connections for cracks and damage (arrows)

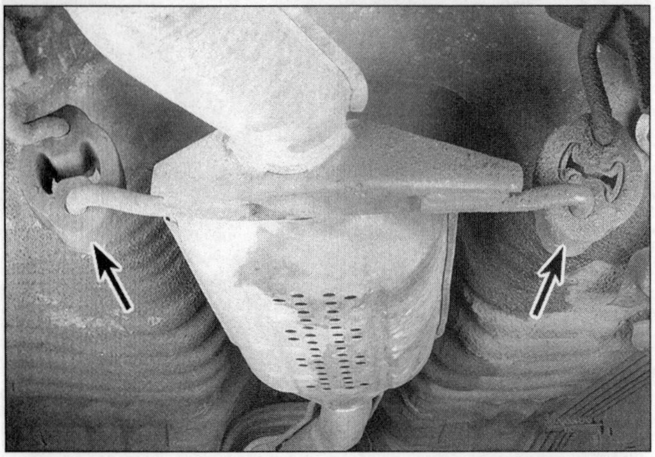

26.4 Be sure to check each exhaust system component rubber hanger (arrows) for damage

27.6 Remove the transaxle drain plug

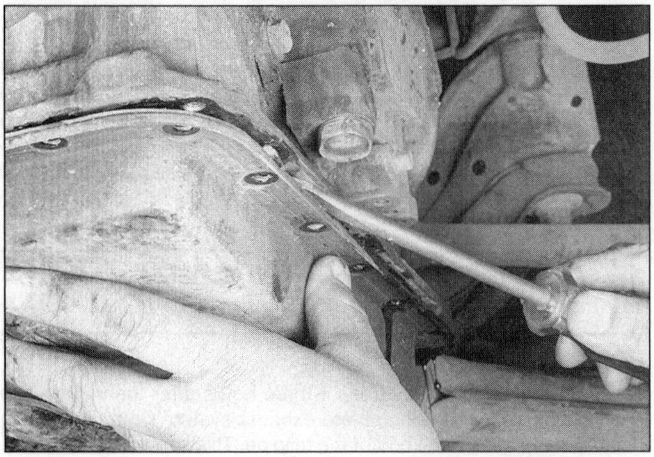

27.9 Pry the pan free and let it hang down so the fluid can drain

27.11 Remove the filter bolts and lower the filter (be careful, there will be some residual fluid)

tem, especially the mounts and hangers. Try to move the pipes, muffler and catalytic converter. If the components can come in contact with the body or suspension parts, secure the exhaust system with new mounts **(see illustration)**.

5 Check the running condition of the engine by inspecting inside the end of the tailpipe. The exhaust deposits here are an indication of engine state-of-tune. If the pipe is black and sooty or coated with white deposits, the engine is in need of a tune-up, including a thorough fuel system inspection.

27 Automatic transaxle fluid and filter change (every 30,000 miles or 24 months)

Refer to illustrations 27.6, 27.9, 27.11, 27.13

1 At the specified time intervals, the automatic transaxle fluid should be drained and replaced.

2 Before beginning work, purchase the specified transmission fluid (see *Recommended fluids and lubricants* at the front of this Chapter).

3 Other tools necessary for this job include jackstands to support the vehicle in a raised position, wrenches, drain pan capable of holding at least eight quarts, newspapers and clean rags.

4 The fluid should be drained immediately after the vehicle has been driven. Hot fluid is more effective than cold fluid at removing built up sediment. **Warning:** *Fluid temperature can exceed 350-degrees F in a hot transaxle. Wear protective gloves.*

5 After the vehicle has been driven to warm up the fluid, raise it and support it securely on jackstands.

6 Position a drain pan under the transaxle drain plug and remove the plug **(see illustration)**. Allow the oil to completely drain, then re-install the plug and tighten it to the torque listed in this Chapter's Specifications.

7 Move the drain pan under the transaxle pan and remove the rear and side pan mounting bolts.

8 Loosen the front pan bolts approximately four turns.

9 Carefully pry the transmission pan loose with a screwdriver, allowing the fluid to drain **(see illustration)**. Once the fluid has drained, remove the remaining bolts and lower the pan.

10 Remove the remaining bolts, pan and gasket. Carefully clean the gasket surface of the transmission to remove all traces of the old gasket and sealant.

11 Remove the oil strainer/filter retaining bolts and lower the filter from the transaxle **(see illustration)**. Be careful when lowering the filter as it contains residual fluid.

12 Place the new filter in position, and install the bolts. Tighten the bolts to the torque listed in this Chapter's Specifications.

13 Carefully clean the gasket surfaces of the fluid pan, removing all traces of old gasket material. Wash the pan in clean solvent and dry it with compressed air. Be sure to clean the metal filings from the magnet **(see illustration)**.

14 Install a new gasket, place the fluid pan in position and install the bolts in their original positions. Tighten the bolts to the torque listed in this Chapter's Specifications.

15 Lower the vehicle.

16 With the engine off, add new fluid to the transaxle through the

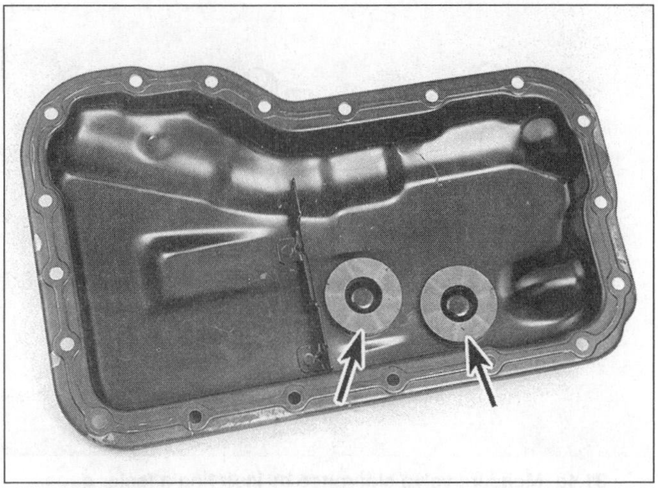

27.13 Wash the pan in clean solvent and remove metal filings from the magnet (arrow)

29.2 Grasp the hose securely and pull the PCV valve out of the cover

dipstick tube (see *Recommended fluids and lubricants* for the recommended fluid type and capacity). Use a funnel to prevent spills. It is best to add a little fluid at a time, continually checking the level with the dipstick (see Section 9). Allow the fluid time to drain into the pan.

17 Start the engine and shift the selector into all positions from P through L, then shift into P and apply the parking brake.

18 With the engine idling, check the fluid level. Add fluid up to the Cool level on the dipstick.

28 Manual transaxle lubricant change (every 30,000 miles or 24 months)

1 At the specified time intervals, the manual transaxle lubricant should be drained and replaced.

2 Before beginning work, purchase the specified lubricant (see *Recommended fluids and lubricants* at the front of this Chapter) and a new drain plug washer/seal.

3 Other tools necessary for this job include jackstands to support the vehicle in a raised position, wrenches, drain pan capable of holding at least four quarts, newspapers and clean rags.

4 The oil should be drained immediately after the vehicle has been driven. Hot oil is more effective than cold oil at removing built up sediment. **Warning:** *Oil temperature can exceed 350-degrees F in a hot transaxle. Wear protective gloves.*

5 After the vehicle has been driven to warm up the oil, disconnect the speedometer cable and remove the speedometer driven gear assembly.

6 Raise the vehicle and support it securely on jackstands. Make sure it is safely supported and as level as possible.

7 Move the necessary equipment under the vehicle, being careful not to touch any of the hot exhaust components.

8 Place the drain pan under the transaxle drain plug and loosen the drain plug.

9 Carefully unscrew the drain plug and washer with your fingers. Be careful not to burn yourself on the oil.

10 Allow the oil to drain completely. Clean the drain plug then reinstall it with a new washer. Tighten the drain plug to the torque listed in this Chapter's Specifications.

11 Lower the vehicle.

12 With the engine off, add new oil to the transaxle through the speedometer driven gear case hole (see *Recommended fluids and lubricants* at the front of this Chapter for oil type and transaxle capacity). Use a funnel to prevent spills. It is best to add a little oil at a time, continually checking the level (see Section 18).

13 Install the speedometer driven gear assembly and reconnect the speedometer cable.

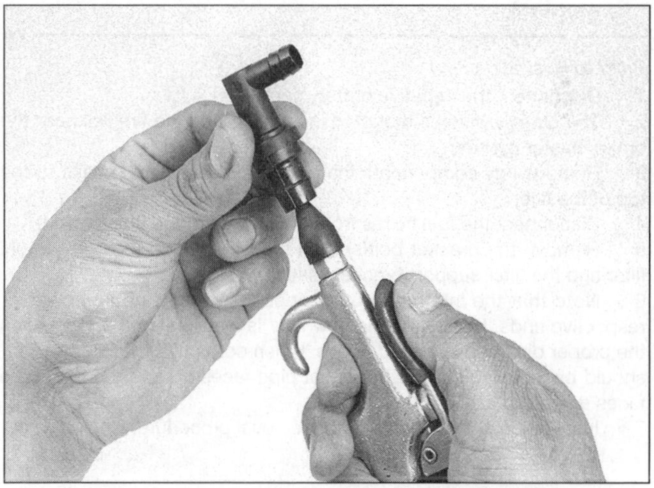

29.4 To check the PVC valve, first attach a clean section of hose to the cylinder head side of the valve and blow through it - air should pass through easily - then blow through the intake manifold side of the valve and verify that air passes through with difficulty

29 Positive Crankcase Ventilation (PCV) valve and hose check and replacement (every 30,000 miles or 24 months)

Refer to illustrations 29.2 and 29.4

1 The PCV valve and hose is located in the valve cover.

2 Pull the PCV valve from the cover **(see illustration).**

3 With the engine idling at normal operating temperature, place your finger over the end of the valve. If there's no vacuum at the valve, check for a plugged hose or valve. Replace any plugged or deteriorated hoses.

4 Turn off the engine. Remove the PCV valve from the hose. Connect a clean piece of hose and blow through the valve from the valve cover (cylinder head) end. If air will not pass through the valve in this direction, replace it with a new one **(see illustration).**

5 When purchasing a replacement PCV valve, make sure it's for your particular vehicle and engine size. Compare the old valve with the new one to make sure they're the same.

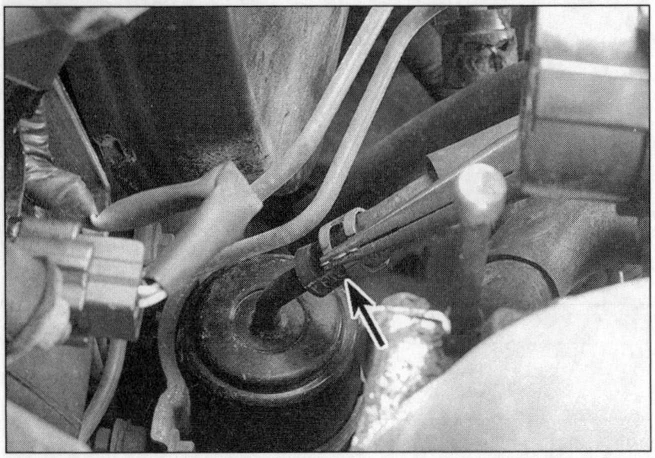

30.4 Disconnect the fuel hoses and remove the filter and bracket

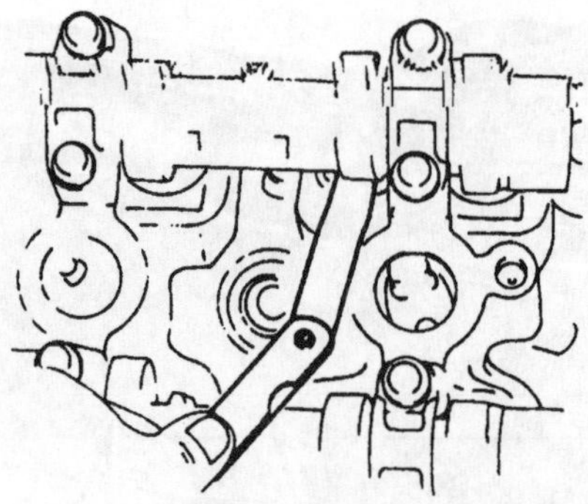

31.4a Measure valve clearance by inserting a feeler gage between the camshaft lobe and valve tappet

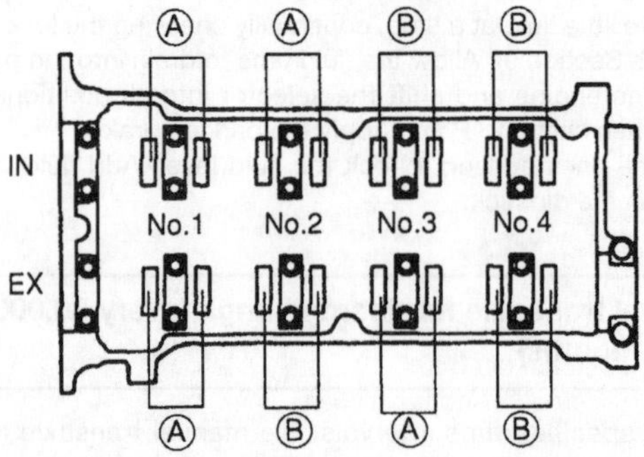

31.4b Valve clearance measurement positions

30 Fuel filter replacement (every 60,000 miles or 48 months)

Refer to illustration 30.4

1 Disconnect the negative battery cable.

2 The canister filter is mounted in a bracket on the firewall near the brake master cylinder.

3 Remove any components that would interfere with access to the top of the filter.

4 Disconnect the fuel hoses from the fuel filter **(see illustration)**.

5 Remove the bracket bolt(s) from the firewall and remove the old filter and the filter support bracket assembly.

6 Note that the inlet and outlet pipes are clearly labeled on their respective ends. Make sure the new filter is installed so that it's facing the proper direction as noted above. When correctly installed, the filter should be installed so that the outlet pipe faces up and the inlet pipe faces down.

7 Installation is the reverse of the removal procedure.

31 Valve clearance check and adjustment (1.5L DOHC and 1997 1.8L DOHC engines only) (every 60,000 miles or 48 months)

1 With the exception of the 1995 and later models with the 1.5 Liter DOHC engine and the 1997 1.8L DOHC engine, all Mazda 323 and Protegé engines are equipped with hydraulic lash adjusters which automatically maintain the correct valve clearance and adjustment is not required. The 1995 and later models with the 1.5 Liter engine and the 1997 1.8L DOHC engine use a tappet and an adjustment shim between the camshaft and valve, and valve clearance is adjusted by changing the shim thickness.

Check

Refer to illustrations 31.4a and 31.4b

2 Remove the valve/camshaft cover (see Chapter 2, Part A)

3 With the engine in a cold condition, measure the valve clearance as follows.

4 Turn the crankshaft clockwise so that the No. 1 piston is at TDC of the compression stroke. Measure the valve clearance at the "A" positions **(see illustrations)**.

5 Compare the measured clearance to that listed in this Chapter's Specifications. If the clearance exceeds specifications the adjustment shim will have to be replaced.

6 Turn the crankshaft 360 degrees clockwise so that the No. 4 piston is at TDC of the compression stroke. Measure the valve clearance at the "B" positions.

7 Again, if the clearance exceeds specifications the adjustment shim will have to be replaced.

Adjustment

8 Valve adjustment requires numerous special fixtures and tools and for this reason it is strongly recommended that you take the vehicle to your dealer's service department to ensure that this critical job is performed correctly.

Chapter 2 Part A Engines

Contents

Specifications

General

Firing order	1-3-4-2
Engine identification (8th character of the Vehicle Identification Number)	
VIN code 4	BP 1.8L Single Overhead Camshaft (SOHC)
VIN code 6	BP 1.8L Double Overhead Camshaft (DOHC)
VIN code X (1994 and earlier)	B6 1.6L Single Overhead Camshaft (SOHC)
VIN code X (1995 and later)	Z5 1.5L Double Over-head Camshaft (DOHC)

Cylinder location and distributor rotation

The blackened terminal shown on the distributor cap indicates the Number One spark plug wire position

Timing belt

Tensioner spring free length	
1.6L SOHC and 1.8L SOHC	2.31 inches
1.5L DOHC	2.80 inches
1.8L DOHC	2.33 inches
Timing belt deflection	
1.6L SOHC and 1.8L SOHC	0.43 to 0.51 inches
1.5L DOHC	0.28 to 0.35 inches
1.8L DOHC	0.36 to 0.45 inches

Camshaft

1.6L SOHC	
Lobe height - intake and exhaust	1.4272 inches minimum
Journal diameter	
Front and rear journals	1.7102 inches minimum
Center journals	1.7098 inches minimum
Out-of-round limit	0.002 inch maximum
Journal oil clearance	0.006 inch maximum
Endplay	0.008 inch maximum
1.8L SOHC	
Lobe height	
Intake	1.4092 inches minimum
Exhaust	1.4202 inches minimum
Journal diameter	
Front and rear journals	1.7102 inches minimum
Center journals	1.7096 inches minimum
Out-of-round limit	0.002 inch maximum
Journal oil clearance	0.006 inch maximum
Endplay	0.008 inch maximum
1.5L DOHC	
Lobe height - intake and exhaust	1.6024 inches minimum
Journal diameter	1.0201 inches minimum
Out-of-round limit	0.0012 inches maximum
Journal oil clearance	0.0033 inches maximum
Endplay	0.0079 inches maximum
1.8L DOHC	
Lobe height	
Intake	1.7281 inches minimum
Exhaust	1.7480 inches minimum
Journal diameter	1.0213 inches minimum
Out-of-round limit	0.002 inch maximum
Journal oil clearance	0.006 inch maximum
Camshaft runout	0.0012 inch maximum
Endplay	0.008 inch maximum
Lifter-to-bore clearance	0.0071 maximum

Oil pump

Driven rotor-to-pump housing clearance	0.0078 inch maximum
Outer rotor-to-body clearance	0.087 inch maximum
Rotor set-to-oil pump housing (side clearance)	0.0055 inch maximum
Oil pump relief valve spring free length	1.791 inches minimum

Rocker arm and shaft (SOHC)

1.6L SOHC	
Outside diameter	0.7070 inch minimum
Oil clearance	0.004 inch maximum
Rocker arm inside diameter	0.7097 inch maximum
1.8L SOHC	
Outside diameter	0.7464 inch minimum
Oil clearance	0.004 inch maximum
Rocker arm inside diameter	
Intake	0.7491 inch maximum
Exhaust	0.7493 inch maximum

Valve clearance

1.6L and 1.8L SOHC, 1996 and earlier 1.8L DOHC	zero lash (hydraulic non-adjustable)
1.5L DOHC	
Intake and exhaust	0.010 to 0.012 inch (cold)
1.8L DOHC (1997 model)	
Intake	0.008 to 0.009 inch (cold)
Exhaust	0.012 to 0.013 inch (cold)

Torque specifications

	Ft-lbs (unless otherwise indicated)
Camshaft bearing cap bolts (1.5L and 1.8L DOHC)	100 to 125 in-lbs
Camshaft idler pulley bolts	
1.6L and 1.8L SOHC	14 to 19
1.5L and 1.8L DOHC	27 to 38
Camshaft seal plate bolts (1.5L and 1.8L DOHC)	69 to 95 in-lbs

Torque specifications	Ft-lbs (unless otherwise indicated)
Camshaft sprocket bolt	36 to 45
Camshaft thrust plate bolt (1.6L SOHC)	69 to 95 in-lbs
Crankshaft pulley bolts	109 to 152 in-lbs
Crankshaft sprocket bolt	116 to 123
Cylinder head bolts	
1.6L and 1.8L SOHC, 1.8L DOHC	56 to 60
1.5L DOHC	
Step 1	13 to 16
Step 2	Tighten an additional 85 to 95 degrees
End plate bolts	69 to 95 in-lbs
Engine mount bolts/nuts	
No. 1 engine mount bracket bolts to engine	50 to 68
No. 1 engine rubber mount through-bolt	48 to 65
No. 1 engine mount to crossmember nut	50 to 65
No. 2 engine mount bracket bolts to engine	28 to 38
No. 2 engine mount bracket to crossmember	28 to 38
No. 3 engine mount bracket to engine	55 to 77
No. 3 engine mount bracket small bolts	14 to 16
No. 3 engine mount bracket nuts	69 to 83
No. 3 engine mount brackets large bolt	50 to 68
No. 4 left (driver's side) engine/transaxle bracket-to-transaxle nuts	50 to 68
No. 4 left (driver's side) engine/transaxle bracket-to-frame bolts	32 to 44
Exhaust manifold bolts/nuts	
1.6L and 1.8L SOHC	12 to 17
1.5L and1.8L DOHC	28 to 34
Exhaust manifold heat shield bolts/nuts	69 to 95 in-lbs
Exhaust pipe bracket bolts	27 to 38
Flywheel cover bolts	
1.6L and 1.8L SOHC	27 to 38
1.5L and 1.8L DOHC	48 to 65
Flywheel/driveplate bolts	71 to 76
Intake manifold bolts	14 to 19
Oil pan Main Bearing Support Plate (MBSP) bolts (all except 1.5L DOHC)	12 to 15
Oil Pan Stiffener bolts (models with separate oil pan)	27 to 38
Oil pan bolts	69 to 95 in-lbs
Oil pump bolts	14 to 19
Oil pump strainer	69 to 95 in-lbs
Rear cover screws	69 to 95 in-lbs
Rocker arm shaft bolts (1.6L and 1.8L SOHC)	16 to 21
Tensioner pulley bolt	
1.6L and 1.8L SOHC	14 to 19
1.5L and 1.8L DOHC	28 to 38
Timing belt idler pulley bolts	
1.6L and 1.8L SOHC	14 to 19
1.5L and 1.8L DOHC	28 to 38
Timing belt cover bolts	70 to 95 in-lbs
Valve cover bolts	
1.6L and 1.8L SOHC	43 to 78 in-lbs
1.5L DOHC	61 to 95 in-lbs
1.8L DOHC	
Two bolts at end of valve cover	69 to 95 in-lbs
Screws on top of valve cover	43 to 78 in-lbs
Water pump pulley	70 to 95 in-lbs

1 General information

This Part of Chapter 2 is devoted to in-vehicle repair procedures for all engines. All information concerning engine removal and installation and engine block and cylinder head overhaul can be found in Part B of this Chapter.

The following repair procedures are based on the assumption that the engine is installed in the vehicle. If the engine has been removed from the vehicle and mounted on a stand, many of the Steps outlined in this Part of Chapter 2 will not apply.

The Specifications included in this Part of Chapter 2 apply only to the procedures contained in this Part. Part B of Chapter 2 contains the Specifications necessary for cylinder head and engine block rebuilding.

Caution: *If the stereo in your vehicle is equipped with an anti-theft system, make sure you have the correct activation code before disconnecting the battery in any of the following procedures.*

2 Repair operations possible with the engine in the vehicle

Many major repair operations can be accomplished without removing the engine from the vehicle.

Clean the engine compartment and the exterior of the engine with some type of degreaser before any work is done. It will make the job easier and help keep dirt out of the internal areas of the engine.

Depending on the components involved, it may be helpful to remove the hood to improve access to the engine as repairs are performed (refer to Chapter 11 if necessary). Cover the fenders to prevent damage to the paint. Special pads are available, but a substitute such as a thick bedspread or blanket will also work.

If vacuum, exhaust, oil or coolant leaks develop, indicating a need for gasket or seal replacement, the repairs can generally be made with the engine in the vehicle. The intake and exhaust manifold gaskets, oil pan gasket, crankshaft oil seals and cylinder head gasket are all accessible with the engine in place.

Exterior engine components, such as the intake and exhaust manifolds, the oil pan, the oil pump, the water pump, the starter motor, the alternator, the distributor and the fuel system components can be removed for repair with the engine in place.

Since the cylinder head can be removed without pulling the engine, camshaft and valve component servicing can also be accomplished with the engine in the vehicle. Replacement of the timing belt and sprockets is also possible with the engine in the vehicle.

In extreme cases caused by a lack of necessary equipment, repair or replacement of piston rings, pistons, connecting rods and rod bearings is possible with the engine in the vehicle. However, this practice is not recommended because of the engine cleaning and other preparation work, such as driveshaft , steering, stabilizer bar, engine mount members that may require partial disassembly or removal for access to the engine.

3 Top Dead Center (TDC) - locating

Refer to illustration 3.8

Note: *The following procedure is based on the assumption that the distributor is correctly installed. If you are trying to locate TDC to install the distributor correctly, piston position must be determined by feeling for compression at the number one spark plug hole, then aligning the ignition timing marks as described in Step 8.*

1 Top Dead Center (TDC) is the highest point in the cylinder that each piston reaches traveling up-and-down as the crankshaft turns. Each piston reaches TDC on the compression stroke and again on the exhaust stroke, but TDC generally refers to piston position on the compression stroke.

2 Positioning the piston(s) at TDC is an essential part of many procedures such as camshaft and timing belt/sprocket removal and distributor removal.

3 Before beginning this procedure, be sure to place the transmission in Neutral and apply the parking brake or block the rear wheels. Also, disable the ignition system by detaching the primary (low voltage) wires from the coil (see Chapter 5). Remove the spark plugs (see Chapter 1).

4 In order to bring any piston to TDC, the crankshaft must be turned using one of the methods outlined below. When looking at the front of the engine, normal crankshaft rotation is clockwise.

a) *The preferred method is to turn the crankshaft with a socket and ratchet attached to the bolt threaded into the front of the crankshaft.*

b) *A remote starter switch, which may save some time, can also be used. Follow the instructions included with the switch. Once the piston is close to TDC, use a socket and ratchet as described in the previous paragraph.*

c) *If an assistant is available to turn the ignition switch to the Start position in short bursts, you can get the piston close to TDC without a remote starter switch. Make sure your assistant is out of the vehicle, away from the ignition switch, then use a socket and ratchet as described in Paragraph a) to complete the procedure.*

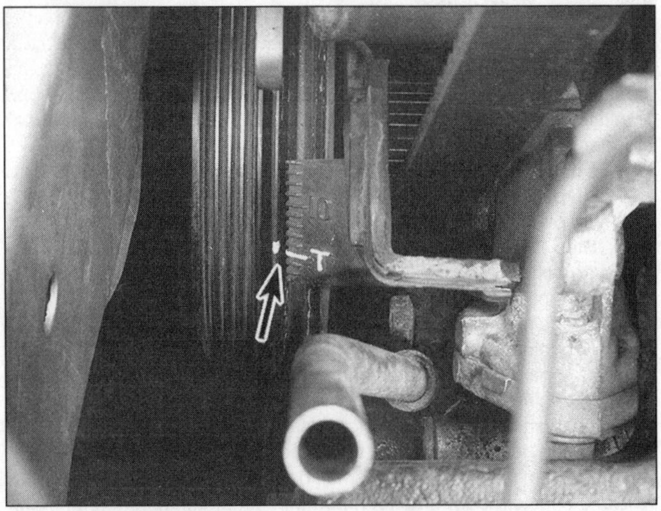

3.8 To bring the number one piston to TDC, align the timing notch on the edge of the crankshaft pulley with the T-degree mark

5 Note the position of the terminal for the number one spark plug wire on the distributor cap. If the terminal is not marked, follow the plug wire from the number one cylinder spark plug to the cap.

6 Use a felt-tip pen or chalk to make a mark on the distributor body and the cap - directly at the terminal.

7 Detach the cap from the distributor and set it aside (see Chapter 1 if necessary).

8 Turn the crankshaft (see Step 3 above) until the notch in the crankshaft sprocket is aligned with the T on the timing plate (located at the front of the engine) **(see illustration)**.

9 Look at the distributor rotor - it should be pointing directly at the mark you made on the distributor body.

10 If the rotor is 180-degrees off, the number one piston is at TDC on the exhaust stroke.

11 To get the piston to TDC on the compression stroke, turn the crankshaft one complete turn (360-degrees) clockwise. The rotor should now be pointing at the mark on the distributor. When the rotor is pointing at the number one spark plug wire terminal in the distributor cap and the ignition timing marks are aligned, the number one piston is at TDC on the compression stroke. **Note:** *If it is impossible to align the ignition timing marks when the rotor is pointing at the mark on the distributor body, the timing belt may have jumped the teeth on the sprockets or may have been installed incorrectly.*

12 After the number one piston has been positioned at TDC on the compression stroke, TDC for any of the remaining pistons can be located by turning the crankshaft and following the firing order. Mark the remaining spark plug wire terminal locations on the distributor body just like you did for the number one terminal, then number the marks to correspond with the cylinder numbers. As you turn the crankshaft, the rotor will also turn. When it's pointing directly at one of the marks on the distributor, the piston for that particular cylinder is at TDC on the compression stroke.

4 Valve cover - removal and installation

Removal

Refer to illustrations 4.4 and 4.5

1 Disconnect the negative cable from the battery.

2 Detach the PCV (Positive Crankcase Ventilation) valve and breather hoses from the valve cover.

4.4 Remove the timing belt cover bolts (SOHC engine shown)

4.5 Remove the valve cover bolts (SOHC engine shown)

1.6L and 1.8L SOHC models

3 Disconnect the spark plug wires from the clips.

4 Remove the two upper bolts from the timing belt cover **(see illustration)**. Loosen, but do not remove the lower timing belt cover bolts.

5 Remove the valve cover bolts **(see illustration)**.

6 Lift the valve cover from the cylinder head. If it sticks, knock it loose with a rubber mallet or a hammer and a block of wood. Don't pry between the sealing surfaces.

7 Visually check the valve cover gasket for damage and to ensure that has not hardened and is still flexible. Save it for reuse if satisfactory.

1.5L and 1.8L DOHC models

8 Label the spark plug cables, then remove them from the spark plugs.

9 Remove the distributor, leaving the spark plug cables connected to the distributor.

10 On a 1.8L DOHC engine, remove the bolts attaching the upper timing belt cover, then remove the cover.

11 Remove the bolts holding the valve cover in place, disconnect any tubing or other connected components and move them out of the way, and remove the valve cover. If the cover sticks, knock it loose with a rubber mallet or a hammer and a block of wood. Do not pry between the sealing surfaces.

Installation

Refer to illustrations 4.12, 4.21a, 4.21b and 4.23

1.6L and 1.8L SOHC models

12 If a new valve cover gasket is being installed, clean the groove of the valve cover. Apply silicone sealant in the groove of the valve cover and press the new gasket into the groove **(see illustration)**.

13 If the valve cover gasket is being reused, remove the gasket, make sure the groove is clean and the gasket is clean. Apply silicone sealant in the groove of the valve cover, and reinstall the gasket.

14 Position the valve cover in place and insert the bolts by hand, starting the threads several turns before using a wrench.

15 Tighten the valve cover bolts/screws in several steps to the torque listed in this Chapter's Specifications.

16 Reinstallation of the remaining parts is the reverse of removal.

17 Run the engine and check for oil leaks.

1.5L and 1.8L DOHC models

18 The mating surfaces of the housing or cylinder head and cover must be clean when the cover is installed. Carefully use a gasket scraper to remove all traces of sealant and old gasket material - be careful to not gouge the gasket surfaces when cleaning. Then clean the mating surfaces with a rag with gasket cleaner or solvent. If there is

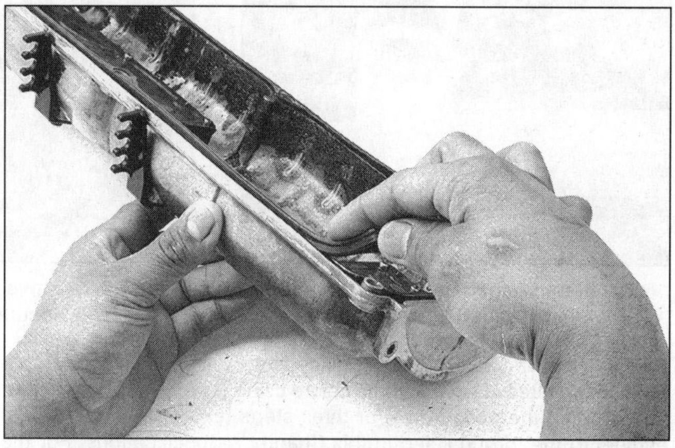

4.12 Press the valve cover gasket into the groove by hand (SOHC engine shown)

residue or oil on the mating surfaces when the cover is installed, oil leaks may develop.

19 If a new valve cover gasket is being installed, apply silicone sealant in the groove of the valve cover and press the new gasket into the groove **(see illustration 4.12)**.

20 If the valve cover gasket is being reused, remove the gasket, make sure the groove is clean and the gasket is clean. Apply silicone sealant in the groove of the valve cover, and reinstall the gasket.

21 Apply a light coating of silicone sealant to the areas shown **(see illustrations)**.

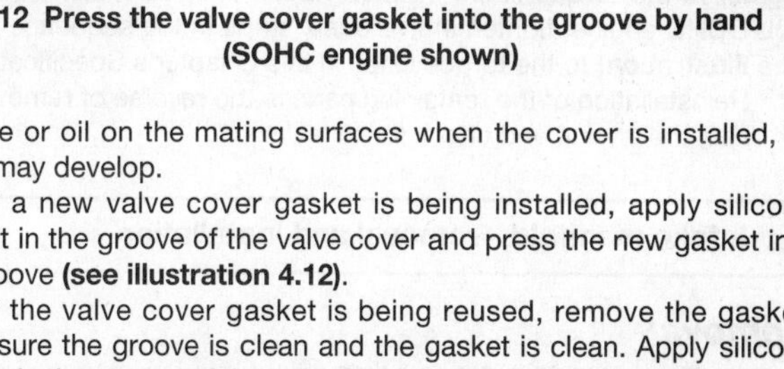

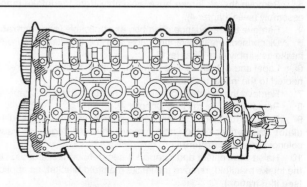

4.21a Apply silicone sealant to the shaded areas on the cylinder head before installing the valve cover (1.8L DOHC)

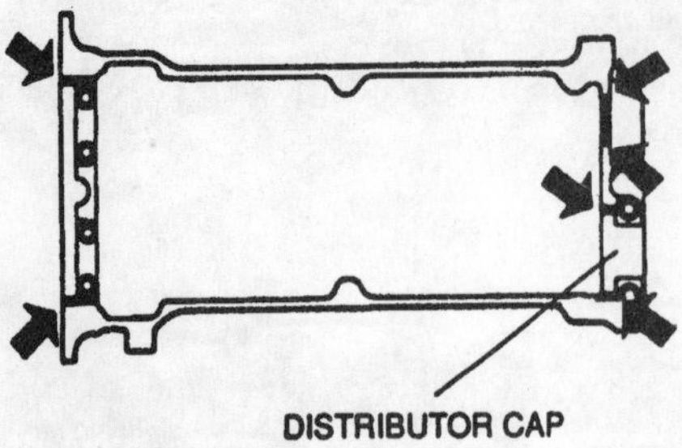

4.21b Apply silicone sealant to the areas shown before installing the valve cover (1.5L DOHC)

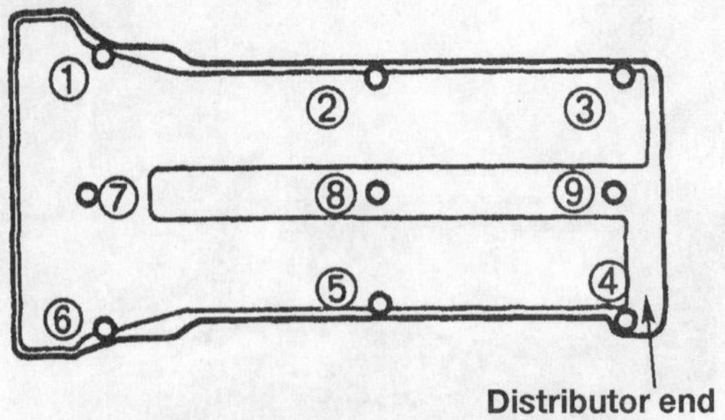

4.23 Valve cover tightening sequence (1.5L DOHC)

5.4 Remove the resonance chamber above the radiator, as applicable

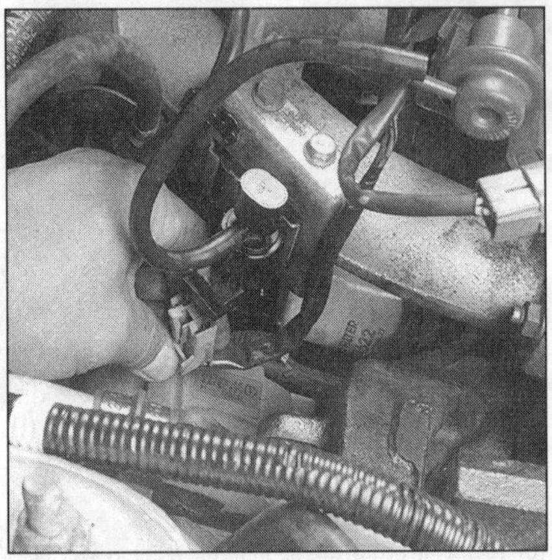

5.9 Remove the fuel regulator vacuum solenoid

5.10 Remove the intake manifold support bracket

22 Position the valve cover in place and insert the bolts by hand, starting the threads several turns before using a wrench.

23 Tighten the bolts in two or three steps (except the 1.5L DOHC engine) to the torque listed in this Chapter's Specifications. For the 1.5L DOHC engine, tighten in five or six steps in the sequence shown **(see illustration)** to the torque listed in this Chapter's Specifications.

24 Reinstallation of the remaining parts is the reverse of removal.

25 Run the engine and check for oil leaks.

5 Intake manifold - removal and installation

Removal

Refer to illustrations 5.4, 5.9 and 5.10

1 Disconnect the negative cable from the battery.

2 Drain the cooling system (see Chapter 1).

3 Remove the air intake hose assembly from the intake manifold assembly (see Chapter 4).

4 Remove the resonance chamber, as applicable **(see illustration)**.

5 Disconnect the accelerator cable and the throttle cable from the intake assembly (see Chapter 4).

6 Label and detach all wire harness, control cables and hoses connected to the intake manifold.

7 Remove the air intake plenum and throttle body (see Chapter 4).

8 Remove the fuel rail (see Chapter 4).

9 Remove the electrical connector and vacuum lines to the fuel regulator vacuum solenoid, and remove the fuel regulator vacuum solenoid **(see illustration)**.

10 Raise the vehicle and support it securely on jackstands. Under the intake manifold, remove the intake manifold bracket, as applicable **(see illustration)**.

11 Remove the intake manifold mounting bolts, while supporting the intake manifold from above the engine.

12 Lower the vehicle if necessary.

13 Remove the intake manifold.

Installation

14 Carefully use a gasket scraper to remove all traces of old gasket material and any sealant from the manifold and cylinder head, then clean the mating surfaces with gasket cleaner or solvent - be careful to not gouge the gasket surfaces when cleaning. If the gasket was leaking, have the manifold checked for warpage at an automotive machine shop and resurfaced if necessary.

15 Install a new gasket, then position the manifold on the head and install the nuts/bolts.

16 Tighten the nuts/bolts in three or four equal steps to the torque listed in this Chapter's Specifications. Work from the center out towards the ends, while alternating upper to lower bolts/nuts to avoid warping the manifold.

17 Reinstall the remaining parts in the reverse order of removal.

18 Before starting the engine, check the throttle linkage for smooth operation.

19 Check coolant level. Run the engine and check for coolant and vacuum leaks.

20 Road test the vehicle and check for proper operation of all accessories, including the cruise control system (if equipped).

6 Exhaust manifold - removal and installation

Refer to illustration 6.3

Warning: *The engine must be completely cool before beginning this procedure.*

Removal

1 Disconnect the negative cable from the battery.

2 Unplug the oxygen sensor electrical connector from the exhaust manifold. If you are installing a new manifold, remove the sensor (see Chapter 6).

3 Remove the heat shield bolts and remove the heat shield from the manifold **(see illustration)**.

6.3 Remove the exhaust manifold heat shield

4 Apply penetrating oil to the exhaust manifold mounting bolts/nuts and to the exhaust pipe nuts.

5 Raise the vehicle and support it securely on jackstands (see Chapter 1).

6 Disconnect the exhaust pipe from the exhaust manifold. Lower the vehicle.

7 Remove the manifold bolts/nuts and detach the manifold from the cylinder head. **Note:** *If any bolts/nuts are difficult to remove, reapply penetrating oil to the bolts/nuts and let them soak for at least 15 minutes. If any bolts or studs break during removal, you may be able to use a vise-grip pliers after the manifold is removed to unscrew the broken bolt/stud. If unable to remove the broken bolt/stud, see your automotive parts store for stud removal tools. Replace any damaged parts with factory parts, or parts specifically designed for exhaust system application.*

Installation

8 Use a scraper to remove all traces of old gasket material and carbon deposits from the manifold and cylinder head mating surfaces. If the gasket was leaking, have the manifold checked for warpage at an automotive machine shop and resurfaced if necessary. **Caution:** *When scraping, be very careful not to gouge or scratch the delicate aluminum cylinder head manifold mounting surface.*

9 Position a new exhaust manifold gasket over the studs on the cylinder head.

10 Install the manifold and thread the mounting bolts/nuts into place.

11 Working from the center out, tighten the bolts/nuts to the torque listed in this Chapter's Specifications in several equal steps.

12 Reinstall the remaining parts in the reverse order of removal. If reinstalling the oxygen sensor, use a special anti-seize thread lubricant available at your automotive parts store.

13 Run the engine and check for exhaust leaks.

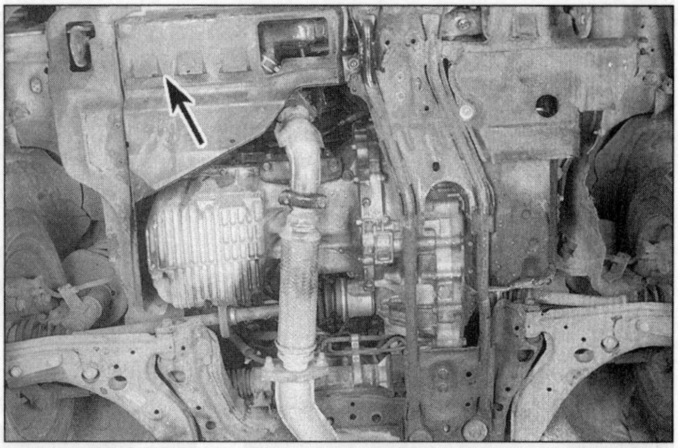

7.3 Remove the undercover splash shield for access to engine

7 Timing belt and sprockets - removal and installation

Removal

1 Disconnect the negative cable from the battery

2 Block the rear wheels and set the parking brake.

1.6L and 1.8L SOHC models

Refer to illustrations 7.3, 7.9, 7.10, 7.12a, 7.12b and 7.15

3 Remove the under cover splash shield **(see illustration).**

4 Remove the power steering and air conditioner drivebelt, if applicable (see Chapter 1).

5 Remove the alternator drivebelt (see Chapter 1). Remove the spark plugs from all cylinders.

6 Remove the water pump pulley bolts and remove the water pump pulley.

7 Remove the four crankshaft pulley bolts.

8 Remove the crankshaft pulley.

9 Remove the crankshaft sprocket center bolt **(see illustration). Note:** *If necessary to prevent the crankshaft from turning, remove the flywheel/driveplate access cover and carefully wedge a screwdriver between the ring gear teeth and the engine block. Do not damage the gear teeth when holding the flywheel/driveplate.*

10 Remove the timing belt guide **(see illustration).** If necessary, carefully pry the guide off using two large screwdrivers or small prybars.

11 Remove the timing belt upper cover and lower cover.

12 Temporarily reinstall the crankshaft sprocket bolt, rotate the engine to align the crankshaft and camshaft sprocket marks **(see illustrations).** The crankshaft sprocket pulley Woodruff key should be fac-

7.9 Remove the center bolt from the crankshaft sprocket using a large socket and ratchet or breaker bar

7.10 Slide the timing belt guide from the crankshaft - if necessary, carefully pry it off using two large screwdrivers or small prybars

7.12a Timing belt camshaft sprocket alignment mark (SOHC engines)

7.12b Timing belt crankshaft sprocket alignment mark (SOHC engines)

7.15 To release the tension on the timing belt, loosen the timing belt tensioner pulley bolt, rotate the pulley away from the belt and retighten the bolt

ing upwards (top).

13 Remove the crankshaft sprocket bolt.

14 If reusing the timing belt, paint match marks on the sprockets and belt and an arrow indicating direction of travel on the belt.

15 Loosen the timing belt tensioner **(see illustration)**, and temporarily tighten the tensioner with the spring fully extended. Remove the timing belt.

16 If it is necessary to remove the camshaft sprocket(s) to replace the seal(s), remove the valve cover (see Section 4). Remove the camshaft sprocket bolt(s) and remove the sprocket(s) from the camshaft(s). Prevent the camshaft from turning by placing a wrench on the hex surface of the camshaft **(see illustration 7.31)**. If it is necessary to remove the crankshaft sprocket, carefully pry it off with two prybars.

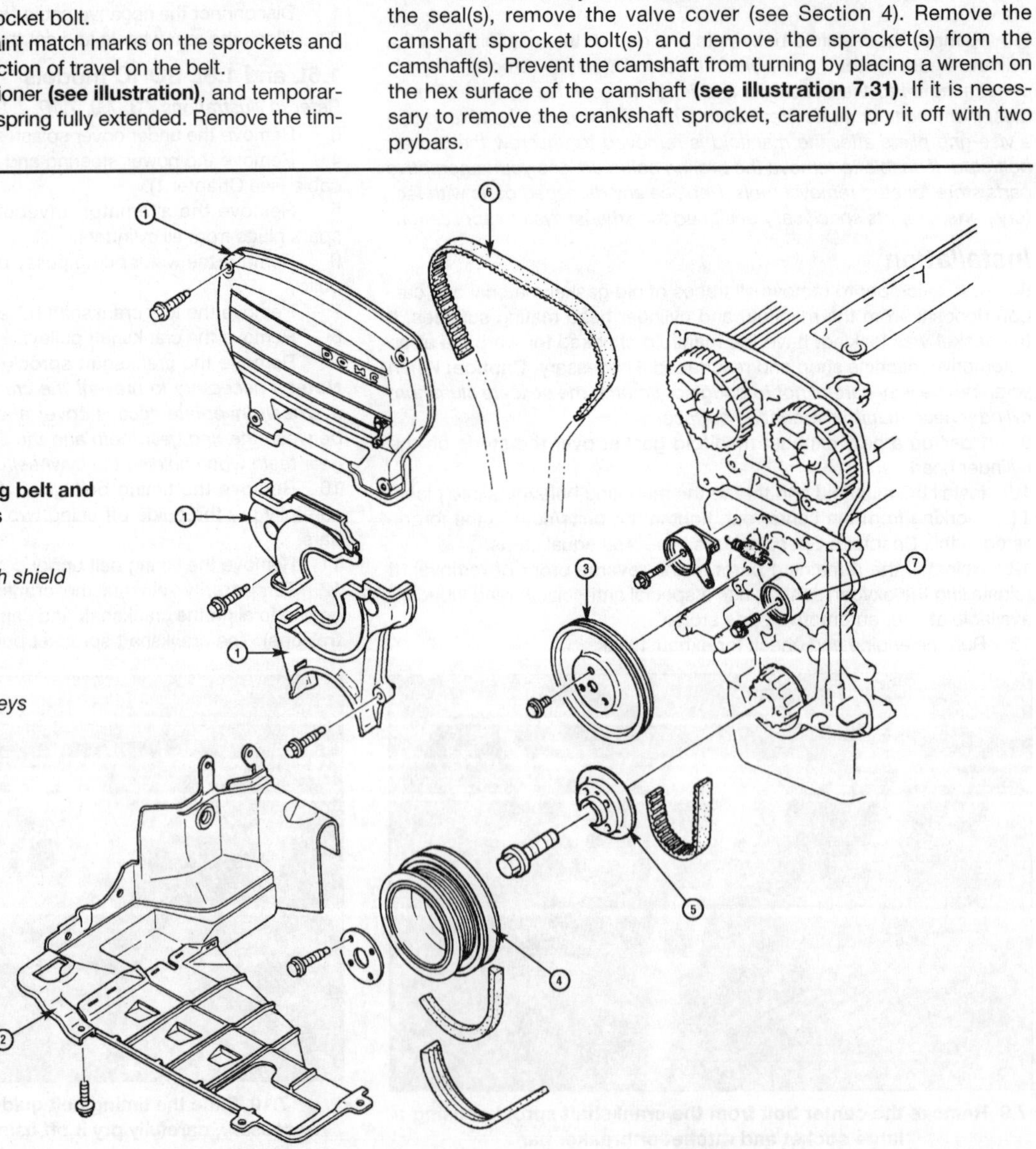

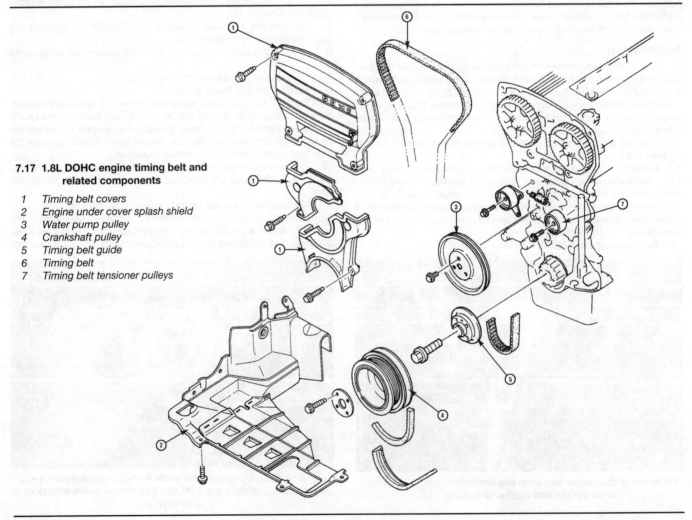

7.17 1.8L DOHC engine timing belt and related components

1 *Timing belt covers*
2 *Engine under cover splash shield*
3 *Water pump pulley*
4 *Crankshaft pulley*
5 *Timing belt guide*
6 *Timing belt*
7 *Timing belt tensioner pulleys*

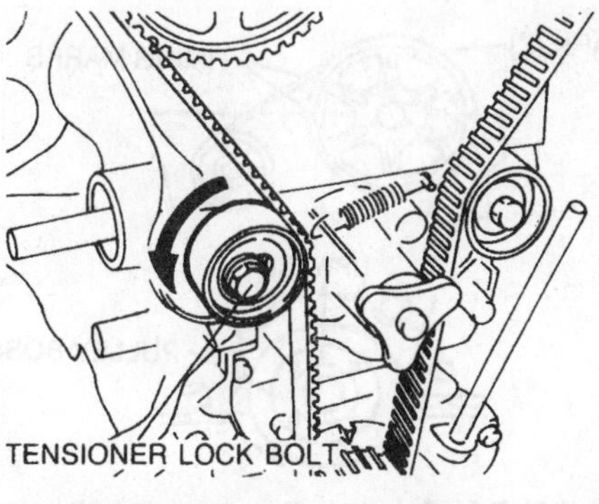

7.29 To release the tension on the timing belt, loosen the timing belt tensioner pulley bolt, rotate the pulley away from the belt and retighten the bolt

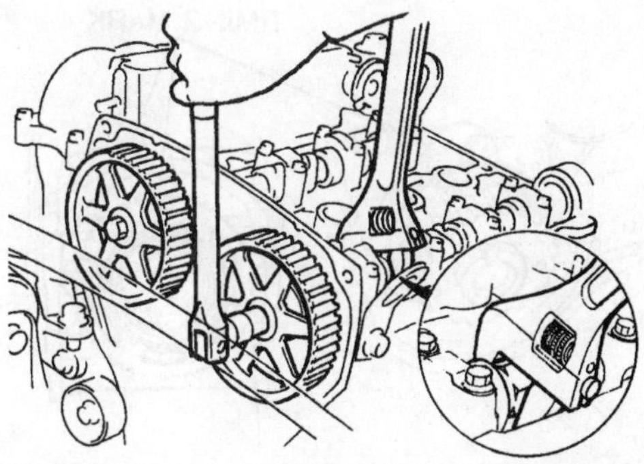

7.31 To remove the camshaft sprocket, hold the camshaft with a wrench on the hex while loosening the sprocket bolt

1.5L and 1.8L DOHC models

Refer to illustrations 7.17, 7.29 and 7.31

17 Remove the engine under cover shield **(see illustration)**.

18 Remove the power steering and/or air conditioning drivebelt (see Chapter 1).

19 Remove the alternator drivebelt (see Chapter 1).

20 Remove the water pump pulley bolts and remove the pulley.

21 Remove the spark plugs from all cylinders.

22 Remove the oil dipstick.

23 Remove the four crankshaft pulley plate bolts and remove the pulley.

24 Remove the timing belt upper cover, middle cover, and lower cover.

25 Remove the crankshaft sprocket center bolt. **Note:** *If necessary to prevent the crankshaft from turning, remove the flywheel/driveplate access cover and carefully wedge a screwdriver between the ring gear teeth and the engine block. Do not damage the gear teeth when holding the flywheel/driveplate.*

26 Remove the timing belt guide **(see illustration 7.10)**.

27 Temporarily reinstall the crankshaft sprocket bolt, and rotate the engine to align the crankshaft and camshaft sprocket marks **(see illustrations 7.41b and 7.41c)**. The timing belt guide dowel pin should be facing upward (top). Remove the crankshaft sprocket bolt.

28 If reusing the timing belt, paint match marks on the pulley and belt and an arrow indicating direction of travel on the belt.

29 Loosen the timing belt tensioner **(see illustration)**. Cover the tensioner with a rag to protect it while prying the tensioner outward with a prybar. Temporarily tighten the tensioner with the spring fully extended.

30 Remove the timing belt.

31 If it is necessary to remove the camshaft sprocket(s) (to replace the seal(s), remove the valve cover (see Section 4). Remove the camshaft sprocket bolt(s) and remove the sprocket(s) from the camshaft(s). Prevent the camshaft from turning by placing a wrench on the hex surface on the shaft **(see illustration)**. If it is necessary to remove the crankshaft sprocket, carefully pry it off with two prybars.

Inspection

Refer to illustrations 7.34, 7.35 and 7.36

Caution: *Do not bend, twist or turn the timing belt inside out. Do not allow it to come in contact with oil, coolant or fuel. Do not use timing belt tension to keep the camshaft or crankshaft from turning when installing the sprocket bolt(s). Do not turn the crankshaft or camshaft more than a few degrees (necessary for tooth alignment) while the timing belt is removed.*

32 Remove the idler pulleys and check the bearings for smooth operation and excessive play. Inspect the spring for damage.

33 If the timing belt was broken during engine operation, the belt may have been fouled by debris or may have been damaged by a defective component in the area of the timing belt; check for belt material in the teeth of the sprockets. Any defective parts or debris in the sprockets must be cleaned out of all the sprockets before installing the new belt or the belt will not mesh properly when installed.

34 If the belt teeth are cracked or pulled off **(see illustration)**, the distributor, water pump, oil pump or camshaft(s) may have seized.

35 If there is noticeable wear or cracks in the belt **(see illustration)**, check to see if there are nicks or burrs on the sprockets.

36 If there is wear or damage on only one side of the belt **(see illustration)**, check the belt guide and the alignment of all sprockets. Also check the oil seals at the front of the engine and replace them if they are leaking.

37 Replace the timing belt with a new one if obvious wear or damage is noted or if it is the least bit questionable. Correct any problems which contributed to belt failure prior to belt installation. **Note:** *We recommend replacing the belt whenever it is removed, since belt failure can lead to expensive engine damage.*

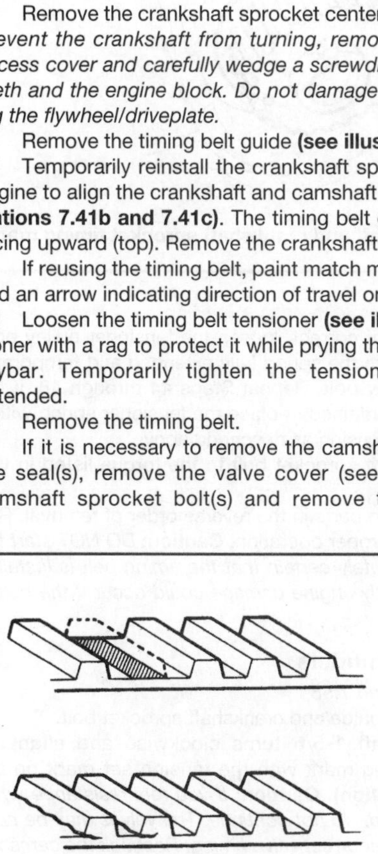

7.34 Check the timing belt for cracked and missing teeth

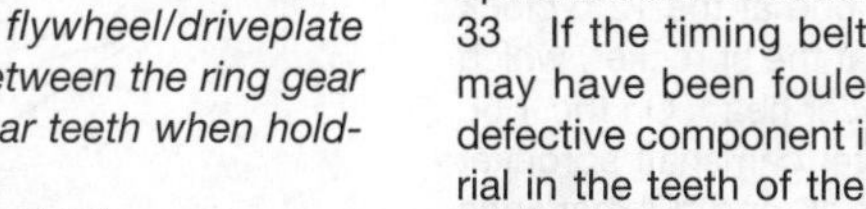

7.35 If the belt is cracked or worn, check the pulleys for nicks and burrs

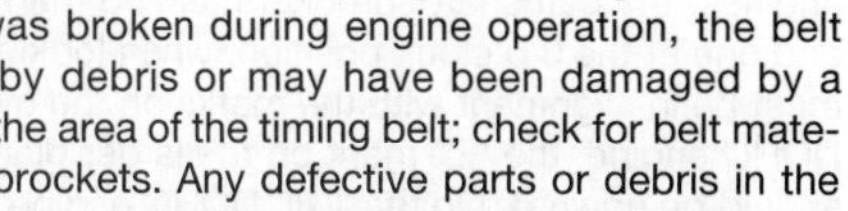

7.36 Wear on one side of the belt indicates pulley misalignment problems

2A

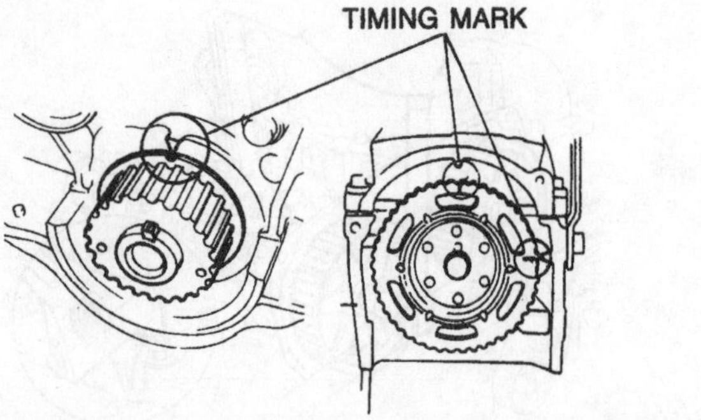

7.41a 1.6L SOHC and 1.8L SOHC camshaft and crankshaft sprocket timing marks

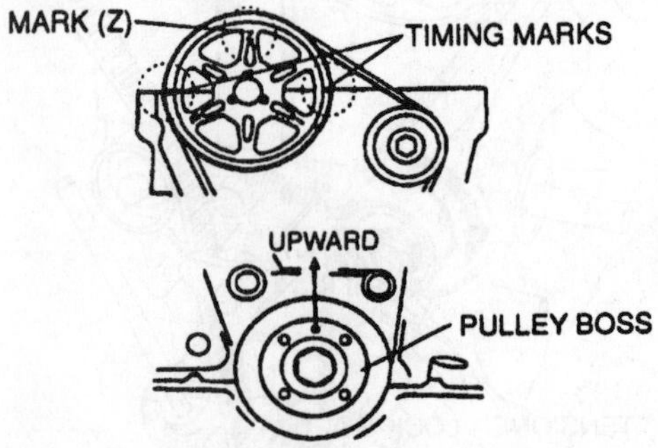

7.41b 1.5L DOHC camshaft and crankshaft sprocket timing marks

Installation

Refer to illustrations 7.41a, 7.41b and 7.41c

38 Remove all dirt and oil from the timing belt area at the front of the engine.

39 If they were removed, install the idler pulleys and tensioner. The idler pulley should be pulled back against spring tension with the spring fully extended and the idler pulley bolt temporarily tightened.

40 If they were removed, install the camshaft(s) and crankshaft sprocket(s). Make sure the sprocket Woodruff key is installed with the tapered side toward the oil pump body. Tighten the sprocket bolt(s) to the torque listed in this Chapter's Specifications, referring to Steps 16 and 31 above.

41 Recheck the camshaft sprocket and crankshaft sprocket timing marks to be sure they are properly aligned **(see illustrations)**. The crankshaft sprocket is aligned with the mark upwards. On SOHC engines, the camshaft sprocket has two marks, one at the 12 o'clock and one at the 3 o'clock position, when looking at the sprocket, which must be in alignment with the marks on the cylinder head. On the 1.5L DOHC engine, the "Z" mark on the larger diameter camshaft sprocket should be upward. On the 1.8L DOHC engine the "I" and "E" markings are upward in alignment with the two notches in the seal plate. **Note:** *If necessary, rotate the camshaft sprocket(s) slightly to achieve proper alignment.*

42 Slip the timing belt over the crankshaft sprocket and camshaft sprocket(s), and position the belt with no looseness on the side opposite the tensioner pulley. If the original belt is being reinstalled, align the marks made during removal with the marks on the sprockets, and be sure to install the timing belt so that it will rotate in the same direction as removed (the direction of rotation was marked during removal).

1.6L and 1.8L SOHC models

43 Install the timing belt guide and crankshaft sprocket bolt.

44 Rotate the crankshaft two turns clockwise, align the crankshaft sprocket timing marks. **Caution:** *If you feel resistance while rotating the engine by hand, do not continue. The valves may be contacting the pistons due to incorrect valve timing. Recheck the camshaft and crankshaft sprockets to be sure they are correctly aligned with their marks.*

45 Verify the camshaft sprocket marks are properly aligned with the marks on the cylinder head **(see illustration 7.41a)**.

46 Loosen the tensioner (idler) pulley bolt to apply tension to the timing belt. **Note:** *The tensioner pulley spring applies the proper tension to the belt.*

47 Tighten the tensioner pulley bolt.

48 Again, rotate the crankshaft two turns clockwise, align the crankshaft sprocket timing marks and verify the camshaft sprocket marks are aligned with the marks on the cylinder head **(see illustration 7.41a)**.

49 Check the timing belt tension by applying moderate force by hand (about 20 pounds force) midway between the crankshaft sprocket and camshaft sprocket (*not* the tensioner pulley side) and measure the belt deflection. Deflection should be approximately 1/2-inch, but not less than 7/16-inch.

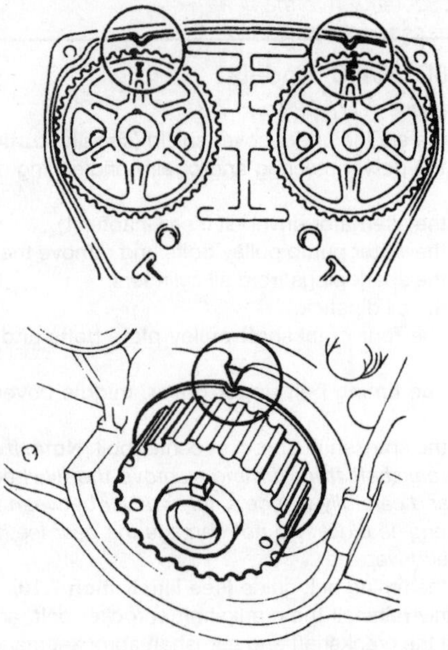

7.41c 1.8L DOHC camshaft and crankshaft sprocket timing marks

50 If belt deflection is *not* correct, loosen the tensioner pulley bolt, set the tensioner pulley with the spring fully extended and temporarily tighten the tensioner pulley bolt. Repeat Steps 44 through 48. If the proper tension is still not obtained, replace the tensioner spring with a new spring and reset belt tension as described above.

51 Tighten the crankshaft sprocket bolt to the torque listed in this Chapter's Specifications.

52 Reinstall the remaining parts in the reverse order of removal. Run the engine and check for proper operation. **Caution:** *DO NOT start the engine until you are absolutely certain that the timing belt is installed correctly. Serious and costly engine damage could occur if the belt is improperly installed.*

1.5L and 1.8L DOHC models

Refer to illustrations 7.54 and 7.58

53 Install the timing belt guide and crankshaft sprocket bolt.

54 Rotate the crankshaft 1-5/6 turns clockwise and align the crankshaft sprocket timing mark with the tension set mark on the engine block **(see illustration)**. **Caution:** *If you feel resistance while rotating the engine by hand, do not continue. The valves may be contacting the pistons due to incorrect valve timing. Recheck the camshaft and crankshaft sprockets to be sure they are correctly aligned with their marks.*

55 Loosen the tensioner pulley bolt and allow the tensioner spring to apply tension to the timing belt. **Note:** *The tensioner pulley spring*

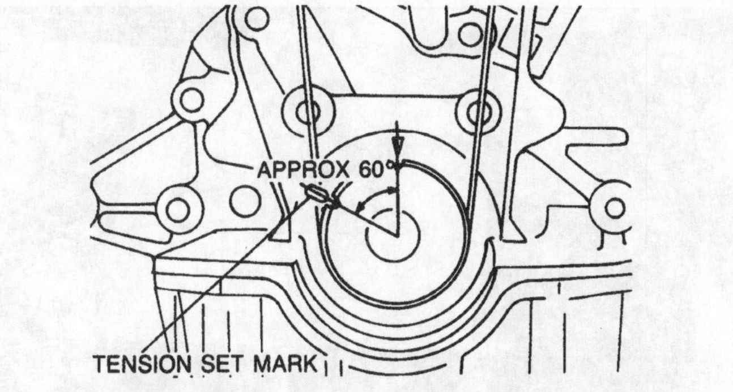

7.54 On 1.5L and 1.8L DOHC engines align the crankshaft sprocket timing mark with the Tension Set Mark

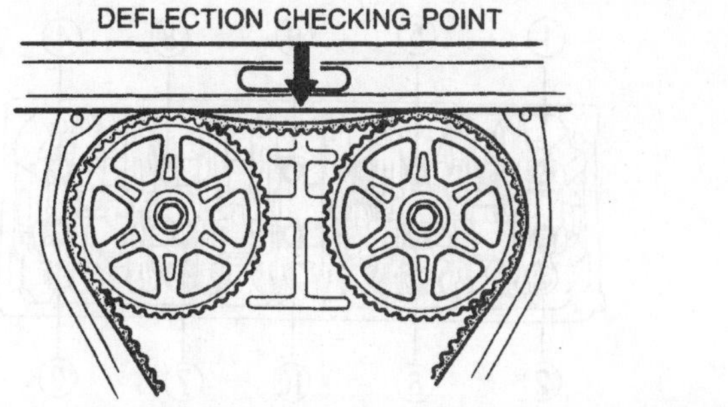

7.58 Check the timing belt deflection at a point midway between the camshaft sprockets (or camshaft sprocket and idler pulley on the 1.5L engine)

applies the proper tension to the belt.

56 Tighten the tensioner pulley bolt.

57 Turn the crankshaft 2-1/6 turns clockwise and verify that the crankshaft sprocket timing mark and the camshaft sprocket timing marks are correctly aligned **(see illustrations 7.41b and 7.41c)**. If the timing marks do not align, remove the timing belt and repeat the installation procedure.

58 Check the timing belt tension by applying moderate force by hand (about 20 pounds force) midway between the camshaft sprockets and measure the belt deflection **(see illustration)**. 1.5L DOHC engine belt deflection should be 9/32 inch to 11/32 inch. 1.8L DOHC engine belt deflection should be 3/8 inch to 7/16 inch.

59 If belt deflection is *not* correct, repeat the installation procedure. If the proper tension is still not obtained, replace the tensioner spring with a new spring and reset belt tension as described above.

60 Tighten the crankshaft sprocket bolt to the torque listed in this Chapter's Specifications.

61 Reinstall the remaining parts in the reverse order of removal. Run the engine and check for proper operation. **Caution:** *DO NOT start the engine until you are absolutely certain that the timing belt is installed correctly. Serious and costly engine damage could occur if the belt is improperly installed.*

8 Camshaft oil seal(s) - replacement

Removal

Refer to illustration 8.5

1 Disconnect the cable from the negative battery terminal.

2 Block the rear wheels and set the parking brake.

3 Position cylinder number one to TDC on the compression stroke (see Section 3).

4 Remove the camshaft sprocket bolt(s) and sprocket(s) (see Section 7). On 1.8L DOHC models, remove the timing belt sprocket rear shield.

5 Carefully pry the camshaft seal out of the bore using a thin screwdriver **(see illustration)**. Or drill a small hole in the seal midway between the camshaft and cylinder head; thread a small screw into the camshaft oil seal one or two threads and use the screw to pull the seal from the bore. **Caution:** *DO NOT nick or scratch the camshaft or seal bore.*

8.5 Carefully pry the camshaft seal out of the bore - DO NOT nick or scratch the camshaft or seal bore

Installation

6 Apply some clean engine oil to the lip of the new camshaft oil seal. Push the seal in slightly by hand.

7 Hold a short length of pipe or tube sized to fit the camshaft oil seal bore against the seal, and lightly tap the seal in, flush to the edge of the camshaft cap or to the depth of the original seal.

8 Reinstall the remaining parts in the reverse order of removal.

9 Run the engine and check for proper operation.

9 Rocker arms, lash adjusters and camshaft(s) - removal, inspection and installation

Removal

Refer to illustration 9.4

1 Remove the valve cover (see Section 4).

2 Remove the distributor (see Chapter 5).

3 Remove the timing belt covers, timing belt, and camshaft sprocket(s) (see Section 7).

4 Measure the thrust clearance (endplay) of the camshaft(s) with a dial indicator **(see illustration)**. If the clearance is greater than the

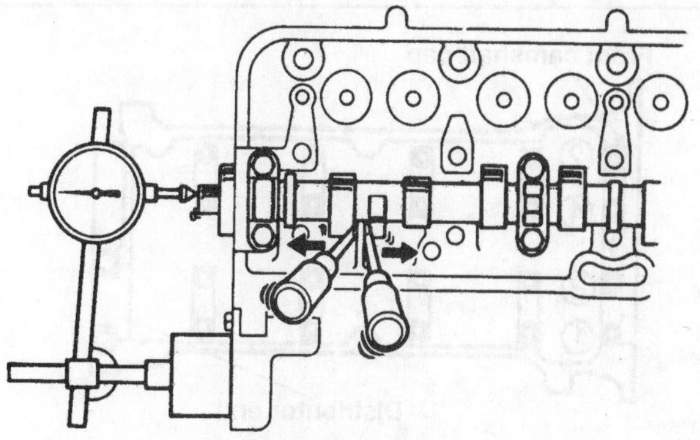

9.4 Pry the camshaft back-and-forth to check the endplay (thrust clearance)

2A

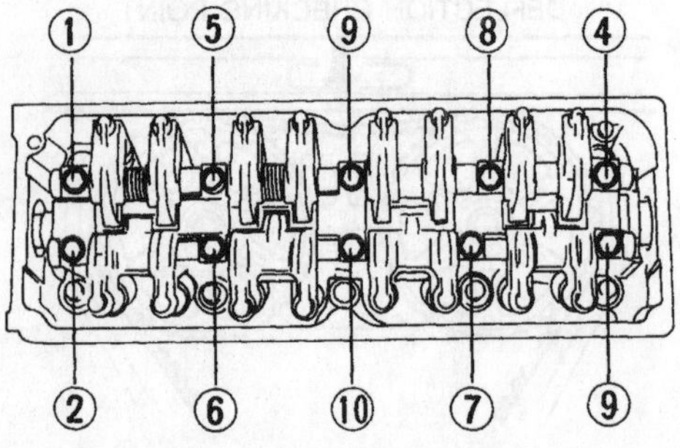

9.6 Loosen the camshaft bearing cap bolts, in several steps, in the sequence shown (SOHC engine)

9.9 Pull the camshaft straight out of the cylinder head

value listed in this Chapter's Specifications, replace the camshaft thrust plate, camshaft, and/or the cylinder head.

1.6L and 1.8L SOHC models

Refer to Illustrations 9.6, 9.7 and 9.9

Note: *The 1.6L and 1.8L SOHC engines use a rocker shaft and rocker arm with hydraulic lash adjusters. The hydraulic lash adjusters eliminate the need for valve lash adjusting screws or shims. After initial installation, no further valve adjustment is necessary.*

5 Number or mark the components before removal to be sure that the parts will be reinstalled in the same location when reassembled.

6 Loosen the rocker arm bolts in the sequence shown **(see illustration)** in two or three steps.

9.7 Mark up a cardboard box or a similar method to store the lifters/shims and bearing caps to relocate for reinstallation

7 Remove the rocker arm and rocker shaft assembly. Mark or otherwise store the rocker arms and springs so for later reinstallation in the same locations from which they were removed **(see illustration).**

8 In order to remove the camshaft without removing the cylinder head from the engine, remove the distributor, the air cleaner assembly and reposition the underhood fuse box.

9 Pull the camshaft straight out of the cylinder head **(see illustration).** Remove the camshaft oil seal.

1.5L and 1.8L DOHC models

Refer to illustrations 9.11a, 9.11b and 9.11c

Note: *The 1990 through 1996 1.8L DOHC engine uses two overhead camshafts to directly-actuate hydraulic valve lifters, which control the valves. After initial installation, no further valve adjustments are necessary. The hydraulic lifters eliminate the need for an adjusting shim. However, the 1.5L DOHC engine and the 1997 model 1.8L DOHC engine use shim-in-bucket type lifters, which do require adjustment by measuring lash and installing new shims of proper thickness. The need to properly mark or store parts for later reinstallation in the same locations from which they were removed is very important* **(see illustration 9.7).**

10 Remove the camshaft sprocket bolts (see Section 7) and remove the sprockets. Remove the timing belt sprocket rear shield.

11 Loosen the camshaft bearing cap bolts in two or three steps in the sequence shown **(see illustrations).** Remove the camshaft bearing caps, marking or packaging to record their locations for correct reinstallation later. To further ensure correct reinstallation later, take note of the factory camshaft cap stamped numbers and direction arrows.

12 Make note how far into the bearing cap the old oil seal is located

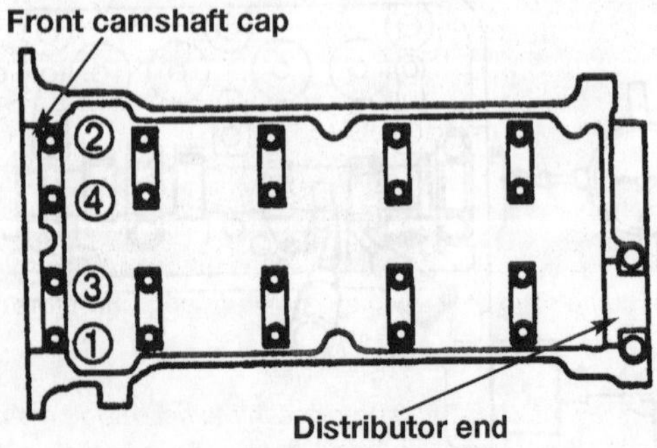

9.11a Loosen the two front camshaft caps in two or three steps in sequence (1.5L DOHC)

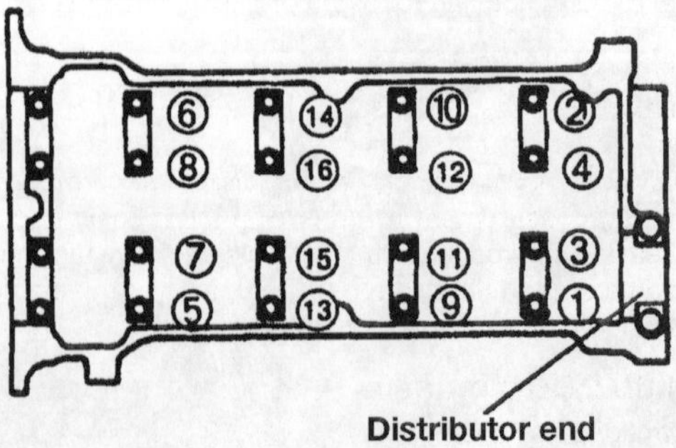

9.11b Loosen the remaining camshaft caps in two or three steps in sequence (1.5L DOHC)

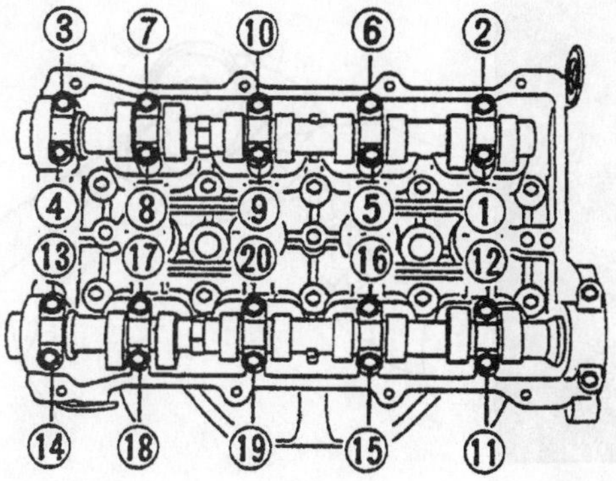

9.11c Loosen the camshaft caps in two or three steps in sequence (1.8L DOHC)

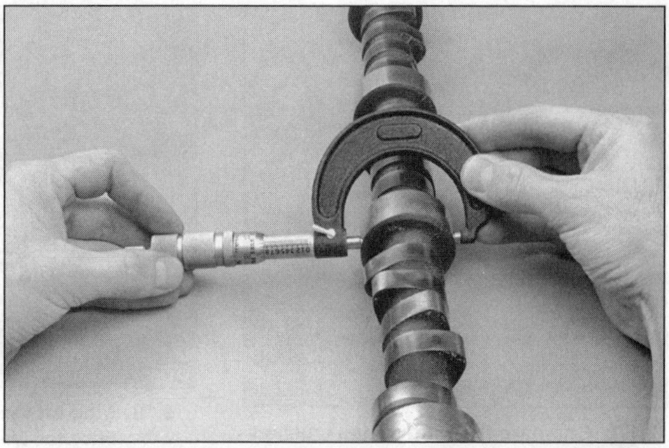

9.16a Measure each journal diameter with a micrometer (if any journal measures less than the specified limit, replace the camshaft)

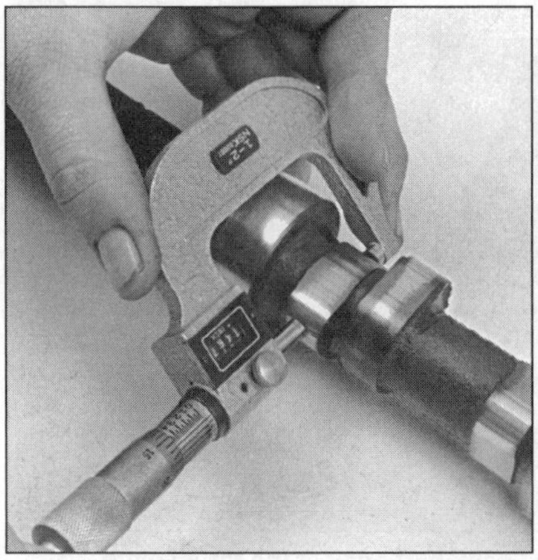

9.16b Measure the lobe heights on the camshaft(s) - if any lobe height is less than the minimum listed in this Chapter's specifications, replace the camshaft

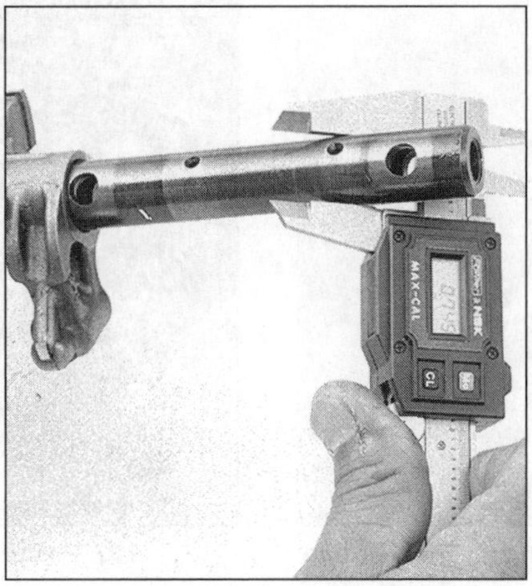

9.16c Measure the rocker arm shaft outer diameter

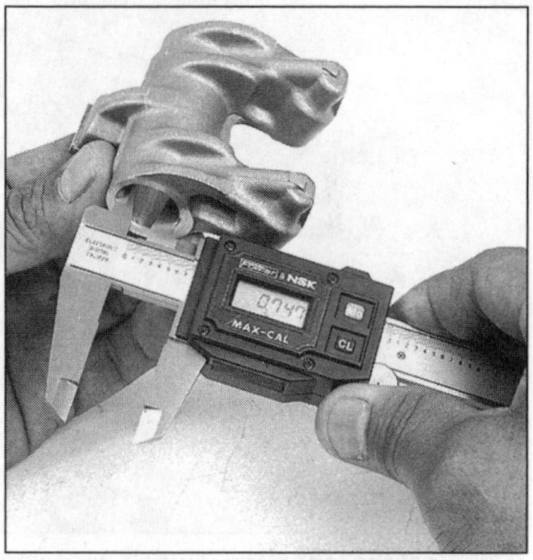

9.16d Measure the rocker arm inside diameter - subtract the shaft outside diameter from the rocker inside diameter to determine the oil clearance

and use this as a guide for installation depth later.

13 Mark the camshafts to ensure proper reinstallation later. Remove the camshafts. Remove the oil seals from the camshafts.

14 Using a magnet or tweezers, as applicable, lift out each valve lifter or shim/bucket lifter and set them in numbered boxes, plastic bags or other containers so they can be reinstalled in the same position during reassembly. **Note:** *Do not scratch the lifters when removing them.*

Inspection

15 Examine all parts, looking for signs of pitting, scoring or scuffing.

1.6L and 1.8L SOHC models

Refer to illustrations 9.16a, 9.16b, 9.16c and 9.16d

16 Measure the camshaft journals and camshaft lobes. Measure each camshaft bore inside diameter and subtract the camshaft journal outside diameter measurement to determine the camshaft journal oil clearance. Measure the rocker arm shaft outside diameter and rocker arm inside diameter **(see illustrations)**. Compare your measurements to the values listed in this Chapter's Specifications.

1.5L and 1.8L DOHC models

Refer to illustrations 9.17a, 9.17b, 9.18 and 9.19

17 Check the oil clearance for each camshaft journal as follows:

a) *Clean the bearing caps and the camshaft journals with cleaning solvent and dry thoroughly.*

9.17a Lay a strip of Plastigage on each camshaft journal

b) *Carefully lay the camshaft(s) in place in the head. Do not install the lifters and do not use any lubrication.*
c) *Lay a strip of Plastigage on each journal* **(see illustration)**.
d) *Install the camshaft bearing caps in the proper locations as removed with the arrows pointing as removed.*

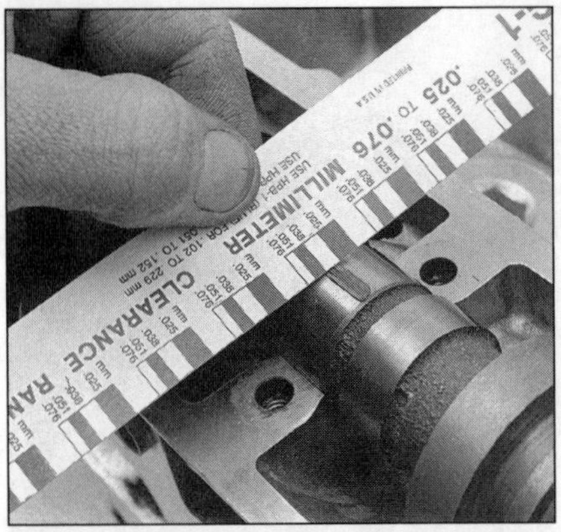

9.17b Compare the width of the crushed Plastigage to the scale on the envelope to determine the oil clearance

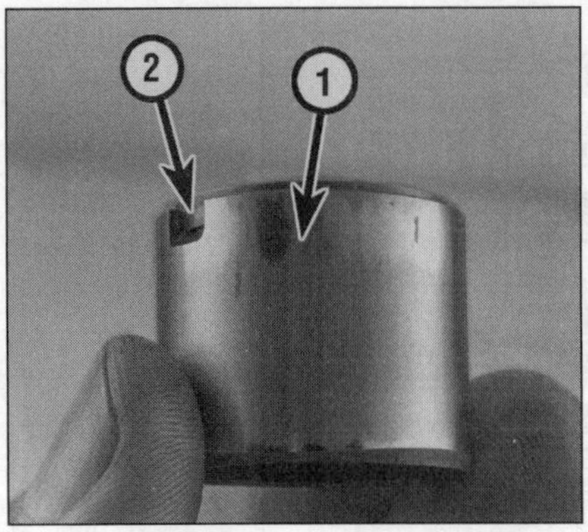

9.18 Wipe off the oil and inspect each lifter for wear and scuffing

1 Lifter wall
2 Shim

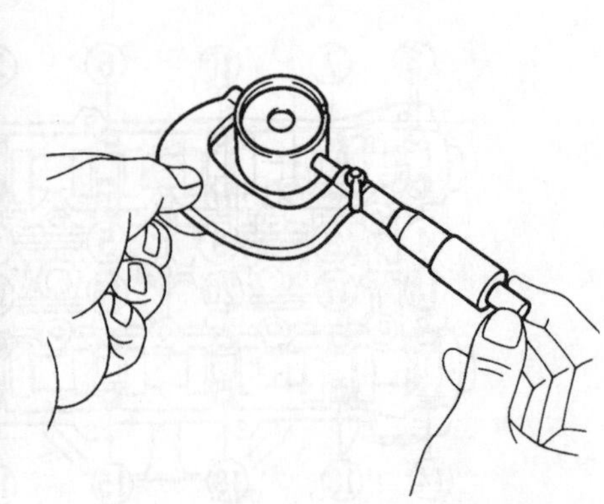

9.19 Use a micrometer to measure lifter diameter

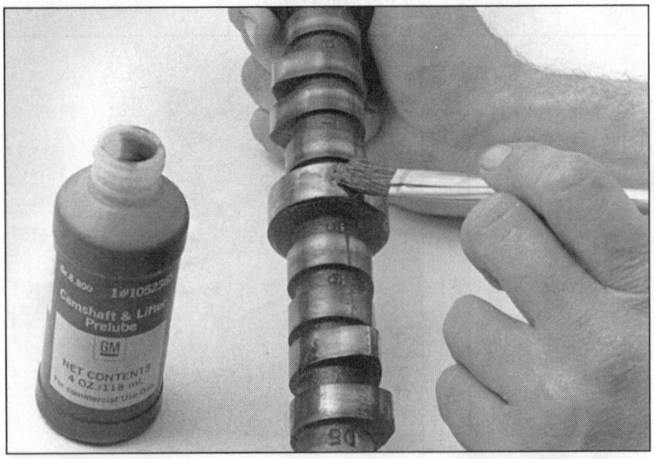

9.26 Coat the lobes and journals with camshaft and lifter prelube

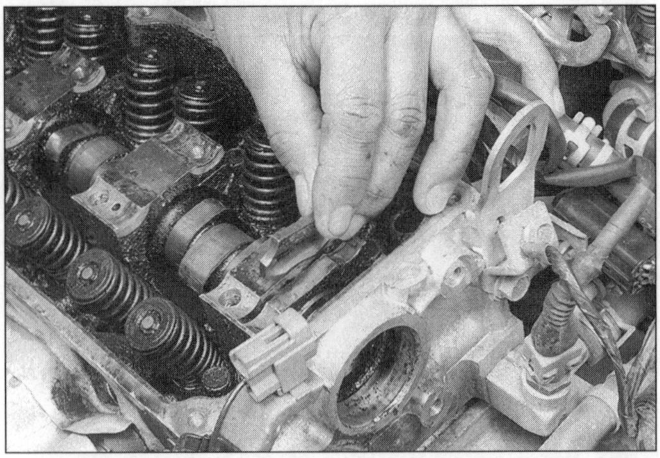

9.27 Position the camshaft against the thrust plate

e) Tighten the bolts IN SEQUENCE **(see illustrations 9.37a and 9.37b)** *to the torque listed in this Chapter's Specifications in two or three steps.* **Note:** *Do not turn the camshaft while the Plastigage is in place.*

f) Remove the camshaft bearing cap bolts IN SEQUENCE **(see illustrations 9.11a, 9.11b, and 9.11c)** *and detach the caps.*

g) Compare the width of the crushed Plastigage (at its widest point) to the scale on the Plastigage envelope **(see illustration).**

h) If the clearance is greater than specified, replace the camshaft and/or cylinder head.

i) Scrape off the Plastigage with your fingernail or the edge of a credit card - do not scratch or nick the journals or bearing caps.

18 On 1.5L and 1997 1.8L DOHC models, inspect each lifter shim surface for scuffing and scoring marks or other surface defects. If defective, replace the shim. **Note:** *You can use the other side of the shim if the lower surface was not previously in contact with the cam lobe.* On 1996 and earlier 1.8L DOHC models, inspect each hydraulic lifter for scuffing and scoring marks **(see illustration).** Press the lifter plunger in by hand, checking for movement. If the lifter plunger moves, replace the lifter.

19 Measure the outside diameter of each lifter and measure the lifter bore diameter. Compare your measurements with the values listed in this Chapter's Specifications **(see illustration)**. Replace any lifter that is worn excessively.

20 Visually examine the camshaft lobes and bearing journals for scoring marks, pitting, galling and evidence of overheating (blue, discolored areas). Look for flaking away of the hardened surface of each lobe.

21 Using a micrometer, measure the diameter of each camshaft journal **(see illustration 9.16a)**. If the diameter of any one journal is less than specified, replace the camshaft.

22 Using a micrometer, measure the height of each lobe **(see illustration 9.16b)**. If the height for any one lobe is less than the specified minimum, replace the camshaft.

23 Replace any parts that are worn beyond specifications.

Installation

1.6L and 1.8L SOHC models

Refer to illustrations 9.26, 9.27 and 9.30

24 Apply clean engine oil to the new camshaft oil seal and the cylinder head camshaft bore.

25 Hold a short length of pipe or tube sized to fit the camshaft oil seal bore against the seal, and lightly tap the seal in, flush to the edge of the cylinder head.

26 Apply camshaft assembly lubricant to the camshaft lobes and bearing journals **(see illustration)**.

27 Install the camshaft in the cylinder head and into position with the thrust plate **(see Illustration)**.

28 If the hydraulic lash adjusters were removed from the rocker arms, or are being replaced, fill the rocker arm cavity with clean engine oil, coat the lash adjusters with clean engine oil, and install them into the rocker arm.

29 Assemble and install the rocker arm assembly as it was removed. On 1.6L SOHC models, make sure that the rocker shaft oil holes face downward. **Note:** *There are two types of rocker arms used on the 1.6L SOHC model; one type is used on cylinders no. 1 and 2, while the other type is used on cylinders no. 3 and 4 - be careful to install them exactly as removed, and if replacing any rocker arms, be sure to obtain the cor-*

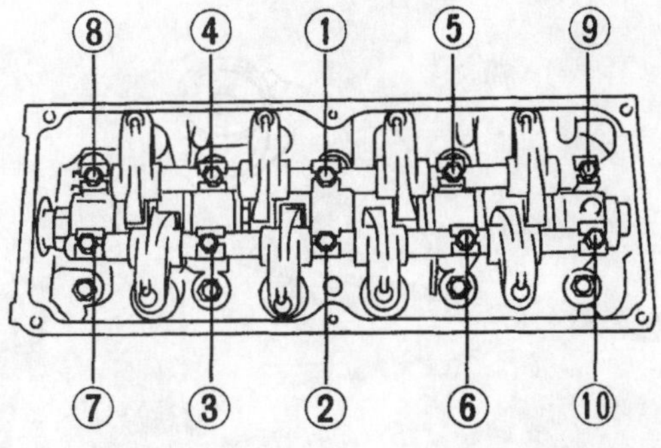

9.30 Rocker arm bolt tightening sequence - SOHC models

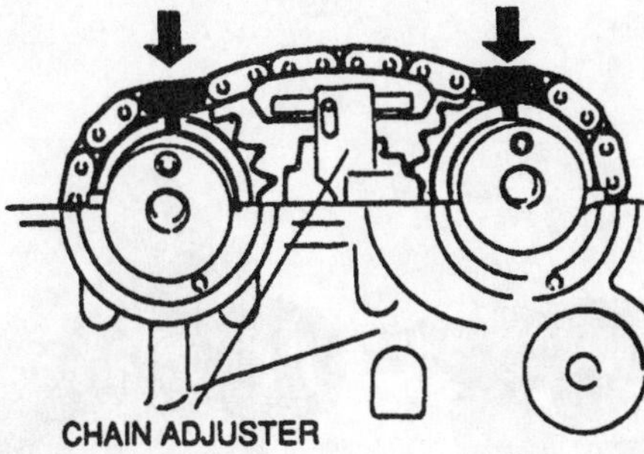

9.35 Install the 1.5L DOHC camshaft drive chain adjuster and chain, with alignment marks as shown

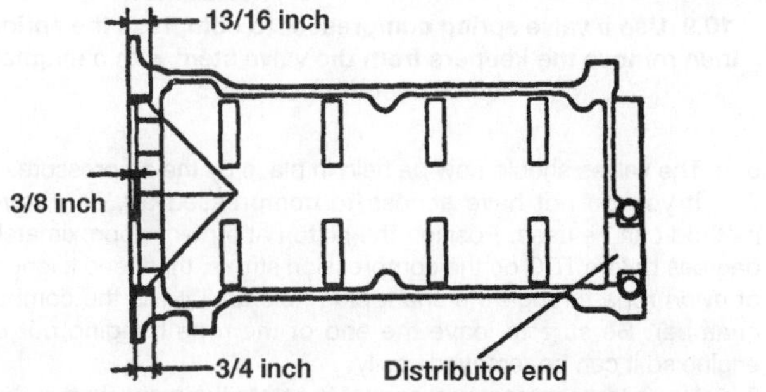

9.36a Apply silicone sealant to the shaded surfaces (1.5L DOHC)

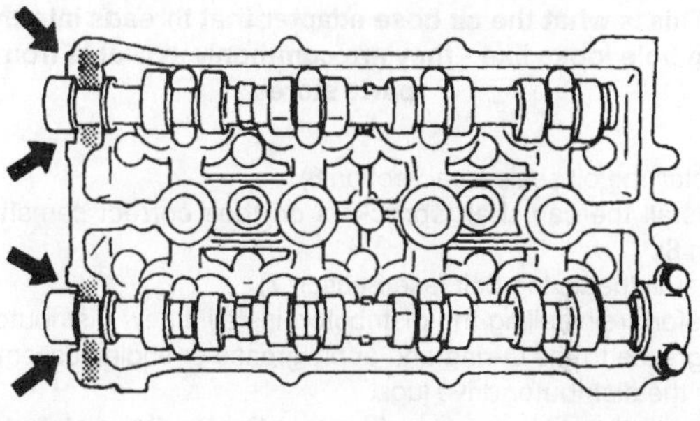

9.36b Apply silicone sealant to the shaded surfaces (1.8L DOHC)

rect parts. On 1.8L SOHC models, make sure the rocker shaft identification mark is facing upward. **Note:** *On 1.8L SOHC models, the installation bolt holes are different on the exhaust and intake shafts. The identification mark is white for Intake and blue for Exhaust.*

30 Tighten the rocker arm bolts to the torque listed in this Chapter's Specifications in several steps and in the recommended sequence **(see Illustration)**.

31 Install the camshaft sprocket (see Section 7) and tighten the bolt to the torque listed in this Chapter's Specifications.

32 Install the timing belt (see Section 7).

33 The remainder of installation is the reverse of the removal procedure.

1.5L and 1.8L DOHC models

Refer to illustrations 9.35, 9.36a and 9.36b

34 Apply engine assembly lubricant or clean engine oil to the hydraulic lifters and install into the lifter bores, install them in their original locations. Check that the lifters travel smoothly in their bores.

35 Apply camshaft assembly lubricant or clean engine oil to the camshaft lobes and bearing journals. Install the camshafts. On the 1.5L DOHC engine, also install the camshaft chain adjuster between the camshafts and align the marks on the camshaft gears and the timing chain **(see illustration)**. Make sure the exhaust camshafts is reinstalled on the exhaust manifold side of the engine, and the intake camshaft is reinstalled on the intake manifold side of the engine. **Note:** *Make sure the correct camshaft is installed on the side that drives the distributor. The camshaft that drives the distributor has a groove or slot for distributor engagement.*

36 Apply silicone sealant to the shaded areas of the bearing caps surfaces as shown **(see illustrations)**.

37 Install the camshaft bearing caps in the proper order as marked when removed, in the stamped numerical order with the arrows pointing as removed. Then tighten the cap bolts in two or three steps IN SEQUENCE **(see illustrations)** to the torque listed in this Chapter's Specifications.

38 Apply clean engine oil to the lips of the new camshaft oil seals

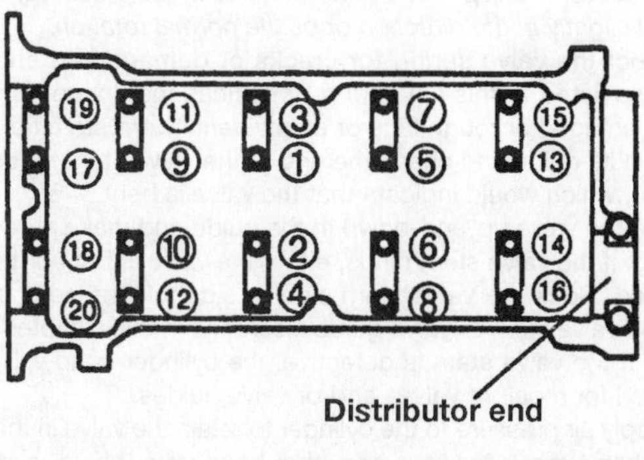

9.37a Camshaft bearing cap bolt tightening sequence - 1.5L DOHC engine

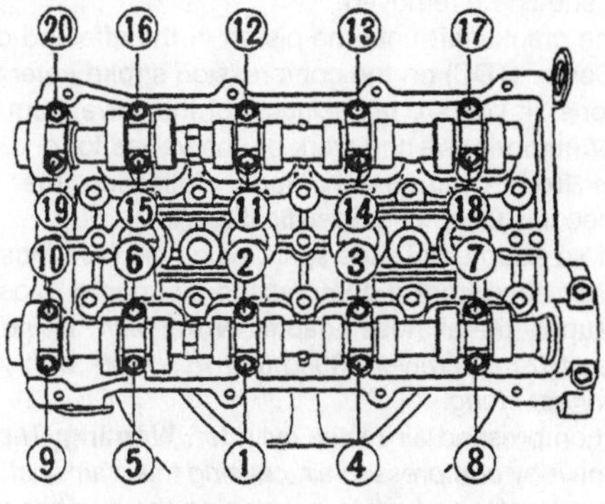

9.37b Camshaft bearing cap bolt tightening sequence - 1.8L DOHC engine

2A

10.4 This is what the air hose adapter that threads into the spark plug hole looks like - they are commonly available from auto parts stores

10.9 Use a valve spring compressor to compress the springs, then remove the keepers from the valve stem with a magnet or small needle-nose pliers

and install the oil seals (see Section 8).

39 Install the camshaft sprockets on their correct camshafts (see Section 8).

40 Install the timing belt (see Section 7).

41 Before reinstalling the distributor, install a new distributor O-ring. Apply grease to the O-ring and apply grease or engine assembly lubricant to the distributor drive lugs.

42 Install the distributor and loosely tighten the distributor timing adjustment bolt(s). Connect the distributor electrical connector.

43 Reinstall the remaining parts in the reverse order of removal.

44 Run the engine and adjust the timing (see Chapter 1). Check the engine for proper operation.

10 Valve springs, retainers and seals - replacement

Refer to illustrations 10.4, 10.9, 10.10, 10.15 and 10.17

Note: *Broken valve springs and defective valve stem seals can be replaced without removing the cylinder head. Two special tools and a compressed air source are normally required to perform this operation, so read through this Section carefully and rent or buy the tools before beginning the job. If compressed air isn't available, a length of nylon rope can be used to keep the valves from falling into the cylinder during this procedure.*

1 Refer to Section 9 and remove the camshaft(s). Remove the valve lifters from the defective valves. Keep the lifters in order so they may be reinstalled in their original location.

2 Remove the spark plug from the cylinder which has the defective component. If all of the valve stem seals are being replaced, all of the spark plugs should be removed.

3 Turn the crankshaft until the piston in the affected cylinder is at Top Dead Center (TDC) on the compression stroke (refer to Section 3 for instructions). If you are replacing all of the valve stem seals, begin with cylinder number one and work on the valves for one cylinder at a time. Move from cylinder-to-cylinder following the firing order sequence (see this Chapter's Specifications).

4 Thread an adapter into the spark plug hole **(see illustration)** and connect an air hose from a compressed air source. Most auto parts stores can supply the air hose adapter. **Note:** *Many cylinder compression gauges utilize a screw-in fitting that may work with your air hose quick-disconnect fitting.*

5 Apply compressed air to the cylinder. **Warning:** *The piston may be forced down by compressed air, causing the crankshaft to turn suddenly. If the wrench used when positioning the number one piston at TDC is still attached to the bolt in the crankshaft pulley end, damage or injury could occur if the crankshaft moves.*

6 The valves should now be held in place by the air pressure.

7 If you do not have access to compressed air, an alternative method can be used. Position the piston at a point approximately 45-degrees before TDC on the compression stroke, then feed a long piece of *nylon* rope through the spark plug hole until it fills the combustion chamber. Be sure to leave the end of the rope hanging out of the engine so it can be removed easily.

8 Use a large ratchet and socket to rotate the crankshaft in the normal direction of rotation (clockwise, when viewed from the front) until slight resistance is felt.

9 Stuff clean shop rags into any cylinder head holes above and below the valves to prevent parts and tools from falling into the engine, then use a valve spring compressor to compress the spring. Remove the keepers with small needle-nose pliers or a magnet **(see illustration). Note:** *Different types of tools are available for compressing the valve springs with the head in place. One type grips the lower spring coils and presses on the retainer as the knob is turned, while the other type uses a bolt or stud and nut for leverage. Both types work well, although the lever type is usually less expensive.*

10 Remove the spring retainer and valve spring (mark the top end of the valve spring for later reinstallation). On 1.5L DOHC and 1.8L DOHC, measure the depth to the upper side of the valve stem oil seal, then remove the oil seal **(see illustration). Note:** *If using air pressure to hold the valve(s) and this fails to hold the valve in the closed position during this operation, the valve face and/or seat is probably damaged. If so, the cylinder head will have to be removed, the alternate procedure for holding the valves described above may be used, or the cylinder head will require removal for additional repair operations.*

11 Wrap a rubber band or tape around the top of the valve stem so the valve won't fall into the combustion chamber, then release the air pressure. **Note:** *If a rope was used instead of air pressure, turn the crankshaft slightly in the direction opposite normal rotation.*

12 Inspect the valve spring for cracks or damage and check free length is as listed in this Chapter's Specifications. Inspect the valve stem for damaged or rough face or an unevenly worn stem tip . Rotate the valve in its guide and check the end of the valve stem for eccentric movement, which would indicate that the valve is bent.

13 Move the valve up-and-down in the guide and make sure there is no binding. If the valve stem binds, either the valve is bent or the guide is damaged. Rock the valve stem side to side; clearance should not exceed the valve stem to valve guide clearance in this Chapter's Specifications. If the valve stem is defective, the cylinder head will have to be removed for repair of valves and/or valve guides.

14 Reapply air pressure to the cylinder to retain the valve in the closed position, then remove the tape or rubber band from the valve stem. If a nylon rope was used instead of air pressure, rotate the crankshaft in the normal direction of rotation until slight resistance is felt.

10.10 Remove the valve guide oil seal with an oil seal removal tool or a pair of pliers

10.15 Gently tap the seal into place with a hammer and a deep socket - measure the depth of oil seal on DOHC engines

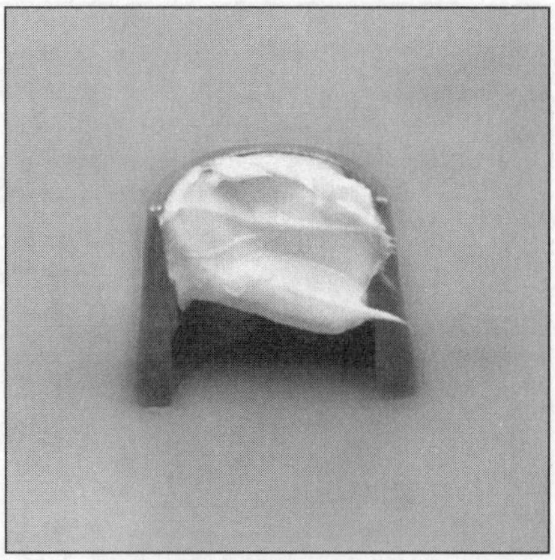

10.17 Apply a small dab of grease to each keeper as shown here before installation - it'll hold them in place on the valve stem as the spring is released

15 Lubricate the valve stem with engine oil or engine assembly lubricant and install a new oil seal using an oil seal installer tool or deep socket **(see illustration)**, measuring the installed depth as necessary. On 1.5L DOHC engines, install the oil seal to the depth measured before seal removal (Step 10 above). On 1.8L DOHC engines, the oil seal is inserted similarly, which should be to a depth such that the upper side of the oil seal is 0.787 inch above the bottom of the oil seal bore.

16 Install the spring in position over the valve. Replace any springs not meeting the inspection above. Be sure the spring is installed as marked during removal (top of the spring is up) and also note that the end of the spring with a closer pitch is toward the cylinder head.

17 Install the valve spring retainer. Compress the valve spring and carefully position the keepers in the groove. Apply a small dab of grease to the inside of each keeper to hold it in place if necessary **(see illustration)**.

18 Remove the pressure from the spring tool and make sure the keepers are seated.

19 Disconnect the compressed air hose and remove the adapter from the spark plug hole. If a nylon rope was used in place of air pressure, pull it out of the cylinder.

20 Refer to Section 9 and install the camshaft(s).

21 Install the rest of the parts in the reverse order of the removal procedure.

22 Start and run the engine, then check for oil leaks and unusual sounds coming from the valve cover area

11 Cylinder head - removal and installation

Refer to illustrations 11.27 and 11.33

Caution: *The engine must be completely cool before beginning this procedure.*

Removal

1 Disconnect the negative cable from the battery and remove the spark plugs.

2 Drain the coolant from the engine block and radiator (see Chapter 1).

3 Drain the engine oil and remove the oil filter (see Chapter 1).

4 Remove the intake air intake tube assembly from the intake plenum (see Chapter 4).

5 Remove the resonance tube above the radiator, (see Section 5) as applicable.

6 Remove the throttle cable (on automatic transmission models) and accelerator cable.

7 Remove the brake vacuum hose, fuel hose, radiator hoses, the purge control vacuum hose (from intake plenum to firewall area), cruise control vacuum hose (as applicable), and the heater hoses. Mark the hoses for later reinstallation.

8 Remove all electrical connectors/wiring harness connections to the cylinder head. Mark the connectors for later reinstallation.

9 Remove water bypass tubing bolts/nuts (where applicable, the bypass tubing is mounted on engine head).

10 Remove the water pump pulley and drive belt.

11 Remove the air intake plenum and the fuel rail (see Chapter 4).

12 Remove the intake manifold (see Section 5).

13 Detach the exhaust pipe from the exhaust manifold. Remove the exhaust manifold (see Section 6).

14 Remove the valve cover (see Section 4).

15 Remove the timing belt covers and the timing belt (see Section 7).

16 Remove the power steering pump and alternator drive belt(s) (see Chapter 5).

17 Remove the alternator/generator brackets.

18 Remove the distributor (see Chapter 5).

19 Unbolt the power steering pump, as applicable, and lay it to the side without disconnecting the hoses (see Chapter 10).

20 Check the cylinder head. Label and detach any remaining components that would interfere with cylinder head removal.

21 Using a breaker bar and the appropriate Allen-head driver or socket, loosen the cylinder head bolts in 1/4-turn increments, loosening in the reverse of the tightening sequence **(see illustration 11.33)** until they can be removed by hand.

22 Lift the cylinder head off the engine block. If it is stuck, very carefully pry up at the transaxle end, away from the head gasket surface.

23 Remove all external components from the head to allow for thorough cleaning and inspection. See Chapter 2, Part B, for cylinder head servicing procedures.

Installation

24 The mating surfaces of the cylinder head and block must be perfectly clean when the head is installed.

25 Use a gasket scraper to remove all traces of carbon and old gasket material, then clean the mating surfaces with lacquer thinner or acetone. If any oil residue is on the mating surfaces when the head is installed, the gasket may not seal correctly and leaks could develop. When working on the block, stuff the cylinders with clean shop rags to prevent the entry of debris. Use a vacuum cleaner to remove material that falls into the cylinders. **Caution:** *Be careful not to gouge the soft aluminum of the cylinder head.*

26 Check the block and head mating surfaces for nicks, deep scratches and other damage. If damage is slight, it can be removed with a file; if it's excessive, machining may be the only alternative.

2A

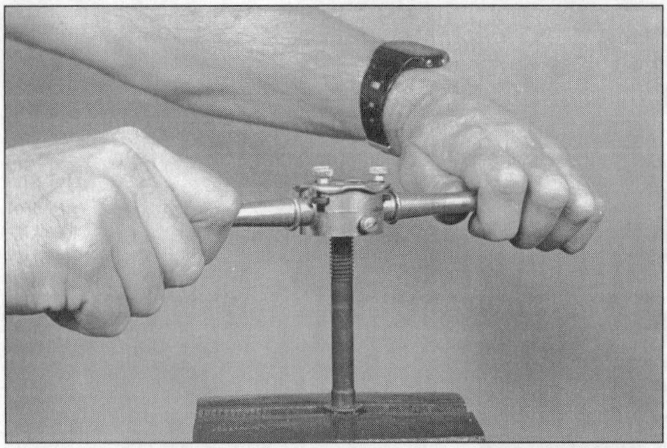

11.27 A die should be used to remove sealant and corrosion from the head bolt threads prior to installation

27 Use a thread die of the correct thread size to chase (clean up) the head bolt threads **(see illustration)**. **Note:** *Cleaning up the threads using a thread die should not cut any metal from the threads. If you observe any metal cuttings while chasing the threads, stop and replace the bolt with a new bolt from an automotive parts store or dealer. Make sure the replacement bolt is a OEM (Original Equipment Manufacturer) replacement cylinder head bolt specifically designed for this engine, and is the correct length and thread type. Discard the defective bolt.* Use a tap of the correct thread size to chase the threads in the head bolt holes, then clean the holes with compressed air - make sure that no residue such as dirt, corrosion, and sealant remains in the holes and the threads are not damaged as this will affect torque readings, which affects the quality of the head installation job. **Warning:** *Wear eye protection when using compressed air!*

28 Install the components that were removed from the head.

29 Position the new gasket over the dowel pins in the block.

30 Carefully set the head on the block without disturbing the gasket.

31 Before installing the head bolts, apply a small amount of clean engine oil to the threads.

32 Install the bolts and tighten them finger tight.

33 Tighten the bolts following the recommended sequence in several steps to the torque listed in this Chapter's Specifications **(see illustration)**.

34 The remaining installation steps are the reverse of removal.

35 Refill the cooling system, install a new oil filter and add oil to the engine (see Chapter 1).

36 Run the engine and check for leaks. Set the ignition timing (see Chapter 5) and road test the vehicle.

37 Frequently recheck coolant level for the first few hundred miles to be sure that no leakage exists.

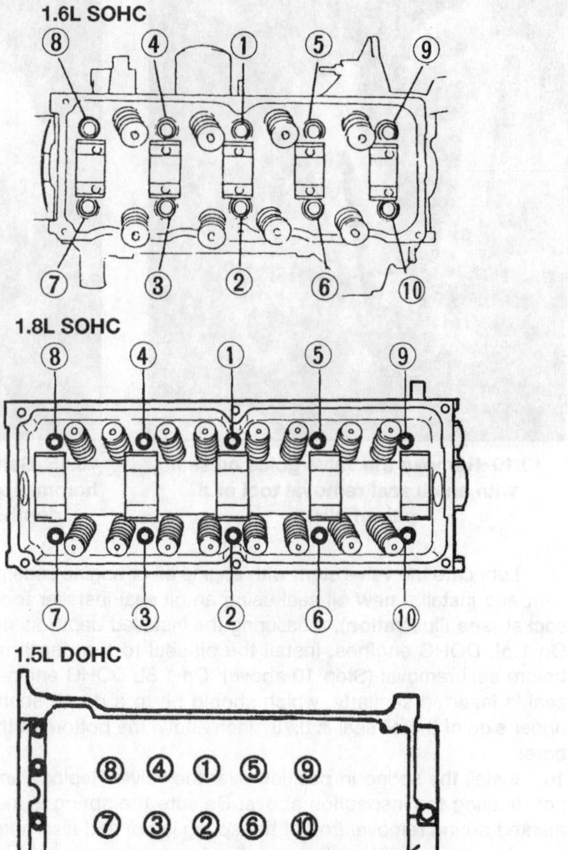

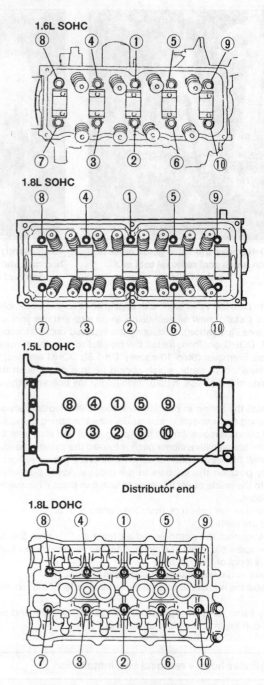

11.33 Cylinder head bolt TIGHTENING sequence

12 Oil pan - removal and installation

Removal

Refer to illustrations 12.5a, 12.5b, 12.7a, 12.7b, 12.7c and 12.7d

1 Disconnect the negative cable from the battery.

2 Set the parking brake and block the rear wheels. Raise the front of the vehicle and support it securely on jackstands.

3 Remove the under cover splash shield(s) from under the engine **(see illustration 7.3)**.

4 Drain the engine oil and remove the oil filter (see Chapter 1).

5 Disconnect the exhaust pipe from the exhaust manifold **(see illustrations)**.

6 Remove the oil pan as follows: **Caution:** *Do not insert the screwdriver or prying tool between the Main Bearing Support Plate (MBSP) and the engine block. Be very careful not to scratch, bend, or otherwise damage the mating surfaces of the oil pan, MBSP, and block or oil leaks could develop.* **Note:** *Oil pan bolts may be of varying sizes. Mark, tag, or store each oil pan bolt/nut with the location removed from the oil pan for correct reinstallation later.*

7 On 1.6L SOHC models, the oil pan may be one piece, or it may be a two-piece design with an Oil Pan Stiffener at the transaxle end of the engine which attaches to the oil pan. Also, this engine has a MBSP between the oil pan and the oil pan, attached at the main journals and the oil pan bolts. If the vehicle you are working on has a two piece oil pan, first remove the oil pan stiffener bolts around the bottom of the transaxle and at the engine block, then remove the oil pan stiffener. Remove the remaining oil pan bolts and then remove the oil pan. If the oil pan is stuck, carefully pry it loose by inserting a screwdriver or small pry bar at the engine block ears located at the transaxle end of the

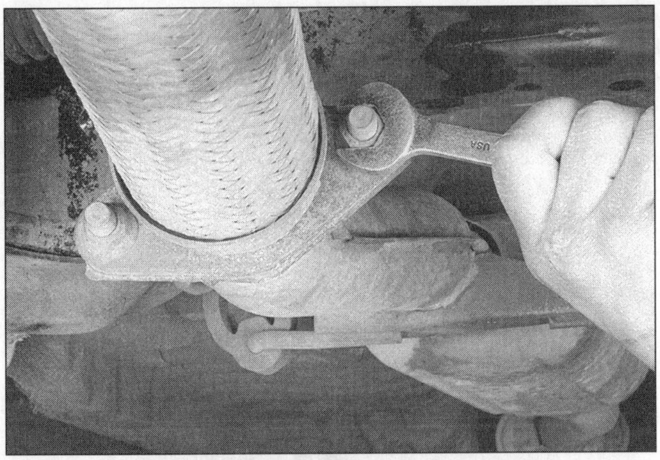

12.5a Remove the exhaust pipe flange connection . . .

12.5b . . . and remove the pipe from the exhaust manifold - remove the catalytic converter if necessary

12.7a Carefully pry the oil pan away from the Main Bearing Support Plate (MBSP) - pry at the engine block ears as shown

12.7b Remove the oil pickup tube/screen assembly

12.7c Remove the MBSP bolts (if equipped)

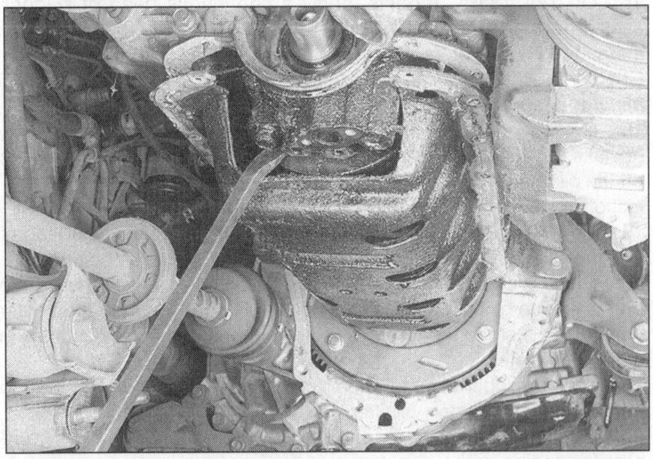

12.7d Carefully pry the MBSP from the engine block by prying against a main bearing journal - DO NOT pry against a rod journal at this step. If the mating surfaces are damaged, oil leaks could develop

engine **(see illustration)**. Do not pry along the oil pan lip and the MBSP. With the oil pan removed, detach the oil strainer from the MBSP **(see illustration)**. Then remove the MBSP bolts **(see illustration)**, and very carefully pry the MBSP against the main bearing journal or at the corners of the MBSP **(see illustration)**. **Caution:** *Do not pry on the rod bearing caps.*

8 On 1.8L SOHC and 1.8L DOHC models, remove the oil pan bolts and then remove the oil pan. If the oil pan is stuck, pry it loose very carefully by inserting a screwdriver or putty knife at the engine block ears at the flywheel end of the engine block. **Caution:** *Do not insert the screwdriver or prying tool at any other area*. Then, remove the MBSP attaching bolts and remove the MBSP, prying as necessary against the main bearing journal or at the corners of the MBSP.

9 On 1.5L DOHC models, remove the oil pan bolts and then remove

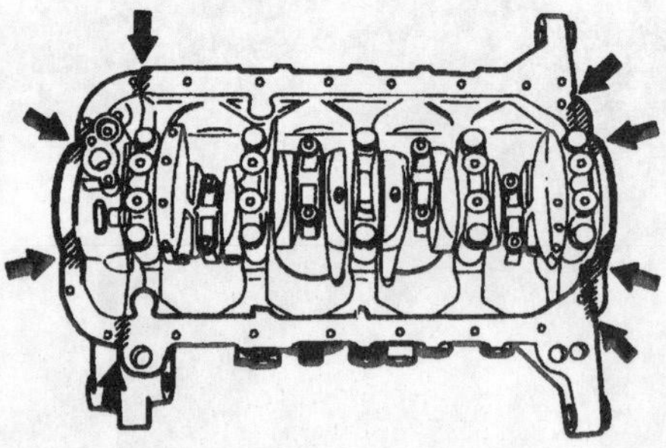

12.13 Apply silicone sealant to the engine block at the shaded areas shown (except 1.5L DOHC engine)

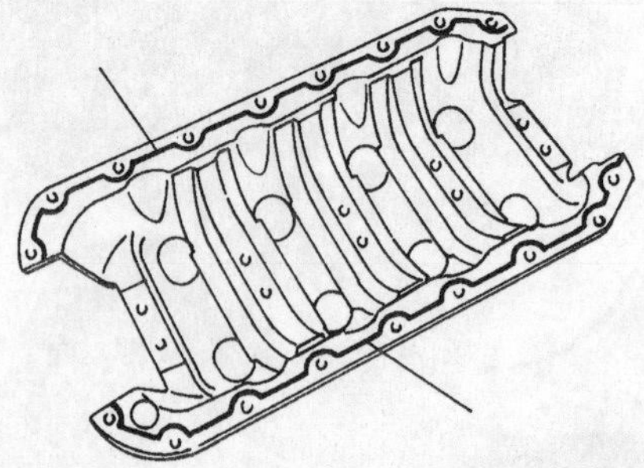

12.14 Apply a bead of silicone sealant to the main bearing support plate or oil pan inside the bolt holes

the oil pan. If the oil pan is stuck, pry it loose carefully by inserting a screwdriver or putty knife at the corners of the oil pan.

Installation

Refer to illustrations 12.13, 12.14 and 12.16

10 Use a scraper to remove all traces of old gasket material and sealant from the block, MBSP, and oil pan. Clean the mating surfaces with gasket cleaner or equivalent solvent, available at automotive parts stores. **Caution:** *Be very careful not to scratch, bend, or otherwise damage the mating surfaces of the pan and block or oil leaks could develop.*

11 Make sure the threaded bolt holes in the block are clean. Visually check the condition of the oil strainer.

12 Check the oil pan flange for cracks or distortion, particularly at the bolting flange.

13 On all except the 1.5L DOHC model, apply silicone sealant to the shaded areas of the engine block **(see illustration)**. **Note:** *The next step must be completed so that the MBSP can be installed within 5 minutes after the sealant in this step was applied.*

14 On all except the 1.5L DOHC model, apply a continuous bead of silicone sealant to the bolting flange (lip) of the MBSP inside the bolt holes **(see illustration)**. Install the MBSP bolts and tighten them to the torque listed in this Chapter's Specification. **Note:** *The MBSP must be installed within 5 minutes of application of the sealant applied in Step 11 above.*

15 On 1.5L DOHC models, apply a continuous bead of silicone sealant to the bolting flange (lip) of the oil pan inside the bolt holes. Install the oil pan bolts and tighten them to the torque listed in this Chapter's Specification. **Note:** *The oil pan must be installed within 5 minutes of application of the sealant.*

16 On all except the 1.5L DOHC model, apply silicone sealant to new gaskets for the oil pump body and rear cover. Install the new gaskets on the oil pump body and rear cover on the engine block, with the projections on the gaskets in the notches **(see illustration)**.

17 On all except the 1.5L DOHC model, apply a continuous bead of silicone sealant to the oil pan bolting flange (lip) inside the bolt holes.

18 On all except the 1.5L DOHC model, carefully position the oil pan on the engine block and install the bolts/nuts. Working from the center out, tighten them to the torque listed in this Chapter's Specifications in three or four steps.

19 The remainder of installation is the reverse of removal. Be sure to add oil and install a new oil filter.

20 Let the silicone sealant set up approximately 12 hours before running the engine.

21 After sufficient time for the silicone sealant to set up, run the engine and check for oil leaks.

13 Front cover - removal and installation

Refer to illustration 13.6

Removal

1 Disconnect the negative battery cable.

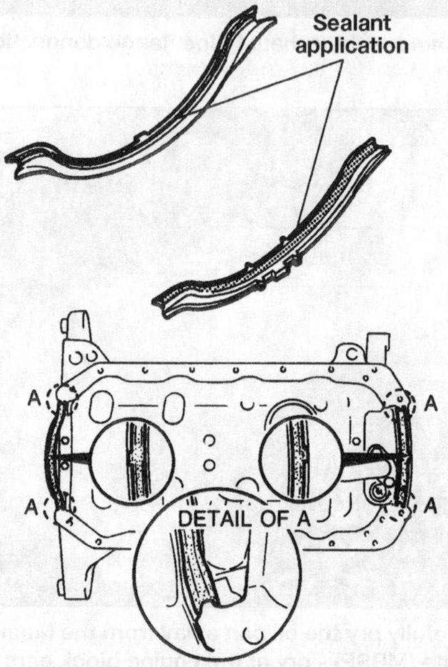

12.16 Location of projections on gasket/seal installation for the oil pump body and the rear cover (except 1.5L DOHC engine)

2 Remove the under cover splash shield.

3 Securely support the front of the vehicle on jackstands, and remove the front passenger side tire for access to the front cover. Remove the alternator (see Chapter 5). Remove the air conditioning compressor (without disconnecting the hoses) and secure it aside (see Chapter 3).

4 Remove the crankshaft pulley, water pump pulley, timing belt covers, timing belt, and timing belt guide (see Section 7).

5 Remove the crankshaft sprocket using two prybars or screwdrivers placed behind the gear to apply even pressure on the gear to slide it off the crankshaft.

6 Remove the front cover bolts/nuts from the engine block **(see illustration)** and separate the front cover from the engine block. You may have to pry carefully between the front main bearing cap and the pump housing with a screwdriver.

Installation

7 Use a scraper to remove all traces of gasket and sealant from the cover and engine block, then clean the mating surfaces with solvent.

8 Install new gasket with a thin coat of silicone sealant on the front cover gasket surface. Reinstall the front cover to the engine block. **Note:** *Be sure the sealant doesn't plug or cover any oil passages.*

9 Install the bolts/nuts, tightening them to the torque listed in this Chapter's Specifications.

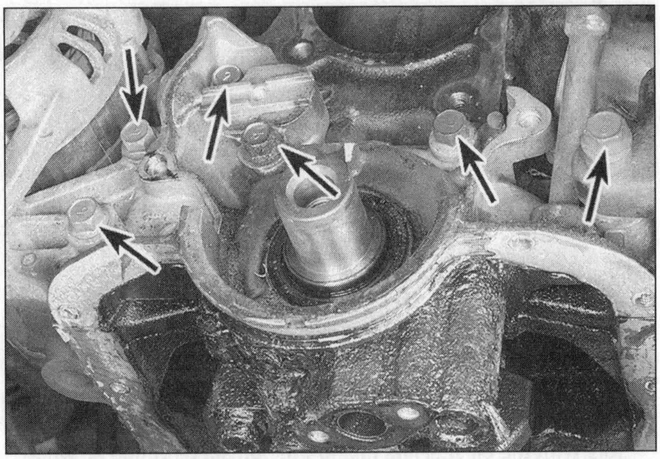

13.6 Remove the bolts (arrows) and separate the front cover from the engine block

10 The remainder of installation is the reverse of the removal procedure.

14 Oil pump - removal, inspection and installation

Refer to illustration 14.2

Note: *If you are replacing the front oil seal only and not removing, inspecting, repairing or replacing the oil pump, the front oil seal can be replaced without oil pump removal as described in Section 15.*

Removal

1 Remove the front cover, which is also the housing for the oil pump assembly (see Section 13).

2 Place the front cover/oil pump on a workbench. Note how far the oil seal is seated in the bore. Using a seal removal tool or a screwdriver taped or wrapped with a rag to protect the pump bore, remove the oil seal from the housing **(see illustration)**. **Caution:** *Do not scratch the housing bore.*

3 Remove the screws that hold the oil pump cover (slotted plate) to the front cover/oil pump housing. Inspect the oil pump cover for distortion or damage.

4 Remove the oil pressure relief valve. Note or mark the direction of the components as installed, then remove the oil pump inner and outer rotors from the housing.

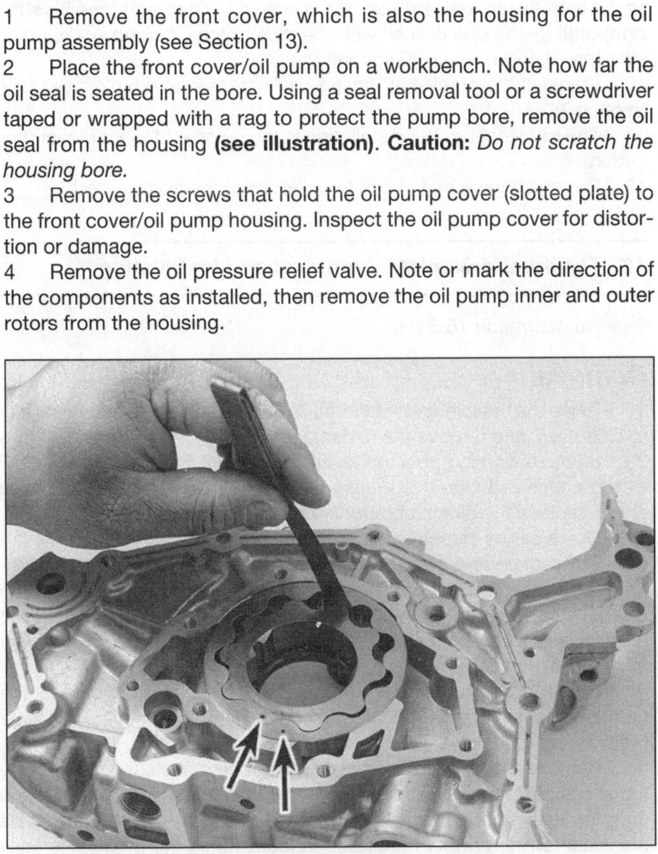

14.5b . . . then measure the clearance between the drive and driven rotor. . .

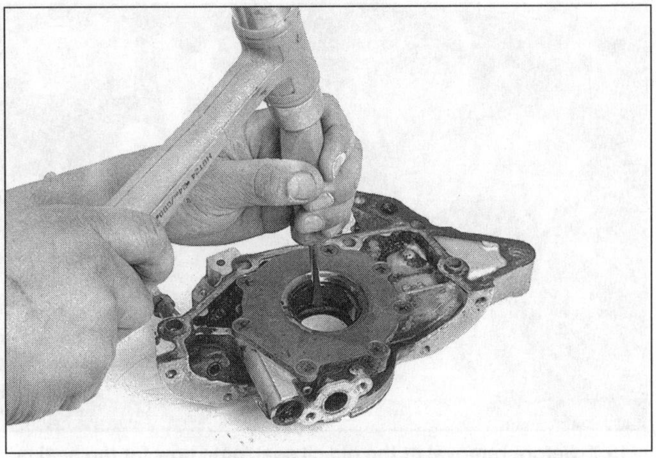

14.2 Remove the front oil seal using screwdriver or punch - wrap the tool tip with tape to protect the oil pump bore

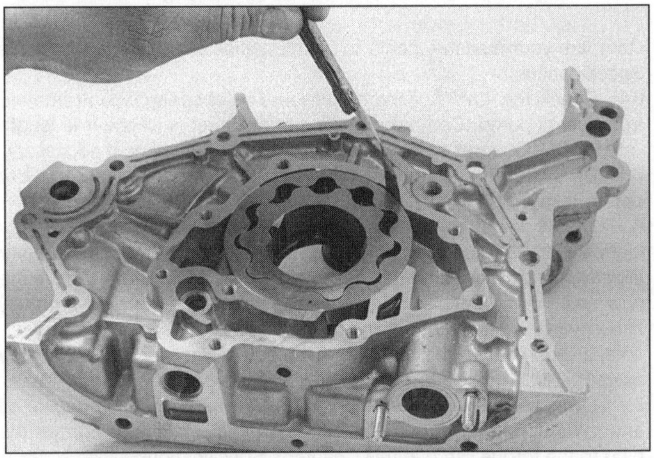

14.5a Measure the clearance between the oil pump driven rotor and the pump housing . . .

Inspection

Refer to illustrations 14.5a, 14.5b and 14.5c

5 Reinstall the oil pump inner and outer rotors into the oil pump housing **(see illustrations)** and measure the clearance of:

a) *The driven rotor-to-pump housing.*
b) *The drive rotor-to-oil pump driven rotor.*
c) *The rotor set-to-oil pump housing endplay clearance.*

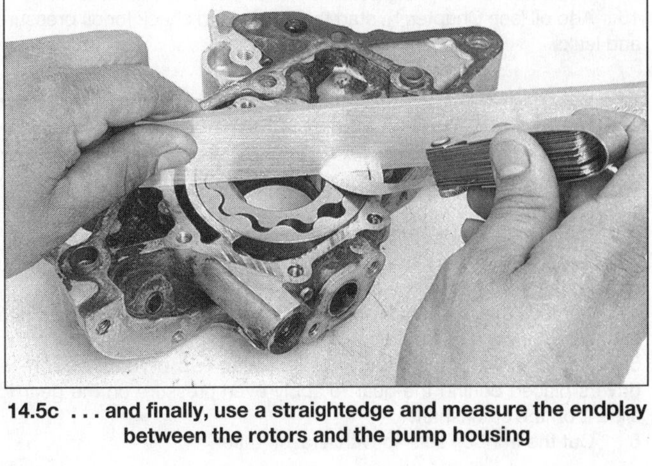

14.5c . . . and finally, use a straightedge and measure the endplay between the rotors and the pump housing

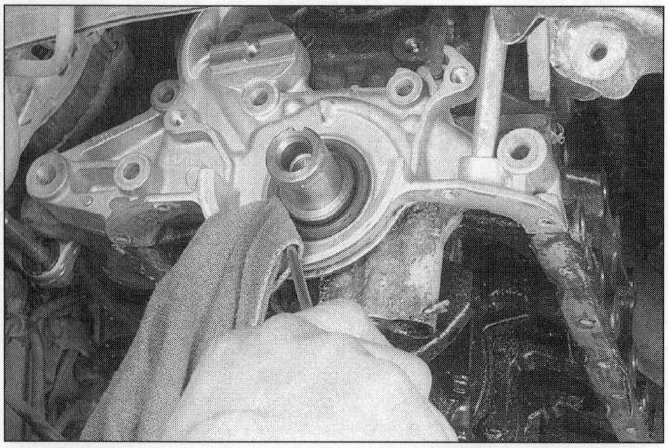

15.7 Before removal of the old oil seal, note how far the seal is seated in the bore and the direction the oil seal lip faces. Remove the front oil seal with a screwdriver taped or wrapped with a rag to protect the crankshaft surface and engine block

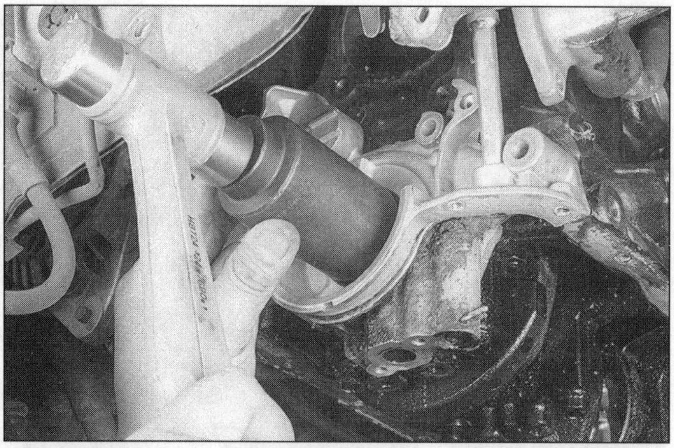

15.9 With the oil seal lips facing the correct direction as when removed, press the oil seal partially into place by hand. Using a large socket or suitable pipe or tubing to fit the seal, tap the seal into the bore until it is flush with the face of the oil pump body, as noted before removal

Compare your measurements to the clearance listed in this Chapter's Specifications.

6 Check the length of the oil pressure relief spring when removed from the oil pump. Compare the length measured with the free length listed in this Chapter's Specifications. Replace the spring if necessary.

7 Be sure the surfaces of the pump housing are clean and dry before reassembly.

8 Lightly coat the outer edge of a new oil seal with engine assembly lubricant or clean engine oil. Using a socket with an outside diameter slightly smaller than the outside diameter of the seal, carefully drive the new seal into place with a hammer. Make sure it's installed squarely and driven in to the same depth as the original. If a socket is not available, a short section of large diameter pipe will also work. Apply engine assembly lubricant to the seal lip surface that contacts the crankshaft.

9 Lubricate the oil pressure relief valve piston with clean engine oil and reinstall the valve components into the pump case. Tighten the plug to the torque listed in this Chapter's Specifications.

10 Lubricate the rotor set with clean engine oil. Reinstall the rotors.

11 Pack the pump cavities with petroleum jelly (this will prime the pump and ensure good suction when the engine is started).

12 Install the cover and tighten the screws to the torque listed in this Chapter's Specifications.

13 It is a good idea to remove the oil pan and inspect the screen at the end of the oil pick-up tube (see Section 12) for any debris that might plug it. Either clean the tube and screen completely or replace it with a new one at this time.

Installation

14 Install the front cover (see Section 13).

15 Reinstall the remaining parts in the reverse order of removal.

16 Add oil (see Chapter 1), start the engine and check for oil pressure and leaks.

15 Crankshaft front oil seal - replacement

Refer to illustrations 15.7 and 15.9

1 Disconnect the negative battery cable.

2 Remove the under cover splash shield.

3 Securely support the front of the vehicle on jackstands, and remove the front passenger side tire for access to the front cover.

4 Remove the crankshaft pulley, timing belt covers, timing belt, and timing belt guide (see Section 7).

5 Remove the crankshaft sprocket using two prybars or screwdrivers placed behind the gear to apply even pressure on the gear to slide it off the crankshaft.

6 Cut the front oil seal lip with a razor knife.

7 Note how far the seal is seated in the bore and the direction the oil seal lip faces (the oil seal should be flush with the face of the oil pump body. Remove the front oil seal with a screwdriver taped or wrapped with a rag to protect the crankshaft surface and engine block **(see illustration)**.

8 Clean the bore in the engine block and clean the crankshaft surface. Coat the outside of the new front oil seal with engine oil. Apply engine assembly lubricant or clean engine oil to the seal lip.

9 Press the oil seal in slightly by hand, with the oil seal lip facing the same direction as removed. Using a seal driver or a socket with an outside diameter slightly smaller than the outside diameter of the front oil seal, carefully tap the new seal into place with a hammer **(see illustration)** until the oil seal is flush with the face of the oil pump body. Make sure the oil seal is installed squarely.

10 Reinstall the crankshaft timing belt sprocket and timing belt (see Section 7).

11 The remainder of the installation is the reverse of the removal procedure.

12 Run the engine and check for oil leaks at the front oil seal.

16 Flywheel/driveplate - removal and installation

Refer to illustration 16.3

Removal

1 Raise the vehicle and support it securely on jackstands, then refer to Chapter 7 and remove the transaxle.

2 If you're working on a model with a manual transaxle, remove the clutch cover and clutch disc (see Chapter 8). Now is a good time to check/replace the clutch components and pilot bearing.

3 Use a center-punch or paint to make alignment marks on the flywheel/driveplate and crankshaft to ensure correct reinstallation alignment later **(see illustration)**. **Note:** *The flywheel can be marked prior to transaxle removal if desired through the access hole at the oil pan /transaxle housing area (1.5L DOHC engine access method may vary from other models).*

4 Remove the bolts that secure the flywheel/driveplate to the crankshaft. If the crankshaft turns, wedge a screwdriver in the ring gear teeth to jam the flywheel.

5 Remove the flywheel/driveplate from the crankshaft. On the automatic transaxle models, also remove the driveplate backing plate and adapter, taking note of which sides of the driveplate the adapter plates are mounted for correct reinstallation later. Since the flywheel is fairly heavy, be sure to support it while removing the last bolt.

6 Clean the flywheel to remove grease and oil. Inspect the surface

16.3 Mark the flywheel/driveplate and the crankshaft so they can be reassembled in the same relative position

for cracks, rivet grooves, burned areas and score marks. Light scoring can be removed with emery cloth. Check for cracked and broken ring gear teeth. Lay the flywheel on a flat surface and use a straightedge to check for warpage. If necessary, take the flywheel to an automotive machine shop to have it resurfaced.

7 Clean and inspect the mating surfaces of the flywheel/driveplate and the crankshaft. If the crankshaft rear seal is leaking, replace it before reinstalling the flywheel/driveplate (see Section 17).

Installation

8 Remove any thread sealant from the crankshaft flywheel bolt holes and bolts. **Caution:** *If all the thread sealant cannot be removed from a bolt, replace that bolt. Do not apply new sealant when installing a new bolt.*

9 For manual transaxle models, position the flywheel at the crankshaft. For automatic transaxle models, position the adapter, driveplate, and backing plate at the crankshaft. Be sure to align the marks made during removal. Before installing the bolts, apply thread sealant to the threads of any bolts except new bolts used.

10 Wedge a screwdriver in the ring gear teeth to keep the flywheel/driveplate from turning as you tighten the bolts to the torque listed in this Chapter's Specifications. Follow a criss-cross pattern and work up to the final torque in three or four steps.

11 The remainder of installation is the reverse of the removal procedure.

17 Rear main oil seal - replacement

Refer to illustrations 17.4 and 17.5

1 The transaxle must be removed from the vehicle for this procedure (see Chapter 7).

2 Remove the flywheel/driveplate (see Section 16).

3 Cut the rear main oil seal lip with a razor knife.

4 Pry out the old seal with a screwdriver taped or wrapped in a rag, or use a seal removal tool to pry the seal out **(see illustration)**.

5 Apply engine oil to the crankshaft seal journal and to the lip of the new seal. Carefully push the new seal part way into place by hand. Carefully tap into place using a flat punch, large socket, or a suitable short pipe or tubing of the correct diameter until the oil seal is flush with the edge of the rear cover **(see illustration)**.

6 Reinstall the flywheel/driveplate (see Section 16).

7 The remaining steps are the reverse of removal.

18 Engine mounts - check and replacement

1 Engine mounts seldom require attention, but broken or deteriorated mounts should be replaced immediately or the added strain placed on the driveline components may cause damage or wear. **Warning:** *Do not remove any engine mounts or components of engine mounts if the engine is not properly supported as described. DO NOT place any part of your body directly under the engine when performing engine mount work and when the engine is supported only by a jack!*

17.4 The quick way to replace the rear main oil seal is to simply pry the old one out . . .

17.5 . . . then lubricate the crankshaft journal and the lip of the new seal with engine oil and tap the new seal into place - the seal lip is stiff and can be easily damaged during installation if you are not careful

Check

2 During the check, the engine must be raised slightly to remove the weight from the mounts.

3 Raise the vehicle and support it securely on jackstands, then position a jack with a block of wood under the engine oil pan or use an engine support fixture from above. Carefully raise the engine just enough to take the weight off the mounts. **Warning:** *DO NOT place any part of your body under the engine when it's supported only by a jack! Support the engine just enough to take the weight off the engine mounts but without lifting the weight of the car from the jackstands*

4 Check the mounts to see if the rubber is cracked, hardened or separated from the metal portion. Occasionally, the rubber will split down the center.

5 Check for relative movement between the mounts and the engine or frame, using a large screwdriver or prybar to attempt to move the mounts. If movement is noted, lower the engine and tighten the mount fasteners.

6 Rubber preservative liquid, available from any automotive parts store, should be applied to the engine mounts (and other chassis rubber components) to help protect from deterioration.

2A

18.8a Transaxle/engine mounts are attached to this crossmember which is removable

18.8b Reinstall the transaxle/engine mounts by attaching the mount brackets to the transaxle

Replacement

Refer to illustrations 18.8a, 18.8b, 18.9 and 18.10

7 Disconnect the negative battery cable from the battery, then raise the vehicle and support it securely on jackstands (if not already done). Support the engine as described in Step 3.

8 Replace the transaxle/engine mounts No. 1 and 2 as follows:

- *a) Detach the engine mount nuts located on the bottom of the engine mount crossmember **(see illustration)**.*
- *b) Remove the engine mount through bolts/nuts to detach from the rubber mount from the mount bracket.*
- *c) Remove the crossmember mounting bolts and remove the crossmember for access.* **Warning:** Do not remove the crossmember if the engine is not supported as described above.
- *d) Reinstall the transaxle/engine mounts by attaching the mount brackets to the transaxle **(see illustration)**, installing the mount through-bolts, washers and nuts, and then installing the crossmember.*
- *e) Tighten all bolts/nuts to the torque listed in this Chapter's Specifications.*

9 Replace the engine mount No. 3 (located on the right side, near the engine timing belt cover) as follows **(see illustration)**:

- *a) Remove the through-bolt nut and washer and withdraw the through-bolt from the frame bracket.*
- *b) Detach the dynamic damper block on the top of the engine mount by removing the bolt and nut (except 1.5L DOHC engine).*
- *c) Remove the engine mount bracket nuts and remove the engine mount.*
- *d) Reinstall the right side engine mount by installing the mount bracket onto the vehicle frame, inserting the through-bolt to connect the engine bracket, and using a new washer, install the washer and nut.*
- *e) Install the dynamic damper and its bolt and nut (except 1.5L DOHC engine).*
- *f) Tighten all bolts and nuts to the torque listed in this Chapter's Specifications.*

10 Replace engine mount No. 4 (located at the left side of the engine compartment at the battery tray area, attaching the transaxle/engine to the vehicle body) as follows **(see illustration)**:

- *a) Remove the battery and battery tray.*
- *b) Remove the engine mount bracket bolts/nuts at the engine bracket.*
- *c) Remove the engine mount bolts/nuts at the vehicle body bracket.*
- *d) Remove the engine mount.*
- *e) Reinstall the left side engine mount by installing the mount bracket onto the vehicle frame, install a new washers (except 1.5L DOHC engine) and install the nut(s). Tighten the left side engine mount bracket-to-vehicle body bolts to the torque listed in this Chapter's Specifications in several steps and in the following sequence (except 1.5L DOHC engine): Tighten one of the bolts closest to the rubber mount first, then using a criss-cross pattern, tighten the remaining bolts and nuts.*

18.9 Engine mount on the right side below the engine timing belt cover is removed by detaching the through-bolt. The bracket is removed by removing the dynamic damper block (on top of the engine mount, except 1.5L DOHC engine) and removing the nuts securing the bracket to the vehicle body

1 *Engine mount No. 3 through-bolt*
2 *Engine mount Dynamic damper*
3 *Engine mount bracket nuts*

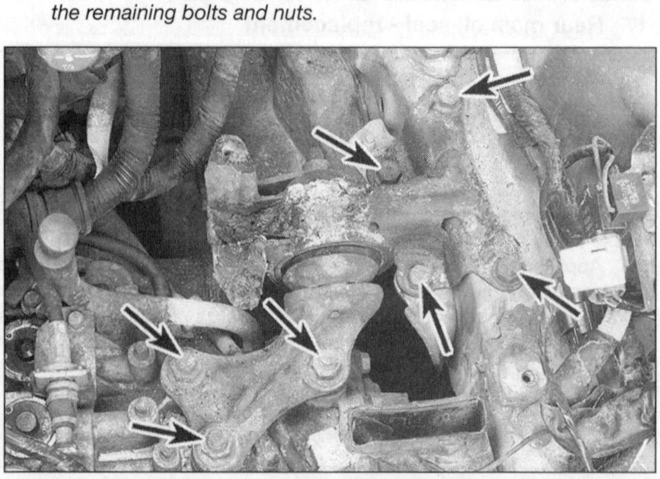

18.10 Transaxle/engine mount at the left (driver's) side of the engine - a bolt torque sequence is necessary for the bracket to the vehicle body (except 1.5L DOHC engine)

Chapter 2 Part B
General engine overhaul procedures

Contents

2B

Specifications

General

Displacement	
1.6L SOHC	97 cubic inches
1.8L SOHC	112 cubic inches
1.8L DOHC	112 cubic inches
1.5L DOHC	91 cubic inches
Cylinder compression pressure @ 300 rpm	
1.6L SOHC (except California)	
Standard	192 psi
Minimum	125 psi
1.6L SOHC (California)	
Standard	185 psi
Minimum	142 psi
1.8L SOHC	
Standard	173 psi
Minimum	121 psi
1.8L DOHC	
Standard	182 psi
Minimum	128 psi
1.5L DOHC	
Standard	195 psi
Minimum	146 psi
Oil pressure (all engines - warm)	
1000 rpm	29 to 42 psi
3000 rpm	43 to 56 psi

Cylinder head

Warpage limits	
Block surface	
1.6L SOHC	0.006 inch
1.8L SOHC and 1.8L DOHC	0.004 inch
1.5L DOHC	0.006 inch
Manifold surfaces (all engines)	0.006 inch

Valves and related components

Valve margin thickness (minimum)	
1.6L SOHC (except California)	
Intake	0.031 inch
Exhaust	0.043 inch
1.6L SOHC (California), 1.8L SOHC and 1.8L DOHC	
Intake	0.035 inch
Exhaust	0.039 inch
1.5L DOHC	
Intake	0.043 inch
Exhaust	0.047 inch
Valve stem diameter	
1.6L SOHC (except California)	
Intake	0.2745 to 0.2749 inch
Exhaust	0.2743 to 0.2748 inch
1.6L SOHC (California), 1.8L SOHC and 1.8L DOHC	
Intake	0.2351 to 0.2356 inch
Exhaust	0.2349 to 0.2354 inch
1.5L DOHC	
Intake	0.2154 to 0.2159 inch
Exhaust	0.2152 to 0.2157 inch
Valve stem-to-guide clearance	
Intake (all engines)	
Standard	0.0010 to 0.0023 inch
Service limit	0.008 inch
Exhaust (all engines)	
Standard	0.0012 to 0.0025 inch
Service limit	0.008 inch
Valve spring	
Out-of-square limit	
1.6L SOHC (except California)	
Intake	0.060 inch
Exhaust	0.060 inch
1.6L SOHC (California)	
Intake	0.063 inch
Exhaust	0.059 inch
1.8L SOHC	
Intake	0.063 inch
Exhaust	0.060 inch
1.8L DOHC	
Intake	0.064 inch
Exhaust	0.064 inch
1.5L DOHC - Intake and Exhaust	0.052 inch
Free length (minimum)	
1.6L SOHC (except California)	
Intake	1.398 inches
Exhaust	1.400 inches
1.6L SOHC (California)	
Intake	1.540 inches
Exhaust	1.500 inches
1.8L SOHC	
Intake	1.535 inches
Exhaust	1.476 inches
1.8L DOHC	
Intake	1.555 inches
Exhaust	1.555 inches
1.5L DOHC	
Compressed height, spring force	29 to 32 lbs (Measure spring force at 1.24 inches)

Crankshaft and connecting rods

Connecting rod journal	
Diameter	
All except 1.5L DOHC	1.7693 to 1.7699 inches
1.5L DOHC	1.5725 to 1.5730 inches
Out-of-round limits (all engines)	0.0020 inch
Runout limits (all engines)	0.0016 inch
Main bearing journal (all engines)	
Diameter	1.9661 to 1.9667 inches
Out-of-round	0.0020 inch
Runout limit	0.0016 inch
Main Bearing oil clearance (all engines)	
Standard	0.0007 to 0.0014 inch
Service limit	0.004 inch
Connecting rod oil clearance	
1.6L SOHC and 1.8L SOHC	
Standard	0.0011 to 0.0026 inch
Service limit	0.004 inch
1.8L DOHC	
Standard	0.0008 to 0.0026 inch
Service limit	0.004 inch
1.5L DOHC	
Standard	0.0012 to 0.0039 inch
Service limit	0.004 inch
Connecting rod side clearance (all engines)	
Standard	0.0044 to 0.0103 inch
Service limit	0.012 inch
Crankshaft endplay (all engines)	
Standard	0.0032 to 0.0111 inch
Service limit	
All except 1.5L DOHC	0.012 inch
1.5L DOHC	0.010 inch
Thrust washer thickness	0.0985 to 0.1003 inch

Engine block

Deck warpage limit (all engines)	0.0060 inch
Cylinder bore diameter	
1.6L SOHC	
Standard	3.0709 to 3.0716 inches
Oversize 1	3.0810 to 3.0812 inches
Oversize 2	3.0908 to 3.0910 inches
1.8L SOHC and 1.8L DOHC	
Standard	3.2678 to 3.2684 inches
Oversize 1	3.2778 to 3.2780 inches
Oversize 2	3.2877 to 3.2879 inches
1.5L DOHC	2.9646 to 2.9638 inches
Oversize 1	2.9745 to 2.9751 inches
Oversize 2	2.9843 to 2.9849 inches
Taper and out-of-round limits	
All except 1.5L DOHC	0.0007 inch
1.5L DOHC	0.0006 inch

Pistons and rings

Piston diameter	
1.6L SOHC	
Standard	3.0691 to 3.0698 inches
Oversize 1	3.0792 to 3.0794 inches
Oversize 2	3.0890 to 3.0892 inches
1.8L SOHC and 1.8L DOHC	
Standard	3.2659 to 3.2666 inches
Oversize 1	3.2761 to 3.2762 inches
Oversize 2	3.2859 to 3.2860 inches
1.5L DOHC	2.9632 to 2.9638 inches
Oversize 1	2.9730 to 2.9737 inches
Oversize 2	2.9828 to 2.9835 inches
Piston-to-bore clearance	
Standard	
All except 1.5L DOHC	0.0016 to 0.0020 inch
1.5L DOHC	0.0012 to 0.0016 inch

2B

Pistons and rings (continued)

Piston-to-bore clearance (continued)	
Service limit	
All except 1.5L DOHC	0.0060 inch
1.5L DOHC	0.0039 inch
Piston ring end gap	
No. 1 (top) compression ring (all engines)	
Standard	0.006 to 0.011 inch
Service limit	0.039 inch
No. 2 (middle) compression ring	
Standard	
1.6L SOHC (except California), 1.8L SOHC and 1.8L DOHC	0.006 to 0.011 inch
1.6L SOHC (California)	0.012 to 0.017 inch
1.5L DOHC	0.010 to 0.015 inches
Service limit	0.039 inch
Oil ring (all engines)	
Standard	0.008 to 0.027 inches
Service limit	0.039 inch
Piston ring groove clearance	
No. 1 (top) compression ring	
Standard	
1.6L SOHC	0.0012 to 0.0027 inch
1.8L SOHC and 1.8L DOHC	0.0012 to 0.0025 inch
1.5L DOHC	0.0014 to 0.0025 inch
Service limit (all engines)	0.006 inch
No. 2 (middle) compression ring	
Standard	
All except 1.5L DOHC	0.0012 to 0.0027 inch
1.5L DOHC	0.0012 to 0.0025 inch
Service limit (all engines)	0.006 inch

Torque specifications*

	Ft-lbs (unless otherwise indicated)
Main bearing cap bolts (all engines)	40 to 43
Connecting rod cap nuts/bolts	
All engines (except 1.5L DOHC)	35 to 36
1.5L DOHC engine	22 to 25
1.8L SOHC and 1.8L DOHC oil jets	104 to 156 in-lbs

***Note:** *Refer to Part A for additional torque specifications.*

1 General information

Included in this portion of Chapter 2 are the general overhaul procedures for the cylinder head(s) and internal engine components.

The information ranges from advice concerning preparation for an overhaul and the purchase of replacement parts to detailed, step-by-step procedures covering removal and installation of internal engine components and the inspection of parts.

The following Sections have been written based on the assumption that the engine has been removed from the vehicle. For information concerning in-vehicle engine repair, as well as removal and installation of the external components necessary for the overhaul, see Chapter 2A and Section 8 of this Chapter.

The Specifications included in this Part are only those necessary for the inspection and overhaul procedures which follow. Refer to Chapter 2, Part A for additional Specifications.

2 Engine overhaul - general information

Refer to illustrations 2.4a and 2.4b

It's not always easy to determine when, or if, an engine should be completely overhauled, as a number of factors must be considered.

High mileage is not necessarily an indication that an overhaul is needed, while low mileage doesn't preclude the need for an overhaul. Frequency of servicing is probably the most important consideration. An engine that's had regular and frequent oil and filter changes, as well as other required maintenance, will most likely give many thousands of miles of reliable service. Conversely, a neglected engine may require an overhaul very early in its life.

Excessive oil consumption is an indication that piston rings, valve seals and/or valve guides are in need of attention. Make sure that oil leaks aren't responsible before deciding that the rings and/or guides are bad. Perform a cylinder compression check to determine the extent of the work required (see Section 4). Also check the vacuum readings under various conditions (see Section 3).

Check the oil pressure with a gauge installed in place of the oil pressure sending unit **(see illustrations)** and compare it to this Chapter's Specifications. If it's extremely low, the bearings and/or oil pump are probably worn out.

Loss of power, rough running, knocking or metallic engine noises, excessive valve train noise and high fuel consumption rates may also point to the need for an overhaul, especially if they're all present at the same time. If a complete tune-up doesn't remedy the situation, major mechanical work is the only solution.

An engine overhaul involves restoring the internal parts to the specifications of a new engine. During an overhaul, the piston rings are replaced and the cylinder walls are reconditioned (re-bored and/or honed). If a re-bore is done by an automotive machine shop, new oversize pistons will also be installed. The main bearings, connecting rod bearings and camshaft bearings are generally replaced with new ones and, if necessary, the crankshaft may be reground to restore the journals. Generally, the valves are serviced as well, since they're usually in less-than-perfect condition at this point. While the engine is being overhauled, other components, such as the distributor, starter and alternator, can be rebuilt as well. The end result should be a like new engine that will give many trouble free miles. **Note:** *Critical cooling system components such as the hoses, drivebelts, thermostat and water*

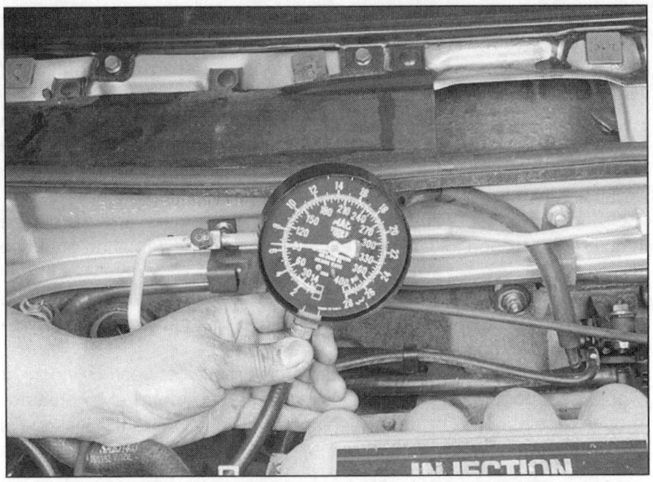

2.4a The oil pressure can be checked by removing the sending unit and installing a pressure gauge in its place

2.4b The oil pressure sending unit (arrow) is located in the right front corner of the engine block, near the oil filter

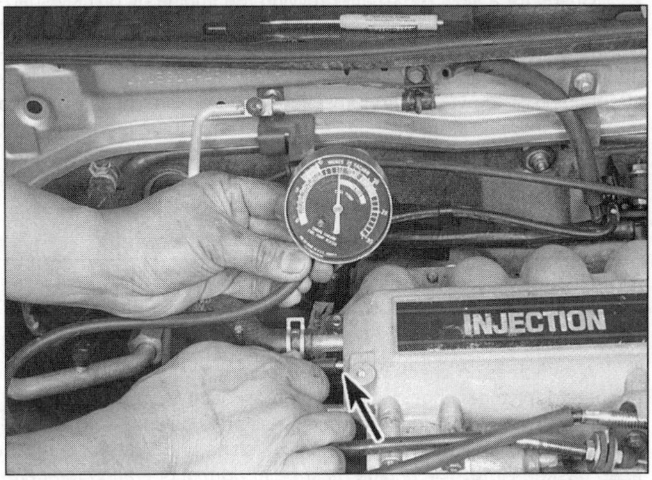

3.4 The vacuum gauge is easily attached to this unused port (arrow) on the intake manifold

pump should be replaced with new parts when an engine is overhauled. The radiator should be checked carefully to ensure that it isn't clogged or leaking (see Chapter 3). *If you purchase a rebuilt engine or short block, some rebuilders will not warranty their engines unless the radiator has been professionally flushed. Also, we don't recommend overhauling the oil pump - always install a new one when an engine is rebuilt.*

Before beginning the engine overhaul, read through the entire procedure to familiarize yourself with the scope and requirements of the job. Overhauling an engine isn't difficult, but it is time-consuming. Plan on the vehicle being tied up for a minimum of two weeks, especially if parts must be taken to an automotive machine shop for repair or reconditioning. Check on availability of parts and make sure that any necessary special tools and equipment are obtained in advance. Most work can be done with typical hand tools, although a number of precision measuring tools are required for inspecting parts to determine if they must be replaced. Often an automotive machine shop will handle the inspection of parts and offer advice concerning reconditioning and replacement. **Note:** *Always wait until the engine has been completely disassembled and all components, especially the engine block, have been inspected before deciding what service and repair operations must be performed by an automotive machine shop.* Since the block's condition will be the major factor to consider when determining whether to overhaul the original engine or buy a rebuilt one, never purchase parts or have machine work done on other components until the block has been thoroughly inspected. As a general rule, time is the primary cost of an overhaul, so it doesn't pay to install worn or substandard parts.

As a final note, to ensure maximum life and minimum trouble from a rebuilt engine, everything must be assembled with care in a spotlessly-clean environment.

3 Vacuum gauge diagnostic checks

Refer to illustration 3.4

A vacuum gauge provides valuable information about what is going on in the engine at a low-cost. You can check for worn rings or cylinder walls, leaking head or intake manifold gaskets, incorrect carburetor adjustments, restricted exhaust, stuck or burned valves, weak valve springs, improper ignition or valve timing and ignition problems.

Unfortunately, vacuum gauge readings are easy to misinterpret, so they should be used in conjunction with other tests to confirm the diagnosis.

Both the absolute readings and the rate of needle movement are important for accurate interpretation. Most gauges measure vacuum in inches of mercury (in-Hg). As vacuum increases (or atmospheric pressure decreases), the reading will increase. Also, for every 1,000 foot increase in elevation above sea level, the gauge readings will decrease about one inch of mercury.

Connect the vacuum gauge directly to intake manifold vacuum, not to ported (above the throttle plate) vacuum **(see illustration)**. Be sure no hoses are left disconnected during the test or false readings will result.

Before you begin the test, allow the engine to warm up completely. Block the wheels and set the parking brake. With the transmission in neutral (or Park, on automatics), start the engine and allow it to run at normal idle speed. **Warning:** *Carefully inspect the fan blades for cracks or damage before starting the engine. Keep your hands and the vacuum tester clear of the fan and do not stand in front of the vehicle or in line with the fan when the engine is running.*

Read the vacuum gauge; an average, healthy engine should normally produce between 17 and 22 inches of vacuum with a fairly steady needle.

Refer to the following vacuum gauge readings and what they indicate about the engines condition:

1 A low steady reading usually indicates a leaking gasket between the intake manifold and carburetor or throttle body, a leaky vacuum hose, late ignition timing or incorrect camshaft timing. Check ignition timing with a timing light and eliminate all other possible causes, utilizing the tests provided in this Chapter before you remove the timing belt cover to check the timing marks.

2 If the reading is three to eight inches below normal and it fluctu-

ates at that low reading, suspect an intake manifold gasket leak at an intake port or a faulty injector.

3 If the needle has regular drops of about two to four inches at a steady rate the valves are probably leaking. Perform a compression or leak-down test to confirm this.

4 An irregular drop or down-flick of the needle can be caused by a sticking valve or an ignition misfire. Perform a compression or leak-down test and read the spark plugs.

5 A rapid vibration of about four in-Hg vibration at idle combined with exhaust smoke indicates worn valve guides. Perform a leak-down test to confirm this. If the rapid vibration occurs with an increase in engine speed, check for a leaking intake manifold gasket or head gasket, weak valve springs, burned valves or ignition misfire.

6 A slight fluctuation, say one inch up and down, may mean ignition problems. Check all the usual tune-up items and, if necessary, run the engine on an ignition analyzer.

7 If there is a large fluctuation, perform a compression or leak-down test to look for a weak or dead cylinder or a blown head gasket.

8 If the needle moves slowly through a wide range, check for a clogged PCV system, incorrect idle fuel mixture, throttle body or intake manifold gasket leaks.

9 Check for a slow return after revving the engine by quickly snapping the throttle open until the engine reaches about 2,500 rpm and let it shut. Normally the reading should drop to near zero, rise above normal idle reading (about 5 in.-Hg over) and then return to the previous idle reading. If the vacuum returns slowly and doesn't peak when the throttle is snapped shut, the rings may be worn. If there is a long delay, look for a restricted exhaust system (often the muffler or catalytic converter). An easy way to check this is to temporarily disconnect the exhaust ahead of the suspected part and redo the test.

4 Compression check

Refer to illustration 4.6

1 A compression check will tell you what mechanical condition the upper end (pistons, rings, valves, head gasket[s]) of your engine is in. Specifically, it can tell you if the compression is down due to leakage caused by worn piston rings, defective valves and seats or a blown head gasket. **Note:** *The engine must be at normal operating temperature and the battery must be fully charged for this check.*

2 Begin by cleaning the area around the spark plugs before you remove them (compressed air should be used, if available, otherwise a small brush or even a bicycle tire pump will work). The idea is to prevent dirt from getting into the cylinders as the compression check is being done.

3 Remove all of the spark plugs from the engine (see Chapter 1).

4 Block the throttle wide open.

5 Detach the coil wire from the center of the distributor cap and ground it on the engine block. Use a jumper wire with alligator clips on each end to ensure a good ground. It is also a good idea to pull the EFI fuse from the fuse panel to disable the fuel pump during the compression test.

6 Install the compression gauge in the spark plug hole **(see illustration)**.

7 Crank the engine over at least seven compression strokes and watch the gauge. The compression should build up quickly in a healthy engine. Low compression on the first stroke, followed by gradually increasing pressure on successive strokes, indicates worn piston rings. A low compression reading on the first stroke, which doesn't build up during successive strokes, indicates leaking valves or a blown head gasket (a cracked head could also be the cause). Deposits on the undersides of the valve heads can also cause low compression. Record the highest gauge reading obtained.

8 Repeat the procedure for the remaining cylinders and compare the results to this Chapter's Specifications.

9 Add some engine oil (about three squirts from a plunger-type oil can) to each cylinder, through the spark plug hole, and repeat the test.

10 If the compression increases after the oil is added, the piston rings are definitely worn. If the compression doesn't increase significantly, the leakage is occurring at the valves or head gasket. Leakage past the valves may be caused by burned valve seats and/or faces or warped, cracked or bent valves.

11 If two adjacent cylinders have equally low compression, there's a strong possibility that the head gasket between them is blown. The appearance of coolant in the combustion chambers or the crankcase would verify this condition.

12 If one cylinder is 20-percent lower than the others, and the engine has a slightly rough idle, a worn exhaust lobe on the camshaft could be the cause.

13 If the compression is unusually high, the combustion chambers are probably coated with carbon deposits. If that's the case, the cylinder head should be removed and decarbonized.

14 If compression is way down or varies greatly between cylinders, it would be a good idea to have a leak-down test performed by an automotive repair shop. This test will pinpoint exactly where the leakage is occurring and how severe it is.

5 Engine removal - methods and precautions

If you've decided that an engine must be removed for overhaul or major repair work, several preliminary steps should be taken.

Locating a suitable place to work is extremely important. Adequate work space, along with storage space for the vehicle, will be needed. If a shop or garage isn't available, at the very least a flat, level, clean work surface made of concrete or asphalt is required.

Cleaning the engine compartment and engine before beginning the removal procedure will help keep tools clean and organized.

An engine hoist or A-frame will also be necessary. Make sure the equipment is rated in excess of the combined weight of the engine and transaxle. Safety is of primary importance, considering the potential hazards involved in lifting the engine out of the vehicle.

If the engine is being removed by a novice, a helper should be available. Advice and aid from someone more experienced would also be helpful. There are many instances when one person cannot simultaneously perform all of the operations required when lifting the engine out of the vehicle.

Plan the operation ahead of time. Arrange for or obtain all of the tools and equipment you'll need prior to beginning the job. Some of the equipment necessary to perform engine removal and installation safely and with relative ease are (in addition to an engine hoist) a heavy duty floor jack, complete sets of wrenches and sockets as described in the front of this manual, wooden blocks and plenty of rags and cleaning solvent for mopping up spilled oil, coolant and gasoline. If the hoist

4.6 A compression gauge with a threaded fitting for the spark plug hole is preferred over the type that requires hand pressure to maintain the seal - be sure to block open the throttle valve as far as possible during the compression check!

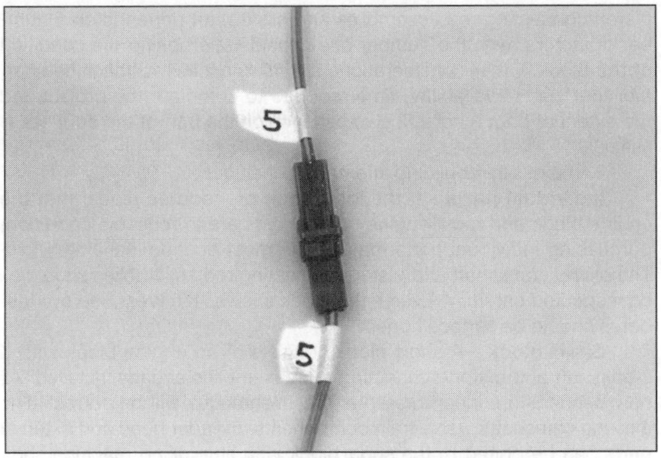

6.7 Label both ends of each wire and hose before disconnecting it

must be rented, make sure that you arrange for it in advance and perform all of the operations possible without it beforehand. This will save you money and time.

Plan for the vehicle to be out of use for quite a while. A machine shop will be required to perform some of the work which the do-it-yourselfer can't accomplish without special equipment. These shops often have a busy schedule, so it would be a good idea to consult them before removing the engine in order to accurately estimate the amount of time required to rebuild or repair components that may need work.

Always be extremely careful when removing and installing the engine. Serious injury can result from careless actions. Plan ahead, take your time and a job of this nature, although major, can be accomplished successfully.

6 Engine - removal and installation

Refer to illustrations 6.7, 6.24 and 6.25

Note 1: *Read through the entire Section before beginning this procedure. The factory recommends removing the engine and transaxle from the top as a unit, then separating the engine from the transaxle on the shop floor.* **Note 2:** *The following sequence for engine removal and replacement can be utilized for all SOHC and DOHC engines covered in this manual. The steps may be varied to accommodate combinations of accessories.*

Removal

Warning: *Some models are equipped with airbags. The airbag is armed and can deploy (inflate) anytime the battery is connected. To prevent accidental deployment (and possible injury), turn the ignition key to LOCK and disconnect the negative battery cable whenever working near airbag components. After the battery is disconnected, wait at least two minutes before beginning work (the system has a back-up capacitor that must fully discharge). See Chapter 12 for more information.*

1 Relieve the fuel system pressure (see Chapter 4).

2 Disconnect the negative cable from the battery. **Caution:** *If the stereo in your vehicle is equipped with an anti-theft system, make sure you have the correct activation code before disconnecting the battery.*

3 Place protective covers on the fenders and cowl and remove the hood (see Chapter 11).

4 Raise the vehicle and support it securely on jackstands.

5 Drain the cooling system, engine oil, transaxle oil and remove the drivebelts (see Chapter 1).

6 Remove the hood and front wheels.

7 Clearly label, then disconnect all vacuum lines, coolant and emissions hoses, wiring harness connectors, ground straps and fuel lines. Masking tape and/or a touch up paint applicator work well for marking items **(see illustration)**. Take instant photos or sketch the locations of components and brackets.

8 Remove the air cleaner housing assembly and the resonance chamber (see Chapter 4).

9 Remove the engine undercover to provide access to the bottom of the engine (see Chapter 2A).

10 Remove the battery bracket, the battery cover, the battery, the battery carrier and the battery duct.

11 Disconnect the accelerator cable.

12 Remove the windshield washer tank and coolant reservoir tank.

13 Disconnect the heater hoses.

14 Remove the cooling fan(s) the radiator hoses and the radiator (see Chapter 3)

15 Release the residual fuel pressure in the tank by removing the gas cap, then detach the fuel lines connecting the engine to the chassis (see Chapter 4). Plug or cap all open fittings.

16 On power steering-equipped vehicles, unbolt the power steering pump. If clearance allows, tie the pump aside without disconnecting the hoses. If necessary, remove the pump (see Chapter 10).

17 On air-conditioned models, unbolt the compressor and set it aside. Do not disconnect the refrigerant hoses. **Note:** *Wire the compressor out of the way with a coat hanger, don't let the compressor hang on the hoses.*

18 Disconnect the throttle linkage, transmission Throttle Valve(TV) linkage, speedometer cable, and speed control cable, if equipped, from the engine (see Chapter 4).

19 Disconnect the clutch release cylinder, the shift control rod and cable and the extension bar (see Chapter 8).

20 Disconnect the front exhaust pipe, the stabilizer, the tie-rod end and the driveshaft (see Chapter 10).

21 Attach a lifting sling to the engine. Position a hoist and connect the sling to it. Take up the slack until there is slight tension on the hoist.

22 Recheck to be sure nothing except the mounts are still connecting the engine to the vehicle or to the transaxle. Disconnect and label anything still remaining.

23 Support the transaxle with a floor jack. Place a block of wood on the jack head to prevent damage to the transaxle. Remove the dynamic damper, the mount brackets, and the engine support bracket. **Warning:** *Do not place any part of your body under the engine/transaxle when it's supported only by a hoist or other lifting device.*

24 Slowly lift the engine and transaxle out of the vehicle **(see illustration)**. It may be necessary to pry the mounts away from the frame brackets.

6.24 Attach the engine hoist as shown. Lift the engine high enough to clear the vehicle, then move it away and lower the hoist - the engine can be removed with the transaxle still attached

6.25 Lower the engine outside of the vehicle, remove the driveplate, and attach the engine to a suitable workstand

25 Move the engine away from the vehicle and carefully lower the hoist until the engine can be set on the floor; or remove the flywheel/driveplate and mount the engine on an engine stand **(see illustration). Note:** *On automatic transaxle-equipped models, mark the front and rear spacer plates and keep them with the driveplate.*
26 On automatic transaxle-equipped models, remove the torque converter-to-driveplate fasteners (see Chapter 7B) and push the converter back slightly into the bellhousing.
27 Remove the engine-to-transaxle bolts and separate the engine from the transaxle (see Chapter 7A). The torque converter should remain in the transaxle.

Installation

28 Check the engine/transaxle mounts. If they're worn or damaged, replace them.
29 On manual transaxle-equipped models, inspect the clutch components (see Chapter 8) and on automatic models inspect the converter seal and bushing.
30 On automatic transaxle-equipped models, apply a dab of grease to the nose of the converter. Make sure the converter is completely seated on the transaxle input shaft and the front pump splines. To do this, push in on the converter and turn it, feeling for a "clunk" - it may even "clunk" more than once. If you feel nothing, the converter is already completely seated.
31 Carefully guide the transaxle into place, following the procedure outlined in Chapter 7. **Caution:** *Do not use the bolts to force the engine and transaxle into alignment. It may crack or damage major components.*
32 Install the engine-to-transaxle bolts and tighten them to the torque listed in the Chapter 7 Specifications.
33 Attach the hoist to the engine and carefully lower the engine/transaxle assembly into the engine compartment.
34 Install the mount bolts and tighten them securely.
35 Reinstall the remaining components and fasteners in the reverse order of removal.
36 Add coolant, oil, power steering and transmission fluids as needed (see Chapter 1).
37 Run the engine and check for proper operation and leaks. Shut off the engine and recheck the fluid levels.

7 Engine rebuilding alternatives

The do-it-yourselfer is faced with a number of options when performing an engine overhaul. The decision to replace the engine block, piston/connecting rod assemblies and crankshaft depends on a number of factors, with the number one consideration being the condition of the block. Other considerations are cost, access to machine shop facilities, parts availability, time required to complete the project and the extent of prior mechanical experience on the part of the do-it-yourselfer.

Some of the rebuilding alternatives include:

Individual parts - If the inspection procedures reveal that the engine block and most engine components are in reusable condition, purchasing individual parts may be the most economical alternative. The block, crankshaft and piston/connecting rod assemblies should all be inspected carefully. Even if the block shows little wear, the cylinder bores should be surface honed.

Short block - A short block consists of an engine block with a crankshaft and piston/connecting rod assemblies already installed. All new bearings are incorporated and all clearances will be correct. The existing camshafts, valve train components, cylinder head and external parts can be bolted to the short block with little or no machine shop work necessary.

Long block - A long block consists of a short block plus an oil pump, oil pan, cylinder head, valve cover, camshaft and valve train components, timing sprockets and chain or gears and timing cover. All components are installed with new bearings, seals and gaskets incorporated throughout. The installation of manifolds and external parts is all that's necessary.

Give careful thought to which alternative is best for you and discuss the situation with local automotive machine shops, auto parts dealers and experienced rebuilders before ordering or purchasing replacement parts.

8 Engine overhaul - disassembly sequence

Refer to illustration 8.5

1 It's much easier to disassemble and work on the engine if it's mounted on a portable engine stand. A stand can often be rented quite cheaply from an equipment rental yard. Before the engine is mounted on a stand, the flywheel/driveplate and rear oil seal retainer should be removed from the engine.
2 If a stand isn't available, it's possible to disassemble the engine with it blocked up on the floor. Be extra careful not to tip or drop the engine when working without a stand.
3 If you're going to obtain a rebuilt engine, all external components must come off first, to be transferred to the replacement engine, just as they will if you're doing a complete engine overhaul yourself. These include:

Alternator and brackets
Emissions control components
Distributor, spark plug wires and spark plugs
Thermostat and housing cover
Water pump
EFI components
Intake/exhaust manifolds
Oil filter
Engine mounts
Clutch and flywheel/driveplate
Engine rear plate

Note: *When removing the external components from the engine, pay close attention to details that may be helpful or important during installation. Note the installed position of gaskets, seals, spacers, pins, brackets, washers, bolts and other small items.*
4 If you're obtaining a short block, which consists of the engine block, crankshaft, pistons and connecting rods all assembled, then the cylinder head, oil pan and oil pump will have to be removed as well from your engine so that your short block can be turned in to the rebuilder as a core. See *Engine rebuilding alternatives* for additional information regarding the different possibilities to be considered.
5 If you're planning a complete overhaul, the engine must be disassembled and the internal components removed **(see illustration)**. The

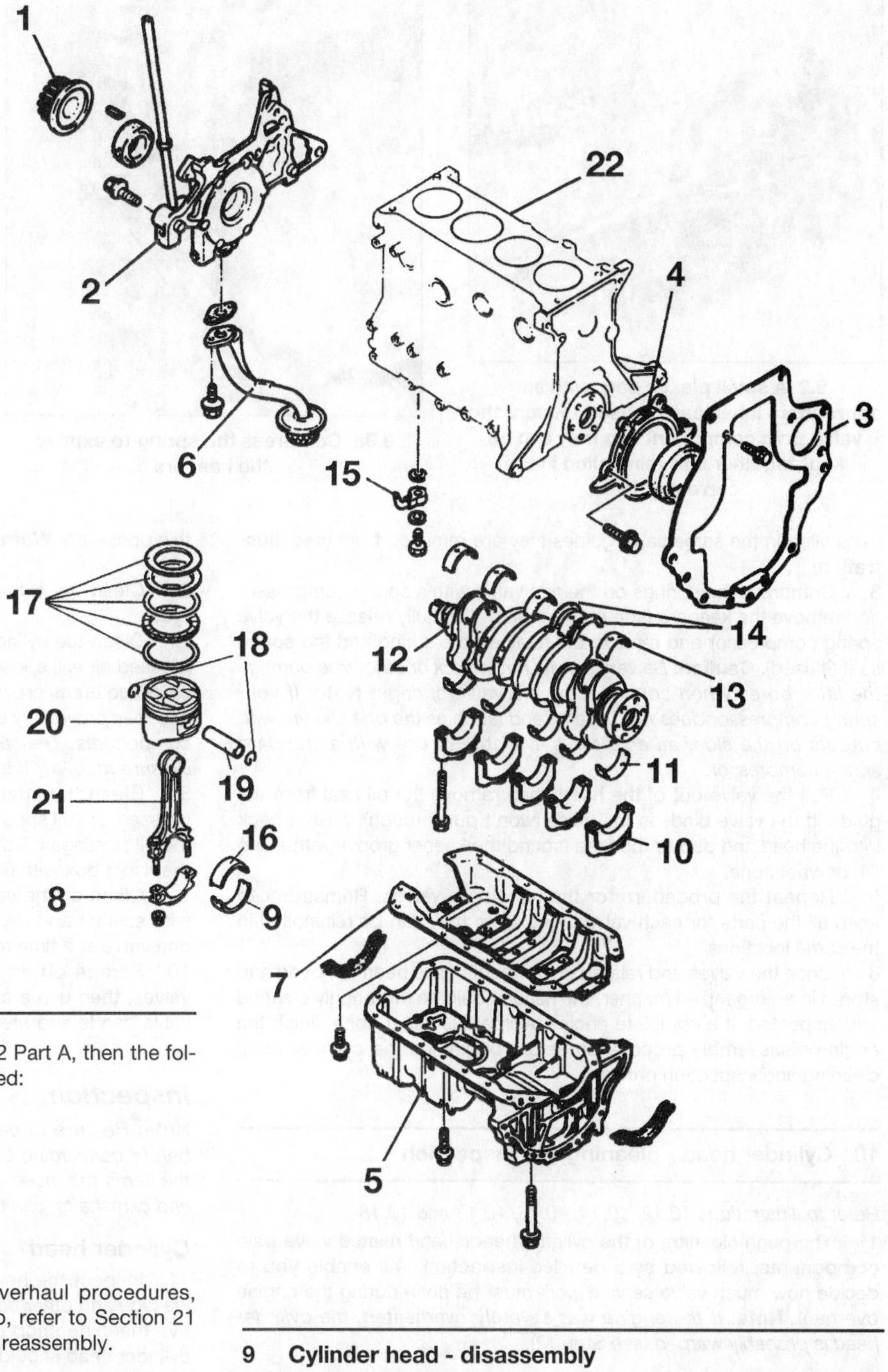

8.5 Four-cylinder engine lower end components - exploded view

1 *Crankshaft timing belt sprocket*
2 *Front cover (oil pump assembly)*
3 *Rear cover end plate*
4 *Rear cover*
5 *Oil pan*
6 *Oil pump pickup tube & screen*
7 *Main Bearing Support Plate (MBSP)*
8 *Connecting rod cap*
9 *Lower connecting rod bearing*
10 *Main bearing cap*
11 *Lower main bearing*
12 *Crankshaft*
13 *Upper main bearing*
14 *Thrust bearings*
15 *Oil jet assembly (one per cylinder)*
16 *Upper connecting rod bearing*
17 *Piston ring set*
18 *Piston pin clips*
19 *Piston wrist pin*
20 *Piston*
21 *Connecting rod*
22 *Cylinder block*

2B

engine cylinder head is first removed in Chapter 2 Part A, then the following engine block components are disassembled:

Oil pan
Main bearing support plate
Front cover (oil pump assembly)
Rear cover
Piston/connecting rod assemblies
Crankshaft rear oil seal retainer
Crankshaft and main bearings

6 Before beginning the disassembly and overhaul procedures, make sure the following items are available. Also, refer to Section 21 for a list of tools and materials needed for engine reassembly.

Common hand tools
Small cardboard boxes or plastic bags for storing parts
Gasket scraper
Ridge reamer
Micrometers
Telescoping gauges
Dial indicator set
Valve spring compressor
Cylinder surfacing hone
Piston ring groove-cleaning tool
Electric drill motor
Tap and die set
Wire brushes
Oil gallery brushes
Cleaning solvent

9 Cylinder head - disassembly

Refer to illustrations 9.2, 9.3a and 9.3b

Note: *New and rebuilt cylinder heads are commonly available for most engines at dealerships and auto parts stores. Due to the fact that some specialized tools are necessary for the disassembly and inspection procedures, and replacement parts may not be readily available, it may be more practical and economical for the home mechanic to purchase a replacement head rather than taking the time to disassemble, inspect and recondition the original.*

1 Cylinder head disassembly involves removal of the intake and exhaust valves and related components. It's assumed that the lifters and camshafts have already been removed (see Part A as needed).

2 Before the valves are removed, arrange to label and store them, along with their related components, so they can be kept separate and

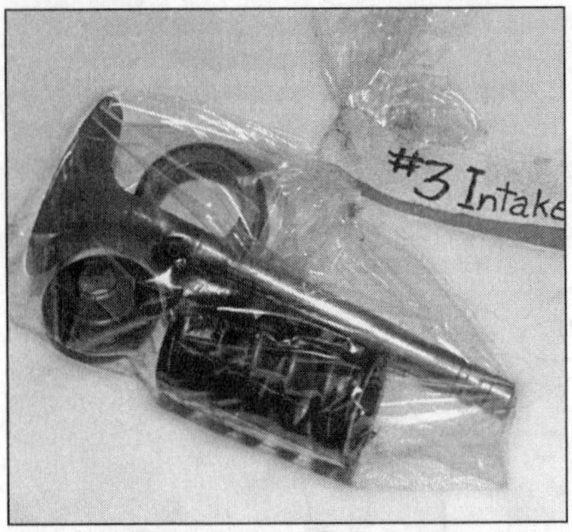

9.2 A small plastic bag, with an appropriate label, can be used to store the valve train components so they can be kept together and reinstalled in the correct guide

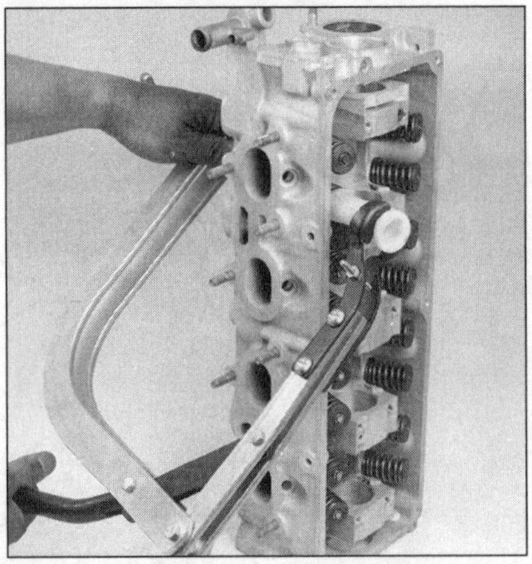

9.3a Compress the spring to expose the keepers

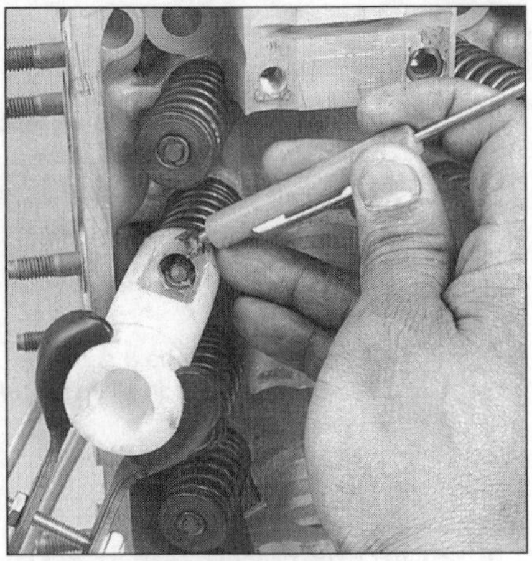

9.3b Remove the keepers with a small magnetic screwdriver or needle-nose pliers

reinstalled in the same valve guides they are removed from **(see illustration)**.

3 Compress the springs on the first valve with a spring compressor and remove the keepers **(see illustrations)**. Carefully release the valve spring compressor and remove the retainer, the spring and the spring seat (if used). **Caution:** *Be very careful not to nick or otherwise damage the lifter bores when compressing the valve springs.* **Note:** *If your spring compressor does not have an end (such as the one shown) with cutouts on the side, an adapter is available to use with a standard spring compressor.*

4 Pull the valve out of the head, then remove the oil seal from the guide. If the valve binds in the guide (won't pull through), push it back into the head and deburr the area around the keeper groove with a fine file or whetstone.

5 Repeat the procedure for the remaining valves. Remember to keep all the parts for each valve together so they can be reinstalled in the same locations.

6 Once the valves and related components have been removed and stored in an organized manner, the head should be thoroughly cleaned and inspected. If a complete engine overhaul is being done, finish the engine disassembly procedures before beginning the cylinder head cleaning and inspection process.

10 Cylinder head - cleaning and inspection

Refer to illustrations 10.12, 10.14, 10.16, 10.17 and 10.18

1 Thorough cleaning of the cylinder head(s) and related valve train components, followed by a detailed inspection, will enable you to decide how much valve service work must be done during the engine overhaul. **Note:** *If the engine was severely overheated, the cylinder head is probably warped* (see Step 12).

Cleaning

2 Scrape all traces of old gasket material and sealing compound off the head gasket, intake manifold and exhaust manifold sealing surfaces. Be very careful not to gouge the cylinder head. Special gasket-removal solvents that soften gaskets and make removal much easier are available at auto parts stores.

3 Remove all built up scale from the coolant passages.

4 Run a stiff wire brush through the various holes to remove deposits that may have formed in them. If there are heavy rust deposits in the water passages, the bare head should be professionally cleaned at a machine shop.

5 Run an appropriate-size tap into each of the threaded holes to remove corrosion and thread sealant that may be present. If compressed air is available, use it to clear the holes of debris produced by this operation. **Warning:** *Wear eye protection when using compressed air!*

6 Clean the exhaust and intake manifold stud threads with a wire brush.

7 Clean the cylinder head with solvent and dry it thoroughly. Compressed air will speed the drying process and ensure that all holes and recessed areas are clean. **Note:** *Decarbonizing chemicals are available and may prove very useful when cleaning cylinder heads and valve train components. They are very caustic and should be used with caution. Be sure to follow the instructions on the container.*

8 Clean the lifters with solvent and dry them thoroughly. Compressed air will speed the drying process and can be used to clean out the oil passages. Don't mix them up during the cleaning process; keep them in a box with numbered compartments.

9 Clean all the valve springs, spring seats, keepers and retainers with solvent and dry them thoroughly. Work on the components from one valve at a time to avoid mixing up the parts.

10 Scrape off any heavy deposits that may have formed on the valves, then use a motorized wire brush to remove deposits from the valve heads and stems. Again, make sure the valves don't get mixed up.

Inspection

Note: *Be sure to perform all of the following inspection procedures before concluding that machine shop work is required. Make a list of the items that need attention. The inspection procedures for the lifters and camshafts, can be found in Part A.*

Cylinder head

11 Inspect the head very carefully for cracks, evidence of coolant leakage and other damage. If cracks are found, check with an automotive machine shop concerning repair. If repair isn't possible, a new cylinder head should be obtained.

12 Using a straightedge and feeler gauge, check the head gasket mating surface for warpage **(see illustration)**. If the warpage exceeds the limit found in this Chapter's Specifications, it can be resurfaced at an automotive machine shop.

13 Examine the valve seats in each of the combustion chambers. If they're pitted, cracked or burned, the head will require valve service that's beyond the scope of the home mechanic.

14 Check the valve stem-to-guide clearance with a small hole gauge and micrometer, or a dial indicator. Also, check the valve stem deflection with a dial indicator attached securely to the head **(see illustration)**. The valve must be in the guide and approximately 1/16-inch off the seat. The total valve stem movement indicated by the gauge needle must be noted, then divided by two to obtain the actual clearance value. If it exceeds the stem-to-guide clearance limit found in this Chapter's Specifications, the valve guides should be replaced. After

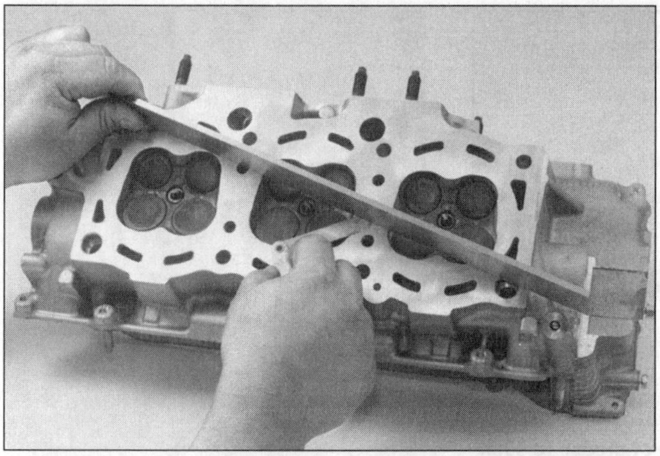

10.12 **Check the cylinder head gasket surfaces for warpage by trying to slip a feeler gauge under the precision straightedge (see the Specifications for the maximum warpage allowed and use a feeler gauge of that thickness)**

this is done, if there's still some doubt regarding the condition of the valve guides they should be checked by an automotive machine shop (the cost should be minimal). **Note:** *Most home mechanics will not have a precision small bore gauge, but your local machine shop can measure the guides for you.*

Valves

15 Carefully inspect each valve face for uneven wear, deformation, cracks, pits and burned areas. Check the valve stem for scuffing and galling and the neck for cracks. Rotate the valve and check for any obvious indication that it's bent. Look for pits and excessive wear on the end of the stem. The presence of any of these conditions indicates the need for valve service by an automotive machine shop.

16 Measure the margin width on each valve **(see illustration)**. Any valve with a margin narrower than that listed in this Chapter's Specifications will have to be replaced with a new one.

Valve components

17 Check each valve spring for wear (on the ends) and pits. Measure the free length and compare it to this Chapter's Specifications **(see illustration)**. Any springs that are shorter than specified have sagged and should not be re-used. The tension of all springs should be pressure checked with a special fixture before deciding that they're suitable for use in a rebuilt engine (take the springs to an automotive machine shop for this check).

18 Stand each spring on a flat surface and check it for squareness **(see illustration)**. If any of the springs are distorted or sagged, replace all of them with new parts.

19 Check the spring retainers and keepers for obvious wear and cracks. Any questionable parts should be replaced with new ones, as extensive damage will occur if they fail during engine operation.

20 Any damaged or excessively worn parts must be replaced with new ones.

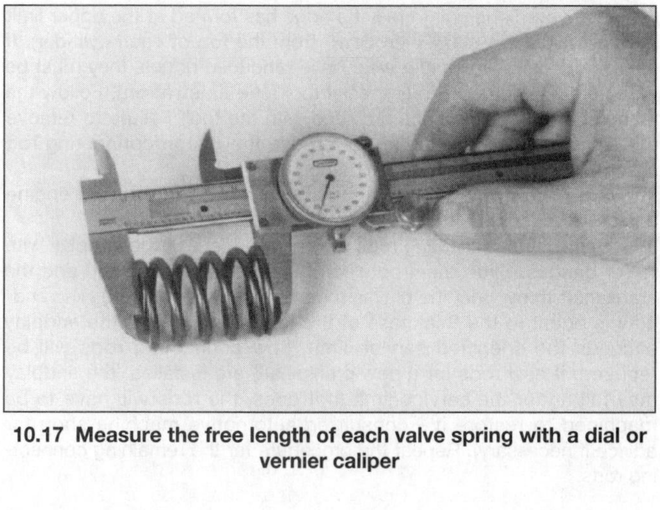

10.17 **Measure the free length of each valve spring with a dial or vernier caliper**

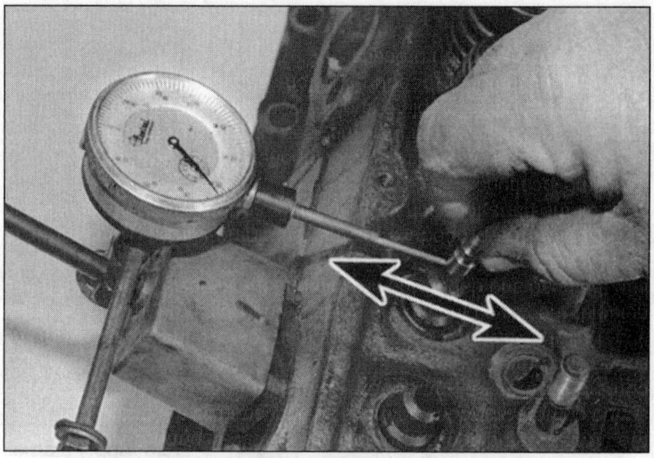

10.14 **A dial indicator can be used to determine the valve stem-to-guide clearance**

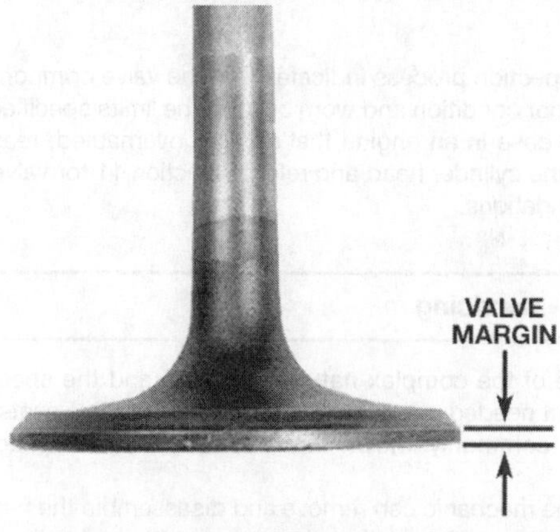

10.16 **The margin width on each valve must be as specified (if no margin exists, the valve cannot be re-used)**

10.18 **Check each valve spring for squareness**

12.3 Gently tap the valve seals into place with a deep socket and hammer

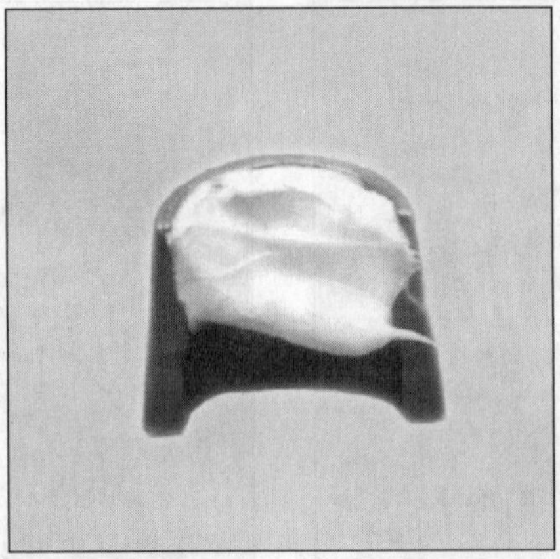

12.6 Apply a small dab of grease to each keeper before installation - it'll hold them in place on the valve stem as the spring is released

13.1 A ridge reamer is required to remove the ridge from the top of each cylinder - do this before removing the pistons!

21 If the inspection process indicates that the valve components are in generally poor condition and worn beyond the limits specified, which is usually the case in an engine that's being overhauled, reassemble the valves in the cylinder head and refer to Section 11 for valve servicing recommendations.

11 Valves - servicing

1 Because of the complex nature of the job and the special tools and equipment needed, servicing of the valves, the valve seats and the valve guides, commonly known as a valve job, should be done by a professional.

2 The home mechanic can remove and disassemble the head(s), do the initial cleaning and inspection, then reassemble and deliver them to a dealer service department or an automotive machine shop for the actual service work. Doing the inspection will enable you to see what condition the head(s) and valvetrain components are in and will ensure that you know what work and new parts are required when dealing with an automotive machine shop.

3 The dealer service department, or automotive machine shop, will remove the valves and springs, recondition or replace the valves and valve seats, recondition the valve guides, check and replace the valve springs, spring retainers and keepers (as necessary), replace the valve seals with new ones, reassemble the valve components and make sure the installed spring height is correct. The cylinder head gasket surface will also be resurfaced if it's warped.

4 After the valve job has been performed by a professional, the head(s) will be in like new condition. When the heads are returned, be sure to clean them again before installation on the engine to remove any metal particles and abrasive grit that may still be present from the valve service or head resurfacing operations. Use compressed air, if available, to blow out all the oil holes and passages.

12 Cylinder head - reassembly

Refer to illustrations 12.3 and 12.6

1 Regardless of whether or not the head was sent to an automotive machine shop for valve servicing, make sure it's clean before beginning reassembly. Note that there are several small core plugs (also called freeze plugs or expansion plugs) in the head. These should be replaced whenever the engine is overhauled or the cylinder head is reconditioned (see Section 15 for the replacement procedure).

2 If the head was sent out for valve servicing, the valves and related components will already be in place. Begin the reassembly procedure with Step 8.

3 Install new seals on each of the valve guides. **Note:** *Intake and exhaust valves require different seals - DO NOT mix them up!* Gently tap each intake valve seal into place until it's seated on the guide **(see illustration)**. **Caution:** *Don't hammer on the valve seals once they're seated or you may damage them. Don't twist or cock the seals during installation or they won't seat properly on the valve stems.*

4 Beginning at one end of the head, lubricate and install the first valve. Apply moly-base grease or clean engine oil to the valve stem.

5 Drop the spring seat or shim(s) over the valve guide and set the valve spring and retainer in place.

6 Compress the springs with a valve spring compressor and carefully install the keepers in the upper groove, then slowly release the compressor and make sure the keepers seat properly. Apply a small dab of grease to each keeper to hold it in place if necessary **(see illustration)**.

7 Repeat the procedure for the remaining valves. Be sure to return the components to their original locations - don't mix them up!

8 Tap the end of the valve stem lightly two or three times with a plastic hammer to verify that the keepers are all fully seated.

13 Pistons/connecting rods - removal

Refer to illustrations 13.1, 13.3, 13.4 and 13.6

Note: *Prior to removing the piston/connecting rod assemblies, remove the cylinder head(s), the oil pan and the oil pump pick-up tube by referring to the appropriate Sections in Chapter 2A.*

1 Use your fingernail to feel if a ridge has formed at the upper limit of ring travel (about 1/4-inch down from the top of each cylinder). If carbon deposits or cylinder wear have produced ridges, they must be completely removed with a special tool **(see illustration)**. Follow the manufacturer's instructions provided with the tool. Failure to remove the ridges before attempting to remove the piston/connecting rod assemblies may result in piston damage.

2 After the cylinder ridges have been removed, turn the engine upside-down so the crankshaft is facing up.

3 Before the connecting rods are removed, check the endplay with feeler gauges. Slide them between the first connecting rod and the crankshaft throw until the play is removed **(see illustration)**. The endplay is equal to the thickness of the feeler gauge(s). If the endplay exceeds the specified service limit, new connecting rods will be required. If new rods (or a new crankshaft) are installed, the endplay may fall under the service limit (if it does, the rods will have to be machined to restore it - consult an automotive machine shop for advice if necessary). Repeat the procedure for the remaining connecting rods.

13.3 Check the connecting rod side clearance with a feeler gauge as shown here

13.4 The connecting rods and caps should be marked to indicate which cylinder they're installed in - if they aren't, mark them with a center punch or scribe to avoid confusion during reassembly

4 Check the connecting rods and caps for identification marks. If they aren't plainly marked, use a small center punch to make the appropriate number of indentations on each rod and cap (1, 2, 3, etc., depending on the engine type and cylinder they're associated with) **(see illustration)**.

5 Loosen each of the connecting rod cap nuts 1/2-turn at a time until they can be removed by hand. Remove the number one connecting rod cap and bearing insert. Don't drop the bearing insert out of the cap.

6 Slip a short length of plastic or rubber hose over each connecting rod cap bolt to protect the crankshaft journal and cylinder wall as the piston is removed **(see illustration)**.

7 Remove the bearing insert and push the connecting rod/piston assembly out through the top of the engine. Use a wooden hammer handle to push on the upper bearing surface in the connecting rod. If resistance is felt, double-check to make sure that all of the ridge was removed from the cylinder.

8 Repeat the procedure for the remaining cylinders. **Note:** *Turn the crankshaft as needed to put the rod to be removed close to parallel with the cylinder bore, i.e. don't try to drive it out while at a large angle to the bore.*

9 After removal, reassemble the connecting rod caps and bearing inserts in their respective connecting rods and install the cap nuts/bolts finger tight. Leaving the old bearing inserts in place until reassembly will help prevent the connecting rod bearing surfaces from being accidentally nicked or gouged.

10 Don't separate the pistons from the connecting rods (see Section 18 for additional information).

14 Crankshaft removal

Refer to illustrations 14.1 and 14.3

Note: *The crankshaft can be removed only after the engine has been removed from the vehicle. It's assumed that the flywheel or driveplate, crankshaft sprocket, timing belt, oil pan, oil pick-up tube, oil pump and piston/connecting rod assemblies have already been removed. The rear main oil seal and retainer must be removed from the block before proceeding with crankshaft removal.*

1 Before the crankshaft is removed, check the endplay. Mount a dial indicator with the stem in line with the crankshaft and touching end of the crank **(see illustration)**.

2 Push the crankshaft all the way to the rear and zero the dial indicator. Next, pry the crankshaft to the front as far as possible and check the reading on the dial indicator. The distance that it moves is the endplay. If it's greater than specified, check the crankshaft thrust surfaces for wear. If no wear is evident, new thrust washers should correct the endplay.

3 If a dial indicator is not available, feeler gauges can be used. Gently pry or push the crankshaft all the way to the front of the engine. Slip feeler gauges between the crankshaft and the front face of the num-

2B

13.6 To prevent damage to the crankshaft journals and cylinder walls, slip sections of hose over the rod bolts before removing the pistons

14.1 Checking crankshaft endplay with a dial indicator

14.3 Checking crankshaft endplay with a feeler gauge

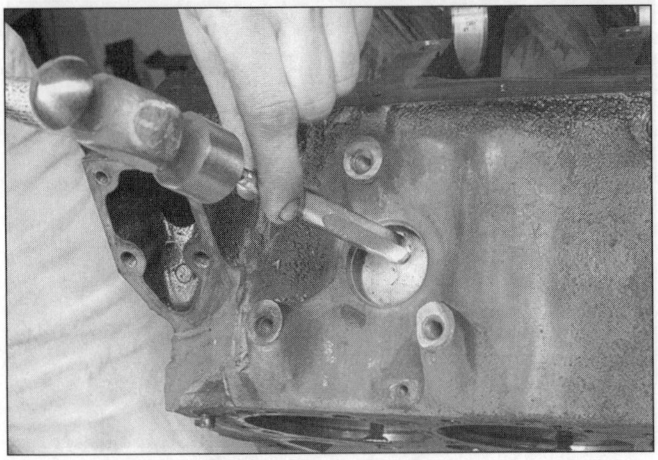

15.1a A hammer and a large punch can be used to knock the core plugs sideways in their bores

15.1b Pull the core plugs from the block with pliers

ber 4 (thrust) main bearing to determine the clearance **(see illustration).**

4 Check the main bearing caps to see if they're marked to indicate their locations. They should be numbered consecutively from the front of the engine to the rear. If they aren't, mark them with number stamping dies or a center punch. Main bearing caps generally have a cast-in arrow, which points to the front of the engine. Loosen the main bearing cap bolts 1/4-turn at a time each, in the reverse order of the recommended tightening sequence **(see illustration 23.12)**, until they can be removed by hand.

5 Gently tap the caps with a soft-face hammer, then separate them from the engine block. If necessary, use the bolts as levers to remove the caps. Try not to drop the bearing inserts if they come out with the caps.

6 Carefully lift the crankshaft out of the engine. It may be a good idea to have an assistant available, since the crankshaft is quite heavy. With the bearing inserts in place in the engine block and main bearing caps or cap assembly, return the caps to their respective locations on the engine block and tighten the bolts finger tight.

15 Engine block - cleaning

Refer to illustrations 15.1a, 15.1b, 15.6, 15.8 and 15.10

Caution: *The core plugs (also known as freeze or soft plugs) may be difficult or impossible to retrieve if they're driven completely into the block coolant passages.*

1 Using the blunt end of a punch, tap in on the outer edge of the core plug to turn the plug sideways in the bore. Then using pliers, pull the core plug from the engine block **(see illustrations).**

2 Using a gasket scraper, remove all traces of gasket material from the engine block. Be very careful not to nick or gouge the gasket sealing surfaces.

3 Remove the main bearing caps or cap assembly and separate the bearing inserts from the caps and the engine block. Tag the bearings, indicating which cylinder they were removed from and whether they were in the cap or the block, then set them aside.

4 Remove all of the threaded oil gallery plugs from the block. The plugs are usually very tight - they may have to be drilled out and the holes retapped. Use new plugs when the engine is reassembled.

5 If the engine is extremely dirty, it should be taken to an automotive machine shop to be steam cleaned or hot tanked.

6 After the block is returned, clean all oil holes, oil galleries, and oil jets **(see illustration)** one more time. Brushes specifically designed for this purpose are available at most auto parts stores. Flush the passages with warm water until the water runs clear, dry the block thoroughly and wipe all machined surfaces with a light, rust preventive oil. If you have access to compressed air, use it to speed the drying process and to blow out all the oil holes and galleries. **Warning:** *Wear eye protection when using compressed air!*

15.6 After the block is returned, clean all oil holes, oil galleries and oil jets (arrow)

7 If the block is not extremely dirty or sludged up, you can do an adequate cleaning job with hot soapy water and a stiff brush. Take plenty of time and do a thorough job. Regardless of the cleaning method used, be sure to clean all oil holes and galleries very thoroughly, dry the block completely and coat all machined surfaces with light oil.

8 The oil jet and the threaded holes in the block must be clean to ensure accurate torque readings during reassembly. Run the proper size tap into each of the holes to remove rust, corrosion, thread sealant or sludge and restore damaged threads **(see illustrations)**. If possible, use compressed air to clear the holes of debris produced by this operation. Now is a good time to clean the threads on the head bolts and the main bearing cap bolts as well.

9 Reinstall the main bearing caps and tighten the bolts finger tight.

10 After coating the sealing surfaces of the new core plugs with Permatex no. 2 sealant, install them in the engine block **(see illustration)**. Make sure they are driven in straight and seated properly or leakage could result. Special tools are available for this purpose, but a large socket, with an outside diameter that will just slip into the core plug, a 1/2-inch drive extension and a hammer will work just as well.

11 Apply non-hardening sealant (such as Permatex no. 2 or Teflon pipe sealant) to the new oil gallery plugs and thread them into the holes in the block. Make sure they are tightened securely.

12 If the engine isn't going to be reassembled right away, cover it with a large plastic trash bag to keep it clean.

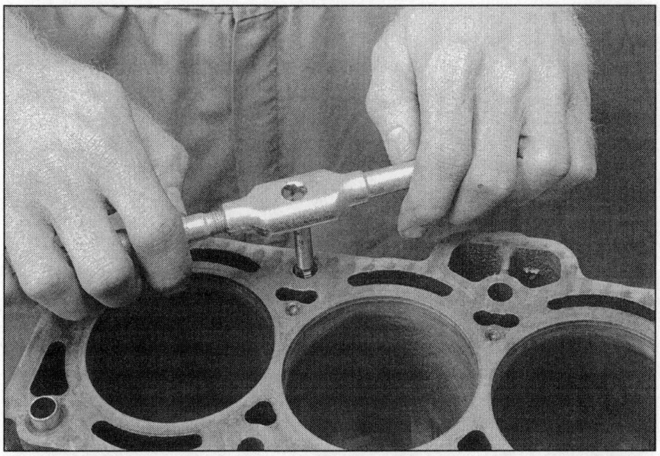

15.8 All bolt holes in the block - particularly the main bearing cap and head bolt holes - should be cleaned and restored with a tap (be sure to remove debris from the holes after this is done)

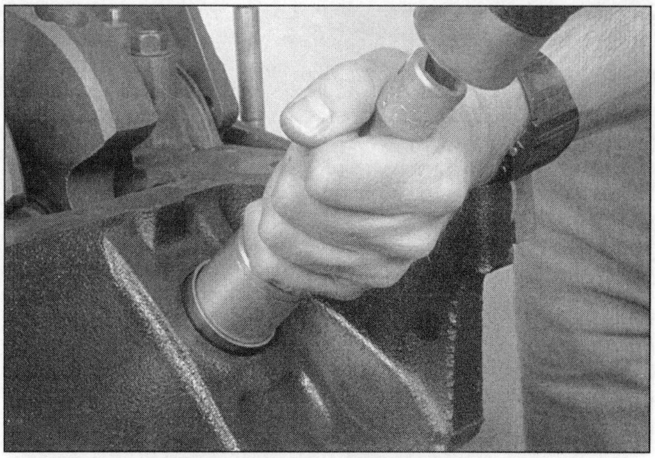

15.10 A large socket on an extension can be used to drive the new core plugs into the bores

16 Engine block - inspection

Refer to illustrations 16.4a, 16.4b, 16.4c and 16.9

1 Before the block is inspected, it should be cleaned as described in Section 15.

2 Visually check the block for cracks, rust and corrosion. Look for stripped threads in the threaded holes. It's also a good idea to have the block checked for hidden cracks by an automotive machine shop that has the special equipment to do this type of work, especially if the vehicle had a history of overheating or using coolant. If defects are found, have the block repaired, if possible, or replaced.

3 Check the cylinder bores for scuffing and scoring.

4 Check the cylinders for taper and out-of-round conditions as follows **(see illustrations)**:

5 Measure the diameter of each cylinder at the top (just under the ridge area), center and bottom of the cylinder bore, parallel to the crankshaft axis.

6 Next, measure each cylinder's diameter at the same three locations perpendicular to the crankshaft axis.

7 The taper of each cylinder is the difference between the bore diameter at the top of the cylinder and the diameter at the bottom. The out-of-round specification of the cylinder bore is the difference

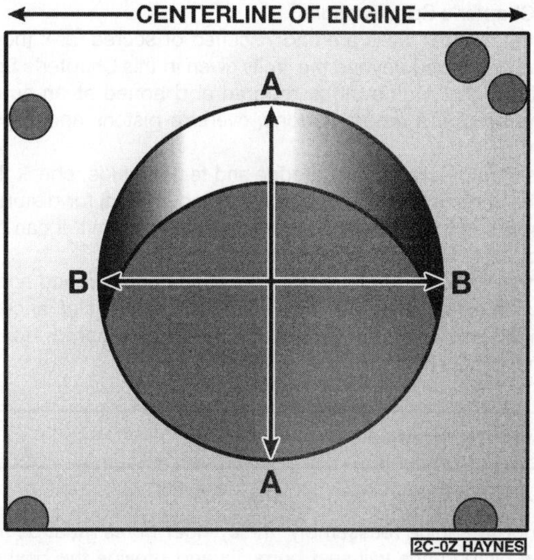

16.4a Measure the diameter of each cylinder at a right angle to engine centerline (A), and parallel to engine centerline (B) - out-of-round is the difference between A and B; taper is the difference between A and B at the top of the cylinder and A and B at the bottom of the cylinder

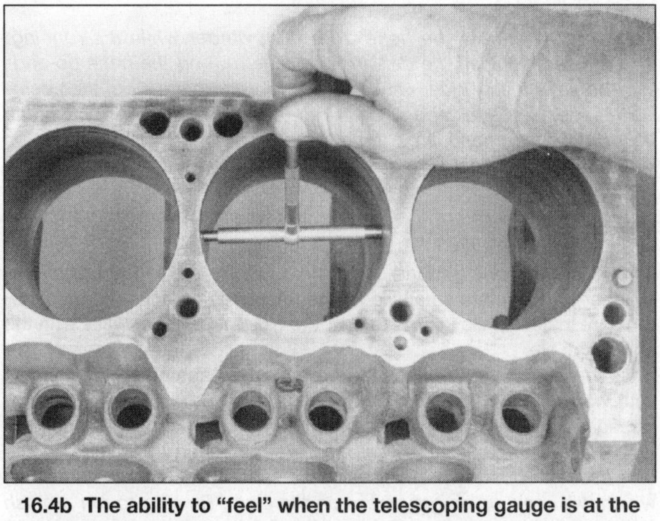

16.4b The ability to "feel" when the telescoping gauge is at the correct point will be developed over time, so work slowly and repeat the check until you're satisfied that the bore measurement is accurate

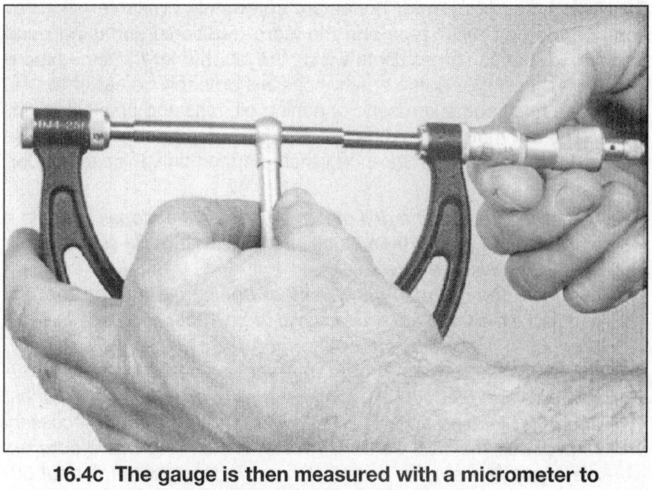

16.4c The gauge is then measured with a micrometer to determine the bore size

2B

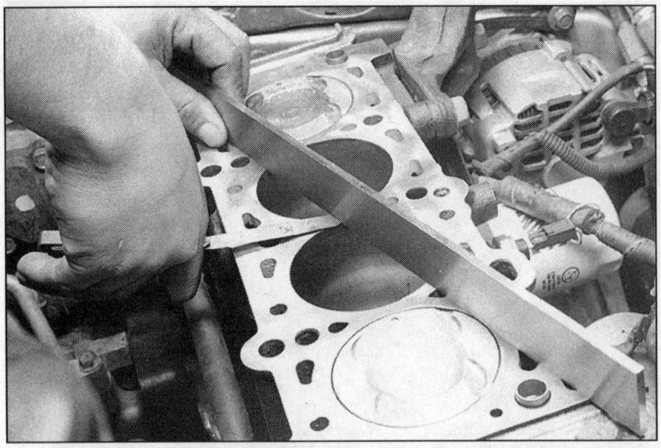

16.9 Check the block deck for distortion with a precision straightedge and feeler gauges

17.3a A "bottle brush" hone will produce better results if you have never done cylinder honing before

between the parallel and perpendicular readings. Compare your results to this Chapter's Specifications.

8 If the cylinder walls are badly scuffed or scored, or if they're out-of-round or tapered beyond the limits given in this Chapter's Specifications, have the engine block rebored and honed at an automotive machine shop. If a rebore is done, oversize pistons and rings will be required.

9 Using a precision straightedge and feeler gauge, check the block deck (the surface that mates with the cylinder head) for distortion **(see illustration)**. If it's distorted beyond the specified limit, it can be resurfaced by an automotive machine shop.

10 If the cylinders are in reasonably good condition and not worn to the outside of the limits, and if the piston-to-cylinder clearances can be maintained properly, then they don't have to be rebored. Honing is all that's necessary (Section 17).

17 Cylinder honing

Refer to illustrations 17.3a and 17.3b

1 Prior to engine reassembly, the cylinder bores must be honed so the new piston rings will seat correctly and provide the best possible combustion chamber seal. **Note:** *If you don't have the tools or don't want to tackle the honing operation, most automotive machine shops will do it for a reasonable fee.*

2 Before honing the cylinders, install the main bearing caps or cap assembly (without bearing inserts) and tighten the bolts to the specified torque.

3 Two types of cylinder hones are commonly available - the flex hone or "bottle brush" type and the more traditional surfacing hone with spring-loaded stones. Both will do the job, but for the less-experienced mechanic the "bottle brush" hone will probably be easier to use. You'll also need some kerosene or honing oil, rags and an electric drill motor. The drill motor should be operated at a steady, slow speed. Use a large 1/2-inch drill or a 3/8-inch variable-speed drill. Proceed as follows:

a) *Mount the hone in the drill motor, compress the stones and slip it into the first cylinder* **(see illustration)**. **Warning:** *Be sure to wear safety goggles or a face shield!*

b) *Lubricate the cylinder with plenty of honing oil, turn on the drill and move the hone up-and-down in the cylinder at a pace that will produce a fine crosshatch pattern on the cylinder walls. Ideally, the crosshatch lines should intersect at approximately a 60-degree angle* **(see illustration)**. *Be sure to use plenty of lubricant and don't take off any more material than is absolutely necessary to produce the desired finish.* **Note:** *Piston ring manufacturers may specify a smaller crosshatch angle than the traditional 60-degrees - read and follow any instructions included with the new rings.*

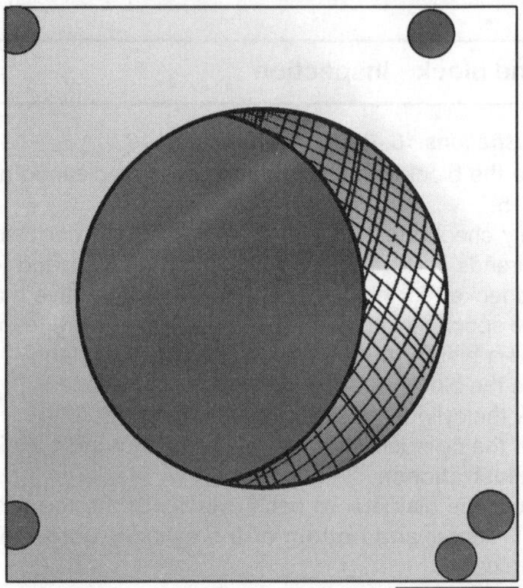

17.3b The cylinder hone should leave a smooth, crosshatch pattern with the lines intersecting at approximately a 60-degree angle

c) *Don't withdraw the hone from the cylinder while it's running. Instead, shut off the drill and continue moving the hone up-and-down in the cylinder until it comes to a complete stop, then compress the stones and withdraw the hone. If you're using a "bottle brush" type hone, stop the drill motor, then turn the chuck in the normal direction of rotation while withdrawing the hone from the cylinder.*

d) *Wipe the oil out of the cylinder and repeat the procedure for the remaining cylinders.*

4 After the honing job is complete, chamfer the top edges of the cylinder bores with a small file so the rings won't catch when the pistons are installed. Be very careful not to nick the cylinder walls with the end of the file.

5 The entire engine block must be washed again very thoroughly with warm, soapy water to remove all traces of the abrasive grit produced during the honing operation. **Note:** *The bores can be considered clean when a lint-free white cloth - dampened with clean engine oil - used to wipe them out doesn't pick up any more honing residue, which will show up as gray areas on the cloth. Be sure to run a brush through all oil holes and galleries and flush them with running water.*

6 After rinsing, dry the block and apply a coat of light rust preventive oil to all machined surfaces. Wrap the block in a plastic trash bag to keep it clean and set it aside until reassembly.

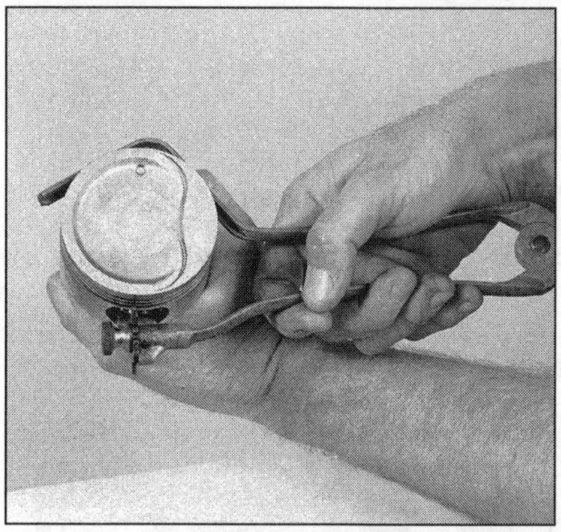

18.4a The piston ring grooves can be cleaned with a special tool, as shown here . . .

18.4b . . . or a section of a broken ring

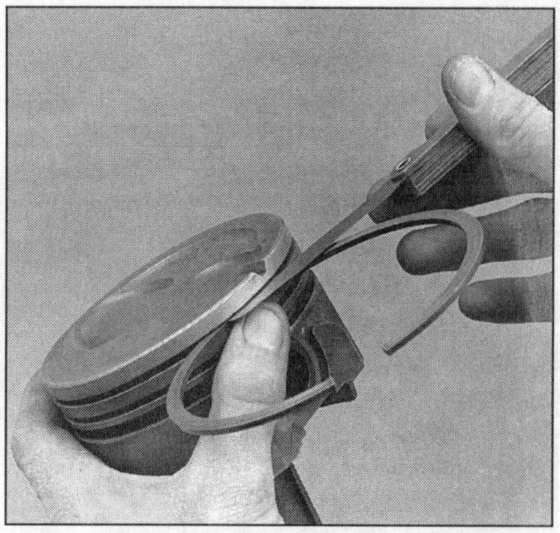

18.10 Check the ring groove clearance with a feeler gauge at several points around the groove

18 Pistons/connecting rods - inspection

Refer to illustrations 18.4a, 18.4b, 18.10 and 18.11

1 Before the inspection process can be carried out, the piston/connecting rod assemblies must be cleaned and the original piston rings removed from the pistons. **Note:** *Always use new piston rings when the engine is reassembled.*

2 Using a piston ring installation tool, carefully remove the rings from the pistons. Be careful not to nick or gouge the pistons in the process.

3 Scrape all traces of carbon from the top of the piston. A hand-held wire brush or a piece of fine emery cloth can be used once the majority of the deposits have been scraped away. Do not, under any circumstances, use a wire brush mounted in a drill motor to remove deposits from the pistons. The piston material is soft and may be eroded away by the wire brush.

4 Use a piston ring groove-cleaning tool to remove carbon deposits from the ring grooves. If a tool isn't available, a piece broken off the old ring will do the job. Be very careful to remove only the carbon deposits - don't remove any metal and do not nick or scratch the sides of the ring grooves **(see illustrations)**.

5 Once the deposits have been removed, clean the piston/rod assemblies with solvent and dry them with compressed air (if available). Make sure the oil return holes in the back sides of the ring grooves and the oil hole in the lower end of each rod are clear.

6 If the pistons and cylinder walls aren't damaged or worn excessively, and if the engine block is not rebored, new pistons won't be necessary. Normal piston wear appears as even vertical wear on the piston thrust surfaces and slight looseness of the top ring in its groove. New piston rings, however, should always be used when an engine is rebuilt.

7 Carefully inspect each piston for cracks around the skirt, at the pin bosses and at the ring lands.

8 Look for scoring and scuffing on the thrust faces of the skirt, holes in the piston crown and burned areas at the edge of the crown. If the skirt is scored or scuffed, the engine may have been suffering from overheating and/or abnormal combustion, which caused excessively high operating temperatures. The cooling and lubrication systems should be checked thoroughly. A hole in the piston crown is an indication that abnormal combustion (preignition) was occurring. Burned areas at the edge of the piston crown are usually evidence of spark knock (detonation). If any of the above problems exist, the causes must be corrected or the damage will occur again. The causes may include intake air leaks, incorrect air/fuel mixture, incorrect ignition timing and EGR system malfunctions.

9 Corrosion of the piston, in the form of small pits, indicates that coolant is leaking into the combustion chamber and/or the crankcase. Again, the cause must be corrected or the problem may persist in the rebuilt engine.

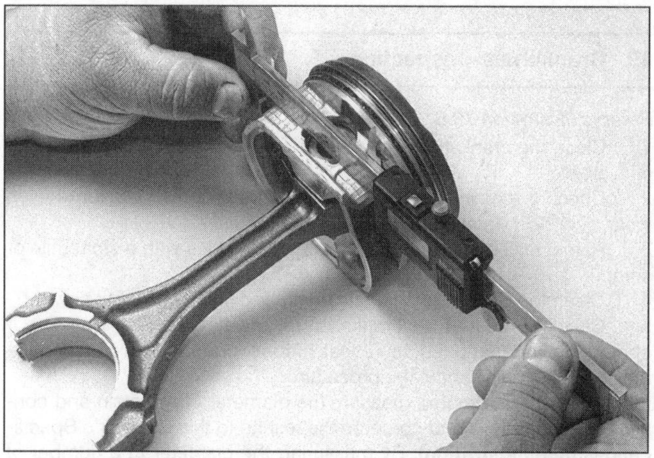

18.11 Measure the piston diameter at a 90-degree angle to the piston pin, at the bottom of the piston pin area - a precision caliper may be used if a micrometer isn't available

10 Measure the piston ring groove clearance by laying a new piston ring in each ring groove and slipping a feeler gauge in beside it **(see illustration)**. Check the clearance at three or four locations around each groove. Be sure to use the correct ring for each groove - they are different. If the clearance is greater than that listed in this Chapter's Specifications, new pistons will have to be used.

11 Check the piston-to-bore clearance by measuring the bore (see Section 16) and the piston diameter. Make sure the pistons and bores are correctly matched. Measure the piston across the skirt, at a 90-degree angle to the piston pin **(see illustration)**. Subtract the piston diameter from the bore diameter to obtain the clearance. If it's greater than specified, the block will have to be rebored and new pistons and rings installed.

12 Check the piston-to-rod clearance by twisting the piston and rod in opposite directions. Any noticeable play indicates excessive wear, which must be corrected.

13 If the pistons must be removed from the connecting rods for any reason, the rods should be taken to an automotive machine shop, to be checked for bend and twist, since automotive machine shops have special equipment for this purpose.

14 Check the connecting rods for cracks and other damage. Temporarily remove the rod caps, lift out the old bearing inserts, wipe the rod and cap bearing surfaces clean and inspect them for nicks, gouges and scratches. After checking the rods, replace the old bearings, slip the caps into place and tighten the nuts finger tight. **Note:** *If the engine is being rebuilt because of a connecting rod knock, be sure to install new rods.*

2B

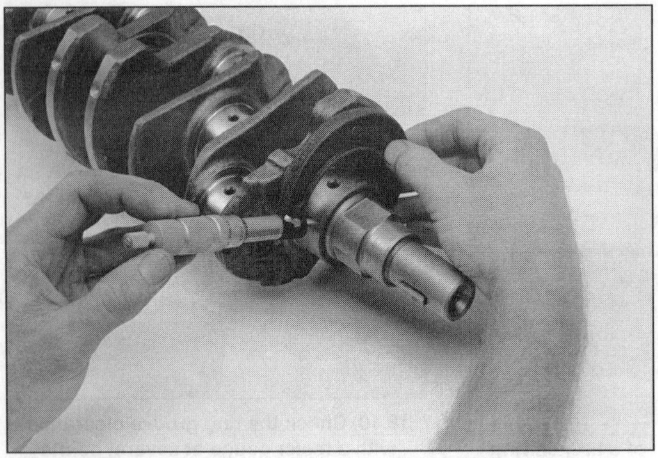

19.6 **Measure the diameter of each crankshaft journal at several points to detect taper and out-of-round conditions**

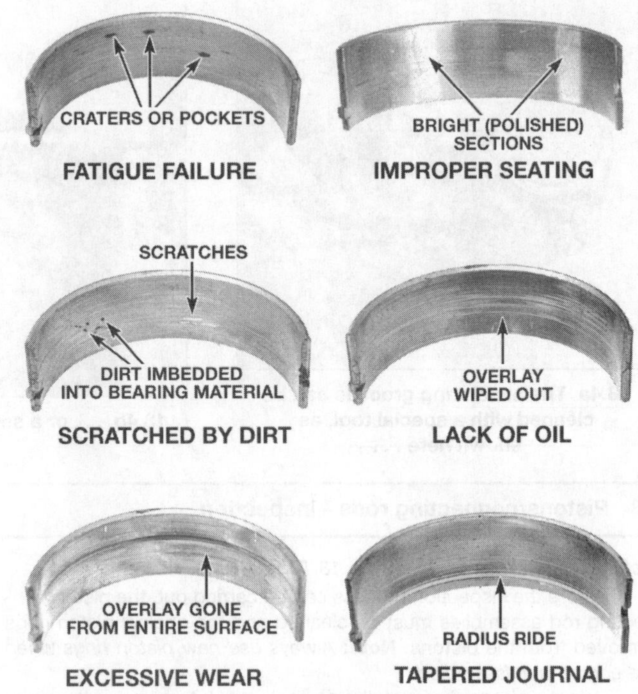

20.1 When inspecting the main and connecting rod bearings, look for these problems

19 Crankshaft - inspection

Refer to illustration 19.6

1 Clean the crankshaft with solvent and dry it with compressed air (if available).

2 Check the main and connecting rod bearing journals for uneven wear, scoring, pits and cracks.

3 Remove all burrs from the crankshaft oil holes with a stone, file or scraper.

4 Clean the oil holes with a stiff brush and flush them with solvent.

5 Check the rest of the crankshaft for cracks and other damage. It should be magnafluxed to reveal hidden cracks - an automotive machine shop will handle the procedure.

6 Using a micrometer, measure the diameter of the main and connecting rod journals and compare the results to this Chapter's Specifications **(see illustration)**. By measuring the diameter at a number of points around each journal's circumference, you'll be able to determine whether or not the journal is out-of-round. Take the measurement at each end of the journal, near the crank throws, to determine if the journal is tapered. Crankshaft runout should be checked also, but large V-blocks and a dial indicator are needed to do it correctly. If you don't have the equipment, have a machine shop check the runout.

7 If the crankshaft journals are damaged, tapered, out-of-round or worn beyond the limits given in the Specifications, have the crankshaft reground by an automotive machine shop. Be sure to use the correct size bearing inserts if the crankshaft is reconditioned.

8 Check the oil seal journals at each end of the crankshaft for wear and damage. If the seal has worn a groove in the journal, or if it's nicked or scratched, the new seal may leak when the engine is reassembled. In some cases, an automotive machine shop may be able to repair the journal by pressing on a thin sleeve. If repair isn't feasible, a new or different crankshaft should be installed.

9 Refer to Section 20 and examine the main and rod bearing inserts.

20 Main and connecting rod bearings - inspection and selection

Inspection

Refer to illustration 20.1

1 Even though the main and connecting rod bearings should be replaced with new ones during the engine overhaul, the old bearings should be retained for close examination, as they may reveal valuable information about the condition of the engine **(see illustration)**.

2 Bearing failure occurs because of lack of lubrication, the presence of dirt or other foreign particles, overloading the engine and corrosion. Regardless of the cause of bearing failure, it must be corrected before the engine is reassembled to prevent it from happening again.

3 When examining the bearings, remove them from the engine block, the main bearing caps, the connecting rods and the rod caps and lay them out on a clean surface in the same general position as their location in the engine. This will enable you to match any bearing problems with the corresponding crankshaft journal.

4 Dirt and other foreign particles get into the engine in a variety of ways. It may be left in the engine during assembly, or it may pass through filters or the PCV system. It may get into the oil, and from there into the bearings. Metal chips from machining operations and normal engine wear are often present. Abrasives are sometimes left in engine components after reconditioning, especially when parts are not thoroughly cleaned using the proper cleaning methods. Whatever the source, these foreign objects often end up embedded in the soft bearing material and are easily recognized. Large particles will not embed in the bearing and will score or gouge the bearing and journal. The best prevention for this cause of bearing failure is to clean all parts thoroughly and keep everything spotlessly clean during engine assembly. Frequent and regular engine oil and filter changes are also recommended.

5 Lack of lubrication (or lubrication breakdown) has a number of interrelated causes. Excessive heat (which thins the oil), overloading (which squeezes the oil from the bearing face) and oil leakage or throw off (from excessive bearing clearances, worn oil pump or high engine speeds) all contribute to lubrication breakdown. Blocked oil passages, which usually are the result of misaligned oil holes in a bearing shell, will also oil starve a bearing and destroy it. When lack of lubrication is the cause of bearing failure, the bearing material is wiped or extruded from the steel backing of the bearing. Temperatures may increase to the point where the steel backing turns blue from overheating.

6 Driving habits can have a definite effect on bearing life. Low speed operation in too high a gear (lugging the engine) puts very high loads on bearings, which tends to squeeze out the oil film. These loads cause the bearings to flex, which produces fine cracks in the bearing

Main journal diameter undersize

mm {in}

Bearing size	Journal diameter
0.25 {0.01} undersize	49.704—49.708 {1.9569—1.9570}
0.50 {0.02} undersize	49.454—49.458 {1.9470—1.9471}
0.75 {0.03} undersize	49.204—49.208 {1.9372—1.9373}

Crankpin journal diameter undersize

mm {in}

Bearing size	Journal diameter
0.25 {0.01} undersize	44.690—44.706 {1.7595—1.7600}
0.50 {0.02} undersize	44.440—44.456 {1.7496—1.7502}
0.75 {0.03} undersize	44.190—44.206 {1.7398—1.7403}

20.9 Select undersized main and rod journal bearings according to this chart - except 1.5L DOHC engine

face (fatigue failure). Eventually the bearing material will loosen in pieces and tear away from the steel backing. Short trip driving leads to corrosion of bearings because insufficient engine heat is produced to drive off the condensed water and corrosive gases. These products collect in the engine oil, forming acid and sludge. As the oil is carried to the engine bearings, the acid attacks and corrodes the bearing material.

7 Incorrect bearing installation during engine assembly will lead to bearing failure as well. Tight-fitting bearings leave insufficient bearing oil clearance and will result in oil starvation. Dirt or foreign particles trapped behind a bearing insert result in high spots on the bearing which lead to failure.

Selection

Refer to illustration 20.9

8 If the original bearings are worn or damaged, or if the oil clearances are incorrect (see Section 23 or 25), the following procedures should be used to select the correct new bearings for engine reassembly. However, if the crankshaft has been reground, new undersize bearings must be installed - the following procedure should not be used if undersize bearings are required! The automotive machine shop that reconditions the crankshaft will provide or help you select the correct size bearings. Regardless of how the bearing sizes are determined, use the oil clearance, measured with Plastigage, as a guide to ensure the bearings are the right size.

Main bearings

9 If you need to use a STANDARD size main bearing, install one that is the same size as the original bearing listed in the specifications in the front of this Chapter. If the diameter is less than the minimum, have a qualified engine machine shop grind the journals to match standard undersize bearings **(see illustration)**. There are three different sizes of undersized main bearings.

Connecting rod bearings

10 If you need to use a STANDARD size rod bearing, install one that is the same size as the original bearing listed in the specifications in the from of this Chapter. If the diameter is less than the minimum, grind the journals to match standard undersize bearings **(see illustration 20.9)**. There are three different sizes of undersized rod bearings.

All bearings

11 Remember, the oil clearance is the final judge when selecting new bearing sizes. If you have any questions or are unsure which bearings to use, get help from a dealer parts or service department.

21 Engine overhaul - reassembly sequence

1 Before beginning engine reassembly, make sure you have all the necessary new parts, gaskets and seals as well as the following items on hand:

Common hand tools
A 1/2-inch drive torque wrench
Piston ring installation tool
Piston ring compressor
Short lengths of rubber or plastic hose to fit over connecting rod bolts
Plastigage
Feeler gauges
A fine-tooth file
New engine oil
Engine assembly lube or moly-base grease
Camshaft installation lube
Gasket sealant
Thread locking compound

2 In order to save time and avoid problems, engine reassembly must be done in the following general order:

Piston rings (Part B)
Crankshaft and main bearings (Part B)
Piston/connecting rod assemblies (Part B)
Rear main (crankshaft) oil seal (Part B)
Cylinder head and lifters (Part A)
Camshafts (Part A)
Oil pump (Part A)
Timing belt and sprockets (Part A)
Timing belt covers (Part A)
Oil pick-up (Part A)
Oil pan (Part A)
Intake and exhaust manifolds (Part A)
Valve cover (Part A)
Flywheel/driveplate (Part A)

22 Piston rings - installation

Refer to illustrations 22.3, 22.4, 22.9a, 22.9b and 22.12

1 Before installing the new piston rings, the ring end gaps must be checked. It's assumed that the piston ring groove clearance has been checked and verified correct (see Section 18).

2 Lay out the piston/connecting rod assemblies and the new ring sets so the ring sets will be matched with the same piston and cylinder during the end gap measurement and engine assembly.

3 Insert the top (number one) ring into the first cylinder and square it up with the cylinder walls by pushing it in with the top of the piston **(see illustration)**. The ring should be near the bottom of the cylinder, at the lower limit of ring travel.

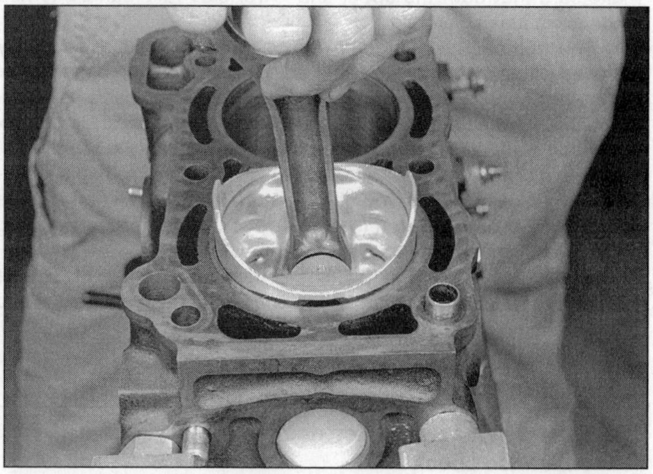

22.3 When checking piston ring end gap, the ring must be square in the cylinder bore (this is done by pushing the ring down with the top of a piston as shown)

2B

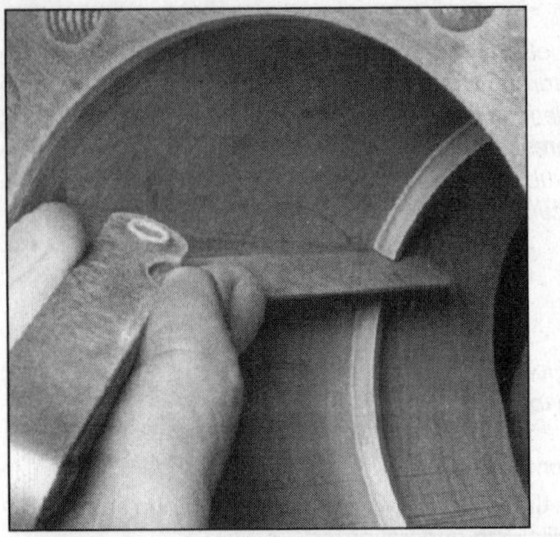

22.4 With the ring square in the cylinder, measure the end gap with a feeler gauge

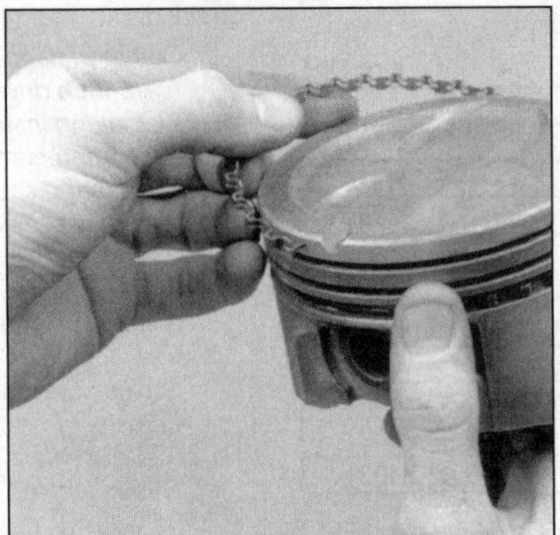

22.9a Install the spacer/expander in the oil control ring groove

22.9b DO NOT use a piston ring installation tool when installing the oil ring side rails

4 To measure the end gap, slip feeler gauges between the ends of the ring until a gauge equal to the gap width is found **(see illustration)**. The feeler gauge should slide between the ring ends with a slight amount of drag. Compare the measurement to that found in this Chapter's Specifications. If the gap is larger or smaller than specified, double-check to make sure you have the correct rings before proceeding.

5 If the gap is too small, replace the rings - DO NOT file the ends to increase the clearance.

6 Excess end gap is not critical unless it's greater than the service limit listed in this Chapter's Specifications. Again, double-check to make sure you have the correct rings for your engine.

7 Repeat the procedure for each ring that will be installed in the first cylinder and for each ring in the remaining cylinders. Remember to keep rings, pistons and cylinders matched up.

8 Once the ring end gaps have been checked/corrected, the rings can be installed on the pistons.

9 The oil control ring (lowest one on the piston) is usually installed first. It's composed of three separate components. Slip the spacer/expander into the groove **(see illustration)**. If an anti-rotation tang is used, make sure it's inserted into the drilled hole in the ring groove. Next, install the lower side rail. Don't use a piston ring installation tool on the oil ring side rails, as they may be damaged. Instead, place one end of the side rail into the groove between the spacer/expander and the ring land, hold it firmly in place and slide a finger around the piston while pushing the rail into the groove **(see illustration)**. Next, install the upper side rail in the same manner.

10 After the three oil ring components have been installed, check to make sure that both the upper and lower side rails can be turned smoothly in the ring groove.

11 The number two (middle) ring is installed next. It's usually stamped with a mark which must face up, toward the top of the piston. **Note:** *Always follow the instructions printed on the ring package or box - different manufacturers may require different approaches. Do not mix up the top and middle rings, as they have different cross sections.*

12 Use a piston ring installation tool and make sure the ring's identification mark is facing the top of the piston, then slip the ring into the middle groove on the piston **(see illustration)**. Don't expand the ring any more than necessary to slide it over the piston.

13 Install the number one (top) ring in the same manner. Make sure the mark is facing up. Be careful not to confuse the number one and number two rings.

14 Repeat the procedure for the remaining pistons and rings.

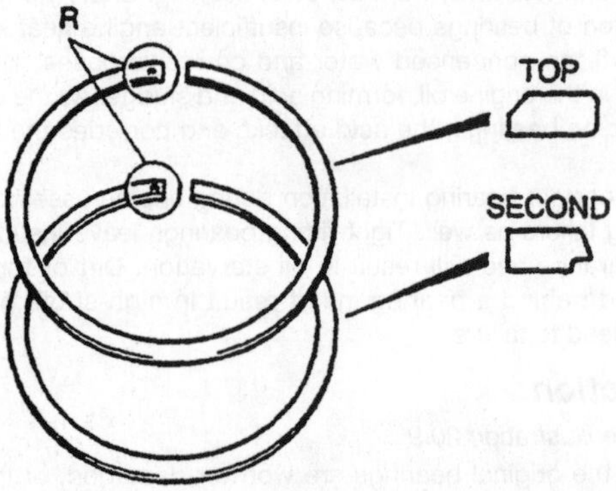

22.12 Install the compression rings with a ring expander - the mark must face up

23 Crankshaft - installation and main bearing oil clearance check

Refer to illustrations 23.10, 23.12, 23.14, 23.19a, 23.19b and 23.19c

1 Crankshaft installation is the first major step in engine reassembly. It's assumed at this point that the engine block and crankshaft have been cleaned, inspected and repaired or reconditioned.

2 Position the engine with the bottom facing up.

3 Remove the main bearing cap bolts and lift out the caps. Lay the caps out in the proper order.

4 If they're still in place, remove the old bearing inserts from the block and the main bearing caps. Wipe the main bearing surfaces of the block and caps with a clean, lint free cloth. They must be kept spotlessly clean!

Main bearing oil clearance check

5 Clean the back sides of the new main bearing inserts and lay the bearing half with the oil groove in each main bearing saddle in the block. Lay the other bearing half from each bearing set in the corresponding main bearing cap. Make sure the tab on each bearing insert fits into the recess in the block or cap. Also, the oil holes in the block must line up with the oil holes in the bearing insert. **Caution:** *Do not hammer the bearings into place and don't nick or gouge the bearing faces. No lubrication should be used at this time.*

6 The thrust bearings (washers) must be installed in the number four cap and saddle.

7 Clean the faces of the bearings in the block and the crankshaft main bearing journals with a clean, lint free cloth. Check or clean the oil holes in the crankshaft, as any dirt here can go only one way - straight through the new bearings.

8 Once you're certain the crankshaft is clean, carefully lay it in position in the main bearings.

9 Before the crankshaft can be permanently installed, the main bearing oil clearance must be checked.

23.10 Lay the Plastigage strips (arrow) on the main bearing journals, parallel to the crankshaft centerline

23.12 Main bearing cap bolt tightening sequence

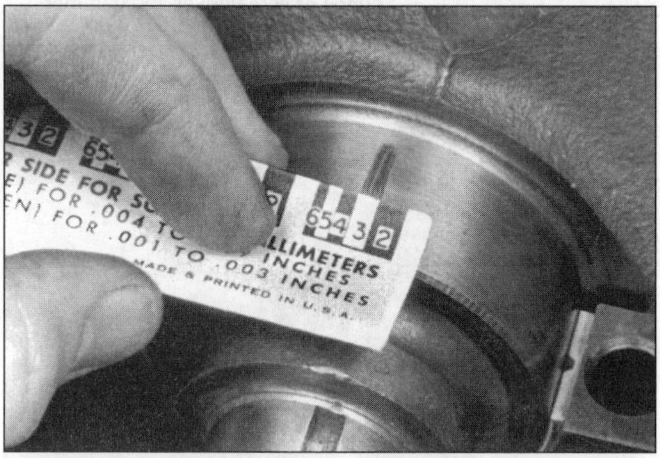

23.14 Compare the width of the crushed Plastigage to the scale on the envelope to determine the main bearing oil clearance (always take the measurement at the widest point of the Plastigage) - be sure to use the correct scale; standard and metric scales are included

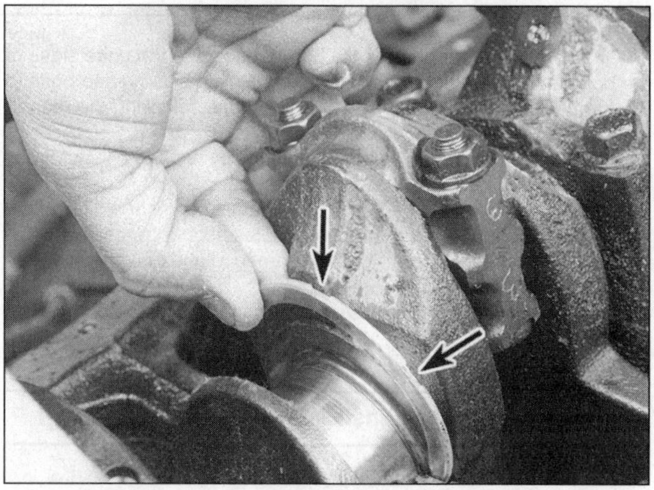

23.19a Insert the thrust washer into position with the oil grooves facing OUT (arrow)

10 Trim several pieces of the appropriate size Plastigage (they must be slightly shorter than the width of the main bearings) and place one piece on each crankshaft main bearing journal, parallel with the journal axis **(see illustration)**.

11 Clean the faces of the bearings in the caps and install the caps in their respective positions (don't mix them up) with the arrows pointing toward the front of the engine. Don't disturb the Plastigage. Apply a light coat of oil to the bolt threads and the under- sides of the bolt heads, then install them.

12 Following the recommended sequence **(see illustration)**, tighten the main bearing cap bolts, in three steps, to the torque listed in this Chapter's Specifications. Do not rotate the crankshaft at any time during this operation!

13 Remove the bolts and carefully lift off the main bearing caps. Keep them in order. Don't disturb the Plastigage or rotate the crankshaft. If any of the main bearing caps are difficult to remove, tap them gently from side-to-side with a soft-face hammer to loosen them.

14 Compare the width of the crushed Plastigage on each journal to the scale printed on the Plastigage envelope to obtain the main bearing oil clearance **(see illustration)**. Check the Specifications to make sure it's correct.

15 If the clearance is not as specified, the bearing inserts may be the wrong size (which means different ones will be required - see Section 20). Before deciding that different inserts are needed, make sure that no dirt or oil was between the bearing inserts and the caps or block when the clearance was measured. If the Plastigage is noticeably wider at one end than the other, the journal may be tapered (see Section 19).

16 Carefully scrape all traces of the Plastigage material off the main bearing journals and/or the bearing faces. Don't nick or scratch the bearing faces.

Final crankshaft installation

17 Carefully lift the crankshaft out of the engine. Clean the bearing faces in the block, then apply a thin, uniform layer of clean moly-base grease or engine assembly lube to each of the bearing surfaces. Coat the thrust washers as well.

18 Lubricate the crankshaft surfaces that contact the oil seals with multi-purpose grease, engine assembly lube or clean engine oil.

19 Make sure the crankshaft journals are clean, then lay the crankshaft back in place in the block. Clean the faces of the bearings in the caps, then apply lubricant to them. Install the caps in their respective positions with the arrows pointing toward the front of the engine. **Note:** *Be sure to install the thrust washers with the number 4 main journal.* The upper (block side) thrust washers can be rotated into position around the crank with the crank in the block, with the thrust washer grooves facing OUT. The tanged lower thrust washers should be placed on the caps with their grooves OUT and the tangs fitting into the cap slots **(see illustrations)**.

23.19b Rotate the thrust washer into position

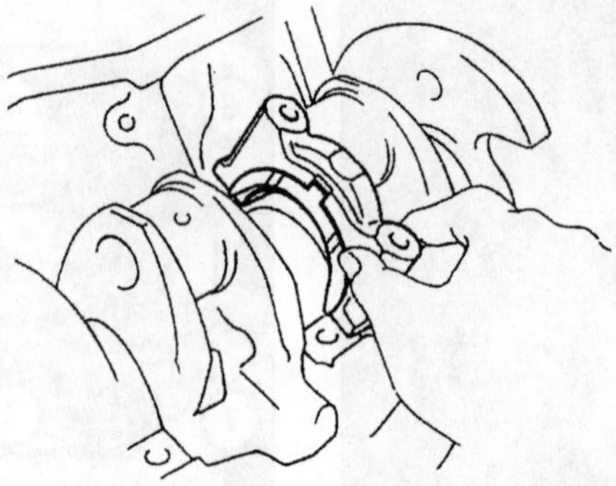

23.19c Install the thrust washer in the number four cap with the oil grooves facing OUT

24.3 After removing the retainer from the block, support it on a couple of wood blocks and drive out the old seal with a punch or screwdriver and hammer

20 Apply a light coat of oil to the bolt threads and the undersides of the bolt heads, then install them. Tighten all main bearing cap bolts to the torque listed in this Chapter's Specifications, following the recommended sequence.

21 Rotate the crankshaft a number of times by hand to check for any obvious binding.

22 Check the crankshaft endplay with a feeler gauge or a dial indicator as described in Section 14. The endplay should be correct if the crankshaft thrust faces aren't worn or damaged and new thrust washers have been installed.

23 Install a new rear main oil seal, then bolt the retainer to the block (see Section 24).

24 Rear main oil seal - installation

Refer to illustrations 24.3 and 24.5

1 The crankshaft must be installed first and the main bearing caps bolted in place, then the new seal should be installed in the retainer and the retainer bolted to the block.

2 Check the seal contact surface on the crankshaft very carefully for scratches and nicks that could damage the new seal lip and cause oil leaks. If the crankshaft is damaged, the only alternative is a new or different crankshaft.

3 The old seal can be removed from the retainer by driving it out from the back side with a hammer and punch **(see illustration)**. Be sure to note how far it's recessed into the bore before removing it; the new seal will have to be recessed an equal amount. Be very careful not to scratch or otherwise damage the bore in the retainer or oil leaks could develop.

4 Make sure the retainer is clean, then apply a thin coat of engine oil to the outer edge of the new seal. The seal must be pressed squarely into the bore, so hammering it into place isn't recommended. If you don't have access to a press, sandwich the housing and seal between two smooth pieces of wood and press the seal into place with the jaws of a large vise. The pieces of wood must be thick enough to distribute the force evenly around the entire circumference of the seal. Work slowly and make sure the seal enters the bore squarely.

5 As a last resort, the seal can be tapped into the retainer with a hammer. Use a block of wood to distribute the force evenly and make sure the seal is driven in squarely **(see illustration)**.

6 The seal lips must be lubricated with clean engine oil or multi-purpose grease before the seal/retainer is slipped over the crankshaft and bolted to the block, using a new gasket.

7 Tighten the bolts a little at a time to the torque listed in the Chapter 2A Specifications.

24.5 Drive the new seal into the retainer with a wood block or a section of pipe, if you have one large enough - make sure you don't cock the seal in the retainer bore

25 Pistons/connecting rods - installation and rod bearing oil clearance check

Refer to illustrations 25.3, 25.5, 25.9, 25.11, 25.13 and 25.17

1 Before installing the piston/connecting rod assemblies, the cylinder walls must be perfectly clean, the top edge of each cylinder must be chamfered, and the crankshaft must be in place.

2 Remove the cap from the end of the number one connecting rod (refer to the marks made during removal). Remove the original bearing inserts and wipe the bearing surfaces of the connecting rod and cap with a clean, lint-free cloth. They must be kept spotlessly clean.

Connecting rod bearing oil clearance check

3 Clean the back side of the new upper bearing insert, then lay it in place in the connecting rod. Make sure the tab on the bearing fits into the recess in the rod so the oil holes line up **(see illustration)**. Don't hammer the bearing insert into place and be very careful not to nick or gouge the bearing face. Don't lubricate the bearing at this time.

4 Clean the back side of the other bearing insert and install it in the rod cap. Again, make sure the tab on the bearing fits into the recess in the cap, and don't apply any lubricant. It's critically important that the mating surfaces of the bearing and connecting rod are perfectly clean and oil free when they're assembled.

5 Position the piston ring gaps at staggered intervals around the

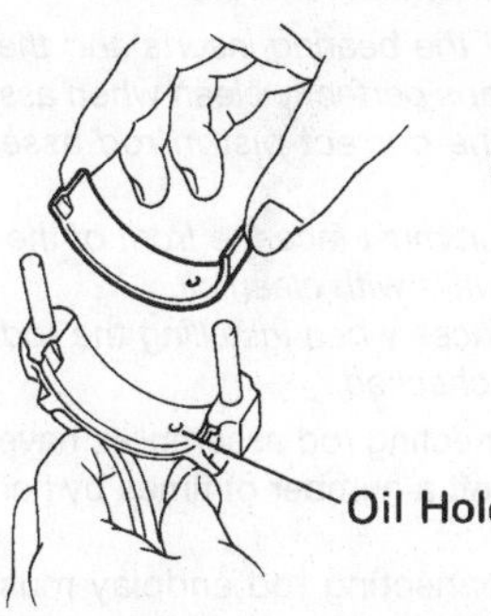

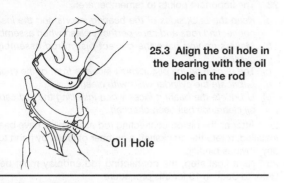

25.3 Align the oil hole in the bearing with the oil hole in the rod

piston **(see illustration)**.

6 Slip a section of plastic or rubber hose over each connecting rod cap bolt.

7 Lubricate the piston and rings with clean engine oil and attach a piston ring compressor to the piston. Leave the skirt protruding about 1/4-inch to guide the piston into the cylinder. The rings must be compressed until they're flush with the piston.

8 Rotate the crankshaft until the number one connecting rod journal is at BDC (bottom dead center) and apply a coat of engine oil to the cylinder wall.

9 With the dimple on top of the piston **(see illustration)** facing the front of the engine, gently insert the piston/connecting rod assembly into the number one cylinder bore and rest the bottom edge of the ring compressor on the engine block.

10 Tap the top edge of the ring compressor to make sure it's contacting the block around its entire circumference.

11 Gently tap on the top of the piston with the end of a wooden hammer handle **(see illustration)** while guiding the end of the connecting rod into place on the crankshaft journal. The piston rings may try to pop out of the ring compressor just before entering the cylinder bore, so keep some downward pressure on the ring compressor. Work slowly, and if any resistance is felt as the piston enters the cylinder, stop immediately. Find out what's hanging up and fix it before proceeding. **Caution:** *Do not, for any reason, force the piston into the cylinder - you might break a ring and/or the piston.*

12 Once the piston/connecting rod assembly is installed, the connecting rod bearing oil clearance must be checked before the rod cap is permanently bolted in place.

13 Cut a piece of the appropriate size Plastigage slightly shorter than the width of the connecting rod bearing and lay it in place on the number one connecting rod journal, parallel with the journal axis **(see illustration)**.

14 Clean the connecting rod cap bearing face, remove the protective hoses from the connecting rod bolts and install the rod cap. Make sure

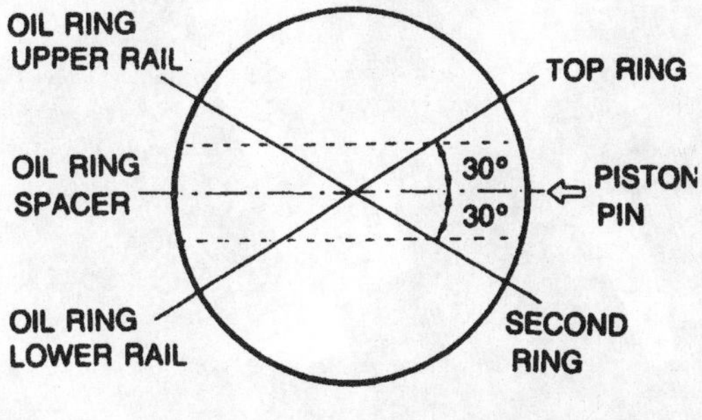

25.5 Ring end gap positions - stagger the ring end gaps around the piston, as shown, before installing the pistons

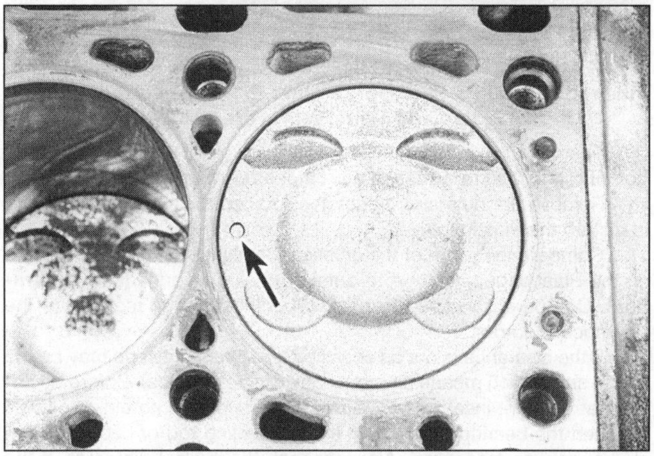
25.9 Check to assure the mark on the piston (arrow) and the mark on the connecting rod are aligned towards the front of the engine

the mating mark on the cap is on the same side as the mark on the connecting rod. Check the cap to make sure the front mark is facing the timing belt end of the engine.

15 Apply a light coat of oil to the undersides of the nuts, then install and tighten them to the torque listed in this Chapter's Specifications, working up to it in three steps. Use a thin-wall socket to avoid erroneous torque readings that can result if the socket is wedged between the rod cap and nut. If the socket tends to wedge itself between the nut and the cap, lift up on it slightly until it no longer contacts the cap.

25.11 The piston can be driven (gently) into the cylinder bore with the end of a wooden or plastic hammer handle

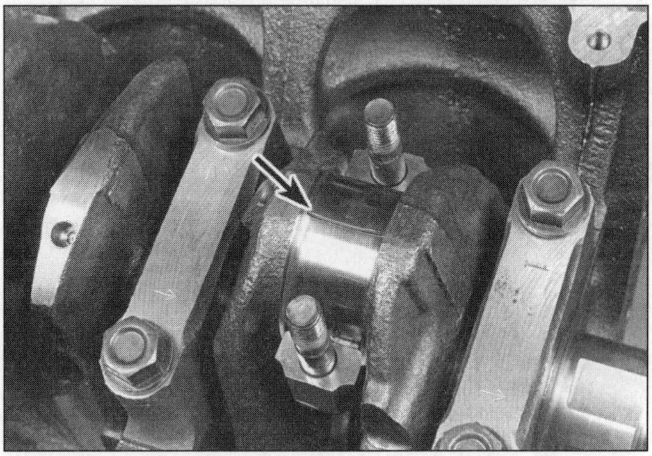
25.13 Lay the Plastigage strips on each rod bearing journal, parallel to the crankshaft centerline

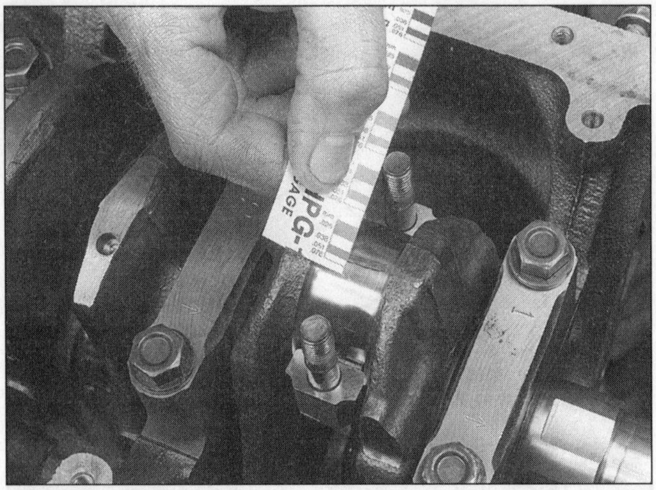

25.17 Measure the width of the crushed Plastigage to determine the rod bearing oil clearance (be sure to use the correct scale - standard and metric scales are included)

Do not rotate the crankshaft at any time during this operation.

16 Remove the nuts and detach the rod cap, being very careful not to disturb the Plastigage.

17 Compare the width of the crushed Plastigage to the scale printed on the Plastigage envelope to obtain the oil clearance **(see illustration)**. Compare it to this Chapter's Specifications to make sure the clearance is correct.

18 If the clearance is not as specified, the bearing inserts may be the wrong size (which means different ones will be required). Before deciding that different inserts are needed, make sure that no dirt or oil was between the bearing inserts and the connecting rod or cap when the clearance was measured. Also, recheck the journal diameter. If the Plastigage was wider at one end than the other, the journal may be tapered (refer to Section 19).

Final connecting rod installation

19 Carefully scrape all traces of the Plastigage material off the rod journal and/or bearing face. Be very careful not to scratch the bearing, use your fingernail or the edge of a credit card to remove the Plastigage.

20 Make sure the bearing faces are perfectly clean, then apply a uniform layer of clean moly-base grease or engine assembly lube to both of them. You'll have to push the piston higher into the cylinder to expose the face of the bearing insert in the connecting rod, be sure to slip the protective hoses over the rod bolts first.

21 Slide the connecting rod back into place on the journal, remove the protective hoses from the rod cap bolts, install the rod cap and tighten the nuts to the torque listed in this Chapter's Specifications. Again, work up to the torque in three steps.

22 Repeat the entire procedure for the remaining pistons/connecting rods.

23 The important points to remember are:

- a) *Keep the back sides of the bearing inserts and the insides of the connecting rods and caps perfectly clean when assembling them.*
- b) *Make sure you have the correct piston/rod assembly for each cylinder.*
- c) *The dimple on the piston must face the front of the engine.*
- d) *Lubricate the cylinder walls with clean oil.*
- e) *Lubricate the bearing faces when installing the rod caps after the oil clearance has been checked.*

24 After all the piston/connecting rod assemblies have been properly installed, rotate the crankshaft a number of times by hand to check for any obvious binding.

25 As a final step, the connecting rod endplay must be checked. Refer to Section 13 for this procedure.

26 Compare the measured endplay to this Chapter's Specifications to make sure it's correct. If it was correct before disassembly and the original crankshaft and rods were reinstalled, it should still be right. If new rods or a new crankshaft were installed, the endplay may be inadequate. If so, the rods will have to be removed and taken to an automotive machine shop for resizing.

26 Initial start-up and break-in after overhaul

Warning: *Have a fire extinguisher handy when starting the engine for the first time.*

1 Once the engine has been installed in the vehicle, double-check the engine oil and coolant levels.

2 With the spark plugs out of the engine and the ignition system and fuel pump disabled (see Section 4), crank the engine until oil pressure registers on the gauge or the light goes out.

3 Install the spark plugs, hook up the plug wires and restore the ignition system and fuel pump functions (see Section 4).

4 Start the engine. It may take a few moments for the fuel system to build up pressure, but the engine should start without a great deal of effort.

5 After the engine starts, it should be allowed to warm up to normal operating temperature. While the engine is warming up, make a thorough check for fuel, oil and coolant leaks.

6 Shut the engine off and recheck the engine oil and coolant levels.

7 Drive the vehicle to an area with minimum traffic, accelerate from 30 to 50 mph, then allow the vehicle to slow to 30 mph with the throttle closed. Repeat the procedure 10 or 12 times. This will load the piston rings and cause them to seat properly against the cylinder walls. Check again for oil and coolant leaks.

8 Drive the vehicle gently for the first 500 miles (no sustained high speeds) and keep a constant check on the oil level. It is not unusual for an engine to use oil during the break-in period.

9 At approximately 500 to 600 miles, change the oil and filter.

10 For the next few hundred miles, drive the vehicle normally. Do not pamper it or abuse it.

11 After 2000 miles, change the oil and filter again and consider the engine broken in.

Chapter 3
Cooling, heating and air conditioning systems

3

Contents

Specifications

General

Radiator cap pressure rating	10.7 to 14.9 psi
Thermostat rating	188 to 193 degrees F
Refrigerant type	
1994 and earlier	R-12
1995 and later	R-134a
Refrigerant capacity	
1994 and earlier	28.2 ounces
1995 and later	21.2 ounces

Torque specifications

	Ft-lbs (unless otherwise indicated)
Thermostat housing bolts	14 to 19
Water pump-to-block bolts	14 to 19
Radiator drain plug (1995 and later)	6 to 10 in-lbs

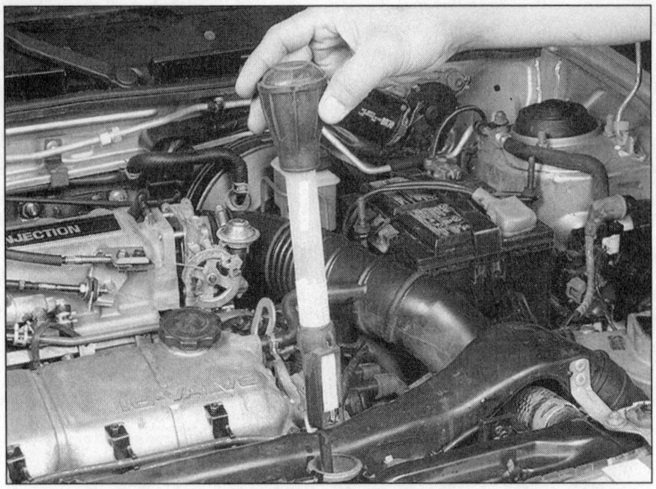

2.4 An inexpensive hydrometer can be used to test the condition of your coolant - also available are antifreeze test strips

3.7 Disconnect the electrical connector from the thermoswitch located in the thermostat housing

1 General information

Engine cooling system

All vehicles covered by this manual employ a pressurized engine cooling system with thermostatically-controlled coolant circulation. An impeller type water pump mounted on the front of the block pumps coolant through the engine. The coolant flows around each cylinder and toward the rear of the engine. Cast-in coolant passages direct coolant around the intake and exhaust ports, near the spark plug areas and in proximity to the exhaust valve guides.

A wax-pellet type thermostat is located in the thermostat housing at the transaxle end of the engine. During warm up, the closed thermostat prevents coolant from circulating through the radiator. When the engine reaches normal operating temperature, the thermostat opens and allows hot coolant to travel through the radiator, where it is cooled before returning to the engine.

The cooling system is sealed by a pressure-type radiator cap. This raises the boiling point of the coolant, and the higher boiling point of the coolant increases the cooling efficiency of the radiator. If the system pressure exceeds the cap pressure-relief value, the excess pressure in the system forces the spring-loaded valve inside the cap off its seat and allows the coolant to escape through the overflow tube into a coolant reservoir. When the system cools, the excess coolant is automatically drawn from the reservoir back into the radiator.

The coolant reservoir does double duty as both the point at which fresh coolant is added to the cooling system to maintain the proper fluid level and as a holding tank for overheated coolant.

This type of cooling system is known as a closed design because coolant that escapes past the pressure cap is saved and reused.

Heating system

The heating system consists of a blower fan and heater core located within the heater box under the right end of the dashboard, the inlet and outlet hoses connecting the heater core to the engine cooling system and the heater/air conditioning control head on the dashboard. Hot engine coolant is circulated through the heater core. When the heater mode is activated, a flap door opens to expose the heater box to the passenger compartment. A fan switch on the control head activates the blower motor, which forces air through the core, heating the air.

Air conditioning system

The air conditioning system consists of a condenser mounted in front of the radiator, an evaporator mounted adjacent to the heater core, a compressor mounted on the engine, a filter-drier which contains a high pressure relief valve and the plumbing connecting all of the above.

A blower fan forces the warmer air of the passenger compartment through the evaporator core (similar to a radiator in reverse), transferring the heat from the air to the refrigerant. The liquid refrigerant boils off into low pressure vapor, taking the heat with it when it leaves the evaporator. The compressor keeps refrigerant circulating through the system, pumping the warmed coolant through the condenser where it is cooled and then circulated back to the evaporator.

2 Antifreeze - general information

Refer to illustration 2.4

Warning: *Do not allow antifreeze to come in contact with your skin or painted surfaces of the vehicle. Rinse off spills immediately with plenty of water. Antifreeze is highly toxic if ingested. Never leave antifreeze lying around in an open container or in puddles on the floor; children and pets are attracted by it's sweet smell and may drink it. Check with local authorities about disposing of used antifreeze. Many communities have collection centers which will see that antifreeze is disposed of safely. Never dump used antifreeze on the ground or into drains.*

Note: *Non-toxic antifreeze is now manufactured and available at local auto parts stores, but even these types should be disposed of properly.*

1 The cooling system should be filled with a water/ethylene-glycol based antifreeze solution, which will prevent freezing down to at least -20 degrees F, or lower if local climate requires it. It also provides protection against corrosion and increases the coolant boiling point.

2 The cooling system should be drained, flushed and refilled every 30,000 miles or every two years (see Chapter 1). The use of antifreeze solutions for periods of longer than two years is likely to cause damage and encourage the formation of rust and scale in the system. If your tap water is "hard," i.e. contains a lot of dissolved minerals, use distilled water with the antifreeze.

3 Before adding antifreeze to the system, check all hose connections, because antifreeze tends to search out and leak through very minute openings. Engines do not normally consume coolant. Therefore, if the level goes down, find the cause and correct it.

4 The exact mixture of antifreeze-to-water you should use depends on the relative weather conditions. The mixture should contain at least 50 percent antifreeze, but should never contain more than 70 percent antifreeze. Consult the mixture ratio chart on the antifreeze container before adding coolant. Hydrometers are available at most auto parts stores to test the ratio of antifreeze to water **(see illustration)** or antifreeze test strips are available instead of the hydrometer gauge. Use antifreeze which meets the vehicle manufacturer's specifications.

3.10 The thermostat is installed with the spring end into the cylinder head and the bypass hole up

3 Thermostat - check and replacement

Warning: *Do not attempt to remove the radiator cap, coolant or thermostat until the engine has cooled completely.*

Check

1 Before assuming the thermostat is responsible for a cooling system problem, check the coolant level (Chapter 1), drivebelt tension (Chapter 1) and temperature gauge (or light) operation.
2 If the engine takes a long time to warm up (as indicated by the temperature gauge or heater operation), the thermostat is probably stuck open. Replace the thermostat with a new one.
3 If the engine runs hot, use your hand to check the temperature of the lower radiator hose. If the hose is not hot, but the engine is, the thermostat is probably stuck in the closed position, preventing the coolant inside the engine from traveling through the radiator. Replace the thermostat. **Caution:** *Do not drive the vehicle without a thermostat. The computer may stay in open loop and emissions and fuel economy will suffer.*
4 If the lower radiator hose is hot, it means that the coolant is flowing and the thermostat is open. Consult the Troubleshooting Section at the front of this manual for further diagnosis.

Replacement

Refer to illustrations 3.7 and 3.10

5 Disconnect the negative cable from the battery.
6 Drain the coolant from the radiator (see Chapter 1).
7 Disconnect the thermoswitch electrical connector from the thermostat cover located at the left end of the cylinder head **(see illustration)**.
8 Loosen the radiator hose clamp and remove the radiator hose from the thermostat cover. **Note:** *The radiator hose can be left attached to the thermostat cover, unless the thermostat cover itself is to be replaced.*
9 Detach the thermostat cover from the engine. Be prepared for some coolant to spill as the gasket seal is broken.
10 Remove the thermostat, noting the direction in which it was installed in the block **(see illustration)**.
11 Remove the gasket and thoroughly clean the sealing surfaces.
12 Install the thermostat with the spring end toward the engine, and with the small bypass hole in the thermostat at the high point (top).
13 Fit a new gasket, aligning the gasket with the bolt holes in the block. On 1995 and later models, install the gasket with the print side facing the cylinder head.
14 Installation is the reverse of removal. Tighten the thermostat cover fasteners to the torque listed in this Chapter's Specifications.
15 Refill the cooling system, run the engine and check for leaks and proper operation.

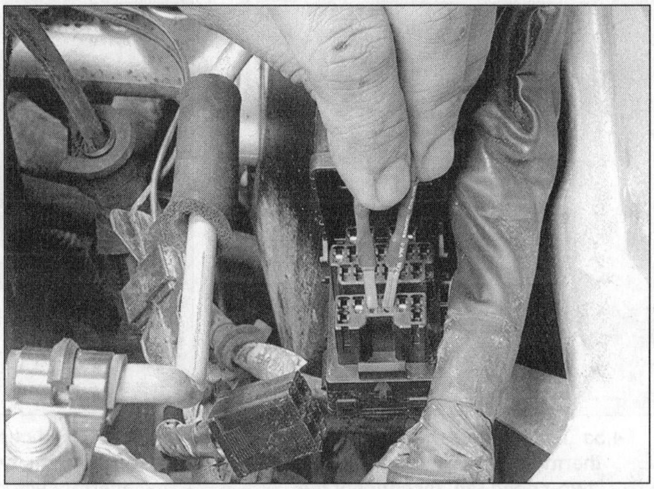

4.1 Check the radiator fan operation by connecting a jumper wire between the Diagnosis Connector TFA terminal and ground terminal (1990 through 1994 models)

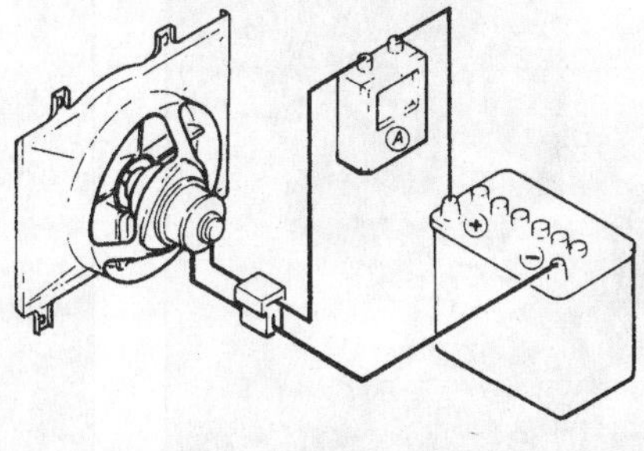

4.2 Disconnect the radiator fan electrical connector and connect fused jumper wires directly to the positive and negative terminals of the battery

4 Engine cooling fan and circuit - check and replacement

Warning: *To avoid possible injury, keep clear of the fan blades, as they may start turning at any time!*

Check

Refer to illustrations 4.1, 4.2 and 4.5

1 Install a jumper wire across the fan test (TFA) terminal and the ground (GND) terminal of the diagnosis connector, located on the engine compartment firewall **(see illustration)**. With the ignition key ON, the fan should now operate. If the fan does not operate, check the fan system components including the fan relay, fan thermoswitch, and fan motor itself.
2 To test an inoperative fan motor (one that doesn't come on when the engine gets hot or when the air conditioner is on), first check the fuses and/or fusible links (see Chapter 12). Then disconnect the electrical connector at the fan motor and use fused jumper wires to connect the fan directly to the battery **(see illustration)**. If the fan still does not work, replace the fan motor. Some 1994 and earlier 1.8L models with an automatic transaxle are equipped with a two speed fan. Fans with a four-prong connector are a two-speed fan. Be sure to check both fan speeds of two-speed fans by connecting both positive (+) connectors and negative (-) connectors to the test battery using fused jumper wires. **Warning:** *Do not allow the test clips to contact each other or any metallic part of the vehicle.*
3 If the fan motor tested OK in the previous test but is still inoperative, then the fault lies in the fuse, relays, thermoswitch or wiring. The relays and thermoswitch can be tested as described below. **Note:** *On 1995 and later models, the cooling fan relay is controlled by the PCM*

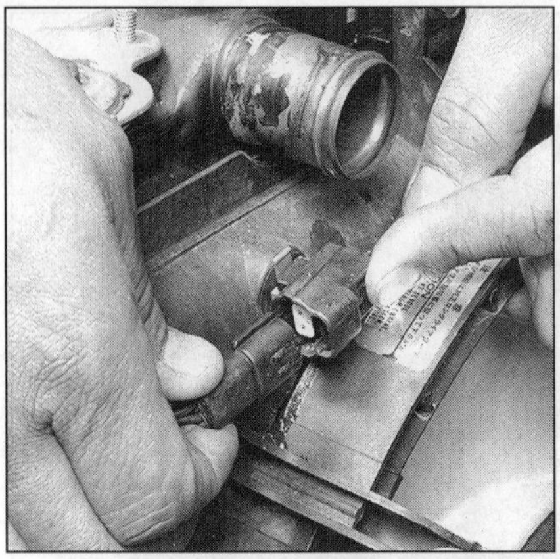

4.5a To test the second radiator fan thermoswitch, on models with a two-speed fan, disconnect the electrical connector . . .

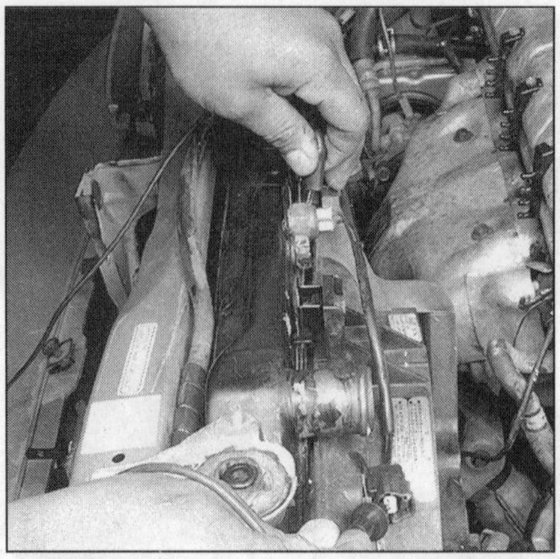

4.5b . . . and check for continuity by touching the two terminals in the thermoswitch connector with the probes of an ohmmeter

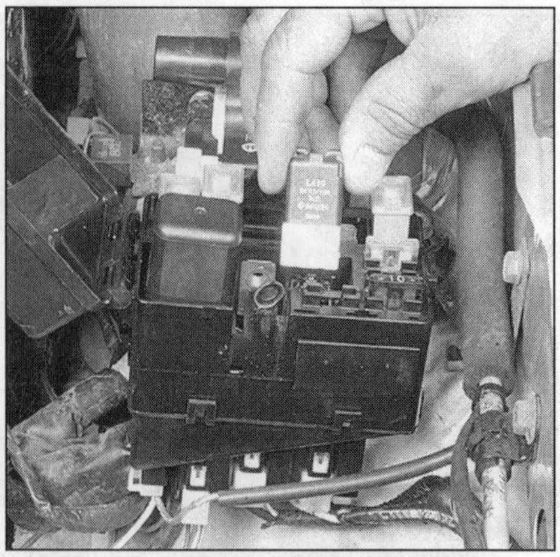

4.7a Cooling fan relay No. 1 is located in the main fuse block (1990 through 1994 model shown)

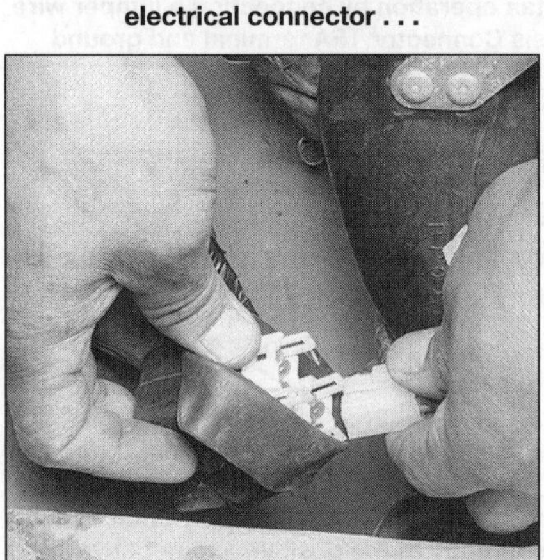

4.7b Cooling fan relays No. 2 and No. 3 are located on a separate bracket in front of the main relay box on the fender (1990 through 1994 model shown)

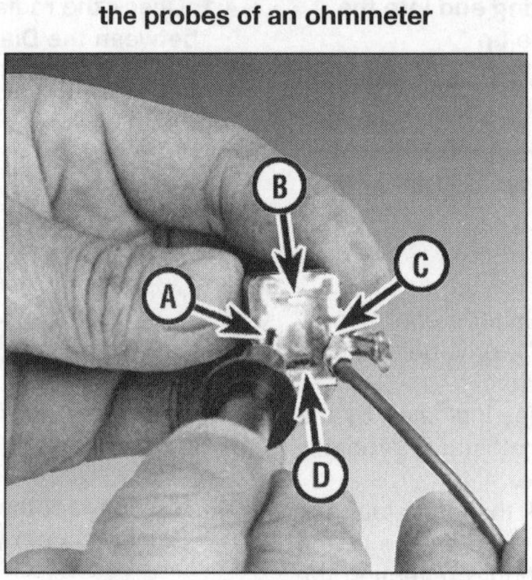

4.8a No. 1 cooling fan relay (Type 1) terminal guide for continuity test (1990 through 1994 shown)

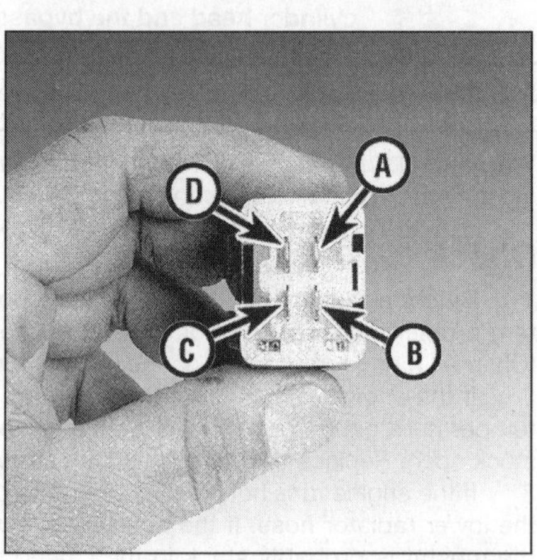

4.8b No. 2 fan relay (Type 2) and No. 3 fan relay (Type 2) terminal guide for continuity test (1990 through 1994 shown)

with information supplied by the engine coolant temperature sensor. See Chapter 6 for testing the coolant temperature sensor. If the fan motor, relay and related circuits all test good and the cooling fan fails to operate normally, the fault may lie with the PCM. Have the PCM diagnosed by a dealer service department or other qualified repair facility.

4 On all 1990 through 1994 models, fan thermoswitch can be tested for continuity with an ohmmeter. Disconnect the wiring connector **(see illustration 3.7)** and attach one lead of the ohmmeter to the electrical connector prong on the thermoswitch, and the other lead to the body of the thermoswitch. When the engine is cold (below 194-degrees F) there should be NO continuity. When the engine is hot (above 207-degrees F), there should be continuity. Replace the thermoswitch if necessary (see Section 9).

5 On 1990 through 1994 models with a two speed fan, the second fan thermoswitch actuates relays No. 2 and No. 3. Test the thermoswitch for continuity with an ohmmeter by disconnecting the fan thermoswitch wiring connector and attaching the ohmmeter leads to the two terminals in the thermoswitch connector **(see illustrations)**. When the engine is cold (below 205-degrees F) there should be NO continuity. When the engine is hot (above 221-degrees F), there should be continuity.

6 Replace the thermoswitch if necessary (see Section 9).

Relay check

Refer to illustrations 4.7a, 4.7b, 4.8a, 4.8b and 4.8c

7 On all models, locate number 1 fan relay in the main relay box **(see illustration)**. On models with a two speed cooling fan, locate the No. 2 fan relay and the No. 3 fan relay located forward of the main relay box (No. 2 fan relay is closest to the inner fender, while the No. 3 fan relay is mounted inboard of the No. 2 fan relay) **(see illustration)**.

8 Remove the cooling fan relays, beginning with the No. 1 fan relay. Using an ohmmeter, test for continuity. On 1994 and earlier models, two types of relays are used by the manufacturer, and the terminals are numbered differently. Be sure to test the relay as shown **(see illustrations)**. With no voltage applied, there should be NO continuity between terminals A and C. There should be continuity between terminals B and

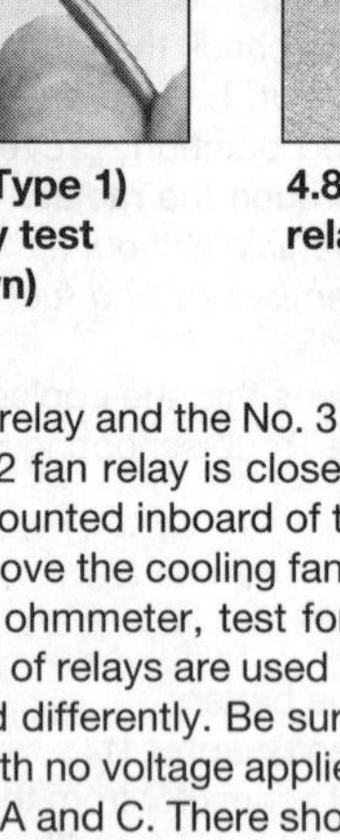

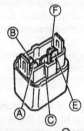

4.8c 1995 and later fan relay terminal guide and continuity table

○—○: Continuity B+: Battery positive voltage

Step \ Terminal	A	B	C	E	F
1	○	○	○		○
2	B+	Ground	○	○	

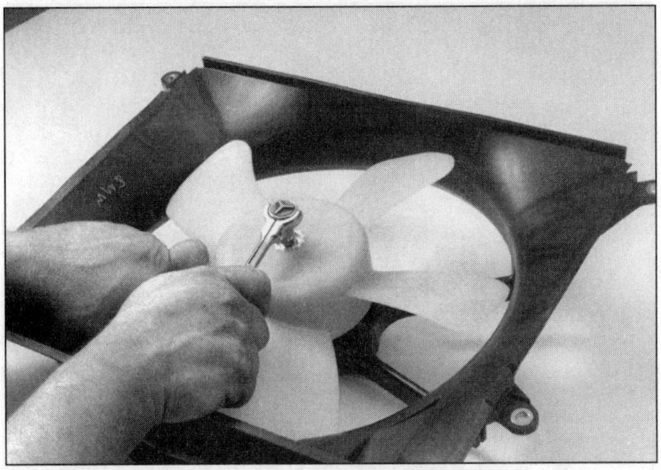

4.16 **Hold the cooling fan blades and remove the fan retaining nut**

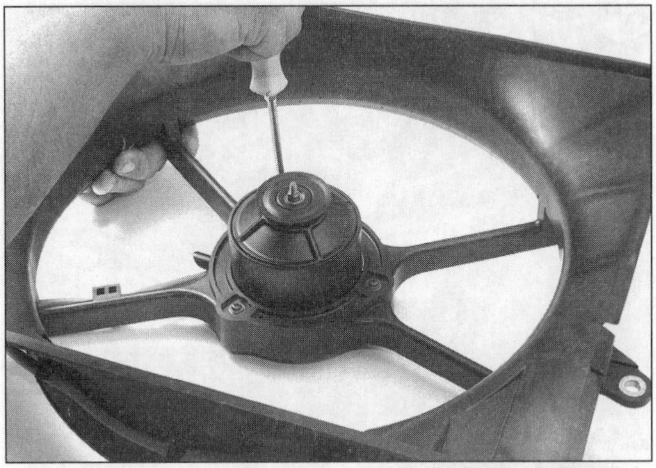

4.17 **Remove the screws retaining the motor to the shroud**

D. With battery voltage applied across terminals B and D, there should be continuity between terminals A and C. On 1995 and later models, remove the fan relay and test the relay as shown **(see illustration)**.

9 If the fan relays, thermoswitch and fan motors all test good, take the vehicle to a dealer service department or other qualified repair facility for further diagnosis, due to the complexity and variety of the circuits involved.

Fan replacement

Refer to illustrations 4.16 and 4.17

10 Disconnect the negative battery cable.

11 Drain the cooling system (see Chapter 1) below the level of the upper radiator hose.

12 On 1990 through 1994 models, remove the resonance chamber.

13 Disconnect the wiring connector at the fan motor.

14 Loosen the radiator upper hose clamps and remove the upper hose.

15 Unbolt the fan shroud and lift the fan shroud from the engine compartment. On 1995 and later models, move the coolant fan assembly to the side after removing the bolts and remove the radiator (see Section 5). Remove the fan assembly.

16 While holding the fan blades, remove the fan retaining nut **(see illustration)**. Remove the fan from the fan motor.

17 Remove the fan motor from the fan shroud **(see illustration)**.

18 Installation is the reverse of removal. When installing the fan shroud and the resonance chamber, tighten the mounting bolts securely.

5 Radiator and coolant reservoir - removal and installation

Warning: *Do not start this procedure until the engine is completely cool.*

Radiator

Refer to illustrations 5.8, 5.9a, 5.9b and 5.10

1 Disconnect the negative battery cable.

2 Drain the engine coolant into a container (see Chapter 1).

3 On 1990 through 1994 models, remove the resonance chamber **(see illustration 4.12)**.

4 Disconnect the wiring connector at the fan motor.

5 On 1990 through 1994 models with a two speed fan, disconnect the wiring connector at the fan thermoswitch.

6 Disconnect the coolant reservoir hose from the radiator filler neck. Then remove the coolant reservoir.

7 Loosen the radiator hose clamps and remove both the upper and lower hoses.

8 If equipped with an automatic transaxle, disconnect the oil cooler hose from the radiator **(see illustration)**. Place a drip pan to catch the transmission fluid and cap the fittings.

9 Remove the fan retaining bolts and lift out the fan assembly **(see illustrations)**. On 1995 and later models, move the fan assembly to the side while the radiator is removed. **Note:** *The bottom of the radiator is retained, without bolts, by the radiator support frame.*

5.8 Remove the automatic transaxle cooler lines

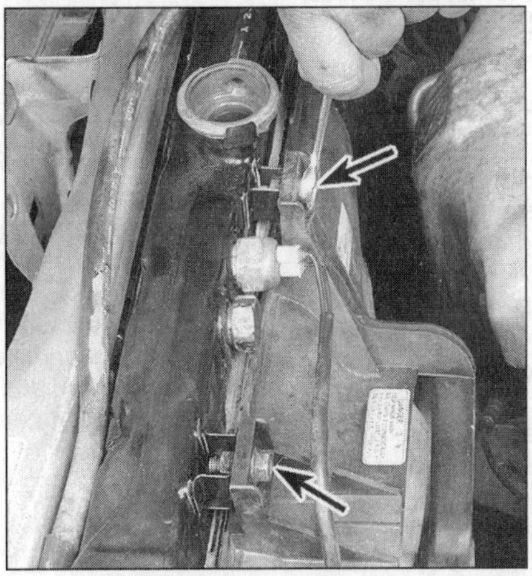

5.9a Remove the radiator fan assembly bolts . . .

5.9b . . . and lift out the radiator fan assembly

3

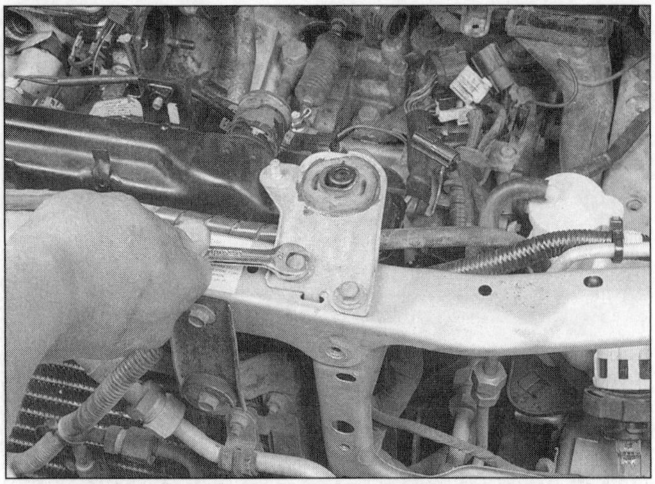

5.10a Remove the two radiator upper mounting assemblies and . . .

5.10b . . . remove the radiator carefully. Retrieve the lower mounts - they must be in place on the bottom of the radiator when the radiator is reinstalled

10 Detach and lift out the radiator **(see illustration)**. Be aware of dripping fluids and the sharp fins.
11 On 1995 and later models, the cooling fan and fan shroud can now be removed, if necessary (see Section 4).
12 With the radiator removed, it can be inspected for leaks, damage and internal blockage. If in need of repairs, have a professional radiator shop or dealer service department perform the work as special techniques are required.
13 Bugs and dirt can be cleaned from the radiator with compressed air and a soft brush. Don't bend the cooling fins as this is done. **Warning:** *Wear eye protection when using compressed air.*
14 Installation is the reverse of the removal procedure. Be sure the bottom of the radiator is located properly. When installing the radiator fan shroud and the resonance chamber, tighten the mounting bolts securely.
15 After installation, fill the cooling system with the proper mixture of antifreeze and water. Refer to Chapter 1 if necessary.
16 Start the engine and check for leaks. Allow the engine to reach normal operating temperature, indicated by both radiator hoses becoming hot. Recheck the coolant level and add more if required.
17 On automatic transaxle equipped models, check and add automatic transmission fluid as needed.

Coolant reservoir

Refer to illustration 5.18

18 Unbolt the coolant reservoir and lift it out of engine compartment **(see illustration).**
19 Pour the coolant into a container. Wash out and inspect the reservoir for cracks and chafing. Replace it if damaged.
20 Installation is the reverse of removal.

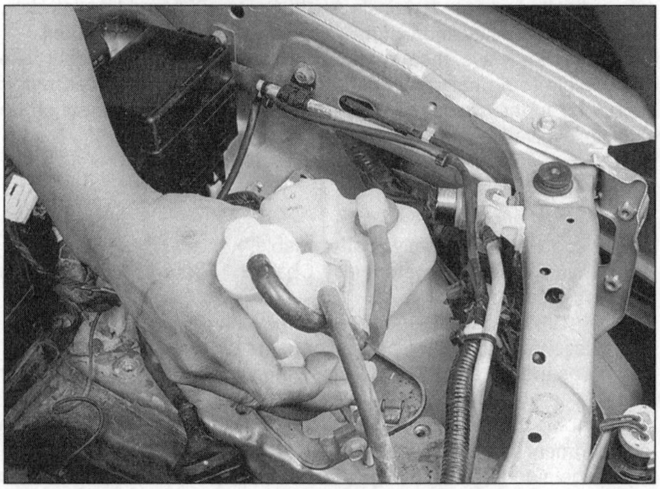

5.18 Remove the reservoir bottle

6 Water pump - check

1 A failure in the water pump can cause serious engine damage due to overheating. If the pump is defective, it should be replaced with a new or rebuilt unit
2 Remove the timing belt cover(s) (see Chapter 2A).
3 Water pumps are equipped with weep or vent holes. If a failure occurs in the pump seal, coolant will leak from the hole. In most cases you'll need a flashlight to find the hole on the water pump from underneath to check for leaks. On 1.8L DOHC engines any water coming from this hole is vented to the outside of the timing belt cover on the back side of the engine in order to not damage the timing belt.
4 Check the water pump shaft bearing for wear by grasping the pump hub and gently rocking the hub and shaft from side to side. If any looseness is apparent, excessive water pump shaft/bearing wear is possible.
5 If the water pump shaft bearings fail there may be a howling sound at the drivebelt end of the engine while it's running. Don't mistake drivebelt slippage, which causes a squealing sound, for water pump bearing failure. If a squealing sound is heard, check belt condition and belt tension.

7 Water pump - removal and installation

Refer to illustration 7.7

Warning: *Wait until the engine is completely cool before beginning this procedure. Do not allow antifreeze to come in contact with your skin or painted surfaces of the vehicle. Rinse off spills immediately with plenty of water. Antifreeze is highly toxic if ingested. Never leave antifreeze lying around in an open container or in puddles on the floor; children and pets are attracted by it's sweet smell and may drink it. Check with local authorities about disposing of used antifreeze. Many communities have collection centers which will see that antifreeze is disposed of safely.*

Removal

1 Disconnect the negative battery cable from the battery.
2 Drain the cooling system (see Chapter 1). If the coolant is relatively new or in good condition, save it and reuse it.

7.7 After removing the front covers and timing belt, remove the water pump mounting bolts (arrows) and remove the water pump

8.3 Location of the temperature gauge sending unit (arrow)

3 Remove the water pump drivebelt, pulley, timing belt cover(s) and timing belt (see Chapter 2A).
4 Remove the water inlet pipe and gasket from the water pump.
5 On 1990 through 1994 models, remove the water bypass pipe and O-ring, located on the water inlet pipe.
6 On 1990 through 1994 1.8L DOHC models, remove the oil level gauge (dipstick) tube clamp located at the engine block.
7 Remove the water pump mounting bolts **(see illustration)** and detach the water pump from the engine. If the water pump is stuck, gently tap it with a soft-faced hammer to break the seal.

Installation

8 Clean the bolt threads and the threaded holes in the engine to remove corrosion and sealant.
9 Remove all traces of old gasket material from the sealing surfaces.
10 Compare the new water pump to the old one to make sure they are identical.
11 Apply a thin film of silicone sealant to the new gasket and install it on the water pump.
12 Carefully mate the water pump to the engine.
13 Install the water pump mounting bolts. Tighten them to the torque listed in this Chapter's Specifications. Don't over-tighten them or the pump may be damaged.
14 Reinstall all parts removed for access to the water pump.
15 Refill the cooling system (see Chapter 1) and check the timing belt tension (see Chapter 2A). Run the engine and check for leaks.

8 Coolant temperature gauge sending unit - check and replacement

Refer to illustration 8.3

Warning: *Do not start this procedure until the engine is completely cool.*

Check

1 If the coolant temperature gauge is inoperative, check the fuses first (see Chapter 12).
2 If the temperature gauge indicates excessive temperature after running awhile, see the *Troubleshooting Section* in the front of the manual.
3 If the temperature gauge indicates HOT as soon as the engine is started cold, disconnect the electrical connector at the coolant gauge sending unit, located in the engine compartment **(see illustration).** If the gauge reading drops, replace the sending unit. If the reading remains high, the wire to the gauge may be shorted to ground or the gauge is faulty.
4 If the coolant temperature gauge fails to show any indication after the engine has been warmed up, (approximately 10 minutes) and the fuses are good, shut off the engine. Disconnect the electrical connector at the sending unit and, using a jumper wire, connect the wire to a clean ground on the engine. Briefly turn on the ignition without starting the engine. If the gauge now indicates HOT, replace the sending unit.
5 Additionally, the sending unit may be checked for resistance using an ohmmeter; with the engine coolant hot, resistance should be 190 to 260 ohms.
6 If the gauge fails to respond, the circuit may be open or the temperature gauge may be faulty.

Replacement

7 Drain the coolant (see Chapter 1).
8 Disconnect the wiring connector from the sending unit.
9 Using a deep socket or a wrench, remove the sending unit.
10 Install the new sending unit, and tighten it securely. Do not use thread sealer as it may electrically insulate the sending unit. Connect the electrical connector.
11 Refill the cooling system and check for coolant leakage and proper gauge operation.

9 Radiator cooling fan thermoswitch - replacement

Note: *1990 through 1994 models use either one of two cooling fan thermoswitches to control the operation of the cooling fan. On 1.8L engines with an automatic transaxle, the second thermoswitch controls the high speed operation of the dual-speed fan. See Section 4 for information on checking the thermoswitches. On 1995 and later models, the cooling fan relay is controlled by the PCM with information supplied by the engine coolant temperature sensor, see Chapter 6 for information on the coolant temperature sensor.*

1 Drain the cooling system (see Chapter 1).
2 To replace the main radiator cooling fan thermoswitch, disconnect the electrical connector and unscrew the switch from the thermostat housing **(see illustration 3.7)**.
3 Install the new switch with a new O-ring and tighten it securely. Connect the electrical connector and refill the cooling system.
4 To replace the secondary radiator cooling fan thermoswitch on models with a two-speed fan, remove the radiator resonance chamber. Disconnect the electrical connector and remove the radiator fan thermoswitch and gasket **(see illustration 4.5)**. Install the new radiator fan thermoswitch with a new gasket. Tighten the radiator thermoswitch securely. Connect the radiator thermoswitch electrical connector.
5 Install the radiator resonance chamber. Tighten the fasteners securely.
4 Refill the cooling system.

3

10 Blower motor and circuit - check and component replacement

Refer to illustrations 10.1, 10.2, 10.6a, 10.6b and 10.6c

1 On 1990 through 1994 models, if heater blower fan is inoperative, first check heater circuit breaker, located above the underdash fuse box **(see illustration)**. The heater circuit breaker is a 30A fuse with a reset button feature. On 1995 and later models, check the 40A fuse located in the underdash fuse box (see Chapter 12).

2 If the reset button is OUT on 1990 through 1994 models, or if the fuse is blown on 1995 and later models, first check for a short circuit in the blower wiring by disconnecting the electrical connector at the blower. Check for any shorts (continuity) between the blower electrical connector **(see illustration)** and any convenient body ground. Replace or repair the harness if necessary.

3 On 1990 through 1994 models, depress the reset button to reset the heater circuit breaker.

4 Measure the voltage at the heater blower motor as follows:

a) *Remove the glove box for access to the blower.*
b) *Turn the ignition switch on, and turn the blower switch to the Position 4 (high speed).*
c) *Using a voltmeter, test the blower motor terminal wires.*
d) *The voltage should measure 12-volts. If 12-volts is present and the blower doesn't run, replace the blower (see Section 11).*

5 With the voltmeter still connected to the blower electrical connector, turn the blower switch down to Position 3, Position 2, and finally, Position 1, checking the voltage is lower at each lower position of the blower switch. Replace the resistor assembly if necessary.

6 Further checks of the resistors can be made by removing the resistor assembly and checking terminal continuity as follows **(see illustrations)**:

a) *On 1990 through 1994 models, if no continuity is measured between resistor assembly terminals A and B, A and C, and A and D, replace the resistor assembly.*
b) *On 1995 and 1996 models, if no continuity is measured between resistor assembly terminals A and C, C and E, and C and D, replace the resistor assembly.*
c) *On 1997 models, if no continuity is measured between resistor assembly terminals A and C, B and C, and B and D, replace the resistor assembly.*

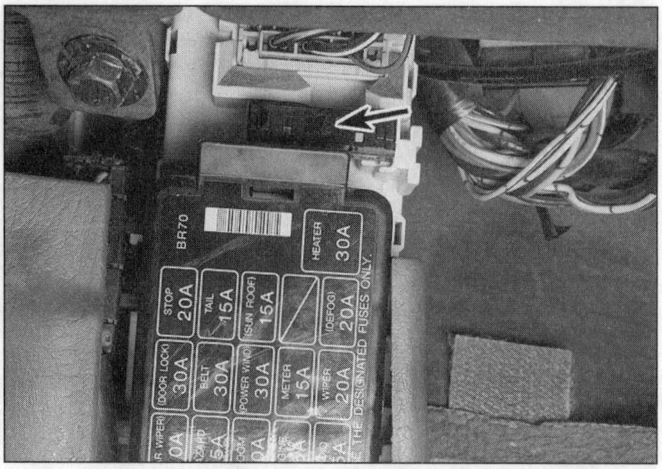

10.1 On 1990 through 1994 models, check the circuit breaker reset button (arrow), located above the fuse box

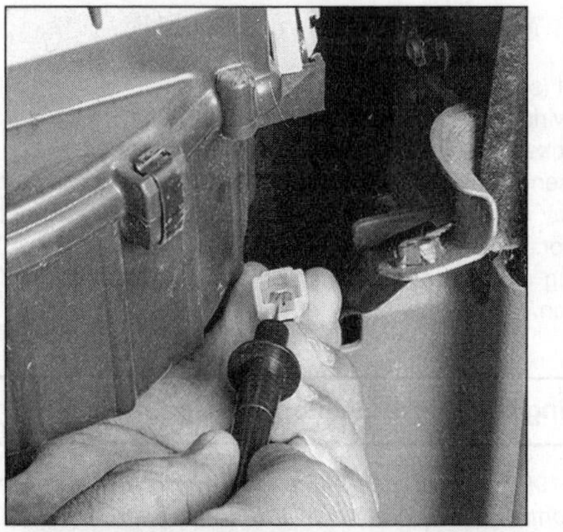

10.2 With the blower motor electrical connector disconnected, check for shorts between the electrical connector and any convenient chassis ground. If no shorts are found, reconnect the blower electrical connector to the blower terminal for additional tests

10.6a Remove the blower motor resistor assembly mounting screws . . .

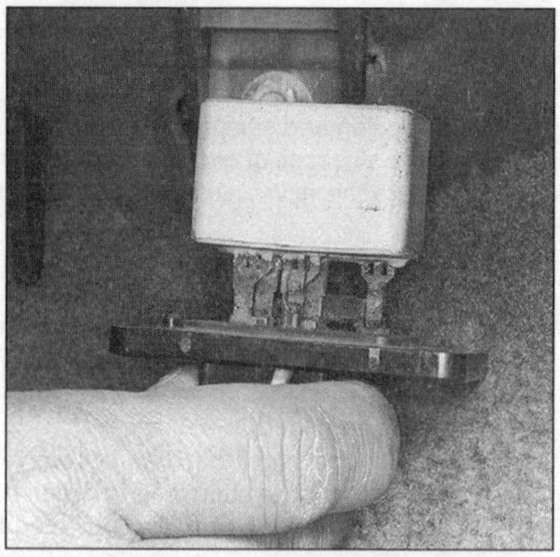

10.6b . . . and withdraw the resistor assembly to test continuity

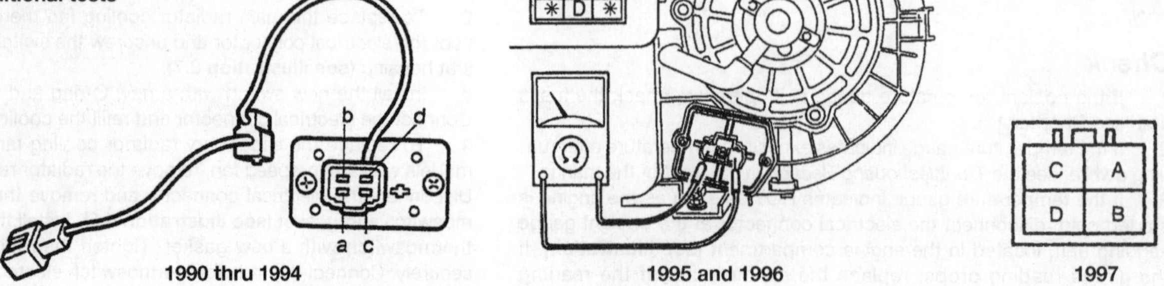

10.6c Blower resistor terminal guide

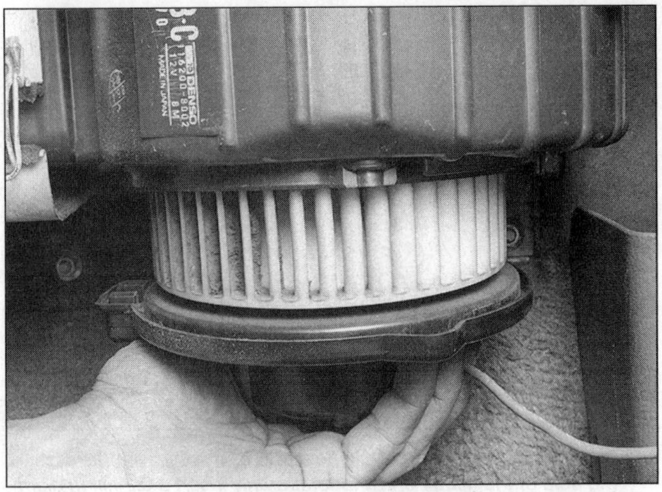
11.4 Remove the blower motor from the housing

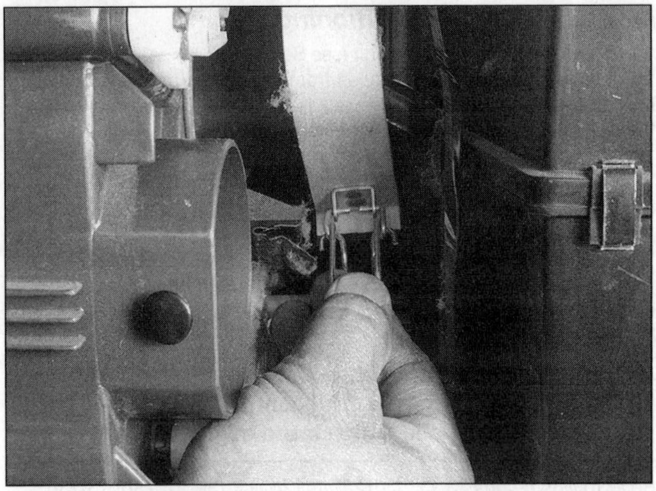
12.5 Unlatch the heater unit seal plate

11 Blower motor - removal and installation

Refer to illustration 11.4

1 Remove the trim panel underneath the glove box.
2 Disconnect the electrical connector from the blower motor.
3 Remove the three screws retaining the blower motor to the housing.
4 Withdraw the blower motor straight down and out of the housing **(see illustration)**.
5 To remove the blower fan, remove the fastener from the shaft and withdraw the fan from the motor.
6 Installation is the reverse of removal.

12 Heater core - replacement

Warning 1: *1995 and later models are equipped with airbags. The airbag is armed and can deploy (inflate) anytime the battery is connected. To prevent accidental deployment (and possible injury), turn the ignition key to LOCK and disconnect the negative battery cable whenever working near airbag components. After the battery is disconnected, wait at least two minutes before beginning work (the system has a back-up capacitor that must fully discharge). For more information see Chapter 12.*
Warning 2: *The air conditioning system is under high pressure. Do not loosen any hose fittings or remove any components until the system has been discharged. Air conditioning refrigerant should be properly discharged into an EPA-approved recovery/recycling unit by a dealer service department or an automotive air conditioning repair facility. Always wear eye protection when disconnecting air conditioning system fittings.*

1 If equipped with air conditioning, have the refrigerant discharged and recovered by a qualified repair facility.
2 Disconnect the cable from the negative battery terminal.
3 Drain the engine coolant (see Chapter 1).
4 Remove the instrument panel (Refer to Chapter 11).

Models without air conditioning

Refer to illustrations 12.5, 12.6 and 12.9

5 Remove the seal plate on the right side of the heater unit by unlatching the seal plate latch **(see illustration)**.
6 Disconnect the heater hoses from the heater core by unlocking the hose connections at the firewall **(see illustration)**. Keep plenty of towels or rags on the carpeting to catch any coolant that may drip.
7 Remove the three nuts from the studs retaining the heater unit to the dash.
8 Remove the heater unit from the dash. The seal plate will come out with the heater unit as an assembly.
9 Remove the heater core from the heater unit **(see illustration)**.
10 Reassembly is the reverse of removal. When installing the heater hoses on the heater core, make sure the hose connectors are securely locked.

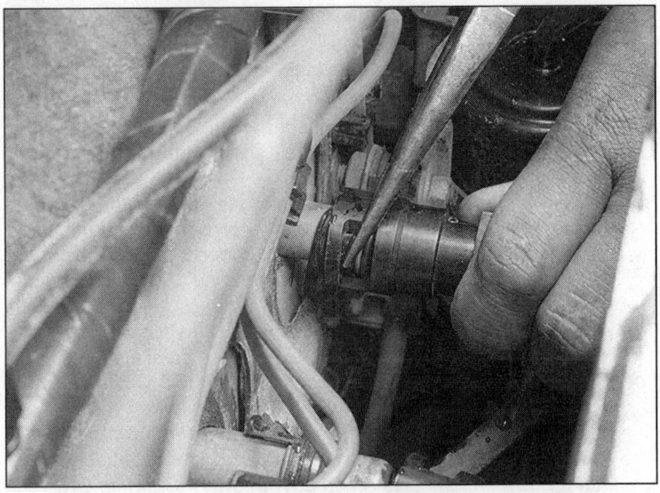
12.6 Disconnect the heater hose from the heater unit by unlocking the hose connector

12.9 Remove the heater core from of the heater unit

Models with air conditioning

11 Remove the evaporator unit (see Section 18).

12 Disconnect the heater hoses from the heater core by unlocking the hose connections at the firewall. Keep plenty of towels or rags on the carpeting to catch any coolant that may drip inside.

13 Disconnect the heater electrical connectors.

14 Remove the three nuts from the studs retaining the heater unit to the dash.

15 Remove the heater unit from the dash.

16 Remove the heater core from the heater unit.

17 Reassembly is the reverse of removal. When installing the heater hoses on the heater unit, check the hose connectors are securely locked.

13 Heater and air conditioning control assembly - removal, installation, check and adjustment

Refer to illustrations 13.11, 13.12a, 13.12b, 13.13a, 13.13b, 13.13c and 13.13d

Warning: *1995 and later models are equipped with airbags. The airbag is armed and can deploy (inflate) anytime the battery is connected. To prevent accidental deployment (and possible injury), turn the ignition key to LOCK and disconnect the negative battery cable whenever working near airbag components. After the battery is disconnected, wait at least two minutes before beginning work (the system has a back-up capacitor that must fully discharge). For more information see Chapter 12.*

Note: *Two types on control systems are used on the models covered by this manual; a manual "wire type" control system and an electronic "logic type" system. Logic controls can be distinguished from the wire type control by the type of control unit at the dashboard. Logic controls have a series of push buttons for the heater and air conditioning operation, a fan switch, and a lever for air mix. Logic controls use only one air MIX wire plus electrical switches for the remaining heater and air conditioning functions. Electrically-driven actuators are used at the blower unit and the heater units instead of mechanical levers.*

Removal and installation

1 Disconnect the negative battery cable.

2 Remove the side panel below the dash on the passenger side (see Chapter 11).

3 Remove the underdash panel on the passenger side.

4 Remove the center heater and radio control panel (see Chapter 11).

5 Remove the instrument cluster bezel (see Chapter 11).

6 Remove the glove box (see Chapter 11).

7 Remove the glove box cover inside the dash (see Chapter 11).

8 On models with manual wire type controls, disconnect the heater control wires behind the heater control (MODE wire, MIX wire, and REC-FRESH wire, as applicable). Remove the heater control assembly.

9 On models with electronic "Logic" type controls, disconnect the heater air MIX wire, the control unit retaining screws, and as the control unit is pulled out, disconnect the two electrical connectors. Remove the heater/air conditioning control assembly.

10 Installation is the reverse of the removal procedure. When installation of the heater/air conditioning control assembly is complete, connect and adjust the heater control wires as follows.

Check and adjustment

11 On 1990 through 1994 models with wire-type controls:

a) *To connect and adjust the REC-FRESH wire, set the REC-FRESH lever to the Fresh position, connect the REC-FRESH wire to the REC-FRESH door, set the door to FRESH position and clamp the wire in place. Check the lever moves its full stroke.*

b) *To connect and adjust the MIX wire, set the MIX lever to the COLD position, connect the MIX wire to the MIX door, set the door to the COLD position and clamp the wire in place. Check the lever moves its full stroke.*

c) *To connect and adjust the MODE wire, set the MODE lever to the DEFROST position, remove the MODE wire from Clip A* **(see illustration)**. *Align the set pin hole at B of the link with the matching hole of the heater unit and temporarily insert a 0.24 inch diameter set pin. Use either a 15/64-inch diameter drill bit or a Letter B diameter drill bit as a 0.24-inch diameter set pin. Holding the MODE wire housing and with the wire straight , push the MODE wire into Clip A. Check the operation of the MODE lever. If the result is not correct, pull the MODE wire approximately 1/16-inch toward the heater unit link. Remove the set pin that was installed for adjustment.*

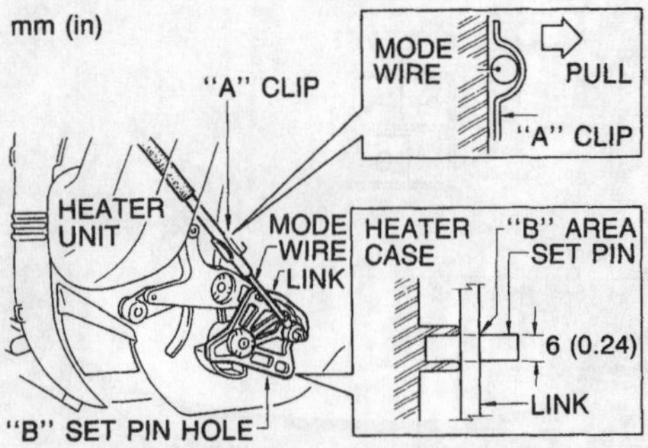

13.11 On 1990 through 1994 models, remove the heater MODE wire from Clip A. Insert a 0.24-inch set pin in hole B and complete the MODE wire adjustment

12 On 1995 and 1996 models with wire-type controls:

a) *Adjust the airflow MODE wire by setting the MODE lever to DEFROSTER, connect the wire at the heater, set the MODE wire link to DEFROSTER and insert a screwdriver at the set hole near the bottom of the unit, clamp the MODE wire and verify that the MODE control lever on the dashboard moves full stroke.*

b) *Adjust the air MIX wire by setting the temperature control lever to MAX COLD, connect the wire at the heater, set the air mix link to MAX COLD and insert a screwdriver at the set hole. Clamp the air MIX wire and verify that the temperature control lever on the dashboard moves full stroke.*

c) *Adjust the air INTAKE wire by setting the REC/FRESH lever to FRESH, connecting the air INTAKE wire to the air intake link at the heater, set the air INTAKE link to FRESH and clamp the wire in place. Verify the REC/FRESH lever on the dashboard moves full stroke.*

d) *To check control unit switches, access the back of the control unit and backprobe the fan switch electrical connector, the A/C switch electrical connector, and the heater unit electrical connector, checking for continuity between connector terminals as shown* **(see illustrations)**.

e) *Disconnect the fan switch electrical connector and check for continuity between fan switch terminals as shown in the illustration. Replace the fan switch if defective.*

13 On 1995 and later models with logic controls:

a) *Check and adjust the MIX wire as above.*

b) *To check the fan switch, disconnect the fan switch electrical connector and check for continuity as shown* **(see illustrations)**. *Replace fan switch if defective.*

c) *To check the REC switch, disconnect the REC switch electrical connector. Connect a 1 K-ohm resistor between terminals C and F* **(see illustrations)** *of the switch, connect the vehicle battery to terminal F and battery ground to terminal J. Connect a voltmeter between terminals C and J. With the REC switch ON, voltage should be 1-volt or less. With the REC switch OFF, 12-volts should be present. Replace the control unit if defective.*

d) *To check the FRESH switch, disconnect the REC switch electrical connector. Connect a 1 K-ohm resistor between terminals A and F* **(see illustrations)** *of the switch, connect the vehicle battery to terminal F and battery ground to terminal J. Connect a voltmeter between terminals A and J. With the REC switch ON, voltage should be 1-volt or less. With the REC switch OFF, 12-volts should be present. Replace the control unit if defective.*

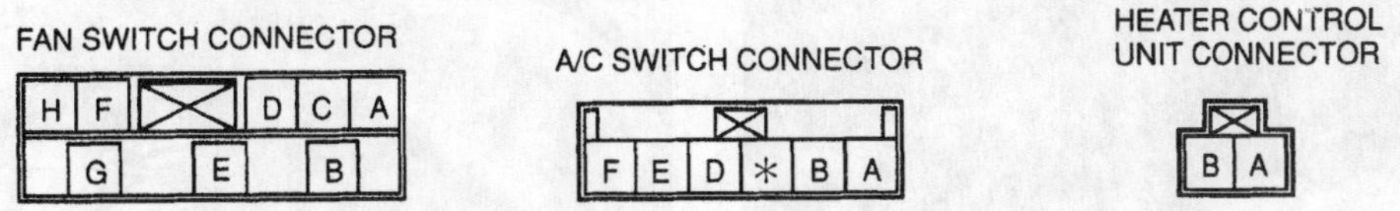

O—O: Continuity

Switch position \ Terminal	Fan switch A	Fan switch B	Fan switch C	Fan switch D	Fan switch E	Fan switch F	Fan switch G	Fan switch H	A/C switch A	A/C switch B	A/C switch D	A/C switch E	A/C switch F	Heater control unit A	Heater control unit B
Constant	O		O	O					O	O	O	O	O	O	O
OFF															
1		O		O											
2		O				O		O							
3		O			O			O							
4		O					O	O							

13.12a Terminal guide and continuity table for 1995 and later models with wire type controls

e) To check the MODE switch, disconnect the REC switch electrical connector. Connect a 1 K-ohm resistor between terminals J and L **(see illustrations)** *of the control unit, connect the vehicle battery to terminal F and battery ground to terminal J, connect a jumper wire between terminals J and R, connect a voltmeter between terminals J and L; voltage should measure 12-volts. Replace the control unit if defective.*

f) Connect a 1 K-ohm resistor between terminals J and N **(see illustrations)** *of the control unit, connect the vehicle battery to terminal F and battery ground to terminal J, connect a jumper wire between terminals J and P, connect a voltmeter (DC voltage setting) between terminals J and N; voltage should measure 12-volts. Replace the control unit if defective.*

g) Connect a 1 K-ohm resistor between terminals J and L **(see illustrations)** *of the control unit, connect the vehicle battery to terminal F and battery ground to terminal J, connect a jumper wire between terminals J and L, connect a voltmeter between terminals J and L; voltage should measure 1-volt or less. Replace the control unit if defective.*

O—O: Continuity

A/C switch	D	E
OFF		
ON	O	O

13.12b Terminal guide and continuity table for wire type control fan switch

h) Connect a 1 K-ohm resistor between terminals J and N **(see illustrations)** *to the control unit, connect the vehicle battery to terminal F and battery ground to terminal J, connect a jumper wire between terminals J and R, connect a voltmeter between terminals J and N; voltage should measure 1-volt or less. Replace the control unit if defective.*

i) Check the continuity of terminals listed **(see illustrations)** *while pressing the mode switch to the positions shown. Replace the control unit if defective.*

j) Check the continuity of the A/C switch terminals **(see illustrations)**, *pressing the A/C switch to ON and OFF positions. Replace the control unit if defective.*

O—O: Continuity

Switch position \ Terminal	B	D	E	F	G	H
OFF						
1	O	O				
2	O			O		O
3	O		O			O
4	O				O	O

13.13a Fan switch terminal guide and continuity table for 1995 and later with logic control

O—O: Continuity

Switch \ Terminal	J	T	S	Q	O	M
VENT	O	O				
BI–LEVEL	O		O			
HEAT	O			O		
HEAT/DEF	O				O	
DEFROSTER	O					O

13.13c MODE switch continuity table for 1995 and later with logic control

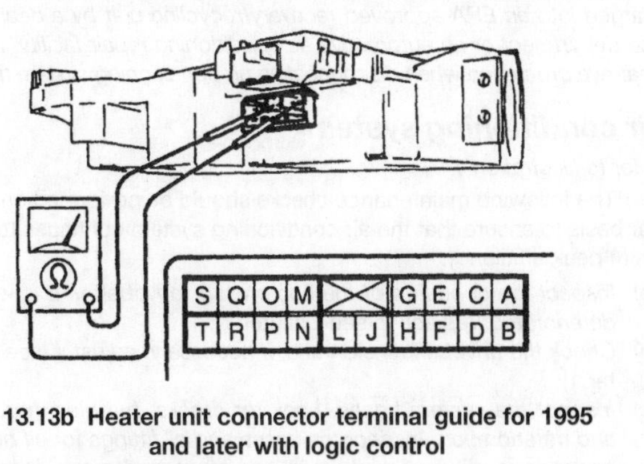

13.13b Heater unit connector terminal guide for 1995 and later with logic control

O—O: Continuity

A/C switch \ Terminal	B	D
OFF		
ON	O	O

13.13d A/C switch continuity table for 1995 and later with logic control

3

14.1 The fins of the condenser can be cleaned with a fin comb - use the side of the tool with the correct fins-per-inch spacing for your core

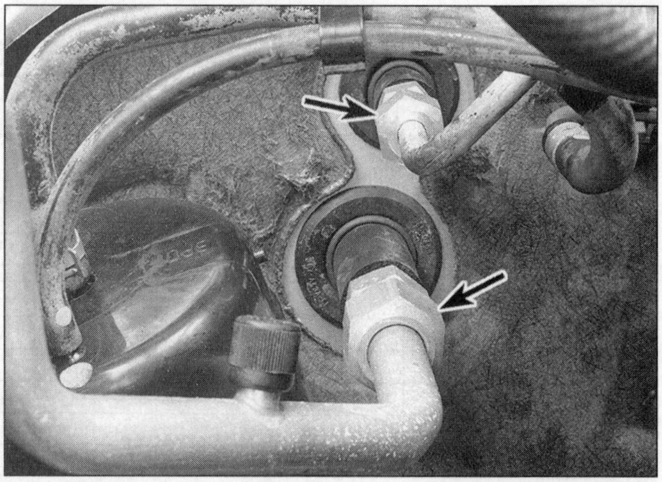

14.9 With the system operating, the evaporator outlet line (large tubing) should feel slightly cooler than the inlet line (small tubing)

14 On 1997 models with wire-type controls:

a) *Adjust the airflow MODE wire by setting the MODE lever to VENT, connect the wire at the heater, set the MODE wire link at the heater to VENT and insert a screwdriver at the set hole near the bottom of the unit. Clamp the MODE wire and verify that the MODE control lever on the dashboard moves full stroke.*
b) *Adjust the air MIX wire by setting the temperature control lever to MAX HOT, connect the wire at the heater, set the air mix link to MAX HOT and insert a screwdriver at the set hole. Clamp the air MIX wire and verify that the HOT-COLD control lever on the dashboard moves full stroke.*
c) *Adjust the air INTAKE wire the same as the 1995 through 1996 wire type controls above.*

14 Air conditioning and heating system - check and maintenance

Warning: *The air conditioning system is under high pressure. Do not loosen any hose fittings or remove any components until the system has been discharged. Air conditioning refrigerant should be properly discharged into an EPA-approved recovery/recycling unit by a dealer service department or an automotive air conditioning repair facility. Always wear eye protection when disconnecting air conditioning system fittings.*

Air conditioning system

Refer to illustration 14.1

1 The following maintenance checks should be performed on a regular basis to ensure that the air conditioning system continues to operate at peak efficiency:

a) *Inspect the condition of the compressor drivebelt. If it is worn or deteriorated, replace it* (see Chapter 1).
b) *Check the drivebelt tension and, if necessary, adjust it* (see Chapter 1).
c) *Inspect the system hoses. Look for cracks, bubbles, hardening and deterioration. Inspect the hoses and all fittings for oil bubbles or seepage. If there is any evidence of wear, damage or leakage, replace the hose(s).*
d) *Inspect the condenser fins for leaves, bugs and any other foreign material that may have embedded itself in the fins. Use a "fin comb" or compressed air to remove debris from the condenser* **(see illustration)**.
e) *Make sure the system has the correct refrigerant charge.*

2 It's a good idea to operate the system for about ten minutes at least once a month. This is particularly important during the winter months because long term non-use can cause hardening, and subsequent failure, of the seals.

3 Leaks in the air conditioning system are best spotted when the system is brought up to operating temperature and pressure, by running the engine with the air conditioning ON for five minutes. Shut the engine off and inspect the air conditioning hoses and connections. Traces of oil usually indicate refrigerant leaks.

4 Because of the complexity of the air conditioning system and the special equipment required to effectively work on it, accurate troubleshooting of the system should be left to a professional technician.

5 If the air conditioning system doesn't operate at all, check the fuse panel and the air conditioning relay, located in the fuse/relay box in the engine compartment. Refer to Sections 4, 9 and 11 for electrical checks of heating/air conditioning system components.

6 The most common cause of poor cooling is simply a low system refrigerant charge. If a noticeable drop in cool air output occurs, the following quick check will help you determine if the refrigerant level is low. For more complete information on the air conditioning system, refer to the *Haynes Automotive Heating and Air Conditioning Manual*.

Checking the refrigerant charge

Refer to illustrations 14.9, 14.10 and 14.11

7 Warm the engine up to normal operating temperature.

8 With the engine at fast idle, place the air conditioning temperature selector at the coldest setting and put the blower at the highest setting. Open the doors (to make sure the air conditioning system doesn't cycle off as soon as it cools the passenger compartment).

9 With the compressor engaged, the clutch will make an audible click and the center of the clutch will rotate. After the system reaches operating temperature, feel the two pipes connected to the evaporator at the firewall **(see illustration)**.

10 The pipe leading from the condenser outlet to the evaporator (small tubing) should be cold, and the evaporator outlet line (the larger tubing that leads back to the compressor) should be slightly colder (3 to 10 degrees F). If the evaporator outlet is considerably warmer than the inlet, the system needs a charge. Insert a thermometer in the center air distribution duct while operating the air conditioning system **(see illustration)** - the temperature of the output air should be 35 to 40 degrees F below the ambient air temperature (down to approximately 40 degrees F). If the ambient (outside) air temperature is very high, say 110 degrees F, the duct air temperature may be as high as 60 degrees F, but generally the air conditioning is 35 to 40 degrees F cooler than the ambient air. If the air isn't as cold as it used to be, the system probably needs a charge. Further inspection or testing of the system is beyond the scope of the home mechanic and should be left to a professional.

11 Inspect the sight glass. If the refrigerant looks foamy when running, it's low **(see illustration)**. When ambient temperatures are very hot, bubbles may show in the sight glass even with the proper amount

14.10 Check the temperature of the output air in the center register with a thermometer - it should be 35 to 40 degrees below the ambient air temperature

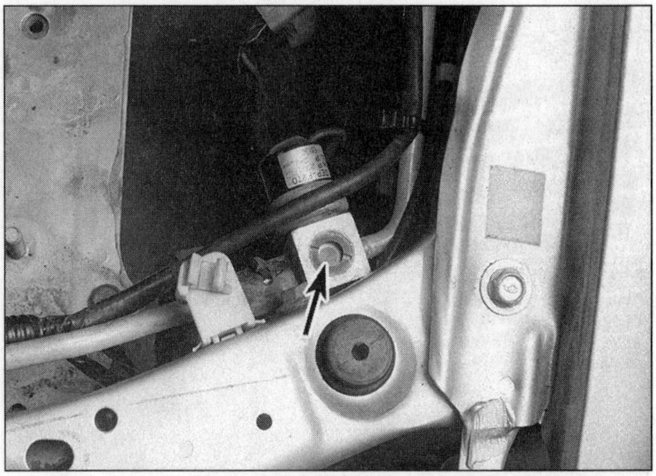

14.11 The sight glass is located on top of the receiver/drier (1990 through 1994 shown)

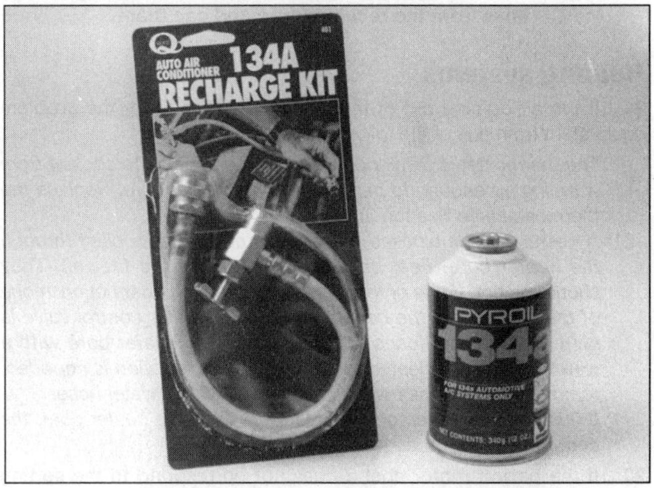

14.13 Refrigerant kit for R-134 recharging

of refrigerant. With the proper amount of refrigerant, when the air conditioning is turned off, the sight glass should show refrigerant that foams, then clears.

Adding refrigerant

Caution: *Refrigerant has changed from the use of R-12 through 1994 models, to the "environmentally friendly" R-134a used in 1995 and later models. The two refrigerants are NOT compatible. Even after purging and evacuating an R-12 system, there is enough residual oil and refrigerant in the hoses and components that simply filling the system with R-134a cannot be done. Special fittings and manifold gauge sets are used on the different refrigerant types so that an accidental hook-up of the two systems cannot be made. When replacing entire components, additional refrigerant oil should be added equal to the amount that is removed with the component being replaced. Refrigerant oils, just like refrigerant R-12 vs. R-134a, are not compatible. Be sure to read the can before adding any oil to the system, to make sure it is compatible with the type of system being repaired.*

Note: *Because of Federal regulations by the Environmental Protection Agency, R-12 refrigerant is not available for home-mechanic use, however, cans of R-134 refrigerant are commonly available in auto parts stores. Models with R-12 systems will have to be serviced at a dealership or air conditioning shop.*

1994 and earlier models

12 Because of Federal regulations implemented by the Environmental Protection Agency, R-12 refrigerant is not available for home-mechanic use. Model years 1990 through 1994 use R-12 refrigerant. Have the system discharged, evacuated, charged and leak tested by a qualified shop. Use only refrigerant oil compatible with your system. Refrigerant oils for use with refrigerant R-12 are not compatible with other oils.

1995 and later models

Refer to illustration 14.13

13 Buy an automotive charging kit at an auto parts store **(see illustration)**. A charging kit includes a 14-ounce can of R-134a refrigerant, a tap valve and a short section of hose that can be attached between the tap valve and the system low side service valve . The system low side service valve (charging port) is located on the larger air conditioning tubing line going to the firewall **(see illustration 14.9)**. Because one can of refrigerant may not be sufficient to bring the system charge up to the proper level, it's a good idea to buy a couple of additional cans. Try to find at least one can that contains red refrigerant dye. If the system is leaking, the red dye will leak out with the refrigerant and help you pinpoint the location of the leak.

14 Connect the charging kit by following the manufacturer's instructions. Back off the valve handle on the charging kit and screw the kit onto the refrigerant can, making sure first that the O-ring or rubber seal inside the threaded portion of the kit is in place. **Warning:** *Wear protective eye wear when dealing with pressurized refrigerant cans.*

15 Remove the dust cap from the low-side charging port and attach the quick-connect fitting on the kit hose. **Warning:** *DO NOT hook the charging kit hose to the system high side! The fittings on the charging kit are designed to fit only on the low side of the system.*

16 Warm the engine to normal operating temperature and turn on the air conditioner. Keep the charging kit hose away from the fan and other moving parts.

17 Turn the valve handle on the kit until the stem pierces the can, then back the handle out to release the refrigerant. You should be able to hear the rush of gas. Add refrigerant to the low side of the system until both the outlet and the evaporator inlet pipe feel about the same temperature. Allow stabilization time between each addition. **Warning:** *Never add more than two cans of refrigerant to the system. The can may tend to frost up, slowing the procedure. Wrap a shop towel wet with hot water around the bottom of the can to keep it from frosting.*

18 If you have an accurate thermometer, you can place it in the center air conditioning duct inside the vehicle to monitor the air temperature. A charged system that is working properly, should output air down to approximately 40 degrees F.

19 When the can is empty, turn the valve handle to the closed position and release the connection from the low-side port. Replace the dust cap.

20 Remove the charging kit from the can and store the kit for future use with the piercing valve in the UP position, to prevent inadvertently piercing the can on the next use.

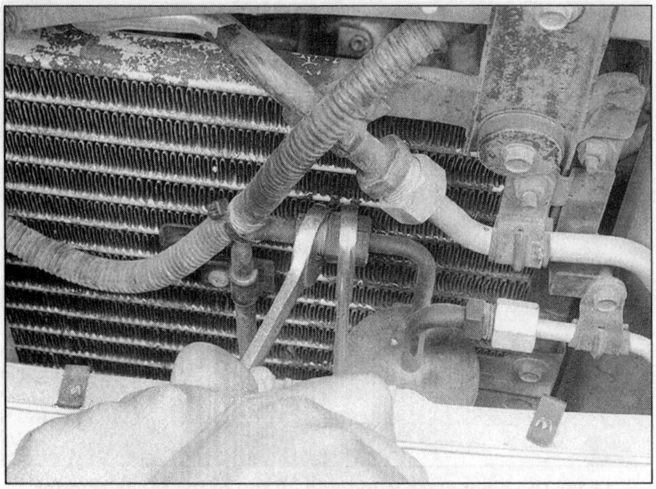

15.3 After the system has been discharged, remove the refrigerant line clamp bolt and disconnect the two refrigerant lines from the receiver/drier and cap them

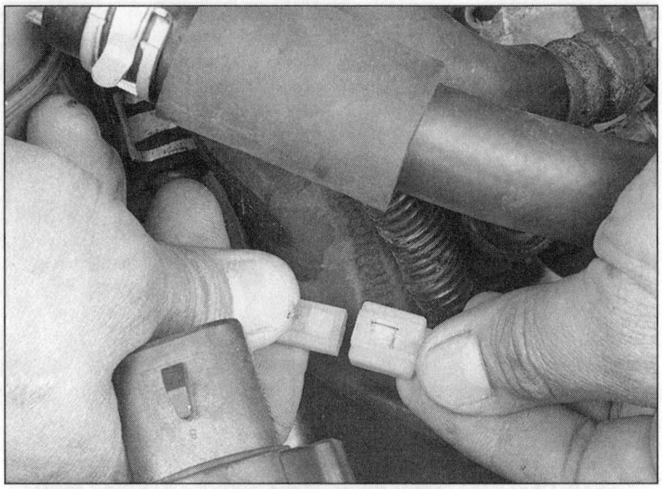

16.5 Disconnect the wiring harness connector at the compressor

Heating systems

21 If the air coming out of the heater vents isn't hot, the problem could stem from any of the following causes:

- a) *The thermostat is stuck open, preventing the engine coolant from warming up enough to carry heat to the heater core. Replace the thermostat* (see Section 3).
- b) *A heater hose is blocked, preventing the flow of coolant through the heater core. Feel both heater hoses at the firewall. They should be hot. If one of them is cold, there is an obstruction in one of the hoses or in the heater core, or the heater control valve is shut. Detach the hoses and back flush the heater core with a water hose. If the heater core is clear but circulation is impeded, remove the two hoses and flush them out with a water hose.*
- c) *If flushing fails to remove the blockage from the heater core, the core must be replaced.* (see Section 12).

22 If the blower motor speed does not correspond to the setting selected on the blower switch, the problem could be a bad fuse, circuit, switch, blower motor resistor or motor (see Sections 10 and 11).

23 If there isn't any air coming out of the vents:

- a) *Turn the ignition ON and activate the fan control. Place your ear at the heating/air conditioning register (vent) and listen. Most motors are audible. Can you hear the motor running?*
- b) *If you can't (and have already verified that the blower switch and the blower motor resistor are good), the blower motor itself is probably bad* (see Section 10).

24 If the carpet under the heater core is damp, or if antifreeze vapor or steam is coming through the vents, the heater core is leaking. Remove it (see Section 12) and install a new unit (most radiator shops will not repair a leaking heater core).

25 Inspect the drain hose from the heater/air conditioning assembly located under the vehicle; make sure it is not clogged.

15 Air conditioning receiver/drier - removal and installation

Refer to illustration 15.3

Warning: *The air conditioning system is under high pressure. Do not loosen any hose fittings or remove any components until the system has been discharged. Air conditioning refrigerant should be properly discharged into an EPA-approved recovery/recycling unit by a dealer service department or an automotive air conditioning repair facility. Always wear eye protection when disconnecting air conditioning system fittings.*

1 Have the refrigerant discharged and recovered by a qualified repair facility.

2 On 1990 through 1994 models, refer to Chapter 11 and remove the radiator grille. On 1995 and later models, remove the driver's side undercar splash shield and fender mud guard.

3 On 1995 and later models, remove the receiver/drier pressure switch electrical connector. Then, for all models, remove the refrigerant line clamp bolt and disconnect the refrigerant lines from the receiver/drier **(see illustration)**. Cap the open fittings to prevent entry of moisture.

4 Remove the receiver/drier mounting bolts and remove the receiver/drier.

5 Installation is the reverse of removal. Replace any O-rings with new ones specifically for the type of refrigerant in your system and lubricate them with refrigerant oil prior to installation. **Warning:** *Do not apply compressor oil to the fitting nuts.* Tighten the receiver/drier inlet and outlet fittings securely.

6 Have the system evacuated, charged and leak tested by the shop that discharged it. If the receiver was replaced, have them add about 0.3 ounces of new refrigerant oil to the high pressure side of the compressor. Use only refrigerant oil compatible with your system.

16 Air conditioning compressor - removal and installation

Refer to illustrations 16.5 and 16.6

Warning: *The air conditioning system is under high pressure. Do not loosen any hose fittings or remove any components until the system has been discharged. Air conditioning refrigerant should be properly discharged into an EPA-approved recovery/recycling unit by a dealer service department or an automotive air conditioning repair facility. Always wear eye protection when disconnecting air conditioning system fittings.*

1 Have the refrigerant discharged and recovered by a qualified repair facility.

2 Disconnect the negative cable from the battery.

3 Remove the undercover and splash shield on the passenger side from under the vehicle.

4 Remove the drivebelt from the compressor (see Chapter 1).

5 Disconnect the refrigerant lines and compressor electrical connector **(see illustration)**.

6 Unbolt the compressor and lift it from the vehicle **(see illustration)**.

7 If a new or rebuilt compressor is being installed, follow the directions supplied with the compressor regarding the proper level of refrigerant oil prior to installation.

8 Installation is the reverse of removal. Tighten the compressor mounting bolts securely. Replace any O-rings with new ones specifically for the type of refrigerant in your system and lubricate them with refrigerant oil prior to installation. **Warning:** *Do not apply compressor oil to the fitting nuts.* Tighten the refrigerant line bolts securely.

9 Have the system evacuated, recharged and leak tested by the shop that discharged it.

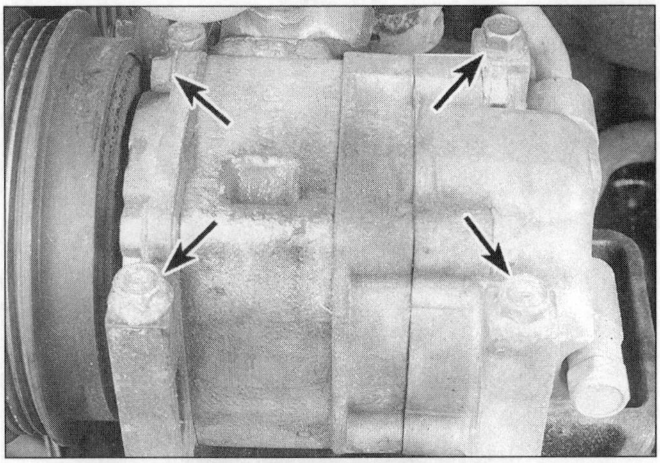

16.6 Remove the compressor mounting bolts (arrows) and remove the compressor

17 Air conditioning condenser- removal and installation

Warning: *The air conditioning system is under high pressure. Do not loosen any hose fittings or remove any components until the system has been discharged. Air conditioning refrigerant should be properly discharged into an EPA-approved recovery/recycling unit by a dealer service department or an automotive air conditioning repair facility. Always wear eye protection when disconnecting air conditioning system fittings.*

1 Have the refrigerant discharged and recovered by a qualified repair facility.

2 Refer to Chapter 11 and remove the radiator grille.

3 On 1990 through 1994 models, remove the receiver/drier (see Section 15).

4 Remove the undercover shield from under the vehicle. Insert a fin protector such as a sheet of cardboard between the radiator and condenser.

5 On 1990 through 1994 models, remove the radiator (see Section 5).

6 Disconnect the condenser inlet and outlet fittings. Immediately cap the open fittings to keep moisture and contamination out of the system.

7 Remove the condenser.

8 Check the condenser for cracks, damage, refrigerant leakage, bent fins, and distorted or damaged condenser inlet and outlet. Repair or replace the condenser as necessary.

9 Installation is the reverse of removal. Replace any O-rings with new ones specifically for the type of refrigerant in your system and lubricate them with refrigerant oil prior to installation. **Warning:** *Do not apply compressor oil to the fitting nuts. Tighten the condenser inlet and outlet fittings securely.*

10 Have the system evacuated, recharged and leak tested by the shop that discharged it. If the condenser was replaced, have the shop add about 0.9 ounces of new refrigerant oil for 1990 through 1994 models, or 0.5 ounces of new refrigerant oil for 1995 and later models, to the high pressure side of the compressor. Use only refrigerant oil compatible with your system.

18 Air conditioning evaporator and expansion valve - removal and installation

Refer to illustrations 18.2, 18.8, 18.11 and 18.15

Warning 1: *1995 and later models are equipped with airbags. The airbag is armed and can deploy (inflate) anytime the battery is connected. To prevent accidental deployment (and possible injury), turn the ignition key to LOCK and disconnect the negative battery cable whenever working near airbag components. After the battery is disconnected, wait at least two minutes before beginning work (the system has a back-up capacitor that must fully discharge). For more information see Chapter 12.*

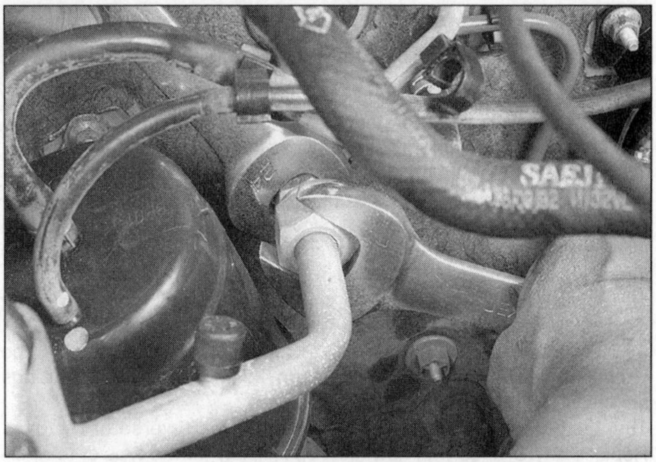

18.2 Use a back-up wrench when disconnecting the air conditioning lines at the firewall

18.8 Unlatch the seal plates on each side of the evaporator cooling unit

Warning 2: *The air conditioning system is under high pressure. Do not loosen any hose fittings or remove any components until the system has been discharged. Air conditioning refrigerant should be properly discharged into an EPA-approved recovery/recycling unit by a dealer service department or an automotive air conditioning repair facility. Always wear eye protection when disconnecting air conditioning system fittings.*

1 Have the refrigerant discharged and recovered by a qualified repair facility.

2 Disconnect the air conditioning lines at the firewall; use a back-up wrench to prevent damage the fittings **(see illustration)**. Cap the open fittings after disassembly to prevent the entry of air or dirt.

3 Remove the glove box (see Chapter 11). Remove the glove box cover inside the dash.

4 Remove the side panel from the dash on the passenger side.

5 Remove the underdash panel on the passenger side.

6 On 1995 and later models, remove the cooling unit duct. Disconnect the air INTAKE wire from the blower unit link.

7 On 1990 through 1994 models, disconnect the evaporator cooling unit electrical connector.

8 Unlatch the seal plates on each side of the evaporator cooling unit **(see illustration)**.

9 Remove the evaporator cooling unit nuts from the mounting studs at the firewall.

10 Remove the evaporator cooling unit.

11 Separate the lower and upper cooling unit housings **(see illustration)**.
12 Remove the evaporator.
13 Disconnect the expansion valve fittings and remove the expansion valve from the evaporator. Immediately cap the open fittings to keep moisture and contamination out of the system.
14 On 1990 through 1994 models, if necessary, remove the air conditioning thermoswitch from the upper cooling unit housing.
15 On 1995 and later models, if necessary, remove the air conditioning thermoswitch from the evaporator core and replace in the same location as removed.
16 Check the evaporator core and fittings for cracks or any other damage. Replace the evaporator if necessary.
17 Reinstall the expansion valve, replacing the gaskets on the expansion valve. Tighten the expansion valve inlet and outlet fittings securely.
18 Evaporator cooling unit installation is the reverse of removal. Replace any O-rings with new ones specifically for the type of refrigerant in your system and lubricate them with refrigerant oil prior to installation. **Warning:** *Do not apply compressor oil to the fitting nuts.* Tighten the evaporator cooling unit inlet and outlet fittings securely.
19 Have the system evacuated, charged and leak tested by the shop that discharged it. If the evaporator is replaced with a new unit, add 1.5 ounces of new refrigerant oil the high pressure side of the compressor. Use only refrigerant oil compatible with your system.

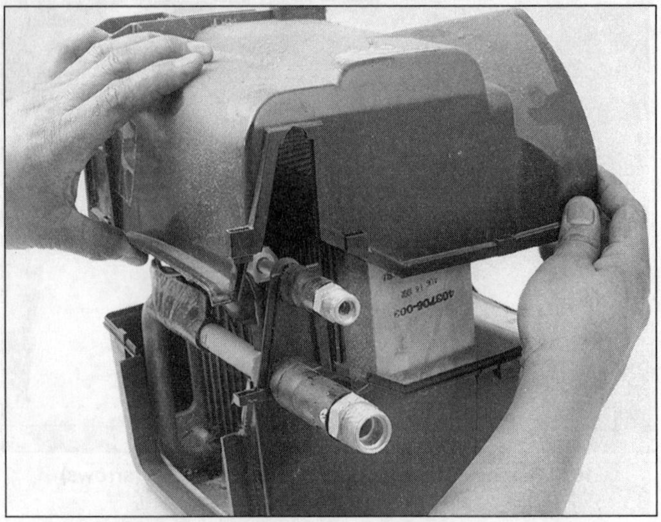

18.11 Remove the cooling unit housing clips, separate the two halves of the cooling unit housing and remove the evaporator core

Chapter 4
Fuel and exhaust systems

Contents

Specifications

Fuel system

Fuel pressure	
Fuel pump pressure (maximum)	
1990 and 1991	64 to 85 psi
1992 through 1994	64 to 92 psi
1995 and later	72 to 93 psi
Ignition ON, engine not running	38 to 46 psi
Engine idling	
1990 through 1994	30 to 37 psi
1995 and later	29 to 34 psi
Engine idling (vacuum hose from pressure regulator disconnected)	
1990 through 1994	38 to 46 psi
1995 and later	40 to 45 psi
Fuel system hold pressure (minimum)	21 psi
Fuel injector resistance	12 to 16 ohms
Idle Air Control (IAC) valve resistance	
1990 through 1994	11 to 13 ohms
1995 and later	10.7 to 12.3 ohms
Accelerator cable freeplay	
1990 through 1994	3/64 to 1/8 inch
1995 and later	3/64 to 3/32 inch

Idle Speed

All models	700 to 800 rpm

Torque specification

	Ft-lbs
Throttle body mounting bolts	14 to 19
Fuel rail mounting bolts	14 to 19
Air intake plenum bolts/nuts	14 to 18

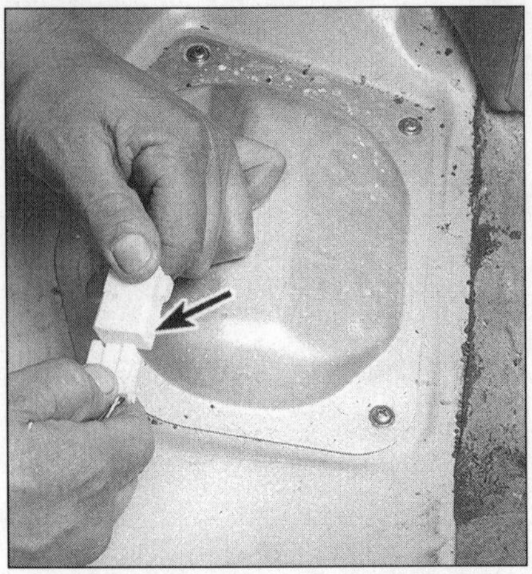

2.5 Unplug the fuel pump connector (arrow)

3.1 Connect a jumper wire to the GND and F/P terminals of the diagnostic connector

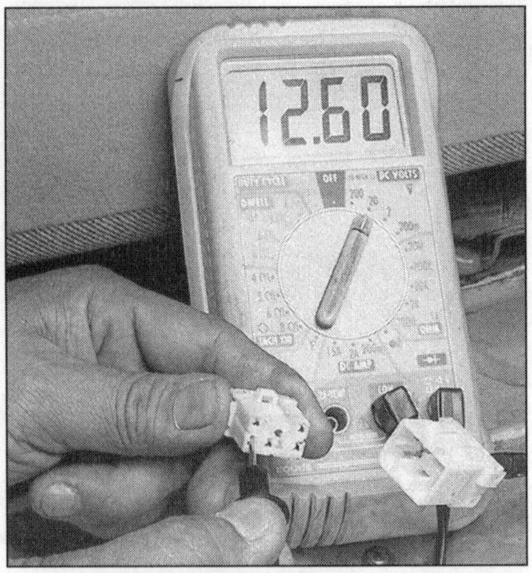

3.7 Check for battery voltage at the fuel pump electrical connector

1 General information

The fuel system consists of a fuel tank, an electric fuel pump (located in the fuel tank), an EFI/fuel pump relay, fuel injectors, a fuel pressure regulator, an air cleaner assembly and a throttle body unit. All models covered by this manual are equipped with the Multi Point Fuel Injection (MPFI) system.

Multi Point Fuel Injection (MPFI) system

Multi point fuel injection uses timed impulses to sequentially inject the fuel directly into the intake port of each cylinder. The injectors are controlled by the Powertrain Control Module (PCM). The PCM monitors various engine parameters and delivers the exact amount of fuel, in the correct sequence, into the intake ports. The 1.8L DOHC engine is also equipped with a Variable Inertia Charging System (VICS) which effectively varies the length of the intake air path, yielding higher torque and a wider torque band. The throttle body serves only to control the amount of air passing into the system. Because each cylinder is equipped with an injector mounted immediately adjacent to the intake valve, much better control of the fuel/air mixture ratio is possible.

Fuel pump and lines

Fuel is circulated from the fuel tank to the fuel injection system, and back to the fuel tank, through a pair of metal lines running along the underside of the vehicle. An electric fuel pump is attached to the fuel level sending unit inside the fuel tank. All excess fuel is routed back to the fuel tank through a separate return line.

The fuel pump will operate as long as the engine is cranking or running and the PCM is receiving ignition reference pulses from the electronic ignition system (see Chapter 5). If there are no reference pulses, the fuel pump will shut off after 2 or 3 seconds.

Exhaust system

The exhaust system includes an exhaust manifold fitted with an exhaust oxygen sensor, a catalytic converter, an exhaust pipe, and a muffler.

The catalytic converter is an emission control device added to the exhaust system to reduce pollutants. A single-bed converter is used in combination with a three-way (reduction) catalyst. Refer to Chapter 6 for more information regarding the catalytic converter.

2 Fuel pressure relief

Refer to illustration 2.5

Warning: *Gasoline is extremely flammable, so take extra precautions when you work on any part of the fuel system. Don't smoke or allow open flames or bare light bulbs near the work area, and don't work in a garage where a natural gas-type appliance (such as a water heater or a clothes dryer) with a pilot light is present. Since gasoline is carcinogenic, wear latex gloves when there's a possibility of being exposed to fuel, and, if you spill any fuel on your skin, rinse it off immediately with soap and water. Mop up any spills immediately and do not store fuel-soaked rags where they could ignite. The fuel system is under constant pressure, so, if any fuel lines are to be disconnected, the fuel pressure in the system must be relieved first. When you perform any kind of work on the fuel system, wear safety glasses and have a Class B type fire extinguisher on hand.*

1 Before servicing any fuel system component, you must relieve the fuel pressure to minimize the risk of fire or personnel injury.

2 Remove the fuel filler cap - this will relieve any pressure built up in the tank.

3 Remove the rear seat cushion (see Chapter 11).

4 On 1995 and later models remove the fuel pump access cover.

5 Disconnect the fuel pump electrical connector **(see illustration)**.

6 Start the engine and wait for the engine to stall, then turn the ignition key to OFF.

7 The fuel system is now depressurized. **Note:** *Place a rag around the fuel line before removing any hose clamp or fitting to prevent any residual fuel from spilling onto the engine.*

8 Connect the fuel pump electrical connector.

9 Install the rear seat cushion (see Chapter 11).

3 Fuel pump/fuel pressure - check

Warning: *Gasoline is extremely flammable, so take extra precautions when you work on any part of the fuel system. See the Warning in Section 2.*

Fuel pump operation check

Refer to illustrations 3.1, 3.7 and 3.9

1 Connect the diagnostic connector terminals F/P and GND with a jumper wire **(see illustration)**.

2 Remove the fuel filler cap.

3 Turn the ignition switch to ON (but do not start the engine).

4 The fuel pump is now activated. Listen for fuel pump noises from the fuel tank (under the rear seat).

5 Turn the ignition switch OFF.

6 Remove the jumper wire. Close the cap on the test connector.

7 If the fuel pump did not operate, measure the voltage between the fuel pump connector wire B/P and ground. You should read full battery voltage **(see illustration)**.

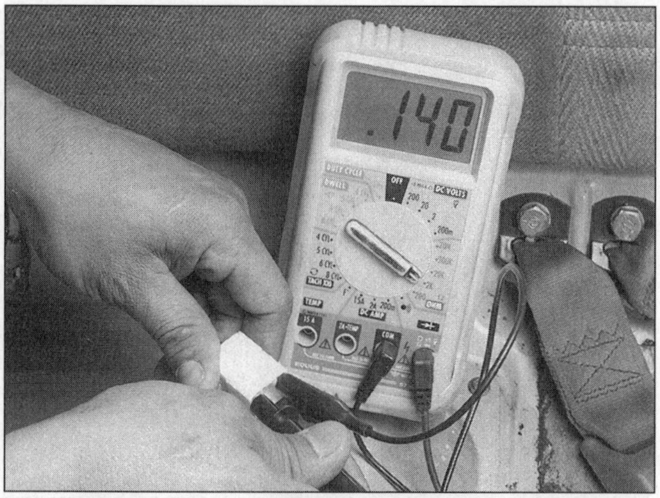

3.9 Check for continuity between B/P and B terminals of the fuel pump connector

8 If not correct, check the EFI 30-amp fuse and the circuit opening/fuel pump relays (see Steps 32 through 38).
9 If the relay checks correctly, check for continuity between fuel pump connector terminals B/P and B (on the pump side) **(see illustration)**.
10 If there is no continuity, check the pump's ground circuit for continuity and repair it as necessary.
11 If there is still no continuity, replace the fuel pump (see Section 5).
12 Reconnect the cable to the battery.

Fuel pressure check

Refer to illustration 3.13

13 Using a T-fitting, install the fuel pressure gauge in the main fuel hose going from the top of the fuel filter to the engine **(see illustration)**.
14 Perform the pressure check procedure (see Steps 1 through 4) and compare your readings to the pressures in this Chapter's Specifications.

a) *If the pressure is high, check for a restricted fuel return line. If the line is clear, replace the pressure regulator.*
b) *If the pressure is low, pinch the fuel return line. If the pressure goes up, replace the fuel pressure regulator. If the pressure does not increase, check the fuel feed line, the fuel pump and the fuel filter.*

15 Remove the jumper wire from the diagnostic connector.
16 Start the engine and with the engine idling:

a) *Measure the fuel pressure and compare your reading to the fuel pressure listed in this Chapter's Specifications.*
b) *If the pressure is not as specified, check the vacuum sensing hose and fuel pressure regulator (see Steps 18 through 22).*

17 Stop the engine and verify that the fuel pressure remains above the minimum system hold pressure listed in this Chapter's Specifications for five minutes after the engine is turned off. If the pressure bleeds down, the fuel pressure regulator, the fuel pump or a fuel injector may be leaking.

Fuel pressure regulator check

Refer to illustration 3.18

18 Disconnect the pressure regulator vacuum hose and plug the supply hose or pipe. Connect a hand-held vacuum pump to the regulator. Start the engine and read the fuel pressure gauge without vacuum applied to the fuel pressure regulator. Apply vacuum to the regulator and check the fuel pressure again **(see illustration)**. The fuel pressure should decrease as vacuum increases.
19 Reconnect the vacuum hose to the regulator and check the fuel

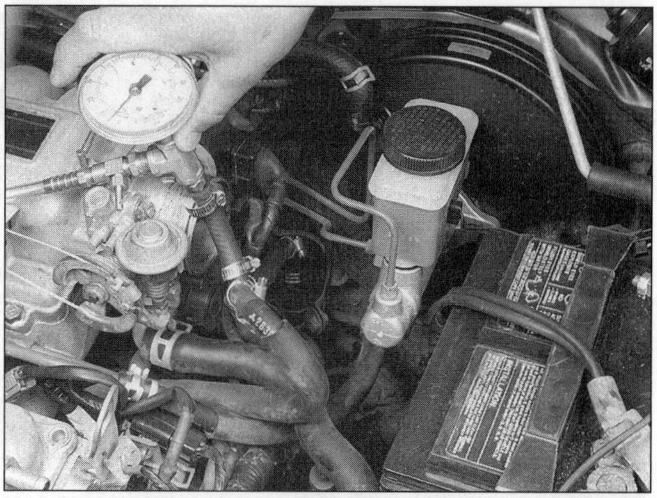

3.13 Measure the fuel pump pressure at the fuel filter

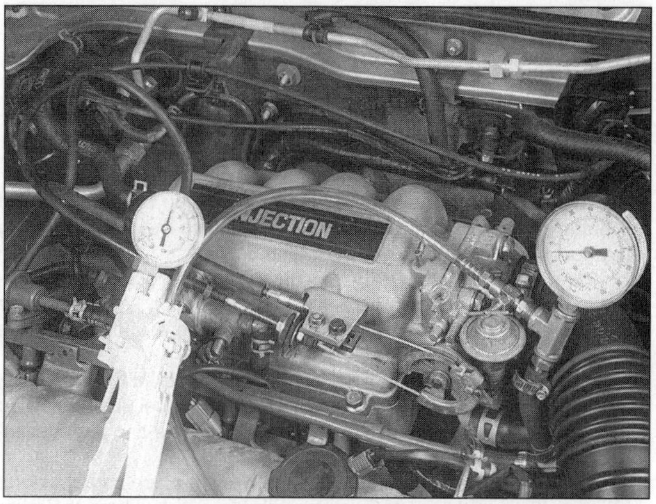

3.18 First check the fuel pressure without vacuum applied to the fuel pressure regulator (arrow) and then with vacuum applied - fuel pressure should DECREASE as vacuum INCREASES

pressure at idle, comparing your reading with the value listed in this Chapter's Specifications. Disconnect the vacuum hose and watch the gauge - the pressure should increase as soon as the hose is disconnected. If the pressure at idle was too high (with the hose connected), connect a vacuum gauge and check for vacuum in the supply line. If there is no reading on the gauge, check the air intake plenum and intake manifold for a vacuum leak.
20 If the fuel pressure is LOW, pinch the fuel return line shut and watch the gauge. If the pressure doesn't rise, the fuel pump is defective or there is a restriction in the fuel feed line. If the pressure rises sharply, replace the fuel pressure regulator (see Section 13).
21 If the indicated fuel pressure is too high, relieve the fuel pressure (see Section 2), disconnect the fuel return line and blow through it to check for blockage. If there is no blockage, replace the fuel pressure regulator (see Section 13).
22 If the fuel pressure does not fluctuate as described in Step 19, and vacuum is present at the hose, replace the fuel pressure regulator (see Section 13).
23 Depressurize the fuel system (see Section 2). Carefully remove the fuel pressure gauge. Be sure to cover the fitting with a rag before loosening it.
24 Wipe up any spilled gasoline.
25 Start the engine and check for leaks.

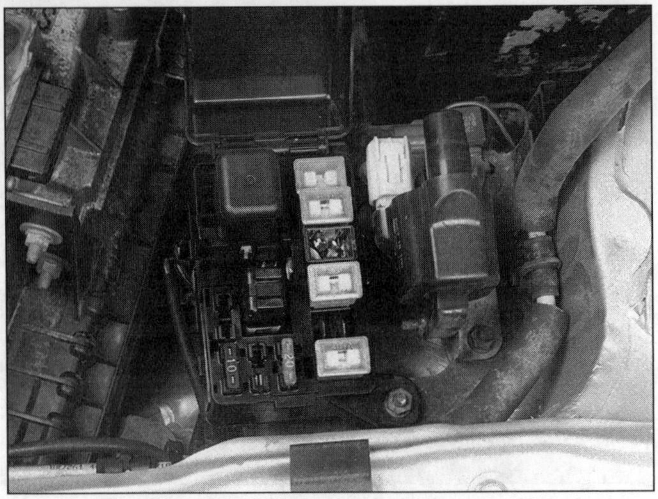

3.27 Remove the EFI main relay (arrow)

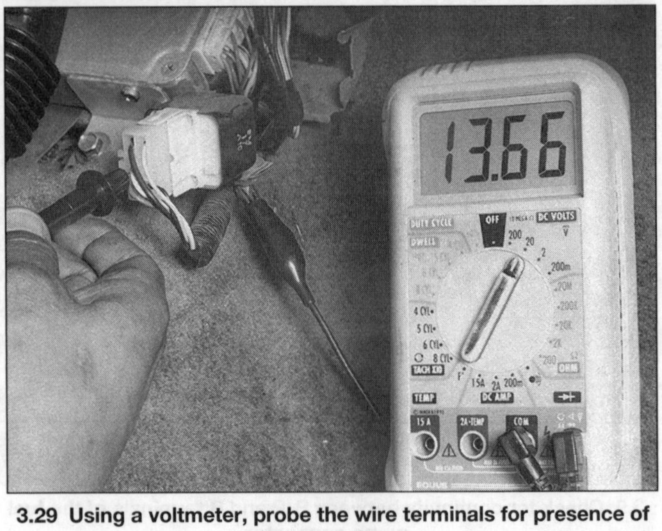

3.29 Using a voltmeter, probe the wire terminals for presence of battery voltage

EFI main relay, circuit opening relay (1990 through 1992 models) and fuel pump relay checks (1993 and later models)

Voltage checks

Refer to illustrations 3.27 and 3.29

26 There are two relays involved in the fuel pump circuit. First, test for battery voltage to the EFI main relay and then the circuit opening relay (fuel pump relay on 1993 and later models).

27 Remove the EFI main relay from the main fuse block **(see illustration)** in the engine compartment and with the ignition key ON (engine not running), check for battery voltage across the A and B terminals **(see illustration 3.32)**.

28 If battery voltage is present, insert the relay back in the fuse block and check for battery voltage at the circuit opening/fuel pump relay. To access the relay you will have to remove the console and the passenger side wall (see Chapter 11).

29 Leave the circuit opening/fuel pump relay in place and check for battery voltage at the relay by probing the terminals where the wires enter the connector. The following conditions should exist.

a) *For 1990 through 1994 models, with the ignition switch ON there should be full battery voltage at the LIGHT GREEN and WHITE/RED STRIPE wire terminals* **(see illustration)**.
b) *For 1995 and later models, with the ignition switch ON there should be full battery voltage at the two WHITE/RED STRIPE wire terminals.*

30 If battery voltage is present at the relay connectors, check the relays.

EFI main relay

Refer to illustration 3.32

31 Verify that the relay clicks when turning the ignition switch from OFF to ON and back to OFF, then remove the EFI main relay **(see illustration 3.35)** from the fuse block.

32 Using an ohmmeter check for continuity across A and B **(see illustration)**. Check that there is no continuity across terminals C and D.

33 Apply battery voltage across terminals A and B. Using an ohmmeter, check across terminals C and D. Continuity should exist. If the test results are incorrect, replace the relay.

Circuit opening relay (1990 through 1992 models) and fuel pump relay (1993 and 1994 models)

Refer to illustration 3.34

34 Using an ohmmeter, check the resistance between the terminals:

a) *Between STA and E1, there should be 21 to 43 ohms*
b) *Between B and Fc, there should be 109 to 226 ohms*
c) *Between B and Fp there should be infinite resistance*

35 Apply battery voltage across terminals STA and E1. Using an ohmmeter, check for continuity across terminals +B and Fp. Continuity should exist. If the test results are incorrect, replace the relay.

Fuel pump relay (1995 and later models)

Refer to illustration 3.36

36 Using an ohmmeter, check for continuity across terminals A and B **(see illustration)**; there should be continuity. Check that there is no continuity across terminals C and E.

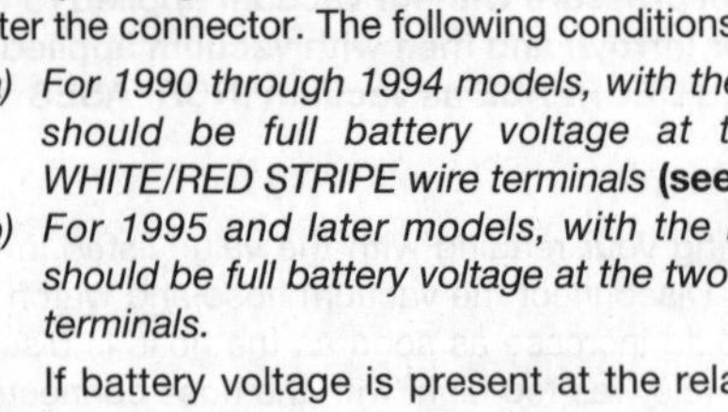

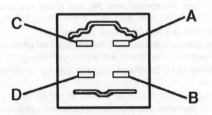

3.32 EFI main relay terminal identification (1990 through 1994 models)

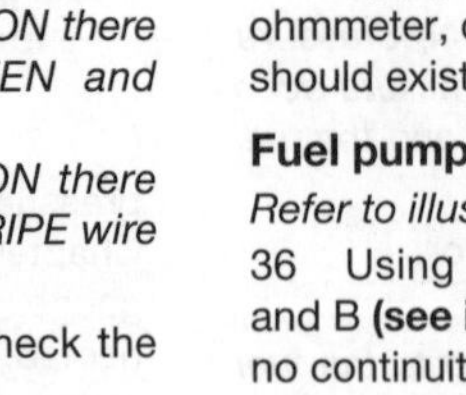

3.34 Circuit opening relay/fuel pump relay terminal identification

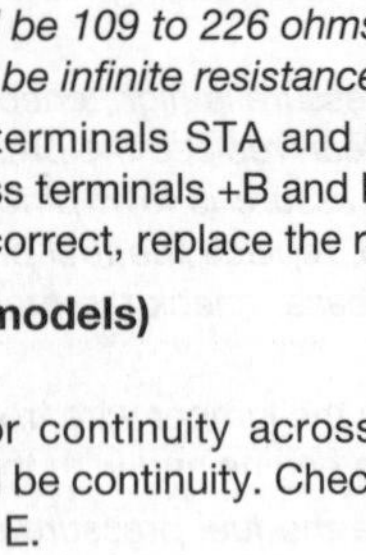

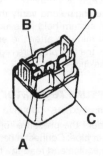

3.36 Fuel pump relay terminal identification (1995 and later models)

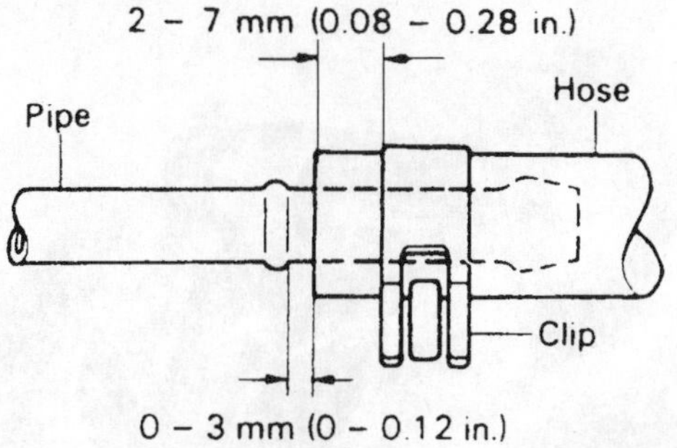

4.6 When attaching a section of rubber hose to a metal fuel line, be sure to overlap the hose as shown, secure it to the line with a new hose clamp of the proper type

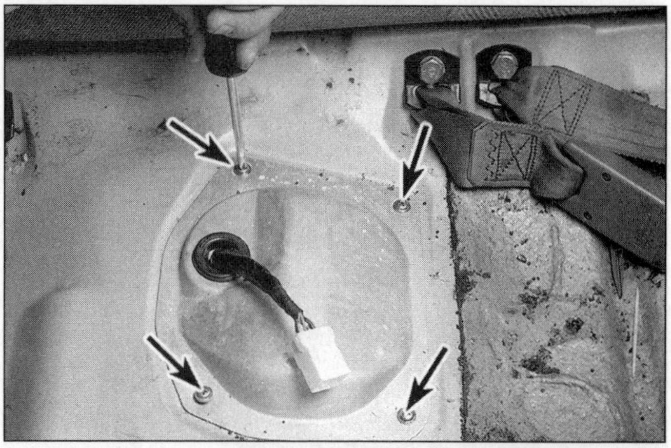

5.4 Remove the access cover screws (arrows) and pull up the cover

5.5a Unplug the fuel pump electrical connector . . .

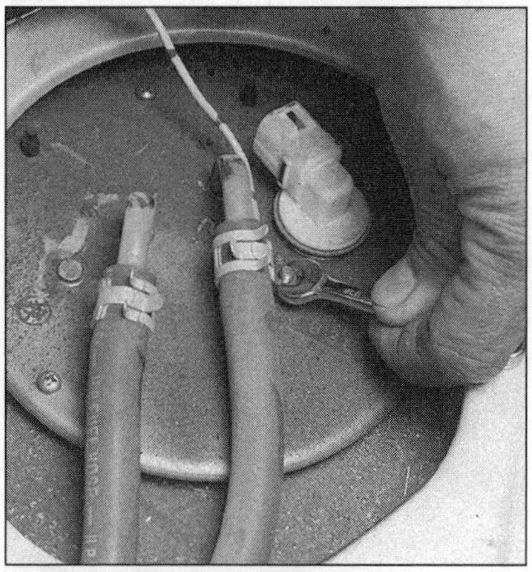

5.5b . . . then remove the terminal nut and wire on the top of the pump

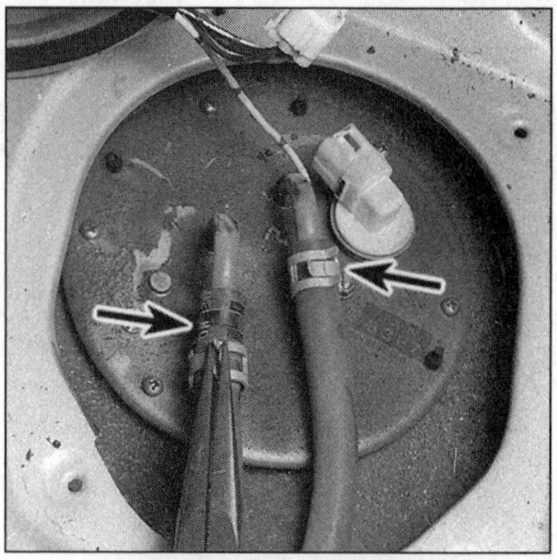

5.6 Disconnect the at the fuel supply hose (right arrow) and fuel return hose (left arrow)

37 Apply battery voltage across terminals A and B. Using an ohmmeter, check for continuity across terminals C and E **(see illustration 3.44)**. Continuity should exist. If the test results are incorrect, replace the relay.

4 Fuel lines and fittings - inspection and replacement

Warning: *Gasoline is extremely flammable, so take extra precautions when you work on any part of the fuel system. See the Warning in Section 2.*

Inspection

1 Once in a while, you will have to raise the vehicle to service or replace some component (an exhaust pipe hanger, for example). Whenever you work under the vehicle, always inspect fuel lines and all fittings and connections for damage or deterioration.

2 Check all hoses and pipes for cracks, kinks, deformation or obstructions.

3 Make sure all hoses and pipe clips attach their associated hoses or pipes securely to the underside of the vehicle.

4 Verify all hose clamps attaching rubber hoses to metal fuel lines or pipes are snug enough to assure a tight fit between the hoses and pipes.

Replacement

Refer to illustration 4.6

5 If you must replace any damaged sections, use original equipment replacement hoses or pipes constructed from exactly the same material as the section you are replacing. Do not install substitutes constructed from inferior or inappropriate material or you could cause a fuel leak or a fire.

6 Always, before detaching or disassembling any part of the fuel line system, note the routing of all hoses and pipes and the orientation of all clamps and clips to assure that replacement sections are installed in exactly the same manner. When attaching hoses to metal lines, overlap them as shown **(see illustration)**.

7 Before detaching any part of the fuel system, be sure to relieve the fuel line and tank pressure (see Section 2).

5 Fuel pump - removal and installation

Refer to illustrations 5.4, 5.5a, 5.5b, 5.6, 5.7, 5.8 and 5.9

Warning: *Gasoline is extremely flammable, so take extra precautions when you work on any part of the fuel system. See the Warning in Section 2.*

1 Remove the fuel tank cap. Depressurize the fuel system (see Section 2).

2 Disconnect the cable from the negative terminal of the battery.

3 Remove the rear seat cushion (see Chapter 11).

4 Remove the fuel pump access cover **(see illustration)**.

5 Unplug the electrical connector and disconnect the wire attached to the top of the fuel pump **(see illustrations)**.

6 Disconnect the fuel supply and return hoses from the pump **(see illustration)**.

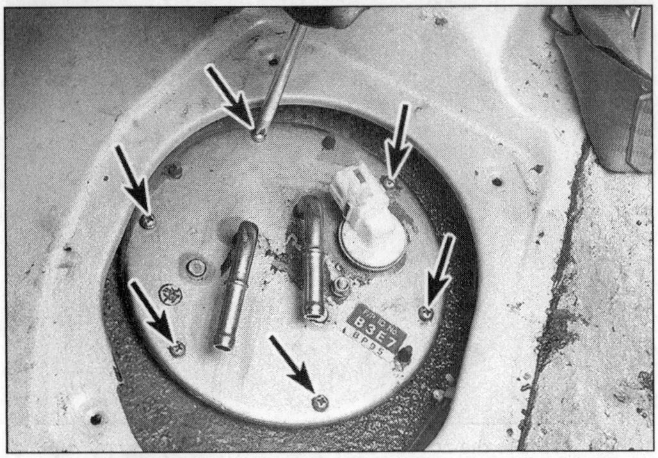

5.7 Remove the screws (arrows) securing the pump in the fuel tank

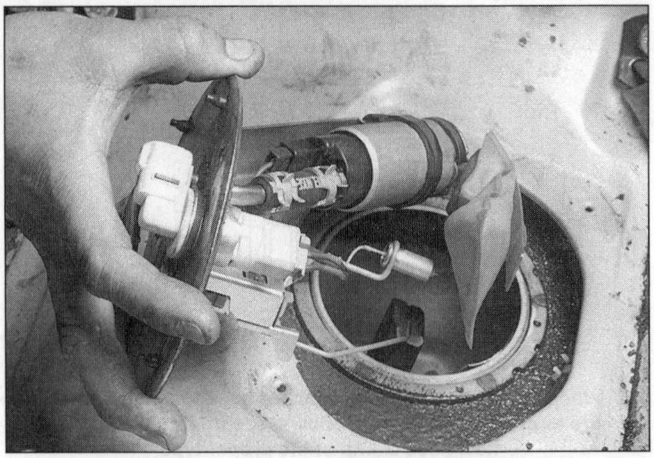

5.8 Lift the fuel pump assembly from the fuel tank at an angle so as not to damage the inlet screen or float arm

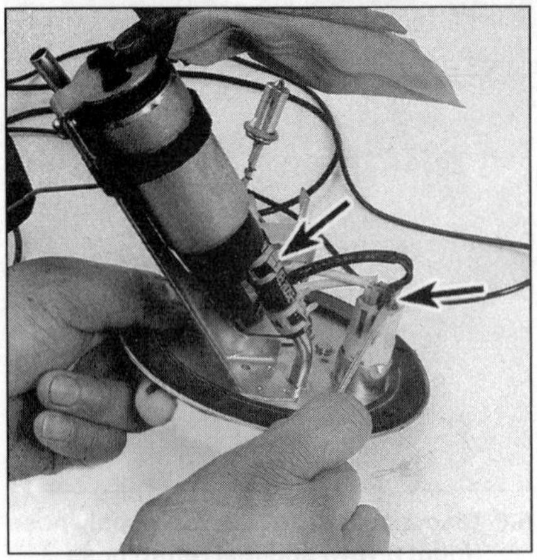

5.9 Disconnect the fuel pump electrical connector and the hose clamp (arrows)

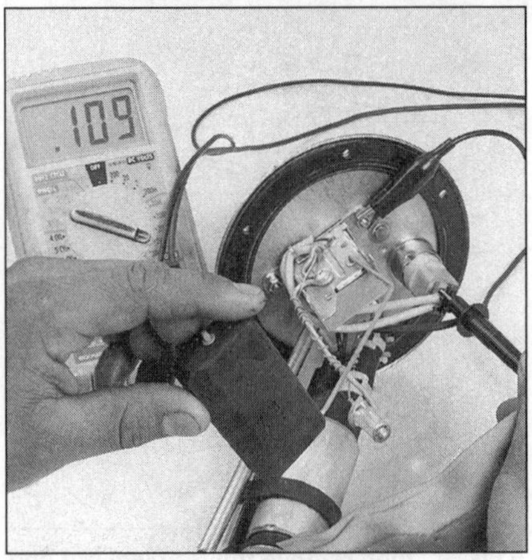

6.3a Resistance with the float arm down (tank empty) should be about 110 ohms

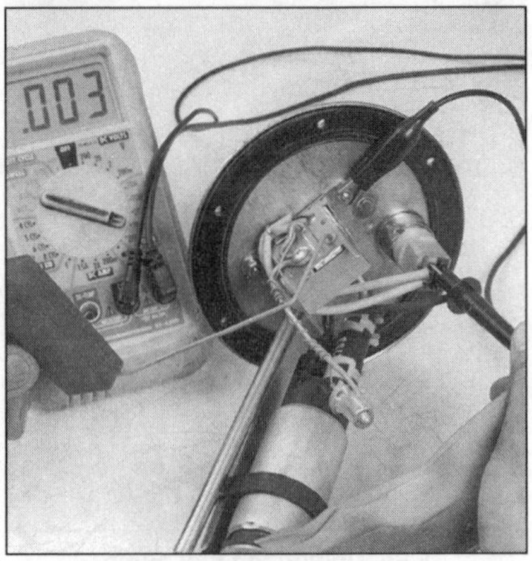

6.3b Resistance with the float arm up (tank full) should be 2 to 4 ohms

7 Remove the fuel pump retaining screws **(see illustration)**.

8 Carefully lift the fuel pump assembly out of the fuel tank **(see illustration)**.

9 Disconnect the electrical connector and move the hose clamp clear of the pump fitting **(see illustration)**.

10 Remove the band securing the pump to the bracket.

11 Remove the bracket at the bottom of the pump with the rubber mount.

12 Remove the fuel pump.

13 Remove the sock filter from the bottom of the pump and inspect it for contamination. If it is dirty, replace it.

14 Installation is the reverse of removal. Install a new O-ring set (O-ring, cap and spacer) at the hose connection and a new tank seal during installation. **Note:** *After installing the fuel pump to the bracket, pull the pump down so it is seated tightly against the pad on the bottom of the bracket, then position the hose clamps.*

6 Fuel level sending unit - check and replacement

Warning: *Gasoline is extremely flammable, so take extra precautions when you work on any part of the fuel system. See the Warning in Section 2.*

Check

Refer to illustrations 6.3a and 6.3b

1 The fuel level sending unit is part of the fuel pump assembly mounted in the fuel tank.

2 Remove the fuel pump assembly (see Section 5).

3 Using an ohmmeter, check the resistance of the sending unit with the float arm completely down (tank empty) and with the arm up (tank full) **(see illustrations)**. The resistance should change steadily from 110 ohms to approximately 2 to 4 ohms.

4 If the readings are incorrect, replace the sending unit.

Replacement

Refer to illustrations 6.6 and 6.7

5 Remove the fuel pump assembly from the fuel tank (see Section 5).

6 Disconnect the electrical connection to the fuel level sending unit **(see illustration)**.

7 Remove the nut securing the sending unit bracket and separate the sending unit from the assembly **(see illustration)**.

8 Installation is the reverse of removal.

7 Fuel tank - removal and installation

Refer to illustrations 7.6, 7.9a, 7.9b and 7.10

Warning: *Gasoline is extremely flammable, so take extra precautions when you work on any part of the fuel system. See the Warning in Section 2.*

1 This procedure is much easier to perform if the fuel tank is empty. Some models may have a drain plug for this purpose. If for some rea-

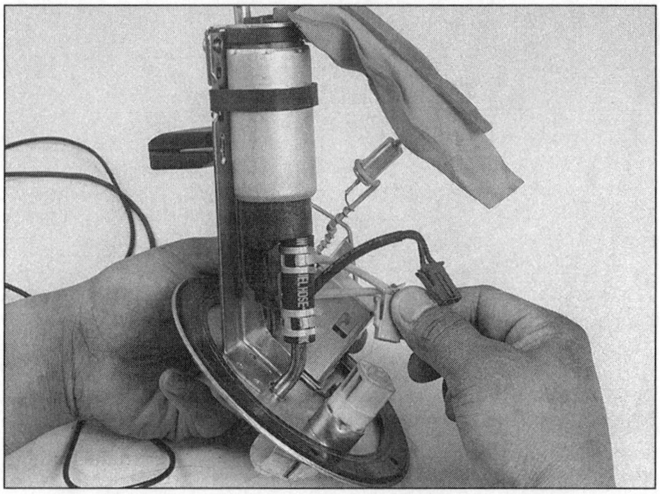

6.6 Disconnect the sending unit electrical connector

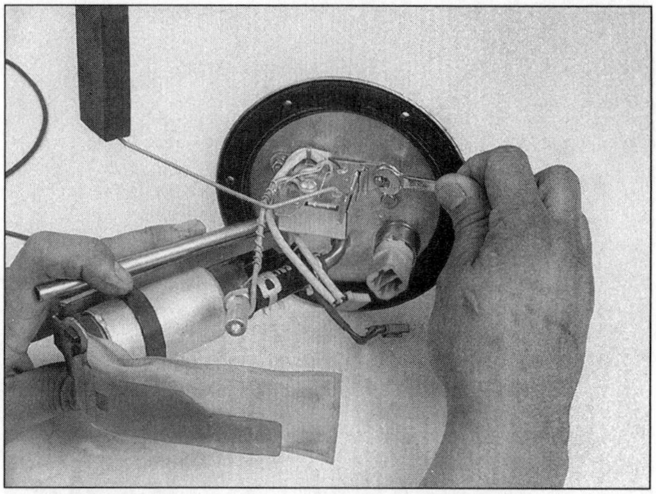

6.7 Remove the sending unit retaining nut

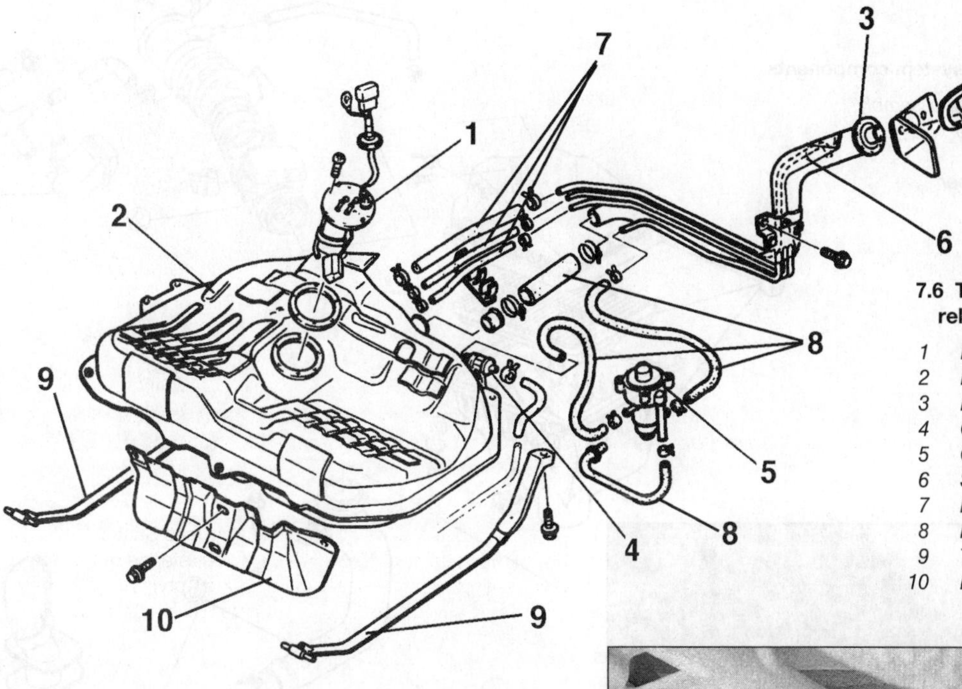

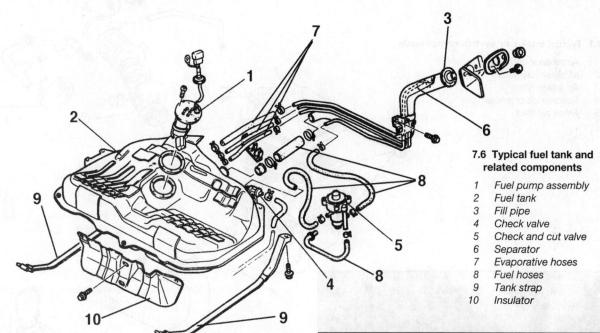

7.6 Typical fuel tank and related components

1. *Fuel pump assembly*
2. *Fuel tank*
3. *Fill pipe*
4. *Check valve*
5. *Check and cut valve*
6. *Separator*
7. *Evaporative hoses*
8. *Fuel hoses*
9. *Tank strap*
10. *Insulator*

son the drain plug can't be removed, postpone the job until the tank is empty or siphon the fuel into an approved container using a siphoning kit (available at most auto parts stores). **Warning:** *Do not start the siphoning action by mouth!*

2 Remove the fuel filler cap to relieve fuel tank pressure. Relieve the fuel system pressure (see Section 2)

3 Detach the cable from the negative terminal of the battery.

4 If the tank is full or nearly full, drain the fuel into an approved container.

5 Raise the vehicle and place it securely on jackstands.

6 Familiarize yourself with the layout of the fuel tank assembly before proceeding **(see illustration)**.

7 Remove the insulator from the front of the fuel tank. Refer to Section 5 and disconnect the fuel pump hoses and electrical connectors.

8 Support the fuel tank with a floor jack. Place a sturdy plank between the jack head and the fuel tank to protect the tank.

9 Disconnect the fuel lines and the evaporative hoses at the tank **(see illustrations)**. **Note:** *Be sure to plug the hoses to prevent leakage*

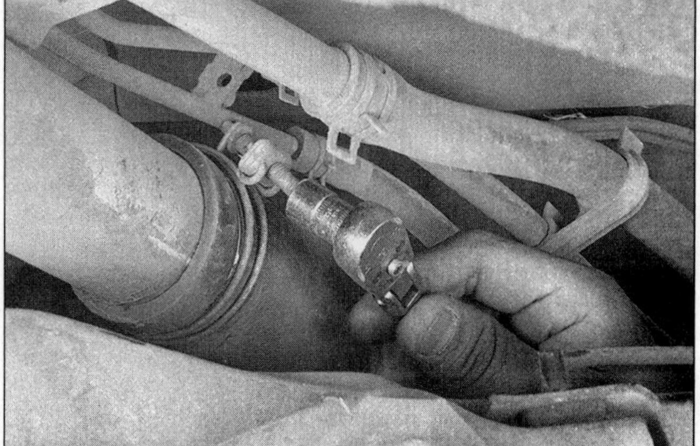

7.9a Loosen the clamp that retains the fuel filler hose

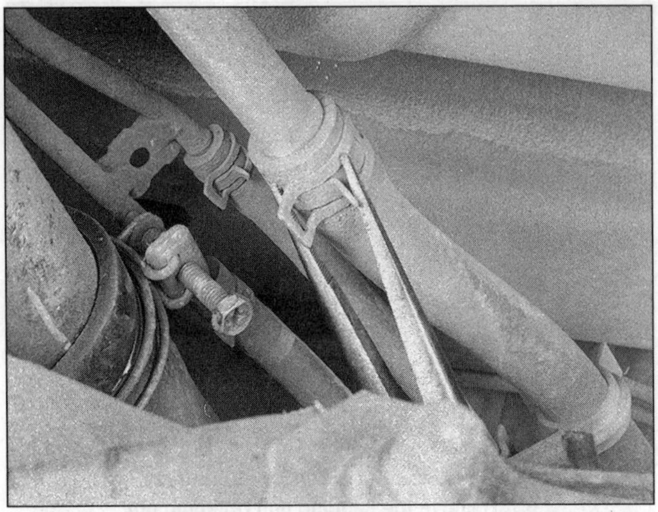

7.9b Loosen the clamp and detach the fuel evaporative hoses from the tank

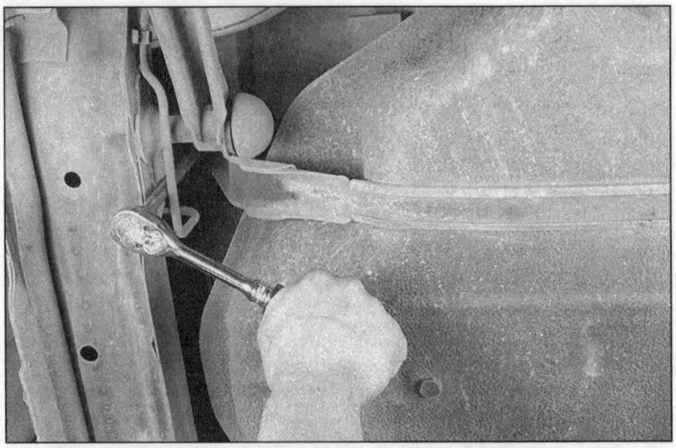

7.10 Remove the fuel tank strap bolts (arrows) from the body

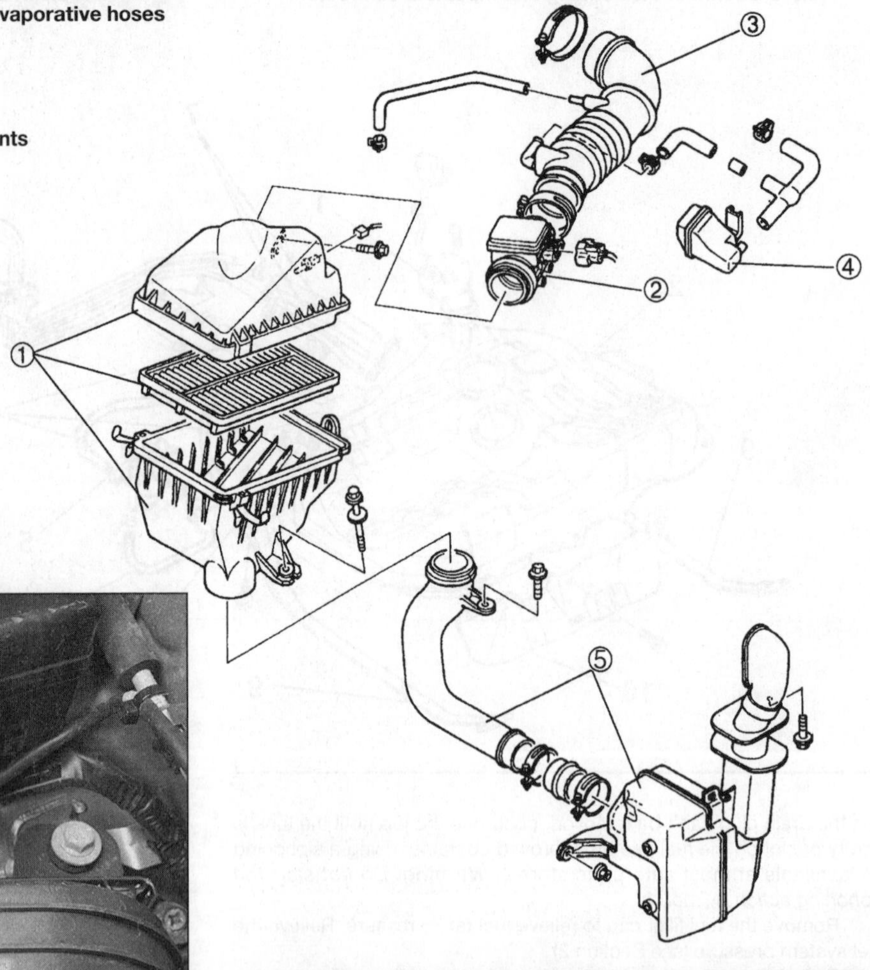

9.1 Typical intake air system components

1. *Air cleaner and filter assembly*
2. *Mass airflow sensor*
3. *Air intake hose*
4. *Resonance chamber*
5. *Fresh air duct*

9.2 Release the electrical connector lock tabs and unplug the connector

and contamination of the fuel system.

10 Remove the bolts from the fuel tank retaining straps **(see illustration)**.

11 Remove the tank from the vehicle.

12 Installation is the reverse of removal.

8 Fuel tank cleaning and repair - general information

1 Any repairs to the fuel tank or filler neck should be carried out by a professional who has experience in this critical and potentially dangerous work. Even after cleaning and flushing of the fuel system, explosive fumes can remain and ignite during repair of the tank.

2 If the fuel tank is removed from the vehicle, it should not be placed in an area where sparks or open flames could ignite the fumes coming out of the tank. Be especially careful inside garages where a natural gas-type appliance is located, because the pilot light could cause an explosion.

9.3 Remove the clamp and separate the hose from the valve cover

9.4 Loosen the clamp and pull the air intake hose from the throttle body

9.5 Loosen the clamp and pull the air intake hose from the resonance chamber

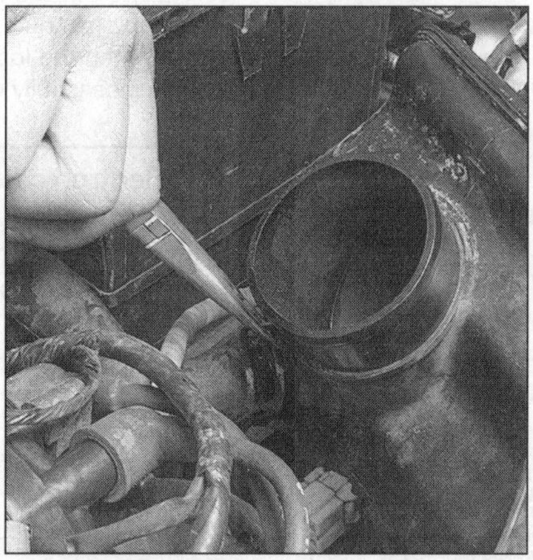

9.6 Disconnect the smaller air hose from the resonance chamber

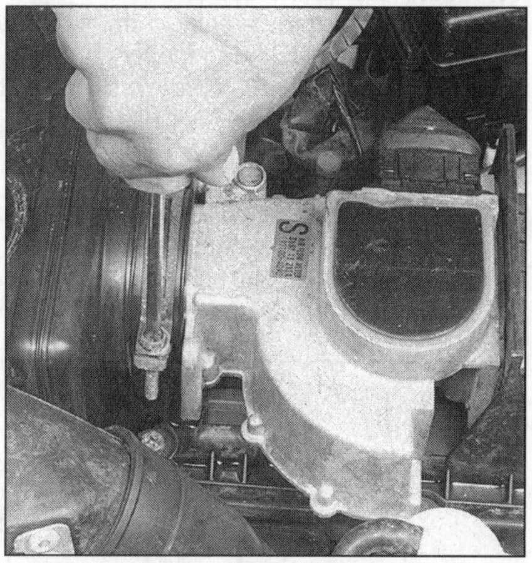

9.7 Loosen the hose clamp at the air filter and remove the resonance chamber

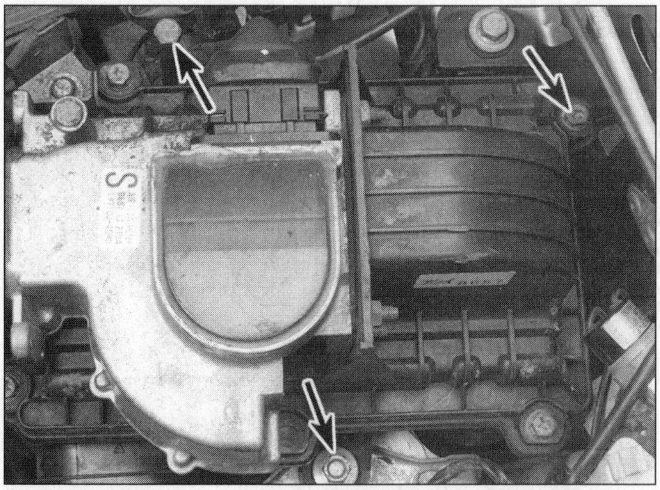

9.8 Remove the air cleaner housing mounting bolts

9 Air cleaner assembly - removal and installation

Refer to illustrations 9.1, 9.2, 9.3, 9.4, 9.5, 9.6, 9.7 and 9.8

1 Familiarize yourself with the intake air system components before proceeding **(see illustration)**.

2 Disconnect the mass airflow sensor electrical connector **(see illustration)**.

3 Locate the hose going from the air intake to the valve cover and disconnect it from the valve cover **(see illustration)**.

4 Loosen the air intake hose clamp at the throttle body and detach the air intake hose **(see illustration)**.

5 Loosen the air intake hose clamp at the resonance chamber and remove the hose **(see illustration)**.

6 Use a needle-nose pliers to release the clamp on the small hose at the resonance chamber and disconnect the hose **(see illustration)**.

7 Loosen the hose clamp at the air cleaner housing and remove the resonance chamber **(see illustration)**.

8 Remove the attaching bolt(s) **(see illustration)** and remove the air cleaner assembly from the engine compartment.

9 Installation is the reverse of removal.

10 Accelerator cable - removal, installation and adjustment

Refer to illustrations 10.2 and 10.3

Removal

1 Detach the cable from the negative terminal of the battery.

2 Loosen the locknut on the threaded portion of the throttle cable at

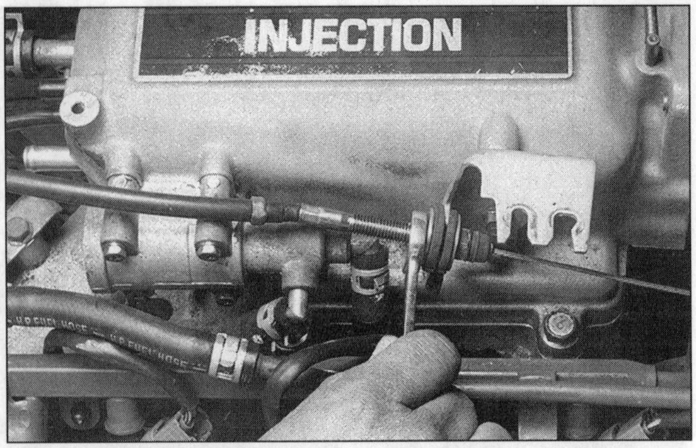

10.2 Loosen the locknuts on the accelerator cable

10.3 Rotate the throttle lever and remove the cable end from the slot

the plenum **(see illustration)**.

3 Rotate the throttle lever and slip the throttle cable end out of the slot in the lever **(see illustration)**.

4 Detach the throttle cable from the accelerator pedal and release the cable guide attached to the firewall.

5 From the engine compartment side of the firewall, pull the cable through the firewall.

Installation and adjustment

6 Installation is the reverse of removal. Make sure the cable casing grommet seats properly in the firewall.

7 To adjust the cable, fully depress the accelerator pedal and check that the throttle is fully opened.

8 Measure the play in the accelerator and compare your measurement to that listed in this Chapter's Specifications.

9 If the throttle is not fully opened and/or if the play is incorrect, loosen the locknuts, and adjust the cable.

10 Tighten the locknuts and recheck the adjustment. Make sure the throttle closes fully when the pedal is released.

11 Electronic Fuel Injection (EFI) system - general information

Refer to illustrations 11.1a and 11.1b

1 These models are equipped with an Electronic Fuel Injection (EFI)

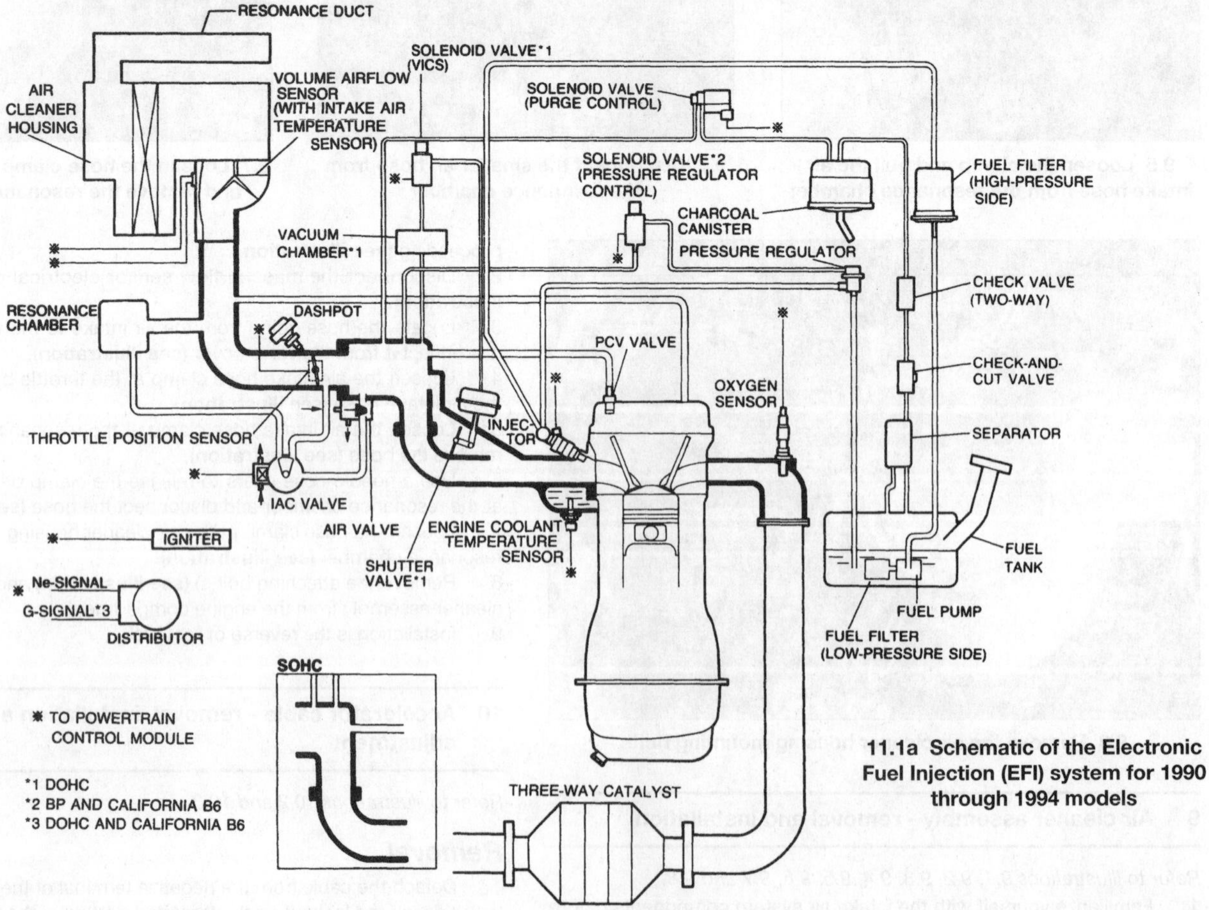

11.1a Schematic of the Electronic Fuel Injection (EFI) system for 1990 through 1994 models

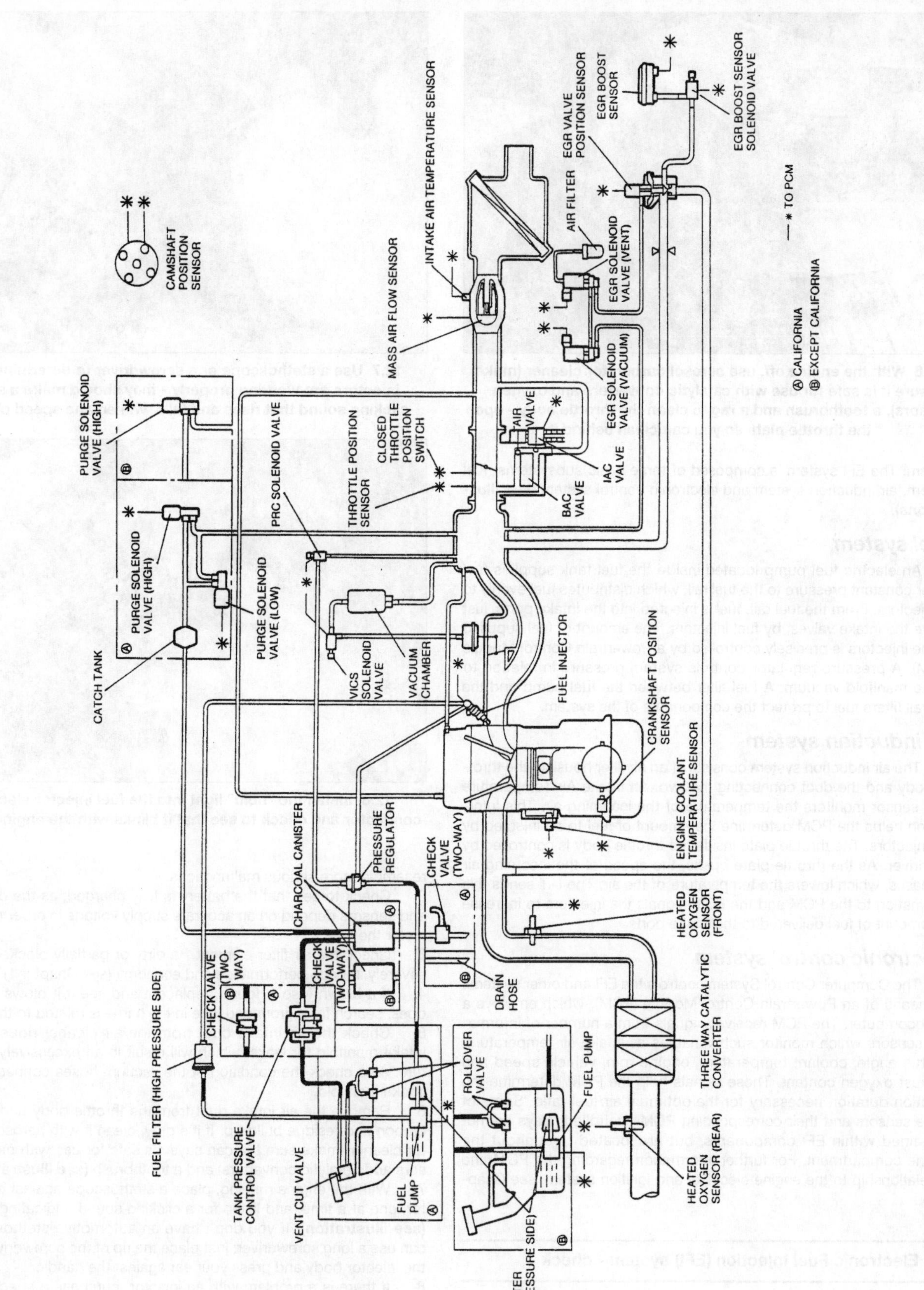
CAMSHAFT POSITION SENSOR
INTAKE AIR TEMPERATURE SENSOR
MASS AIR FLOW SENSOR
AIR FILTER
EGR VALVE POSITION SENSOR
EGR BOOST SENSOR
EGR BOOST SENSOR SOLENOID VALVE
EGR SOLENOID VALVE (VENT)
EGR SOLENOID VALVE (VACUUM)
— * TO PCM
Ⓐ CALIFORNIA
Ⓑ EXCEPT CALIFORNIA
PURGE SOLENOID VALVE (HIGH)
PURGE SOLENOID VALVE (HIGH)
PURGE SOLENOID VALVE (LOW)
CATCH TANK
PRC SOLENOID VALVE
THROTTLE POSITION SENSOR
CLOSED THROTTLE POSITION SWITCH
AIR VALVE
IAC VALVE
BAC VALVE
VICS SOLENOID VALVE
VACUUM CHAMBER
FUEL INJECTOR
CRANKSHAFT POSITION SENSOR
ENGINE COOLANT TEMPERATURE SENSOR
CHARCOAL CANISTER
PRESSURE REGULATOR
CHECK VALVE (TWO-WAY)
CHECK VALVE (TWO-WAY)
CHECK VALVE (TWO WAY)
HEATED OXYGEN SENSOR (FRONT)
DRAIN HOSE
FUEL FILTER (HIGH PRESSURE SIDE)
CHECK VALVE
THREE WAY CATALYTIC CONVERTER
ROLLOVER VALVE
FUEL PUMP
VENT CUT VALVE
TANK PRESSURE CONTROL VALVE
FUEL PUMP
HEATED OXYGEN SENSOR (REAR)
FUEL FILTER (LOW PRESSURE SIDE)

11.1b Schematic of the Electronic Fuel Injection (EFI) system for 1995 and later models

4

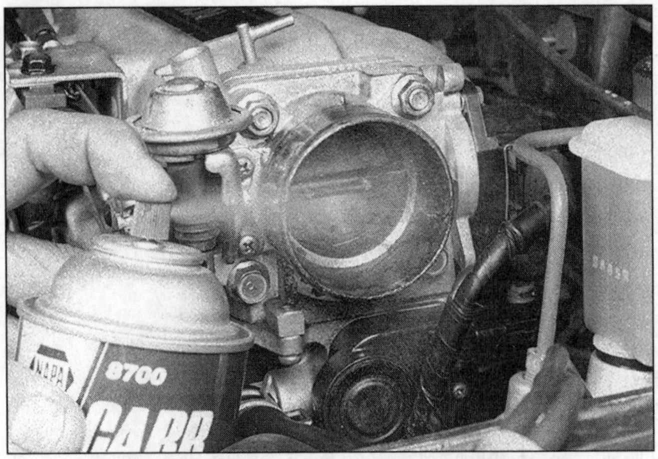

12.6 With the engine off, use aerosol carburetor cleaner (make sure it is safe for use with catalytic converters and oxygen sensors), a toothbrush and a rag to clean the throttle body - open the throttle plate so you can clean behind it

system. The EFI system is composed of three basic subsystems: fuel system, air induction system and electronic control system **(see illustrations)**.

Fuel system

2 An electric fuel pump located inside the fuel tank supplies fuel under constant pressure to the fuel rail, which distributes fuel evenly to all injectors. From the fuel rail, fuel is injected into the intake ports, just above the intake valves, by fuel injectors. The amount of fuel supplied by the injectors is precisely controlled by a Powertrain Control Module (PCM). A pressure regulator controls system pressure in relation to intake manifold vacuum. A fuel filter between the fuel pump and the fuel rail filters fuel to protect the components of the system.

Air induction system

3 The air induction system consists of an air filter housing, the throttle body and the duct connecting the two. An Intake Air Temperature (IAT) sensor monitors the temperature of the incoming air. This information helps the PCM determine the amount of fuel to be injected by the injectors. The throttle plate inside the throttle body is controlled by the driver. As the throttle plate opens, the speed of the incoming air increases, which lowers the temperature of the air. The IAT sends this information to the PCM and the PCM signals the injectors to increase the amount of fuel delivered to the intake ports.

Electronic control system

4 The Computer Control System controls the EFI and other systems by means of an Powertrain Control Module (PCM), which employs a microcomputer. The PCM receives signals from a number of information sensors which monitor such variables as intake air temperature, throttle angle, coolant temperature, engine rpm, vehicle speed and exhaust oxygen content. These signals help the PCM determine the injection duration necessary for the optimum air/fuel ratio. Some of these sensors and their corresponding PCM-controlled relays are not contained within EFI components, but are located throughout the engine compartment. For further information regarding the PCM and its relationship to the engine electrical and ignition system, see Chapter 6.

12 Electronic Fuel Injection (EFI) system - check

Refer to illustrations 12.6, 12.7, 12.8 and 12.9

1 Check the ground wire connections for tightness. Check all wiring and electrical connectors that are related to the system. Loose electrical connectors and poor grounds can cause many problems that

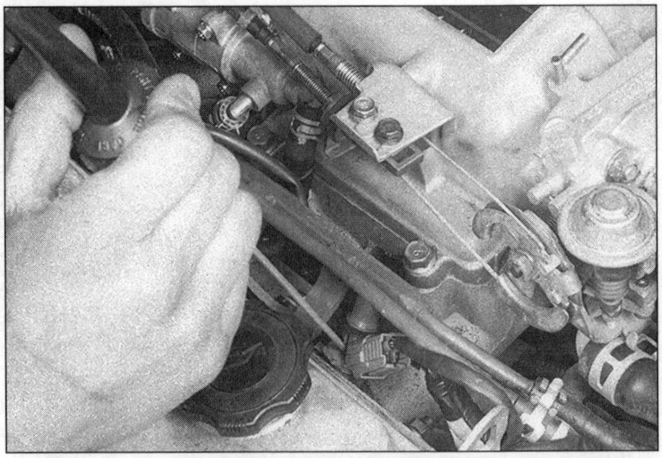

12.7 Use a stethoscope or a screwdriver to determine if the injectors are working properly - they should make a steady clicking sound that rises and falls with engine speed changes

12.8 Install the "noid" light into the fuel injector electrical connector and check to see that it blinks with the engine running

resemble more serious malfunctions.

2 Check to see that the battery is fully charged, as the control unit and sensors depend on an accurate supply voltage in order to properly meter the fuel.

3 Check the air filter element - a dirty or partially blocked filter will severely impede performance and economy (see Chapter 1).

4 If a blown fuse is found, replace it and see if it blows again. If it does, search for a grounded wire in the harness related to the system.

5 Check the air intake duct from the air cleaner housing to the intake manifold for leaks, which will result in an excessively lean mixture. Also check the condition of the vacuum hoses connected to the intake manifold.

6 Remove the air intake duct from the throttle body and check for carbon and residue build-up. If it's dirty, clean it with aerosol carburetor cleaner (make sure the can says it's safe for use with oxygen sensors and catalytic converters) and a toothbrush **(see illustration)**.

7 With the engine running, place a stethoscope against each injector, one at a time, and listen for a clicking sound, indicating operation **(see illustration)**. If you don't have an automotive stethoscope you can use a long screwdriver; just place the tip of the screwdriver against the injector body and press your ear against the handle.

8 If there is a problem with an injector, purchase a special injector test light ("noid" light) and install it into the injector electrical connector **(see illustration)**. Start the engine and make sure that each injector connector flashes the noid light. This will test for the proper voltage signal to the injector.

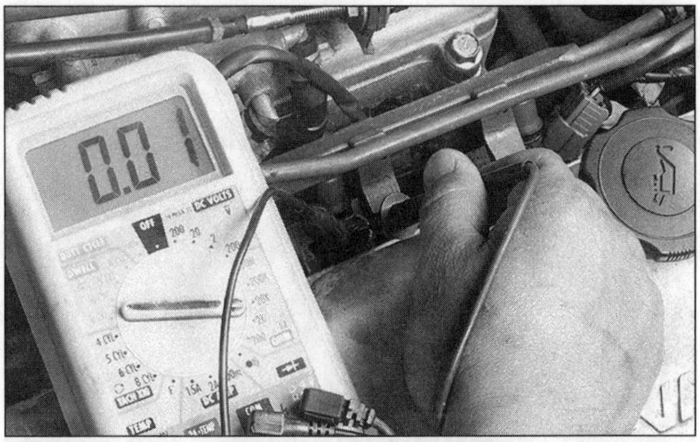
12.9 Using an ohmmeter, measure the resistance across the terminals of the injector

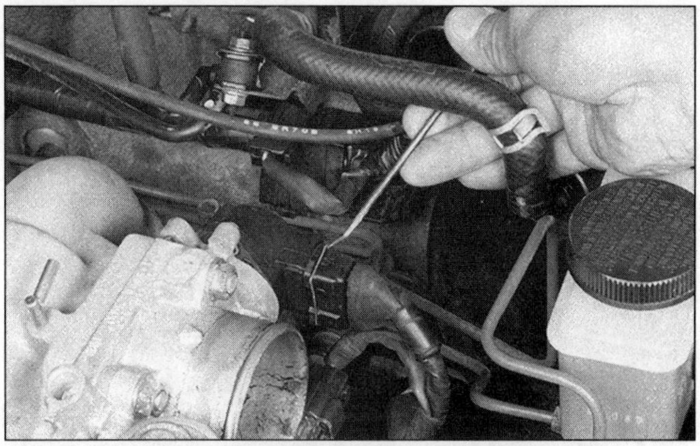
13.9 Loosen the TPS connector with a probe or small screwdriver, then disconnect the TPS connector

13.10 A typical throttle body is retained by four bolts/nuts (arrows)

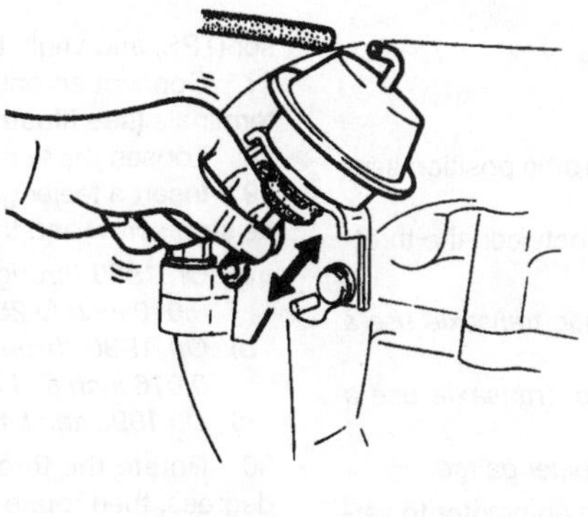
13.16 Actuator rod should move in and out smoothly

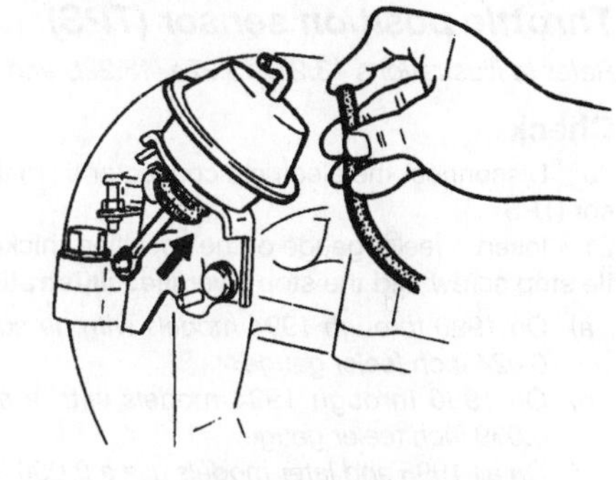
13.18 You should be able to feel the vacuum with your finger

9 With the engine OFF and the fuel injector electrical connectors disconnected, measure the resistance of each injector **(see illustration)**. Compare the measured resistance to the values listed in this Chapter's Specifications. Out of range injectors are probably faulty.
10 The remainder of the system checks should be left to a dealer service department or other qualified repair shop, as there is a chance that the control unit may be damaged if not performed properly.

13 Electronic Fuel Injection (EFI) system - component check and replacement

Warning: *Gasoline is extremely flammable, so take extra precautions when you work on any part of the fuel system. See the Warning in Section 2.*

Throttle body

Refer to illustrations 13.9 and 13.10

Check

1 Verify that the throttle linkage operates smoothly when the throttle lever is moved from fully closed to fully open.
2 Check the throttle body for wear and deposits. **Note:** *Do not remove the thin seal coating from the throttle valves or bore.*

Replacement

Warning: *Wait until the engine is completely cool before beginning this procedure.*
3 Detach the cable from the negative terminal of the battery.
4 Loosen the hose clamps and remove the air intake duct.
5 Detach the accelerator cable from the throttle lever (see Section 10).
6 If your vehicle is equipped with an automatic transmission, detach the throttle valve cable from the throttle linkage (see Chapter 7B), detach the cable bracket from the engine and set the cable and bracket aside.
7 Clearly label, then detach, all vacuum hoses from the throttle body.
8 Clearly label, then detach, all coolant hoses from the throttle body. Plug the coolant hoses to prevent coolant loss.
9 Disconnect the electrical connector from the throttle position sensor (TPS) **(see illustrations)**.
10 Remove the four throttle body mounting bolts **(see illustration)**.
11 Detach the throttle body and gasket from the intake manifold.
12 Using a soft brush and carburetor cleaner, thoroughly clean the throttle body casting, then blow out all passages with compressed air. **Caution:** *Do not clean the throttle position sensor with anything. Just wipe it off carefully with a clean, soft cloth.*
13 Installation of the throttle body is the reverse of removal.
14 Be sure to tighten the throttle body mounting bolts to the torque listed in this Chapter's Specifications.

Variable Intake Control System (VICS) shutter valve actuator (1.8L DOHC engine only)

Refer to illustrations 13.16 and 13.18

Check

15 Remove the vacuum hose from the actuator located on the opposite end of the plenum from the throttle body.
16 Verify that the actuator rod can move in and out smoothly **(see illustration)**.
17 Start the engine and run it at idle.
18 Place a finger over the end of the vacuum hose and verify that there is vacuum **(see illustration)**.
19 Install the vacuum hose and verify that the rod is pulled inward.

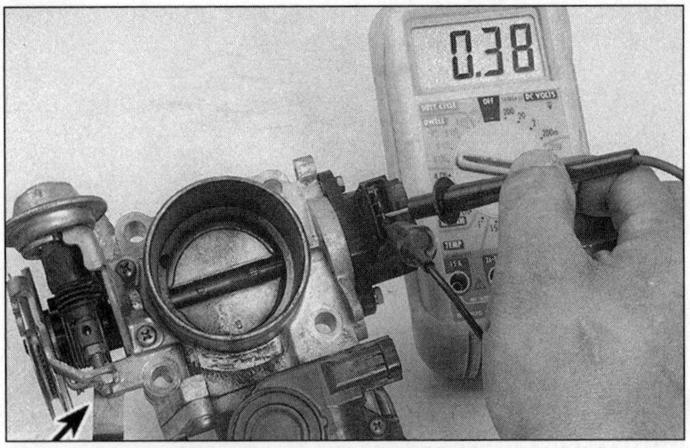

13.21 Insert a feeler gauge of the required thickness between the throttle stop screw and stop lever (arrow)

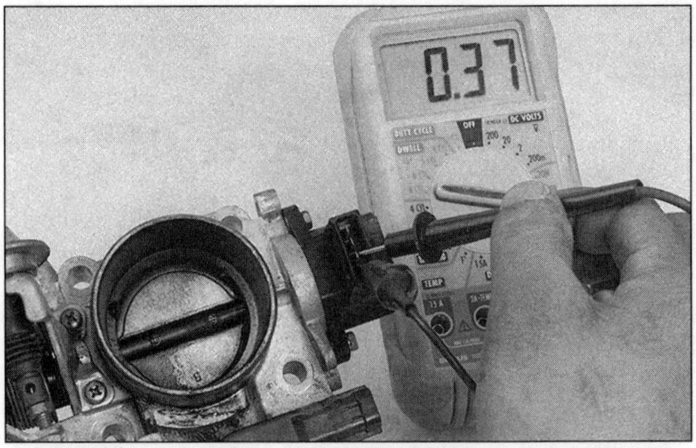

13.22a On 1990 through 1994 models there should be no continuity between the lower TPS terminals with the feeler gauge in place

Throttle position sensor (TPS)

Refer to illustrations 13.21, 13.22a, 13.22b and 13.28

Check

20 Disconnect the electrical connector from the throttle position sensor (TPS).

21 Insert a feeler gauge of the specified thickness between the throttle stop screw and the stop lever **(see illustration)**.

- *a) On 1990 through 1994 models with an automatic transaxle use a 0.024 inch feeler gauge.*
- *b) On 1990 through 1994 models with a manual transaxle use a 0.039 inch feeler gauge.*
- *c) On all 1995 and later models use a 0.050 inch feeler gauge.*

22 With the correct feeler gauge in position, use an ohmmeter to verify that there is no continuity between the specified terminal pairs **(see illustrations)**.

- *a) The two lower terminals (E and IDL) on all 1990 through 1994 models, regardless of transaxle type.*
- *b) Terminals A and B on 1995 and later models.*

23 On 1990 through 1994 models with an automatic transaxle, connect the ohmmeter probes to the 2nd terminal from the top and the lowest terminal. Then slowly rotate the throttle lever toward the wide-open position; there should be no continuity until the throttle reaches the wide-open position. In the closed throttle position there should be less than 1 K-ohm of resistance and at the wide-open position approximately 5 K-ohm resistance.

24 On 1990 through 1994 models with a manual transaxle, connect the ohmmeter probes to the top two terminals. Then slowly rotate the throttle lever toward the wide-open position; there should be no continuity until the throttle reaches the wide-open position.

25 If the continuity and/or resistance is not as specified, adjust the TPS.

Adjustment

26 Disconnect the electrical connector from the throttle position sensor (TPS) and verify that the throttle valve is in the closed position.

27 Connect an ohmmeter between the throttle position sensor lower terminals **(see illustration 13.22a and 13.22b)**.

28 Loosen the two TPS attaching screws **(see illustration)**.

29 Insert a feeler gauge of the specified thickness between the throttle stop screw and the stop lever:

- *a) On 1990 through 1994 models with an automatic transaxle use a 0.010 inch (0.25 mm) feeler gauge.*
- *b) On 1990 through 1994 models with a manual transaxle use a 0.016 inch (0.4 mm) feeler gauge.*
- *c) On 1995 and later models use a 0.006 inch (0.15 mm) feeler gauge.*

30 Rotate the throttle position sensor clockwise approximately 30 degrees, then rotate it back (counterclockwise) until there is continuity.

31 Replace the feeler gauge with a gauge of the specified thickness and verify that there is no continuity:

- *a) On 1990 through 1994 models with an automatic transaxle use a 0.016 inch (0.4 mm) feeler gauge.*
- *b) On 1990 through 1994 models with a manual transaxle use a 0.027 inch (0.7 mm) feeler gauge.*
- *c) On 1995 and later models use a 0.020 inch (0.50 mm) feeler gauge.*

32 If there is continuity, repeat Steps 29 through 31.

33 Tighten the two attaching screws. **Note:** *Do not move the TPS from the set position when tightening the screws.*

34 If you cannot successfully adjust the TPS, replace it.

Replacement

35 If adjustment doesn't bring the sensor within specifications, disconnect it, remove the screws and replace it with a new one, then adjust it as described in Steps 26 through 33.

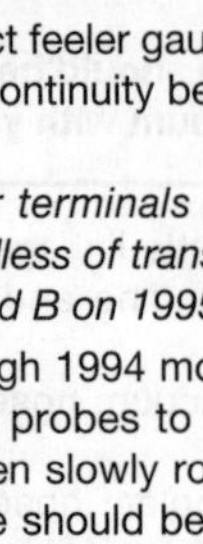

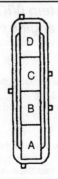

13.22b Typical TPS terminal configuration on 1995 and later models

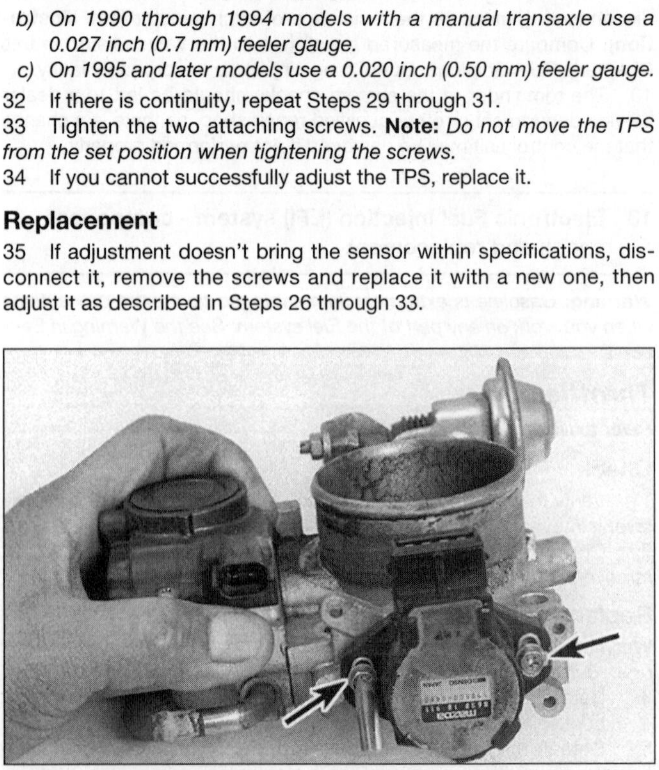

13.28 Loosen the two screws (arrows) holding the TPS in place

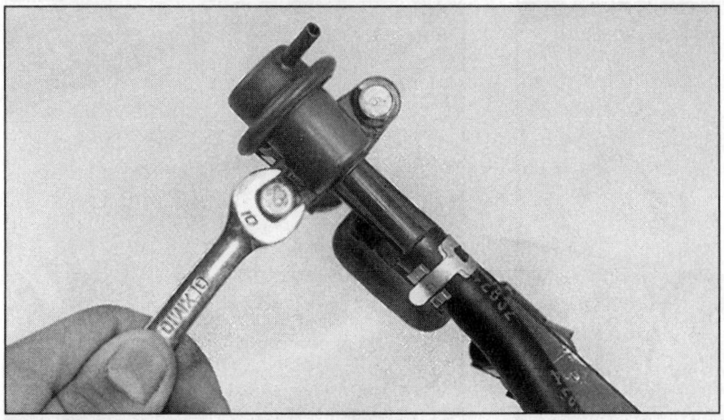

13.41 To remove the fuel pressure regulator from the fuel rail, detach the fuel return hose, remove the two regulator bolts and separate the regulator from the fuel rail (fuel rail removed from engine for clarity)

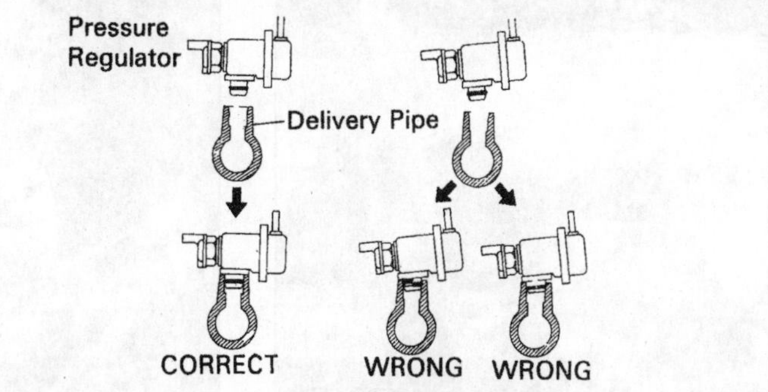

13.42 If the fuel pressure regulator is cocked during installation, it will not seal properly

Fuel pressure regulator

Check

36 Refer to the fuel pump/fuel pressure check procedure (see Section 3).

Replacement

Refer to illustrations 13.41 and 13.42

37 Relieve the fuel pressure (see Section 2) and detach the cable from the negative terminal of the battery.
38 Detach the vacuum sensing hose from the regulator.
39 Place a metal container or shop towel under the fuel return hose.
40 Slide the clamp down the hose and remove the fuel return hose from the regulator.
41 Remove the pressure regulator mounting bolts **(see illustration)** and detach the pressure regulator from the fuel rail.
42 Use a new O-ring and make sure that the pressure regulator is installed properly on the fuel rail **(see illustration)**.
43 The remainder of installation is the reverse of removal.

Idle air control (IAC) valve

Note: *The minimum idle speed is pre-set at the factory and should not require adjustment under normal operating conditions; however if the throttle body has been replaced or you suspect the minimum idle speed has been tampered with (for example, if the idle speed screw was removed from the throttle body) have the vehicle checked by a dealer service department or a qualified automotive repair shop.*

Check

Refer to illustration 13.47

44 Apply the parking brake, shift the transaxle to Neutral (manual) or Park (automatic) and block the drive wheels. Install the lead of a tachometer to the IG (-) terminal on the diagnostic test connector. Start the engine and allow it to reach normal operating temperature. Check the idle speed and compare it to the idle speed listed in this Chapter's Specifications.
45 Check if a click sound is heard and the engine speed increases to approximately 1,200 rpm when the IAC valve is disconnected at idle. If the engine speed does not increase replace the IAC.
46 Disconnect the IAC valve electrical connector.
47 Measure the resistance between the two terminals **(see illustration)**. Compare your results to the IAC valve resistance in this Chapter's Specifications.
48 If the resistance is not as specified, replace the IAC valve.
49 Connect the IAC valve electrical connector.

Replacement

Refer to illustration 13.51

50 Remove the throttle body (see Steps 3 through 11).
51 Remove the mounting screws and detach the IAC valve and gasket **(see illustration)**.
52 Installation of the IAC valve is the reverse of removal. Be sure to use a new gasket when installing the IAC valve.

4

Fuel rail and fuel injectors

Check

53 Refer to the fuel injection system checking procedure (see Section 12).

Replacement

Refer to illustrations 13.57a, 13.57b, 13.57c, 13.58a, 13.58b, 13.61, 13.62a, 13.62b, 13.63, 13.64a, 13.64b and 13.64c

54 Relieve the fuel pressure (see Section 2).
55 Detach the cable from the negative terminal of the battery (see the **Caution** at the beginning of this Section).

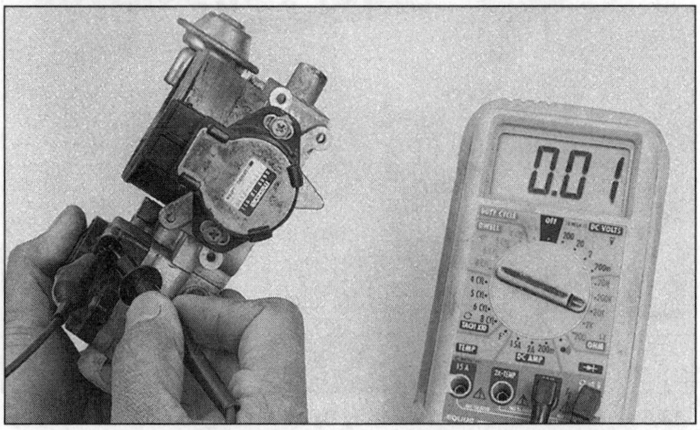

13.47 Using an ohmmeter, check the resistance across the IAC valve terminals

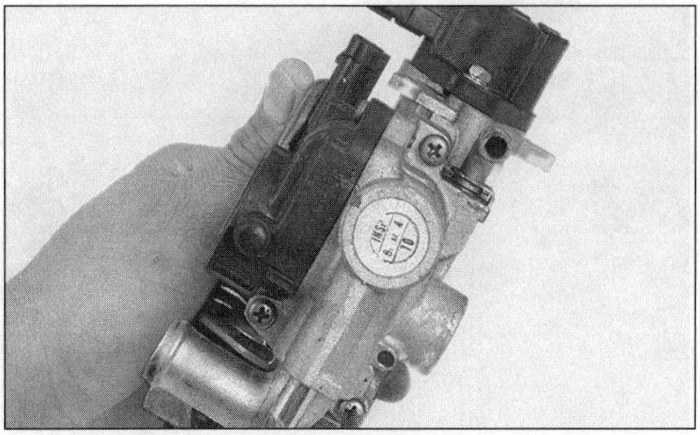

13.51 Remove the screws that retain the IAC valve to the throttle body

13.57a Release the hose clamps with pliers and slide the clamps down the hose

13.57b Remove the air valve mounting screws (arrows)

13.57c Remove the air valve

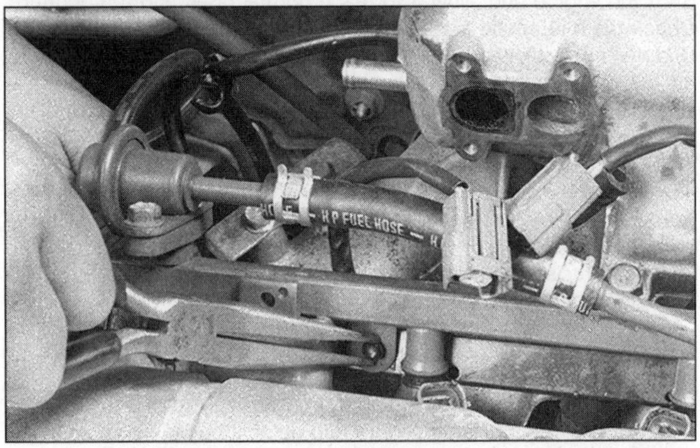

13.58a Release the fuel injection harness clips

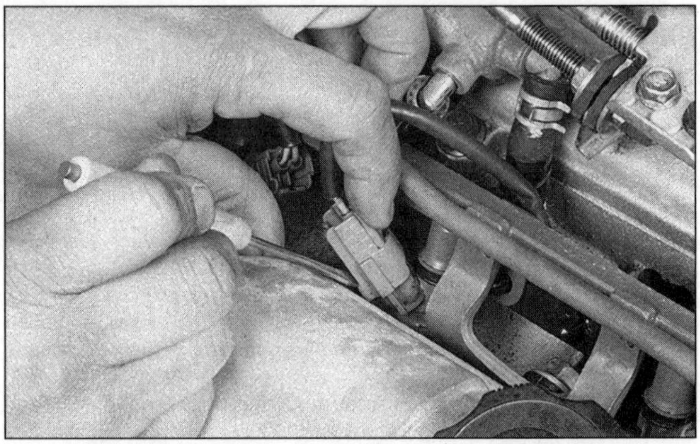

13.58b Disconnect the injector electrical connectors

56 Remove the PCV hose from the cylinder head and intake manifold.

57 Remove the hose clamps/hoses from the air valve, then remove the air valve from the side of the air intake plenum **(see illustrations)**.

58 Carefully mark each injector and its electrical connector with a felt pen or paint, then carefully release the 2 harness clips and remove the connectors **(see illustrations)** from each injector and set the wire harness aside. **Note:** *Use a small flat blade screwdriver to release the connectors lock lever while gently pulling the connector.*

59 Detach the vacuum sensing hose from the fuel pressure regulator.

60 Disconnect the fuel lines from the fuel pressure regulator and the fuel rail.

61 Remove the fuel rail mounting bolts **(see illustration)**.

62 Remove the fuel rail with the fuel injectors attached and if you intend to reuse the injectors number the injector and its position on the rail so you can re-install them in the same position **(see illustrations)**.

63 Remove the fuel injectors from the fuel rail **(see illustration)** and set them aside in a clearly labeled storage container. **Note:** *The seals sometimes stick on the injectors when removed.*

64 If you intend to re-use the same injectors, replace the grommets and O-rings **(see illustrations)**.

65 Installation of the fuel injectors is the reverse of removal.

66 Tighten the fuel rail mounting bolts to the torque listed in this Chapter's Specifications.

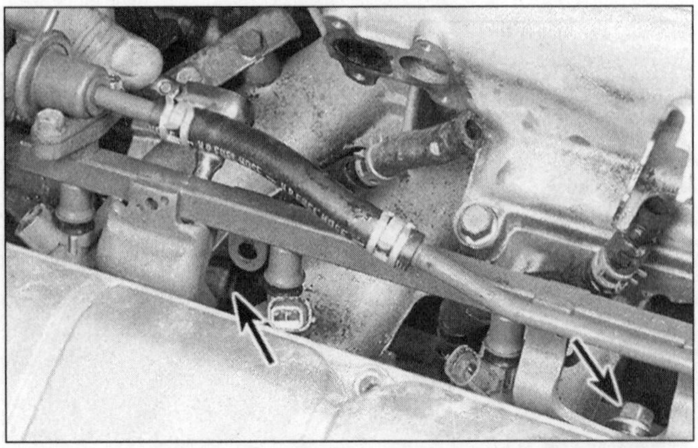

13.61 Remove the bolts (arrows) that retain the fuel rail to the intake manifold

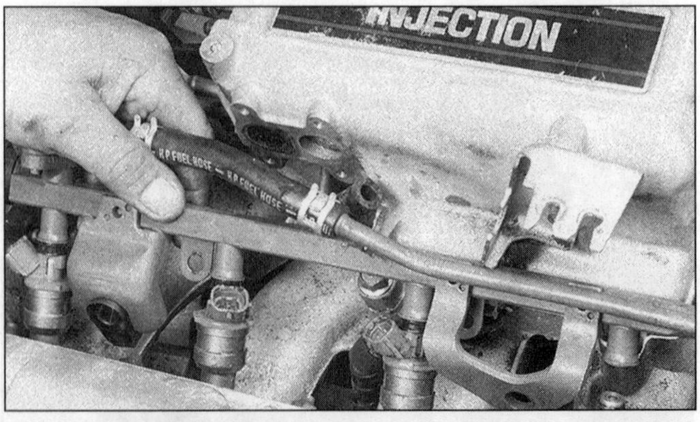

13.62a Lift the fuel rail assembly from the engine. Beware of any fuel that may spill out of the fuel pressure regulator or fuel rail while you are lifting it out

13.62b Number each injector and its rail position

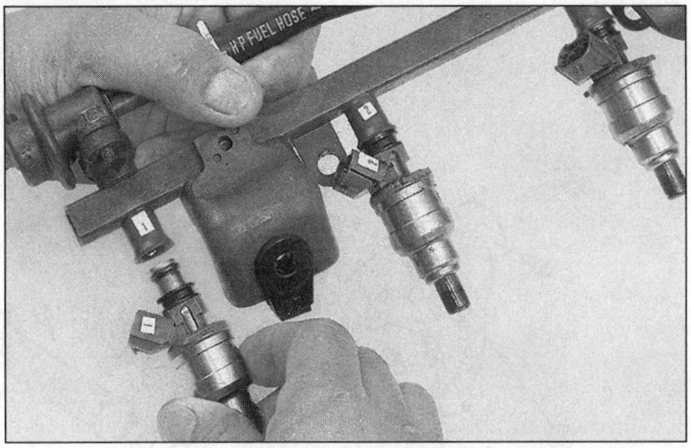

13.63 Gently pull on the injectors to remove them from the rail

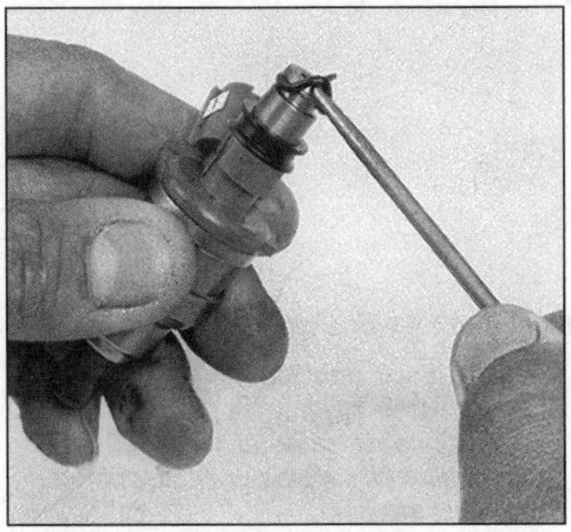

13.64a Remove the O-ring from the injector

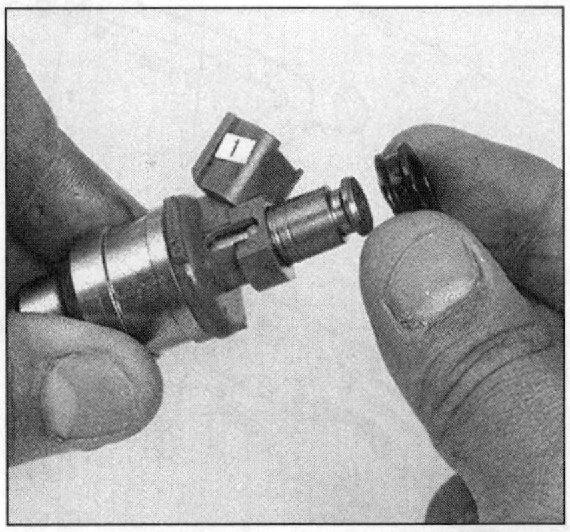

13.64b Remove the grommet from the top of the injector

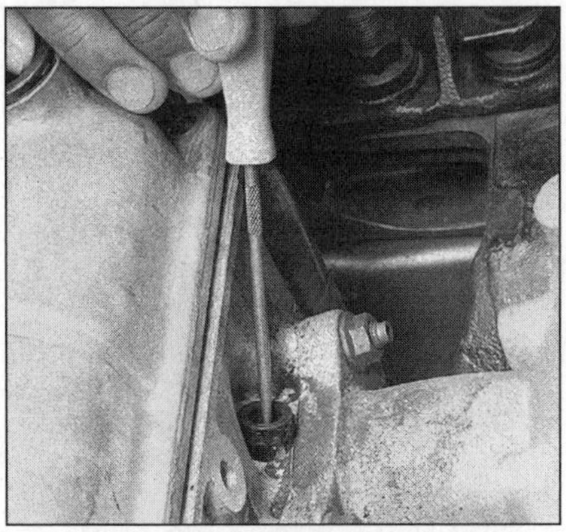

13.64c Remove the insulator from the bores in the intake manifold

Air intake plenum

Removal

Refer to illustrations 13.72 and 13.73

Warning: *Wait until the engine is completely cool before beginning this procedure.*

67 Detach the cable from the negative terminal of the battery.

68 Detach the accelerator cable (see Section 10) and the throttle cable (see Chapter 7) from the plenum and throttle body assembly.

69 On the 1.8 L DOHC engine, disconnect the vacuum hose from the VICS vacuum chamber to the plenum and the vacuum hose attached to the VICS shutter valve on the plenum.

70 Clearly label, then detach, any other vacuum lines connected to the air intake plenum.

71 Detach the throttle body assembly from the plenum (see Step 10 and 11).

72 Remove the air intake plenum upper retaining bolts and nuts **(see illustration)**. **Note:** *Models with the 1.6L SOHC engine have 1 bolt and 2 nuts; models with the 1.8L SOHC engine have 2 bolts and 2 nuts; and models with the 1.8L DOHC engine have 5 bolts and 2 nuts.*

73 Raise the vehicle and support it securely, then from under the vehicle, remove the bolts going from the intake manifold into the air intake plenum **(see illustration)**. **Note:** *Models with the 1.6L SOHC engine have 3 bolts underneath; models with the 1.8L SOHC engine*

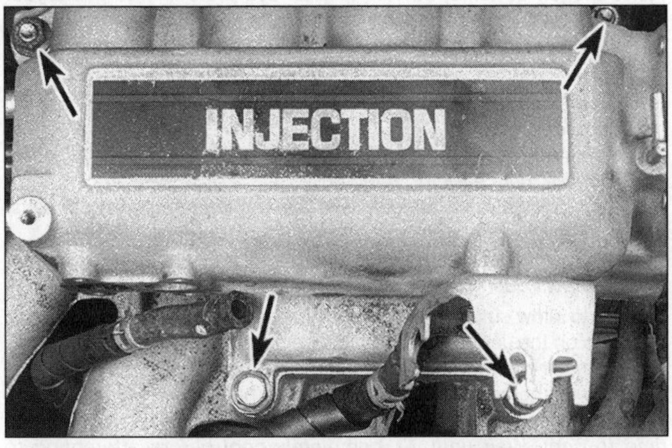

13.72 Remove the upper bolts/nuts (arrows) that fasten the air intake plenum to the intake manifold

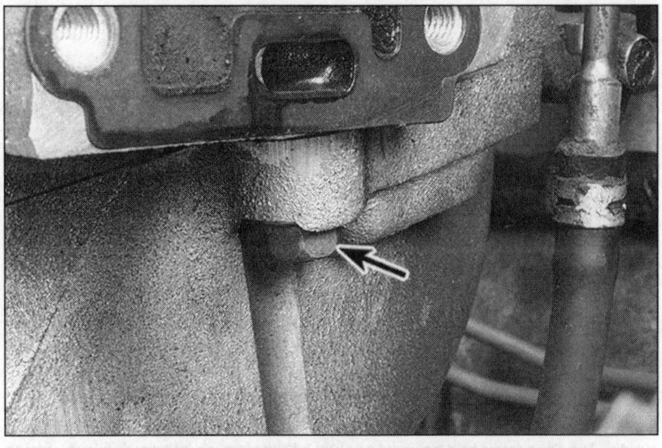

13.73 Remove the bolt (arrow) from the underside of the intake manifold

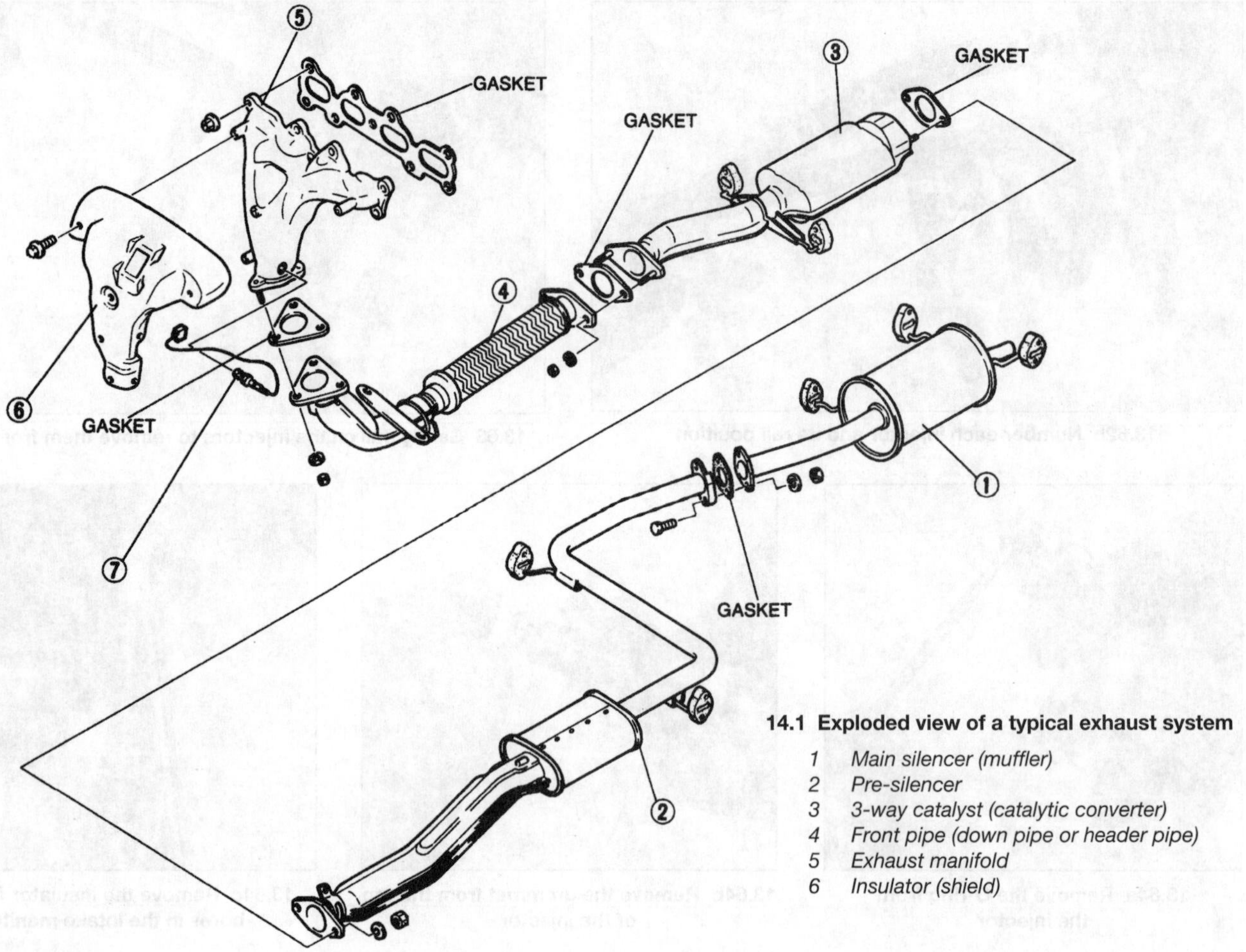

14.1 Exploded view of a typical exhaust system

1 *Main silencer (muffler)*
2 *Pre-silencer*
3 *3-way catalyst (catalytic converter)*
4 *Front pipe (down pipe or header pipe)*
5 *Exhaust manifold*
6 *Insulator (shield)*

have 5 bolts underneath; and Models with the 1.8L DOHC engine have 4 bolts underneath.

74 Lift the air intake plenum off the lower intake manifold.

Installation

75 Be sure to clean and inspect the mounting surface of the lower intake manifold (see Chapter 2A) and the air intake plenum before positioning the new gasket onto the lower intake mounting face. Install the air intake plenum onto the intake manifold. Ensure the gasket remains in place. Install the upper intake manifold retaining bolts and tighten the bolts/nuts to the torque listed in this Chapter's Specifications. Installation is otherwise the reverse of removal.

14 Exhaust system servicing - general information

Refer to illustration 14.1

Warning: *Inspection and repair of exhaust system components should be done only after the system components have cooled completely.*

1 The exhaust system consists of the exhaust manifold, catalytic converter, the muffler, the tailpipe and all connecting pipes, brackets, hangers and clamps. The exhaust system is attached to the body with mounting brackets and rubber hangers **(see illustration)**. If any of these parts are damaged or deteriorated, excessive noise and vibration will be transmitted to the body.

2 Conducting regular inspections of the exhaust system will keep it safe and quiet. Look for any damaged or bent parts, open seams, holes, loose connections, excessive corrosion or other defects which could allow exhaust fumes to enter the vehicle. Deteriorated exhaust system components should not be repaired - they should be replaced with new parts.

3 If the exhaust system components are extremely corroded or rusted together, they will probably have to be cut from the exhaust system. The convenient way to accomplish this is to have a muffler repair shop remove the corroded sections with a cutting torch. If, however, you want to save money by doing it yourself and you don't have an oxygen/acetylene welding outfit with a cutting torch, simply cut off the old components with a hack-saw. If you have compressed air, special pneumatic cutting chisels can also be used. If you do decide to tackle the job at home, be sure to wear eye protection to guard your eyes from metal chips and work gloves to protect your hands.

4 Here are some simple guidelines to apply when repairing the exhaust system:

a) *Work from the back to the front when removing exhaust system components.*
b) *Apply penetrating oil to the exhaust system component fasteners to make them easier to remove.*
c) *Use new gaskets, hangers and clamps when installing exhaust system components.*
d) *Apply anti-seize compound to the threads of all exhaust system fasteners during reassembly.*

Be sure to allow sufficient clearance between newly installed parts and all points on the underbody to avoid overheating the floor pan and possibly damaging the interior carpet and insulation. Pay particularly close attention to the catalytic converter and its heat shield. **Warning:** *The catalytic converter operates at very high temperatures and takes a long time to cool. Wait until it's completely cool before attempting to remove the converter. Failure to do so could result in serious burns.*

Chapter 5
Engine electrical systems

Contents

Specifications

Ignition timing

With test terminals TEN and GND of the Data Link Connector connected with a jumper wire	
1.6L SOHC	6 to 8 degrees BTDC
1.8L SOHC	4 to 6 degrees BTDC
1.8L DOHC	9 to 11 degrees BTDC
1.5L DOHC (without jumper wire)	9 to 11 degrees BTDC

Ignition coil resistance (cold)

Primary resistance	
1994 and earlier	0.81 to 0.99 ohms
1995 and later	0.49 to 0.73 ohms
Secondary resistance	
1994 and earlier	10.0 to 16.0 K-ohms
1995 and later	20.0 to 31.0 K-ohms

Charging system

Charging voltage	14.1 to 14.7 volts
Standard amperage	
All lights and accessories turned off	Less than 12 amps
Headlights (hi-beam) and heater blower motor turned on	65 amps or more at 2,500 to 3,000 rpm
Alternator brush length	
Standard	
All except 1.5L DOHC	0.846 inch
1.5L DOHC	0.790 inch
Minimum	
All except 1.5L DOHC	0.315 inch
1.5L DOHC	0.20 inch

Torque specifications

	Ft-lbs
Alternator mounting bolts	
Adjusting bolt	12 to 16
Pivot bolt	24 to 33
Distributor mounting bolt	14 to 18
Starter mounting bolts	24 to 33

1 General information

The engine electrical systems include all ignition, charging and starting components. Because of their engine related functions, these components are discussed separately from chassis electrical devices such as the lights, the instruments, etc. (which are included in Chapter 12).

Always observe the following precautions when working on the electrical systems:

a) *Be extremely careful when servicing engine electrical components. They are easily damaged if checked, connected or handled improperly.*
b) *Never leave the ignition switch on for long periods of time (10 minutes maximum) with the engine off.*
c) *Don't disconnect the battery cables while the engine is running.*
d) *Maintain correct polarity when connecting a battery cable from another vehicle during jump starting.*

Always disconnect the negative cable first and hook it up last or the battery may be shorted by the tool being used to loosen the cable clamps.

Caution: *If the stereo in your vehicle is equipped with an anti-theft system, make sure you have the correct activation code before disconnecting the battery in any of the following procedures.*

It's also a good idea to review the safety-related information regarding the engine electrical systems located in the *Safety First* section near the front of this manual before beginning any operation included in this Chapter.

2 Battery - emergency jump starting

Refer to the Booster battery (jump) starting procedure at the front of this manual.

3 Battery - removal and installation

Refer to illustration 3.1

1 Beginning with the negative battery cable **(see illustration)**, disconnect both cables from the battery terminals.
2 Remove the battery hold-down clamp.
3 Lift out the battery. Be careful, it's heavy.
4 While the battery is out, inspect the carrier (tray) for corrosion.
5 If you are replacing the battery, make sure that you get one that is identical, with the same dimensions, amperage rating, cold cranking amperage rating, etc., as the original.
6 Installation is the reverse of removal.

4 Battery cables - check and replacement

1 Periodically inspect the entire length of each battery cable for damage, cracked or burned insulation and corrosion. Poor battery cable connections can cause starting problems and decreased engine performance.
2 Check the cable-to-terminal connections at the ends of the cables for cracks, loose wire strands and corrosion. The presence of white, fluffy deposits under the insulation at the cable terminal connection is a sign that the cable is corroded and should be replaced. Check the terminals for distortion, missing mounting bolts and corrosion.
3 When removing the cables, always disconnect the negative cable first and hook it up last or the battery may be shorted by the tool used to loosen the cable clamps. Even if only the positive cable is being replaced, be sure to disconnect the negative cable from the battery first (see Chapter 1 for further information regarding battery cable removal).
4 Disconnect the old cables from the battery, then trace each of them to their opposite ends and detach them from the starter solenoid and ground terminals. Note the routing of each cable to ensure correct installation.
5 If you are replacing either or both of the old cables, take them with you when buying new cables. It is vitally important that you replace the cables with identical parts. Cables have characteristics that make them easy to identify: positive cables are usually red, larger in cross-section and have a larger diameter battery post clamp; ground cables are usually black, smaller in cross-section and have a slightly smaller diameter clamp for the negative post.
6 Clean the threads of the solenoid or ground connection with a wire brush to remove rust and corrosion. Apply a light coat of battery terminal corrosion inhibitor, or petroleum jelly, to the threads to prevent future corrosion.
7 Attach the cable to the solenoid or ground connection and tighten the mounting nut/bolt securely.
8 Before connecting a new cable to the battery, make sure that it reaches the battery post without having to be stretched.
9 Connect the positive cable first, followed by the negative cable.

5 Ignition system - general information and precautions

Refer to illustrations 5.2a and 5.2b

1 The electronic ignition system includes the ignition switch, the battery, the igniter (1994 and earlier models), the ignition coil, the primary (low voltage) and secondary (high voltage) coils, the distributor

3.1 To remove the battery, detach the negative battery cable first, then the positive cable, remove the hold-down strap nuts and bolts and remove the hold-down strap

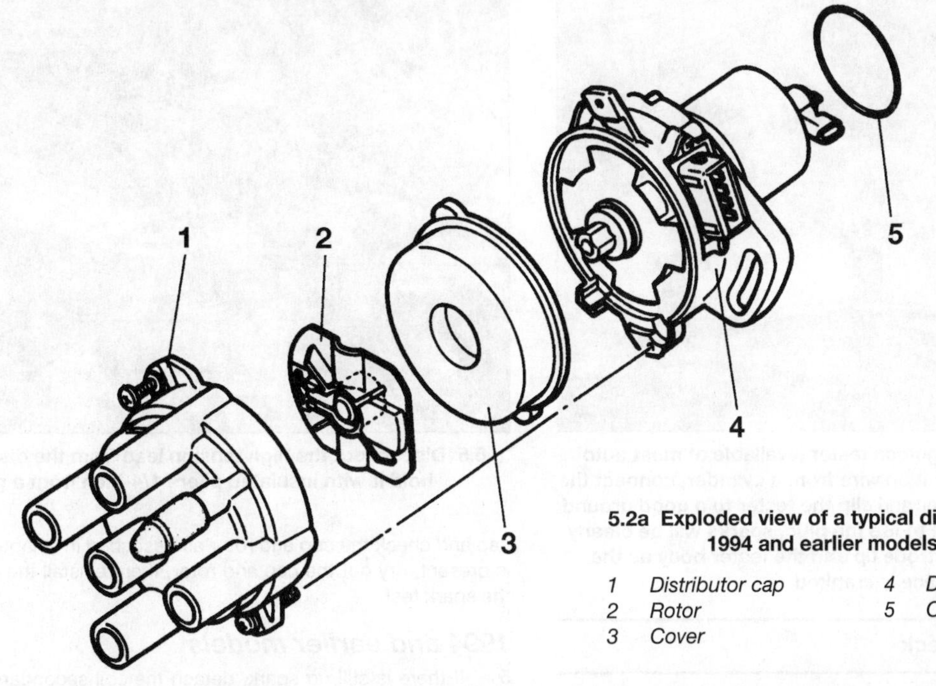

5.2a Exploded view of a typical distributor - 1994 and earlier models

1 *Distributor cap*
2 *Rotor*
3 *Cover*
4 *Distributor*
5 *O-ring*

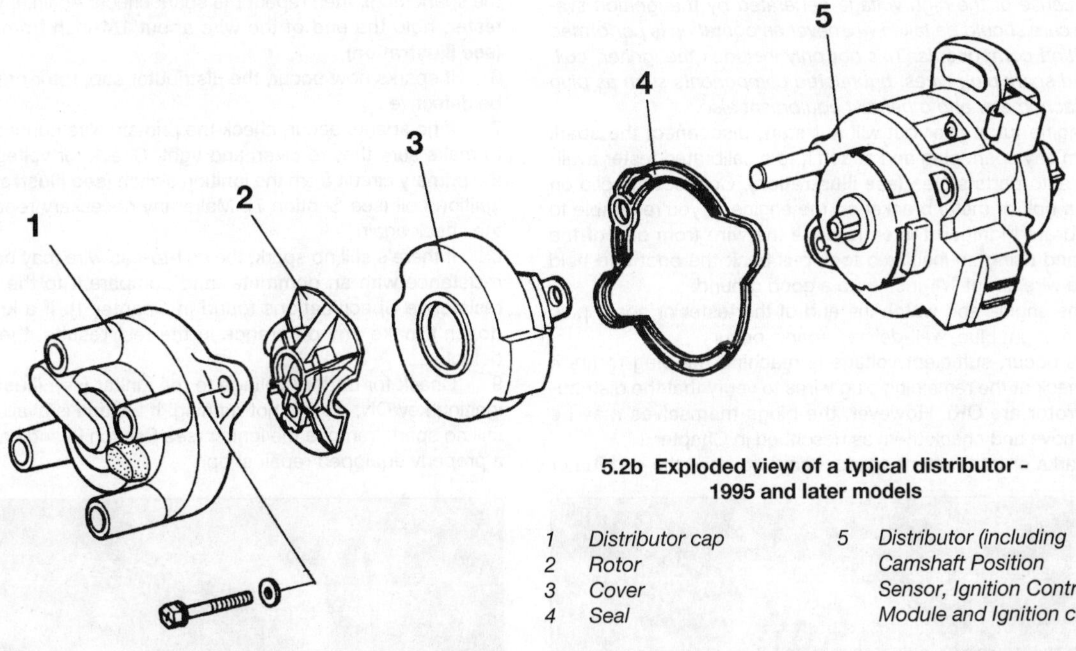

5.2b Exploded view of a typical distributor - 1995 and later models

1 *Distributor cap*
2 *Rotor*
3 *Cover*
4 *Seal*
5 *Distributor (including Camshaft Position Sensor, Ignition Control Module and Ignition coil)*

and the spark plugs. The ignition system is controlled by the Powertrain Control Module (PCM). Using data provided by information sensors which monitor various engine functions (such as rpm, intake air volume, engine temperature, etc.), the PCM ensures a perfectly timed spark under all conditions. **Note:** *In 1995 and later models the igniter and the coil have been integrated into the distributor body, now called the ignition control module and ignition coil.*

2 The electronic ignition systems are divided into two groups: External ignition coil distributor (1994 and earlier models) and the internal ignition coil distributor. (1995 and later models) which also include the ICM **(see illustrations)**. When diagnosing the electronic ignition system, be sure to make all the necessary ignition system checks before replacing any components, as they are expensive and usually non-returnable.

3 When working on the ignition system, take the following precautions:

a) *Do not keep the ignition switch on for more than 10 seconds if the engine will not start.*
b) *Always connect a tachometer in accordance with the manufacturer's instructions. Some tachometers may be incompatible with this ignition system. Consult a dealer service department before buying a tachometer for use with this vehicle.*
c) *Never allow the ignition coil terminals to touch ground. Grounding the coil could result in damage to the igniter and/or the ignition coil.*
d) *Do not disconnect the battery when the engine is running.*
e) *On 1994 and earlier models, make sure the igniter is properly grounded.*

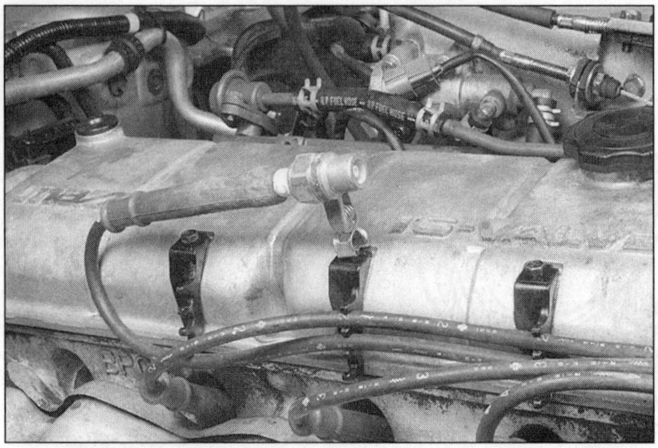

6.1 **To use a calibrated ignition tester (available at most auto parts stores), remove an ignition wire from a cylinder, connect the spark plug boot to the tester and clip the tester to a good ground - if there is enough voltage to fire the plug, sparks will be clearly visible between the electrode tip and the tester body as the engine is cranked**

6 Ignition system - check

Refer to illustrations 6.1, 6.5, 6.7 and 6.9

Warning: *Because of the high voltage generated by the ignition system, extreme care should be taken whenever an operation is performed involving ignition components. This not only includes the igniter, coil, distributor and spark plug wires, but related components such as plug connectors, tachometer and other test equipment also.*

1 If the engine turns over but will not start, disconnect the spark plug wire from any spark plug and attach it to a calibrated tester available at most auto parts stores **(see illustration)**. Connect the clip on the tester to a bolt or metal bracket on the engine. If you're unable to obtain a calibrated ignition tester, remove the wire from one of the spark plugs and using an insulated tool, pull back the boot and hold the end of the wire about 1/4-inch from a good ground.

2 Crank the engine and watch the end of the tester or spark plug wire to see if a bright blue, well-defined sparks occur.

3 If sparks occur, sufficient voltage is reaching the plug to fire it (repeat the check at the remaining plug wires to verify that the distributor cap and rotor are OK). However, the plugs themselves may be fouled, so remove and check them as described in Chapter 1.

4 If no sparks or intermittent sparks occur, remove the distributor cap and check the cap and rotor as described in Chapter 1. If moisture is present, dry out the cap and rotor, then reinstall the cap and repeat the spark test.

6.5 **Disconnect the high tension lead from the distributor and hold it with insulated pliers 1/4-inch from a ground**

1994 and earlier models

5 If there is still no spark, detach the coil secondary wire from the distributor cap and hook it up to the tester (re-attach the plug wire to the spark plug), then repeat the spark check. Again, if you don't have a tester, hold the end of the wire about 1/4-inch from a good ground **(see illustration)**.

6 If sparks now occur, the distributor cap, rotor or plug wire(s) may be defective.

7 If no sparks occur, check the primary wire connections at the coil to make sure they're clean and tight. Check for voltage to the coil on the primary circuit from the ignition switch **(see illustration)**. Check the ignition coil (see Section 7). Make any necessary repairs, then repeat the check again.

8 If there's still no spark, the coil-to-cap wire may be bad (check the resistance with an ohmmeter and compare it to the spark plug wire resistance Specifications found in Chapter 1). If a known good wire doesn't make any difference in the test results, the igniter may be defective .

9 Check for battery voltage to the igniter **(see illustration)** with the ignition key ON, engine not running. If voltage is available and there is still no spark, remove the igniter (see Section 8) and have it checked at a properly equipped repair shop.

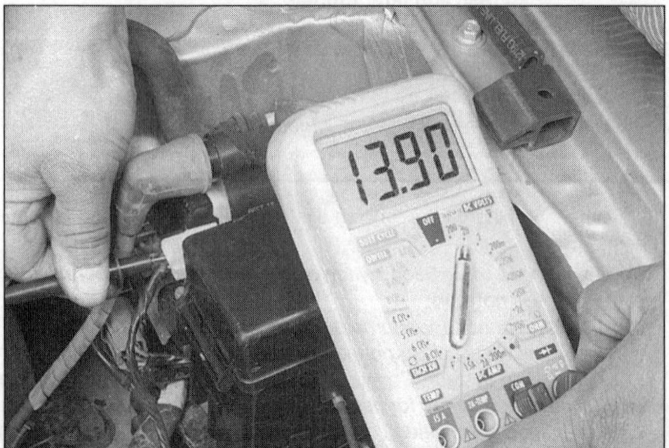

6.7 **Check for battery voltage to the positive side (+) of the ignition coil**

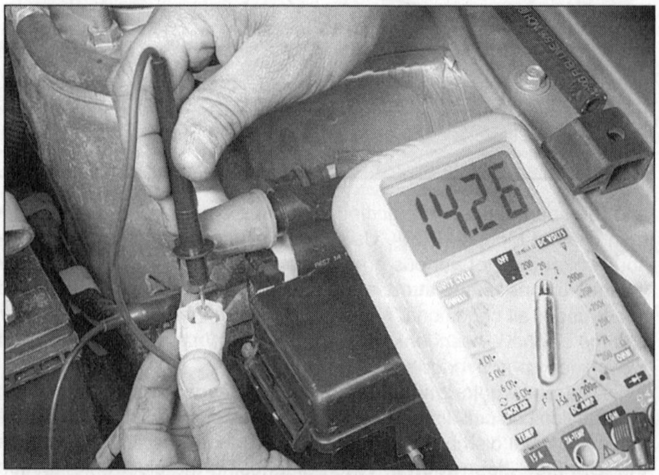

6.9 **Disconnect the igniter electrical connector and with the ignition key ON (engine not running), check for battery voltage to the igniter**

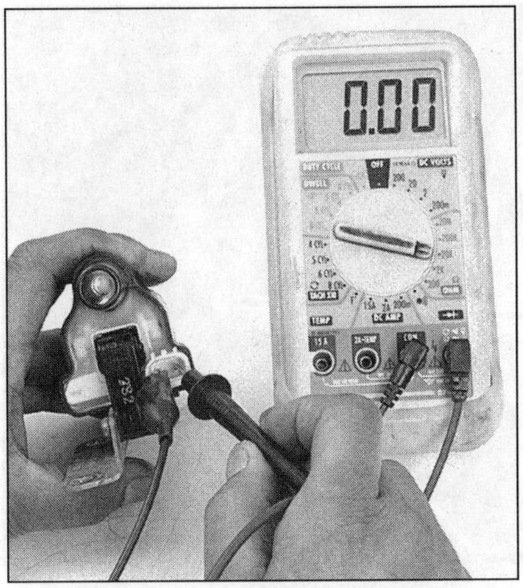

7.5 Connect an ohmmeter between the two terminals of the ignition coil electrical connector to measure the primary coil winding resistance

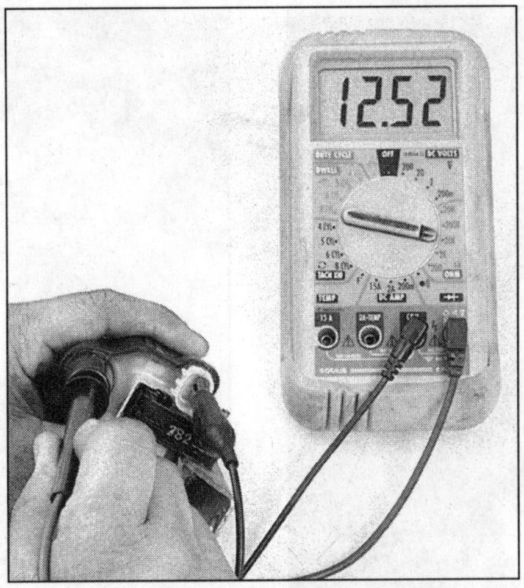

7.6 Connect an ohmmeter between one terminal of the connector and the high-tension tower to measure the resistance of the secondary coil winding

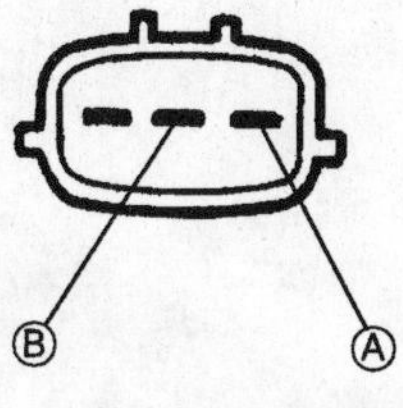

7.9 Distributor 3-pin connector terminal identification

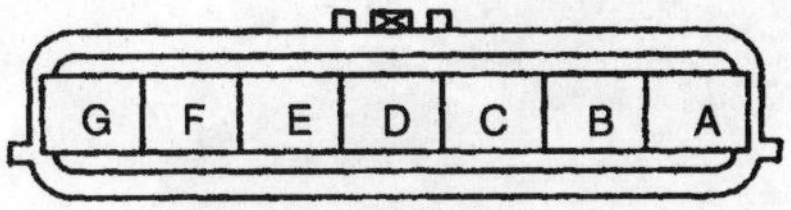

7.12 Distributor 7-pin connector terminal identification

1995 and later models

10 Check the ignition coil, ignition control module-related voltages (3 volts when idling at no load), wiring harness, and distributor connector.

11 If all of these are normal and no firing is observed, replace the distributor.

7 Ignition coil - check and replacement

Check

Refer to illustrations 7.5 and 7.6

1 Perform the ignition system checks as described in Section 6.

2 Crank the engine and verify that a strong blue spark is visible at the coil wire or spark plug wire.

1994 and earlier models

3 If there is no spark, disconnect the connector from the ignition coil **(see illustration 6.7)** and check for voltage at the positive (+) terminal of the connector with the ignition switch in the ON position.

4 If there is no battery voltage, check the main fuse, ignition switch, and wiring harness.

5 Use an ohmmeter to measure the resistance of the primary coil winding **(see illustration)**. If not within specifications identified in this Chapter's Specifications, replace the coil.

6 Use an ohmmeter to measure the resistance of the secondary coil winding **(see illustration)**. If not within the specifications listed in this Chapter's Specifications, replace the coil.

1995 and later models

Refer to illustrations 7.9 and 7.12

7 Perform the ignition system checks as described in Section 6.

8 On all 1995 models and 1996 1.5L DOHC California models, disconnect the 3-pin connector from the distributor.

9 Using an ohmmeter, measure the primary coil resistance between terminals A and B on the distributor **(see illustration)**. Measure the secondary coil resistance between terminal A and the distributor body.

10 Replace the distributor if the resistance is not within the values listed in this Chapter's specifications.

11 On 1996 models (except 1.5L DOHC California models) and all 1997 models, disconnect the 7-pin connector from the distributor.

12 Using an ohmmeter, measure the primary coil resistance between terminals A and B on the distributor **(see illustration)**. Measure the secondary coil resistance between terminal G and the distributor body.

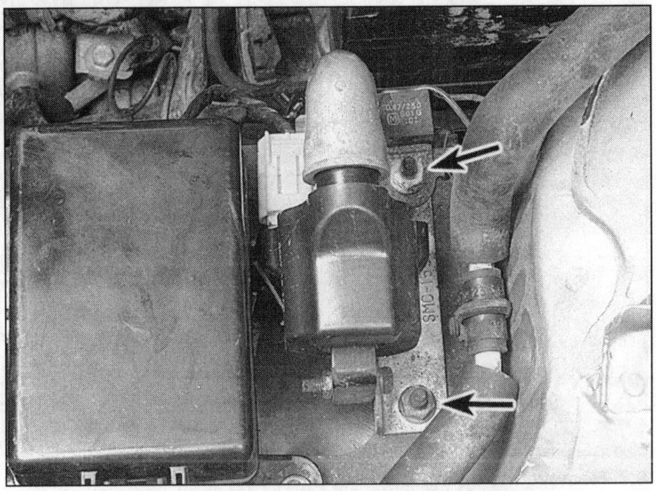

7.17 Remove the coil mounting bolts (arrows)

13 Replace the distributor if the resistance is not within the values listed in this Chapter's specifications.

Replacement

Refer to illustration 7.17

Note: *The coil is replaceable on 1994 and earlier models only. On 1995 and later models, replace the complete distributor assembly.*

14 Detach the cable from the negative terminal of the battery.

15 Remove the heat shield from the coil.

16 Label and disconnect the wires from the coil terminals.

17 remove the coil mounting screws **(see illustration)**.

18 Installation is the reverse of removal.

8 Igniter (1994 and earlier models) - replacement

Refer to illustration 8.3

Note: *A special igniter checker is required to check the function of the igniter. Some automotive parts store will perform the check for you.*

1 Detach the cable from the negative terminal of the battery.

2 Disconnect the electrical connector from the igniter.

3 Remove the screws from the bracket assembly and remove the

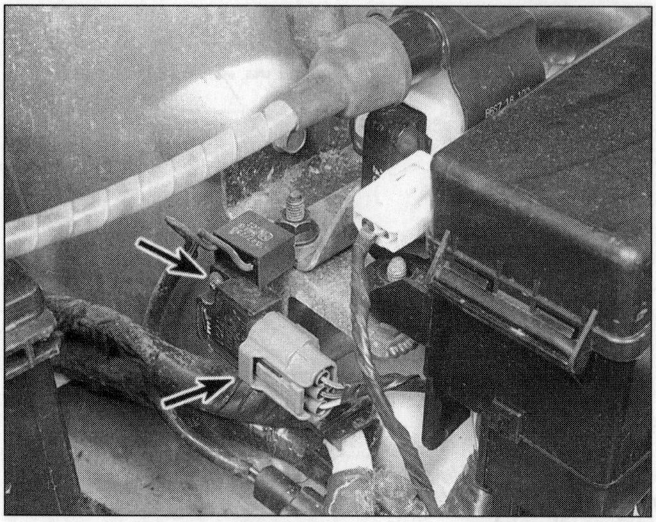

8.3 Remove the screws (arrows) from the bracket assembly and remove the igniter/bracket assembly

9.5 Make a mark on the edge of the distributor base (arrow) directly below the rotor tip and in line with it. Also mark the distributor base and the engine block (arrow) to ensure that the distributor can be reinstalled correctly

9.7 Remove the distributor hold-down bolt and pull the distributor straight out

igniter and bracket assembly from the engine compartment **(see illustration)**.

4 Installation is the reverse of removal.

9 Distributor - removal and installation

Removal

Refer to illustrations 9.5 and 9.7

1 Detach the cable from the negative battery terminal.

2 Look for a raised "1" on the distributor cap. This marks the location for the number one cylinder spark plug wire terminal. If the cap does not have a mark for the number one terminal, locate the number one spark plug and trace the wire back to the terminal on the cap.

3 Remove the distributor cap (see Chapter 1) and turn the engine over until the rotor is pointing toward the number one spark plug terminal (see locating TDC procedure in Chapter 2A).

4 Disconnect and label the electrical connectors from the distributor.

5 Make a mark on the edge of the distributor base directly below the rotor tip and in line with it. Also, mark the distributor base and the engine block to ensure that the distributor is installed correctly **(see illustration)**.

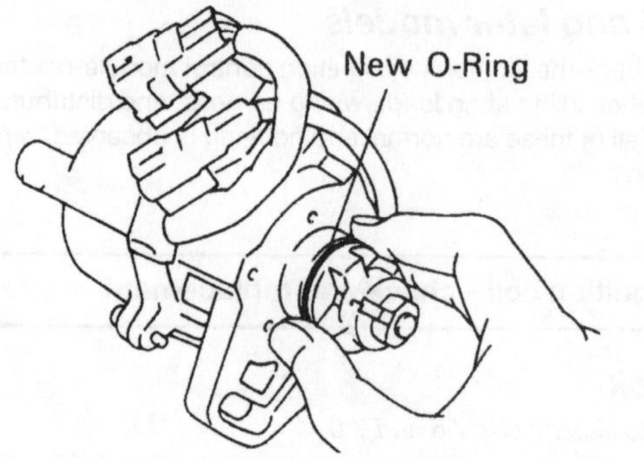

9.8 Install a new O-ring onto the distributor housing

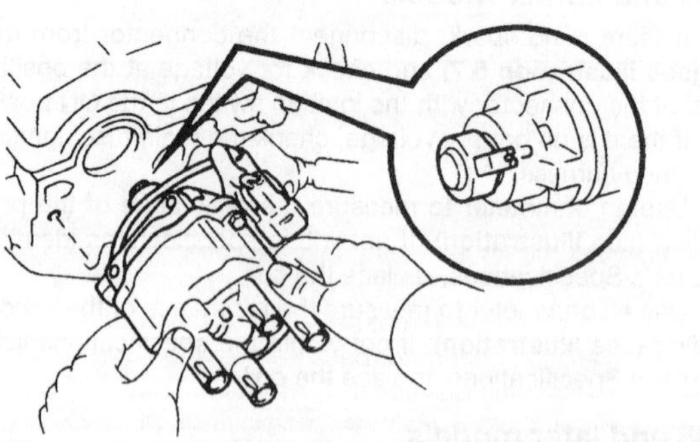

9.9 Align the cut-out portion of the coupling with the groove in the housing

6 If equipped with collar bolts, loosen but do not remove the two bolts in the distributor collar. This will give the distributor shaft clearance.

7 Remove the distributor hold-down bolt **(see illustration)**, then pull the distributor straight out to remove it. **Caution:** *DO NOT turn the crankshaft while the distributor is out of the engine, or the alignment marks will be useless.*

Installation

Refer to illustrations 9.8 and 9.9

Note: *If the crankshaft has been moved while the distributor is out,*

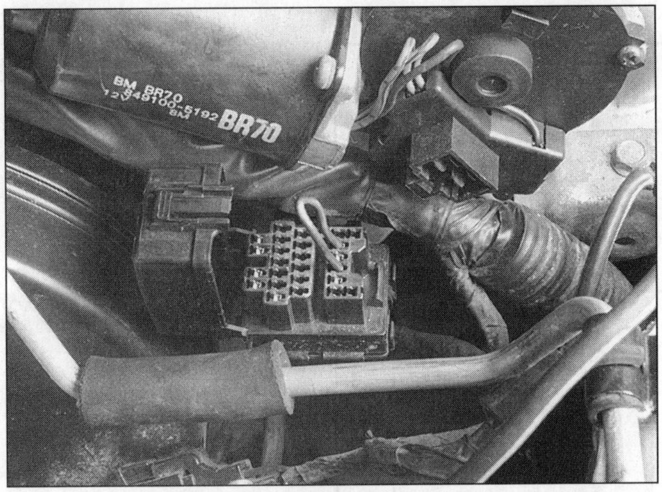

10.2 Attach a jumper wire between terminals TEN and GND of the test connector

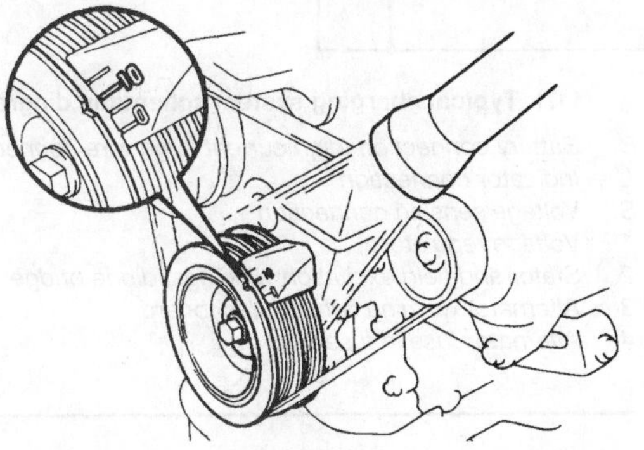

10.5 Point the timing light at the timing marks with the engine at idle

locate Top Dead Center (TDC) for the number one piston (see Chapter 2A) *and position the distributor and the rotor accordingly.*

8 Install a new O-ring onto the distributor housing **(see illustration)**.

9 Align the cut-out portion of the coupling with the groove in the housing **(see illustration)**.

10 Insert the distributor into the engine in exactly the same relationship to the block that it was in when removed.

11 If the distributor does not seat completely, recheck the alignment marks between the distributor base and the block to verify that the distributor is in the same position it was in before removal. Also check the rotor to see if it's aligned with the mark you made on the edge of the distributor base.

12 Loosely install the distributor hold-down bolt(s).

13 Install the distributor cap and connect the electrical connectors.

14 Check the ignition timing (see Section 10) and tighten the distributor hold-down bolt securely.

10 Ignition timing - check and adjustment

Refer to illustrations 10.2, 10.3 and 10.5

Note: *The following ignition timing procedure applies to most models covered by this manual. However, if the procedure specified on the VECI label of your vehicle differs from this one, use the procedure found on the VECI label.*

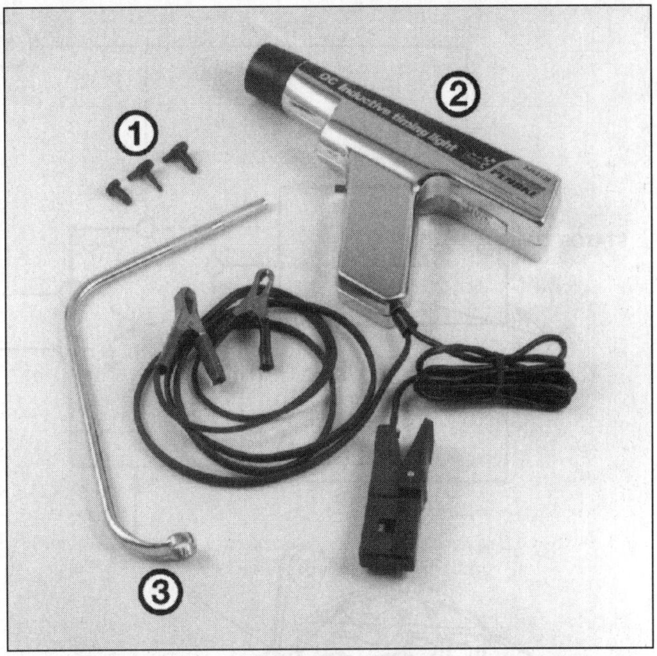

10.3 Tools needed to check and adjust the ignition timing

1 ***Vacuum plugs*** - *Vacuum hoses will, in most cases, have to be disconnected and plugged. Molded plugs in various shapes and sizes are available for this*

2 ***Inductive pick-up timing light*** - *Flashes a bright, concentrated beam of light when the number one spark plug fires. Connect the leads according to the instructions supplied with the light*

3 ***Distributor wrench*** - *On some models, the hold-down bolt for the distributor is difficult to reach and turn with conventional wrenches or sockets. A special wrench like this must be used*

1 Connect a tachometer according to the manufacturer's specifications.

2 Locate the diagnostic connector and insert a jumper wire between terminals TEN and GND **(see illustration). Note:** *This step is not necessary on the 1995 and later models.*

3 With the ignition switch off, connect a timing light according to the manufacturer's specifications **(see illustration)**. Most timing lights are powered by the battery. Also, an inductive style pick-up is installed onto the number one cylinder spark plug wire.

4 Locate the timing marks on the pointer index and the crankshaft pulley.

5 Start the engine and allow it to warm up to normal operating temperature (upper radiator hose hot). Verify that the engine idle is correct (750 rpm with an automatic transaxle and 700 rpm with a manual transaxle). Aim the timing light at the index pointer **(see illustration)**. The mark on the crankshaft pulley should line up with the timing indicator. If necessary, loosen the distributor hold-down bolt and slowly rotate the distributor until the timing marks align. Tighten the hold-down bolt and recheck the timing.

6 Remove the jumper wire from the diagnostic connector and confirm that the ignition timing advances to 12 to 22-degrees BTDC.

7 Turn the engine off and remove the tachometer and the timing light.

11 Charging system - general information and precautions

Refer to illustration 11.1

The charging system includes the alternator, an internal voltage regulator, a charge indicator, the battery and the wiring between all the

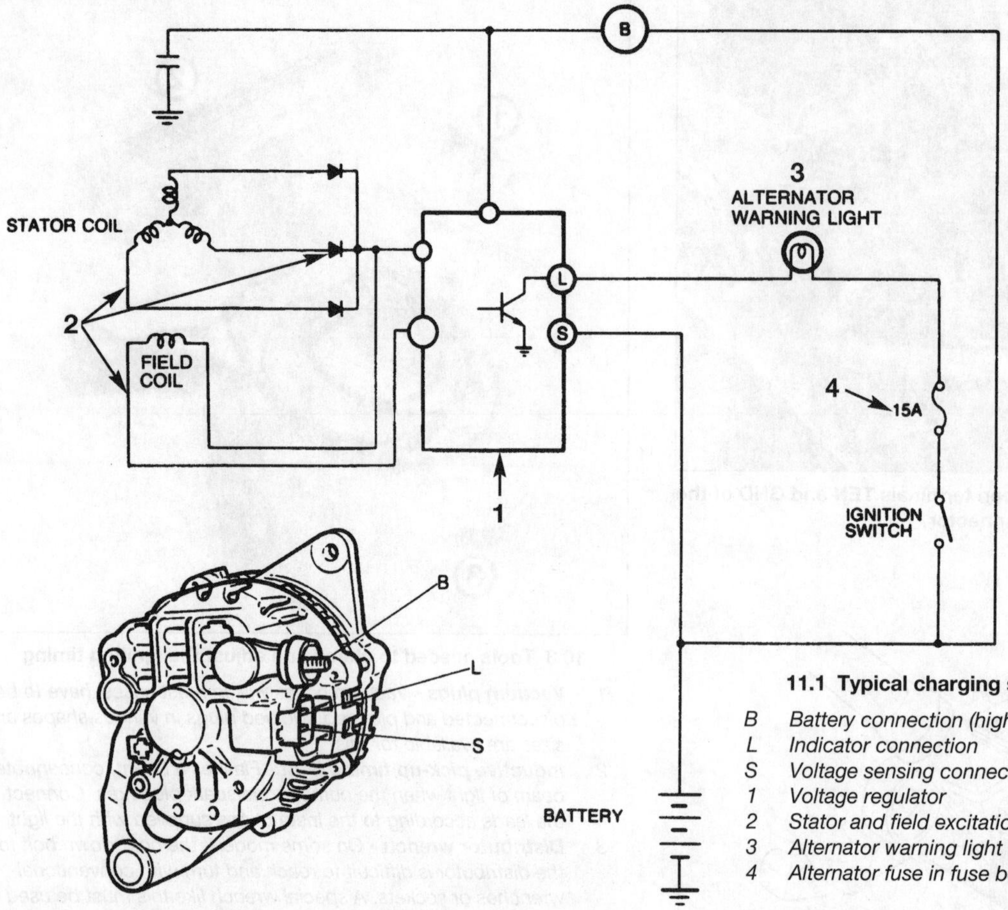

11.1 Typical charging system schematic diagram

B Battery connection (high current large wire connection)
L Indicator connection
S Voltage sensing connection
1 Voltage regulator
2 Stator and field excitation windings, diode bridge
3 Alternator warning light on dashboard
4 Alternator fuse in fuse box

components **(see illustration)**. The charging system supplies electrical power for the ignition system, the lights, the radio, etc. The alternator is driven by a drivebelt at the front of the engine.

The purpose of the voltage regulator is to limit the alternator's voltage to a preset value. This prevents power surges, circuit overloads, etc., during peak voltage output.

The charging system doesn't ordinarily require periodic maintenance. However, the drivebelt, battery and wires and connections should be inspected at the intervals outlined in Chapter 1.

The dashboard warning light should come on when the ignition key is turned to Start, then should go off immediately. If it remains on, there is a malfunction in the charging system. Some vehicles are also equipped with a voltage gauge. If the voltage gauge indicates abnormally high or low voltage, check the charging system (see Section 12).

Be very careful when making electrical circuit connections to a vehicle equipped with an alternator and note the following:

a) *When reconnecting wires to the alternator from the battery, be sure to note the polarity.*
b) *Before using arc welding equipment to repair any part of the vehicle, disconnect the wires from the alternator and the battery terminals.*
c) *Never start the engine with a battery charger connected.*
d) *Always disconnect both battery leads before using a battery charger.*
e) *The alternator is driven by an engine drivebelt which could cause serious injury if your hand, hair or clothes become entangled in it with the engine running.*
f) *Because the alternator is connected directly to the battery, it could arc or cause a fire if overloaded or shorted out.*
g) *Wrap a plastic bag over the alternator and secure it with rubber bands before steam cleaning the engine.*

12 Charging system - check

Refer to illustrations 12.7 and 12.8

1 If a malfunction occurs in the charging circuit, don't automatically assume that the alternator is causing the problem. First check the following items:

a) *Check the drivebelt tension and its condition. Replace it if worn or deteriorated.*
b) *Make sure the alternator mounting and adjustment bolts are tight.*
c) *Inspect the alternator wiring harness and the electrical connectors at the alternator and voltage regulator. They must be in good condition and tight.*
d) *Check the large main fuse in the engine compartment. If it's burned, determine the cause, repair the circuit and replace the fuse (the vehicle won't start and/or the accessories won't work if the fuse blows).*
e) *Check all the fuses that are in series with the charging system circuit. The location of these fuses may vary from year and model but the designations are the same.*
f) *Start the engine and check the alternator for abnormal noises (a shrieking or squealing sound indicates a bad bushing).*
g) *Check the specific gravity of the battery electrolyte. If it's low, charge the battery (doesn't apply to maintenance free batteries).*
h) *Make sure that the battery is fully charged (one bad cell in a battery can cause overcharging by the alternator).*
i) *Disconnect the battery cables (negative first, then positive). Inspect the battery posts and the cable clamps for corrosion. Clean them thoroughly if necessary* (see Chapter 1). *Reconnect the positive cable, then the negative cable.*

2 Using a voltmeter, check the battery voltage with the engine off. It

Terminal	Ign : on (V)	Idle (V)
B	B+	14.1—14.7
L	Approx. 1	14.1—14.7
S	B+	14.1—14.7

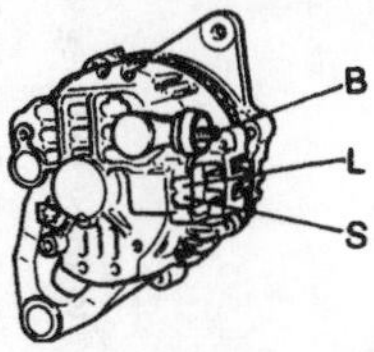

12.7 Check the voltages at the alternator terminals with the ignition On (engine not running) and at idle

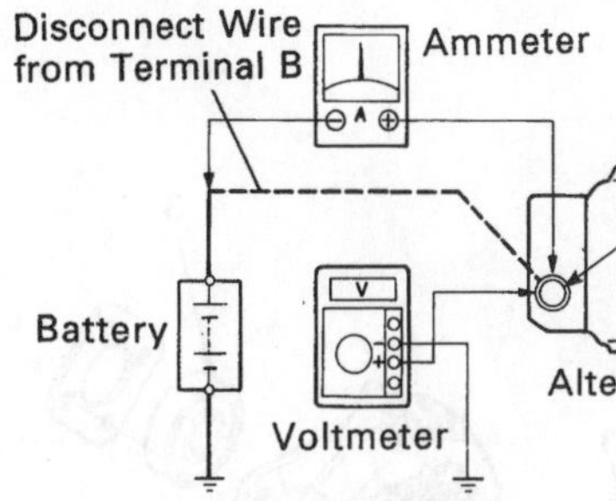

12.8 Hook up an ammeter as shown to check the alternator output

should be approximately 12 volts.

3 Start the engine and check the battery voltage again. It should now be approximately 13.5 to 15.1 volts.

4 Turn on the headlights. The voltage should drop and then come back up, if the charging system is working properly.

5 If the voltage reading is greater than the specified charging voltage, replace the voltage regulator (see Section 14).

6 If the voltmeter reading is less than standard voltage, check the regulator and alternator as follows.

7 Remove the cover from the alternator. Start the engine and check if voltages at alternator terminals as specified in the accompanying illustration **(see illustration)**.

a) If the voltmeter readings are greater than standard voltage, replace the regulator.

b) If the voltmeter reading is less than standard voltage, check the alternator (or have it checked by a dealer service department if you do not have an ammeter).

8 If you have an ammeter, hook it up to the charging system as shown **(see illustration)**. If you do not have an ammeter, you can also use an inductive-type current indicator. This device is inexpensive, readily available at auto parts stores and accurate enough to perform simple amperage checks like the following test.

9 With the engine running at 2,000 rpm, check the reading on the ammeter with all accessories and lights off, then again with the high-beam headlights on and the heater blower switch turned to the HI position. Compare your readings to the standard amperage listed in this Chapter's Specifications.

10 If the ammeter reading is less than standard amperage, repair or replace the alternator.

13 Alternator - removal and installation

Removal

Refer to illustrations 13.6, 13.7 and 13.12

1 Detach the cable from the negative terminal of the battery.

2 Remove the power steering pressure line brace, if equipped.

3 Remove the EGR solenoid valve bracket, if equipped.

4 Detach the electrical connector from the alternator **(see illustration)**.

5 Loosen the alternator adjustment, pivot and lock bolts **(see illustration)** and detach the drivebelt.

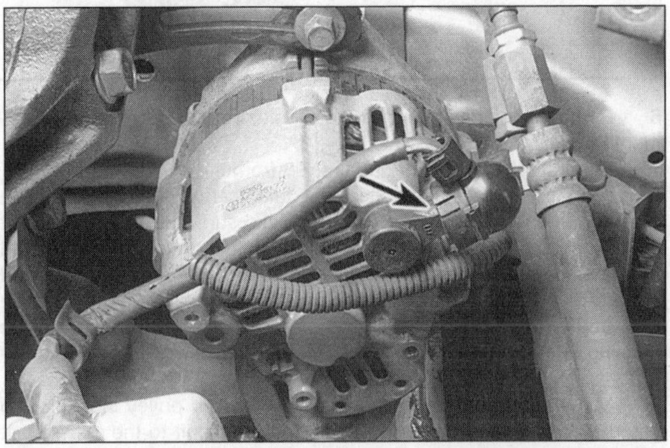

13.4 Detach the electrical connector from the alternator (arrow)

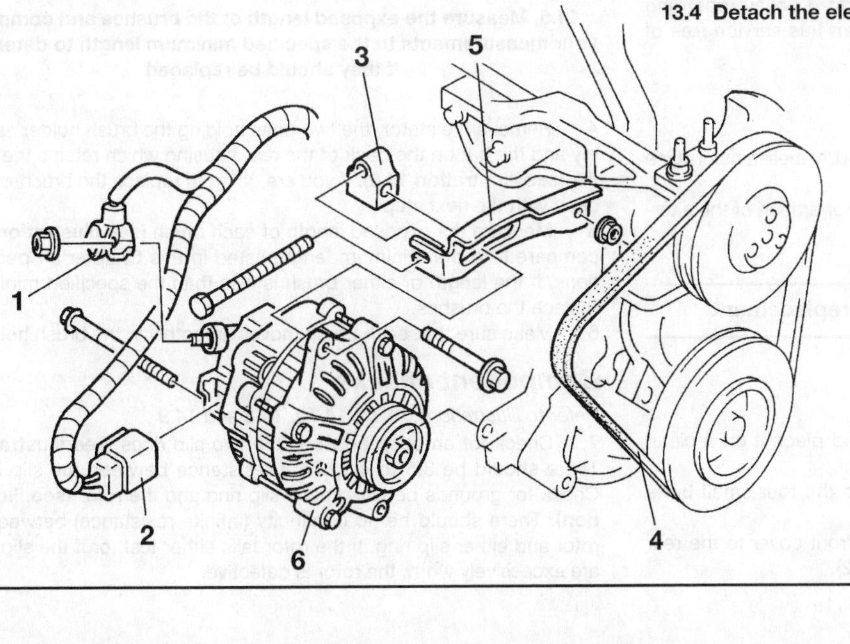

13.5 Alternator installation details

1 *Terminal wire B*
2 *Alternator connector (terminals L and S)*
3 *Belt tensioner*
4 *Drive belt*
5 *Alternator adjusting arm/bracket*
6 *Alternator*

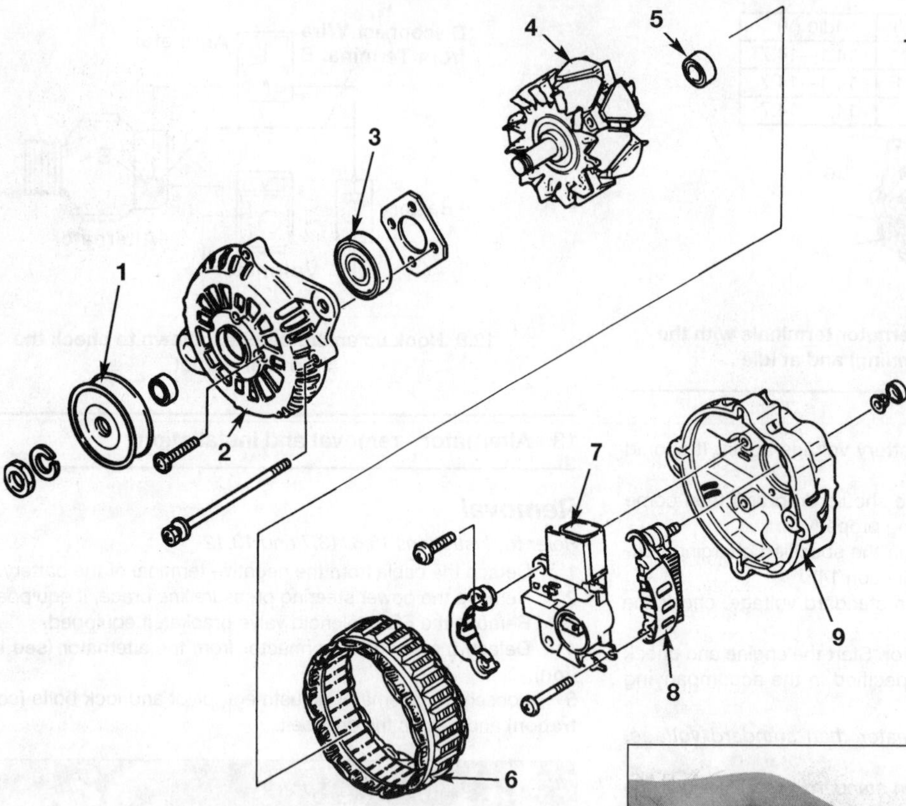

14.2 Exploded view of an alternator

1 *Pulley*
2 *Front cover*
3 *Bearing*
4 *Rotor*
5 *Bearing*
6 *Stator*
7 *Brush holder*
8 *Rectifier*
9 *Rear cover*

6 Remove the adjustment and lock bolts from the alternator adjustment bracket.

7 Separate the alternator and bracket from the engine.

8 If you are replacing the alternator, take the old alternator with you when purchasing a replacement unit. Make sure that the new/rebuilt unit is identical to the old alternator. Look at the terminals - they should be the same in number, size and locations as the terminals on the old alternator. Finally, look at the identification markings - they will be stamped in the housing or printed on a tag or plaque affixed to the housing. Make sure that these numbers are the same on both alternators.

9 Many new/rebuilt alternators do not have a pulley installed, so you may have to switch the pulley from the old unit to the new/rebuilt one. When buying an alternator, find out the store policy regarding installation of pulleys - some stores will perform this service free of charge.

Installation

10 Install in the reverse order of installation

11 After the alternator is installed, adjust the drivebelt tension (see Chapter 1).

12 Check the charging voltage to verify proper operation of the alternator (see Section 13).

14 Alternator components - check and replacement

Disassembly

Refer to illustrations 14.2 and 14.5

1 Remove the alternator (see Section 13) and place it on a clean workbench.

2 Remove the nut, lock-washer, pulley, and the four small bolts located behind the pulley **(see illustration)**.

3 Remove the four large bolts that hold the front cover to the rear housing and separate them **(see illustration 14.2)**.

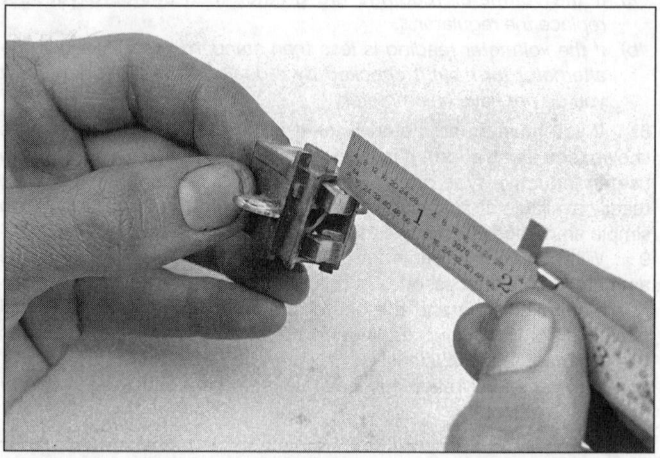

14.5 Measure the exposed length of the brushes and compare your measurements to the specified minimum length to determine if they should be replaced

4 Remove the stator, the two bolts holding the brush holder assembly and the nut on the back of the rear housing which retains the rectifier **(see illustration 14.2)**. If you are going to replace the brushes, proceed with the next step.

5 Measure the exposed length of each brush **(see illustration)** and compare it to the minimum length listed in this Chapter's Specifications. If the length of either brush is less than the specified minimum, replace the brushes.

6 Make sure that each brush moves smoothly in the brush holder.

Component checks

Refer to illustrations 14.7a, 14.7b, 14.8 and 14.9

7 Check for an open between the two slip rings **(see illustration)**. There should be 3.5 to 4.5 ohms resistance between the slip rings. Check for grounds between each slip ring and the rotor **(see illustration)**. There should be no continuity (infinite resistance) between the rotor and either slip ring. If the rotor fails either test, or if the slip rings are excessively worn, the rotor is defective.

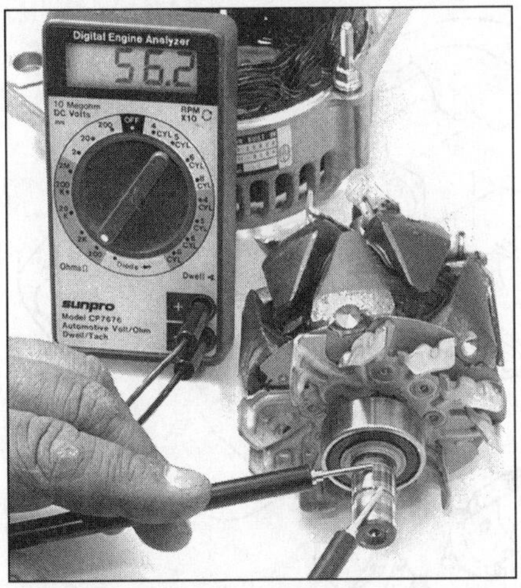

14.7a Continuity should exist between the rotor slip rings

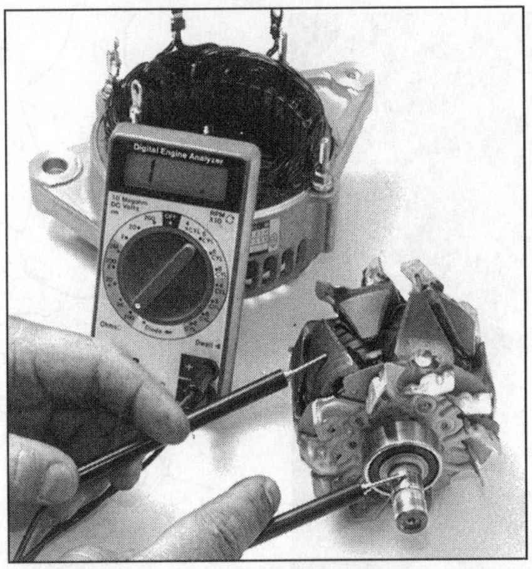

14.7b Check the continuity between the rotor and the slip rings. There should be NO continuity

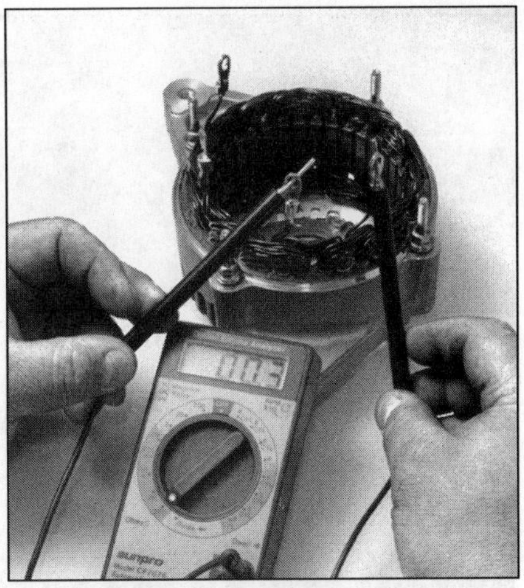

14.8 Check for continuity between the stator windings

8 Check for opens between each end terminal of the stator windings **(see illustration)**. If either reading is open (infinite resistance), the stator is defective. Check for a grounded stator winding between each stator terminal and the frame. If there's continuity between any stator winding and the frame, the stator is defective.

9 Using an ohmmeter, check the rectifier as shown **(see illustration)**. Replace the rectifier if it fails any of the tests.

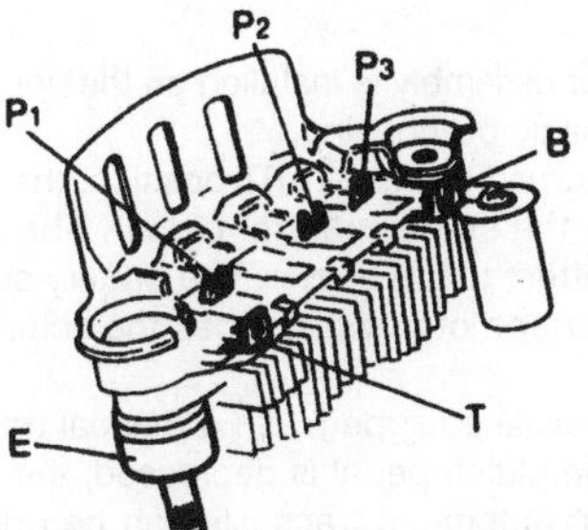

14.9 Rectifier terminal guide and continuity chart - connect the probes of an ohmmeter to the indicated terminals and check for continuity

Negative	Positive	Continuity
E	P1, P2, P3	Yes
B		No
T		No
P1, P2, P3	E	No
	B	Yes
P1, P2, P3	T	Yes

Reassembly

Refer to illustration 14.11

10 Install the components in the reverse order of removal, noting the following:

11 Install the brush holder by depressing each brush with a small screwdriver to clear the shaft **(see illustration)**.

15 Starting system - general information and precautions

Refer to illustration 15.2

1 The sole function of the starting system is to turn over the engine quickly enough to allow it to start.

2 The starting system consists of the battery, the starter motor, the starter solenoid and the electrical circuit connecting the components. The solenoid is mounted directly on the starter motor **(see illustration)**.

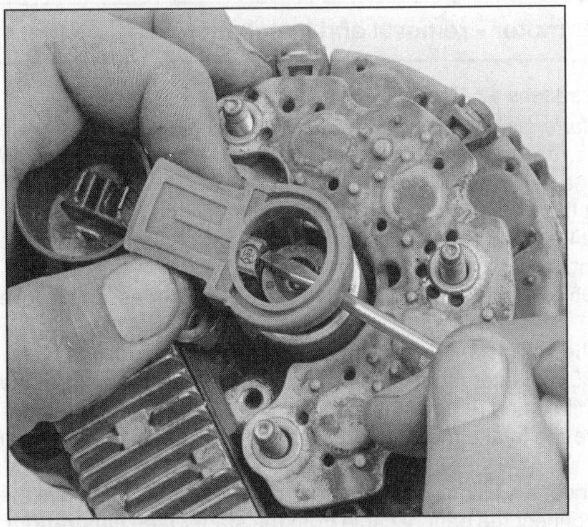

14.11 To facilitate installation of the brush holder, depress each brush with a small screwdriver to clear the shaft

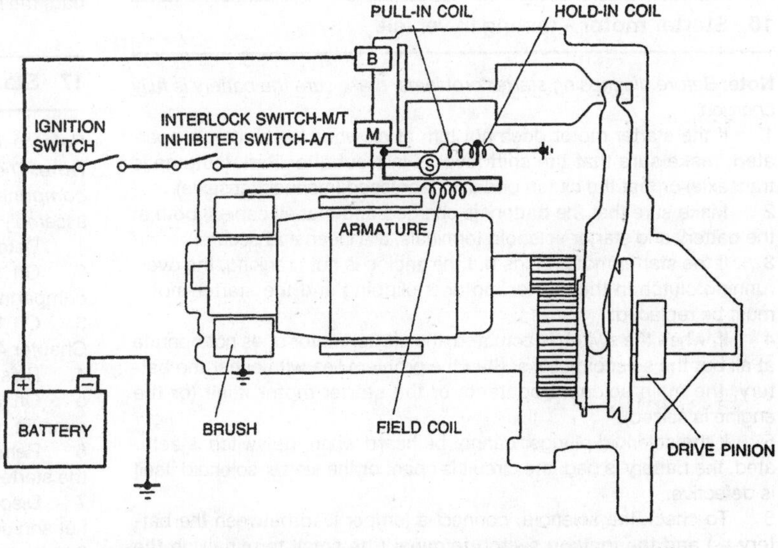

15.2 Wiring schematic of a typical starter/solenoid assembly

5

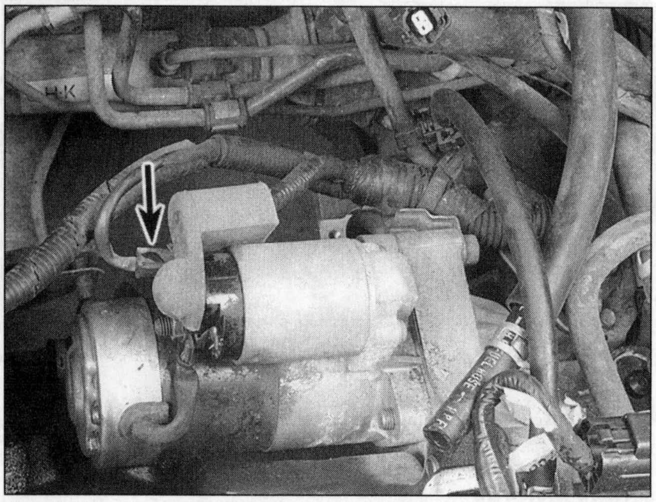

17.7 Disconnect the solenoid electrical connector and remove the battery cable from the starter

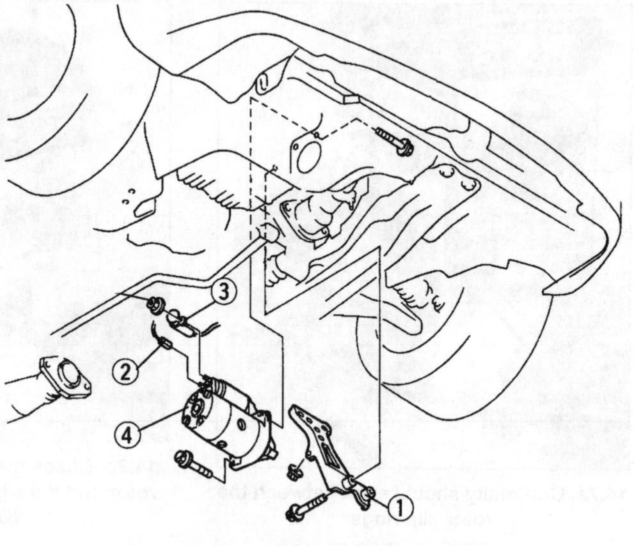

17.8 Starter motor installation details

1 Intake manifold support bracket
2 Terminal S connector
3 Terminal B connector
4 Starter

3 The solenoid/starter motor assembly is installed on the upper part of the engine, next to the transaxle bellhousing.

4 When the ignition key is turned to the START position, the starter solenoid is actuated through the starter control circuit. The starter solenoid then connects the battery to the starter. The battery supplies the electrical energy to the starter motor, which does the actual work of cranking the engine.

5 The starter motor on a vehicle equipped with a manual transaxle can be operated only when the clutch pedal is depressed; the starter on a vehicle equipped with an automatic transaxle can be operated only when the transaxle selector lever is in Park or Neutral.

6 Always observe the following precautions when working on the starting system:

a) *Excessive cranking of the starter motor can overheat it and cause serious damage. Never operate the starter motor for more than 15 seconds at a time without pausing to allow it to cool for at least two minutes.*
b) *The starter is connected directly to the battery and could arc or cause a fire if mishandled, overloaded or short circuited.*
c) *Always detach the cable from the negative terminal of the battery before working on the starting system.*

16 Starter motor - testing in vehicle

Note: *Before diagnosing starter problems, make sure the battery is fully charged.*

1 If the starter motor does not turn at all when the switch is operated, make sure that the shift lever is in Neutral or Park (automatic transaxle) or that the clutch pedal is depressed (manual transaxle).

2 Make sure that the battery is charged and that all cables, both at the battery and starter solenoid terminals, are clean and secure.

3 If the starter motor spins but the engine is not cranking, the overrunning clutch in the starter motor is slipping and the starter motor must be replaced.

4 If, when the switch is actuated, the starter motor does not operate at all but the solenoid clicks, then the problem lies with either the battery, the main solenoid contacts or the starter motor itself (or the engine is seized).

5 If the solenoid plunger cannot be heard when the switch is actuated, the battery is bad, the circuit is open, or the starter solenoid itself is defective.

6 To check the solenoid, connect a jumper lead between the battery (+) and the ignition switch terminal (the small terminal) on the solenoid. If the starter motor now operates, the solenoid is OK and the problem is in the ignition switch, Neutral start switch or in the wiring.

7 If the starter motor still does not operate, remove the starter/solenoid assembly for disassembly, testing and repair.

8 If the starter motor cranks the engine at an abnormally slow speed, first make sure that the battery is charged and that all terminal connections are tight. If the engine is partially seized, or has the wrong viscosity oil in it, it will crank slowly.

9 Run the engine until normal operating temperature is reached, then disconnect the coil wire from the distributor cap and ground it on the engine.

10 Connect a voltmeter positive lead to the battery positive post and connect the negative lead to the negative post.

11 Crank the engine and take the voltmeter readings as soon as a steady figure is indicated. Do not allow the starter motor to turn for more than 15 seconds at a time. A reading of nine volts or more, with the starter motor turning at normal cranking speed, is normal. If the reading is nine volts or more but the cranking speed is slow, the motor is faulty. If the reading is less than nine volts and the cranking speed is slow, the solenoid contacts are probably burned, the starter motor is bad, the battery is discharged or there is a bad connection.

17 Starter motor - removal and installation

Refer to illustrations 17.7 and 17.8

Note: *The starter/solenoid assembly cannot be repaired using separate components. In the event of failure, exchange the starter/solenoid assembly for a new or rebuilt unit.*

1 Detach the cable from the negative terminal of the battery.

2 On 1994 and earlier models, remove the battery from the engine compartment.

3 On 1995 and later models, remove the air cleaner assembly (see Chapter 4).

4 Raise the vehicle and support it securely on jackstands.

5 On 1995 and later models, disconnect the exhaust pipe from the exhaust manifold and remove the catalytic converter (see Chapter 4).

6 Remove the Intake manifold bracket and the starter bracket from the starter.

7 Disconnect the electrical connector from the solenoid, remove the nut and disconnect the battery cable from the starter **(see illustration)**.

8 Remove starter mounting bolts and remove the starter **(see illustration)**.

9 Installation is the reverse of removal.

Chapter 6
Emissions and engine control systems

Contents

1 General Information

Refer to illustrations 1.1a, 1.1b, 1.6a and 1.6b

1 To minimize pollution of the atmosphere from incompletely burned and evaporating gases and to maintain good driveability and fuel economy, a number of emission control systems are used on these vehicles **(see illustrations)**. They include the:

Positive Crankcase Ventilation (PCV) system
Evaporative Emission Control (EVAP) system
Exhaust Gas Recirculation (EGR) system (1995 and later)
Three-way catalytic converter (TWC) system
Powertrain Control Module (PCM)
Idle Speed Control (ISC) System

2 The Sections in this Chapter include general descriptions, checking procedures within the scope of the home mechanic and component replacement procedures (when possible) for each of the systems listed above.

3 Before assuming an emissions control system is malfunctioning, check the fuel and ignition systems carefully (see Chapters 4 and 5).

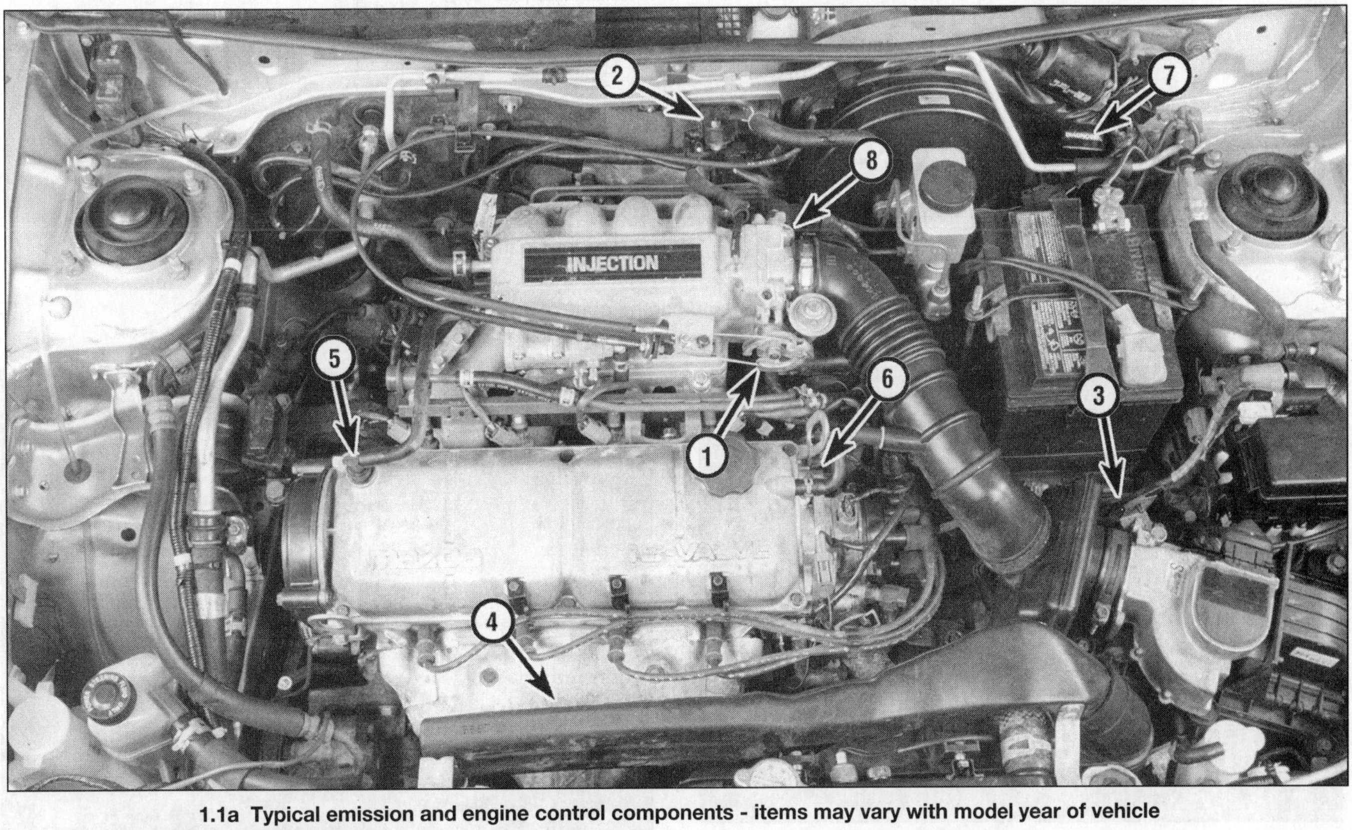

1.1a Typical emission and engine control components - items may vary with model year of vehicle

1 *Idle Speed Control (ISC) valve*
2 *Solenoid valve (purge control)*
3 *Intake Air Temperature (IAT) sensor*
4 *Oxygen sensor (not visible this view)*
5 *Positive Crankcase Ventilation (PCV) valve*
6 *Coolant temperature sensor*
7 *Diagnostic connector*
8 *Throttle position sensor*

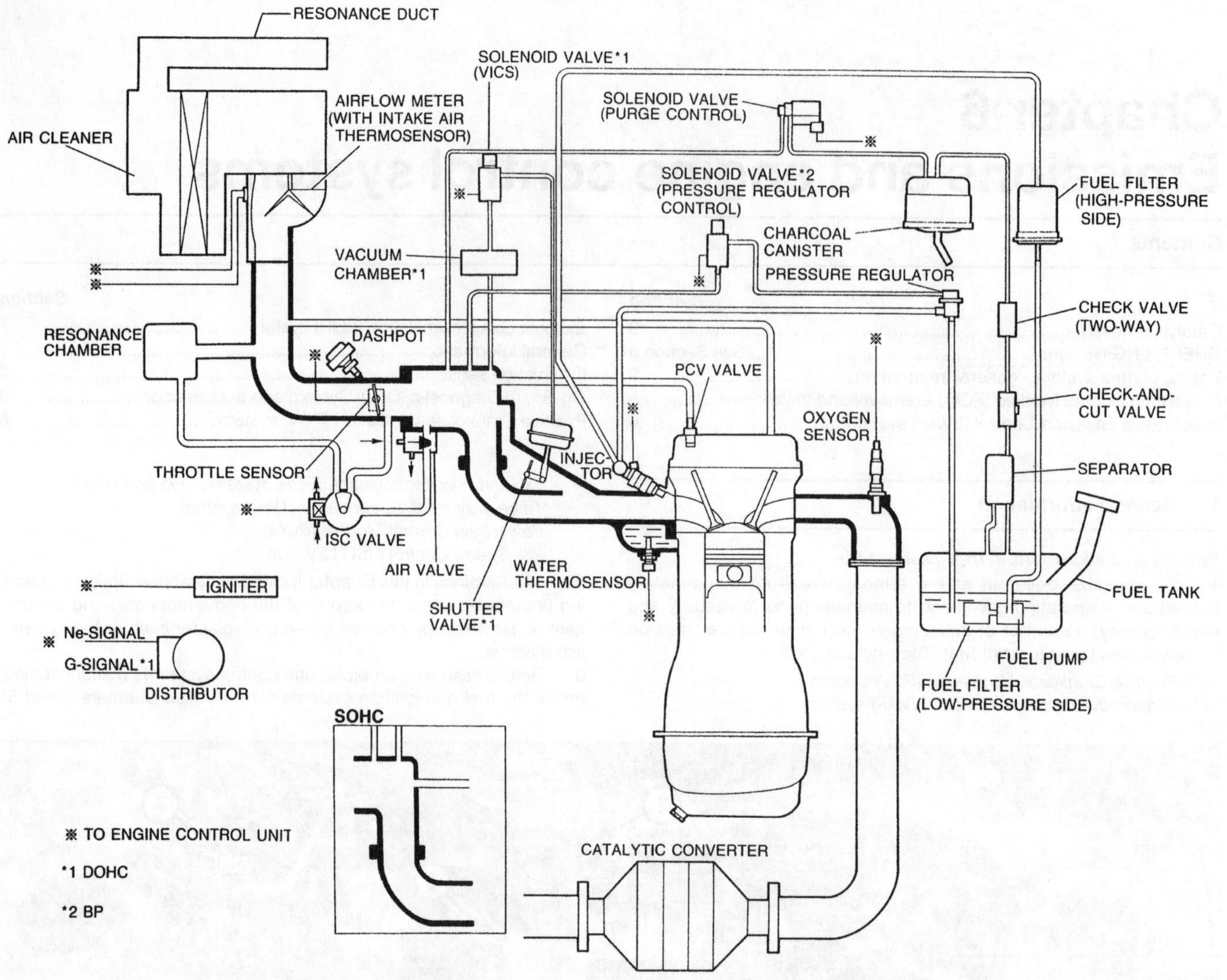

1.1b Typical emissions and engine control systems layout

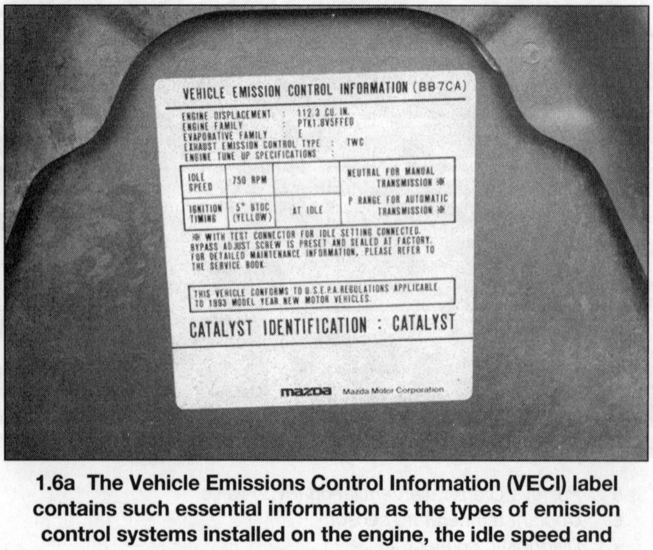

1.6a The Vehicle Emissions Control Information (VECI) label contains such essential information as the types of emission control systems installed on the engine, the idle speed and ignition timing specifications

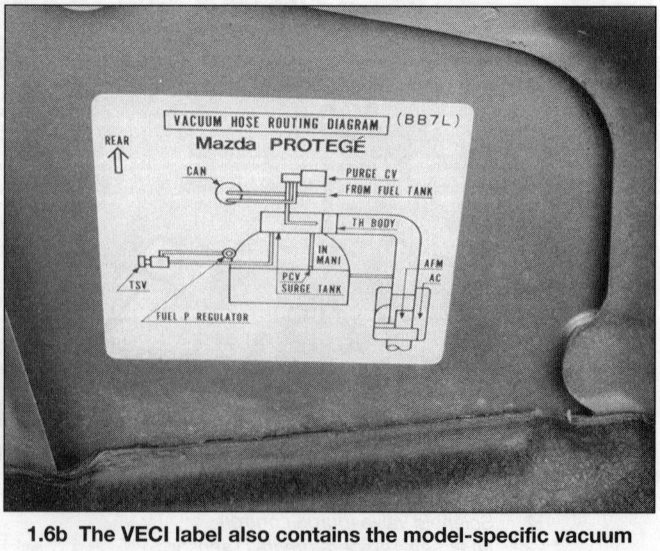

1.6b The VECI label also contains the model-specific vacuum hose routing diagram

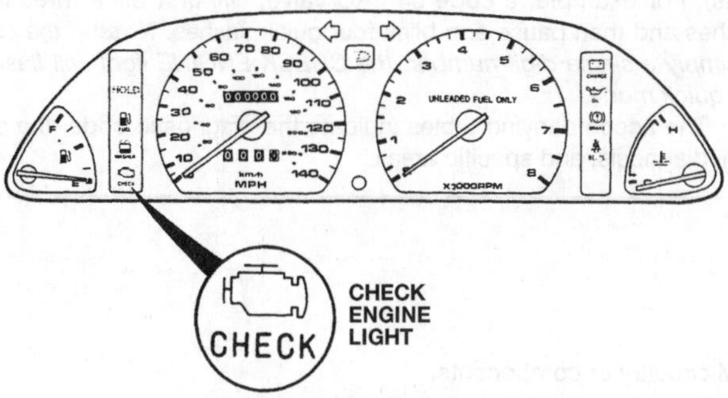

3.1 The CHECK ENGINE light will illuminate if a problem is detected with the engine control system

The diagnosis of some emission control devices requires specialized tools, equipment and training. If checking and servicing become too difficult or if a procedure is beyond the scope of your skills, consult your dealer service department or other repair shop.

4 This doesn't mean, however, that emission control systems are particularly difficult to maintain and repair. You can quickly and easily perform many checks and do most of the regular maintenance at home with common tune-up and hand tools. **Note:** *The most frequent cause of emissions problems is simply a loose or broken electrical connector or vacuum hose, so always check the vacuum hoses and electrical connectors.*

5 Pay close attention to any special precautions outlined in this Chapter. It should be noted that the illustrations of the various systems may not exactly match the system installed on your vehicle because of changes made by the manufacturer during production or from year-to-year.

6 The Vehicle Emissions Control Information (VECI) label and a vacuum hose diagram are located on the hood **(see illustrations)**. These contain important emissions specifications and setting procedures, and a vacuum hose schematic with emissions components identified. When servicing the engine or emissions systems, the VECI label in your particular vehicle should always be checked for up-to-date information.

2 Engine control system - general information

General information

1 The fuel injection system is controlled by means of a microcomputer known as the Powertrain Control Module (PCM).

2 The PCM receives signals from various sensors which monitor changing engine operating conditions such as intake air volume, intake air temperature, coolant temperature, engine rpm, acceleration/deceleration, exhaust oxygen content, etc. These signals are utilized by the PCM to determine the correct fuel injection duration.

3 The system is analogous to the central nervous system in the human body: The sensors (nerve endings) constantly relay signals to the PCM (brain), which processes the data and, if necessary, sends out a command to change the operating parameters of the engine (body).

4 Here's a specific example of how one portion of this system operates: An oxygen sensor, located in the exhaust manifold, constantly monitors the oxygen content of the exhaust gas. If the percentage of oxygen in the exhaust gas is incorrect, an electrical signal is sent to the PCM. The PCM takes this information, processes it and then sends a command to the fuel injection system telling it to change the air/fuel mixture. This happens in a fraction of a second and it goes on continuously when the engine is running. The end result is an air/fuel mixture ratio which is constantly maintained at a predetermined ratio, regardless of driving conditions.

5 In the event of a sensor malfunction, a backup circuit will take over to provide driveability until the problem is identified and fixed.

3.3 To access the diagnostic system, connect the TEN terminal and GND terminal of the Diagnostic Connector with a jumper wire (1994 and earlier models only)

Precautions

6 Follow these steps:

a) *Always disconnect the power by either turning off the ignition switch or disconnecting the battery terminals before unplugging any electrical connectors.*
b) *When installing a battery, be particularly careful to avoid reversing the positive and negative battery cables.*
c) *Do not subject Electronic Fuel Injection components, emissions-related components or the PCM to severe impact during removal or installation.*
d) *Do not be careless during troubleshooting. Even slight terminal contact can invalidate a testing procedure and damage one of the numerous transistor circuits.*
e) *Never attempt to work on the PCM or open the PCM cover. The PCM is protected by a government-mandated extended warranty that will be nullified if you tamper with or damage the PCM.*
f) *If you are inspecting Engine control system components during rainy weather, make sure that water does not enter any part. When washing the engine compartment, do not spray these parts or their electrical connectors with water.*

6

3 On-Board Diagnostic (OBD) System and trouble codes

Refer to illustrations 3.1, 3.3

Note: *This procedure does not include the diagnostic codes or the code extracting procedure for 1995 or later models equipped with the OBD II system. These models require a special SCAN tool to read out the various levels of coded information. Have the 1995 or later models diagnosed by a dealer service department or other qualified repair shop in the event of computer failure.*

1 The PCM (computer) has a built-in self-diagnosis system which detects malfunctions in the system sensors and alerts the driver by illuminating a CHECK ENGINE warning light in the instrument panel **(see illustration)**. The computer stores the failure code until the diagnostic system is cleared by disconnecting the negative battery cable then depressing the brake pedal for a period of five seconds or longer. The warning light goes out automatically when the malfunction is repaired.

2 The CHECK ENGINE warning light should come on when the ignition switch is placed in the On position, this checks the bulb for proper operation. When the engine is started the warning light should go out. If the light remains on, the diagnostic system has detected a malfunction or abnormality in the system.

3 To determine which sensor or system component is malfunctioning, connect a jumper wire between the TEN and GND terminals at the DIAGNOSTIC test connector **(see illustration)** in the engine compartment. Make sure the battery voltage is greater than 11 volts, the transmission is in Neutral, the accessories are off, the throttle valve is closed and the engine is at normal operating temperature, then turn

the ignition switch to the ON position but do not start the engine.
4 The diagnostic code is the number of flashes indicated on the CHECK ENGINE light. If no codes are stored, the CHECK ENGINE light will come on for a few moments, then go out. If any malfunction has been detected, the light will blink the first digit(s) of the code at a long interval(s) and then blink the second digit of the code at short interval(s). For example, a code 34 (IAC valve) will first blink three long flashes and then pause and blink four quick flashes. **Note:** *If the code is simply a single digit number, the CHECK ENGINE light will flash in the quick mode.*
5 The accompanying tables indicate the diagnostic code, the system, diagnosis, and specific areas.

Diagnostic trouble code chart

Note: *Not all codes apply to all models.*

Trouble code	Circuit or system	Corrective action
02	Distributor Ne-signal	Check the distributor and PCM circuitry or components.
03	Distributor G-signal	Check the distributor and PCM circuitry or components.
08	Airflow sensor	Check the airflow sensor circuit from the sensor to the PCM for an open or short circuit or a sensor malfunction.
09	Coolant temperature sensor	Check the coolant temperature sensor circuit for an open or short circuit or a sensor malfunction.
10	Intake air temperature sensor	Check the intake air temperature sensor circuit for an open or short circuit or a sensor malfunction.
12	Throttle position sensor	Check the throttle position sensor circuit for an open or short circuit or a sensor malfunction.
14	Barometric pressure sensor	The barometric pressure sensor is integrated within the PCM. Check the PCM power and ground circuits. If no fault is found with the circuits, replace the PCM.
15	Oxygen sensor	Check the oxygen sensor circuit for an open or short circuit or a sensor malfunction.
17	Oxygen sensor has detected a rich or lean condition	Check the fuel and ignition system performance (i.e. fuel pressure high or low, leaking fuel injectors, inoperative fuel injector, intake air leaks, ignition misfire, etc.).
25	Solenoid valve (fuel pressure regulator)	Check for an open or short circuit from the solenoid valve to the PCM. Check for an open or short circuit from the solenoid valve to the fuel injection main relay. Check for a defective solenoid valve.
26	Solenoid valve (purge control)	Check for an open or short circuit from the solenoid valve to the PCM. Check for an open or short circuit from the solenoid valve to the fuel injection main relay. Check for a defective solenoid valve.
34	IAC valve	Check for an open or short circuit from the IAC valve to the PCM. Check for an open or short circuit from the IAC valve to the fuel injection main relay. Check for a defective IAC valve.
41	Solenoid valve (VICS) (DOHC only)	Check for an open or short circuit from the solenoid valve to the PCM. Check for an open or short circuit from the solenoid valve to the fuel injection main relay. Check for a defective solenoid valve.

Clearing the codes

6 After the self-diagnosis check, remove the jumper wire and close the cover on the DIAGNOSTIC electrical connector. Check the indicated system or component or take the vehicle to a dealer service department to have the malfunction repaired.
7 After repairs have been made, the diagnostic code must be canceled by detaching the cable from the negative terminal of the battery, then depressing the brake pedal for more than 5 seconds.
8 After cancellation, perform a road test and make sure the warning light does not come on. If the original trouble code is repeated, additional repairs are required.

4 Information sensors

Note: *Most of the components described in this Section are protected by a Federally mandated extended warranty. See your dealer for the details regarding your vehicle. Refer to Chapters 4 and 5 for additional information on the location and the diagnostic procedures for the sensors that are not directly covered in this Section.*

Coolant temperature sensor

General description

Refer to illustration 4.1

1 The coolant temperature sensor is a thermistor (a resistor which varies the value of its voltage output in accordance with temperature changes). As the sensor temperature DECREASES, the resistance values will INCREASE. As the sensor temperature INCREASES, the resistance values will DECREASE **(see illustration)**. A failure in this sensor circuit should set a Code 09. This code indicates a failure in the

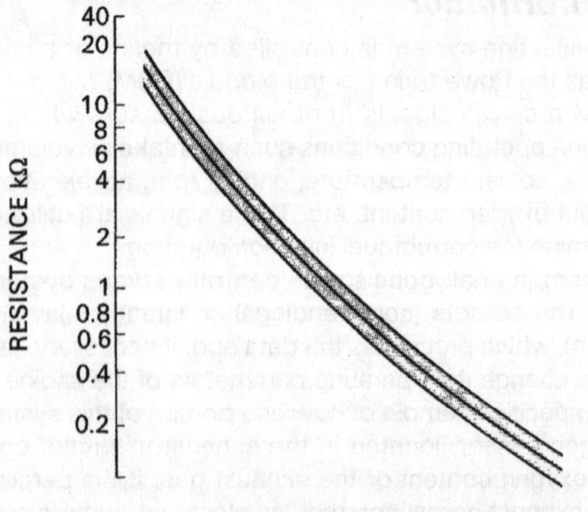

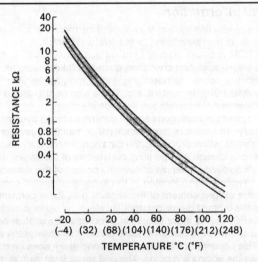

4.1 Compare the indicated resistance values with the temperature specified on this graph - note that as the temperature increases (as the engine warms up) the resistance decreases

4.2a Location of the coolant temperature sensor (arrow)

4.2b To check the coolant temperature sensor, use an ohmmeter to measure the resistance between the two sensor terminals

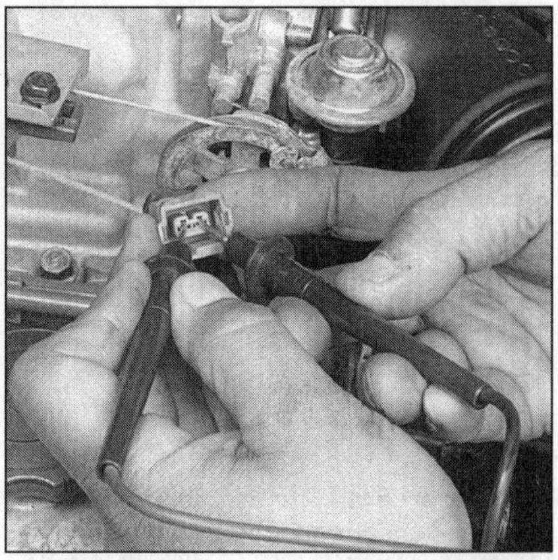

4.3 Use a voltmeter and probe the coolant temperature sensor connector for reference voltage with the ignition key ON (engine not running). It should be approximately 5.0 volts

coolant temperature sensor circuit, so in most cases the appropriate solution to the problem will be either repair of a connector or wire, or replacement of the sensor.

Check

Refer to illustrations 4.2a, 4.2b and 4.3

2 To check the sensor, depress the locking tabs, disconnect the electrical connector **(see illustration)** and measure the resistance across the terminals of the engine-mounted sensor **(see illustration)**. With the engine completely cold (68 degrees F) the resistance should be 2,000 to 3,000 ohms. Next, start the engine and warm it up until it reaches operating temperature (180 degrees F) - the resistance should be 200 to 400 ohms. **Note:** *If necessary, remove the sensor and perform the tests in a pan of heated water to simulate the conditions. Compare the resistance values with the accompanying graph.*

3 If the resistance values of the coolant temperature sensor are correct, check the circuit for the proper signal voltage. Turn the ignition key ON (engine not running) and check for reference voltage **(see illustration)**. It should be approximately 5 volts.

Replacement

4 To remove the sensor, carefully unscrew the sensor. **Caution:** *Handle the coolant sensor with care. Damage to this sensor will affect the operation of the entire fuel injection system.*

5 Before installing the new sensor, wrap the threads with Teflon sealing tape to prevent leakage and thread corrosion.

6 Installation is the reverse of removal.

Oxygen sensor

General description

7 These models are equipped with either a single oxygen sensor system or a dual-stage oxygen sensor system. On dual-stage systems, the main oxygen sensor is mounted ahead of the front catalytic converter and monitors the exhaust gases exiting the engine. The sub oxygen sensor monitors the exhaust gases after they have passed through the front catalytic converter. Each oxygen sensor monitors the oxygen content of the exhaust gas stream. The oxygen content in the exhaust reacts with the oxygen sensor to produce a voltage output which varies from 0.1-volt (high oxygen, lean mixture) to 0.9-volts (low oxygen, rich mixture). The PCM constantly monitors this variable voltage output to determine the ratio of oxygen to fuel in the mixture. The PCM alters the air/fuel mixture ratio by controlling the pulse width (open time) of the fuel injectors. A mixture ratio of 14.7 parts air to 1 part fuel is the ideal mixture ratio for minimizing exhaust emissions, thus allowing the catalytic converter to operate at maximum efficiency. It is this ratio of 14.7 to 1 which the PCM and the oxygen sensor attempt to maintain at all times.

8 The oxygen sensor produces no voltage when the oxygen sensor is below its normal operating temperature of about 600 degrees F. During this initial period before warm-up, the PCM operates in open loop mode.

9 If the engine reaches normal operating temperature and/or has been running for two or more minutes, and if the main oxygen sensor is producing a steady signal voltage below 0.70-volts at 1,500 or more rpm, the PCM will set a Code 15.

10 When there is a problem with the oxygen sensor or its circuit, the PCM operates in the open loop mode - that is, it controls fuel delivery in accordance with a programmed default value instead of feedback information from the oxygen sensor.

11 The proper operation of the oxygen sensor depends on four conditions:

a) ***Electrical*** *- The low voltages generated by the sensor depend upon good, clean connections which should be checked whenever a malfunction of the sensor is suspected or indicated.*
b) ***Outside air supply*** *- The sensor is designed to allow air circulation to the internal portion of the sensor. Whenever the sensor is removed and installed or replaced, make sure the air passages are not restricted.*
c) ***Proper operating temperature*** *- The PCM will not react to the sensor signal until the sensor reaches approximately 600-degrees F. This factor must be taken into consideration when evaluating the performance of the sensor.*
d) ***Unleaded fuel*** *- The use of unleaded fuel is essential for proper operation of the sensor. Make sure the fuel you are using is of this type.*

12 In addition to observing the above conditions, special care must be taken whenever the sensor is serviced.

a) *The oxygen sensor has a permanently attached pigtail and electrical connector which should not be removed from the sensor. Damage to or removal of the pigtail or electrical connector can adversely affect operation of the sensor.*
b) *Grease, dirt and other contaminants should be kept away from the electrical connector and the louvered end of the sensor.*
c) *Do not use cleaning solvents of any kind on the oxygen sensor.*
d) *Do not drop or roughly handle the sensor.*
e) *The silicone boot must be installed in the correct position to prevent the boot from being melted and to allow the sensor to operate properly.*

Check

Refer to illustration 4.13

13 To check the oxygen sensor use a digital voltmeter to monitor the millivolt signal from the oxygen sensor during actual operating conditions. Locate the oxygen sensor electrical connector and backprobe

6

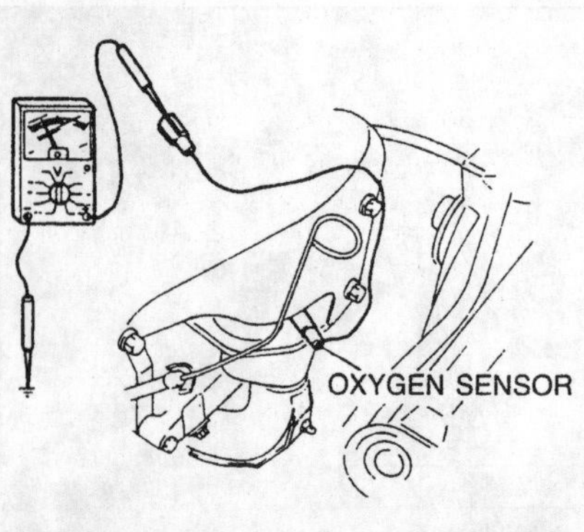

4.13 Insert a pin into the backside of the oxygen sensor connector on the correct terminal and check for a millivolt output signal generated by the sensor

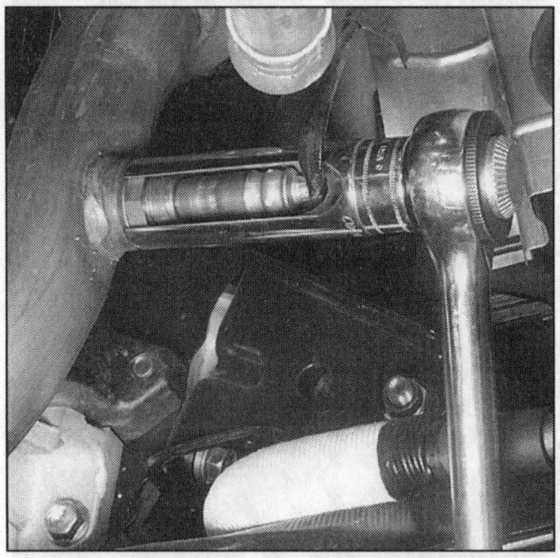
4.21 Slotted sockets are available for easing oxygen sensor removal

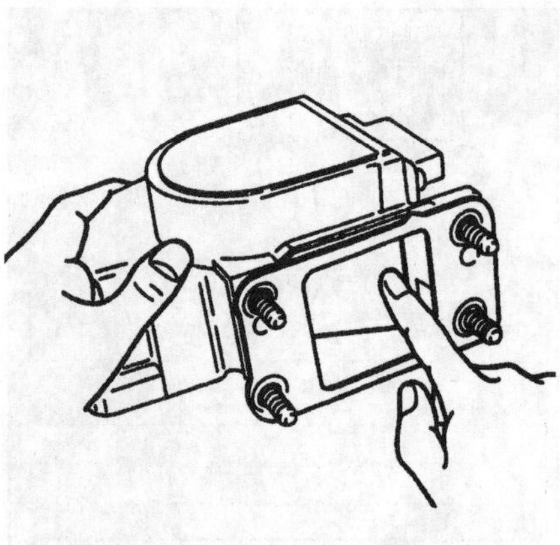
4.29 Check the vane inside the airflow sensor for smooth operation

the sensor wire on the harness side of the oxygen sensor connector **(see illustration)**. To properly backprobe the connector insert a long straight pin (a T-pin is preferred) alongside the wire until the pin contacts the metal wire terminal inside the connector. Connect the positive probe of a voltmeter onto the pin and the negative probe to ground. **Note:** *Refer to the wiring diagrams at the end of Chapter 12 to determine the correct terminals to probe when performing the oxygen sensor checks.*

14 Warm up the engine and monitor the voltage signal of the main oxygen sensor as the engine warms up. Run the engine at 3,000 rpm until the voltmeter indicates approximately 0.55-volt. Increase and decrease the engine speed suddenly several times. Verify that when the speed is increased the meter reads 0.5 to 1.0-volt, and when the speed is decreased it reads zero to 0.4-volt. If the oxygen sensor fails to operate as described, replace it.

15 On models equipped with a heated oxygen sensor, check the oxygen sensor heater as follows: Disconnect the oxygen sensor electrical connector and connect an ohmmeter between the positive and negative terminals on the oxygen sensor side of the connector. It should measure approximately 11.0 to 17.0 ohms. **Note:** *Not all models are equipped with a heated oxygen sensor. Models with heated oxygen sensors will be equipped with a four-wire electrical connector.*

16 Check for proper supply voltage to the oxygen sensor heater. With the ignition key ON (engine not running), check for battery voltage at the positive and negative terminals on the harness side of the connector.

17 To check the heated rear oxygen sensor on 1995 and later models, locate the electrical connector at the catalytic converter and check it in the same manner as the main oxygen sensor.

Replacement

Refer to illustration 4.21

Note: *Because it is installed in the exhaust manifold or pipe, which contracts when cool, the oxygen sensor may be very difficult to loosen when the engine is cold. Rather than risk damage to the sensor (assuming you are planning to reuse it in another manifold or pipe), start and run the engine for a minute or two, then shut it off. Be careful not to burn yourself during the following procedure.*

18 Disconnect the cable from the negative terminal of the battery.

19 Raise the vehicle and place it securely on jackstands.

20 Carefully disconnect the electrical connector from the sensor pigtail lead.

21 Remove the oxygen sensor from the exhaust system **(see illustration)**. **Caution:** *Excessive force may damage the threads.* **Note:** *Some oxygen sensors are threaded directly into the exhaust manifold while others are mounted in the exhaust manifold or pipe with two bolts.*

22 Anti-seize compound must be used on the threads of the sensor to facilitate future removal. The threads of new sensors will already be coated with this compound, but if an old sensor is removed and reinstalled, recoat the threads.

23 Install the sensor and tighten it securely.

24 Reconnect the electrical connector of the pigtail lead to the main engine wiring harness.

25 Lower the vehicle and reconnect the cable to the negative terminal of the battery.

Throttle Position Sensor (TPS)

General description

26 The Throttle Position Sensor (TPS) is located on the end of the throttle shaft on the throttle body (see Chapter 4). By monitoring the output voltage from the TPS, the PCM alters fuel delivery based on throttle valve angle (driver demand). A broken or loose TPS can cause intermittent bursts of fuel from the injector and an unstable idle because the PCM receives a signal that the throttle is moving. All the checks and replacement procedures are covered in Chapter 4.

Airflow sensor/intake air temperature sensor (1994 and earlier models)

General description

Note: *On 1994 and earlier models, the intake air temperature sensor is incorporated into the airflow sensor.*

27 The airflow sensor (located on top of the air cleaner housing) measures the volume or air entering the intake system using a vane-type potentiometer device. As air enters the air by-pass passage, the measuring plate (vane) swings open and allows an electrical device (potentiometer) to vary its voltage signal according to the position of the measuring plate. This information is relayed to the computer and is used to determine the correct amount of fuel to inject into the combustion chamber for the volume of air (load) that is demanded.

28 The intake air temperature sensor is located inside the airflow sensor. This sensor is a resistor which changes value according to the temperature of the air entering the engine. Low temperatures produce a high resistance value (for example, at 68 degrees F the resistance is 2,000 to 3,000 ohms) while high temperatures produce low resistance values (at 176 degrees F the resistance is 200 to 400 ohms **(see illustration 4.43b)**. The PCM supplies approximately 5-volts (reference voltage) to the air temperature sensor. The IAT sensor alters the voltage according to the temperature of the incoming air. The signal voltage sent back to the PCM will be high when the air temperature is cold and low when the air temperature is warm. Any problems with the air temperature sensor will usually set a diagnostic code 10.

Check

Refer to illustrations 4.29 and 4.30

29 Remove the airflow sensor and check the body for cracks or damage, with your finger, press the vane in and make sure it moves smoothly and does not bind **(see illustration)**.

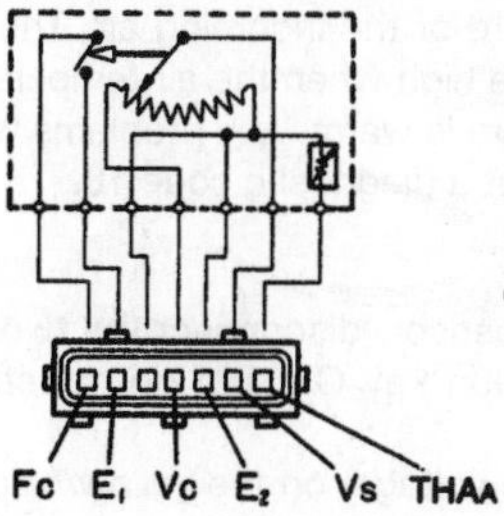

4.30 Airflow sensor and intake air temperature sensor terminal guide and continuity chart - 1994 and earlier models

Terminal	Resistance (Ω)	
	Closed throttle position	Wide open throttle
E2 ↔ Vs	20—600	20—1,000
E2 ↔ Vc	200—400	
E2 ↔ THAA (Intake air temperature sensor)	−20°C {−4°F}: 13.6—18.4 KΩ 20°C { 68°F}: 2.21—2.69 kΩ 60°C {140°F}: 493—667Ω	
E1 ↔ Fc	∞	0

30 Using the accompanying terminal guide and chart **(see illustration)**, measure the resistance of the airflow meter on the designated terminals with the vane in the closed throttle position, then in the open throttle position. Measure the resistance of the intake air temperature sensor and compare it with the chart. If the values are not as specified, replace the sensor.

Replacement

31 Disconnect the electrical connector from the sensor.
32 Remove the intake duct from the sensor and remove the sensor and air cleaner housing top cover from the vehicle.
33 Remove the screws retaining the sensor to the housing and remove the sensor.
34 Installation is the reverse of removal.

Airflow sensor (1995 and later models)

General description

35 The airflow sensor is located in the air intake duct. The sensor uses a hot wire sensing element to measure the amount of air entering the intake system. The air passing over the hot wire causes it to cool. Consequently, this change in temperature can be converted into an analog voltage signal to the PCM which in turn, calculates the required fuel injector pulse width.

Check

36 Disconnect the electrical connector from the airflow sensor and check for battery voltage on the white/red wire terminal with the ignition key On. Check for continuity to ground on the black wire terminal. Repair the circuits if necessary.
37 Reconnect the connector and using a straight pin, backprobe the light green/blue wire terminal, on most models (refer to the wiring diagrams at the end of Chapter 12).
38 With the ignition On, there should be approximately 2.0 volts present. Start the engine and allow it to idle, the voltmeter should now read 1.0 to 2.5 volts. If the voltage is not as specified check the connectors and the circuit from the PCM to the airflow sensor. If the connectors and circuit are good, replace the airflow sensor.

Replacement

39 Disconnect the electrical connector from the sensor.
40 Loosen the hose clamp and remove the intake duct from the sensor.
41 Remove the screws attaching the sensor to the air cleaner housing and remove the sensor.
42 Installation is the reverse of removal.

Intake Air Temperature (IAT) sensor (1995 and later models)

General description

Refer to illustrations 4.43a and 4.43b

43 The intake air temperature (IAT) sensor is located inside the air cleaner housing. This sensor is a resistor which changes value according to the temperature of the air entering the engine. Low temperatures produce a high resistance value (for example, at 68 degrees F the resistance is 2,000 to 3,000 ohms) while high temperatures produce low resistance values (at 176 degrees F the resistance is 200 to 400 ohms **(see illustrations)**. The PCM supplies approximately 5-volts (reference voltage) to the air temperature sensor. The IAT sensor alters the

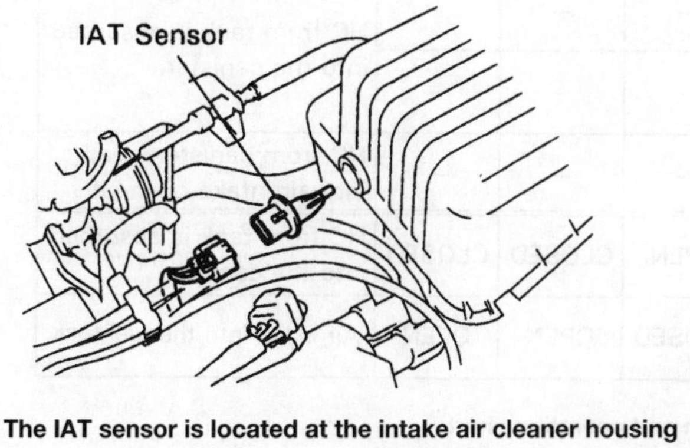

4.43a The IAT sensor is located at the intake air cleaner housing

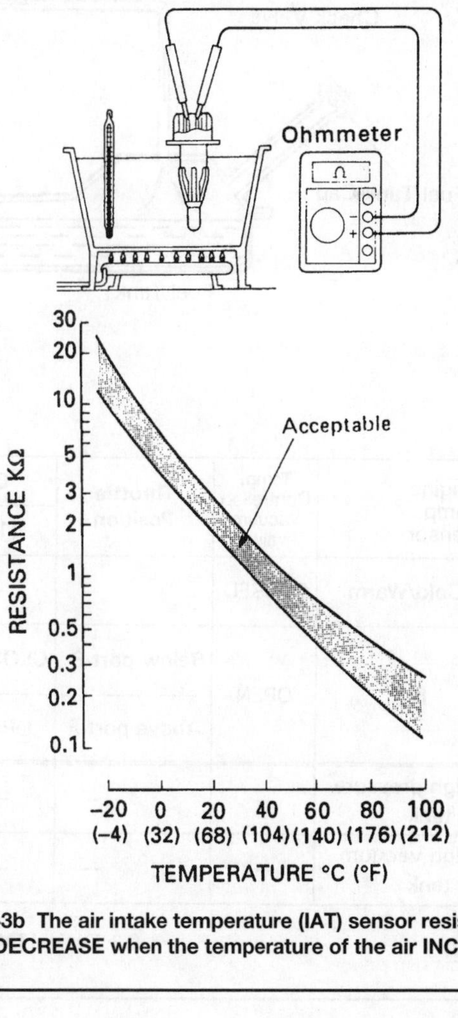

4.43b The air intake temperature (IAT) sensor resistance will DECREASE when the temperature of the air INCREASES

5.3 The PCM is located behind the center console - CAREFULLY disconnect the electrical connectors before removal of mounting hardware

voltage according to the temperature of the incoming air. The signal voltage sent back to the PCM will be high when the air temperature is cold and low when the air temperature is warm. Any problems with the air temperature sensor will usually set a diagnostic code 10.

Check

44 To check the air temperature sensor, disconnect the two prong electrical connector. Turn the ignition key ON, but do not start the engine.

45 Measure the voltage (reference voltage) on the yellow/black wire terminal. The VOM should read approximately 5-volts.

46 If the reference voltage is not correct, have the PCM diagnosed by a dealer service department or other repair shop.

47 Measure the resistance across the air temperature sensor terminals . The resistance should be HIGH when the air temperature is LOW. Next, start the engine and let it idle. Wait awhile and let the engine reach operating temperature. Turn the ignition OFF, disconnect the air temperature sensor and measure the resistance across the terminals. The resistance should be LOW when the air temperature is HIGH. If the sensor does not exhibit this change in resistance, replace the sensor.

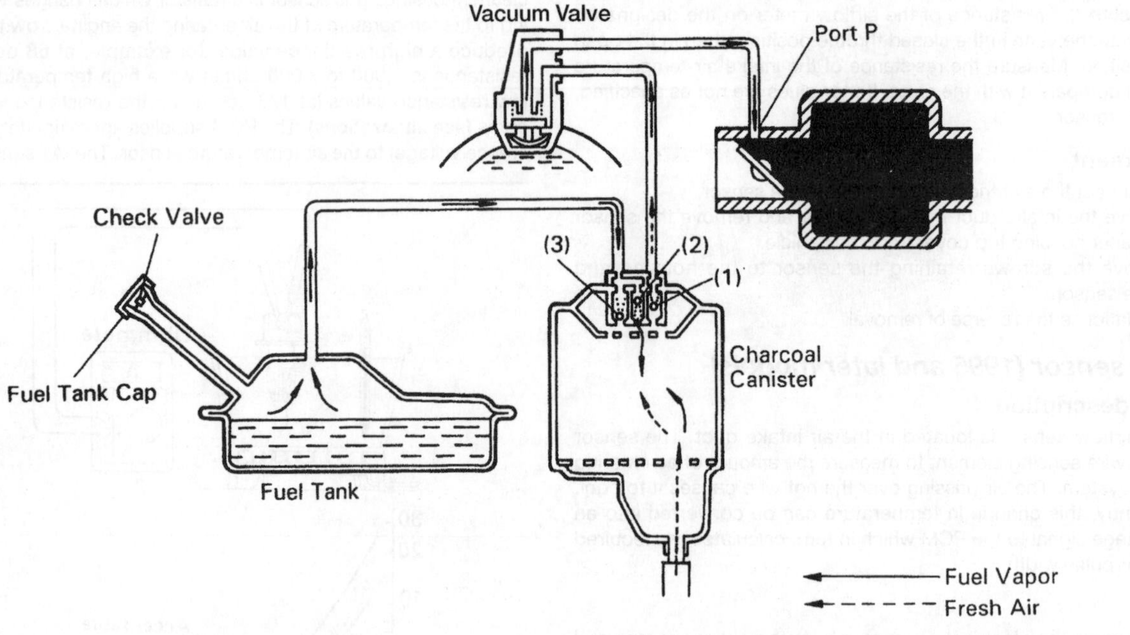

Engine Temp. Sensor	Temp. Controlled Vacuum Valve	Throttle Position	Canister Check Valve (1)	Canister Check Valve (2)	Canister Check Valve (3)	Check Valve in Cap	Evaporated Fuel (HC)
Cold/Warm	CLOSED	—	—	—	—	—	HC from tank is absorbed into the canister.
Hot	OPEN	Below port P	CLOSED	—	—	—	
		Above port P	OPEN	—	—	—	HC from canister is led into air intake chamber.
High pressure in tank		—	—	OPEN	CLOSED	CLOSED	HC from tank is absorbed into the canister.
High vacuum in tank		—	—	CLOSED	OPEN	OPEN	Air is led into the fuel tank.

6.2 Typical EVAP system and operation chart

6.10 Apply air pressure into the charcoal canister purge control valve inlet side

6.11 Apply air pressure to port A on the temperature controlled vacuum valve

Replacement

48 Disconnect the electrical connector from the sensor.
49 Detach the sensor from the air cleaner housing.
50 Install the sensor and connect the electrical connector.

Crankshaft Position Sensor - 1995 and later models

General Description

51 The crankshaft position sensor is located in the timing belt cover near the crankshaft pulley . The crankshaft position sensor relays a signal to the PCM to indicate the exact position (angle) of the crankshaft.

Check

52 Using an ohmmeter, measure the resistance of the crankshaft position sensor . It should be between 500 to 600 ohms depending on the temperature; the warmer the temperature of the sensor, the higher the resistance value. If the resistance is not within the specified range, replace the sensor.
53 Using a feeler gauge measure the air gap between the crankshaft pulley and the crankshaft position sensor. The gap specification should be 0.020 to 0.059 inch (0.5 to 1.5 mm). If not as specified, replace the crankshaft pulley or the crankshaft position sensor.

Replacement

54 To replace the sensor, remove the engine undercover, disconnect the electrical connector and remove the bolts from the crankshaft position sensor.
55 Installation is the reverse of removal.

5 Powertrain Control Module (PCM) - removal and installation

Refer to illustration 5.3

1 Disconnect the negative cable from the battery .
2 Remove the front and rear center console (see Chapter 11).
3 Carefully disconnect the electrical connectors from the PCM **(see illustration)**. Each connector has a locking tab which must be disengaged before the connector is unplugged.
4 Remove the nuts and bolts from the PCM brackets.
5 Lift the PCM from the vehicle.
6 Installation is the reverse of removal.
7 Securely tighten the PCM retaining fasteners during installation.

6 Evaporative Emission Control (EVAP) system

General description

Refer to illustration 6.2

1 This system is designed to trap and store fuel that evaporates from the fuel tank, throttle body and intake manifold that would normally enter the atmosphere in the form of hydrocarbon (HC) emissions.
2 The Evaporative Emission Control (EVAP) system consists of a charcoal-filled canister, the lines connecting the canister to the fuel tank, a temperature controlled vacuum valve and a check valve **(see illustration)**.
3 Fuel vapors are transferred from the fuel tank and throttle body to a canister where they are stored when the engine isn't running. When the engine is running, the fuel vapors are purged from the canister by intake airflow and consumed in the normal combustion process.
4 The charcoal canister is equipped with a check valve that incorporates three check balls. Depending upon the running conditions and the pressure in the fuel tank, the check balls open and close the passageways to the vacuum valve (consequently the throttle body) and fuel tank.

Check

Refer to illustrations 6.10 and 6.11

5 Poor idle, stalling and poor driveability can be caused by an inoperative check valve, a damaged canister, split or cracked hoses or hoses connected to the wrong fittings. Check the fuel filler cap for a damaged or deformed gasket (see Chapter 1).
6 Evidence of fuel loss or fuel odor can be caused by liquid fuel leaking from fuel lines, a cracked or damaged canister, an inoperative check valve, disconnected, misrouted, kinked, deteriorated or damaged vapor or control hoses.
7 Inspect each hose attached to the canister for kinks, leaks and cracks along its entire length. Repair or replace as necessary.
8 Look for fuel leaking from the bottom of the canister. If fuel is leaking, replace the canister and check the hoses and hose routing.
9 Inspect the canister. If it's cracked or damaged, replace it.
10 Check for a clogged filter or a stuck check valve. Using low pressure compressed air, blow into the canister tank pipe **(see illustration)**. Air should flow freely from the other pipes. If a problem is found, replace the canister.
11 Check the operation of the temperature controlled vacuum valve. With the engine completely cold, use a hand-held pump and direct air into port A **(see illustration)**. Air should not pass through the valve. Now warm the engine to operating temperature (above 129 degrees F)

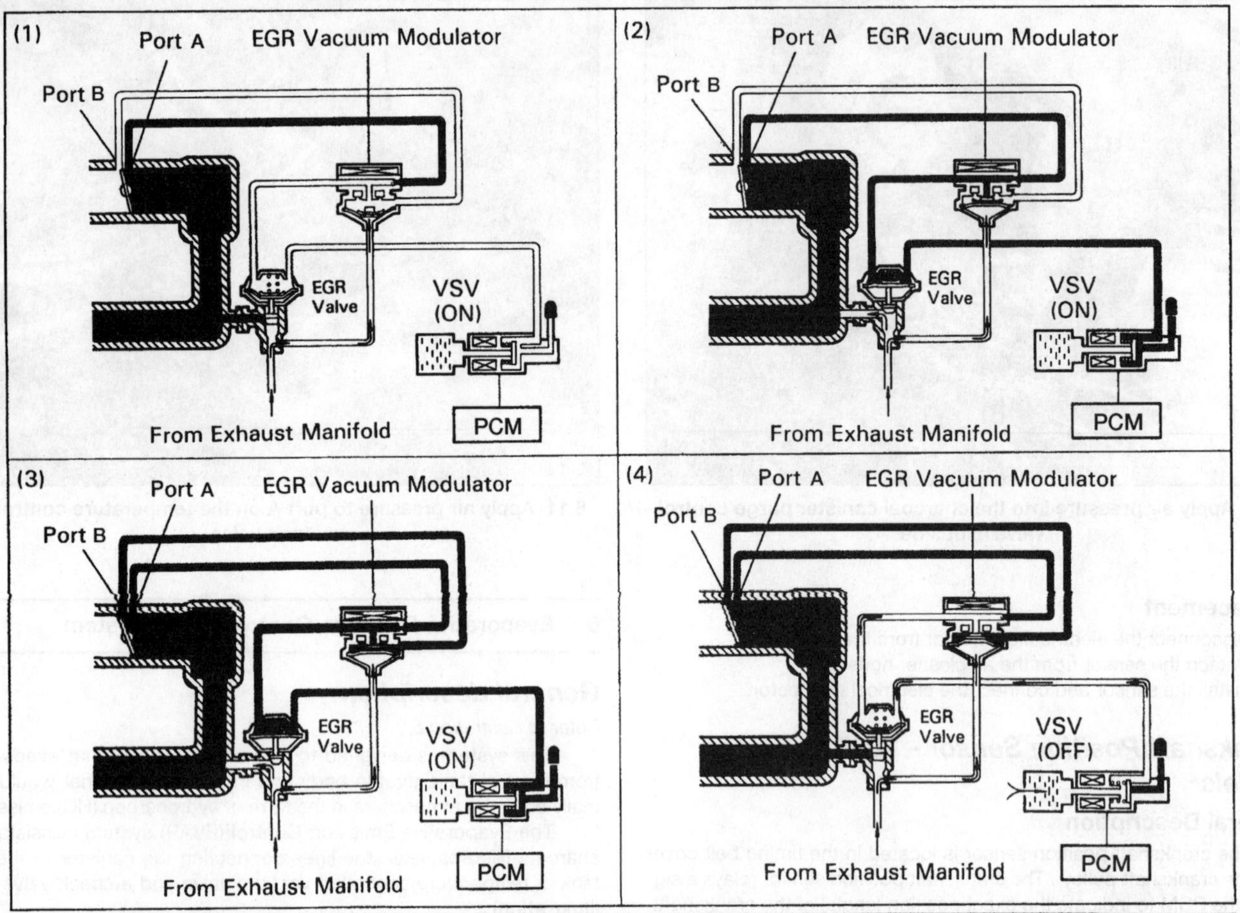

To reduce NOx emissions, part of the exhaust gases are recirculated through the EGR valve to the intake manifold to lower the maximum combustion temperature.

Engine Temp. Sensor	RPM	VSV	Throttle Position	Pressure in the EGR Valve Pressure Chamber	EGR Vacuum Modulator	EGR Valve	Exhaust Gas
COLD	ANY	**** OFF	—	—	—	CLOSED	Not recirculated
WARM/ HOT	LOW		—	—	—	CLOSED	Not recirculated
		*** ON	Below port A	—	—	CLOSED	Not recirculated
			Between port A and port B (1) LOW	* Pressure constantly alternating between low and high	OPENS passage to atmosphere	CLOSED	Not recirculated
			(2) HIGH		CLOSES passage to atmosphere	OPEN	Recirculated
			Above port B (3) HIGH	**	CLOSES passage to atmosphere	OPEN	Recirculated (increase)
	HIGH	(4) OFF	—	—	—	CLOSED	Not recirculated

Remarks: * Pressure increase → Modulator closes → EGR valve opens → Pressure drops
EGR valve closes ← Modulator opens ←

** When the throttle valve is positioned above port R, the EGR vacuum modulator will close the atmosphere passage and open the EGR valve to increase the exhaust gas, even if the exhaust pressure is insufficiently low.

*** VSV switched ON when product of engine speed multiplied by vacuum sensor valve exceeds a specified valve.

**** If terminals TE1 and E1 of data link connector 1 are connected, the VSV switches ON.

7.1 Typical EGR system and operation chart - 1995 and later

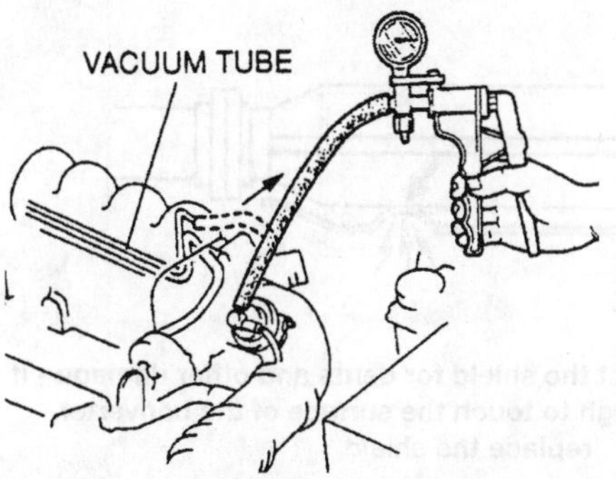

7.4 Vacuum should remain steady and the engine should run rough

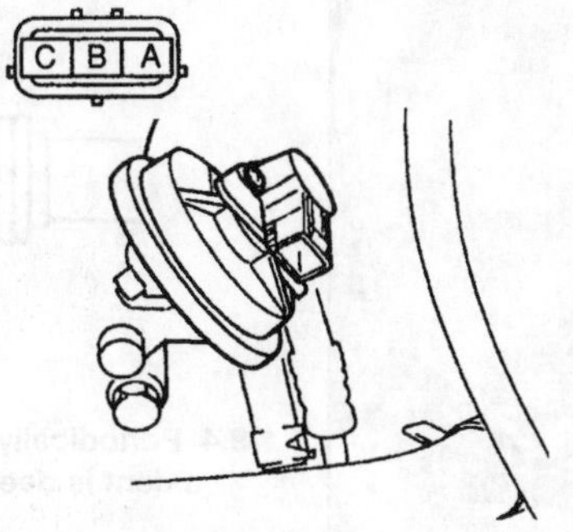

7.7 EGR valve position sensor connector details

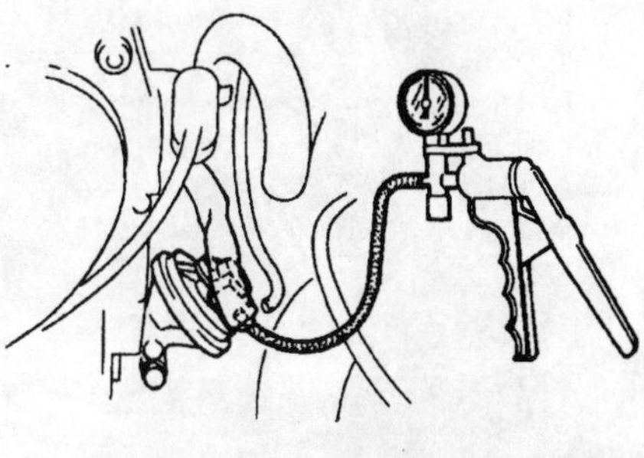
7.9 Vacuum applied to EGR for position sensor voltage check

and observe that air passes through the valve. Replace the valve if the test results are incorrect.

Charcoal canister replacement

12 Clearly label, then detach the vacuum hoses from the canister.
13 Remove the mounting clamp bolts, lower the canister with the bracket, disconnect the hoses from the check valve and remove it from the vehicle.
14 Installation is the reverse of removal.

7 Exhaust Gas Recirculation (EGR) system

General description

Refer to illustration 7.1

1 To reduce oxides of nitrogen emissions, some of the exhaust gases are recirculated through the EGR valve to the intake manifold to lower combustion temperatures **(see illustration).**
2 The EGR system consists of the EGR valve, the EGR modulator, vacuum switching valve (VSV), the Powertrain Control Module (PCM) and the EGR gas temperature sensor.

Check

EGR valve

Refer to illustration 7.4

3 Start the engine and allow it to idle.
4 Detach the vacuum hose from the EGR valve and attach a hand-held vacuum pump in its place **(see illustration).**
5 Apply vacuum to the EGR valve. Vacuum should remain steady and the engine should run poorly.

a) *If the vacuum does not remain steady and the engine does not run poorly, replace the EGR valve and recheck it.*
b) *If the vacuum remains steady but the engine does not run poorly, remove the EGR valve and check the valve and the intake manifold for blockage. Clean or replace parts as necessary and recheck.*

EGR valve position sensor

Refer to illustrations 7.7 and 7.9

6 Disconnect the EGR valve position sensor connector.
7 Measure the resistance between terminals A and B at the sensor connector with an ohmmeter **(see illustration).** The meter reading should be 2.7 K-ohms. If not as specified, replace the EGR valve.
8 Connect the EGR valve position sensor connector.
9 Disconnect the vacuum hose from the EGR valve and install a vacuum pump at the valve **(see illustration).**
10 Turn ignition switch on and measure the voltage at terminal B of the connector **(see illustration 7.7).**
11 Voltmeter should read approximately 0.8 volts with no vacuum applied and approximately 5.0 volts with 5.0 in-Hg applied.
12 If not as specified, inspect the harness and connector between the EGR valve and the PCM terminal.
13 If the harness and connector are OK, replace the EGR valve.

8 Positive Crankcase Ventilation (PCV) system

General information

Refer to illustration 8.1

1 The Positive Crankcase Ventilation (PCV) system reduces hydrocarbon emissions by scavenging crankcase vapors. It does this by circulating fresh air from the air cleaner through the crankcase, where it mixes with blow-by gases and is then rerouted through a PCV valve to the intake manifold **(see illustration).**
2 The main components of the PCV system are the PCV valve, a fresh air intake and the vacuum hoses connecting these components to the engine.
3 To maintain idle quality, the PCV valve restricts the flow when the intake manifold vacuum is high. If abnormal operating conditions (such as piston ring problems) arise, the system is designed to allow excessive amounts of blow-by gases to flow back through the crankcase vent tube into the air cleaner to be consumed by normal combustion.
4 This system directs the blow-by into the throttle body which, over time, can cause an oily residue build up in the area near the throttle plate. Consequently, it is a good idea to periodically clean this residue from the throttle body. Refer to Chapter 4 for this cleaning procedure.

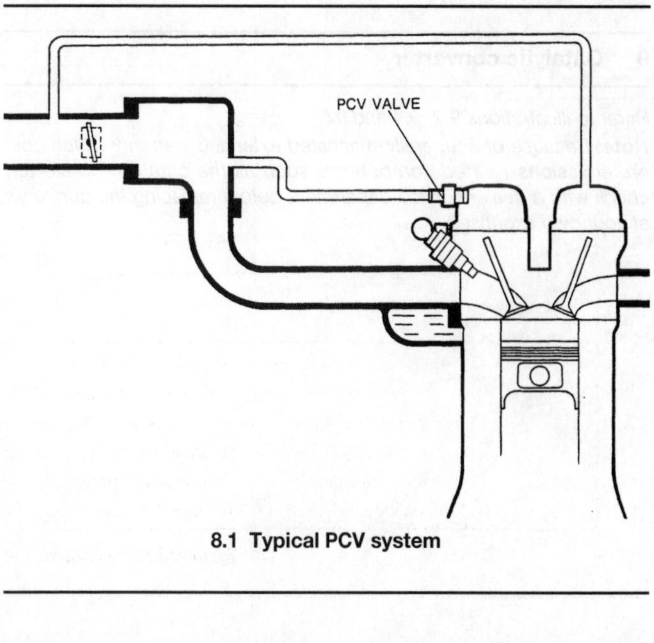

8.1 Typical PCV system

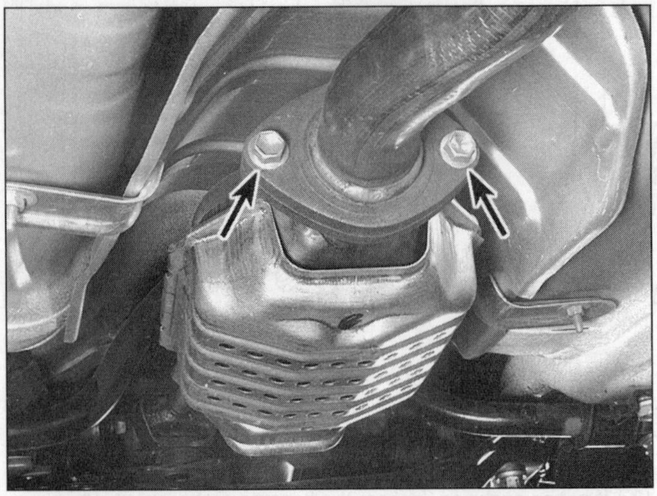

9.2 Let the catalytic converter cool - then spray penetrating lubricant onto the catalytic converter mounting bolts before attempting to unscrew them

Check

5 To check the valve, first pull it out of the grommet in the valve cover and shake the valve. It should rattle, indicating that it's not clogged with deposits. If the valve does not rattle, replace it with a new one.

6 Start the engine and allow it to idle, then place your finger over the valve opening. If vacuum is felt, the PCV valve is working properly. If no vacuum is felt, the PCV valve may be bad or the hose may be plugged. Also, check for vacuum leaks at the valve, filler cap and all the hoses.

Replacement

7 Pull straight up on the valve to remove it. Check the rubber grommet for cracks and distortion. If it's damaged, replace it.

8 If the valve is clogged, the hose is also probably plugged. Remove the hose and clean it with solvent.

9 After cleaning the hose, inspect it for damage, wear and deterioration. Make sure it fits snugly on the fittings.

10 If necessary, install a new PCV valve.

11 Install the clean PCV hose. Make sure that the PCV valve and hose are secure.

9 Catalytic converter

Refer to illustrations 9.2, 9.4 and 9.5

Note: *Because of a federally-mandated extended warranty which covers emissions-related components such as the catalytic converter, check with a dealer service department before replacing the converter at your own expense.*

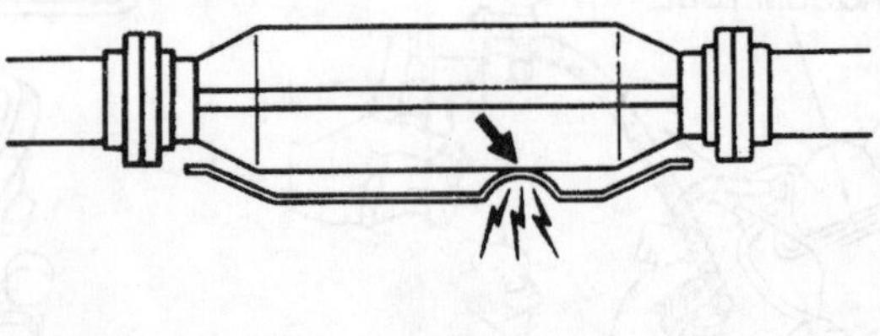

9.4 Periodically inspect the shield for dents and other damage - if a dent is deep enough to touch the surface of the converter, replace the shield

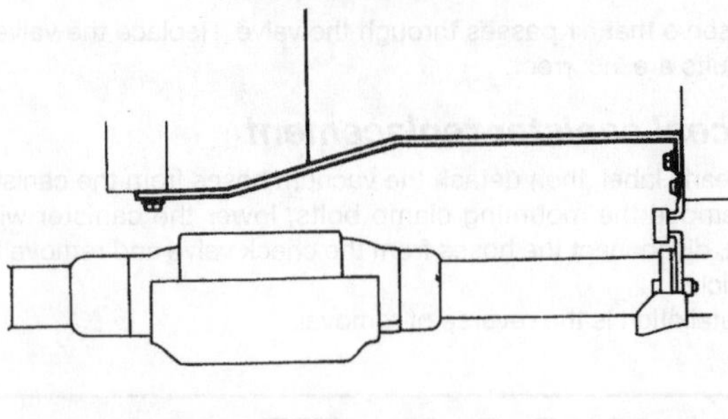

9.5 Periodically inspect the heat insulator to make sure there is adequate clearance between it and the converter

General description

1 To reduce hydrocarbon, carbon monoxide and oxides of nitrogen emissions, all vehicles are equipped with a three-way catalyst system which oxidizes and reduces these chemicals, converting them into harmless nitrogen, carbon dioxide and water.

2 The catalytic converter is mounted in the exhaust system much like a muffler **(see illustration)**.

Check

3 Periodically inspect the catalytic converter-to-exhaust pipe mating flanges and bolts. Make sure that there are no loose bolts and no leaks between the flanges.

4 Look for dents in or damage to the catalytic converter protector **(see illustration)**. If any part of the protector is damaged or dented enough to touch the converter, repair or replace it.

5 Inspect the heat insulator for damage. Make sure that there is adequate clearance between the heat insulator and the catalytic converter **(see illustration)**.

Replacement

6 To replace the catalytic converter, refer to Chapter 4.

Chapter 7 Part A
Manual transaxle

Contents

Specifications

Torque specifications

Torque specifications	**Ft-lbs** (unless otherwise indicated)
Back-up light switch	15 to 21
Transaxle-to-engine bolts	48 to 65
Engine mount-to-support subframe nuts	28 to 38
Support subframe-to-vehicle frame bolts	48 to 65
No. 4 engine mount-to-transaxle bolts	50 to 68
Shifter extension bar-to-transaxle nut	28 to 34
Shifter control rod-to-transaxle change rod bolt	12 to 16

1 General information

The vehicles covered by this manual are equipped with a 5-speed manual transaxle or 4-speed automatic transaxle. Information on the manual transaxle is included in this Part of Chapter 7. Service procedures for the automatic transaxle are contained in Chapter 7, Part B.

The manual transaxle is a compact, two-piece, lightweight aluminum alloy housing containing both the transmission and differential assemblies. A F5M-R transaxle is used with the 1.6L and 1.8L SOHC engines and a G5M-R unit is used with the 1.8L DOHC engine for 1990 through 1992 model years. The 1993 and 1994 transaxles were designated as F25M-R for SOHC engines and G25M-R for the DOHC engine. The 1995 and later models use the F25M-R transaxle for both the 1.5L and the 1.8L DOHC engines. All transaxles are virtually identical except for different gear ratios.

Because of the complexity, unavailability of replacement parts and special tools necessary, internal repair procedures for the manual transaxle are beyond the scope of this manual. For readers who wish to tackle a transaxle rebuild, a brief *Manual transaxle overhaul, general information* Section is provided. The bulk of information in this Chapter is devoted to removal and installation procedures.

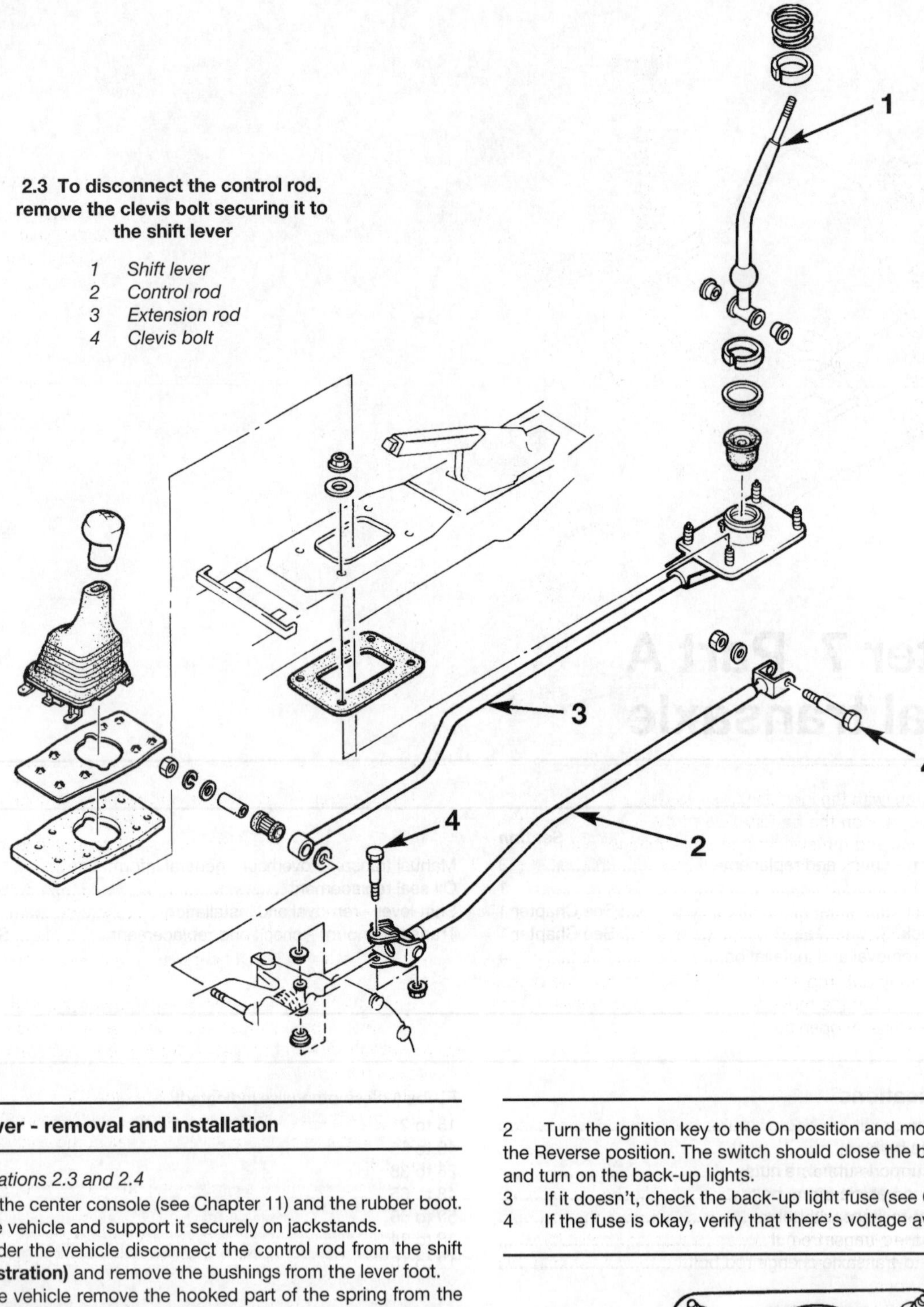

2.3 To disconnect the control rod, remove the clevis bolt securing it to the shift lever

1. *Shift lever*
2. *Control rod*
3. *Extension rod*
4. *Clevis bolt*

2 Shift lever - removal and installation

Refer to illustrations 2.3 and 2.4

1 Remove the center console (see Chapter 11) and the rubber boot.

2 Raise the vehicle and support it securely on jackstands.

3 From under the vehicle disconnect the control rod from the shift lever **(see illustration)** and remove the bushings from the lever foot.

4 Inside the vehicle remove the hooked part of the spring from the bracket groove **(see illustration)** then remove the spring and upper ball seat.

5 Remove the shift lever.

6 Installation is the reverse of removal.

3 Back-up light switch - check and replacement

Check

1 The back-up light switch is located on the front side, near the bottom of the transaxle case.

2 Turn the ignition key to the On position and move the shift lever to the Reverse position. The switch should close the back-up light circuit and turn on the back-up lights.

3 If it doesn't, check the back-up light fuse (see Chapter 12).

4 If the fuse is okay, verify that there's voltage available on the bat-

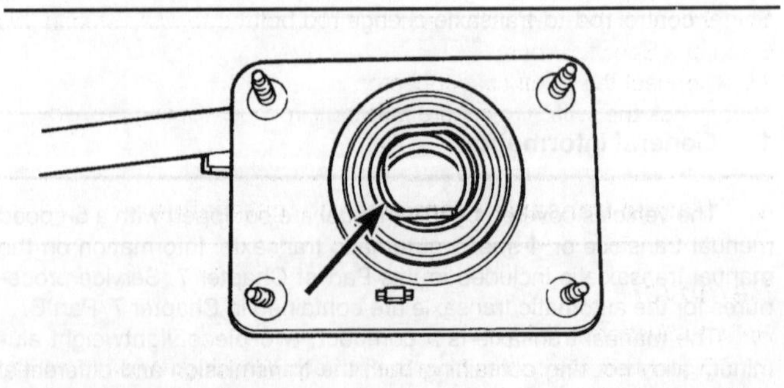

2.4 Remove the spring from the bracket with a needle nose pliers

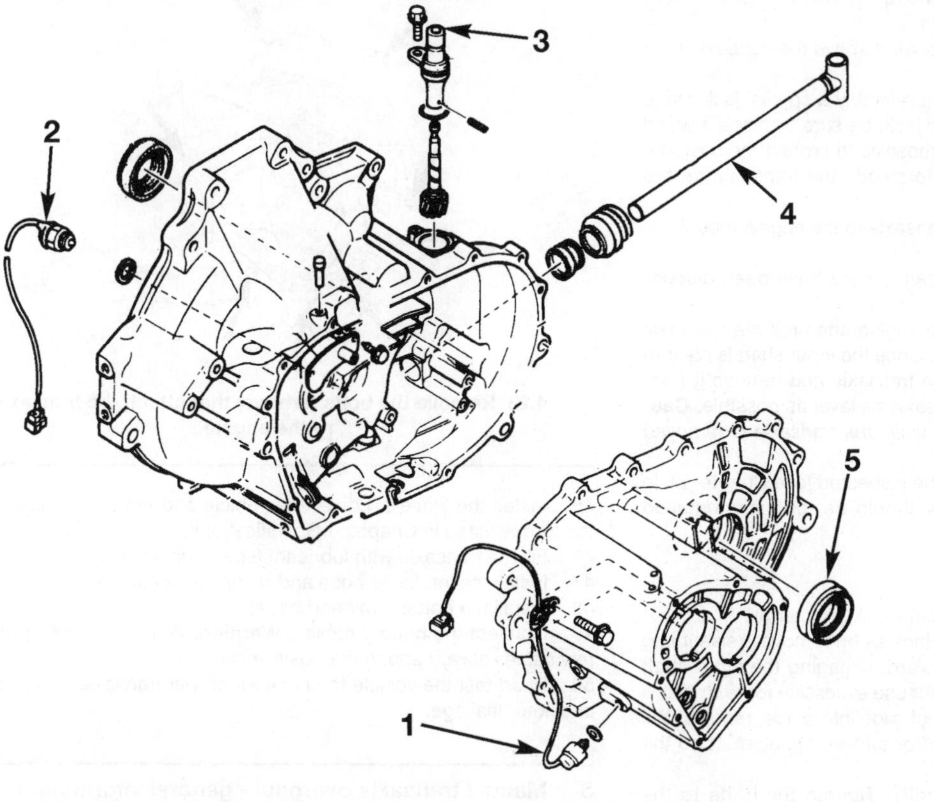

3.8 Transaxle external components

1 Back-up light switch
2 Neutral switch
3 Speedometer drive gear
4 Control rod
5 Oil seal

tery side of the switch (with the ignition turned to On).

5 If there's no voltage on the battery side of the switch, check the wire between the fuse and the switch; if there is voltage, put the shift lever in reverse and see if there's voltage on the ground side of the switch.

6 If there's no voltage on the ground side of the switch, replace the switch (see below); if there is voltage, note whether one or both back-up lights are out.

7 If only one bulb is out, replace it; if they're both out, the bulbs could be the problem, but it's more likely that the wire between the switch and the bulbs has an open somewhere.

Replacement

Refer to illustration 3.8

8 Unplug the electrical connector in the harness to the back-up light switch **(see illustration)**.

9 Unscrew and remove the old switch.

10 To test the new switch before installation, simply check continuity across the switch terminals: with the plunger depressed, there should be continuity; with the plunger free, there should be no continuity.

11 Screw in the new switch and tighten it to the torque listed in this Chapter's Specifications.

12 Connect the electrical connector.

13 Check the switch to ensure that the circuit is working properly.

4 Manual transaxle - removal and installation

Removal

Refer to illustration 4.23

1 Disconnect the cables from the battery. **Warning:** *When removing the battery cables always detach the negative cable first and hook it up last.*

2 Remove the battery and battery tray.

3 Remove the intake air hose and resonance chamber (see Chapter 4).

4 Set the parking brake and move the gear shift lever into the neutral position.

5 Loosen the front wheel lug nuts no more than 1/4 turn, then raise the vehicle and support it securely on jackstands. Remove the wheels.

6 Remove the starter (see Chapter 5).

7 Drain the transaxle lubricant into a suitable container (see Chapter 1).

8 Separate the driveaxle(s) from the transaxle and remove the intermediate shaft if so equipped (see Chapter 8). Support the end of the driveaxle with a wire or rope. **Note:** *It is not necessary to remove the driveaxles from the hub.*

9 Remove the stabilizer bar (see Chapter 10).

10 Remove the clutch release cylinder (see Chapter 8).

11 Unplug the backup light switch pigtail at the connector **(see illustration 3.8)**.

12 Unplug the neutral switch pigtail at the connector **(see illustration 3.8)**.

13 Locate the electrical system ground cable on the clutch pipe bracket near the top of the transaxle. Remove the cable lug bolt and detach the ground cable.

14 Detach any wire harness clamps from the engine and/or transaxle and set the harnesses aside.

15 Disconnect the shifter extension bar from the transaxle and support the bar with a wire **(see illustration 2.3)**.

16 Disconnect the shifter control rod from the transaxle and support the rod with a wire **(see illustration 2.3)**.

17 Support the engine. This can be done from above by using an engine hoist, or by placing a jack (with a wood block as an insulator) under the engine oil pan. The engine must be securely supported at all times while the transaxle is out of the vehicle.

18 Remove the engine support subframe **(see Chapter 7B, illustration 4.24)**.

19 Remove the front exhaust pipe assembly (see Chapter 4).

20 Remove the No. 1 engine mount located at the rear side of the transaxle toward the firewall, and remove the No. 2 engine mount located on the front side of the transaxle.

21 Remove the No. 4 engine mount located above the transaxle near the battery/battery tray area.

22 Support the transaxle with a jack (preferably a special jack made for this purpose). If you're using a floor jack, be sure to place a wood block between the lifting pad and the transaxle to protect the cast aluminum housing. Safety chains will help steady the transaxle on the jack.

23 Remove the bolts attaching the transaxle to the engine **(see illustration)**.

24 Make a final check that all wires and hoses have been disconnected from the transaxle.

25 Lower the left (driver's) end of the engine, then roll the transaxle and jack toward the side of the vehicle. Once the input shaft is clear of the splines in the clutch hub, lower the transaxle and remove it from under the vehicle. Try to keep the transaxle as level as possible. **Caution:** *Do not depress the clutch pedal while the transaxle is removed from the vehicle.*

26 The clutch components can now be inspected (see Chapter 8). In most cases, new clutch components should be routinely installed whenever the transaxle is removed.

Installation

27 If removed, install clutch components (see Chapter 8).

28 With the transaxle secured to the jack as on removal, raise it into position and then carefully slide it forward, engaging the input shaft with the splines in the clutch hub. Do not use excessive force to install the transaxle - if the input shaft does not slide into place, readjust the angle of the transaxle so it is level and/or turn the input shaft so the splines engage properly with the clutch.

29 Install the transaxle-to-engine bolts. Tighten the bolts to the torque listed in this Chapter's Specifications.

30 Remove the transaxle support jack.

31 Install the back, No. 4 engine mount (located above the transaxle, near the battery tray area) on the transaxle. Loosely tighten/snug the bolts.

32 Install the front, No. 2 engine mount on the transaxle, and make sure the rear, No. 1 engine mount is attached to the transaxle. Tighten the bolts securely.

33 Install the front exhaust pipe (down pipe or header pipe) assembly (see Chapter 4).

34 Install the engine mount crossmember bolts and nuts to the body attachment points and then install and tighten the engine mount bolts/nuts. Tighten to the torque listed in this Chapter's Specifications.

35 Tighten the rear, No. 4 engine mount-to-transaxle bolts to the torque listed in this Chapter's Specifications, following the torque sequence given in Chapter 2A.

36 Remove the engine support jack or hoist.

37 Install the shifter extension bar and control rod. Tighten the extension bar nut and control rod bolt to the torque listed in this Chapter's Specifications.

38 Attach any wire harness clamps removed from the engine and/or transaxle.

39 Attach the electrical system ground to the clutch pipe bracket and tighten the bolt securely.

40 Reconnect the neutral switch and backup switch pigtails.

41 Install the clutch release cylinder (see Chapter 8).

42 Install the stabilizer bar (see Chapter 10).

43 Install the driveaxle(s) in the transaxle and the intermediate shaft if so equipped (see Chapter 8).

44 Install the starter (see Chapter 5).

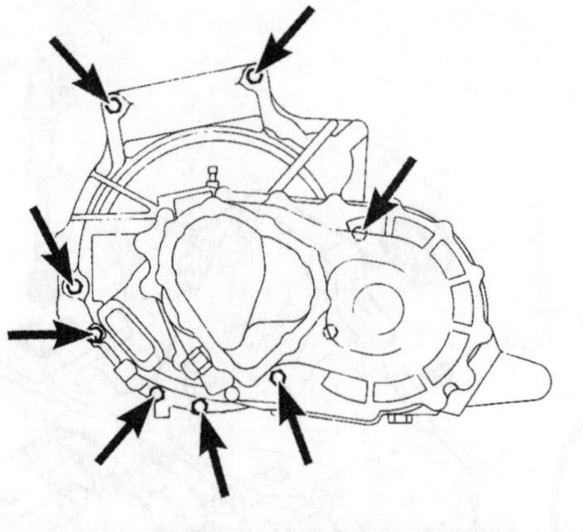

4.23 Remove the bolts (arrows) that attach the transaxle to the engine

45 Install the wheels. Lower the vehicle and tighten the lug nuts to the torque listed in Chapter 1 Specifications.

46 Fill the transaxle with lubricant (see Chapter 1).

47 Install the intake air hose and resonance chamber.

48 Install the battery tray and battery.

49 Connect the battery cables. **Warning:** *When connecting the battery cables always attach the positive cable first.*

50 Road test the vehicle to check for proper transaxle operation and check for leakage.

5 Manual transaxle overhaul - general information

1 Overhauling a manual transaxle is a difficult job for the do-it-yourselfer. It involves the disassembly and reassembly of many small parts. Numerous clearances must be precisely measured and, if necessary, changed with select-fit spacers and snap-rings. As a result, if transaxle problems arise, it can be removed and installed by a competent do-it-yourselfer, but overhaul should be left to a transmission repair shop. Rebuilt transaxles may be available - check with your dealer parts department and auto parts stores. At any rate, the time and money involved in an overhaul is almost sure to exceed the cost of a rebuilt unit.

2 Nevertheless, it's not impossible for an inexperienced mechanic to rebuild a transaxle if the manufactures shop manuals and special tools are available and the job is done in a deliberate step-by-step manner so nothing is overlooked.

3 The tools necessary for an overhaul include internal and external snap-ring pliers, a bearing puller, a slide hammer, a set of pin punches, a dial indicator and possibly a hydraulic press. In addition, a large, sturdy workbench and a vise or transaxle stand will be required.

4 During disassembly of the transaxle, make careful notes of how each piece comes off, where it fits in relation to other pieces and what holds it in place. Your notes plus the manufacturer's shop manual which contains exploded views to illustrate where the parts will make it much easier to get the transaxle back together.

5 Before taking the transaxle apart for repair, it will help if you have some idea what area of the transaxle is malfunctioning. Certain problems can be closely tied to specific areas in the transaxle, which can make component examination and replacement easier. Refer to the *Troubleshooting* section at the front of this manual for information regarding possible sources of trouble.

Chapter 7 Part B
Automatic transaxle

Contents

Specifications

Oil Pressure (engine idling)

Throttle cable, specified pressure	62 to 81 psi
Throttle cable, adjustment pressure	71 psi

Torque specifications

	Ft-lbs (unless otherwise indicated)
Torque converter-to-driveplate bolts	26 to 36
Transaxle-to-engine bolts	
1990 through 1994 models	48 to 65
1995 and later models	41 to 59
Engine oil pan-to-transaxle bolts	28 to 38
Control valve body bolts	70 to 94 in-lbs
Engine mount-to-support subframe nuts	28 to 38
Support subframe-to-vehicle frame bolts	48 to 65
Transverse subframe-to-vehicle frame bolts	69 to 97

1 General information

All vehicles covered in this manual are equipped with either a 5-speed manual transaxle or a 4-speed automatic transaxle. All information on the automatic transaxle is included in this Part of Chapter 7. Information for the manual transaxle can be found in Part A of this Chapter.

The 4-speed automatic transaxle is electronically controlled with fourth gear being an overdrive gear. Shifts are attained by the use of shift solenoids, which are controlled by the Powertrain Control Module. The transaxles utilize a lock-up torque converter.

Because of the complexity of the automatic transaxles and the specialized equipment necessary to perform most service operations, this Chapter contains only those procedures related to general diagnosis, routine maintenance, adjustment and removal and installation.

If the transaxle requires major repair work, it should be left to a dealer service department or an automotive or transmission repair shop. You can, however, remove and install the transaxle yourself and save the expense, even if the repair work is done by a transmission shop.

7B

2 Diagnosis - general

Note: *Automatic transaxle malfunctions may be caused by five general conditions: poor engine performance, improper adjustments, hydraulic malfunctions, mechanical malfunctions or malfunctions in the computer or its signal network. Diagnosis of these problems should always begin with a check of the easily repaired items: fluid level and condition* (see Chapter 1), *shift linkage adjustment and throttle linkage adjustment. Next, perform a road test to determine if the problem has been corrected or if more diagnosis is necessary. If the problem persists after the preliminary tests and corrections are completed, additional diagnosis should be done by a dealer service department or transmission repair shop. Refer to the* Troubleshooting *section at the front of this manual for information on symptoms of transaxle problems.*

Preliminary checks

1 Drive the vehicle to warm the transaxle to normal operating temperature.

2 Check the fluid level as described in Chapter 1:

- a) *If the fluid level is unusually low, add enough fluid to bring the level within the designated area of the dipstick, then check for external leaks (see below).*
- b) *If the fluid level is abnormally high, drain off the excess, then check the drained fluid for contamination by coolant. The presence of engine coolant in the automatic transmission fluid indicates that a failure has occurred in the internal radiator walls that separate the coolant from the transmission fluid (see Chapter 3).*
- c) *If the fluid is foaming, drain it and refill the transaxle, then check for coolant in the fluid, or a high fluid level.*

3 Check the engine idle speed. **Note:** *If the engine is malfunctioning, do not proceed with the preliminary checks until it has been repaired and runs normally.*

4 Check the throttle valve cable for freedom of movement. Adjust it if necessary (see Section 4). **Note:** *The throttle cable may function properly when the engine is shut off and cold, but it may malfunction once the engine is hot. Check it cold and at normal engine operating temperature.*

5 Inspect the shift cable (see Section 5). Make sure that it's properly adjusted and that the cable operates smoothly.

Fluid leak diagnosis

6 Most fluid leaks are easy to locate visually. Repair usually consists of replacing a seal or gasket. If a leak is difficult to find, the following procedure may help.

7 Identify the fluid. Make sure its transmission fluid and not engine oil or brake fluid (automatic transmission fluid is a deep red color).

8 Try to pinpoint the source of the leak. Drive the vehicle several miles, then park it over a large sheet of cardboard. After a minute or two, you should be able to locate the leak by determining the source of the fluid dripping onto the cardboard.

9 Make a careful visual inspection of the suspected component and the area immediately around it. Pay particular attention to gasket mating surfaces. A mirror is often helpful for finding leaks in areas that are hard to see.

10 If the leak still cannot be found, clean the suspected area thoroughly with a degreaser or solvent, then dry it.

11 Drive the vehicle for several miles at normal operating temperature and varying speeds. After driving the vehicle, visually inspect the suspected component again.

12 Once the leak has been located, the cause must be determined before it can be properly repaired. If a gasket is replaced but the sealing flange is bent, the new gasket will not stop the leak. The bent flange must be straightened.

13 Before attempting to repair a leak, check to make sure that the following conditions are corrected or they may cause another leak. **Note:** *Some of the following conditions cannot be fixed without highly specialized tools and expertise. Such problems must be referred to a transmission shop or a dealer service department.*

Gasket leaks

14 Check the pan periodically. Make sure the bolts are tight, no bolts are missing, the gasket is in good condition and the pan is flat (dents in the pan may indicate damage to the valve body inside).

15 If the pan gasket is leaking, the fluid level or the fluid pressure may be too high, the vent may be plugged, the pan bolts may be too tight, the pan sealing flange may be warped, the sealing surface of the transaxle housing may be damaged, the gasket may be damaged or the transaxle casting may be cracked or porous. If sealant instead of gasket material has been used to form a seal between the pan and the transaxle housing, it may be the wrong sealant.

Seal leaks

16 If a transaxle seal is leaking, the fluid level or pressure may be too high, the vent may be plugged, the seal bore may be damaged, the seal itself may be damaged or improperly installed, the surface of the shaft protruding through the seal may be damaged or a loose bearing may be causing excessive shaft movement.

17 Make sure the dipstick tube seal is in good condition and the tube is properly seated. Periodically check the area around the speedometer gear or sensor for leakage. If transmission fluid is evident, check the O-ring for damage.

Case leaks

18 If the case itself appears to be leaking, the casting is porous and will have to be repaired or replaced.

19 Make sure the oil cooler hose fittings are tight and in good condition.

Fluid comes out vent pipe or fill tube

20 If this condition occurs, the transaxle is overfilled, there is coolant in the fluid, the case is porous, the dipstick is incorrect, the vent is plugged or the drain-back holes are plugged.

3 Oil seal replacement

1 Oil leaks frequently occur due to wear of the driveaxle oil seals and/or the speedometer drive gear oil seal and O-rings. Replacement of these seals is relatively easy, since the repairs can usually be performed without removing the transaxle from the vehicle.

Driveaxle oil seals

Refer to illustrations 3.4 and 3.6

2 The driveaxle oil seals are located on the sides of the transaxle, where the inner ends of the driveaxles are splined into the differential side gears. If you suspect that a driveaxle oil seal is leaking, raise the

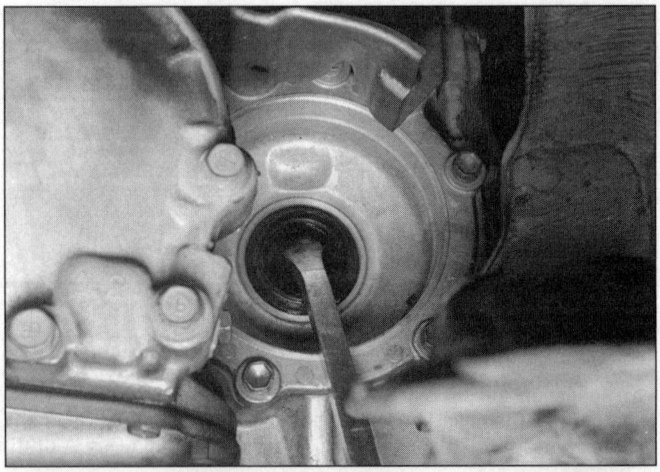

3.4 Carefully pry out the driveaxle oil seal with a seal removal tool or a large screwdriver; make sure you don't damage the seal bore or the new seal may leak

3.6 Use a seal installer, a large socket or a piece of pipe to install the new seal

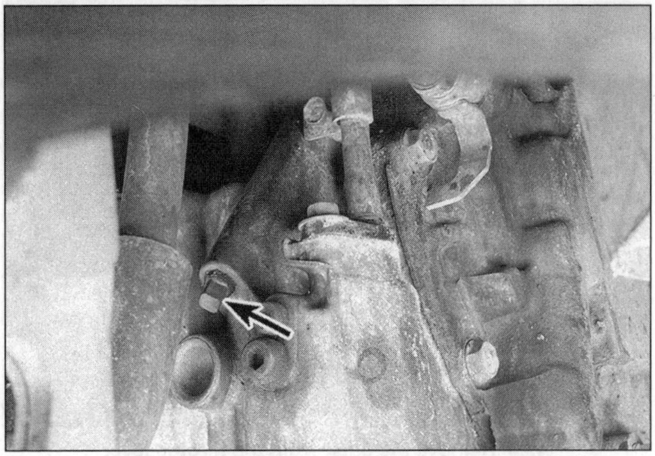

4.4 Remove the square head plug (arrow) on the front side of the transaxle

vehicle and support it securely on jackstands. If the seal is leaking, you'll see lubricant on the side of the transaxle, below the seal.

3 Remove the driveaxle (see Chapter 8).

4 Using a screwdriver or pry bar, carefully pry the oil seal out of the transaxle bore **(see illustration)**.

5 If the oil seal cannot be removed with a screwdriver or pry bar, a special oil seal removal tool (available at auto parts stores) will be required.

6 Using a seal installer, a large section of pipe or a large deep socket as a drift, install the new oil seal. Drive it into the bore squarely and make sure it's completely seated **(see illustration)**. A fully-seated seal should be flush with the surface of the transaxle housing.

7 Lubricate the lip of the new seal with multi-purpose grease, then install the driveaxle (see Chapter 8). Be careful not to damage the lip of the new seal.

4 Throttle cable - check, adjustment and replacement

Note: *The cable adjustment and replacement procedures require a 0 to 100 psi oil pressure gauge and suitable adapters to connect the gauge to the transaxle test port. If you do not have a suitable pressure gauge have the cable adjusted and/or replaced by a dealer service department or other qualified automotive repair shop.*

Check

1 Check the cable and housing for damage.

2 Actuate the accelerator through its full range of travel and ensure it operates smoothly.

3 Replace the throttle cable assembly if necessary.

Adjustment

Refer to illustrations 4.4, 4.7 and 4.10

4 Remove the square-head plug on the front of the transaxle and install a 0 to 100 psi oil pressure gauge in the test port **(see illustration)**.

5 With the shift lever in the Park (P) position, start the engine and let it warm up to normal operating temperature.

6 Check the idle speed adjustment (see Chapter 4) and ensure that it is adjusted correctly.

7 Loosen the bolts securing the throttle cable to the bracket on the front side of the throttle body assembly. **Caution:** *First loosen the bolt on the drivers side (left side; closest to the throttle valve)* **(see illustration)** *and then the bolt on the right side.*

8 Check and ensure that the throttle valve lever is in the closed throttle position.

9 Tighten the left cable bolt **(see illustration 4.7)** securely.

10 Pull the throttle cable toward the right side of the vehicle **(see illustration)** until the line pressure exceeds the specified pressure range listed in this Chapter's Specifications.

11 Push the throttle cable toward the left side of the vehicle until the line pressure decreases to the adjustment pressure listed in this Chapter's Specifications. **Caution:** *If the line pressure will not decrease to the adjustment pressure, tighten bolt 2 with the line pressure at the closest reading to the adjustment pressure.*

12 Tighten the right cable bolt securely.

7B

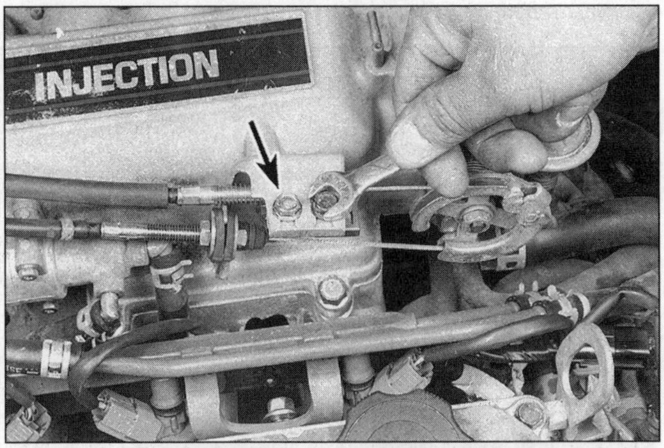

4.7 Loosen the cable mounting bolt on the driver's side first and then the bolt on the right side (arrow)

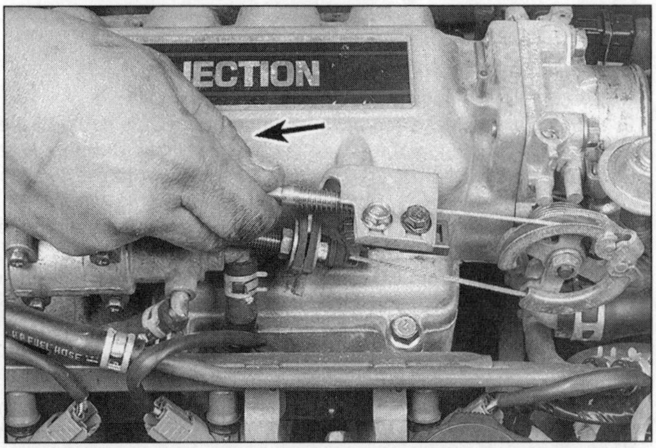

4.10 Pull the throttle cable toward the right side (arrow direction) of the vehicle

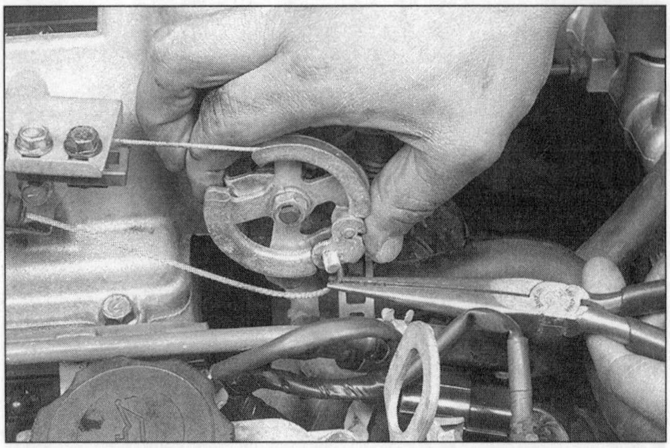

4.20 Remove the cable from the throttle lever

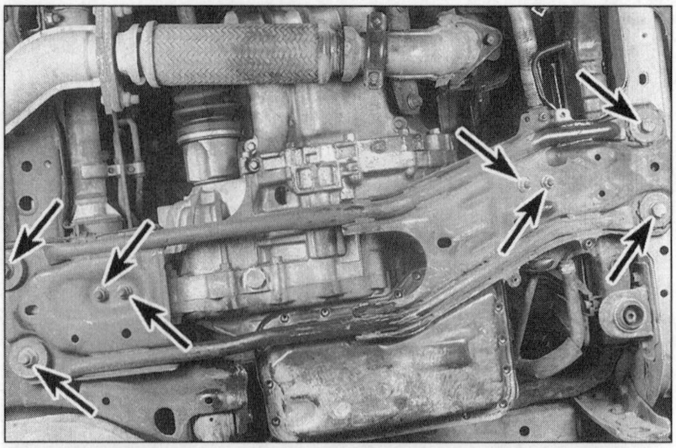

4.24 Remove the engine mount nuts and the nuts and bolts securing the engine support subframe (arrows)

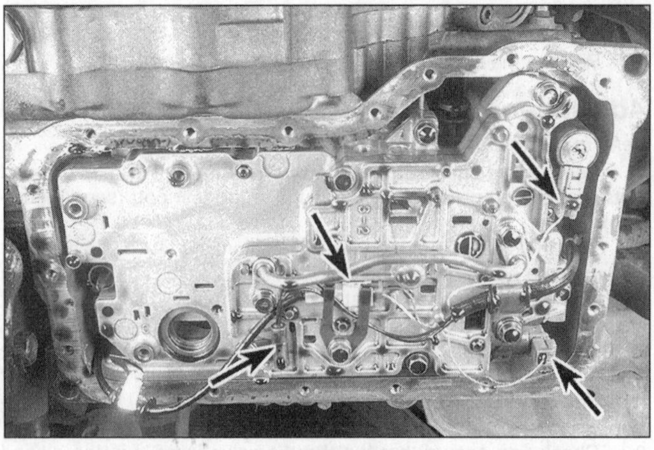

4.26 Disconnect the 4 solenoid connectors (arrows)

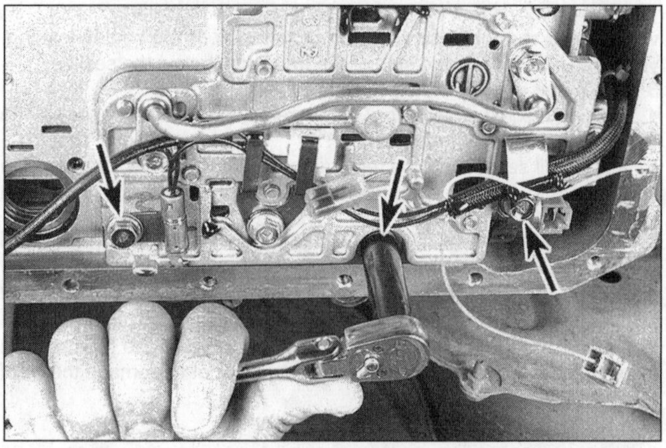

4.27 Loosen then remove the control valve body mounting bolts (there are nine of them - arrows point to three)

13 Stop the engine and ensure that the throttle cable moves smoothly.

14 Restart the engine and accelerate it slightly, then let it run at idle speed.

15 Verify that the line pressure is within the specified pressure range listed in this Chapter's Specifications.

16 If the line pressure is not correct repeat this adjustment procedure.

17 Turn off the engine, remove the pressure gauge and install the square-head plug.

Replacement

Refer to illustrations 4.20, 4.24, 4.26, 4.27, 4.28, 4.29 and 4.33

18 Disconnect the negative cable from the battery.

19 Loosen and remove the bolts securing the throttle cable to the bracket on the front side of the throttle body assembly. **Caution:** *First loosen the bolt on the drivers side (left side; closest to the throttle valve)* **(see illustration 4.7)** *and then the bolt on the right side.*

20 Remove the throttle cable from the bracket and from the throttle lever on the throttle body **(see illustration)**.

21 Loosen the left front wheel lug nuts no more than 1/4 turn, then raise the vehicle and support it securely on jackstands. Remove the wheel and the splash shield.

22 Drain the transaxle lubricant into a suitable container (see Chapter 1).

23 Support the engine. This can be done from above by using an engine hoist, or by placing a jack (with a wood block as an insulator) under the engine oil pan.

24 Remove the engine support subframe **(see illustration)** and on 1995 and later models with the 1.8 Liter DOHC engine remove the transverse subframe.

25 Remove the transaxle oil pan and gasket (see Chapter 1).

26 Disconnect the solenoid connectors **(see illustration)**.

27 Remove the control valve body mounting bolts **(see illustration)** and lower the valve body from the transaxle.

28 Remove the throttle cable from the throttle cam in the transaxle **(see illustration)**.

29 Remove the mounting bolts and throttle cable from the transaxle **(see illustration)**.

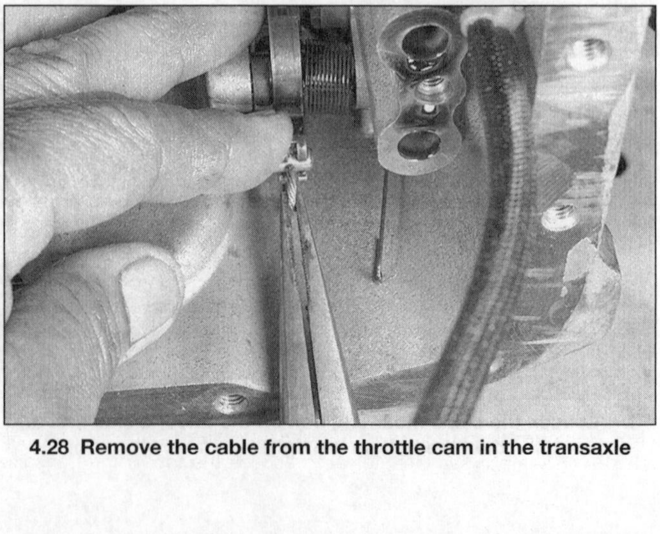

4.28 Remove the cable from the throttle cam in the transaxle

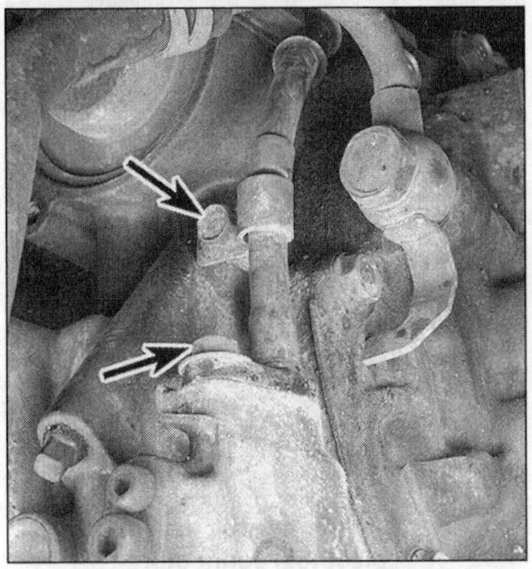

4.29 Remove the cable-to-transaxle mounting bolts (arrows)

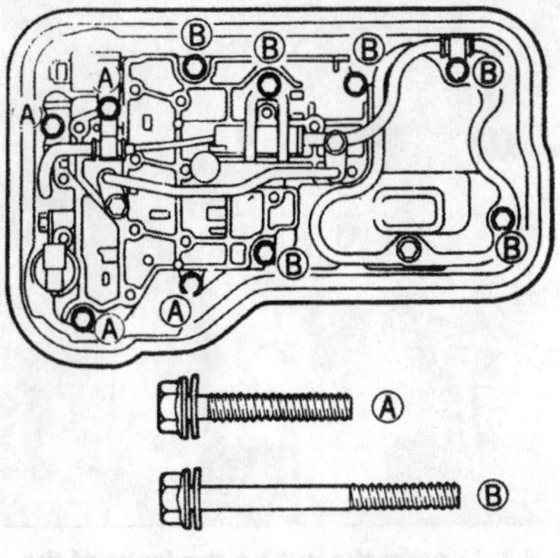

4.33 Install the short bolts (small arrows) and the long bolts (large arrows) in the indicated locations

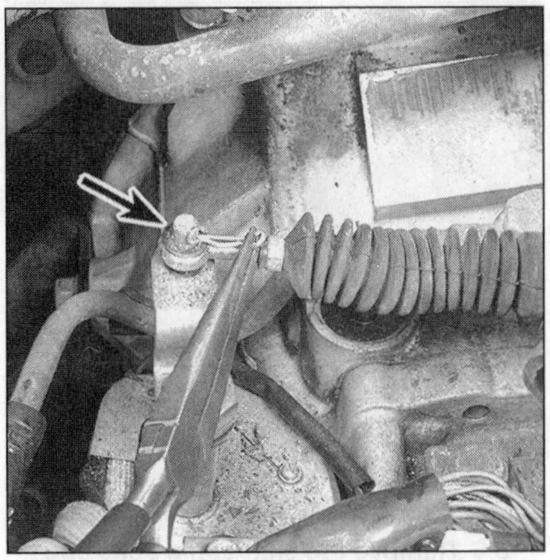

5.2a Remove the retaining clip and the shift cable (arrow) from the shift lever on the transaxle

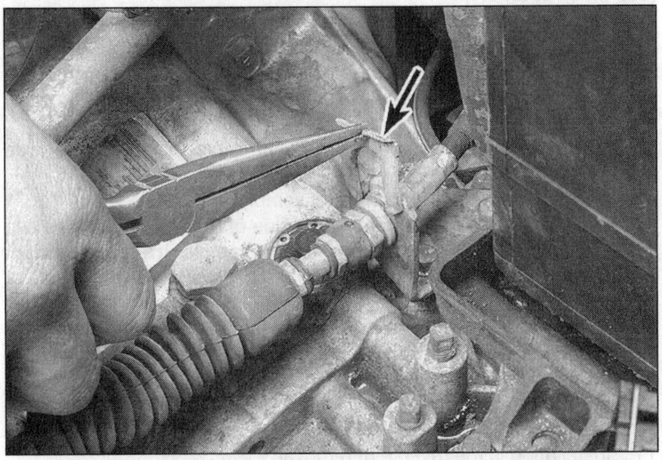

5.2b Remove the bracket clip (arrow) and lift the shift cable off the bracket

5.4 Remove the 4 screws holding the shift indicator panel in place and lift the panel up

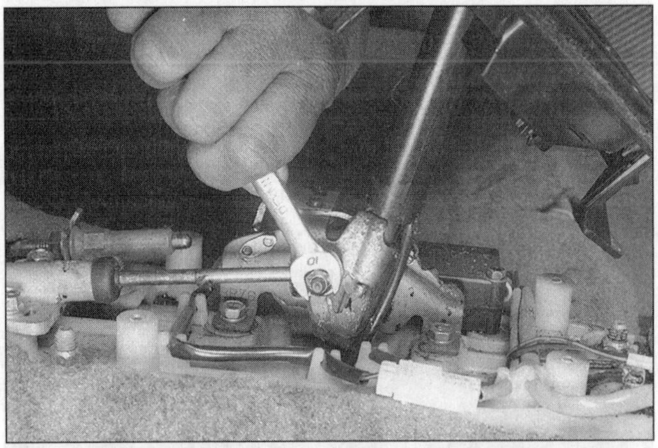

5.5 Remove the retaining nut (arrow) and pull the cable end from the lever

30 Install a new throttle cable to the throttle cam in the transaxle.

31 Connect the throttle cable to the throttle lever on the throttle body.

32 Attach the throttle cable to the transaxle using new bolts and tighten the bolts securely.

33 Install the control valve body tightening the bolts to the torque listed in this Chapter's Specifications. **Caution:** *There are 2 bolt lengths; installing the long bolts in the wrong position could cause severe damage* **(see illustration)**.

34 Reconnect the solenoid connectors.

35 Install the transaxle oil pan (see Chapter 1).

36 Install the engine support subframe. Tighten the bolts to the torque listed in this Chapter's Specifications.

37 Remove the engine support jack or hoist.

38 Connect the battery cables. **Warning:** *When connecting the battery cables always attach the positive cable first.*

39 Fill the transaxle with the proper type and amount of fluid (see Chapter 1).

40 Adjust the throttle cable.

5 Shift cable - removal, installation and adjustment

Removal and installation

Refer to illustrations 5.2a, 5.2b, 5.4, 5.5, and 5.6

1 Remove the battery and battery tray (see Chapter 5) and air cleaner assembly (see Chapter 4) to access the top of the transaxle where the shift cable is attached.

2 Disconnect the shift cable end from the transaxle **(see illustrations)**.

3 Remove the consoles and control box side covers (see Chapter 11).

4 Remove the indicator panel screws and lift up the indicator panel **(see illustration)**.

5 Unscrew the nut securing the shift cable to the shift lever **(see illustration)** and pull the cable end from the lever. **Note:** *With the consoles removed you will see two cables coming into the front of the shift*

5.6 Remove the shift cable bolts and move the cable clear of the shifter mechanism

6.7 Loosen the nut on the front of the shift-lock cable bracket (arrow) to remove the cable from the shift assembly

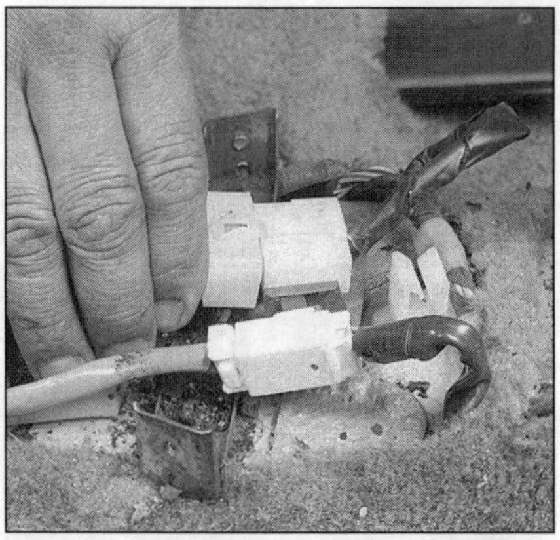

6.8 Unplug the shift assembly electrical connector

mechanism. The shift cable is on the left and the shift-lock cable is on the right.

6 Unscrew the bolts securing the cable to the vehicle **(see illustration)**.

7 Lift the cable clear of the shift lever assembly and carefully pull the cable through grommet in the firewall.

8 Installation is the reverse of removal.

9 When you're done, adjust the shift cable.

Adjustment

10 Move the shift lever to the Park (P) position.

11 Loosen the two cable mounting bolts in front of the shift assembly **(see illustration 5.6)**.

12 While holding the shift lever forward against the stop tighten the shift cable mounting bolts securely.

13 Check the operation of the transaxle in each shift lever position (try to start the engine in each gear - the starter should operate in the Park and Neutral positions only).

6 Shift lever - removal and installation

Removal and installation

Refer to illustrations 6.7, 6.8, 6.9a and 6.9b

1 Disconnect the negative cable from the battery.

2 Remove the consoles and control box side covers (see Chapter 11).

3 Remove the indicator panel screws and lift up the indicator panel **(see illustration 5.4)**.

4 Unscrew the nut securing the shift cable to the shift lever **(see illustration 5.5)** and pull the cable end from the lever. **Note:** *With the consoles removed you will see two cables coming into the front of the shift mechanism. The shift cable is on the left and the shift-lock cable is on the right.*

5 Unscrew the bolts securing the shift cable to the vehicle **(see illustration 5.6)**.

6 Lay the cable clear of the shift assembly.

7 Loosen the nut on the front, cable side of the shift-lock cable and move the cable clear of the shift assembly **(see illustration). Caution:** *Be careful not to turn/loosen the nut on the back, shift assembly side of the bracket.*

8 Disconnect the electrical connectors **(see illustration)**.

9 Remove the 4 nuts that secure the shift assembly to the vehicle **(see illustrations)**.

10 Lift the shift assembly clear of the mounting studs to remove it from the vehicle.

11 Installation is the reverse of removal.

12 Adjust the shift cable (see Section 5).

7 Neutral start switch - check, adjustment and replacement

Adjustment

Refer to illustrations 7.4a and 7.4b

1 If the engine will start with the shift lever in any position other than

6.9a Remove the 2 mounting nuts at the back . . .

6.9b . . . then remove the 2 nuts at the front of the shift assembly

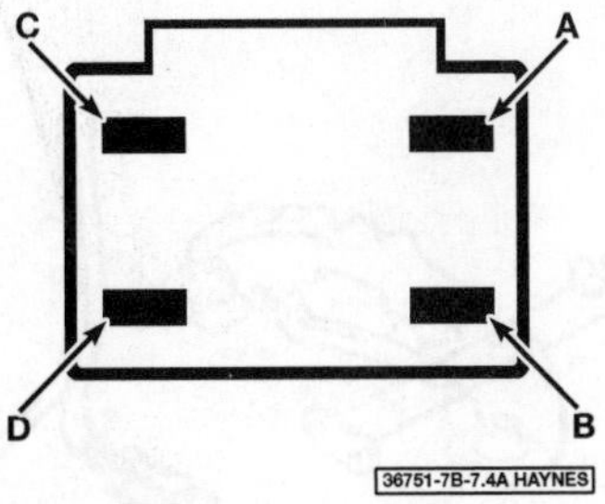

7.4a Touch the ohmmeter leads to connector terminals A and B; there should be continuity when the selector is in the Park and Neutral positions

Park or Neutral, adjust the neutral start switch.

2 Apply the park brake and block the rear wheels. Raise the front of the vehicle and place it securely on jackstands. Shift the transaxle into Neutral.

3 Unplug the electrical connector from the switch and loosen the switch retaining bolts.

4 Touch the ohmmeter leads to the switch terminals inside the electrical connector and rotate the switch until there is continuity between the terminals, indicating that it's now in the Neutral position **(see illustrations)**. Tighten the bolts securely.

Replacement

5 Disconnect the negative cable from the battery.

6 Shift the transaxle into Neutral.

7 Remove the nut and lift off the shift lever.

8 Unplug the electrical connector.

9 Remove the retaining bolts and lift the switch off the shift shaft.

10 To install, line up the flats on the shift shaft with the flats in the switch and push the switch onto the shaft.

11 Position the switch on the transaxle and loosely tighten the bolts.

12 Install the shift lever and follow the adjustment procedure above.

13 Connect the negative battery cable and verify the engine will not start with the shift lever in any position other than Park or Neutral.

8 Shift-lock system - description, check and component replacement

Description

Refer to illustrations 8.1a and 8.1b

1 The shift lock system **(see illustrations)** prevents the shift lever

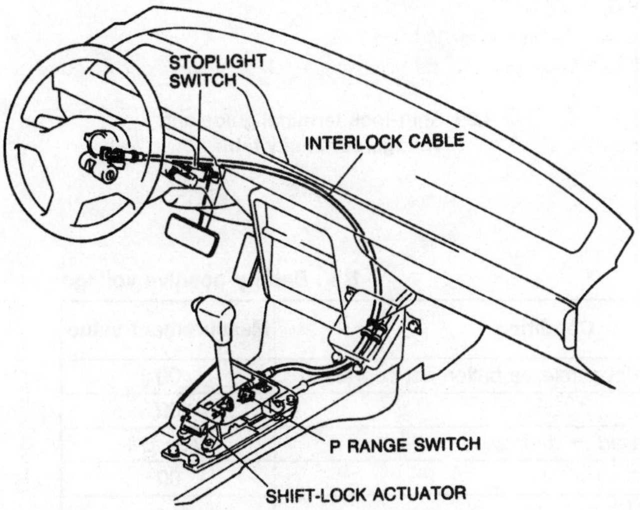

8.1a Shift-lock system components

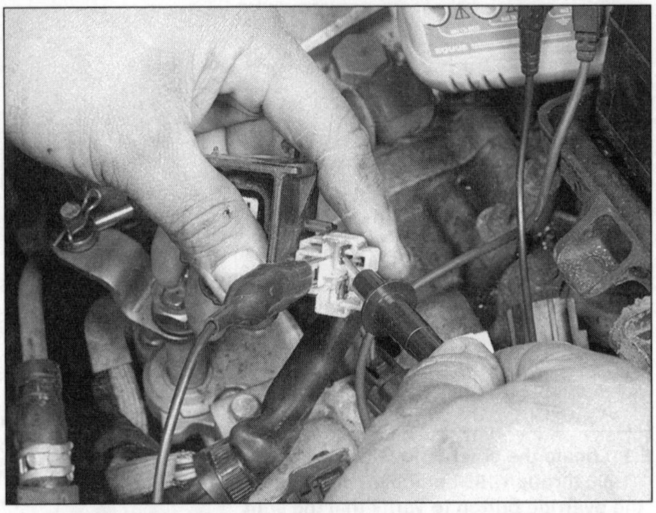

7.4b With the transaxle in Neutral, check continuity with an ohmmeter as shown: loosen the switch retaining bolts, touch the leads of the ohmmeter to the switch terminals inside the electrical connector and rotate the switch until the meter indicates continuity, then tighten the bolts

from being shifted out of the Park (P) position unless the ignition switch is ON and the brake pedal is applied.

Shift-lock

2 Turn the ignition switch ON (engine OFF).

3 Without the brake pedal depressed, verify that the shift lever cannot be shifted from Park (P) position.

4 Depress the brake pedal and verify that the selector lever can be

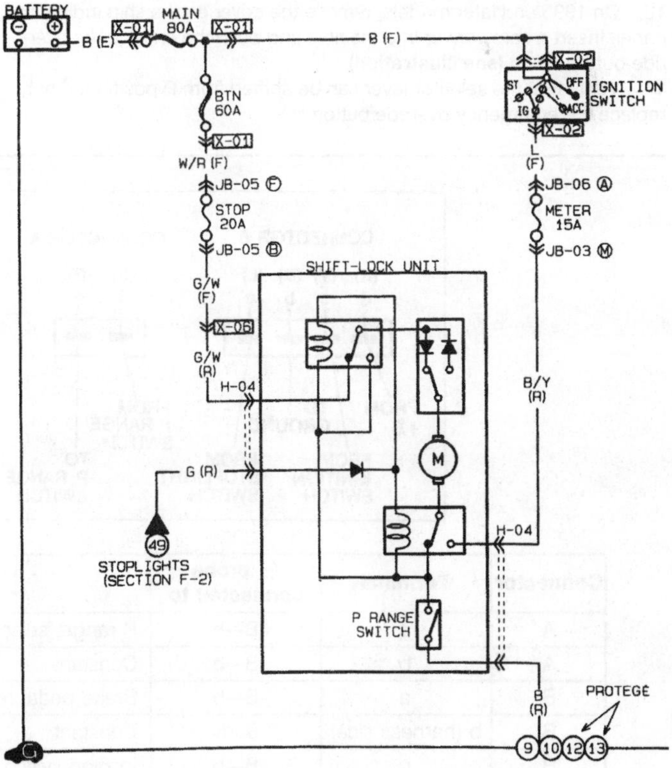

8.1b Shift-lock system electrical schematic

8.9 Locate the emergency override button (1990 through 1994 models) - slide back the override button to verify that the shift selector lever can be shifted from the P position

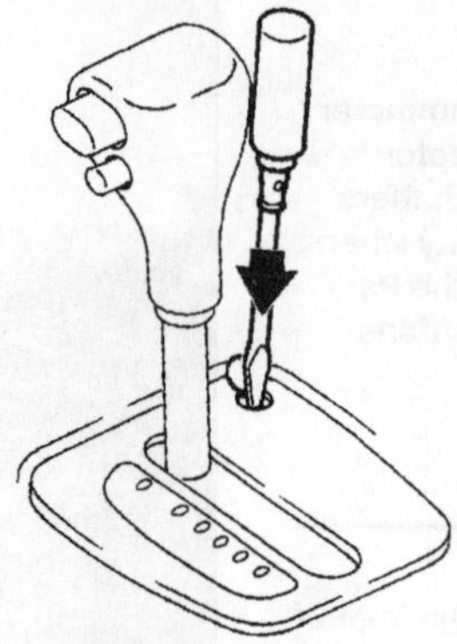

8.10 On 1995 and later models, remove the cover on the shift indicator panel and, using a screwdriver, push down on the emergency override button to actuate it

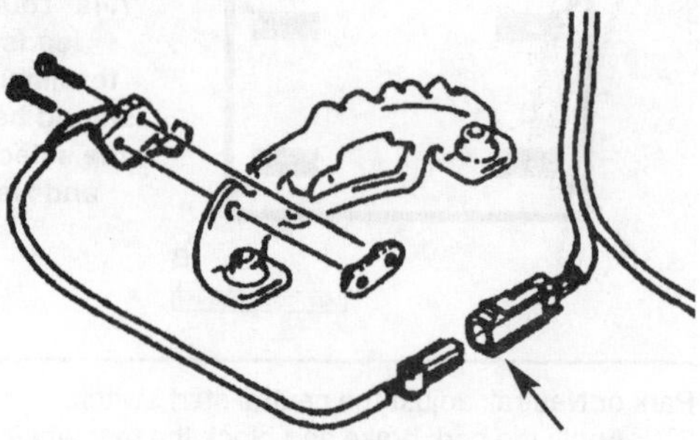

8.19 Disconnect the P-position switch connector (arrow), then check for continuity in Park

shifted from the P position.

5 If the shift-lock does not function correctly, check the P position switch continuity and/or shift-lock actuator terminal voltage and continuity.

Emergency override button

Refer to illustrations 8.9 and 8.10

6 Turn the ignition switch OFF.

7 Verify that the selector lever is in P position.

8 Without the brake pedal depressed, verify that the selector lever cannot be shifted from P position.

9 On 1990 through 1994 models, slide back the emergency override button located on the shift indicator panel **(see illustration).**

10 On 1995 and later models, remove the cover on the shift indicator panel. Insert a screwdriver into the hole and push the emergency override button down **(see illustration).**

11 Verify that the selector lever can be shifted from P position. If not, replace the emergency override button.

Key interlock

12 Turn the ignition switch ON (engine OFF).

13 With the brake pedal depressed, shift the selector lever to R position.

14 Verify that the ignition key cannot be turned to the LOCK position.

15 If ignition switch can be turned to the LOCK position, the ignition switch may need to be replaced.

Park (P) position switch

Refer to illustration 8.19

16 Disconnect the negative cable from the battery. **Caution:** *If the stereo in your vehicle is equipped with an anti-theft system, make sure you have the correct activation code before disconnecting the battery.*

17 Remove the front and rear console (see Chapter 11).

18 Remove the indicator panel screws and lift up the indicator panel **(see illustration 5.4).**

19 Disconnect the P-range switch connector **(see illustration).**

20 Using an ohmmeter check the switch for continuity between the

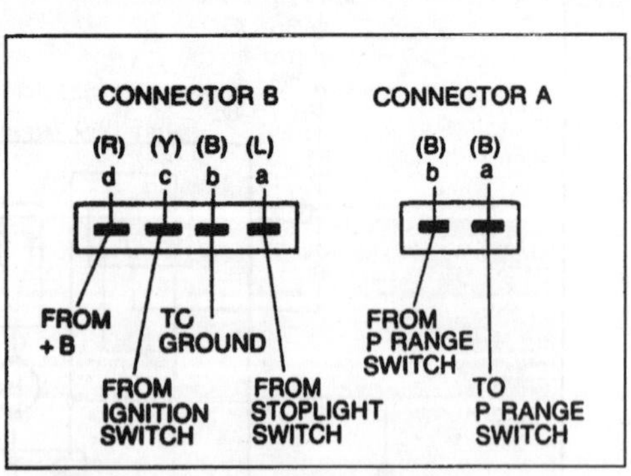

8.29 Shift-lock terminal guide and voltage/continuity table

B+: Battery positive voltage

Connector	Terminal	⊖ probe connected to	Condition	Measurement value
A	a	B—b	P range, selector lever release button not depressed	0Ω
A	b	B—b	Constant	0Ω
B	a	B—b	Brake pedal released → depressed	0V → B+
B	b (harness side)	Body	Constant	0Ω
B	c	B—b	Ignition switch ON	B+
B	d	B—b	Ignition switch OFF	B+

9.1 To check any of the three transaxle mounts, insert a large screwdriver or prybar between the mount and its bracket as shown, and try to lever the mount from side to side or up and down - there should be a little movement, but it should be firm; if the mount moves too easily or looks cracked and torn, replace it

connector terminals with the shift lever in the Park (P) position and the shift lever release button in the released/locked position.

21 Repeat the continuity test with the shift lever release button depressed; depressing the release button should open the switch, breaking continuity.

22 If the switch fails any of these tests, replace it.

23 Reconnect the P-range switch connector.

24 Install the indicator panel.

25 Install the front and rear console.

26 Connect the negative battery cable.

Shift-lock actuator

Refer to illustration 8.29

27 Remove the front and rear console (see Chapter 11).

28 Shift the shift lever to the Park (P) position.

29 Turn the ignition switch ON (engine OFF), and using a Volt-Ohmmeter, check the terminal voltages and continuity **(see illustration)**. **Caution:** *When checking continuity between terminal B (harness side) and ground, disconnect connector B.*

30 If the actuator fails any of these tests, replace it.

31 Turn the ignition switch OFF and install the front and rear console.

9 Transaxle mount - check and replacement

Refer to illustration 9.1

1 Insert a large screwdriver or prybar between the transaxle mount and its bracket and pry the two apart **(see illustration)**.

2 The transaxle mount should not move excessively. If it does, replace the mount.

3 To replace a mount, support the transaxle with a jack, remove the nuts and bolts and remove the mount. It may be necessary to raise the transaxle slightly to provide enough clearance to remove the mount.

4 Installation is the reverse of removal.

10 Automatic transaxle - removal and installation

Removal

Refer to illustrations 10.10, 10.11, 10.12, 10.17, 10.19, 10.21, 10.23 and 10.24

1 Disconnect the cables from the battery. **Warning:** *When removing the battery cables always detach the negative cable first and hook it up last.*

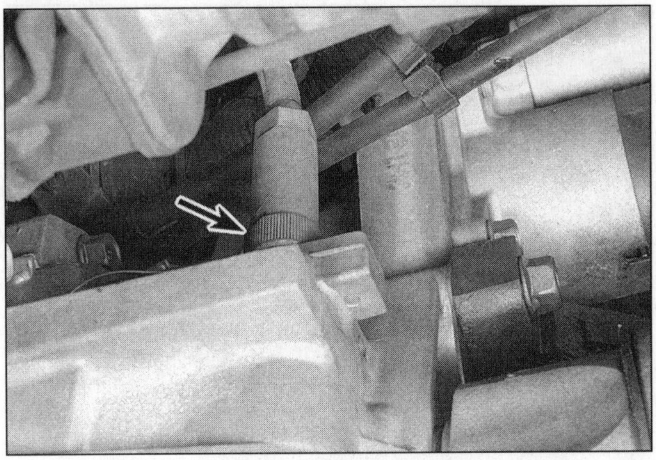

10.10 Disconnect the speedometer cable (arrow) from the transaxle

2 Remove the battery and battery tray.

3 Remove the intake air hose and air cleaner assembly (see Chapter 4).

4 Set the parking brake.

5 Loosen the front wheel lug nuts no more than 1/4 turn, then raise the vehicle and support it securely on jackstands. Remove the wheels and the splash shield(s). **Note:** *All models have a splash shield on the left side of the engine compartment, inside the wheel well; 1995 and later models also have a shield on the right side which must be removed.*

6 Remove the starter (see Chapter 5).

7 Drain the transaxle lubricant into a suitable container (see Chapter 1).

8 Separate the driveaxle(s) from the transaxle and remove the intermediate shaft if so equipped (see Chapter 8). Support the end of the driveaxle with a wire or rope. **Note:** *It is not absolutely necessary to completely remove the driveaxles; you can detach the inner CV joints and suspend them out of the way. However, you'll have more room to work if you remove the driveaxles. And this is a good time to inspect the CV joint boots for tears and deterioration and, if necessary, repack them with new CV joint grease* (see Chapter 8).

9 Remove the stabilizer bar (see Chapter 10).

10 Disconnect the speedometer cable **(see illustration)** (on 1995 and later models disconnect the speed sensor electrical connector and the range switch connector) and shift selector cables (see Section 5).

11 Unplug the neutral start switch and the solenoid valve at the connectors on top of the transaxle **(see illustration)**.

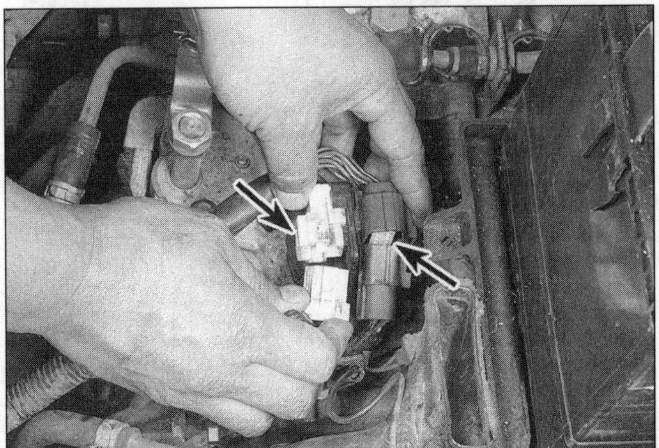

10.11 Unplug the neutral start switch connector (left arrow) and the solenoid valve connector (right arrow) on top of the transaxle

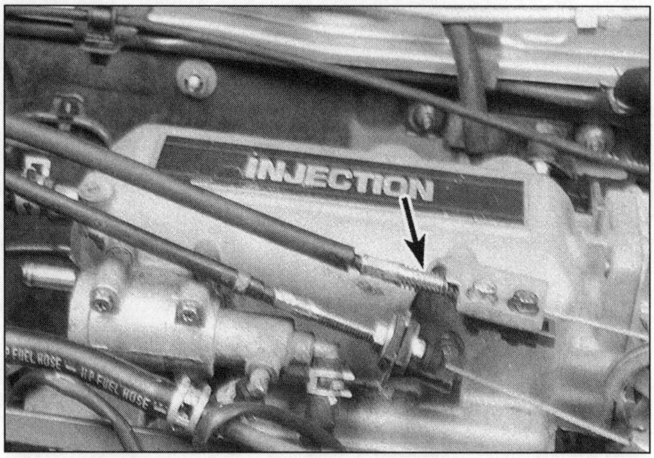

10.12 Clearly mark the throttle cable casing at the mounting bracket (arrow) so it can be reinstalled in its original position

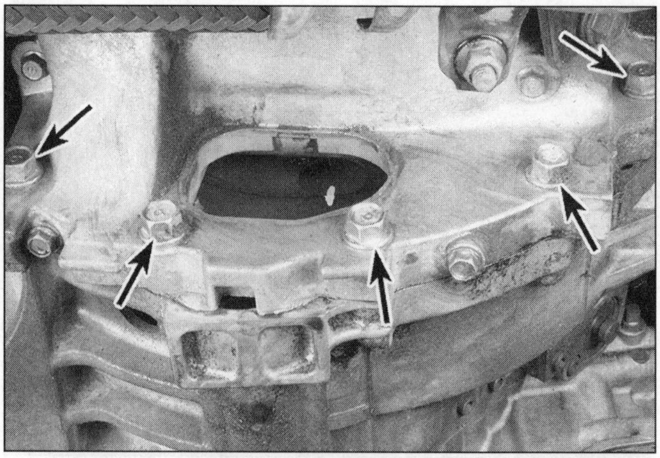

10.17 Remove the engine oil pan-to-transaxle bolts (arrows)

10.19 Remove the bolts securing the No. 2 engine mount to the transaxle

12 Clearly mark the throttle cable casing at the bracket on the throttle body **(see illustration)** so that it can be reinstalled in the same position and remove the throttle cable. **Note:** *It is very important that the casing be reinstalled in the same position on the bracket; otherwise, the transmission will not shift correctly.*
13 Detach any cable or wire harness clamps from the engine and/or transaxle and set the cables and harnesses aside.
14 Support the engine. This can be done from above by using an engine hoist, or by placing a jack (with a wood block as an insulator) under the engine oil pan. The engine must be supported at all times while the transaxle is out of the vehicle.
15 Remove the engine support subframe **(see illustration 4.24)** and on 1995 and later models with the 1.8 Liter DOHC engine remove the transverse subframe.
16 Remove the front exhaust pipe assembly (see Chapter 4).
17 Remove the 5 engine oil pan-to-transaxle bolts **(see illustration).**
18 Remove the No. 1 engine mount located at the rear side of the transaxle, toward the firewall.
19 Remove the No. 2 engine mount located on the front side of the transaxle **(see illustration).**
20 Remove the No. 4 engine mount located above the transaxle near the battery/battery tray area.

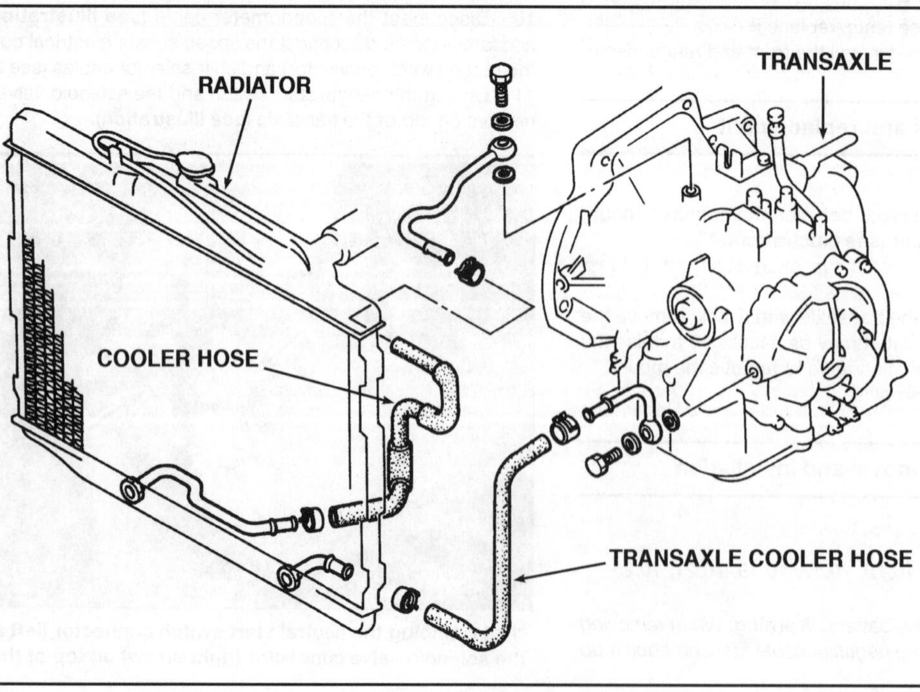

10.21 Locate the transaxle cooler hoses on the side and top of the transaxle and disconnect them

10.23 Mark the relationship of the torque converter to the driveplate (arrow) to ensure proper dynamic balance when it's reattached, then remove all six torque converter bolts (bolt showing in access window) by rotating the crankshaft to bring each bolt to the bottom, where you can get at it

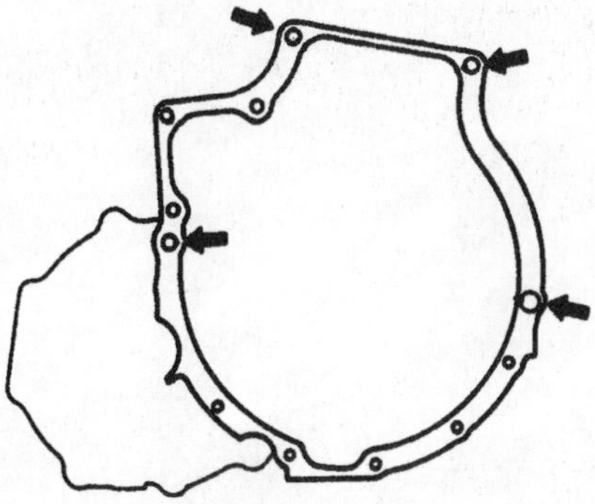

10.24 Remove the remaining transaxle nut and bolts

21 Disconnect the transaxle oil cooler inlet and outlet hoses **(see illustration)**.

22 Support the transaxle with a jack (preferably a special jack made for this purpose). If you're using a floor jack, be sure to place a wood block between the lifting pad and the transaxle to protect the cast aluminum housing. Safety chains will help steady the transaxle on the jack.

23 Remove the torque converter inspection cover. Mark the relationship of the torque converter to the driveplate so they can be installed in the same position **(see illustration)**. Remove the six torque converter mounting bolts. Turn the crankshaft for access to each one in turn.

24 Remove the 4 engine-to-transaxle bolts **(see illustration)**.

25 Make a final check that all wires and hoses have been disconnected from the transaxle.

26 Lower the left (driver's) end of the engine, then roll the transaxle and jack toward the side of the vehicle. Once the input shaft is clear of the splines in the torque converter, lower the transaxle and remove it from under the vehicle. Try to keep the transaxle as level as possible.

27 Move the transaxle to the side to disengage it from the engine block dowel pins and make sure the torque converter is detached from the driveplate. Secure the torque converter to the transaxle so that it will not fall out during removal. Lower the transaxle from the vehicle.

Installation

28 Make sure that the torque converter is securely engaged in the transaxle prior to installation.

29 With the transaxle secured to the jack as on removal, raise it into position and then carefully move it forward. Be sure to keep it level so the torque converter does not slide forward.

30 Move the transaxle carefully into place until the dowel pins are engaged and the torque converter is engaged.

31 Rotate the torque converter to align the bolt holes with the holes in the driveplate. The match marks on the torque converter and driveplate, made during Step 23, must align.

32 Install the 4 bolts securing the transaxle to the engine. Tighten the bolts to the torque listed in this Chapter's Specifications.

33 Install the torque converter-to-driveplate bolts. Tighten them to the torque listed in this Chapter's Specifications. Install the torque converter inspection cover.

34 Install the 5 engine oil pan-to-transaxle bolts. Tighten them to the torque listed in this Chapter's Specifications.

35 Remove the transaxle support jack.

36 Reconnect the transaxle oil cooler inlet and outlet hoses. **Caution:** *The hose ends and tubing they mate with have alignment marks. Be sure to align these marks when sliding the hoses on and that the hoses are fully seated before installing the clamp. Ensure that the hose clamps are positioned so that they do not interfere with any other parts.*

37 Install the engine mounts and tighten the bolts securely.

38 Install the front exhaust pipe assembly (see Chapter 4).

39 Install the engine support subframe and the transverse subframe if so equipped. Tighten the bolts to the torque listed in this Chapter's Specifications.

40 Remove the engine support jack or hoist.

41 Attach any cable or wire harness clamps previously removed from the engine and/or transaxle.

42 Reinstall the throttle cable aligning the mark made during step 12 with the bracket to ensure the cable is installed in the original position.

43 Install and adjust the neutral start switch and the solenoid valve electrical connectors (see Section 7).

44 Connect and adjust the shift cable (see Section 5) and the speedometer cable.

45 Install the stabilizer bar (see Chapter 10).

46 Install and/or connect the driveaxle(s) to the transaxle and the intermediate shaft is so equipped (see Chapter 8).

47 Install the starter (see Chapter 5).

48 Install the wheels. Lower the vehicle and tighten the lug nuts to the torque listed in Chapter 1 Specifications.

49 Fill the transaxle with the proper type and amount of fluid (see Chapter 1).

50 Install the intake air hose and resonance chamber.

51 Install the battery and battery tray.

52 Connect the battery cables. **Warning:** *When connecting the battery cables always attach the positive cable first.*

53 Road test the vehicle to check for proper transaxle operation and check for leakage.

Notes

Chapter 8
Clutch and driveaxles

Contents

Specifications

Clutch

Fluid type	See Chapter 1
Pedal freeplay	See Chapter 1
Driveaxle standard length (1990 through 1994 models)	
1.6L SOHC Engine	
Left driveaxle	25.11 inches
Right driveaxle	36.19 inches
1.8L SOHC Engine	
Left driveaxle	25.20 inches
Right driveaxle	36.17 inches
1.8L DOHC Engine with manual transaxle	
Left driveaxle	24.46 inches
Right driveaxle	24.83 inches
1.8L DOHC Engine with automatic transaxle	
Left driveaxle	25.08 inches
Right driveaxle	24.83 inches
Driveaxle standard length (1995 and later models)	
1.5L DOHC Engine with manual transaxle	
Left driveaxle	25.73 to 26.12 inches
Right driveaxle	23.44 to 23.84 inches
1.5L DOHC Engine with automatic transaxle	
Left driveaxle	25.57 to 25.96 inches
Right driveaxle	23.44 to 23.84 inches
1.8L DOHC Engine with manual transaxle	
Left driveaxle	24.94 to 25.33 inches
Right driveaxle	25.22 to 25.61 inches
1.8L DOHC Engine with automatic transaxle	
Left driveaxle	25.48 to 25.88 inches
Right driveaxle	25.22 to 25.61 inches

Torque specifications

Torque specifications	Ft-lbs
Clutch master cylinder mounting nuts	14 to 18
Clutch pressure plate-to-flywheel bolts	14 to 19
Clutch release cylinder mounting bolts	14 to 17
Driveaxle/hub locknut	174 to 235
Intermediate shaft support bracket bolts	32 to 45
Wheel lug nuts	See Chapter 1

1 General information

The information in this Chapter deals with the components from the rear of the engine to the front wheels, except for the transaxle, which is dealt with in Chapters 7A and 7B. For the purposes of this Chapter, these components are grouped into two categories: clutch and driveaxles. Separate Sections within this Chapter offer general descriptions and checking procedures for both groups.

Since nearly all the procedures covered in this Chapter involve working under the vehicle, make sure it's securely supported on sturdy jackstands or a hoist where the vehicle can be easily raised and lowered.

2 Clutch - description and check

Refer to illustration 2.1

1 All vehicles with a manual transaxle use a single dry plate, diaphragm spring type clutch **(see illustration)**. The clutch disc has a splined hub which allows it to slide along the splines of the transaxle input shaft. The clutch and pressure plate are held in contact by spring pressure exerted by the diaphragm in the pressure plate.

2 The clutch release system is operated by hydraulic pressure. The hydraulic release system consists of the clutch pedal, a master cylinder, a fluid reservoir, the hydraulic line, a slave cylinder which actuates the clutch release lever and the clutch release (or throw-out) bearing.

3 When pressure is applied to the clutch pedal to release the clutch, hydraulic pressure is exerted against the outer end of the clutch release lever. As the lever pivots, the shaft fingers push against the release bearing. The bearing pushes against the fingers of the diaphragm spring of the pressure plate assembly, which in turn releases the clutch plate.

4 Terminology can be a problem regarding the clutch components because common names have in some cases changed from that used by the manufacturer. For example, the driven plate is also called the clutch plate or disc, the pressure plate assembly is sometimes referred to as the clutch cover, the clutch release bearing is sometimes called a throw-out bearing, and the release cylinder is sometimes called the operating or slave cylinder.

5 Other than replacing components that have obvious damage, some preliminary checks should be performed to diagnose a clutch system failure.

a) *The first check should be of the fluid level in the clutch/brake reservoir (see Chapter 1). If the fluid level is low, add fluid as necessary and inspect the hydraulic clutch system for leaks. If the reservoir has run dry, bleed the system (see Section 8) and retest the clutch operation.*
b) *To check "clutch spin down time," run the engine at normal idle speed with the transaxle in Neutral (clutch pedal up - engaged). Disengage the clutch (pedal down), wait several seconds and shift the transaxle into Reverse. No grinding noise should be heard. A grinding noise would most likely indicate a problem in the pressure plate or the clutch disc.*
c) *To check for complete clutch release, run the engine (with the parking brake applied to prevent movement) and hold the clutch pedal approximately 1/2-inch from the floor. Shift the transaxle between 1st gear and Reverse several times. If the shift is not smooth, component failure is indicated. Check the release cylinder pushrod travel. With the clutch pedal depressed completely the release cylinder pushrod should extend substantially. If it doesn't, check the fluid level in the reservoir.*
d) *Visually inspect the clutch pedal bushing at the top of the clutch pedal to make sure there is no sticking or excessive wear.*
e) *Under the vehicle, check that the clutch release lever is solidly mounted on the ball stud.*

3 Clutch components - removal, inspection and installation

Warning: *Dust produced by clutch wear and deposited on clutch components may contain asbestos, which is hazardous to your health. DO NOT blow it out with compressed air and DO NOT inhale it. DO NOT use gasoline or petroleum based solvents to remove the dust. Brake system cleaner should be used to flush the dust into a drain pan. After the clutch components are wiped clean with a rag, dispose of the contaminated rags and cleaner in a labeled, covered container.*

Removal

Refer to illustration 3.6

1 Access to the clutch components is normally accomplished by removing the transaxle, leaving the engine in the vehicle. If, of course, the engine is being removed for major overhaul, then the opportunity should always be taken to check the clutch for wear and replace worn components as necessary. However, the relatively low cost of the clutch components compared to the time and labor involved in gaining access to them warrants their replacement any time the engine or transaxle is removed, unless they are new or in near-perfect condition. The following procedures assume that the engine will stay in place.

2 Remove the release cylinder (see Section 7). Hang it out of the way with a piece of wire - it isn't necessary to disconnect the pipe or hose.

3 Remove the transaxle from the vehicle (see Chapter 7, Part A). Support the engine while the transaxle is out. Preferably, an engine hoist should be used to support it from above. However, if a jack is used underneath the engine, make sure a piece of wood is used between the jack and oil pan to spread the load. **Caution:** *The pick-up for the oil pump is very close to the bottom of the oil pan. If the pan is bent or distorted in any way, engine oil starvation could occur.*

4 The release fork and release bearing can remain attached to the transaxle for the time being.

5 To support the clutch disc during removal, install a clutch alignment tool through the clutch disc hub.

6 Carefully inspect the flywheel and pressure plate for indexing marks. The marks are usually an X, an O or a white letter. If they cannot be found, scribe marks yourself so the pressure plate and the flywheel

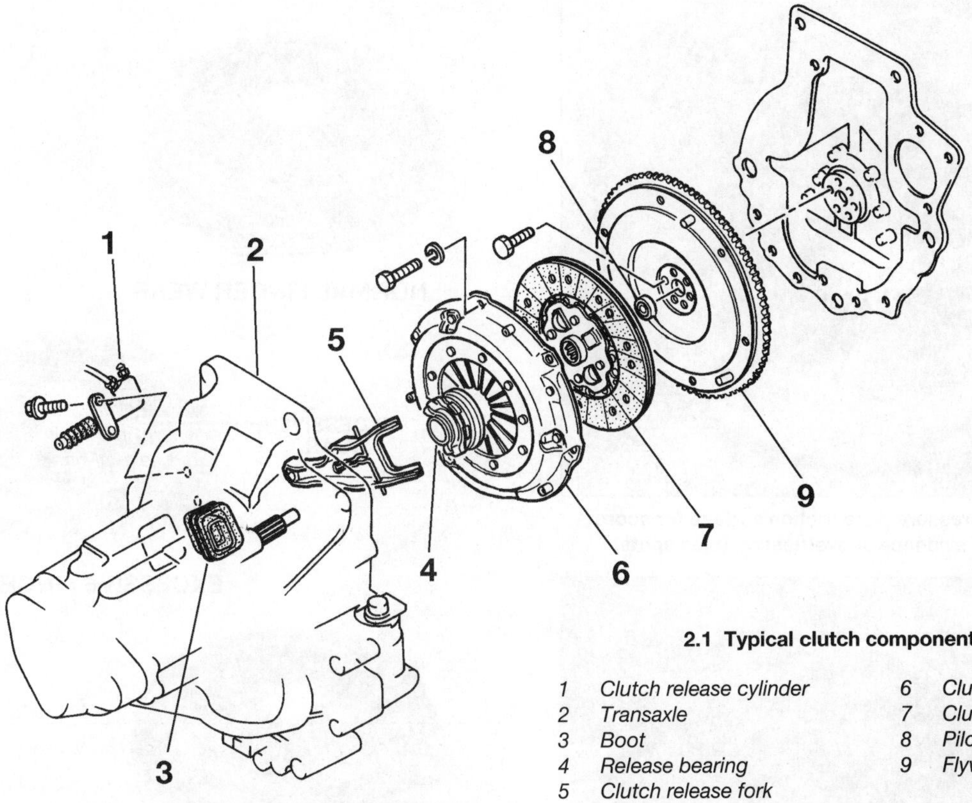

2.1 Typical clutch components

1. *Clutch release cylinder*
2. *Transaxle*
3. *Boot*
4. *Release bearing*
5. *Clutch release fork*
6. *Clutch cover*
7. *Clutch disk*
8. *Pilot bearing*
9. *Flywheel*

3.6 Mark the relationship of the pressure plate to the flywheel (in case you're going to reuse the same pressure plate)

3.10 Examine the clutch disc for evidence of excessive wear, such as smeared friction material, chewed-up rivets, worn hub splines and distorted damper cushions or springs

will be in the same alignment during installation **(see illustration)**.

7 Slowly loosen the pressure plate-to-flywheel bolts. Work in a diagonal pattern and loosen each bolt a little at a time until all spring pressure is relieved. Then hold the pressure plate securely and completely remove the bolts, followed by the pressure plate and clutch disc.

Inspection

Refer to illustrations 3.10, 3.12a and 3.12b

8 Ordinarily, when a problem occurs in the clutch, it can be attributed to wear of the clutch driven plate assembly (clutch disc). However, all components should be inspected at this time.

9 Inspect the flywheel for cracks, heat checking, score marks and other damage. If the imperfections are slight, a machine shop can resurface it to make it flat and smooth. Refer to Chapter 7A or 7B for the flywheel removal procedure.

10 Inspect the lining on the clutch disc. There should be at least 1/16-inch of lining above the rivet heads. Check for loose rivets, distortion, cracks, broken springs and other obvious damage **(see illustration)**. As mentioned above, ordinarily the clutch disc is replaced as a matter of course, so if in doubt about the condition, replace it with a new one.

11 The release bearing should be replaced along with the clutch disc (see Section 4).

3.12a Examine the pressure plate friction surface for score marks, cracks and evidence of overheating (blue spots)

3.14 Center the clutch disc in the pressure plate with a clutch alignment tool

12 Check the machined surface and the diaphragm spring fingers of the pressure plate **(see illustrations)**. If the surface is grooved or otherwise damaged, replace the pressure plate assembly. Also check for obvious damage, distortion, cracking, etc. Light glazing can be removed with emery cloth or sandpaper. If a new pressure plate is indicated, new or factory rebuilt units are available.

Installation

Refer to illustration 3.14

13 Before installation, carefully wipe the flywheel and pressure plate machined surfaces clean. It's important that no oil or grease is on these surfaces or the lining of the clutch disc. Handle these parts only with clean hands.

14 Position the clutch disc and pressure plate with the clutch held in place with an alignment tool **(see illustration)**. Make sure it's installed properly (most replacement clutch plates will be marked "flywheel side" or something similar - if not marked, install the clutch disc with the damper springs or cushion toward the transaxle).

15 Tighten the pressure plate-to-flywheel bolts only finger tight, working around the pressure plate.

16 Center the clutch disc by ensuring the alignment tool is through the splined hub and into the recess in the crankshaft. Wiggle the tool up, down or side-to-side as needed to bottom the tool. Tighten the pressure plate-to-flywheel bolts a little at a time, working in a criss-cross pattern to prevent distortion of the cover. After all of the bolts are snug, tighten them to the torque listed in this Chapter's Specifications. Remove the alignment tool.

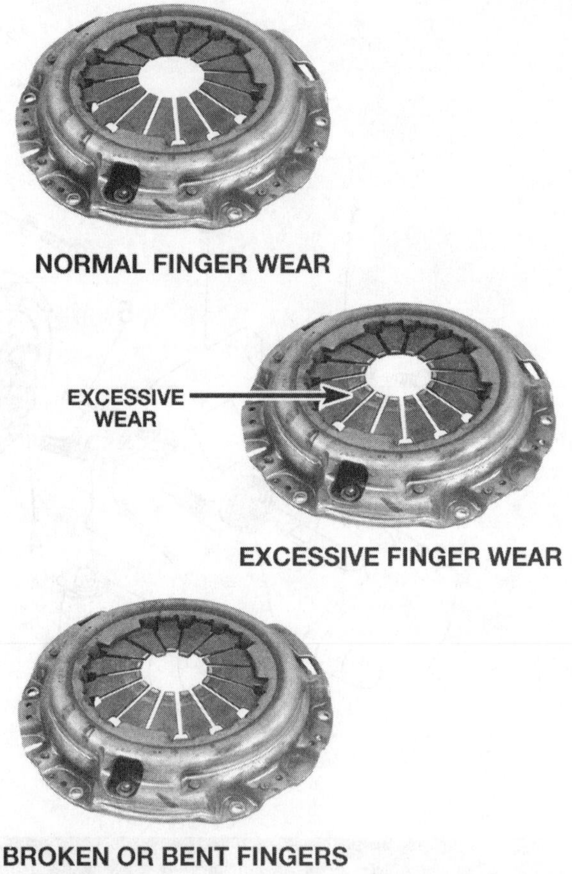

3.12b Replace the pressure plate if any of these conditions are noted

17 Using high-temperature grease, lubricate the inner groove of the release bearing (see Section 4). Also place grease on the release lever contact areas and the transaxle input shaft bearing retainer.

18 Install the clutch release bearing (see Section 4).

19 Install the transaxle, release cylinder and all components removed previously, tightening all fasteners to the proper torque specifications.

4 Clutch release bearing and lever - removal, inspection and installation

Warning: *Dust produced by clutch wear and deposited on clutch components may contain asbestos, which is hazardous to your health. DO NOT blow it out with compressed air and DO NOT inhale it. DO NOT use gasoline or petroleum-based solvents to remove the dust. Brake system cleaner should be used to flush it into a drain pan. After the clutch components are wiped clean with a rag, dispose of the contaminated rags and cleaner in a labeled, covered container.*

Removal

Refer to illustration 4.3

1 Disconnect the negative cable from the battery.

2 Remove the transaxle (see Chapter 7).

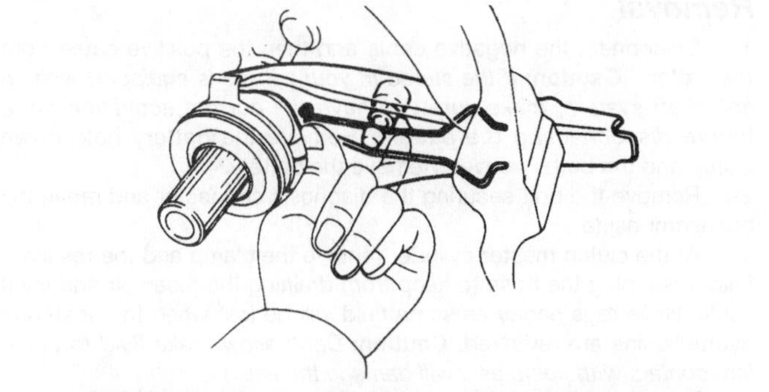

4.3 Reach behind the release lever and disengage the lever from the ball stud by pulling on the retention spring, then remove the lever and bearing

3 Remove the clutch release lever from the ball stud, then remove the bearing from the lever **(see illustration)**.

Inspection

Refer to illustration 4.4

4 Hold the bearing by the outer race and rotate the inner race while applying pressure **(see illustration)**. If the bearing doesn't turn smoothly or if it's noisy, replace the bearing/hub assembly with a new one. Wipe the bearing with a clean rag and inspect it for damage, wear and cracks. Don't immerse the bearing in solvent - it is sealed for life and soaking or dipping in solvent would ruin it. Also check the release lever for cracks and bends.

Installation

Refer to illustrations 4.5 and 4.6

5 Fill the inner groove of the release bearing with high-temperature grease. Also apply a light coat of the same grease to the transaxle input shaft splines and the front bearing retainer **(see illustration)**.

6 Lubricate the release lever ball socket, lever ends and release cylinder pushrod socket with high-temperature grease **(see illustration)**.

7 Attach the release bearing to the release lever.

8 Slide the release bearing onto the transaxle input shaft front bearing retainer while passing the end of the release lever through the opening in the clutch housing. Push the clutch release lever onto the ball stud until it's firmly seated.

9 Apply a light coat of high-temperature grease to the face of the release bearing where it contacts the pressure plate diaphragm fingers.

10 The remainder of installation is the reverse of the removal procedure.

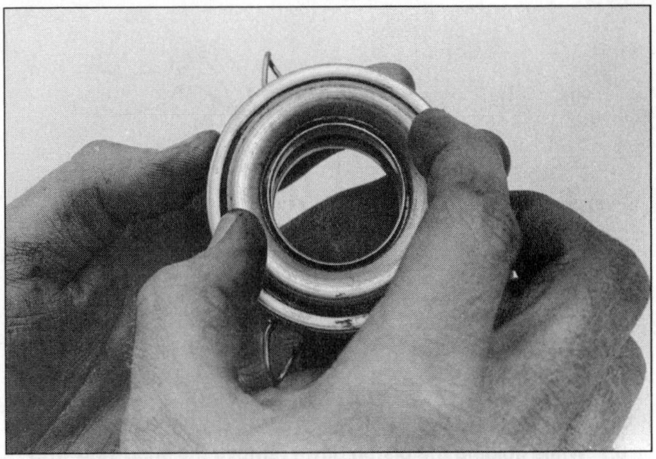

4.4 To check the operation of the bearing, hold it by the outer race and rotate the inner race while applying pressure - the bearing should turn smoothly - if it doesn't, replace it

5 Pilot bearing - inspection and replacement

1 A pilot bearing, pressed into the rear of the crankshaft, supports the front of the transmission input shaft. The needle roller bearing is greased at the factory and does not require additional lubrication. The pilot bearing should be inspected whenever the clutch components are removed. Due to its inaccessibility, if you are in doubt as to its condition, replace it with a new one.

2 Remove the transmission (see Chapter 7, Part A).

3 Remove the clutch components (see Section 3).

4 Inspect the bearing for excessive wear, scoring, lack of grease, dryness or obvious damage (**see illustration 2.1** for location). If any of these conditions are noted, the bearing should be replaced. A flashlight will be helpful to direct light into the recess.

5 The bearing must be pulled from its hole in the crankshaft, gripping the bearing at the rear. Special tools are available, but you may be able to get by with a an alternative tool or fabricated tool. One method that works well is to use a slide-hammer with a small tip that has two adjustable hooks, 180-degrees apart. Such tips are commonly available for slide-hammers, and are often included with better-quality slide-hammer kits. A slide-hammer is a tool with many uses, such as pulling dents from body parts and removing seals; you'll use it later for more things than just removing bushings. If a slide-hammer with the correct hooked tip is not available, try to find a hooked tool that will fit into the bearing hole and hook behind the bearing, then clamp a large pair of locking pliers to the tool and strike the pliers, near the jaws, to pull the bearing out.

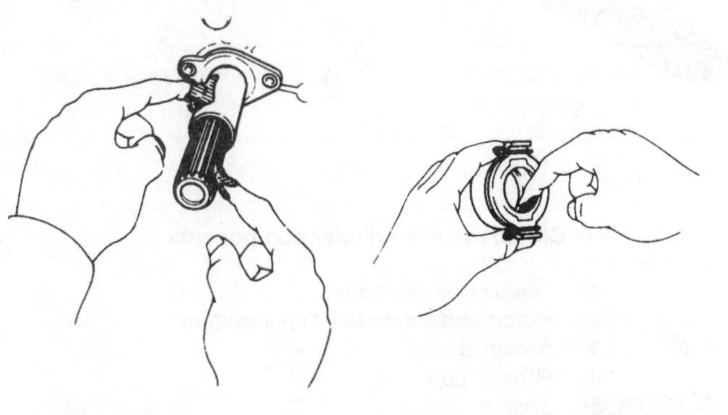

4.5 Apply a light coat of high-temperature grease to the transaxle bearing retainer and also fill the release bearing groove

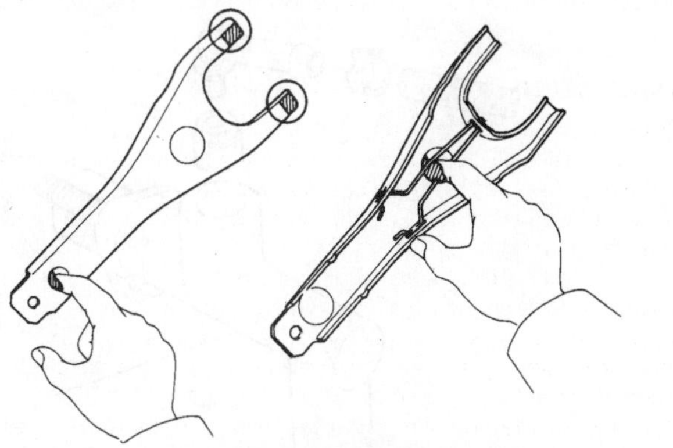

4.6 Apply high temperature grease to the release lever in the areas indicated

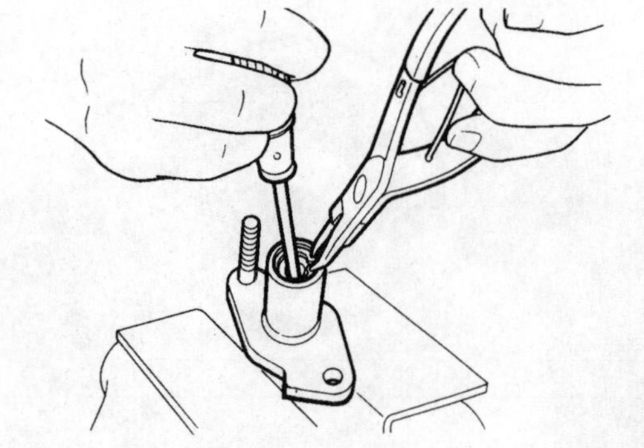

6.7 While holding the piston down remove the snap-ring with snap-ring pliers

6 To install the new bearing, lightly lubricate the outside surface with multi-purpose grease, then drive it into the recess with a hammer and a bearing driver or a clutch alignment tool. Make sure that the bearing seal faces toward the transmission. Don't allow the pilot bearing to become cocked in the bore. Tap it into place until it's flush with the edge of the bearing bore.
7 Lubricate the pilot bearing with high-temperature grease.
8 Install the clutch components (see Section 3).
9 Install the transmission (see Chapter 7, Part A).

6 Clutch master cylinder - removal, overhaul and installation

Note: *Before beginning this procedure, contact local parts stores and dealer service departments concerning the purchase of a rebuild kit or a new master cylinder. Availability and cost of the necessary parts may dictate whether the cylinder is rebuilt or replaced with a new one. If you decide to rebuild the cylinder, inspect the bore as described in Step 10 before purchasing parts.*

Removal

1 Disconnect the negative cable and then the positive cable from the battery. **Caution:** *If the stereo in your vehicle is equipped with an anti-theft system, make sure you have the correct activation code before disconnecting the battery.* Remove the battery hold-down clamp and the battery cover. Remove the battery.
2 Remove the bolt securing the diagnosis connector and move the connector aside.
3 At the clutch master cylinder remove the clamp and the reservoir fluid hose; plug the hose to keep from draining the reservoir and lay it aside. Have rags handy as some fluid will be lost when the hose and hydraulic line are removed. **Caution:** *Don't allow brake fluid to come into contact with paint, as it will damage the finish.*
4 Disconnect the hydraulic line at the clutch master cylinder. If available, use a flare-nut wrench on the fitting, to protect the fitting from being rounded off.
5 From under the dash, remove the nuts which attach the master cylinder to the firewall. Remove the master cylinder, again being careful not to spill fluid from the master cylinder.

Overhaul

Refer to illustrations 6.7 and 6.8

6 Turn the master cylinder over and allow the trapped fluid to drain from the hose/pipe connection into a pan.
7 Place the cylinder in a vise with the piston end up. Push the piston down with a Phillips screwdriver and remove the snap-ring with a snap-ring pliers **(see illustration)**. **Caution:** *Do not damage the push rod contact surface of the piston.*
8 Tap the master cylinder on a block of wood to eject the piston, spacer, primary cup and spring from inside the bore **(see illustration)**. **Note:** *If the rebuild kit supplies a complete piston assembly, ignore the Steps which don't apply.*
9 Carefully remove the seal from the piston.
10 Inspect the bore of the master cylinder for deep scratches, score marks and ridges. The surface must be smooth to the touch. If the bore isn't perfectly smooth, the master cylinder must be replaced with a new or factory rebuilt unit.
11 If the cylinder will be rebuilt, use the new parts contained in the rebuild kit and follow any specific instructions which may have accompanied the rebuild kit. Wash all parts to be re-used with brake cleaner, denatured alcohol or clean brake fluid. DO NOT use petroleum-based solvents.

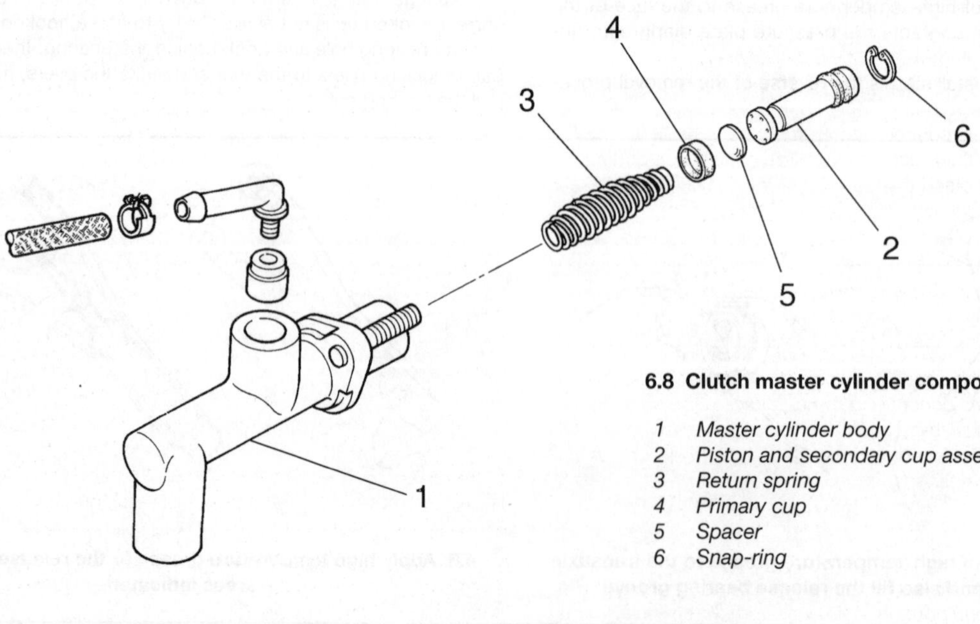

6.8 Clutch master cylinder components

1 *Master cylinder body*
2 *Piston and secondary cup assembly*
3 *Return spring*
4 *Primary cup*
5 *Spacer*
6 *Snap-ring*

7.6 Clutch release cylinder components

1. *Release cylinder body*
2. *Push rod*
3. *Piston and cup assembly*
4. *Spring*
5. *Boot*
6. *Bleeder screw*

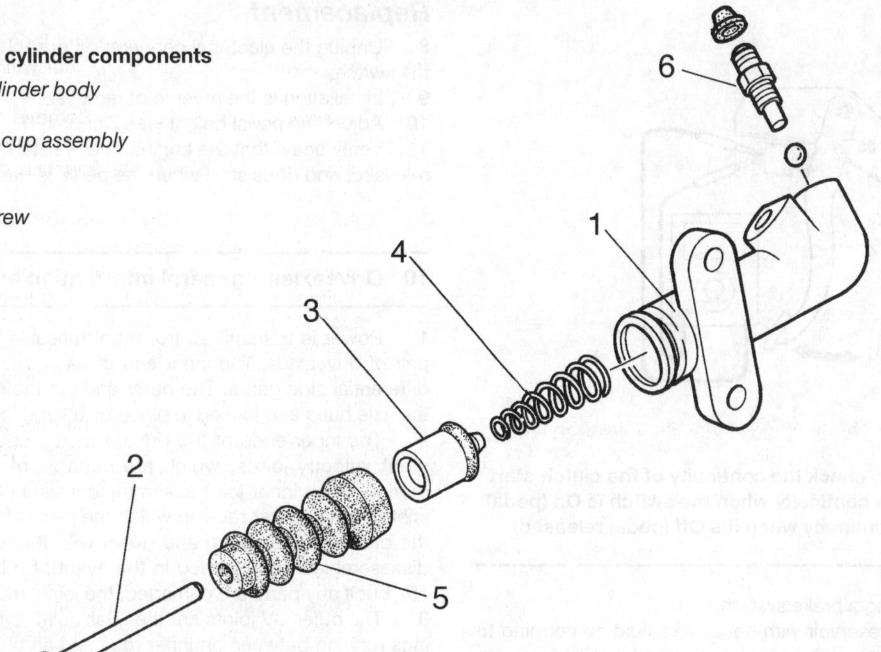

12 Attach a new seal to the piston. The seal lips must face away from the pushrod end of the piston.
13 Lubricate the bore of the cylinder, the spring, primary cup, spacer and piston with plenty of fresh brake fluid.
14 Carefully guide the spring, primary cup, spacer and piston into the cylinder bore.
15 Again place the cylinder in a vise with the piston end up. Push the piston down with a Phillips screwdriver and install a new snap-ring with a snap-ring pliers **(see illustration 6.7)**.

Installation

16 Dab a small amount of grease on the end of the pushrod. Position the master cylinder on the pushrod and against the firewall, installing the mounting nuts finger-tight.
17 Connect the hydraulic line to the master cylinder, moving the cylinder slightly as necessary to thread the fitting properly into the bore. Don't cross-thread the fitting as it's installed.
18 Tighten the mounting nuts and the hydraulic line fitting securely.
19 Reconnect the reservoir hose to the master cylinder.
20 Reinstall the diagnosis connector and the battery.
21 Fill the clutch/brake fluid reservoir with brake fluid conforming to DOT 3 specifications and bleed the clutch system (see Chapter 1).
22 Check the clutch pedal height and freeplay (see Chapter 1).

7 Clutch release cylinder - removal, overhaul and installation

Note: *Before beginning this procedure, contact local parts stores and dealer service departments concerning the purchase of a rebuild kit or a new release cylinder. Availability and cost of the necessary parts may dictate whether the cylinder is rebuilt or replaced with a new one. If it's decided to rebuild the cylinder, inspect the bore as described in Step 8 before purchasing parts.*

Removal

1 Disconnect the negative cable from the battery. **Caution:** *If the stereo in your vehicle is equipped with an anti-theft system, make sure you have the correct activation code before disconnecting the battery.*
2 Raise the vehicle and support it securely on jackstands.
3 Disconnect the hydraulic line at the release cylinder. If available, use a flare-nut wrench on the fitting, which will prevent the fitting from being rounded off. Have a small can and rags handy, as some fluid will be spilled as the line is removed. Cap the fluid line.
4 Remove the release cylinder mounting bolts.
5 Remove the release cylinder.

Overhaul

Refer to illustration 7.6

6 Remove the pushrod and the boot **(see illustration)**.
7 Tap the cylinder on a block of wood to eject the piston and seal. Remove the spring from inside the cylinder.
8 Carefully inspect the bore of the cylinder. Check for deep scratches, score marks and ridges. The bore must be smooth to the touch. If any imperfections are found, the release cylinder must be replaced with a new one.
9 Using the new parts in the rebuild kit, assemble the components using plenty of fresh brake fluid for lubrication. Note the installed direction of the spring and the seal.

Installation

10 Install the release cylinder on the clutch housing. Make sure the pushrod is seated in the release fork pocket.
11 Connect the hydraulic line to the release cylinder. Tighten the connection.
12 Fill the clutch master cylinder with brake fluid (conforming to DOT 3 specifications).
13 Bleed the system (see Section 8).
14 Lower the vehicle and connect the negative battery cable.

8 Clutch hydraulic system - bleeding

1 The hydraulic system should be bled of all air whenever any part of the system has been removed or if the fluid level has been allowed to fall so low that air has been drawn into the master cylinder. The pro-

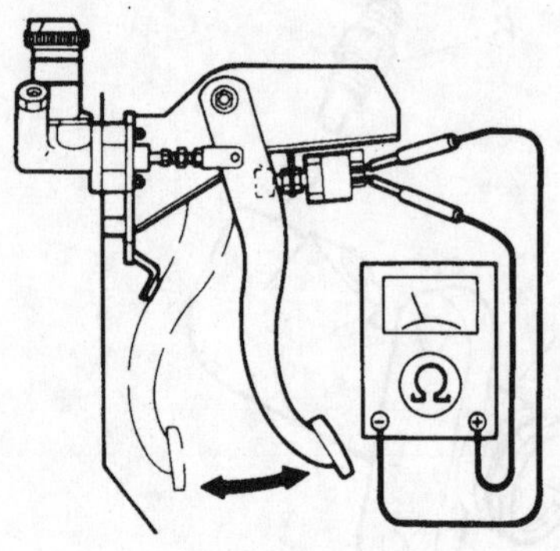

9.5 **Using an ohmmeter, check the continuity of the clutch start switch - there should be continuity when the switch is On (pedal depressed) and no continuity when it's Off (pedal released)**

cedure is similar to bleeding a brake system.

2 Fill the clutch/brake reservoir with new brake fluid conforming to DOT 3 specifications. **Caution:** *Do not re-use any of the fluid coming from the system during the bleeding operation or use fluid which has been inside an open container for an extended period of time.*

3 Raise the vehicle and place it securely on jackstands to gain access to the release cylinder, which is located on the left side of the clutch housing.

4 Locate the bleeder valve on the clutch release cylinder (next to the fitting for the hydraulic fluid line). Remove the dust cap which fits over the bleeder valve and push a length of plastic hose over the valve. Place the other end of the hose into a clear container with about two inches of brake fluid in it. The hose end must be submerged in the fluid.

5 Have an assistant depress the clutch pedal and hold it. Open the bleeder valve on the release cylinder, allowing fluid to flow through the hose. Close the bleeder valve when fluid stops flowing from the hose. Once closed, have your assistant release the pedal.

6 Continue this process until all air is evacuated from the system, indicated by a full, solid stream of fluid being ejected from the bleeder valve each time and no air bubbles in the hose or container. Keep a close watch on the fluid level in the reservoir; if the level drops too low, air will be sucked back into the system and the process will have to be started all over again.

7 Install the dust cap and lower the vehicle. Check carefully for proper operation before placing the vehicle in normal service.

9 Clutch start switch - check and replacement

Check

Refer to illustration 9.5

1 Check the clutch pedal height and freeplay (see Chapter 1).

2 Verify that the engine will not start when the clutch pedal is released. Verify that the engine will start when the clutch pedal is depressed all the way.

3 If the clutch start switch doesn't perform as described, adjust and, if necessary, replace it.

4 Locate the switch on the clutch pedal assembly and unplug the electrical connector.

5 Verify that there is continuity between the clutch start switch terminals when the switch is On (pedal depressed) **(see illustration)**.

6 Verify that no continuity exists between the switch terminals when the switch is Off (pedal released).

7 If the switch fails either of the tests, replace it.

Replacement

8 Unplug the electrical connector. Loosen the locknuts and remove the switch.

9 Installation is the reverse of removal.

10 Adjust the pedal height (see Chapter 1)

11 Verify again that the engine doesn't start when the clutch pedal is released, and does start when the pedal is depressed.

10 Driveaxles - general information and inspection

1 Power is transmitted from the transaxle to the wheels through a pair of driveaxles. The inner end of each driveaxle is splined into the differential side gears. The outer ends of the driveaxles are splined to the axle hubs and locked in place by a large locknut.

2 The inner ends of the driveaxles are equipped with sliding constant velocity joints, which are capable of both angular and axial motion. Each inner joint assembly consists of a tripod bearing and a joint housing (outer race) in which the joint is free to slide in and out as the driveaxle moves up and down with the wheel. The joints can be disassembled and cleaned in the event of a boot failure (see Section 13), but if any parts are damaged, the joints must be replaced as a unit.

3 The outer CV joints are the "Ball Joint" type which have ball bearings running between an inner race and an outer cage, allowing angular but not axial movement. The outer joints should be cleaned, inspected and repacked, but they cannot be disassembled. If an outer joint is damaged, it must be replaced along with the axleshaft (the outer joint and axleshaft are sold as a single component). On vehicles equipped with the 1.8L DOHC engine there is an intermediate/joint shaft between the transaxle and the driveaxle to the right wheel. This shaft is supported by a bracket at the outer end where it mates with the driveaxle.

4 The boots should be inspected periodically for damage and leaking lubricant. Torn CV joint boots must be replaced immediately or the joints can be damaged. Boot replacement involves removal of the driveaxle (see Section 11). **Note:** *Some auto parts stores carry "split" type replacement boots, which can be installed without removing the driveaxle from the vehicle. This is a convenient alternative; however, the driveaxle should be removed and the CV joint disassembled and cleaned to ensure the joint is free from contaminants such as moisture and dirt which will accelerate CV joint wear.* The most common symptom of worn or damaged CV joints, besides lubricant leaks, is a clicking noise in turns, a clunk when accelerating after coasting and vibration at highway speeds. To check for wear in the CV joints and driveaxle shafts, grasp each axle (one at a time) and rotate it in both directions while holding the CV joint housings, feeling for play indicating worn splines or sloppy CV joints. Also check the driveaxle shafts for cracks, dents and distortion.

11 Driveaxle - removal and installation

Removal

Refer to illustrations 11.4, 11.5, 11.10 and 11.11

1 Disconnect the cable from the negative terminal of the battery. **Caution:** *If the stereo in your vehicle is equipped with an anti-theft system, make sure you have the correct activation code before disconnecting the battery.*

2 Set the parking brake.

3 Loosen the front wheel lug nuts 1/4 turn. Using a hammer and punch, unstake the driveaxle hub locknut and loosen it 1/4 turn. Raise the vehicle and support it securely on jackstands. Remove the wheels.

4 Remove the driveaxle hub locknut. To prevent the hub from turning, wedge a prybar between two of the wheel studs and allow the prybar to rest against the ground **(see illustration)**.

5 To loosen the driveaxle from the hub splines, tap the end of the

11.4 Use a large prybar to immobilize the hub while loosening the driveaxle hub nut

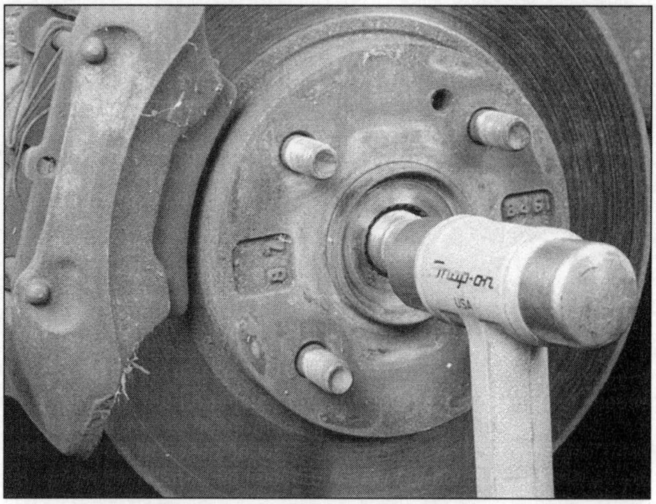

11.5 Using a brass punch, strike the end of the driveaxle sharply with a hammer; when it breaks free, it will move noticeably

11.10 Pull the steering knuckle out and slide the end of the driveaxle out of the hub

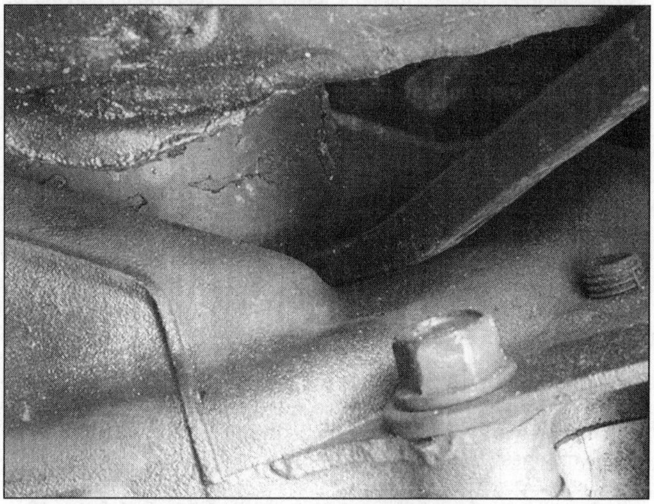

11.11 To separate the inner end of the driveaxle from the transaxle, pry on the CV joint housing like this with a large screwdriver or prybar - you may need to give the prybar a sharp rap with a brass hammer

driveaxle with a soft-faced hammer **(see illustration)** or a hammer and a brass punch. **Note:** *Don't attempt to push the end of the driveaxle through the hub yet. Applying force to the end of the driveaxle, beyond just breaking it loose from the hub, can damage the driveaxle or transaxle. If the driveaxle is stuck in the hub splines and won't move, it may be necessary to remove the brake disc (see Chapter 9) and push it from the hub with a two-jaw puller after Step 9 is performed.*

6 Remove the engine splash shield(s). **Note:** *All models have a splash shield on the left side of the engine compartment, inside the wheel well; 1995 and later models also have a shield on the right side which must be removed.*

7 Remove the nut and bolt securing the stabilizer bar to the control arm (see Chapter 10).

8 Disconnect the tie-rod from the steering knuckle (see Chapter 10).

9 Separate the lower ball joint from the control arm (see Chapter 10).

10 Pull out on the steering knuckle and detach the driveaxle from the hub **(see illustration)**. Don't let the driveaxle hang by the inner CV joint after the outer end has been detached from the steering knuckle, as the inner joint could become damaged. Support the outer end of the driveaxle with a piece of wire, if necessary.

11 Place a drain pan underneath the transaxle to catch the lubricant that will spill out when the driveaxles are removed. Gently pry the inner CV joint out of the transaxle being careful not to damage the dust cover or oil seal **(see illustration)**. On vehicles with an intermediate shaft slide the driveaxle off the shaft.

12 Refer to Chapter 7 for the driveaxle oil seal replacement procedure.

Installation

Refer to illustration 11.13

13 Installation is the reverse of the removal procedure, but with the following additional points:

a) *Install a new clip on the end of the driveaxle inner CV joint, apply molybdenum based grease to the splines and wipe the transaxle oil seal with transaxle oil.*
b) *With the end gap of the clip facing up, push the driveaxle sharply in to seat the clip on the inner CV joint in the groove of the differential side gear.* **Caution:** The sharp edges of the driveaxle snapring can slice or puncture the oil seal.

8

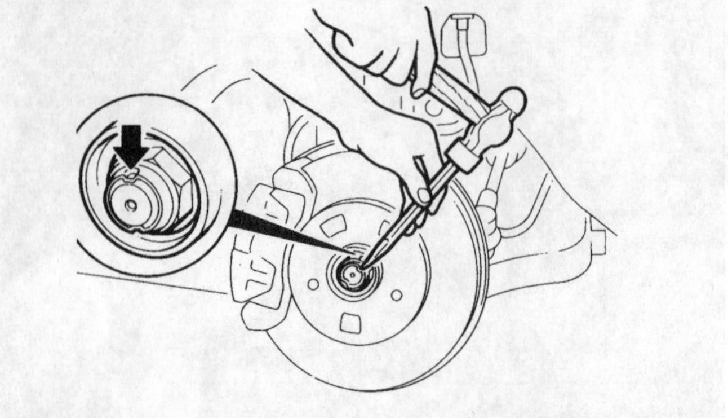

11.13 Tighten the locknut to the specified torque and use a punch to stake the nut so it cannot loosen

c) *Install a new driveaxle hub locknut, tighten it to the torque listed in this Chapter's Specifications and stake the locknut with a punch* **(see illustration)***.*
d) *Install the wheel and lug nuts, lower the vehicle and tighten the lug nuts to the torque listed in the Chapter 1 Specifications.*
e) *Check the transaxle lubricant and add, if necessary, to bring it to the proper level* (see Chapter 1).

12 Intermediate shaft - removal and installation (vehicles with 1.8L DOHC engines only)

Note: *If the shaft does not rotate smoothly and freely by hand, the support bracket bearing will probably need to be replaced. The bearing is pressed into the bracket and should be taken to an automotive machine shop if it needs replacement.*

Removal

1 If you do not plan to service the driveaxle CV joints, it is not necessary to remove the right driveaxle in order to remove the intermediate shaft. In this case follow the procedure in Section 11 with the following changes:

a) *Do not loosen and remove the driveaxle hub locknut and separate the driveaxle from the hub as called out in Steps 3, 4, 5 and 10.*
b) *After separating the driveaxle from the intermediate shaft (Step 11), move the driveaxle clear and support it with a block or wire. Don't let the driveaxle hang by the outer CV joint as the joint could be damaged.*

2 Remove the three bolts securing the intermediate shaft bracket to the vehicle and gently pry/pull the shaft from the transaxle being careful not to damage the oil seal.

Installation

3 Installation is the reverse of the removal procedure:

13 Driveaxle boot replacement and CV joint inspection

Note: *If the CV joints must be overhauled (usually due to torn boots), explore all options before beginning the job. Complete rebuilt driveaxles are available on an exchange basis, which eliminates much time and work. Whichever route you choose to take, check on the cost and availability of parts before disassembling the vehicle.*

1 Remove the driveaxle (see Section 11).

Disassembly

Refer to illustrations 13.3, 13.4, 13.6 and 13.7

2 Mount the driveaxle in a vise with wood-lined jaws (to prevent damage to the axleshaft). Check the CV joint for excessive play in the radial direction, which indicates worn parts. Check for smooth operation throughout the full range of motion for each CV joint. If a boot is torn, disassemble the joint, clean the components and inspect for damage due to loss of lubrication and possible contamination by foreign matter.

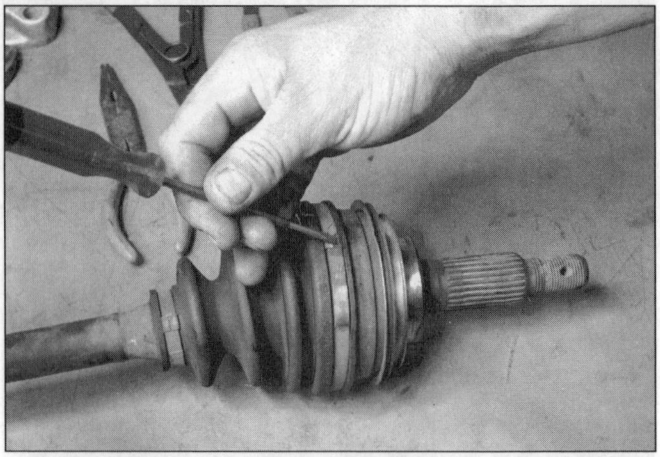

13.3 Lift the tabs on all the boot clamps with a screwdriver, then open the clamps

3 Using a small screwdriver, pry the retaining tabs on the clamps up to loosen them and slide them off **(see illustration)**.

4 Using a screwdriver, carefully pry up on the edge of the outer boot and push it away from the CV joint. Old and worn boots can be cut off. Pull the inner CV joint boot back from the housing and slide the housing from the tripod **(see illustration)**.

5 Mark the tripod and axleshaft to ensure that they are reassembled properly.

6 Remove the tripod joint snap-ring with a pair of snap-ring pliers **(see illustration)**.

7 Use a hammer and a brass punch to drive the tripod joint from the driveaxle **(see illustration)**.

8 If you have not already cut them off, remove both boots. If you're working on a right-side driveaxle, you'll also have to cut off the clamp for the dynamic damper and slide the damper off.

Check

9 Thoroughly clean all components, including the outer CV joint assembly, with solvent until the old CV joint grease is completely removed. Inspect the bearing surfaces of the inner tripods and housings for cracks, pitting, scoring and other signs of wear. It's very difficult to inspect the bearing surfaces of the inner and outer races of the outer CV joint, but you can at least check the surfaces of the ball bearings themselves. If they are in good shape, the races probably are too;

13.4 Remove the boot from the inner CV joint and slide the joint housing from the tripod

13.6 Remove the snap-ring with a pair of snap-ring pliers

13.10a Wrap the splined area of the axleshaft with tape to prevent damage to the boots when removing or installing them

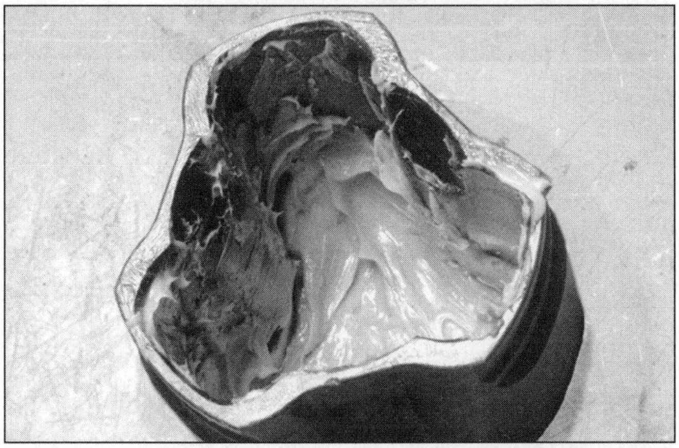

13.10c Place grease at the bottom of the CV joint housing

if they are not, neither are the races. If the inner CV joint is worn, you can buy a new inner CV joint and install it on the old axleshaft; if the outer CV joint is worn, you must purchase a new outer CV joint *and* axleshaft (they are sold preassembled).

Reassembly

Refer to illustrations 13.10a, 13.10b, 13.10c, 13.10d, 13.11, 13.12a, 13.12b and 13.12c

10 Wrap the splines on the end the axleshaft with electrical tape to

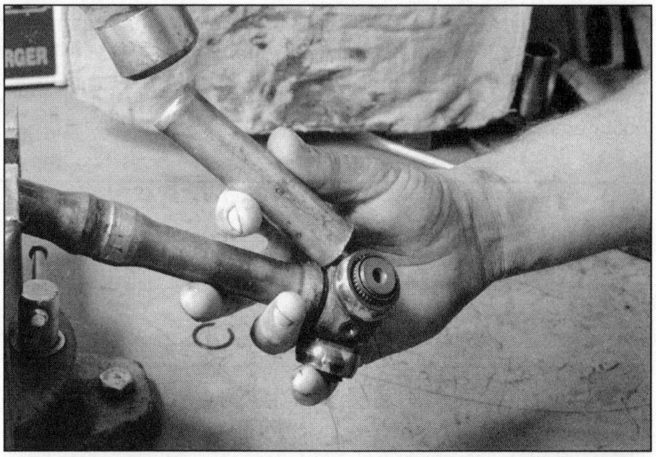

13.7 Drive the tripod joint from the driveaxle with a brass punch and hammer; be careful not to damage the bearing surfaces or the splines on the shaft

13.10b Install the tripod with the recessed portion of the splines facing the axleshaft

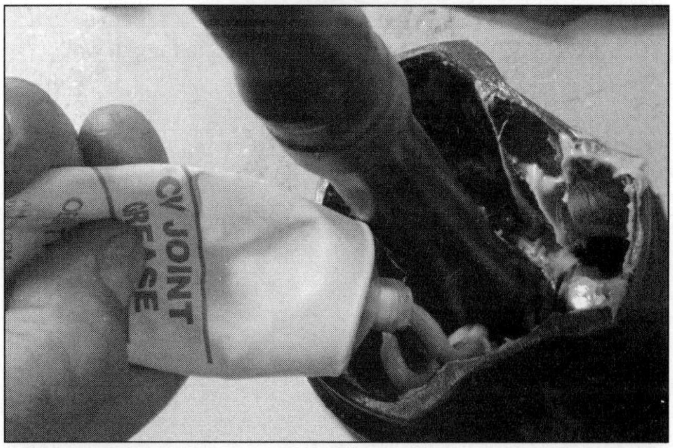

13.10d Install the boot and clamps onto the axleshaft, then insert the tripod into the housing, followed by the rest of the grease

protect the boots from the sharp edges of the splines **(see illustration)**. Slide the clamps and boot(s) onto the axleshaft, then place the tripod on the shaft. **Note:** *If you are working on a right side driveaxle, be sure to install the dynamic damper and a new clamp before installing the inner boot.* Apply grease to the tripod assembly and inside the housing. Insert the tripod into the housing and pack the remainder of the grease around the tripod. **(see illustrations)**.

8

11 Slide the boot into place, making sure both ends seat in their grooves. Adjust the length of the driveaxle to the dimension listed in this Chapter's Specifications **(see illustration)**.

12 Equalize the pressure in the boot, then tighten and secure the boot clamps **(see illustrations)**.

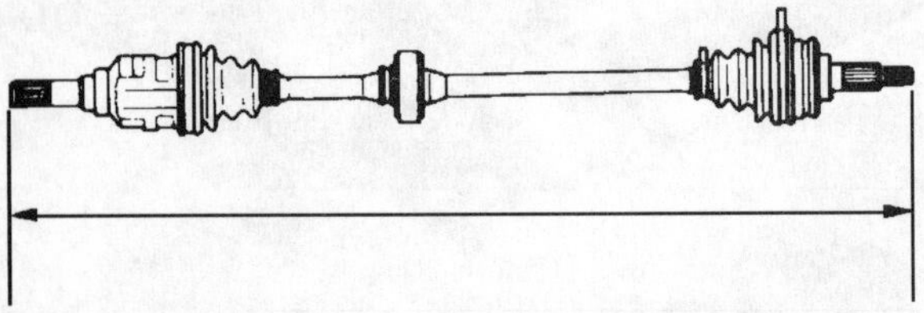

13.11 The driveaxle standard length should be set to the dimension listed in this Chapter's Specifications before the boot clamps are tightened

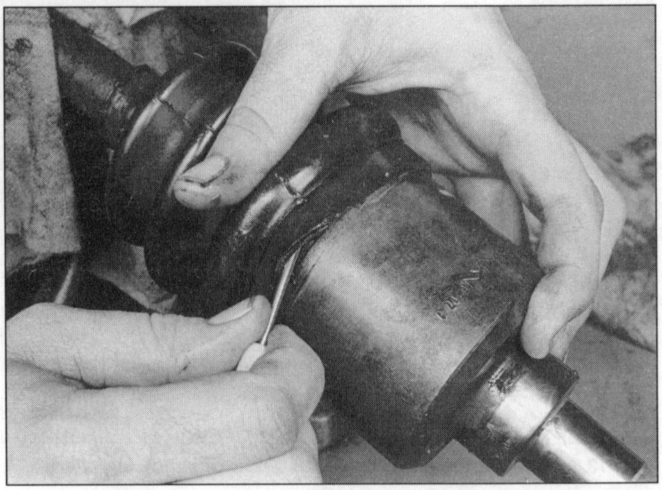

13.12a Equalize the pressure inside the boot by inserting a small, dull screwdriver between the boot and the outer race

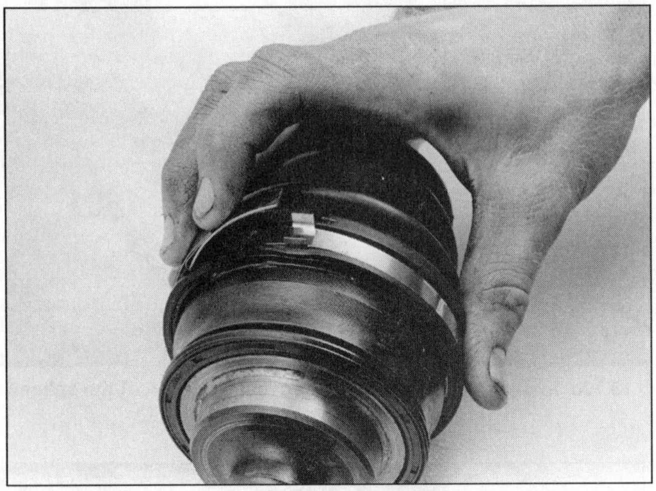

13.12b To install the new clamps, bend the tang down . . .

13.12c . . . then tap the tabs over to hold it in place

Chapter 9 Brakes

Contents

Specifications

General

Brake fluid type	See Chapter 1
Brake pedal height - pedal-to-floor	
1990 through 1994	7-5/8 to 7-3/4 inches
1995 and later	See Section 16
Brake pedal freeplay	
1990 through 1994	5/32 to 1/4 inch
1995 and later	3/16 to 7/16 inch
Brake pedal reserve distance	2-3/4 inches
Brake light switch-to-pedal clearance	See procedure
Power brake booster pushrod-to-master cylinder piston clearance	
1990 through 1994	0.016 to 0.024 inch
1995 and later	0.0039 to 0.0157 inch
ABS sensor to toothed wheel clearance - 1995 and later, front and rear	0.012 to 0.043 inch

Disc brakes

Minimum brake pad thickness	See Chapter 1
Front disc thickness	
Standard	0.87 inch
Minimum*	0.79 inch
Rear disc thickness	
Standard	0.35 inch
Minimum*	
1990 through 1994	0.31 inch
1995 and later	0.276 inch
Disc runout limit (front or rear)	
1990 through 1994	0.004 inch
1995 and later	0.002 inch

Drum brakes

Drum inside diameter	
Standard	
1990 and 1991	9.0 inches
1992	7.90 inches
1993 and later	7.87 inches
Maximum*	
1990 and 1991	9.04 inches
1992 through 1994	7.91 inches
1995 and later	7.93 inches

**Note:* *If different specifications are cast into the disc or drum, they supersede information printed here.*

Parking brake

Parking brake lever travel	5 to 7 clicks

Torque specifications

	Ft-lbs (unless otherwise indicated)
Brake hose-to-caliper banjo bolts	16 to 21
Front caliper mounting bolts	29 to 36
Rear caliper mounting bolts	
1990 through 1994	
Upper bolt	34 to 44
Lower bolt	26 to 28
1995 and later	34 to 44
Master cylinder-to-brake booster nuts	87 to 139 in-lbs
Power brake booster mounting nuts	14 to 18
Wheel cylinder mounting bolts	87 to 112 in-lbs
Wheel lug nuts	See Chapter 1

1 General information

The vehicles covered by this manual are equipped with hydraulically operated front and rear brake systems. The front brakes are disc type and the rear brakes are drum type. Both the front and rear brakes are self-adjusting. The disc brakes automatically compensate for pad wear, while the drum brakes incorporate an adjustment mechanism which is activated as the parking brake is applied.

Hydraulic system

The hydraulic system consists of two separate circuits. The master cylinder has separate reservoirs for the two circuits, and, in the event of a leak or failure in one hydraulic circuit, the other circuit will remain operative. A dual proportioning valve on the firewall provides brake balance between the front and rear brakes.

Power brake booster

The power brake booster, utilizing engine manifold vacuum and atmospheric pressure to provide assistance to the hydraulically operated brakes, is mounted on the firewall in the engine compartment.

Parking brake

The parking brake operates the rear brakes only, through cable actuation. It's activated by a lever mounted in the center console.

Service

After completing any operation involving disassembly of any part of the brake system, always test drive the vehicle to check for proper braking performance before resuming normal driving. When testing the brakes, perform the tests on a clean, dry, flat surface. Conditions other than these can lead to inaccurate test results.

Test the brakes at various speeds with both light and heavy pedal pressure. The vehicle should stop evenly without pulling to one side or the other. Avoid locking the brakes, because this slides the tires and diminishes braking efficiency and control of the vehicle.

Tires, vehicle load and wheel alignment are factors which also affect braking performance.

2 Anti-lock Brake System (ABS) - general information

1 The Anti-lock Brake System (ABS) is designed to maintain vehicle steerability, directional stability and optimum deceleration under severe braking conditions and on most road surfaces. It does this by monitoring the rotational speed of each wheel and controlling the brake line pressure to each wheel during braking. This prevents the wheel from locking up.

Components

Actuator assembly

2 The ABS hydraulic unit consists of an electric hydraulic pump, solenoid valves, flow control valves, buffer and damper chamber, and is located in the engine compartment. The electric pump provides hydraulic pressure to the brakes, modulating brake line pressure during ABS operation, by turning on/off the solenoid valves and opening/closing the flow control valves in the ABS hydraulic unit. The buffer chamber stores hydraulic fluid from the brakes for smooth decrease of pressure. The damper chamber decreases pump noise and vibration. The hydraulic unit is controlled by the ABS control module, located under the dash at the driver's side. A fail-safe mode, operated by the fail-safe relay, mounted in the engine compartment near the left side headlight, returns the brake system to conventional operation if there is a malfunction in the ABS, and the ABS warning light comes ON.

Speed sensors

Refer to illustrations 2.4 and 2.5

3 The speed sensors, which are located at each wheel, generate small electrical pulsations when the toothed sensor rotors are turning, sending a variable voltage signal to the ABS control module indicating wheel rotational speed.

4 The front speed sensors **(see illustration)** are mounted at the front wheel hubs in close relationship to the toothed sensor rotors, which are integral with the outer constant velocity (CV) joints.

5 The rear wheel sensors are bolted to the brake backing plates or axle carriers **(see illustration)**. The sensor rotors are integral with the rear brake hub.

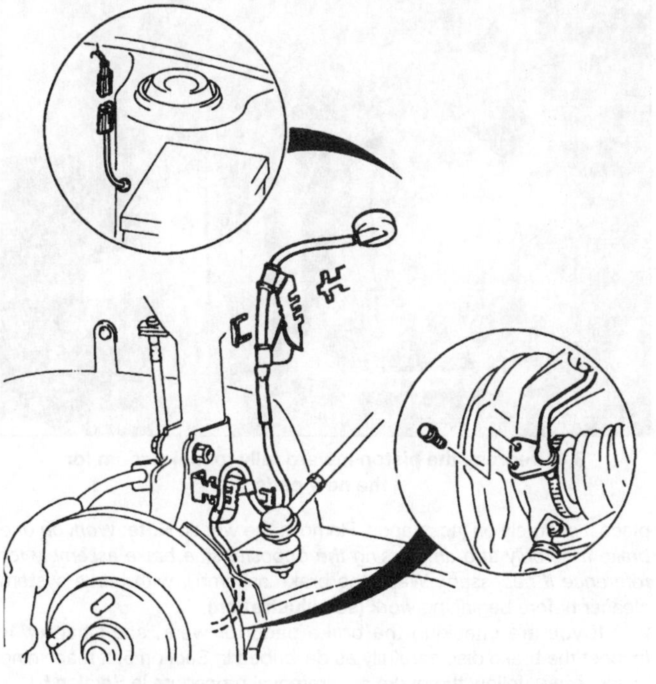

2.4 ABS front wheel speed sensor and sensor rotor

ABS computer

6 The ABS control module, mounted under the dashboard on the driver's side, is the "brain" of the ABS system, in conjunction with the vehicle CPU. The function of the ABS Control Module is to accept and process information received from the wheel speed sensors to control the hydraulic line pressure, avoiding wheel lock up. The ABS Control Module also constantly monitors the system, even under normal driving conditions, to find faults within the system.

7 If a problem develops within the system, an "ABS" light will glow on the dashboard. A diagnostic code will also be stored in the ECU, which, when retrieved by a service technician, will indicate the problem area or component.

Diagnosis and repair

8 If a dashboard warning light comes on and stays on while the vehicle is in operation, the ABS system requires attention. Although a special electronic ABS diagnostic tester is necessary to properly diagnose the system, the home mechanic can perform a few preliminary checks before taking the vehicle to a dealer service department or other repair shop which is equipped with a tester.

- *a) Check the brake fluid level in the reservoir.*
- *b) Check that all electrical connectors are securely connected.*
- *c) Check the fuses.*

Caution: *Do not attempt to use the vehicle until repairs are accomplished.*

9 Additional checks that can be performed to assist you before dealer diagnosis and/or repair, that may help you discuss the problem with the dealer service representatives, are as follows:

With a fully charged vehicle battery, turn the ignition switch ON, and check that the ABS warning light goes out after 2 to 4 seconds.

If the light stays on after 2 to 4 seconds, the ABS control module is detecting a failure and will not activate the ABS hydraulic unit. See the dealer for servicing. Turn the ignition switch OFF.

Carefully jack up the vehicle on a level surface and securely support using jackstands. Shift the transaxle to neutral or N range.

Release the parking brake. Rotate each wheel by hand, making sure that excessive brake drag does not exist.

Locate the Data Link Connector under the hood at the firewall, near the battery, and place a jumper wire between terminals TBS and GND.

Starting with the right front wheel, have an assistant depress the brake pedal while you check that the right front wheel will not rotate by hand.

With the brake pedal still depressed, turn the ignition switch ON and verify that the brake is released momentarily (approximately 1/2 second) and the wheel turns when pressure reduction from the ABS automatically cycles on and off. Perform the same check on the other wheels in order, left front, right rear, and left rear.

If the system tests are satisfactory for momentary brake release (the previous two steps above), then the piping to the ABS hydraulic unit is OK, the braking system including the hydraulic unit is OK, the electrical system (solenoid, ABS motor) in the ABS hydraulic unit is OK, and the ABS control module and its output system including relay, solenoid, wiring harness are OK. Not checked by the above tests are the ABS input system/harness, intermittent failures, and fluid leakage,

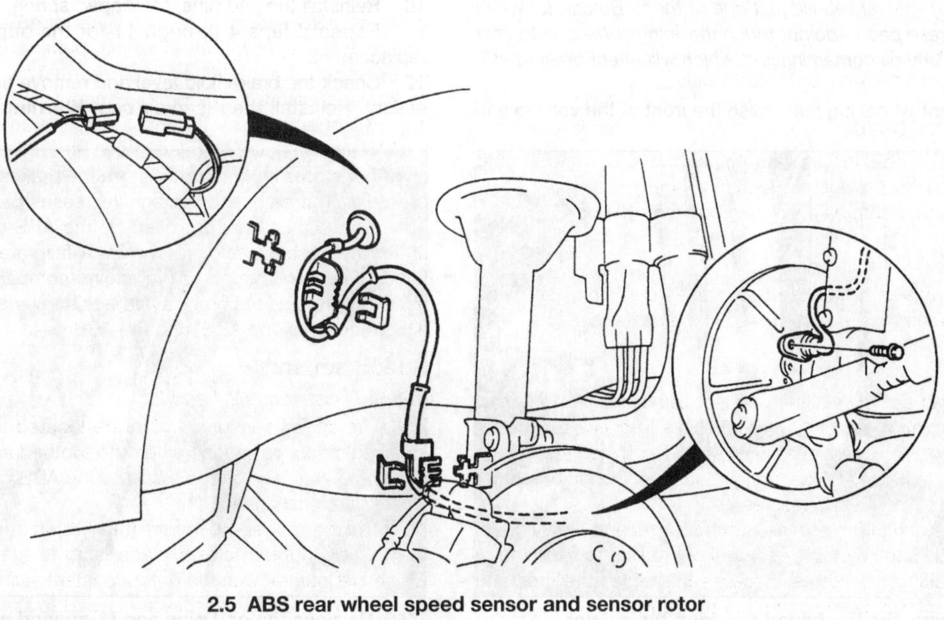

2.5 ABS rear wheel speed sensor and sensor rotor

3.1 Always wash the brakes with brake cleaner before caliper removal

3.4 Depress the piston inward fully to make room for the new pads

and the vehicle should be diagnosed and repaired by a dealer service department or other repair shop. **Caution:** *Do not drive the vehicle until repairs are completed.*

10 The vehicle should be diagnosed and repaired by a dealer service department or other repair shop.

3 Disc brake pads (front) - replacement

Refer to illustrations 3.1, 3.4, 3.5, 3.6, 3.7 and 3.8

Warning: *Dust created by the brake system may contain asbestos, which is harmful to your health. Never blow it out with compressed air and don't inhale any of it. Clean the brake assembly with brake cleaner before any brake work* **(see illustration 3.1)**. *An approved filtering mask should be worn when working on the brakes. Do not, under any circumstances, use petroleum-based solvents to clean brake parts. Use brake system cleaner.*

Note: *If an overhaul is indicated (usually because of fluid leakage), explore all options before beginning the job. New and factory rebuilt calipers are available on an exchange basis, which makes this job quite easy. If you decide to rebuild the calipers, make sure a rebuild kit is available before proceeding. Always rebuild the calipers in pairs (front pair and/or rear pair) - never rebuild just one of them. Be careful when handling the new brake pads - do not touch the lining surface with your fingers to eliminate any oil contamination, which will affect braking efficiency.*

1 Loosen the front wheel lug nuts, raise the front of the vehicle and place it securely on jackstands. Remove the wheel. **Note:** *Work on one brake assembly at a time, using the opposite side brake assembly for reference if necessary.* Wash the brake assembly with brake system cleaner before beginning work **(see illustration)**.

2 If you are checking the brake pads for wear, see Chapter 1. Inspect the brake disc carefully as described in Section 5. If machining is necessary, follow the brake disc removal procedure in Section 5.

3 Open the hood and remove the cap from the brake fluid reservoir.

4 With the old pads in place, press against the pad on the piston side of the caliper, displacing the caliper piston inward fully **(see illustration)**. As the piston is pressed inward, watch the fluid level in the brake fluid reservoir rise, being careful to remove any excess so that fluid will not spill over.

5 Remove the W-shaped clip from the caliper **(see illustration)**.

6 Remove the pad pins and M-shaped spring from the caliper **(see illustration)**.

7 Remove the pads, the anti-squeak shim, the outer shim, and the inner shim **(see illustration)**.

8 Apply a coating of high-temperature brake grease or anti-squeal compound to the brake pad backing plates **(see illustration)**. Be careful to not get any on or near the brake pad friction surfaces.

9 With the caliper piston pushed inward fully, install the new pads with the anti-squeak shim, the outer shim, and the inner shim.

10 Reinstall the pad pins, M-shaped spring, and the W-shaped clip.

11 Repeat Steps 4 through 11 for the opposite wheel brake pad replacement.

12 Check the brake fluid level and remove or add brake fluid as necessary. Reinstall the reservoir cap. **Warning:** *Press the brake pedal*

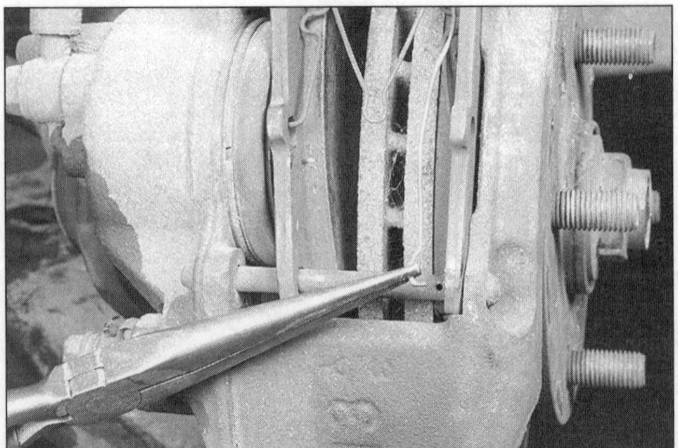

3.5 Remove the W-shaped clip from the caliper

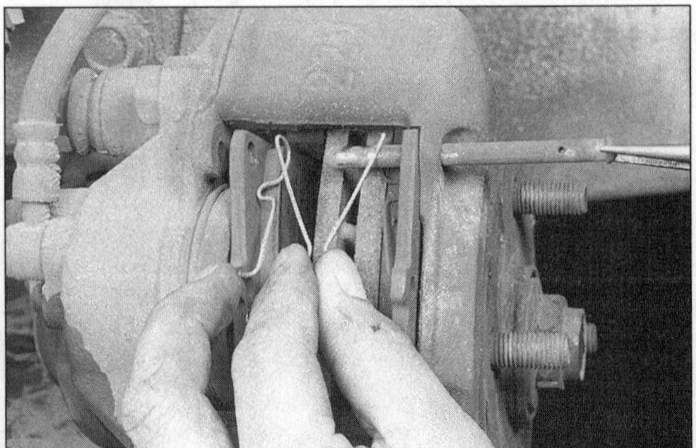

3.6 Remove the pad pins and M-shaped spring from the caliper

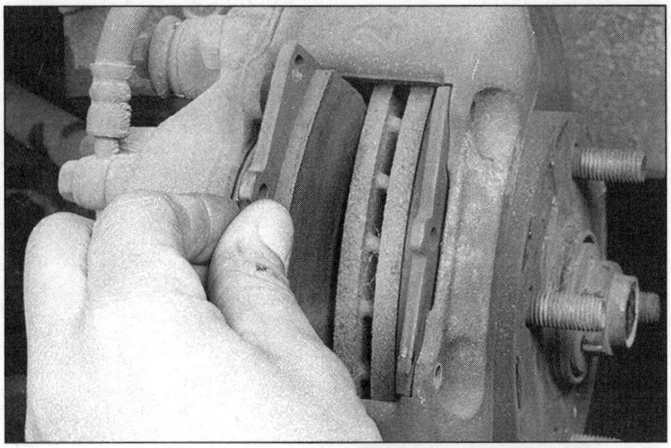

3.7 Remove the pads, the anti-squeak shim, the outer shim, and the inner shim

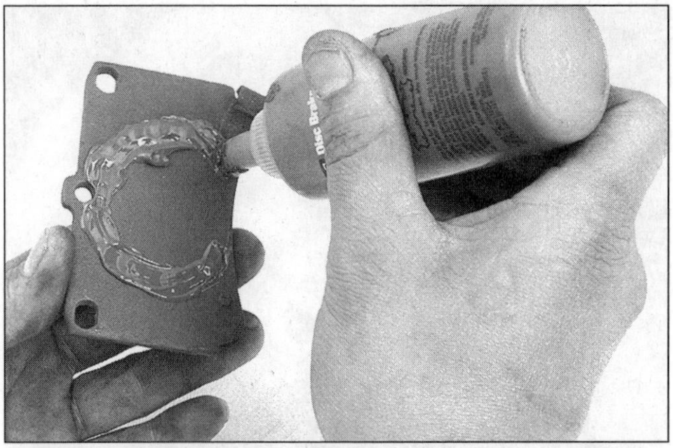

3.8 Apply brake grease or anti-squeal compound to the brake pad backing plates

several times and recheck the brake fluid level in the reservoir before driving the vehicle.

4 Disc brake caliper (front) - removal, overhaul and installation

Warning: *Dust created by the brake system may contain asbestos, which is harmful to your health. Never blow it out with compressed air and don't inhale any of it. An approved filtering mask should be worn when working on the brakes. Do not, under any circumstances, use petroleum-based solvents to clean brake parts. Use brake system cleaner.*

Note: *If an overhaul is indicated (usually because of fluid leakage), explore all options before beginning the job. New and factory rebuilt calipers are available on an exchange basis, which makes this job quite easy. If you decide to rebuild the calipers, make sure a rebuild kit is available before proceeding. Always rebuild the calipers in pairs - never rebuild just one of them.*

Removal

Refer to illustrations 4.2a, 4.2b, 4.7 and 4.8

1 Loosen the front wheel lug nuts, raise the front of the vehicle and place it securely on jackstands. Remove the wheel and prepare for disassembly.

2 Remove the brake hose bolt (banjo bolt) and disconnect the brake hose from the caliper. Plug the brake hose to keep contaminants out of the brake system and to prevent losing any more brake fluid than is necessary **(see illustrations)**. **Note:** *Don't disconnect the hose if you are only removing the caliper for access to other components.*

3 Remove the W-shaped clip from the caliper **(see illustration 3.5)**.

4 Remove the M-shaped spring from the caliper **(see illustration 3.6)**.

5 Remove the pad pins from the caliper **(see illustration 3.6)**.

6 Push the caliper piston inward if necessary **(see illustration 3.4)** to remove the pads, the anti-squeak shim, the outer shim, and the inner shim **(see illustration 3.7)**.

7 Remove the caliper mounting bolts **(see illustration)**.

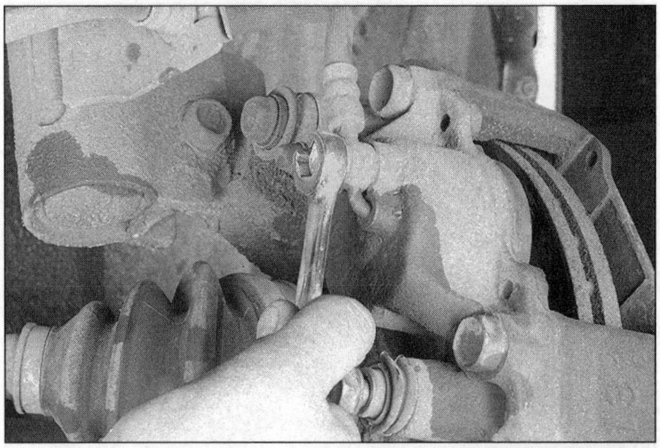

4.2a Remove the brake hose banjo bolt

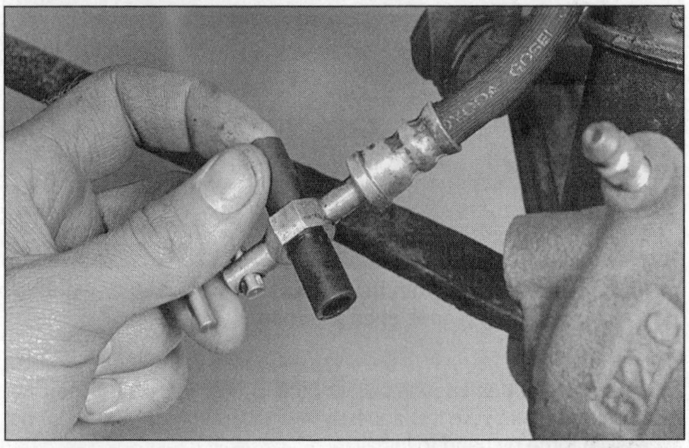

4.2b Using a piece of rubber hose of the appropriate size, plug the brake line; this will prevent brake fluid from leaking out and dirt and moisture from contaminating the fluid in the hose

4.7 Remove the caliper mounting bolts

4.8 Remove the caliper and the two guide plates (not shown)

4.9 Remove the caliper bolt sleeves and boots

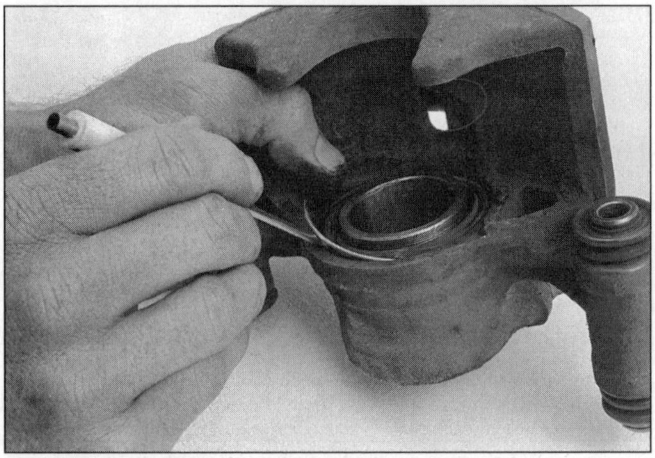

4.11 Using a small screwdriver, remove the cylinder boot set ring

4.13 With the caliper padded to catch the piston, use compressed air to force the piston out of its bore - make sure your hands or fingers are not between the piston and caliper

8 Remove the caliper **(see illustration)** and the two guide plates at the caliper mounting points.

Overhaul

Refer to illustrations 4.9, 4.11, 4.13 and 4.15

9 To overhaul the caliper, remove the bolt sleeves and the boots **(see illustration)**.

10 Remove the rubber cap and bleeder screw.

11 Remove the caliper piston retaining ring and dust boot **(see illustration)**.

12 Before you remove the piston, place a wood block or some rags between the piston and caliper to prevent damage as it is removed.

13 To remove the piston from the caliper, apply compressed air to the brake fluid hose connection on the caliper body **(see illustration)**. Use only enough pressure to ease the piston out of its bore. **Warning:** *Be careful not to place your fingers between the piston and the caliper, as the piston may come out with some force.*

14 Inspect the mating surfaces of the piston and caliper bore wall. If there is any scoring, rust, pitting or bright areas, replace the complete caliper unit with a new one. Crocus cloth can be used to remove light corrosion and stains.

15 If these components are in good condition, remove the piston seal from the caliper bore **(see illustration)**.

16 Wash all the components with brake system cleaner and allow them to dry.

17 To reassemble the caliper, you should already have the correct rebuild kit for your vehicle.

18 Submerge the new piston seal and the piston in brake fluid and install the piston seal in its groove in the caliper bore.

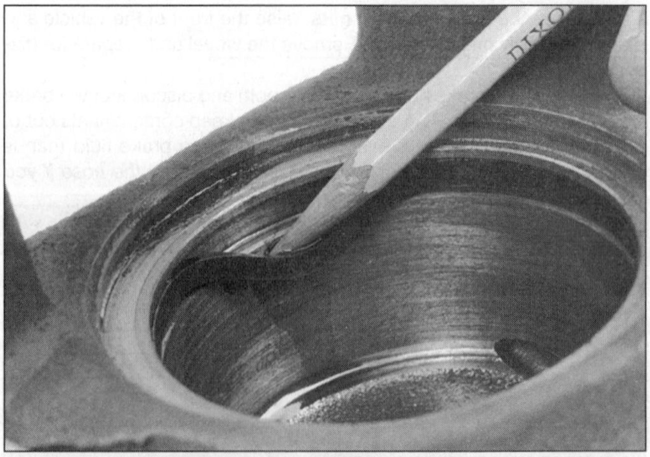

4.15 Remove the seal from the piston using a plastic or wooden tool, such as a pencil

19 Install the piston into the caliper bore. Do not force the piston into the bore, but make sure it is squarely in place, then apply firm (but not excessive) force by hand to install it.

20 Install the new piston dust boot and retaining ring.

21 Reinstall the bleeder screw and rubber cap.

22 Clean the bolt sleeves and lightly coat them with high-tempera-

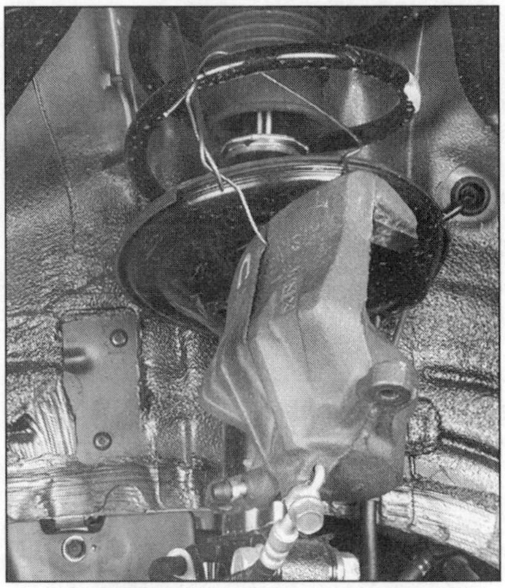

5.2 Hang the caliper with a piece of wire - do not allow the caliper to hang by the brake hose

5.3 The brake pads on this vehicle were obviously neglected, as they wore down to the rivets and cut deep grooves into the disc - wear this severe means the disc must be replaced

5.4a To check disc runout, mount a dial indicator as shown and rotate the disc

ture grease. Reinstall the sleeves and boots.

23 At this time, inspect the brake disc to be sure that it is reusable (see Section 5).

Installation

24 Install the caliper by reversing the removal procedure. Remember to replace the copper sealing washers (gaskets) at the brake hose-to-caliper connection (new washers normally come with the rebuild kit).

25 Bleed the brake circuit according to the procedure in Section 12. Make sure there are no leaks from the hose connections. Test the brakes carefully before returning the vehicle to normal service.

5 Brake disc - inspection, removal and installation

Inspection

Refer to illustrations 5.2, 5.3, 5.4a, 5.4b, 5.5a and 5.5b

1 Loosen the wheel lug nuts, raise the vehicle and support it securely on jackstands. Remove the wheel and install the lug nuts to hold the disc in place. It may be necessary to place washers under the nuts so the disc is held tightly to the hub.

2 Remove the brake caliper as outlined (front brakes see Section 4, rear brakes see Section 9) but it is not necessary to disconnect the brake hose. After removing the caliper bolts, suspend the caliper out of the way with a piece of wire **(see illustration)**.

3 Visually inspect the disc surface for score marks and other damage. Light scratches and shallow grooves are normal after use and may not always be detrimental to brake operation, but deep scoring - over 0.039-inch (1.0 mm) - requires refinishing by an automotive machine shop. Be sure to check both sides of the disc **(see illustration)**. If pulsating has been noticed during application of the brakes, suspect disc runout.

4 To check disc runout, place a dial indicator at a point about 1/2-inch from the outer edge of the disc **(see illustration)**. Set the indicator to zero and rotate the disc slowly by hand. The indicator reading should not exceed the specified allowable runout limit. If it does, the disc must be refinished by an automotive machine shop. **Note:** *The discs should be resurfaced regardless of the dial indicator reading, as this will impart a smooth finish and ensure a perfectly flat surface, eliminating any brake pedal pulsation or other undesirable symptoms related to questionable discs. At the very least, if you elect not to have the discs resurfaced, remove the glaze from the surface with emery cloth or sandpaper, using a swirling motion* **(see illustration)**.

5 It is critical that the disc is not machined to a thickness less than the specified minimum thickness. The minimum wear (or discard)

5.4b Using a swirling motion, remove the glaze from the disc surface with sandpaper or emery cloth

5.5a The minimum wear dimension is cast into the back side of the disc

9

thickness is cast into the inside of the disc **(see illustration)**. The disc thickness can be checked with a micrometer **(see illustration)**.

Removal

6 Remove the lug nuts which were installed to hold the disc in place and remove the disc from the hub. On models equipped with ABS, unplug the electrical connector for the speed sensor, remove the clips fastening the hydraulic brake line to the strut, remove the bolts holding the sensor at the toothed wheel, and remove the sensor.

Installation

7 Place the disc in position over the wheel studs.

8 Install the caliper. Tighten the caliper bolts to the torque listed in this Chapter's Specifications.

5.5b Use a micrometer to measure disc thickness

9 Reinstall the ABS wheel sensor if removed, reinstalling in the reverse order of removal. Make sure the speed sensor-to-toothed rotor clearance is within the range listed in this Chapter's Specifications.

10 Install the wheel, then lower the vehicle to the ground. Tighten the lug nuts to the torque listed in the Chapter 1 Specifications.

11 Check the fluid level in the brake reservoir. Remove or add fluid as needed. Depress the brake pedal a few times to bring the brake pads into contact with the disc. Bleeding won't be necessary unless the brake hose was disconnected from the caliper. Check the operation of the brakes carefully before driving the vehicle.

6 Drum brake shoes - replacement

Refer to illustrations 6.4a through 6.4v

Warning: *Drum brake shoes must be replaced on both wheels (rear) at the same time - never replace the shoes on only one wheel. Also, the dust created by the brake system may contain asbestos, which is harmful to your health. Never blow it out with compressed air and don't*

6.4a Mark the relationship of the drum to the hub, so the drum will retain its dynamic balance after reassembly

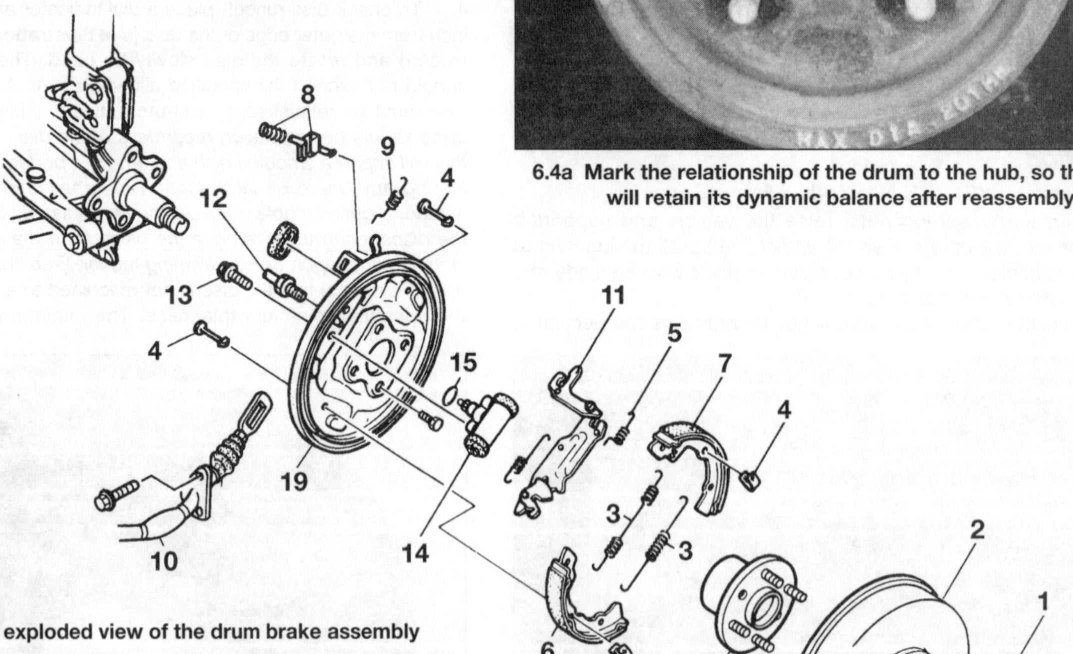

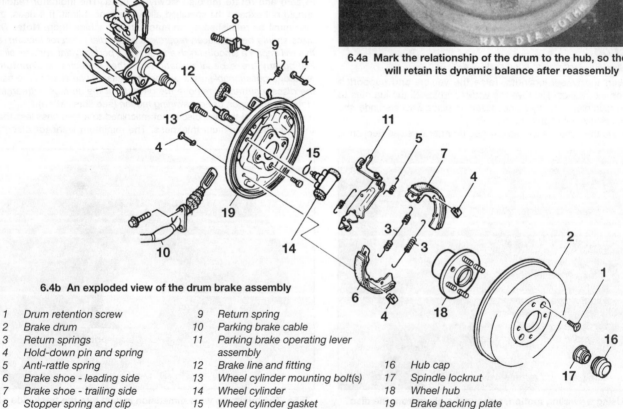

6.4b An exploded view of the drum brake assembly

1 *Drum retention screw*
2 *Brake drum*
3 *Return springs*
4 *Hold-down pin and spring*
5 *Anti-rattle spring*
6 *Brake shoe - leading side*
7 *Brake shoe - trailing side*
8 *Stopper spring and clip*
9 *Return spring*
10 *Parking brake cable*
11 *Parking brake operating lever assembly*
12 *Brake line and fitting*
13 *Wheel cylinder mounting bolt(s)*
14 *Wheel cylinder*
15 *Wheel cylinder gasket*
16 *Hub cap*
17 *Spindle locknut*
18 *Wheel hub*
19 *Brake backing plate*

6.4c Remove the drum retention screws

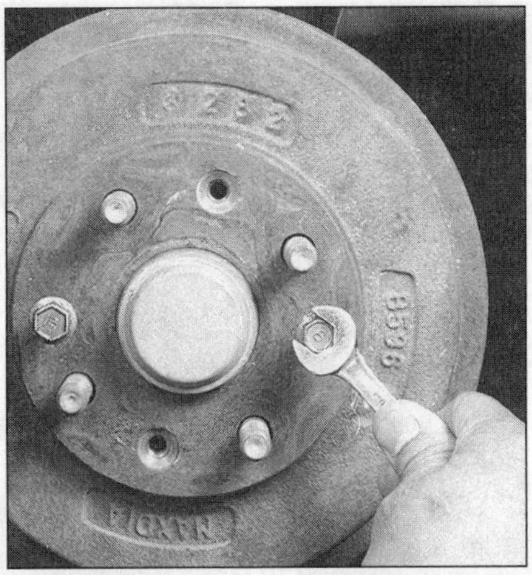

6.4d Thread bolts into the holes provided to unseat the brake drum (if it's stuck) . . .

6.4e . . . and pull the brake drum off

6.4f Before removing anything, place a drain pan under the brake assembly, clean the brake assembly with brake cleaner and allow it to dry; DO NOT USE COMPRESSED AIR TO BLOW OFF BRAKE DUST!

6.4g Unhook the upper return spring from the shoes . . .

6.4h . . . then unhook the lower return spring from the shoes

inhale any of brake dust. An approved filtering mask should be worn when working on the brakes. Do not, under any circumstances, use petroleum-based solvents to clean brake parts. Use brake system cleaner only!

Caution: *Whenever the brake shoes are replaced, the return and hold-down springs should also be replaced. Due to the continuous heating/cooling cycle to which the springs are subjected, spring tension decreases over a period of time and may allow the shoes to drag on the drum and wear at a much faster rate than normal.*

1 Loosen the wheel lug nuts, raise the rear of the vehicle and support it securely on jackstands. Block the front wheels to keep the vehicle from rolling.

2 Release the parking brake.

3 Remove the wheel. If checking brake shoe linings for wear, see Chapter 1. Also, check the brake wheel cylinder for any signs of fluid leakage. If fluid leakage is found, repair the wheel cylinder (see Section 7). **Note:** *All four rear brake shoes at both rear wheels must be replaced at the same time, but to avoid mixing up parts, work on only one brake assembly, and when complete, repair the opposite wheel before driving the vehicle.*

4 Follow the accompanying illustrations for the brake shoe replacement procedure **(see illustrations 6.4a through 6.4v)**. Be sure to stay in order and read the caption under each illustration. **Note:** *If the brake drum cannot be easily pulled off the axle and shoe backing plate assembly, make sure the parking brake is completely released. If the drum still cannot be pulled off, the brake shoes will have to be retracted. This is done by loosening the parking brake cable nut until the parking brake lever at the brake backing plate returns to its stop. The drum should now come off.*

9

6.4i Using a hold-down spring tool or pliers, remove the leading shoe hold-down pin and spring by pushing in and turning the pin 1/4 turn, remove the trailing shoe hold-down pin and spring . . .

6.4j . . . and remove the leading shoe

6.4k Remove the anti-rattle spring from the adjuster and trailing shoe . . .

6.4l . . . and remove the trailing shoe

6.4m Apply high-temperature grease to the shoe contact points on the backing plate

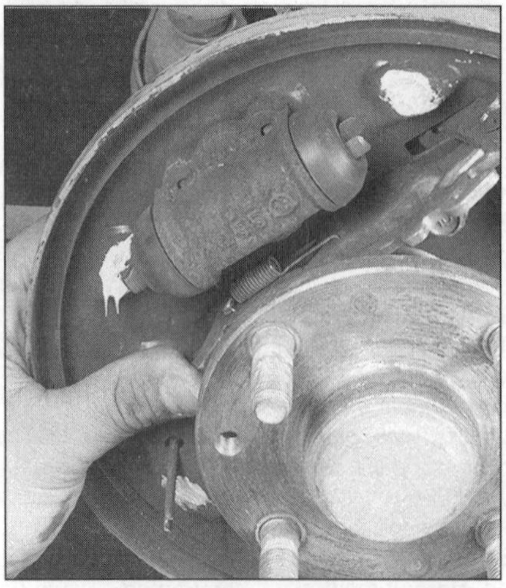

6.4n Push the parking brake operating lever assembly over and hold until . . .

6.4o . . . the trailing brake shoe is installed and then . . .

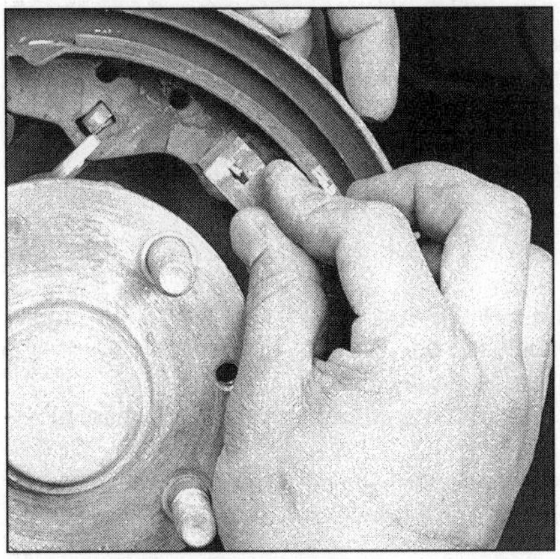

6.4p . . . install the trailing shoe hold-down pin and spring by pushing in and turning the pin 1/4 turn

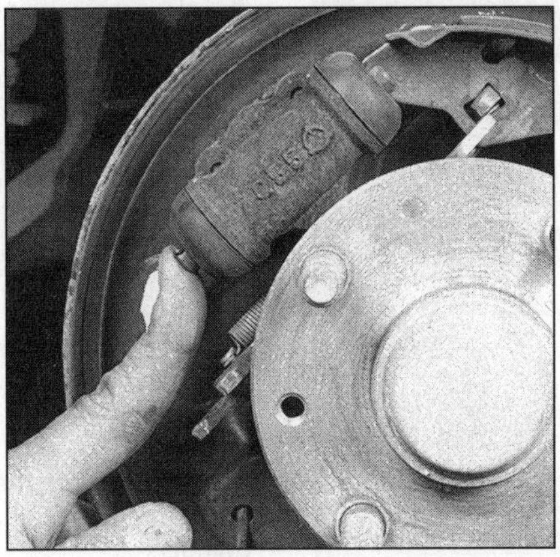

6.4q Depress the wheel cylinder piston on the front side and . . .

6.4r . . . install the leading shoe and its hold-down pin and spring

6.4s Install the lower return spring . . .

6.4t . . . and the upper return spring . . .

6.4u . . . and the anti-rattle spring

6.4v The completed brake assembly looks like this - if you are unsure, remove the wheel and brake drum on the other side of the vehicle and compare

6.5 The maximum drum diameter is cast into the drum

Installation

Refer to illustration 6.5

5 Before reinstalling the brake drum, check it for cracks, score marks, deep scratches and hard spots, which will appear as small discolored areas. If the hard spots cannot be removed with fine emery cloth or if any of the other conditions listed above exist, the drum must be taken to an automotive machine shop to have it resurfaced. **Note:** *Professionals recommend resurfacing the drums each time a brake job is done. Resurfacing will eliminate the possibility of out-of-round drums. If the drums are worn so much that they cannot be resurfaced without exceeding the maximum allowable diameter (stamped into the drum), then new ones will be required* **(see illustration)**. *At the very least, if you elect not to have the drums resurfaced, remove the glaze from the surface with emery cloth or sandpaper, using a swirling motion.*

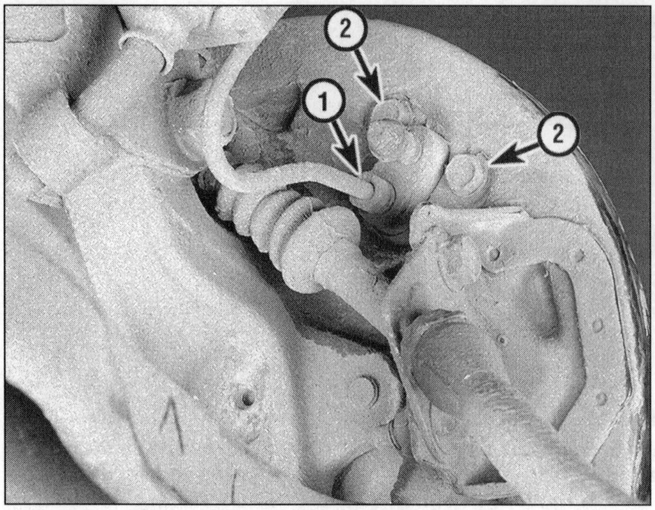

7.4 Disconnect the brake line fitting (1), then remove the two wheel cylinder bolts (2)

6 Before reinstalling the brake drum, have an assistant depress the brake pedal while you check for operation of the automatic adjuster. Install the brake drum on the axle flange.
7 Mount the wheel and install the wheel lug nuts. Make sure the new brake shoes are adjusted so there is no brake drag with the brake pedal released.
8 Lower the vehicle and tighten the lug nuts to the torque listed in the Chapter 1 Specifications.
9 Make a number of forward and reverse stops and operate the parking brake and check for satisfactory pedal action. Check the operation of the brakes carefully before driving the vehicle.

7 Wheel cylinder - removal, overhaul and installation

Note: *If an overhaul is indicated (usually because of fluid leaks or sticky operation), explore all options before beginning the job. New wheel cylinders are available, which makes this job quite easy. If you decide to rebuild the wheel cylinder, make sure a rebuild kit is available before proceeding. Never overhaul only one wheel cylinder - always rebuild both of them. If the wheel cylinder shows evidence of brake fluid leakage, all brake components must be cleaned and the brake shoes must be replaced if contaminated with brake fluid* (see Section 6).

Removal

Refer to illustration 7.4

1 Raise the rear of the vehicle and support it securely on jackstands. Block the front wheels to keep the vehicle from rolling.
2 Remove the brake shoe assembly (see Section 6).
3 Remove all dirt and foreign material from around the wheel cylinder.
4 Disconnect the brake line **(see illustration)** with a flare-nut wrench, if available. Don't pull the brake line away from the wheel cylinder.
5 Remove the wheel cylinder mounting bolts.
6 Detach the wheel cylinder from the brake backing plate and place it on a clean workbench. Immediately plug the brake line to prevent fluid loss and contamination.

Overhaul

Refer to illustration 7.7

7 Remove the bleeder screw, dust boots, piston cups, pistons, spring, and spring caps from the wheel cylinder body **(see illustration)**.
8 Clean the wheel cylinder with brake fluid, denatured alcohol or brake system cleaner. **Warning:** *Do not, under any circumstances, use petroleum-based solvents to clean brake parts!*
9 Use filtered, unlubricated compressed air to dry the wheel cylinder and blow out the passages.
10 Check the bore for corrosion and score marks. Crocus cloth (see your local automotive parts supplier) can be used to remove light corrosion and stains, but the cylinder must be replaced with a new one if the defects cannot be removed easily, or if the bore is scored.
11 Lubricate the wheel cylinder bore, new piston cups and pistons with brake fluid. **Warning:** *Always use fresh brake fluid from a new, previously unopened container.*
12 Assemble the wheel cylinder components. Make sure the piston cup lips face inward.

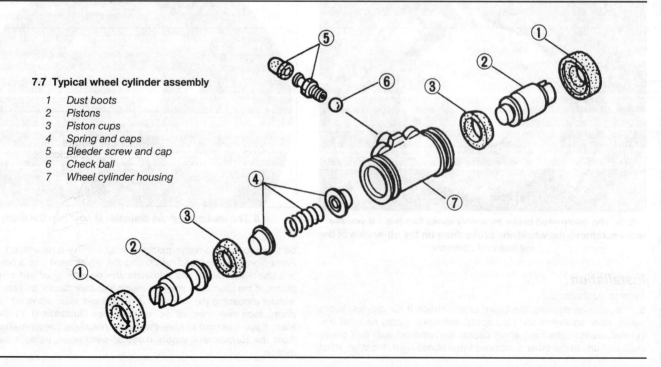

7.7 Typical wheel cylinder assembly

1 *Dust boots*
2 *Pistons*
3 *Piston cups*
4 *Spring and caps*
5 *Bleeder screw and cap*
6 *Check ball*
7 *Wheel cylinder housing*

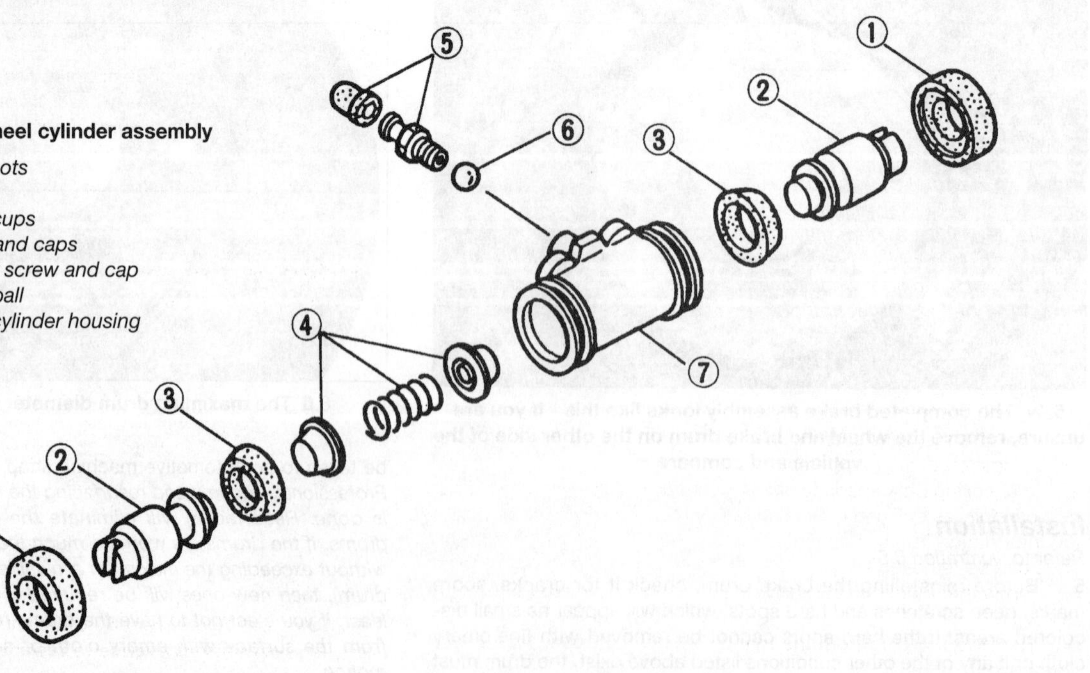

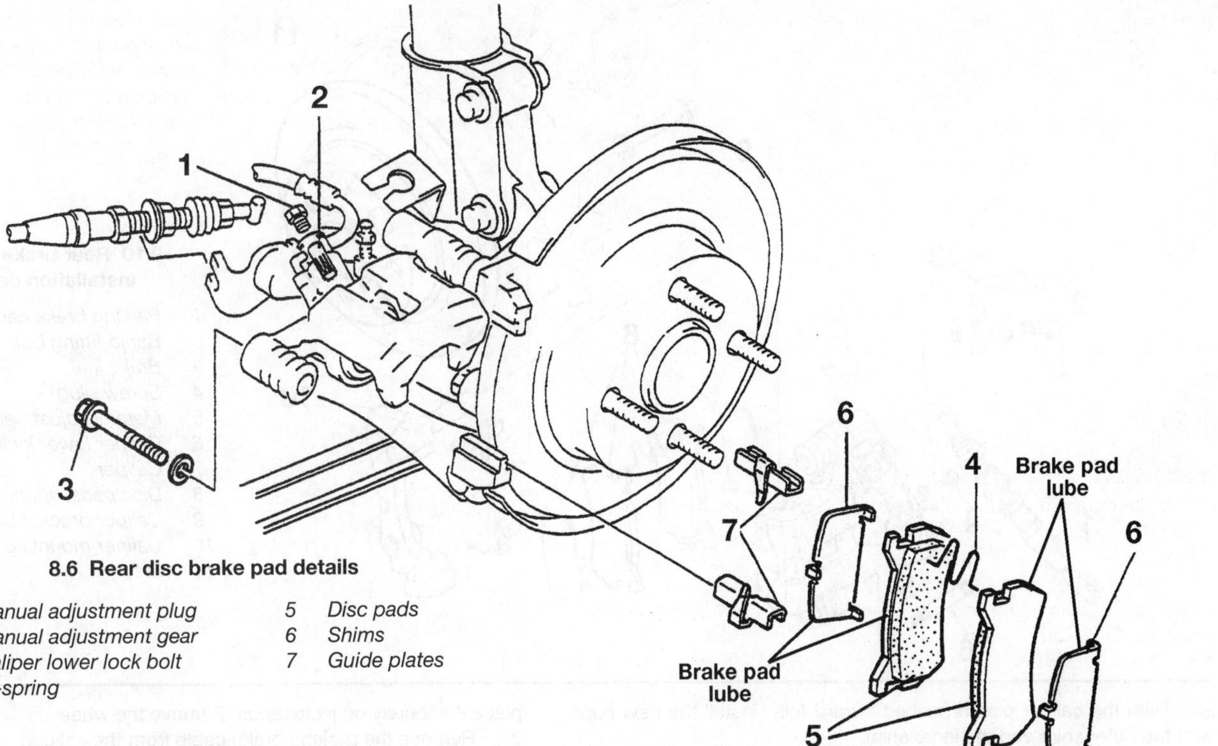

8.6 Rear disc brake pad details

1 *Manual adjustment plug*
2 *Manual adjustment gear*
3 *Caliper lower lock bolt*
4 *M-spring*
5 *Disc pads*
6 *Shims*
7 *Guide plates*

Installation

13 Place the wheel cylinder in position and install the mounting bolts finger tight. Connect the brake line to the cylinder, being careful not to cross-thread the fitting, but do not tighten the brake line at this time.
14 Tighten the wheel cylinder mounting bolts to the torque listed in this Chapter's Specifications.
15 Tighten the brake line securely and install the brake shoe assembly (see Section 6).
16 Bleed the brakes (see Section 10).
17 Check the operation of the brakes carefully before driving the vehicle.

8 Disc brake pads (rear) - replacement

Refer to illustrations 8.6 and 8.7

Warning: *Disc brake pads must be replaced on both rear wheels at the same time - never replace the pads on only one wheel. The dust created by the brake system may contain asbestos, which is harmful to your health. Never blow brake dust out with compressed air and don't inhale any of it. An approved filtering mask should be worn when working on the brakes. Do not, under any circumstances, use petroleum-based solvents to clean brake parts. Use brake system cleaner only!*

1 Remove the cap from the brake fluid reservoir.
2 Loosen the wheel lug nuts, raise the rear of the vehicle and support it securely on jackstands. Block the wheels at the opposite end.
3 Remove the wheels. Work on one brake assembly at a time, using the assembled brake for reference if necessary.
4 If checking brake pads for wear, see Chapter 1. Inspect the brake disc carefully as outlined in Section 5. If machining is necessary, follow the information in that Section to remove the disc, at which time the pads can be removed as well.
5 Open the hood, and carefully remove the cap from the brake fluid reservoir.
6 Remove the plug from the manual adjustment gear screw **(see illustration)**.
7 Pull the brake caliper piston inward by rotating the manual adjustment gear counterclockwise with an Allen wrench **(see illustration)**. As the piston is pulled inward, watch the fluid level in the brake fluid reservoir rise, being careful to remove any excess so the fluid will not spill over.
8 Remove the lower caliper mounting bolt (lock bolt) **(see illustration 8.6)**.
9 Remove the M-shaped spring from the caliper **(see illustration 8.6)**.
10 Slightly loosen the upper caliper mounting bolt, and rotate and swing the caliper up, with the upper mounting bolt remaining in place.
11 Remove the brake pads, shim plates and the caliper guide plates **(see illustration 8.6)**.
12 With the new replacement brake pads ready, apply a light coating of high-temperature brake grease or anti-squeal compound to the brake pad backing plates **(see illustration 3.8)**. Be careful to not get any on or near the brake pad friction surfaces.

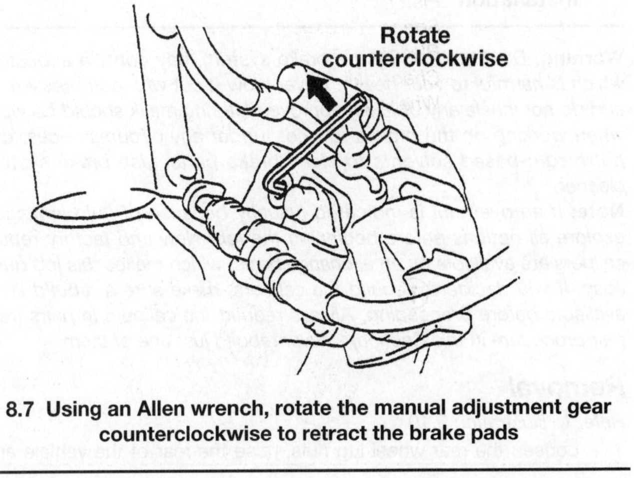

8.7 Using an Allen wrench, rotate the manual adjustment gear counterclockwise to retract the brake pads

9

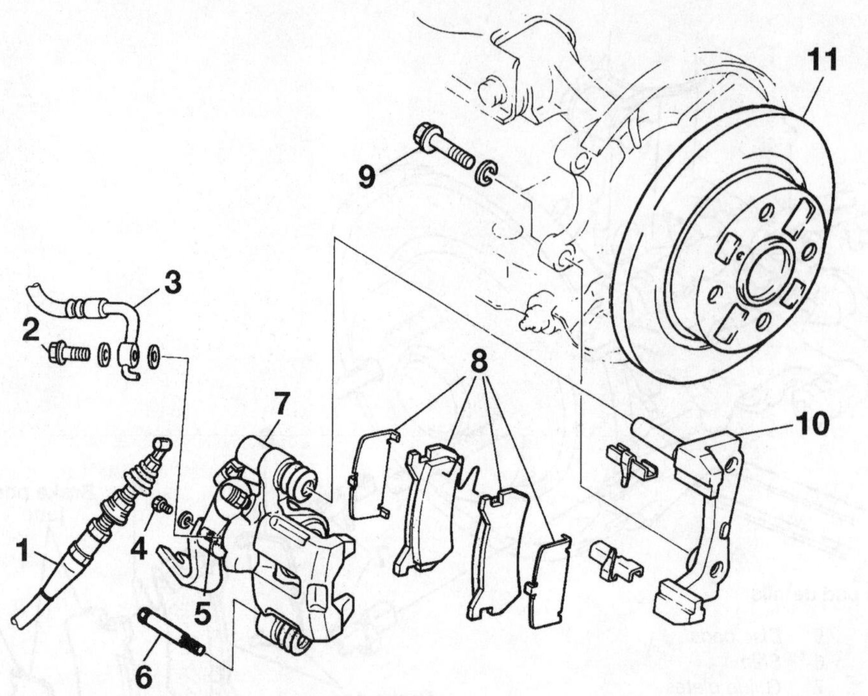

9.10 Rear brake caliper installation details

1. Parking brake cable
2. Banjo fitting bolt
3. Brake line
4. Screw plug
5. Manual adjustment gear
6. Caliper lower lock bolt
7. Caliper
8. Disc pads, springs, shims
9. Caliper bracket bolt
10. Caliper mounting bracket
11. Disc

13 With the caliper piston pushed inward fully, install the new pads with the outer shim and the inner shim.

14 Reinstall the caliper guides and the M-shaped spring **(see illustration 8.6)**.

15 Reinstall the lower caliper mounting bolt (lock bolt) **(see illustration 8.6)**. Tighten the caliper mounting bolts to the torque listed in this Chapter's Specifications.

16 Turn the manual adjustment gear clockwise **(opposite the direction shown in illustration 8.7)** until the caliper piston contacts the brake disc. Then turn the manual adjustment gear 1/3 turn counterclockwise.

17 Reinstall the manual adjustment gear screw plug.

18 Check the brake fluid reservoir level and remove or add brake fluid as necessary. Reinstall the brake fluid reservoir cap.

19 After the job has been completed, firmly depress the brake pedal a few times to bring the pads into contact with the disc. Check the level of the brake fluid, adding some if necessary. Check the operation of the brakes carefully before placing the vehicle into normal service.

20 Repeat Steps 6 through 19 for the opposite wheel brake pad replacement.

9 Disc brake caliper (rear) - removal, overhaul and installation

Warning: *Dust created by the brake system may contain asbestos, which is harmful to your health. Never blow it out with compressed air and do not inhale any of it. An approved filtering mask should be worn when working on the brakes. Do not, under any circumstances, use petroleum-based solvents to clean brake parts. Use brake system cleaner.*

Note: *If an overhaul is indicated (usually because of fluid leakage), explore all options before beginning the job. New and factory rebuilt calipers are available on an exchange basis, which makes this job quite easy. If you decide to rebuild the calipers, make sure a rebuild kit is available before proceeding. Always rebuild the calipers in pairs (rear pair procedure in this Section) - never rebuild just one of them.*

Removal

Refer to illustration 9.10

1 Loosen the rear wheel lug nuts, raise the rear of the vehicle and place it securely on jackstands. Remove the wheel.

2 Remove the parking brake cable from the caliper.

3 Remove the brake hose bolt (banjo bolt) and disconnect the brake hose from the caliper **(see illustration 4.2a)**. Plug the brake hose to keep contaminants out of the brake system and to prevent losing any more brake fluid than is necessary **(see illustration 4.2b)**.

4 Remove the rear disc manual adjustment gear screw plug **(see illustration 8.6)**.

5 Move the brake caliper piston inward by rotating the manual adjustment gear counterclockwise **(see illustration 8.7)**.

6 Remove the lower caliper mounting bolt (lock bolt) **(see illustration 8.6)**.

7 Remove the M-shaped spring from the caliper **(see illustration 8.6)**.

8 Loosen the upper caliper mounting bolt slightly, and rotate the caliper away from the brake disc.

9 Remove the brake pads, shim plates from the side of each pad, and the caliper guide plates **(see illustration 8.6)**.

10 Remove the caliper upper mounting bolt **(see illustration)**, and remove the caliper from the wheel hub.

11 Remove the mounting support from the wheel hub **(see illustration 9.10)**.

12 Remove the brake disc. If the vehicle is equipped with ABS, unplug the speed sensor electrical connector, remove the clips fastening the hydraulic brake line to the strut, remove the bolts holding the sensor at the toothed wheel, and remove the sensor.

Overhaul

13 Due to the complexity of the rear calipers on these models, we do not recommend overhauling them. Replacing them as a pair with rebuilt units will provide better service for less cost.

Installation

14 Install the caliper by reversing the removal procedure. Remember to replace the copper sealing washers (gaskets) at the brake hose-to-caliper connection (new washers normally come with the rebuild kit).

15 If the vehicle is equipped with ABS, reinstall the ABS wheel sensor. Make sure the clearance between the sensor and the toothed rotor is as listed in this Chapter's Specifications.

16 Bleed the brake circuit according to the procedure in Section 12. Make sure there are no leaks from the hose connections. Test the brakes carefully before returning the vehicle to normal service.

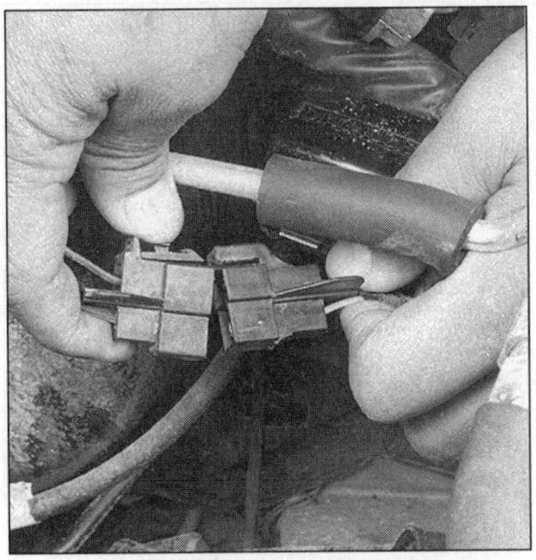

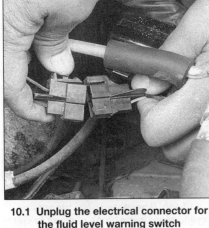

10.1 Unplug the electrical connector for the fluid level warning switch

10.3 Loosen the brake line fittings with a flare-nut wrench

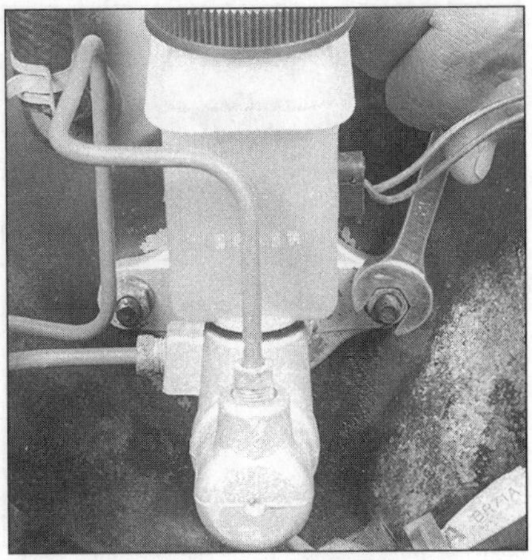

10.5 Remove the master cylinder mounting bolts

10.8a The brake fluid reservoir is retained by a screw

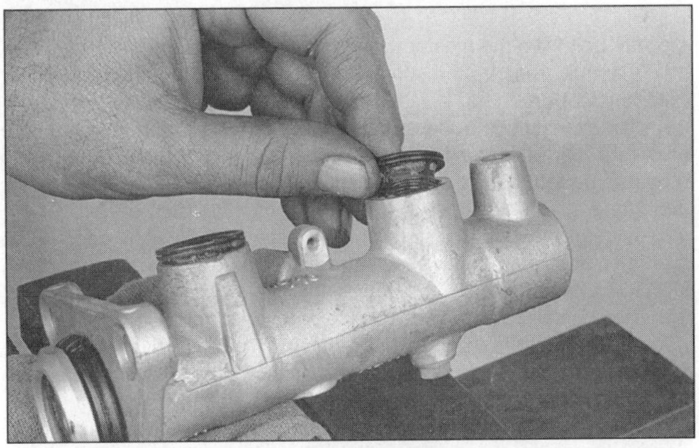

10.8b After the reservoir has been removed, pull the grommets from the master cylinder body; if they're hard, cracked or damaged, or have been leaking, replace them

10 Master cylinder - removal, overhaul and installation

Note: *Before deciding to overhaul the master cylinder, check on the availability and cost of a new or factory rebuilt unit and also the availability of a rebuild kit. If you decide to rebuild the cylinder, inspect the bore as described in Step 12 before purchasing parts.*

Removal

Refer to illustrations 10.1, 10.3 and 10.5

1 Unplug the electrical connector for the fluid level warning switch **(see illustration)**. Check continuity at the level sensor terminals; no continuity should be measured when the fluid level is above MIN.

2 Carefully remove the brake fluid reservoir cap and remove as much fluid as possible from the reservoir with a syringe. Check continuity of the level sensor; continuity should be measured when fluid level is below the MIN level.

3 Place rags under the fittings and prepare caps or plastic bags to cover the ends of the lines once they are disconnected. **Caution:** *Brake fluid will damage paint. Cover all body parts and be careful not to spill fluid during this procedure. Loosen the fittings at the ends of the brake lines where they enter the master cylinder* **(see illustration)**. *To prevent rounding off the flats, use a flare-nut wrench, which wraps around the fitting hex.*

4 Pull the brake lines away from the master cylinder and plug the ends to prevent contamination.

5 Remove the nuts and washers attaching the master cylinder to the power brake booster **(see illustration)**.

6 Pull the master cylinder off the studs to remove it. Again, be careful not to spill the fluid as this is done.

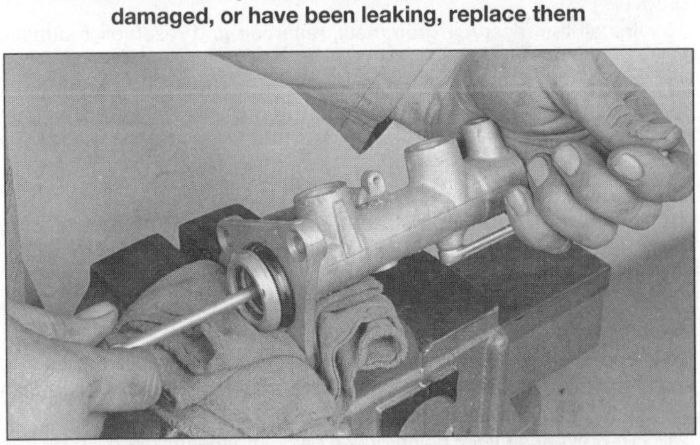

10.9 Using a Phillips screwdriver, depress the pistons, then remove the stopper bolt; be sure to replace the sealing washer for the stopper bolt

Overhaul

Refer to illustrations 10.8a, 10.8b, 10.9, 10.10, 10.11a and 10.11b

7 Before attempting the overhaul of the master cylinder, obtain the proper rebuild kit, which will contain the necessary replacement parts and also any instructions which are specific to your model.

8 Remove the reservoir retaining screw, pull off the reservoir and remove the grommets **(see illustrations)**.

9 Place the cylinder in a vise and use a punch or Phillips screwdriver to depress the pistons until they bottom against the other end of the master cylinder. Hold the pistons in this position and remove the

9

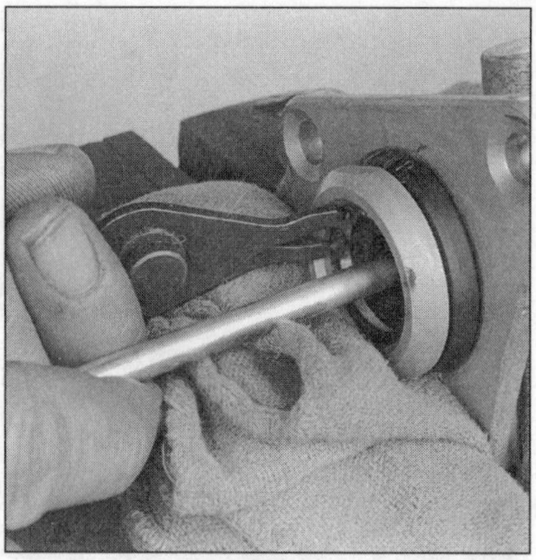

10.10 Depress the pistons again and remove the snap-ring with a pair of snap-ring pliers

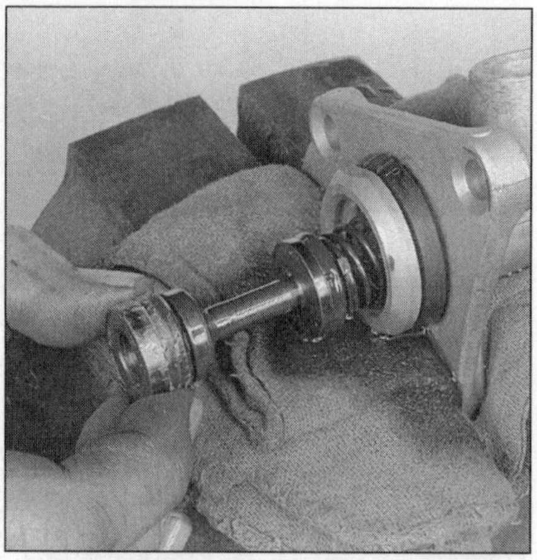

10.11a After the snap-ring has been removed, the primary (No. 1) piston assembly can be removed

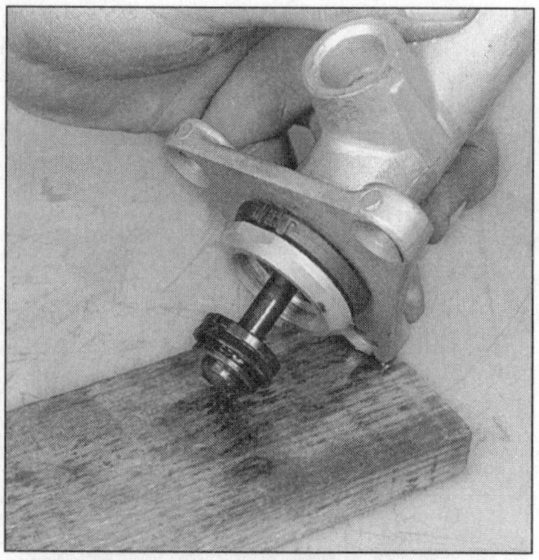

10.11b If necessary, tap the master cylinder against a block of wood to eject the secondary piston

stopper bolt from the master cylinder **(see illustration)**.

10 Carefully remove the snap-ring at the end of the master cylinder **(see illustration)**.

11 The internal components can now be removed from the bore **(see illustrations)**. Make a note of the proper order of the components so they can be returned to their original locations. **Note:** *The two springs are different, so pay particular attention to their installed order.*

12 Carefully inspect the bore of the master cylinder. Any deep score marks or other damage mean that a new master cylinder is required. DO NOT attempt to hone the bore.

13 Replace all parts included in the rebuild kit, following any instructions in the kit. Clean all re-used parts with brake system cleaner. **Warning:** *Do not use any petroleum-based solvents. During reassembly, lubricate all parts liberally with clean, fresh brake fluid.*

14 Push the assembled components into the bore, bottoming them against the end of the master cylinder, then install the stopper bolt.

15 Install the new snap-ring, making sure it's seated properly in the groove.

16 Install the reservoir grommets, reservoir and reservoir mounting screw.

17 Before installing the master cylinder, it should be bench bled. Since you'll have to apply pressure to the master cylinder piston and, at the same time, control flow from the brake line outlets, the master cylinder should be mounted in a vise, with the jaws of the vise clamping on the mounting flange.

18 Insert threaded plugs into the brake line outlet holes and snug them down so no air will leak past them, but not so tight that they cannot be easily loosened.

19 Fill the reservoir with brake fluid of the recommended type (see Chapter 1).

20 Remove one plug and push the piston assembly into the bore to expel the air from the master cylinder. A large Phillips screwdriver can be used to push on the piston assembly.

21 To prevent air from being drawn back into the master cylinder, the plug must be replaced and snugged down before releasing the pressure on the piston.

22 Repeat the procedure until only brake fluid is expelled from the brake line outlet hole. When only brake fluid is expelled, repeat the procedure at the other outlet hole and plug. Be sure to keep the master cylinder reservoir filled with brake fluid to prevent the introduction of any additional air into the master cylinder system while bleeding it.

23 Since high pressure is not involved in the bench bleeding procedure, an alternative to the removal and replacement of the plugs with each stroke of the piston assembly is available. Before pushing in on the piston assembly, remove the plug as described in Step 20. Before releasing the piston, however, instead of replacing the plug, simply put your finger tightly over the hole to keep air from being drawn back into the master cylinder. Wait several seconds for brake fluid to be drawn from the reservoir into the bore, then depress the piston again, removing your finger as brake fluid is expelled. Be sure to put your finger back over the hole each time before releasing the piston, and when the bleeding procedure is complete for that outlet, replace the plug and tighten it before going on to the other port.

Installation

Refer to illustration 10.27

24 Install the master cylinder over the studs on the power brake booster, install the washers, and tighten the nuts only finger-tight at this time. Don't forget to use a new gasket.

25 Thread the brake line fittings into the master cylinder. Since the master cylinder is still loose, it can be moved slightly so the fittings thread in easily by hand. Be careful not to strip the threads as the fittings are tightened.

26 Tighten the master cylinder mounting nuts to the torque listed in this Chapter's Specifications. Tighten the brake line fittings securely using a flare-nut wrench.

27 Fill the master cylinder reservoir with fluid, then bleed the master cylinder and the brake system (see Section 11). To bleed the master cylinder on the vehicle, have an assistant depress the brake pedal and hold it down while you loosen the fitting to allow air and fluid to escape **(see illustration)**. Tighten the fitting, then allow your assistant to return the pedal to its rest position. Repeat this procedure on all fittings until the fluid is free of air bubbles. Check the operation of the brake system carefully before driving the vehicle.

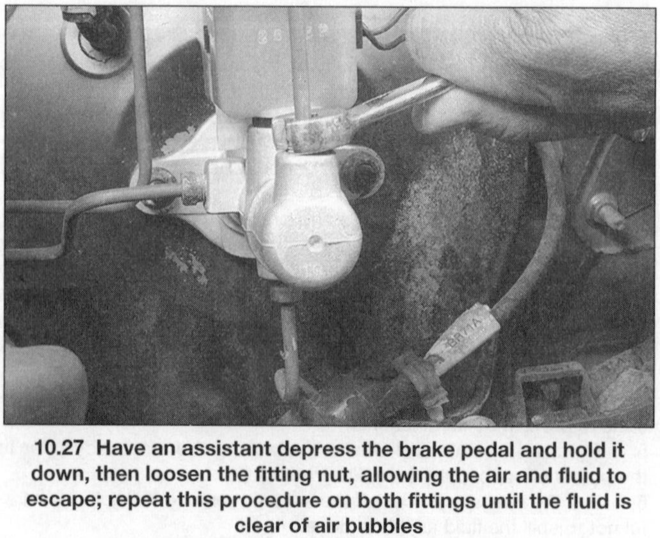

10.27 Have an assistant depress the brake pedal and hold it down, then loosen the fitting nut, allowing the air and fluid to escape; repeat this procedure on both fittings until the fluid is clear of air bubbles

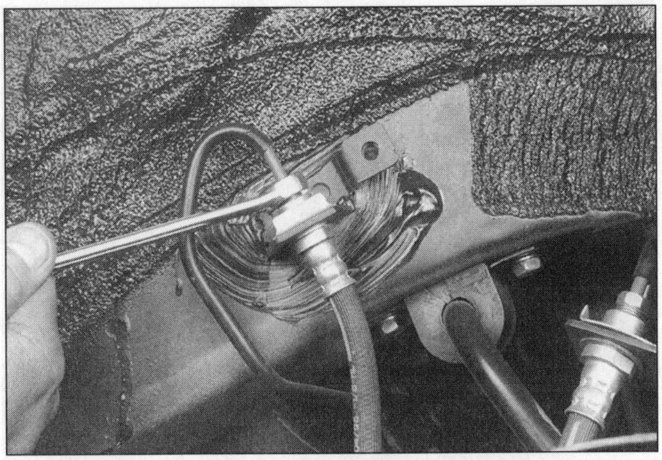

11.3 Unscrew the brake line threaded fitting with a flare-nut wrench to protect the fitting corners from being rounded off

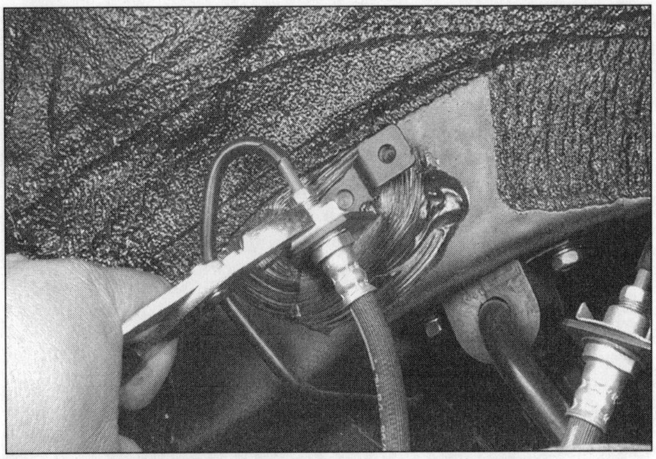

11.4 Pull off the U-clip with a pair of pliers

11 Brake hoses and lines - inspection and replacement

Inspection

1 About every six months, with the vehicle raised and supported securely on jackstands, the rubber hoses which connect the steel brake lines with the front and rear brake assemblies should be inspected for cracks, chafing of the outer cover, leaks, blisters and other damage. These are important and vulnerable parts of the brake system and inspection should be complete. A light and mirror will be helpful for a thorough check. If a hose exhibits any of the above conditions, replace it with a new one.

Replacement

Front brake hose

Refer to illustrations 11.3 and 11.4

2 Loosen the wheel lug nuts, raise the vehicle and support it securely on jackstands. Remove the wheel.

3 At the frame bracket, unscrew the brake line fitting from the hose **(see illustration)**. Use a flare-nut wrench to prevent rounding off the corners and hold the hose fitting with an open-end wrench.

4 Remove the U-clip from the female fitting at the bracket with a pair of pliers **(see illustration)**, then pass the hose through the bracket.

5 At the caliper end of the hose, remove the banjo fitting bolt, then separate the hose from the caliper. Note that there are two copper sealing washers on either side of the fitting - these sealing washers should be replaced with new ones during installation.

6 To install the hose, pass the caliper fitting end through any bracket, as necessary, then connect the fitting to the caliper with the banjo bolt and new copper sealing washers. Make sure the locating lug on the fitting is engaged with the hole in the caliper, then tighten the bolt to the torque listed in this Chapter's Specifications.

7 Push the hose support into the strut bracket and install the U-clip, as necessary. Make sure the hose is not twisted between the caliper and any brackets.

8 Route the hose into the frame bracket, again making sure it is not twisted, then connect the brake line fitting, starting the threads by hand. Install the U-clip, then tighten the fitting securely.

9 Bleed the caliper (see Section 12).

10 Install the wheel and lug nuts, lower the vehicle and tighten the lug nuts to the torque listed in the Chapter 1 Specifications.

Rear brake hose

11 The rear brake hose serves as the flexible connection between two rigid metal lines, one on the body and the other on the suspension. Both ends of the hose are attached to these metal lines with threaded fittings and U-clips. Refer to Steps 2, 3 and 4 above. Be sure to bleed the wheel cylinder when you're done (see Section 12).

Metal brake lines

12 When replacing brake lines, be sure to use the correct parts. Don't use copper tubing for any brake system components. Purchase steel brake lines from a dealer or auto parts store.

13 Prefabricated brake line, with the tube ends already flared and fittings installed, is available at auto parts stores and dealer parts departments. These lines are also bent to the proper shapes.

14 When installing the new line, make sure it is securely supported in the bracket(s) and has plenty of clearance between moving or hot components.

15 After installation, check the master cylinder fluid level and add fluid as necessary. Bleed the brake system (see Section 12) and test the brakes carefully before driving the vehicle in traffic.

12 Brake hydraulic system - bleeding

Refer to illustration 12.8

Warning: *Wear eye protection when bleeding the brake system. If the fluid comes in contact with your eyes, immediately rinse them with water and seek medical attention. Do not get any brake fluid on the brake pads.*

Note: *Bleeding the hydraulic system is necessary to remove any air that manages to find its way into the system when it has been opened during removal and installation of a hose, line, caliper or master cylinder.*

1 If a brake line is disconnected at the brake master cylinder, or if air has entered it due to low fluid level in the brake master cylinder reservoir, start bleeding the brakes at the wheel cylinder or caliper farthest from the brake master cylinder, and move to the next closest wheel cylinder or caliper until all four wheels are bled.

2 If a brake line was disconnected only at a wheel, then only that caliper or wheel cylinder must be bled.

3 If a brake line is disconnected at a fitting located between the master cylinder and any of the brakes, that part of the system served by the disconnected brake line must be bled.

4 Remove any residual vacuum from the brake power booster by applying the brake several times with the engine off.

5 Remove the master cylinder reservoir cover and fill the reservoir with brake fluid. Reinstall the cover. **Note:** *Check the fluid level often during the bleeding operation and add fluid as necessary to prevent the fluid level from falling low enough to allow air bubbles into the master cylinder.*

6 Have an assistant on hand, as well as a supply of new brake fluid, a clear plastic container partially filled with clean brake fluid, a length of plastic, rubber or vinyl tubing to fit over the bleeder valve and a wrench to open and close the bleeder valve.

7 For a brake system bleeding of all four wheels, begin at the right rear wheel; remove the bleeder cap and attach the vinyl hose to the

12.8 When bleeding the brakes, a hose is connected to the bleed screw at the caliper or wheel cylinder and then submerged in brake fluid - air will be seen as bubbles in the tube and container (all air must be expelled before moving to the next wheel)

bleeder valve. Loosen the bleeder valve slightly, then tighten it to a point where it is snug but can still be loosened quickly and easily. If bleeding only specific wheels or portions of the brake system, follow the appropriate Steps below.

8 Place one end of the tubing over the bleeder valve and submerge the other end in brake fluid in the container **(see illustration)**.

9 Have the assistant pump the brakes slowly a few times to get pressure in the system, then hold the pedal down firmly.

10 While the pedal is held down, open the bleeder valve just enough to allow a flow of fluid to leave the valve. Watch for air bubbles to exit the submerged end of the tubing. When the fluid flow slows after a couple of seconds, close the valve and have your assistant release the pedal.

11 Repeat Steps 9 and 10 until no more air is seen leaving the tubing, then tighten the bleeder valve securely and proceed to the left front wheel, the left rear wheel and the right front wheel, in that order, and perform the same procedure. Be sure to check the fluid in the master cylinder reservoir frequently, keeping it about 3/4 full during bleeding. **Note:** *Always use new, fresh brake fluid. Old fluid or fluid from an opened container contains moisture which will deteriorate the brake system components.*

12 At the end of the operation, refill the master cylinder with fluid to the MAX mark on the reservoir.

13 Check the operation of the brakes. The pedal should feel solid when depressed, with no sponginess. If necessary, repeat the entire brake system bleeding. **Warning:** *Do not operate the vehicle if you are in doubt about the effectiveness of the brake system.*

13 Power brake booster - check, removal and installation

Operating check

1 Depress the brake pedal several times with the engine off and make sure there's no change in the pedal reserve distance (distance from the pedal to the floor).

2 Depress the pedal and start the engine. If the pedal goes down slightly, operation is normal.

Airtightness check

3 Start the engine and turn it off after one or two minutes. Depress the brake pedal slowly several times. If the pedal depresses less each time, the booster is airtight.

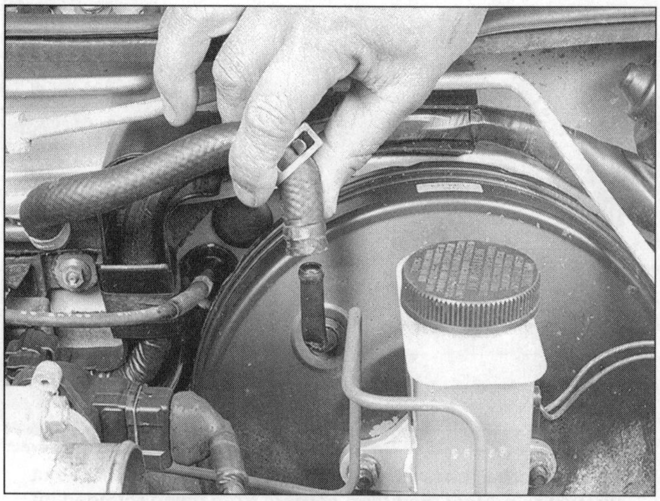

13.6 Detach the hose from the power brake booster; make sure you don't puncture or tear the hose during removal

13.10a To disconnect the power brake booster pushrod from the brake pedal, remove the retaining clip and clevis pin (center arrow); to detach the booster from the firewall, remove the four mounting nuts (arrows, upper right nut not visible in this photo)

4 Depress the brake pedal while the engine is running, then stop the engine with the pedal held depressed. If there is no change in the pedal reserve travel after holding the pedal for 30 seconds, the booster is airtight. **Note:** *If the airtightness check fails in either Step above, first try checking and/or replacing the power brake booster vacuum hose/check valve and repeat the airtightness check.*

Removal

Refer to illustrations 13.6, 13.10a and 13.10b

5 Power brake booster units shouldn't be disassembled. They require special tools not normally found in most automotive repair stations or shops. Because of its critical relationship to brake performance, the booster should be replaced with a new or rebuilt one.

6 Disconnect the vacuum hose/check valve leading from the engine to the booster **(see illustration)**. Be careful not to damage the hose when removing it from the booster fitting.

7 Remove the brake master cylinder (see Section 10).

8 Remove the steering column lower finish panel (see Chapter 11).

9 Remove the pedal return spring.

10 Locate the pushrod clevis connecting the booster to the brake pedal **(see illustrations)**. Remove the cotter pin from the clevis pin with pliers and pull out the clevis pin.

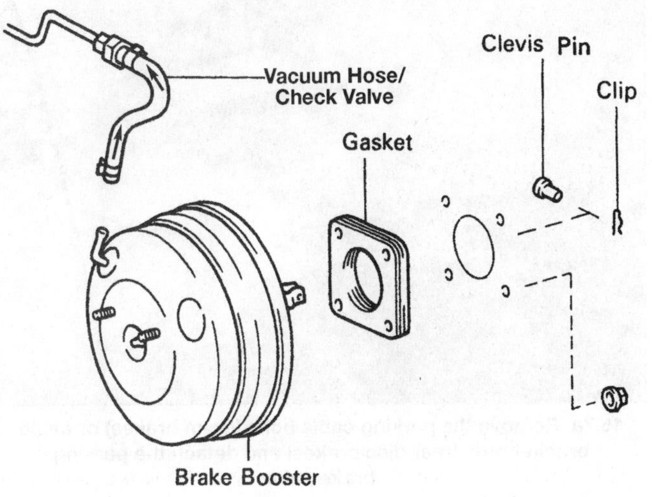

13.10b Power brake booster installation details

11 Remove the four nuts holding the brake booster to the firewall **(see illustration 13.10b)**. You may need a light to see the mounting nuts.

12 Slide the booster straight out from the firewall until the studs clear the holes. Be careful not to tear or damage the brake booster gasket between the firewall and the booster.

Installation

Refer to illustrations 13.15a and 13.15b

13 Installation is basically the reverse of removal. Tighten the booster mounting nuts to the torque listed in this Chapter's Specifications. Be sure to use a new clevis retaining clip if the old clip is loose.

14 When installing the power brake booster vacuum hose/check valve, be sure to install the vacuum hose/check valve with the arrows on the vacuum hose toward the engine.

15 If the power brake booster unit is being replaced, the clearance between the master cylinder piston and the pushrod in the power brake booster must be measured and, if necessary, adjusted. Using a depth micrometer or vernier caliper, measure the distance from the pocket of the primary piston to the master cylinder mounting flange. Next, with the engine running for vacuum applied to the power brake booster (or vacuum applied by a vacuum pump, if desired), measure the distance from the end of the vacuum booster pushrod to the mounting face of the booster where the master cylinder mounting flange seats **(see illustration)**. Subtract the depth of the piston pocket from the protrusion of the pushrod to calculate the clearance and compare your findings with the values listed in this Chapter's Specifications. If not, turn the adjusting screw on the end of the power booster pushrod until the clearance is within the specified limit **(see illustration)**.

16 After the final installation of the master cylinder and brake hoses and lines, the brake pedal height and freeplay must be adjusted and the brake system must be bled. See the appropriate Sections of this Chapter for the procedures.

14 Parking brake - adjustment

Refer to illustration 14.3

1 The parking brake lever, when properly adjusted, should travel five to seven clicks, when a moderate pulling force is applied. If it travels less than the specified minimum number of clicks, the parking brake may not be releasing completely and could cause the rear brakes to drag. If the lever can be pulled up more than the specified maximum number of clicks, the parking brake may not hold adequately on an incline, allowing the car to roll.

2 To gain access to the parking brake cable adjuster, remove the rear console (see Chapter 11).

3 Remove the adjusting nut clip and adjust nut **(see illustration)**. Turn the adjusting nut until the desired travel is attained. Tighten the locknut.

4 Install the rear console.

15 Parking brake cables - replacement

Equalizer-to-brake lever cable

Refer to illustration 15.4

1 Loosen the rear wheel lug nuts, raise the rear of the vehicle and support it securely on jackstands. Block the front wheels. Remove the wheel.

2 Make sure the parking brake is completely released. Remove the console at the parking brake lever (see Chapter 11).

3 Remove the parking brake lever adjusting nut.

4 Under the vehicle, it is best to remove the exhaust and heat shield components in the area of the parking brake cable connection to the

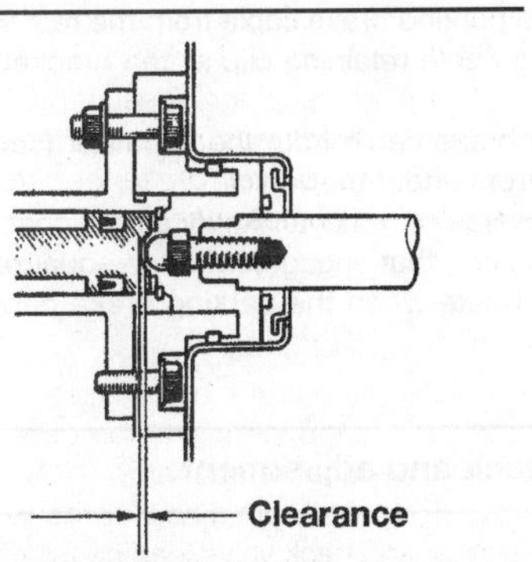

13.15a There should be a slight amount of clearance between the booster pushrod and the master cylinder pushrod; if there is interference between the two, the brakes may drag; if there is too much clearance, there will be excessive brake pedal travel

13.15b To adjust the length of the booster pushrod, hold the serrated portion of the rod with a pair of pliers and turn the adjusting screw in or out, as necessary, to achieve the desired setting

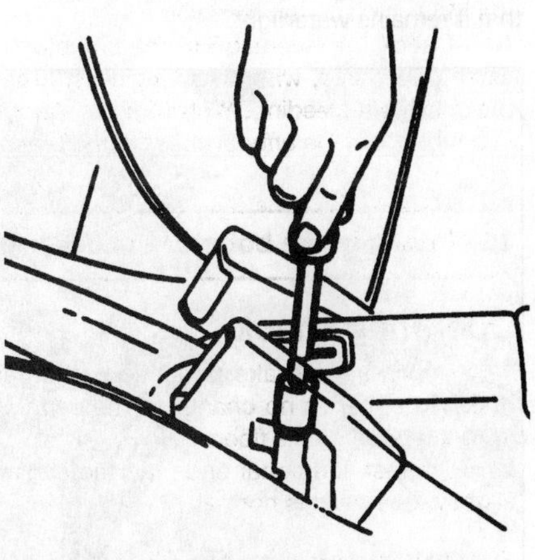

14.3 Remove the cover and turn the adjusting nut until the desired lever travel is obtained

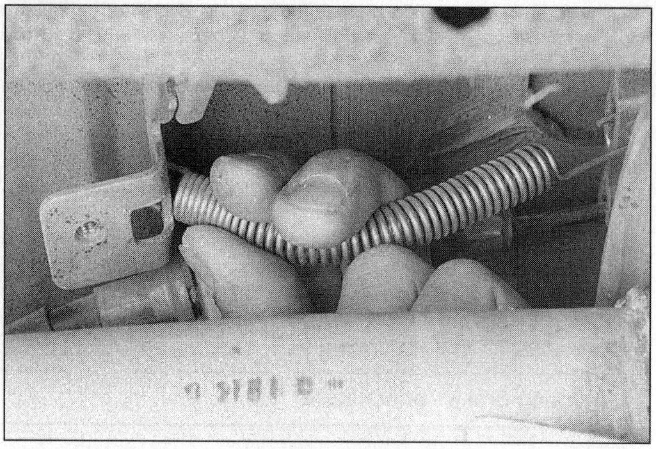

15.4 Under the vehicle, remove the return spring and front parking cable

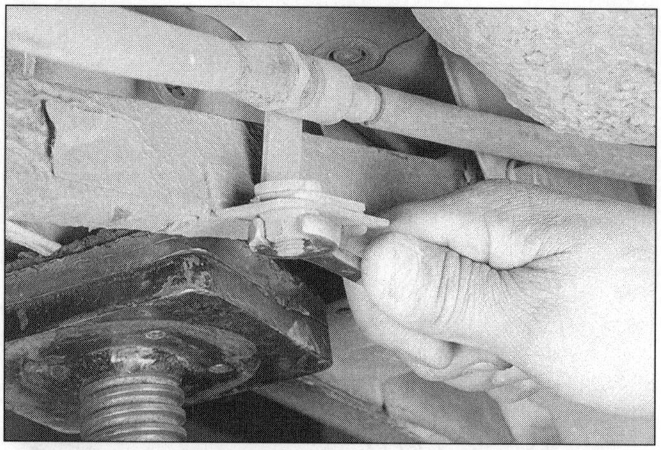

15.7a Remove the parking cable bolts (drum brakes) or cable bracket nuts (rear disc brakes) and detach the parking brake cable

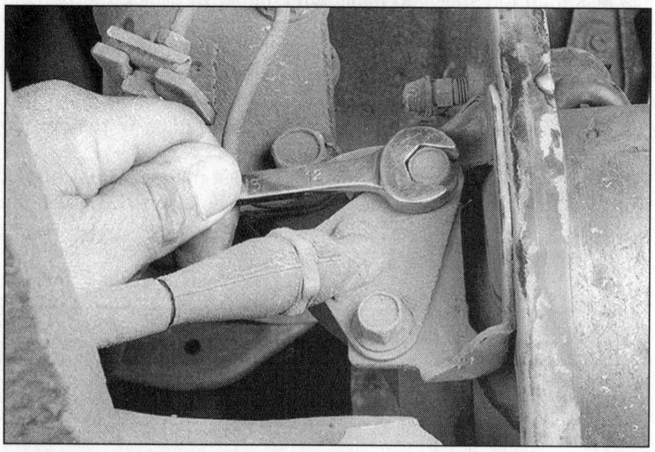

15.7b Remove the cable bolts or nuts at the rear brake assembly

15.8 Remove the retaining clip at the equalizer and detach the forward end of the parking brake cable

parking brake lever. Remove the return spring and front parking cable **(see illustration)**.

5 Pry out the rubber grommet from the floorpan and pull the front parking cable out.

6 Installation is the reverse of removal. Apply a light coat of grease to the portion of the cable end that engages with the equalizer. And coat the sealing edge of the rubber grommet with silicone to ensure that it remains watertight.

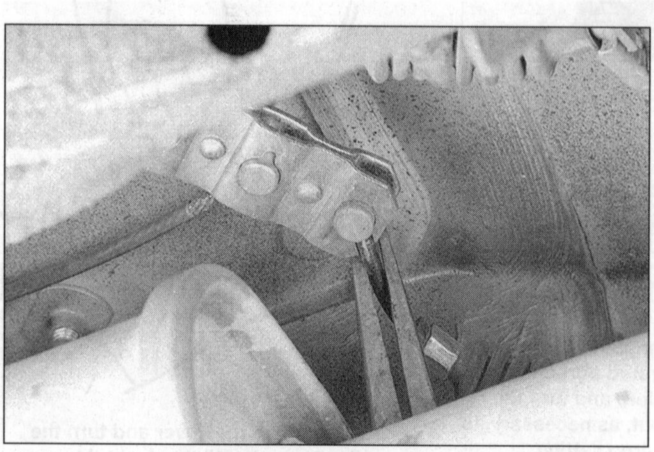

15.9 Twist the cable end until it can be removed from the equalizer

Equalizer-to-parking brake cable

Refer to illustrations 15.7a, 15.7b, 15.8 and 15.9

7 Remove the parking cable mounting bolts (on vehicles with drum brakes) located along the vehicle chassis, or the nuts (on vehicles with rear disc brakes) from the parking brake cable floorpan mounts **(see illustrations)**. Detach the parking brake cable from the rear wheel.

8 Remove the parking cable retaining clip at the bracket end **(see illustration)**.

9 Detach the parking brake cable from the equalizer **(see illustration)**. Pull the cable out from under the vehicle.

10 Installation is the reverse of removal. Apply a light coat of grease to the portion of the cable end that engages with the equalizer.

11 Adjust the parking brake when the parking brake cable is reinstalled (see Section 14).

16 Brake pedal - check and adjustment

Pedal height

Refer to illustration 16.1

1 Measure the pedal height **(see illustration)** and compare your measurement to the pedal height listed in this Chapter's Specifications.

2 If the pedal height is incorrect, adjust it as follows:

3 Unplug the electrical connector from the brake light switch.

4 Loosen the brake light switch locknut and turn the brake switch

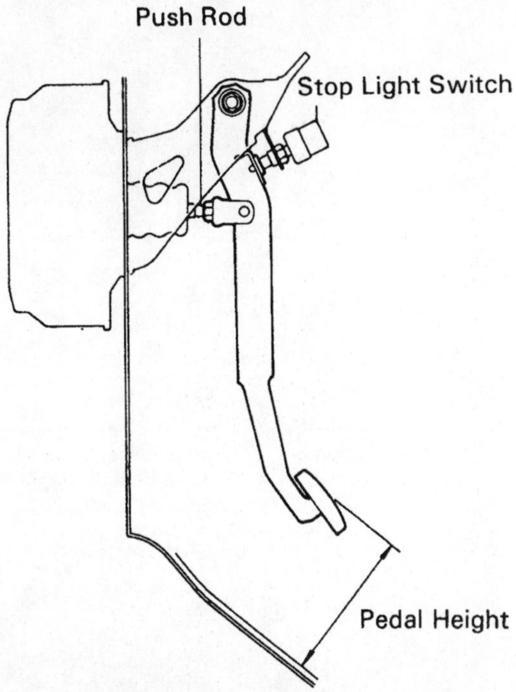

16.1 **Brake pedal height is the distance between the pedal and the firewall when the pedal is released**

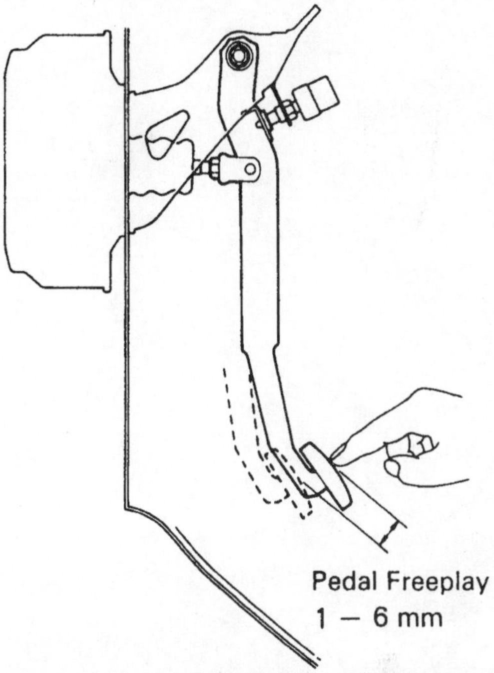

16.15 **Brake pedal freeplay is the distance between the pedal when released and the point at which some resistance is first felt when the pedal is depressed**

until it does not contact the pedal.
5 Loosen the pushrod locknut.
6 Adjust the pedal height by turning the pedal pushrod.
7 Tighten the pushrod locknut.
8 On 1990 to 1994 models, turn the brake light switch until it lightly contacts the pedal stopper. On 1995 and later models, allow a clearance between the adjusting screw and the pedal of 0.004 to 0.039 inches. **Note:** *On 1995 and later, use a new brake light switch assembly each time the brake pedal adjustment is made.*
9 On 1990 through 1994 models, turn the brake light switch an additional 1/2 turn.
10 Tighten the brake light switch locknut.
11 Plug in the brake light switch electrical connector.
12 Check that brake lights come on when the brake pedal is depressed, and go off when the brake pedal is released.
13 Check the pedal freeplay (see below).

Pedal freeplay

Refer to illustration 16.15

14 Stop the engine if it's running, and depress the brake pedal several times until there's no more vacuum left in the booster.
15 Gently press the pedal by hand until you feel some resistance, then measure the distance between the fully released pedal and the point at which you feel resistance **(see illustration)**. Compare your measurement with the pedal freeplay listed in this Chapter's Specifications. If the pedal freeplay is incorrect, adjust it as follows:
16 Adjust the brake pedal pushrod to obtain the specified pedal freeplay, then adjust the brake light switch as described. If the pedal freeplay cannot be adjusted properly, troubleshoot the brake system.

Pedal reserve

17 Start the engine, depress the brake pedal a few times, then press down hard and hold it.
18 Pedal reserve travel is measured from the floor to the top of the pedal while it is held depressed. Compare your measurement to the pedal reserve listed in this Chapter's Specifications.
19 If the pedal reserve is less than specified, check the adjustment of the rear brake shoes, malfunction of the automatic adjuster in rear drum brakes, and/or the power brake booster pushrod-to-master cylinder piston clearance. If the brake pedal feels spongy, bleed the brake system (see Section 12).

17 Brake light switch - check and replacement

Check

1 The brake light switch is located on a bracket at the top of the brake pedal **(see illustration 16.15)**. The switch activates the brake lights at the rear of the vehicle when the pedal is depressed.
2 To check the brake light switch, simply note whether the brake lights come on when the pedal is depressed and go off when the pedal is released. If they do not function correctly, adjust the switch as described in Section 16 (adjusting the switch is part of brake pedal adjustment).
3 If the lights still do not come on, either the switch is not getting voltage, the switch itself is defective, or the circuit between the switch and the lights is defective. There is always the remote possibility that all of the brake light bulbs are burned out, but this is not very likely.
4 Use a voltmeter or test light to verify that there's voltage present at one side of the switch connector. If no voltage is present, troubleshoot the circuit from the switch to the fuse box. If there is voltage present, check for voltage on the other terminal when the brake pedal is depressed. If no voltage is present, replace the switch. If there is voltage present, troubleshoot the circuit from the switch to the brake lights (see the *wiring diagrams* at the end of Chapter 12).

Replacement

5 Disconnect the negative battery cable from the battery.
6 Unplug the electrical connector for the brake light switch.
7 Loosen the brake switch locknut and unscrew the switch from the pedal bracket.
8 Installation is the reverse of removal.
9 Adjust the brake pedal and brake light switch (see Section 16).

Notes

Chapter 10
Suspension and steering systems

Contents

Specifications

Torque specifications

	Ft-lbs (unless otherwise indicated)
Wheel lug nuts	See Chapter 1
Front suspension	
Balljoints	
Balljoint-to-control arm bolt/nuts	69 to 86
Balljoint-to-steering knuckle nut	32 to 41
Control arm	
Front pivot bolt	69 to 93
Rear pivot bolt	69 to 93
Rear pivot nut - 1990 through 1994	69 to 86
Front stabilizer bar	
Bracket bolts	
1990 through 1994	32 to 43
1995 and later	50 to 65
Link nuts	
1990 through 1994	Tighten to 3/4-inch of exposed thread
1995 and later	32 to 44
Front struts	
Strut-to-steering knuckle bolts/nuts	
1990 through 1994	69 to 93
1995 and later	76 to 93
Strut upper mounting nuts	
1990 through 1992	22 to 30
1993 through 1994, 1995 and later	34 to 46
Suspension support-to-piston rod nut	58 to 81
Rear suspension	
Trailing link strut rod **front** nuts/bolts	
1990 through 1994	47 to 68
1995 and later (bolt)	55 to 73
1995 and later - brake cable bracket nut on strut rod	14 to 18
Trailing link strut rod **rear** nuts/bolts	
1990 through 1994	69 to 93
1995 and later (bolt)	69 to 93
Lateral link suspension arm No. 1 & No. 2 **outboard** nut/bolt	
1990 through 1994	63 to 86
1995 and later	64 to 86

Torque specifications (continued)

	Ft-lbs (unless otherwise indicated)
Rear suspension (continued)	
Lateral link suspension arm No. 1 & No. 2 **inboard** nut/bolt	
1990 through 1994	50 to 70
1995 and later - front arm bolt/nut	64 to 86
1995 and later - rear arm cam plate bolt/nut	26 to 39
Rear hub and bearing assembly to rear spindle locknut	130 to 173
Rear drum brake backing plate-to-rear spindle bolts	
1990 through 1994	33 to 43
1995 and later	34 to 49
Rear stabilizer bar	
Link nuts - 1990 through 1994	Tighten to 11/16 inch of exposed thread
Link nuts - 1995 and later	32 to 44
Bushing retainer bolts/nuts	32 to 43
Rear struts	
Strut-to-spindle nuts/bolts	69 to 93
Strut upper mounting nuts	34 to 46
Suspension support-to-piston rod nut	41 to 49
Steering	
Airbag module-to-steering wheel screws (1995 and later only)	70 to 104 in-lbs
Steering gear bracket nuts	28 to 38
Note: *See procedure for torque sequence.*	
Power steering pressure hose banjo nut	
1990 through 1994	12 to 17
1995 and later	18 to 26
Steering wheel nut	29 to 36
Tie-rod ends	
Tie-rod end-to-steering knuckle nut	32 to 41
Tie-rod end locknut	26 to 36
U-joint-to-pinion shaft pinch bolt	14 to 19

1 General information

Refer to illustrations 1.1 and 1.2

The front suspension **(see illustration)** is a MacPherson strut design. The upper end of each strut/coil spring assembly is attached to the vehicle's body strut support. The lower end of the strut assembly is connected to the upper end of the steering knuckle. The steering knuckle is attached to a balljoint mounted on the outer end of the suspension control arm. A stabilizer bar reduces body roll.

The rear suspension **(see illustration)** also utilizes strut/coil spring assemblies. The upper end of each strut is attached to the vehicle body. The lower end of each strut is attached to an axle carrier (spindle). The carrier is located by a pair of suspension arms on each side, and a longitudinally mounted strut rod between the body and each carrier.

The rack-and-pinion steering gear is located behind the engine/transaxle assembly and actuates the tie-rods, which are attached to the steering knuckles. The inner ends of the tie-rods are protected by rubber boots which should be inspected periodically for secure attachment, tears and leaking lubricant.

The manual steering system consists of the steering wheel column, connected by universal joints to the rack and pinion steering gear. The power steering system consists of a belt-driven pump and associated lines and hoses which assists in actuating the rack and pinion steering gear. The power steering pump reservoir should be checked periodically (see Chapter 1). Looseness in the steering can be caused by wear in the steering shaft universal joints, the steering gear, the tie-rod ends, and loose retaining bolts.

Precautions

Frequently, when working on the suspension or steering system components, you may come across fasteners which seem impossible to loosen. These fasteners on the underside of the vehicle are continually subjected to water, road grime, mud, etc., and can become rusted or "frozen," making them extremely difficult to remove. In order to unscrew these stubborn fasteners without damaging them (or other components), be sure to use a generous amount of penetrating oil and allow it to soak in for a while. Using a wire brush to clean exposed threads will also ease removal of the nut or bolt and prevent damage to the threads. Sometimes a sharp blow with a hammer and flat-faced punch (do not use a sharp-pointed or sharp-edged punch) will break the bond between nut and bolt threads, but care must be taken to prevent the punch from slipping off the fastener and ruining the threads. Heating the stuck fastener and surrounding area with a torch sometimes helps too, but this is not recommended because of the obvious dangers associated with heat and flame sources. Long breaker bars and extension, or "cheater," pipes will increase leverage, but never use an extension pipe on a ratchet - the ratcheting mechanism could be damaged. Sometimes tightening the nut or bolt first will help to break it loose. Fasteners that require drastic measures to remove should always be replaced with new ones.

Since most of the procedures dealt with in this Chapter involve jacking up the vehicle and working underneath it, a good pair of jackstands will be needed. A hydraulic floor jack is the preferred type of jack to lift the vehicle, and it can also be used to support certain components during various operations. **Warning:** *Never, under any circumstances, rely on a jack to support the vehicle while working on it. Whenever any of the suspension or steering fasteners are loosened or removed they must be inspected and, if necessary, replaced with new ones of the same part number or of original equipment grade, material strength, size, quality and design. Torque specifications must be followed for proper reassembly and component retention. Never attempt to heat or straighten any suspension or steering components. Instead, replace any bent or otherwise damaged part with a new one.*

1.1 Front suspension and related components

1 Front stabilizer bar link bolt
Note: Stabilizer bar and clamps not shown
2 Support crossmember
3 Control arm
4 Balljoint
5 Strut/coil spring assembly
6 Right driveaxle assembly
7 Left driveaxle assembly
8 Rack-and-pinion steering gear

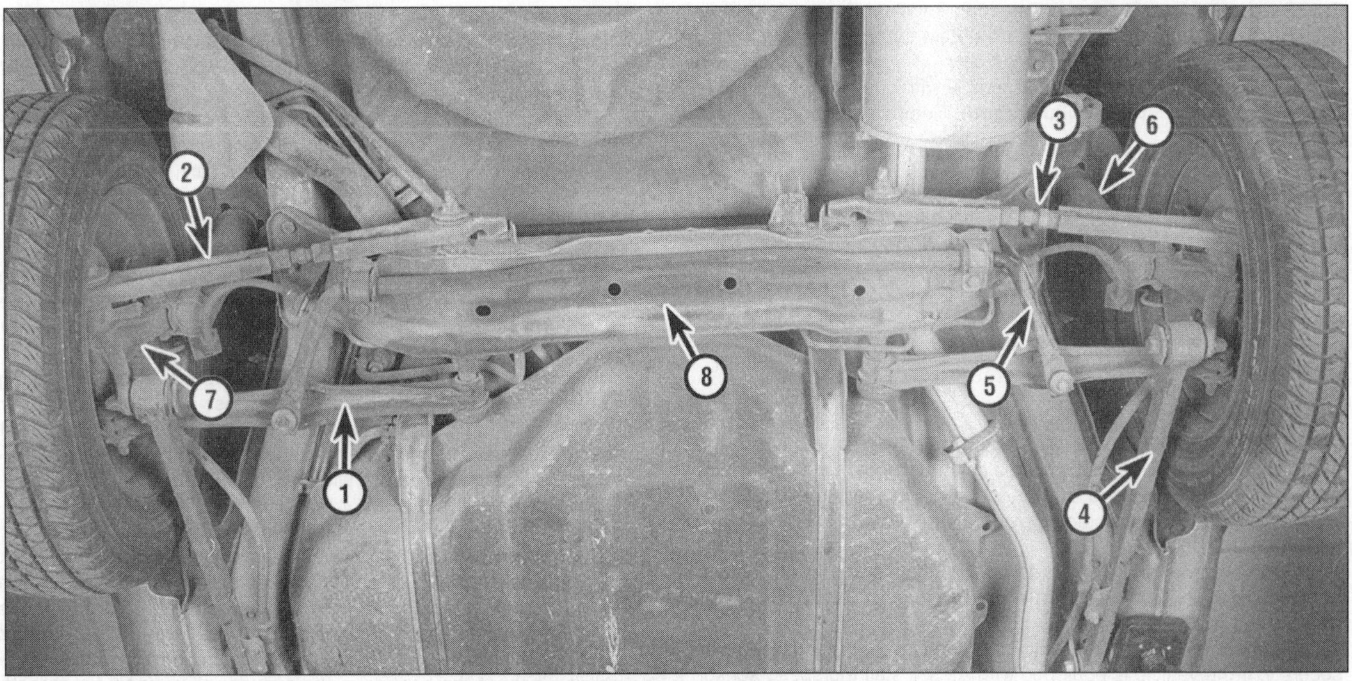

1.2 Rear suspension components

1 Rear lateral suspension arm - No. 1
2 Rear lateral suspension arm - No. 2
3 Rear arm toe adjuster (1990 through 1994; 1995 and later use cam plate adjusters)
4 Strut rod (trailing link)
5 Rear stabilizer bar
6 Strut/coil spring assembly
7 Rear spindle
8 Rear suspension crossmember

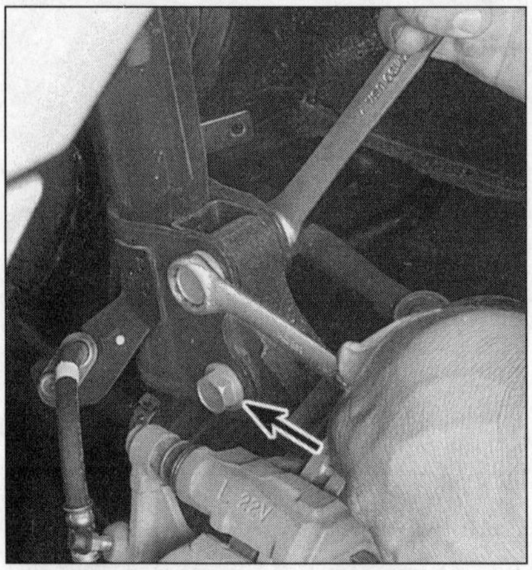

2.3 To detach the strut assembly from the steering knuckle, remove the two nuts, then knock out the bolts with a hammer and flat-nosed punch

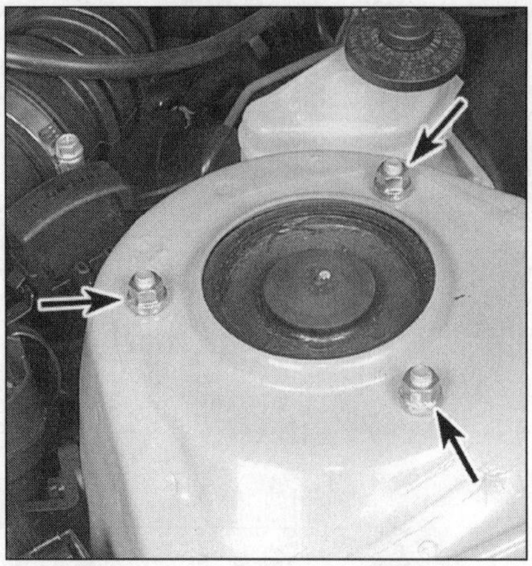

2.5 To detach the upper end of the strut assembly from the body, remove the upper mounting nuts (arrows)

3.3 Install the spring compressor according to the tool manufacturer's instructions and compress the spring until all pressure is relieved from the upper spring seat

2 Strut assembly (front) - removal, inspection and installation

Removal

Refer to illustrations 2.3 and 2.5

1 Loosen the wheel lug nuts, raise the vehicle and support it securely on jackstands. Remove the wheel.

2 Unbolt the brake hose bracket from the strut. If the vehicle is equipped with ABS, detach the speed sensor wiring harness from the strut by removing the clamp bracket bolt.

3 Remove the strut-to-knuckle nuts **(see illustration)** and knock the bolts out with a hammer and punch.

4 Separate the strut from the steering knuckle. Be careful not to overextend the inner CV joint. Also, do not let the steering knuckle fall outward and strain the brake hose.

5 Support the strut and spring assembly with one hand and remove the strut-to-body nuts **(see illustration)**. Remove the assembly out from the fenderwell.

Inspection

6 Check the strut body for leaking fluid, dents, cracks and other obvious damage which would warrant repair or replacement.

7 Check the coil spring for chips or cracks in the spring coating (this will cause premature spring failure due to corrosion). Inspect the spring seat for cuts and general deterioration.

8 If any undesirable conditions exist, proceed to the strut disassembly procedure (see Section 3).

Installation

9 Guide the strut assembly up into the fenderwell and insert the upper mounting studs through the holes in the body. Once the studs protrude, install the nuts to support the strut from falling back downward. The help of an assistant is recommended, as the strut is heavy and awkward.

10 Slide the steering knuckle into the strut flange and insert the two bolts. Install the nuts and tighten them to the torque listed in this Chapter's Specifications.

11 Connect the brake hose bracket to the strut and tighten the bolt securely. If the vehicle is equipped with ABS, install the speed sensor wiring harness bracket.

12 Install the wheel and lug nuts, then lower the vehicle and tighten the lug nuts to the torque listed in the Chapter 1 Specifications.

13 Tighten the upper mounting nuts to the torque listed in this Chapter's Specifications.

14 Drive the vehicle to an alignment shop to have the front end alignment checked, and if necessary, adjusted. **Note:** *When disposing of a used strut assembly, return them to your automotive parts store or dealer - some struts are gas-charged and require special disposal procedures.*

3 Strut/spring assembly - replacement

1 If the struts or coil springs exhibit the telltale signs of wear (leaking fluid, loss of damping capability, chipped, sagging or cracked coil springs) explore all options before beginning any work. The strut/shock absorber assemblies are not serviceable and must be replaced if a problem develops. However, strut assemblies complete with springs may be available on an exchange basis, which eliminates much time and work. Whichever repair/replacement method you choose, check on the cost and availability of parts before disassembling your vehicle. **Warning:** *Disassembling a strut is potentially dangerous and utmost attention must be directed to the job, or serious injury may result. Use only a high-quality spring compressor and carefully follow the manufacturer's instructions furnished with the tool. After removing the coil spring from the strut assembly, set it aside in a safe, isolated area.*

Disassembly

Refer to illustrations 3.3, 3.4, 3.5, 3.6 and 3.7

2 Remove the strut assembly following the procedure described in the previous Section. Mount the strut assembly in a vise. Line the vise jaws with wood or rags to prevent damage to the unit and do not tighten the vise excessively.

3 Following the tool manufacturer's instructions, install the spring compressor (which can be obtained at most auto parts stores or equipment yards on a daily rental basis) on the spring and compress it sufficiently to relieve all pressure from the upper spring seat **(see illustration)**. This can be verified by wiggling the spring.

4 Loosen the piston shaft nut **(see illustration)**. It may be necessary to hold the shaft from turning while loosening the nut.

5 Remove the nut and suspension support **(see illustration)**. Mark the suspension support so that it will be reinstalled with the same side inboard (there is a factory "direction indicator" marking that faces inboard, away from (opposite) the side of the strut with the lower bracket mounting holes; you should mark the orientation when disassembling). Inspect the bearing in the suspension support for smooth operation. If it does not turn smoothly, replace the suspension support. Check the rubber portion of the suspension support for cracking and general deterioration. If there is any separation of the rubber, replace it.

6 Lift the spring seat and upper insulator from the piston shaft **(see illustration)**. Check the rubber spring seat for cracking and hardness, replacing it if necessary.

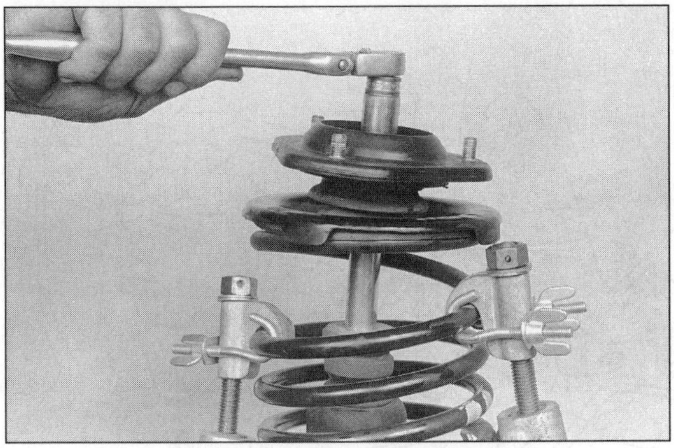

3.4 Remove the piston shaft nut

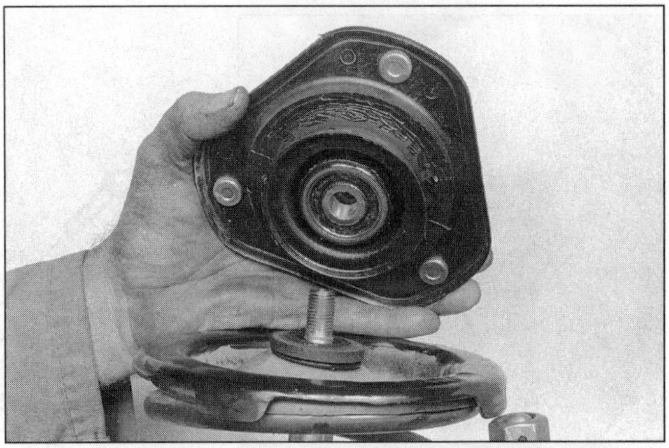

3.5 Lift the suspension support off the piston shaft

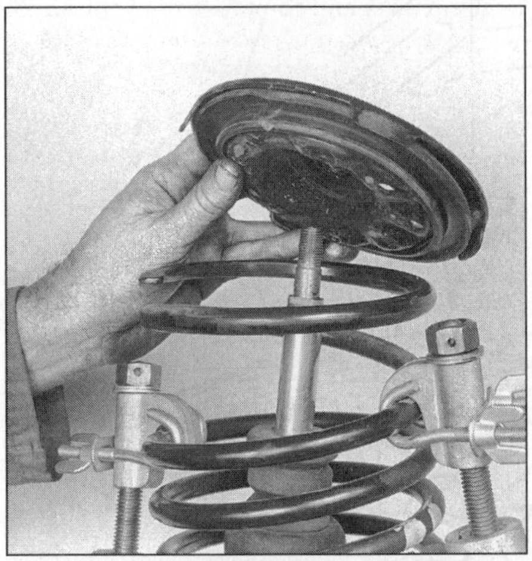

3.6 Remove the spring seat from the piston shaft

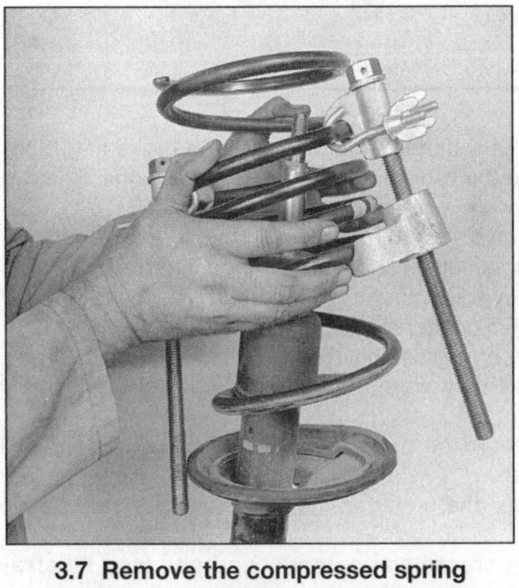

3.7 Remove the compressed spring assembly - keep the ends of the spring pointed away from your body

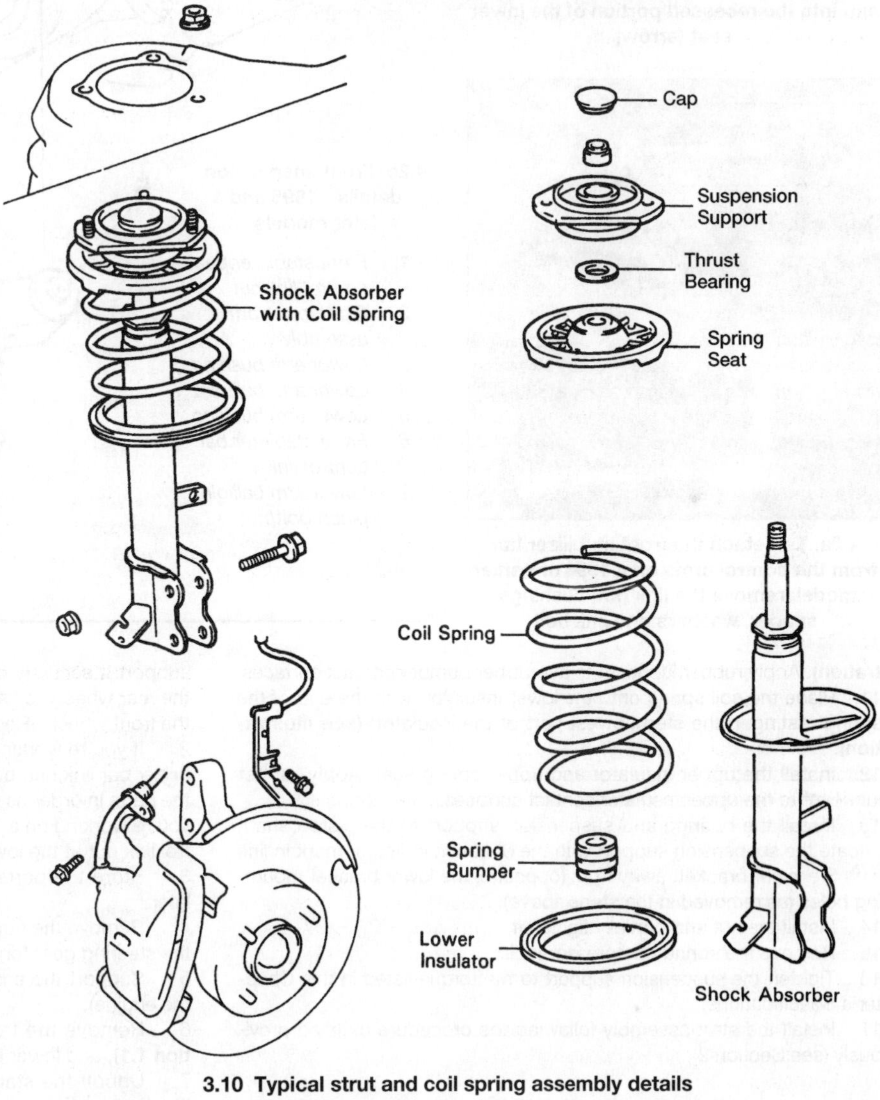

3.10 Typical strut and coil spring assembly details

7 Carefully lift the compressed spring from the assembly **(see illustration)** and set it in a safe place. **Warning:** *Keep the ends of the spring pointed away from your body.*

8 Slide the rubber bumper off the piston shaft.

9 Check the lower insulator (if equipped) for wear, cracking and hardness and replace it if necessary.

Reassembly

Refer to illustrations 3.10 and 3.11

10 If the lower insulator is being replaced, set it into position with the step (dropped portion) seated in the lowest part of the seat. Extend the damper rod to its full length and install the rubber bumper **(see illus-**

10

3.11 When installing the spring, place the end into the recessed portion of the lower seat (arrow)

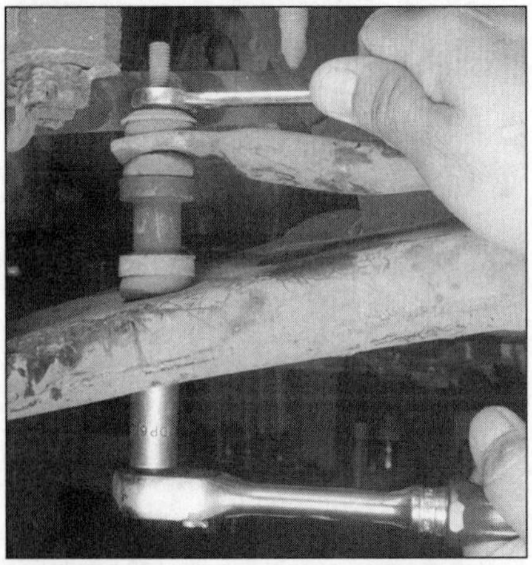

4.2a To detach the front stabilizer bar from the control arms on a 1994 or earlier model, remove the link nut, bushings, spacer, washers and link bolt

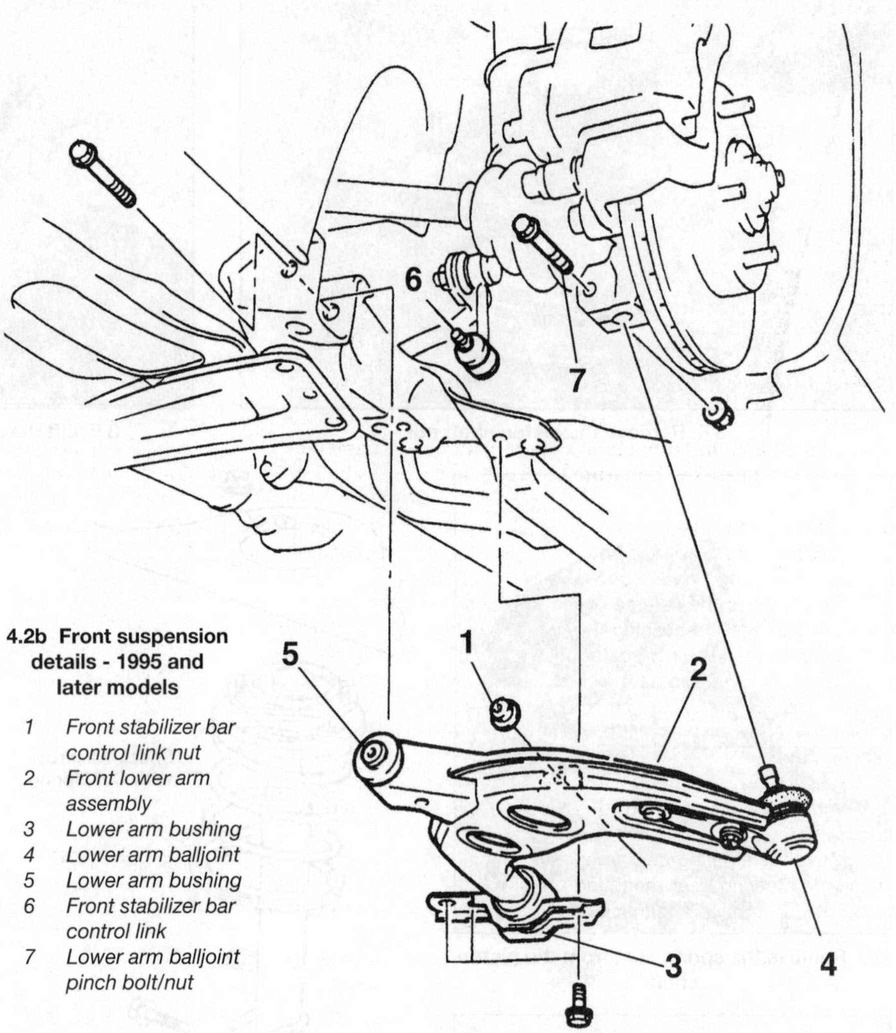

4.2b Front suspension details - 1995 and later models

1 *Front stabilizer bar control link nut*
2 *Front lower arm assembly*
3 *Lower arm bushing*
4 *Lower arm balljoint*
5 *Lower arm bushing*
6 *Front stabilizer bar control link*
7 *Lower arm balljoint pinch bolt/nut*

tration). Apply rubber lubricant to the rubber bumper contact surfaces.

11 Place the coil spring onto the lower insulator, with the end of the spring resting in the step (lowest part of the insulator) **(see illustration)**.

12 Install the upper insulator and upper spring seat. Apply rubber lubricant to the upper insulator contact surfaces.

13 Install the bearing and suspension support to the piston shaft. Locate the suspension support with the direction indicator mark in line with the lower bracket, away from (opposite) the lower bracket mounting holes (as removed in the steps above).

14 Install the nut and partially tighten it.

15 Remove the spring compressor tool.

16 Tighten the suspension support to the torque listed in this Chapter's Specifications.

17 Install the strut assembly following the procedure outlined previously (see Section 2).

4 Stabilizer bar and bushings (front) - removal and installation

Removal

Refer to illustrations 4.2a, 4.2b and 4.7

1 Loosen the front wheel lug nuts. Raise the front of the vehicle and support it securely on jackstands. Apply the parking brake and block the rear wheels to keep the vehicle from rolling off the stands. Remove the front wheels. Remove the engine undercover.

2 If you're working on a 1990 through 1994 model, remove the stabilizer bar link nut, bolt, bushings and washers **(see illustration)**. Store the parts in order as they were mounted, for correct reassembly later. If you're working on a 1995 or later model, remove the stabilizer bar control link nut at the lower arm assembly **(see illustration)**.

3 Store the parts as they were mounted, for correct reassembly later.

4 Remove the nuts from the steering gear (rack and pinion) and pull the steering gear forward.

5 Support the engine (the preferred method is using a hoist above the engine).

6 Remove the front crossmember mounting bolts **(see illustration 1.1)**, and lower the crossmember slowly.

7 Unbolt the stabilizer bar brackets from the crossmember **(see illustration)**.

8 With the stabilizer bar off the vehicle, inspect the bracket bushings. If they are cracked, worn or deteriorated, replace them.

9 Clean the bushing area of the stabilizer bar with a stiff wire brush to remove any rust or dirt.

Installation

10 Apply rubber lubricant to the bushings at the stabilizer bar clamp

4.7 To detach the front stabilizer bar from the crossmember, remove the bolt from the bushing brackets

brackets and at the stabilizer bar ends (attachments to the suspension A-arm). **Caution:** *Do not use petroleum or mineral-based lubricants or brake fluid - they will lead to deterioration of the bushings.*

11 Installation is the reverse of removal. Install the bushings on the stabilizer bar with the bushing flat bottom/split facing the crossmember, and with the bushing located on the stabilizer bar at the installation position line painted on the stabilizer bar. **Note:** *On 1995 and later models, install the stabilizer bar bracket in the direction shown by the arrow marked on the bracket.* Install and tighten the stabilizer bar bracket nuts to the torque listed in this Chapter's Specifications.

12 Raise the crossmember into position. Install and tighten the crossmember bolts to the torque listed in this Chapter's Specifications.

13 Move the steering gear (rack and pinion) back into position and install the steering gear mounting bracket nuts. Tighten the steering gear (rack and pinion) mounting nuts to the torque listed in this Chapter's Specifications.

14 Install the stabilizer bar link bolt, bushings, washers, and nut in the order as removed in the Steps above and tighten to the specified length of exposed thread as listed in this Chapter's Specifications.

5 Control arm - removal, inspection and installation

Removal

Refer to illustration 5.5

1 Loosen the wheel lug nuts on the side to be dismantled, raise the front of the vehicle, support it securely on jackstands and remove the wheel.

2 Remove the stabilizer bar link nut **(see illustrations 4.2a and 4.2b)**, bushings, washers and bolt.

3 Remove the front control arm pivot bolt and washer **(see illustration 1.1)**.

4 Remove the rear control arm pivot bushing clamp bolts **(see illustration 1.1)**. **Note:** *It is not necessary to remove the pivot bushing nut that retains the control arm bushing unless you are replacing the bushing.*

5 Remove the pinch bolt and nut holding the steering knuckle to the lower balljoint **(see illustration)**, then pry the control arm balljoint from the steering knuckle.

6 Remove the control arm.

7 If replacing the lower balljoint, detach the lower balljoint from the control arm.

Inspection

8 Check the control arm for damage or distortion and the bushings for wear, replacing parts as necessary. Do not attempt to straighten a bent control arm.

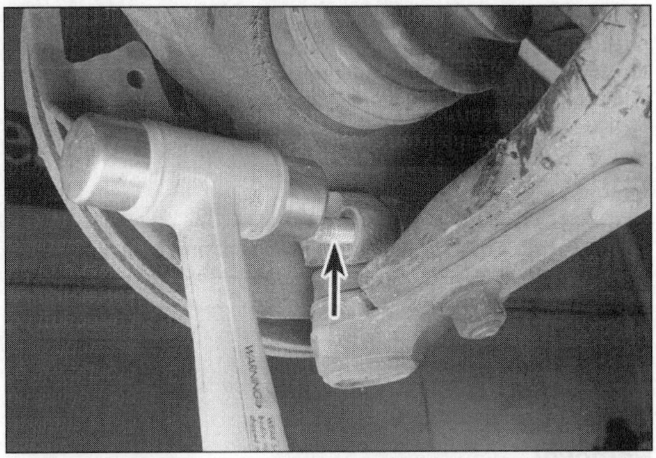

5.5 To detach the control arm from the steering knuckle balljoint, first remove the pinch bolt and nut, drive the bolt out, then pry the balljoint stud from the steering knuckle

Installation

9 Installation is the reverse of removal. Tighten all of the fasteners to the torque values listed in this Chapter's Specifications. **Note:** *Before tightening the pivot bolts, raise the outer end of the control arm with a floor jack to simulate normal ride height.*

10 Install the wheel and lug nuts, lower the vehicle and tighten the lug nuts to the torque listed in the Chapter 1 Specifications.

11 It is a good idea to have the front wheel alignment checked, and if necessary, adjusted after this job has been performed.

6 Balljoints - replacement

Refer to illustration 6.3

1 Loosen the wheel lug nuts, raise the vehicle and support it securely on jackstands. Remove the wheel.

2 Remove the pinch bolt and nut holding the steering knuckle to the lower balljoint. Pry the control arm balljoint from the steering knuckle **(see illustration 5.5)**.

3 Remove the bolt and nuts securing the balljoint to the control arm **(see illustration)**. Separate the balljoint from the control arm with a prybar.

4 To install the balljoint, insert the balljoint threaded stud through the hole in the lower A-arm and install the nut, but do not tighten the nut yet.

6.3 Remove the balljoint bolt and nuts from the control arm and remove the balljoint

5 Install the balljoint mounting bolt and nut. Tighten the balljoint bolt and nuts to the torque listed in this Chapter's Specifications.
6 Insert the balljoint into the steering knuckle fully, and install the pinch bolt and nut. Tighten to the torque listed in this Chapter's Specifications.
7 Install the wheel and lug nuts. Lower the vehicle and tighten the lug nuts to the torque listed in the Chapter 1 Specifications.

7 Steering knuckle and hub - removal and installation

Warning: *Dust created by the brake system may contain asbestos, which is harmful to your health. Never blow it out with compressed air and do not inhale any of it. Do not, under any circumstances, use petroleum-based solvents to clean brake parts. Use brake system cleaner only.*

Removal

1 Loosen the wheel lug nuts, raise the vehicle and support it securely on jackstands. Remove the wheel.
2 Remove the brake caliper and the brake disc (see Chapter 9), and disconnect the brake hose from the strut.
3 If the vehicle is equipped with ABS, remove the wheel speed sensor.
4 Loosen, but don't remove the strut-to-steering knuckle nuts and bolts (see Section 2).
5 Separate the tie-rod end from the steering knuckle arm (see Section 17).
6 Remove the pinch bolt and nut holding the steering knuckle to the lower balljoint **(see illustration 5.5)**. Pry the control arm balljoint from the steering knuckle.
7 Push the driveaxle from the hub as described in Chapter 8. Support the end of the driveaxle with a piece of wire.
8 The strut-to-knuckle bolts can now be removed.
9 Carefully separate the steering knuckle from the strut and lift out the steering knuckle.

Installation

10 Guide the steering knuckle and hub assembly into position, inserting the driveaxle into the hub.
11 Push the steering knuckle into the strut flange and install the bolts and nuts, but do not tighten them yet.
12 Insert the balljoint into the steering knuckle and install the pinch bolt and nut. Tighten the balljoint pinch bolt and nut to the torque listed in this Chapter's Specifications.
13 If you are installing a new balljoint, install it on the control arm (see Section 5), but do not tighten the bolt and nuts yet.
14 Attach the tie-rod to the steering knuckle arm (see Section 17). Tighten the strut bolt nuts, the balljoint-to-control arm bolt and nuts and the tie-rod nut to the torque listed in this Chapter's Specifications. Install a new tie rod nut cotter pin.
15 Place the brake disc on the hub and install the caliper as outlined in Chapter 9.
16 Install the driveaxle/hub nut and tighten it to the torque listed in the Chapter 8 Specifications.
17 Install the wheel and lug nuts.
18 Lower the vehicle and tighten the lug nuts to the torque listed in the Chapter 1 Specifications.

8 Hub and bearing assembly (front) - removal and installation

1 Due to the special tools and expertise required to press the hub and bearing from the steering knuckle, this job should be left to a professional mechanic. However, the steering knuckle and hub may be removed and the assembly taken to a dealer service department or other repair shop. See Section 7 for the steering knuckle and hub removal procedure.

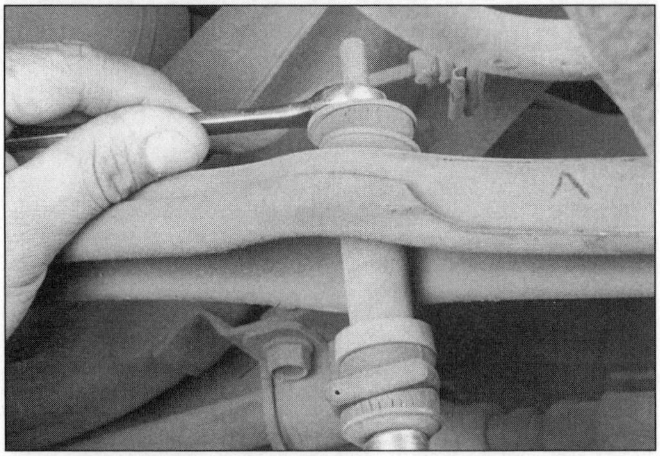

9.2a 1990 through 1994: To detach the rear stabilizer bar, remove the bushing nut, bushings, spacer, washers and bushing bolt (arrow)

9 Stabilizer bar and bushings (rear) - removal and installation

Refer to illustrations 9.2a, 9.2b and 9.3

1 Loosen the rear wheel lug nuts. Raise the rear of the vehicle and place it securely on jackstands. Remove the rear wheels.
2 If you're working on a 1990 through 1994 model, remove the stabilizer bar link nut **(see illustration)**, bolt, bushings and washers. Store the parts in order, for correct reassembly later. If you're working on a 1995 or later model, remove the stabilizer bar control link nut at the strut assembly **(see illustration)**. Store the parts as they were mounted, for correct reassembly later.
3 Unbolt the stabilizer bar bushing clamps from the body **(see illustration)**.
4 The stabilizer bar can now be removed from the vehicle. Pull the bushings off the stabilizer bar using a rocking motion.
5 Check the bushings for wear, hardness, distortion, cracking and other signs of deterioration, replacing them if necessary. Also check the stabilizer bar link bushings for the same conditions, and replace if necessary.
6 Using a wire brush, clean the areas of the bar where the bushings ride. Installation is the reverse of the removal procedure. Apply rubber lubricant to the bushings prior to installation. **Caution:** *Do not use petroleum-based products or brake fluid, as these will damage the rubber.*
7 Install the bushings at the stabilizer bar brackets with the bushing flat bottom/split facing the crossmember, and with the bushing located on the stabilizer bar at the installation position line painted on the stabilizer bar.
8 Install and tighten the stabilizer bar bracket nuts to the torque listed in this Chapter's Specifications.
9 Install the stabilizer bar end bushings, washers, and nut in the order as removed in the Steps above and tighten to the specified length of exposed thread as listed in this Chapter's Specifications.

10 Strut assembly (rear) - removal, inspection and installation

Removal

Refer to illustrations 10.2 and 10.5

1 Loosen the rear wheel lug nuts, raise the rear of the vehicle and support it securely on jackstands. Remove the wheel.
2 Remove the clip and detach the brake hose from the bracket on the strut **(see illustration)**. If the vehicle is equipped with ABS, detach

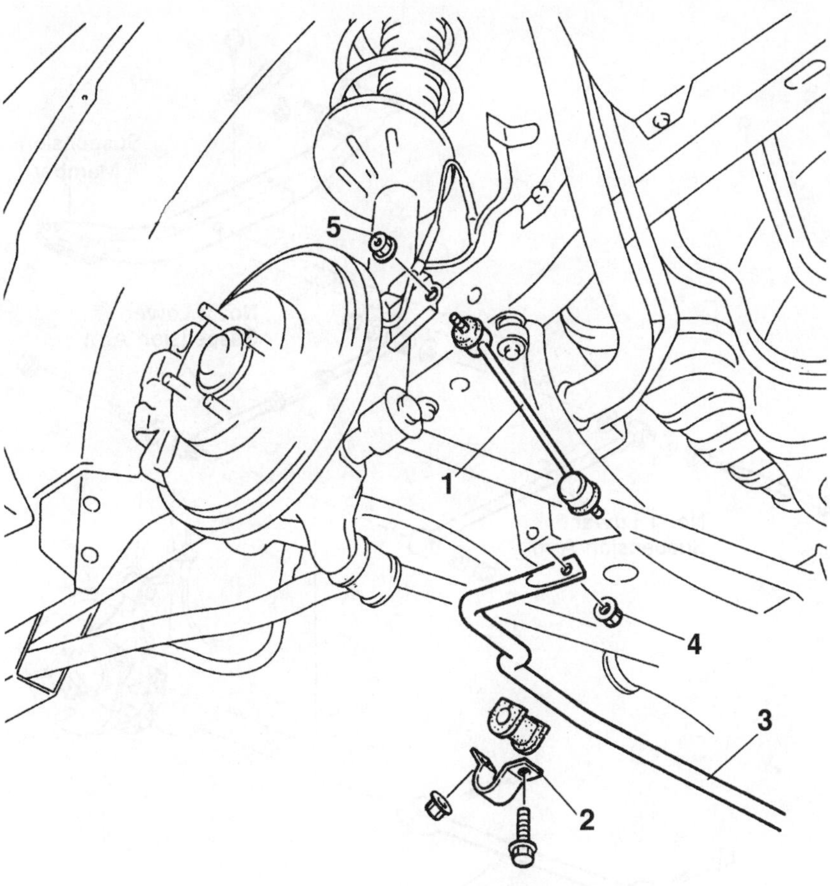

9.2b Rear stabilizer bar details - 1995 and later models

1. *Rear stabilizer bar control link*
2. *Rear stabilizer bar clamp*
3. *Rear stabilizer bar*
4. *Lower control link nut*
5. *Upper control link nut*

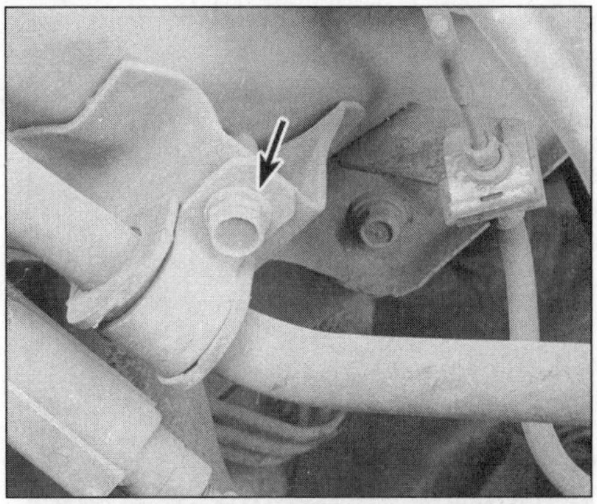

9.3 To detach the rear stabilizer bar from the vehicle body, remove the bolts (arrow) from the bushing brackets (1990 through 1994 model shown)

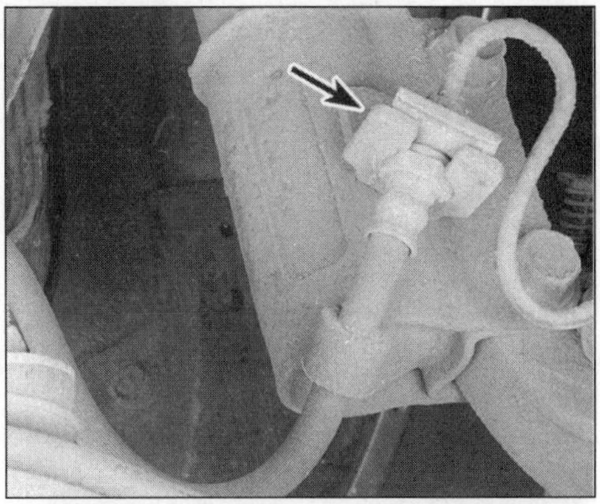

10.2 Remove the clip (arrow) and pass the hose fitting through the slot in the bracket (1990 through 1994 model shown)

the wheel speed sensor wire from the strut.

3 Support the spindle with a floor jack.

4 Remove the strut-to-spindle bolt nuts. Don't let the spindle fall outward, as this could strain the brake hose.

5 Access the upper strut mounting bolts through the trunk on four-door models, and through the passenger compartment/hatch door on two-door models, removing trim as necessary (see Chapter 11). Have an assistant support the strut, then remove the upper strut-to-body mounting nuts **(see illustration)**. Remove the strut assembly.

Inspection

6 Follow the inspection procedures described in Section 2. If you determine that the strut assembly must be disassembled for replacement of the strut or the coil spring, refer to Section 3.

7 When reassembling the strut, make sure the suspension support is aligned as removed, according to the procedure to note the location of the suspension support during disassembly, which is with the two mounting studs lined up with the center of the piston rod.

Installation

8 Maneuver the assembly up into the fenderwell and insert the mounting studs through the holes in the body. Install the nuts, but don't tighten them yet.

9 Push the spindle into the strut lower bracket and install the bolts and nuts, tightening them to the torque listed in this Chapter's Specifications.

10 Attach the brake hose to the strut bracket and install the clip. If the vehicle is equipped with ABS, attach the wheel speed sensor wire to the strut.

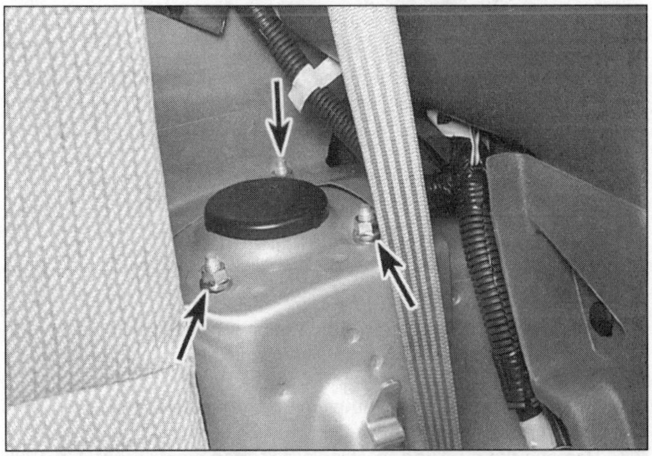

10.5 To detach the upper end of the rear strut from the vehicle, remove these nuts (arrows)

11 Install the wheel and lug nuts, lower the vehicle and tighten the lug nuts to the torque listed in the Chapter 1 Specifications.

12 Tighten the strut upper mounting nuts to the torque listed in this Chapter's Specifications.

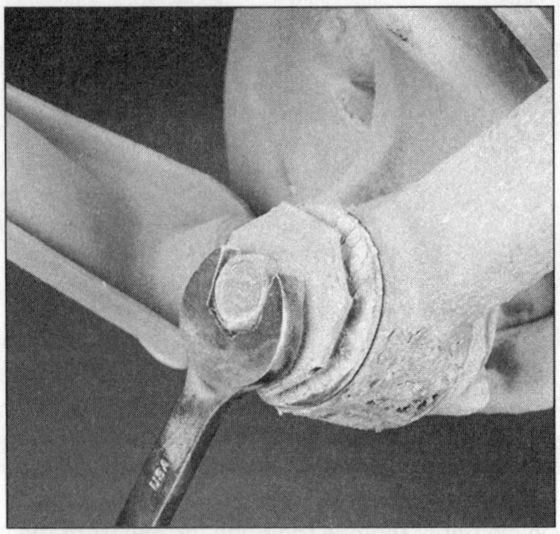

11.3 To detach the rear strut rod from the spindle, remove this bolt - 1990 through 1994 shown

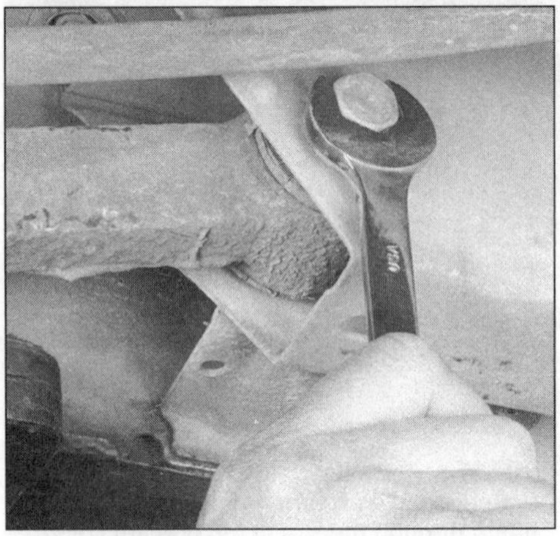

11.4 To disconnect the strut rod from the body, remove this bolt - 1990 through 1994 show

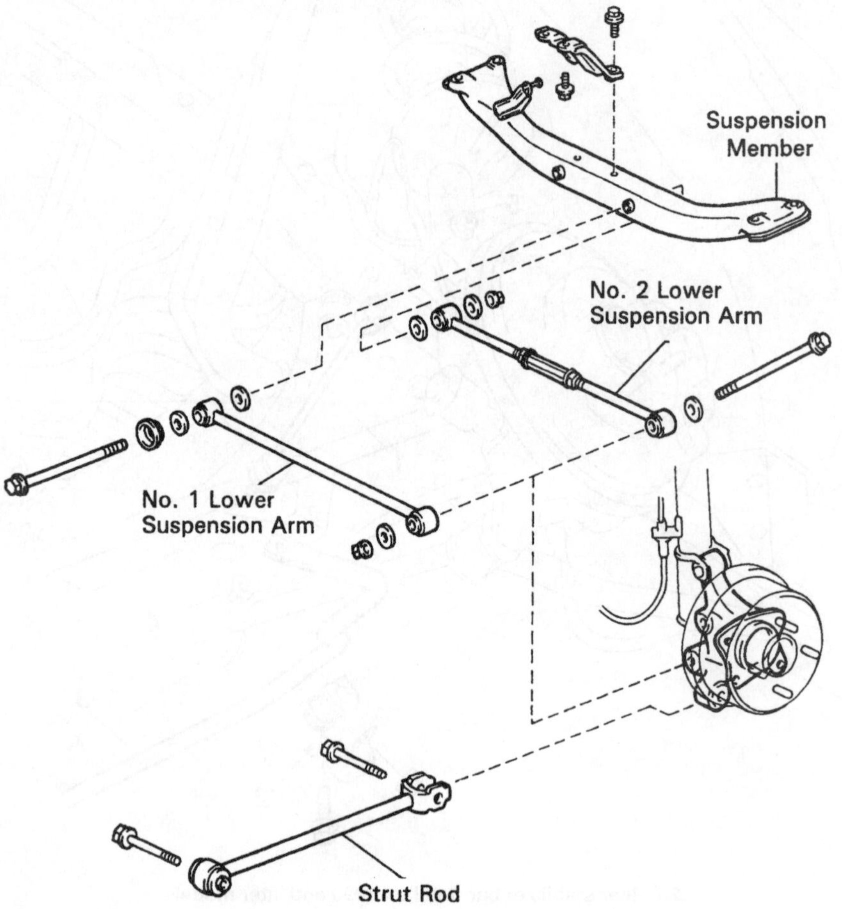

12.1a Rear suspension details - 1990 through 1994 models

13 Repeat Steps 1 through 7 for the other strut.

14 Reinstall any trim removed (see Chapter 11). **Note:** *When disposing of a used strut assembly, return them to your automotive parts store or dealer - some struts are gas charged and require special disposal procedures.*

11 Strut rod - removal and installation

Refer to illustrations 11.3 and 11.4

1 There is one trailing strut rod on each rear wheel, attached with bushings forward of the rear wheel and running back to the rear wheel carrier.

2 Loosen the wheel lug nuts, raise the vehicle and support it securely on jackstands. Remove the wheel.

3 Remove the strut rod-to-spindle bolt **(see illustration)**. On 1995 and later models remove the parking brake cable bracket **(see illustration 12.1b)**.

4 Remove the strut rod-to-body bracket bolt **(see illustration)** and detach the rod from the vehicle.

5 Installation is the reverse of the removal procedure, but don't tighten the bolts until the suspension is raised by a jack to simulate normal ride height. Be sure to tighten the bolts to the torque listed in this Chapter's Specifications.

6 Install the wheel and lug nuts, then lower the vehicle. Tighten the lug nuts to the torque listed in the Chapter 1 Specifications.

12 Suspension arms - removal and installation

Refer to illustrations 12.1a, 12.1b, 12.4 and 12.5

Removal

1 The lateral suspension arms are the two parallel suspension arms mounted on the rear crossmember (two arms for each rear wheel) **(see illustrations)**. Loosen the rear wheel lug nuts, raise the rear of the vehicle and support it securely on jackstands.

2 Block the front wheels and remove the rear wheel.

3 Support the rear wheel carrier with a floor jack. If you're working on a 1995 or later model, mark the suspension arm cam plate settings for proper reinstallation later and remove the crossmember access covers **(see illustration 12.1b)**.

4 Remove the nut, washer, and bolt from the inboard end of the suspension arm at the suspension crossmember **(see illustration)** and remove the bolt.

5 Remove the nut, washer, and bolt from the outboard end of the suspension arm (at the rear spindle) **(see illustration)**.

6 Remove the lateral suspension arms. **Caution:** *On 1990 through 1994 models, DO NOT loosen the locknuts or turn the adjuster on the rear lateral suspension arms; moving this affects the rear wheel toe alignment.*

Installation

7 Installation is the reverse of removal.

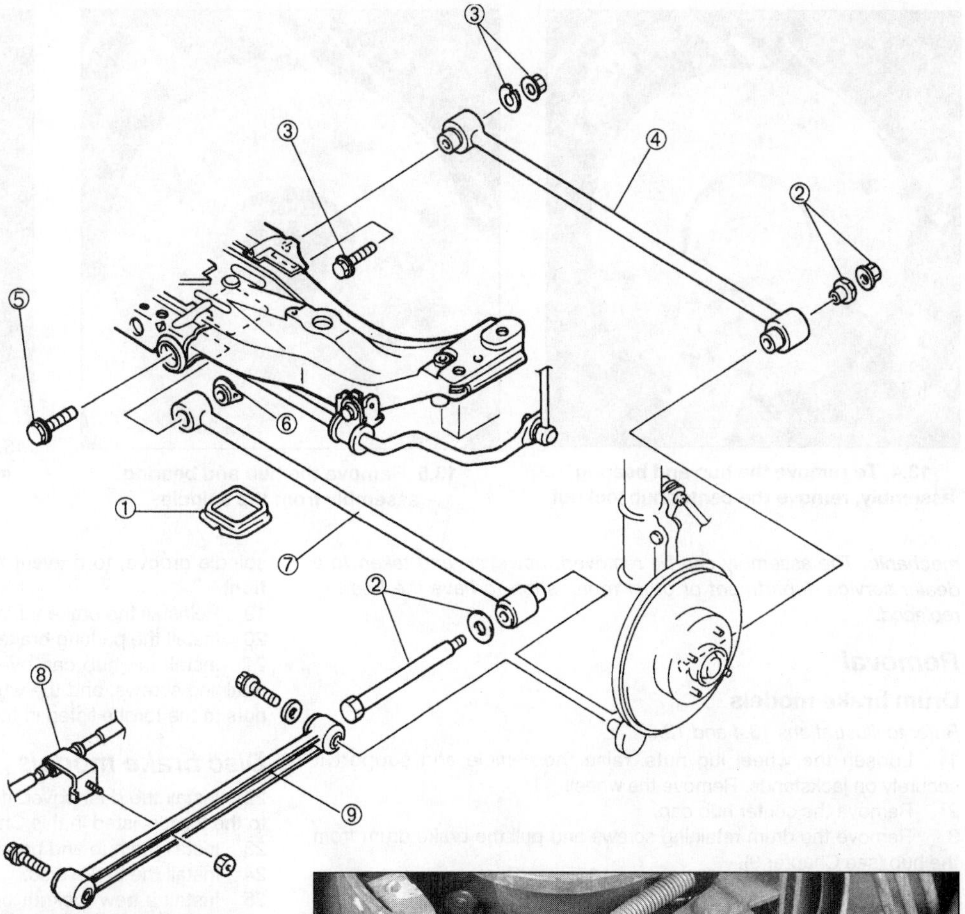

12.1b Rear suspension details - 1995 and later models

1 *Crossmember bolt access caps*
2 *Suspension arm bolts, washers, nuts*
3 *Suspension arm adjusting cam plate, cam bolt, nut*
4 *No. 2 suspension arm (lateral link)*
5 *Suspension arm-to-crossmember bolt, nut*
6 *Suspension arm-to-crossmember bolt, nut*
7 *No. 1 Suspension arm (lateral link)*
8 *Brake cable bracket (on strut rod) and nut*
9 *Strut rod (trailing link)*

12.4 To detach the rear lateral suspension arm from the suspension crossmember, remove the nut and washer - 1990 through 1994 shown

8 If you're working on a 1995 or later model, install the cam plate so the notch faces the same direction as the adjusting cam bolt and align with the marks made prior to removal for proper reinstallation.

9 Using a floor jack, raise the spindle to simulate normal ride height, then tighten all suspension fasteners to the torque listed in this Chapter's Specifications. If you replaced a rear lateral suspension arm (the adjustable lateral suspension arm), have the rear wheel toe adjusted by an alignment shop as soon as you are done.

10 Install the wheel and lug nuts, then lower the vehicle to the ground. Tighten the wheel lug nuts to the torque listed in the Chapter 1 Specifications.

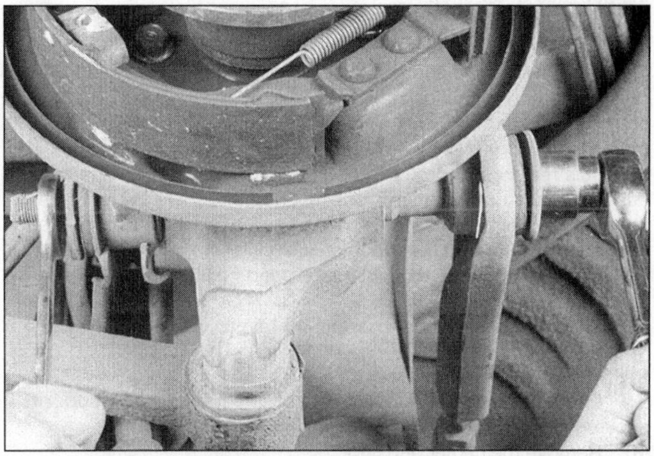

12.5 To detach the rear lateral suspension arms from the spindle, remove the nut and bolt

11 Have the rear wheel alignment checked by a dealer service department or an alignment shop.

13 Hub and bearing assembly and rear brake assembly - removal and installation

Warning: *Dust created by the brake system may contain asbestos, which is harmful to your health. Never blow it out with compressed air and don't inhale any of it. Do not, under any circumstances, use petroleum-based solvents to clean brake parts. Use brake system cleaner only.*

Note: *Due to the special tools required to replace the bearing, the hub and bearing assembly should not be disassembled by the home*

13.4 To remove the hub and bearing assembly, remove the center hub locknut

13.5 Remove the hub and bearing assembly from the spindle

13.18 Stake (punch) the locknut lip down into the spindle groove, to prevent the locknut from loosening

mechanic. The assembly can be removed, however, and taken to a dealer service department or other repair shop to have the bearing replaced.

Removal

Drum brake models

Refer to illustrations 13.4 and 13.5

1 Loosen the wheel lug nuts, raise the vehicle and support it securely on jackstands. Remove the wheel.

2 Remove the center hub cap.

3 Remove the drum retaining screws and pull the brake drum from the hub (see Chapter 9).

4 Using a hammer and punch, unstake the hub locknut. Remove the hub locknut at the rear hub spindle **(see illustration)**.

5 Remove the hub and bearing assembly from its seat and from the brake assembly **(see illustration)**.

6 On 1990 through 1994 models, the rear axle hub can be removed from the bearing to allow replacement of the bearing. Due to the special tools required to do this, you'll have to take the hub and bearing assembly to an automotive machine shop and have the old bearing pulled off the hub and a new bearing pressed on (you can re-use the hub itself, as long as it is in good condition).

7 On 1995 and later models the hub and bearing must be replaced as an assembly.

8 For brake backing plate assembly removal, see Section 14.

Disc brake models

9 Loosen the wheel lug nuts, raise the vehicle and support it securely on jackstands. Remove the wheel.

10 Remove the center hub cap.

11 Using a hammer and punch, unstake the hub locknut. Remove the hub locknut at the rear hub spindle.

12 Remove the brake caliper and brake disc (see Chapter 9).

13 Remove the hub and bearing assembly from the spindle.

14 Refer to Steps 6 and 7 above.

15 Remove the dust cover if necessary.

Installation

Rear drum brake models

Refer to illustration 13.18

16 Check that the brake assembly mounting bolts are tightened onto the rear spindle assembly to the torque listed in this Chapter's Specifications.

17 Install the hub and bearing assembly on the spindle and install a new locknut. Tighten the locknut to the torque listed in this Chapter's Specifications.

18 Using a punch and hammer, stake the locknut lip down into the spindle groove, to prevent the locknut from loosening **(see illustration)**.

19 Reinstall the brake tubing to the brake assembly.

20 Install the parking brake cable.

21 Install the hub cap over the locknut, the brake drum and drum retaining screws, and the wheel. Lower the vehicle and tighten the lug nuts to the torque listed in the Chapter 1 Specifications.

Disc brake models

22 Install the dust cover, if removed, and tighten the mounting bolts to the torque listed in this Chapter's Specifications.

23 Install the hub and bearing assembly on the spindle.

24 Install the brake disc.

25 Install a new locknut on the spindle. Tighten the locknut to the torque listed in this Chapter's Specifications.

26 Using a punch and hammer, stake the locknut lip down into the spindle groove, to prevent the locknut from loosening **(see illustration 13.18)**.

27 Install the center hub cap.

28 Install the brake caliper (see Chapter 9).

29 Install the wheel. Lower the vehicle and tighten the lug nuts to the torque listed in the Chapter 1 Specifications.

14 Rear spindle - removal and installation

Warning: *Dust created by the brake system may contain asbestos, which is harmful to your health. Never blow it out with compressed air and don't inhale any of it. Do not, under any circumstances, use petroleum-based solvents to clean brake parts. Use brake system cleaner only.*

Removal

Drum brake models

1 Loosen the wheel lug nuts, raise the vehicle and support it securely on jackstands. Remove the wheel.

2 Remove the center hub cap.

3 Unstake the locknut and remove the hub locknut at the rear hub spindle **(see illustration 13.4)**.

4 Remove the drum retaining screws and pull the brake drum from the hub (see Chapter 9).

5 Remove the hub and bearing assembly from its seat, maneuvering it out through the brake assembly.

6 Remove the brake line and the brake backing plate bolts, then remove the brake assembly from the rear spindle. It is not necessary to disassemble the brake shoe assembly or disconnect the parking brake cable from the backing plate. Suspend the backing plate and brake

assembly from the coil spring with a piece of wire. **Note:** *If removing the rear brake backing plate assembly completely, detach the parking brake cable* (see Chapter 9).
7 If you're working on a 1995 or later model, remove the wheel speed sensor from its spindle mount.
8 Support the spindle with a jack. Remove the suspension strut-to-spindle bolts.
9 Remove the trailing arm-to-spindle nut and washer and remove the lateral strut-to-spindle bolt.
10 Remove the spindle.

Disc brake models

11 Loosen the wheel lug nuts, raise the vehicle and support it securely on jackstands. Remove the wheel.
12 Remove the center hub cap.
13 Unstake the locknut and remove the hub locknut at the rear hub spindle.
14 Remove the brake caliper and brake disc (see Chapter 9). It is not necessary to disconnect the brake hose or detach the parking brake cable. Suspend the backing plate and brake assembly from the coil spring with a piece of wire.
15 Remove the hub and bearing assembly from its seat.
16 Remove the dust cover if necessary.
17 If you're working on a 1995 or later model, remove the wheel speed sensor from the spindle.
18 Support the spindle with a jack. Remove the suspension strut-to-spindle bolts (see Section 10).
19 Remove the trailing arm-to-spindle nut and washer and remove the lateral strut-to-spindle bolt (see Section 12).
20 Remove the spindle.

Installation

Drum brake models

21 Inspect the spindle for cracks, deformation and signs of wear. If it is worn out, replace it with a new spindle.
22 Installation is the reverse of removal **(see illustration 13.3)**.
23 Install the suspension arm bolt/nut and the strut rod bolts and nuts. Raise the spindle to simulate normal ride height, then tighten the fasteners to the torque values listed in this Chapter's Specifications.
24 If you're working on a 1995 or later model, reattach the wheel speed sensor to the spindle.
25 Remove the floor jack from under the spindle. Attach the brake assembly to the spindle, and tighten the brake assembly mounting bolts to the torque listed in this Chapter's Specifications. Install a new locknut. Tighten the locknut to the torque listed in this Chapter's Specifications and stake the locknut into the spindle groove **(see illustration 13.18)**.
26 Install the hub/bearing.
27 Connect the brake line.
28 Install the rear brake drum (see Chapter 9).
29 Install the wheel and lug nuts.
30 Lower the vehicle and tighten the lug nuts to the torque listed in the Chapter 1 Specifications.

Disc brake models

31 Inspect the spindle for cracks, deformation and signs of wear. If it is worn out, replace it with a new spindle.
32 Installation is the reverse of removal.
33 Install the suspension arm bolt/nut and the strut rod bolts and nuts. Raise the spindle to simulate normal ride height, then tighten the fasteners to the torque values listed in this Chapter's Specifications.
34 Remove the floor jack from under the spindle.
35 If you're working on a 1995 or later model, reattach the wheel speed sensor to the spindle.
36 Install the dust cover and tighten the mounting bolts to the torque listed in this Chapter's Specifications.
37 Install the hub and bearing assembly on the spindle. Install a new locknut on the spindle. Tighten the locknut to the torque listed in this Chapter's Specifications.
38 Using a punch and ball peen hammer, stake the locknut lip down into the spindle groove, to prevent the locknut from loosening **(see illustration 13.18)**.
39 Install the center hub cap. Remove the jack from under the spindle.
40 Install the brake disc. Install the brake disc retaining screws and tighten them to the torque listed in this Chapter's Specifications.
41 Install the brake caliper (see Chapter 9).
42 Install the wheel. Lower the vehicle and tighten the lug nuts to the torque listed in the Chapter 1 Specifications.

15 Steering system - general information

1 All models are equipped with rack-and-pinion steering. The steering gear is bolted to the engine cradle and operates the steering knuckles via tie-rods. The inner ends of the tie-rods are protected by rubber boots which should be inspected periodically for secure attachment, tears and leaking lubricant.
2 On models with power steering, the power assist system consists of a belt-driven pump and associated lines and hoses. The fluid level in the power steering pump reservoir should be checked periodically (see Chapter 1).
3 The steering wheel operates the steering shaft, which actuates the steering gear through universal joints. Looseness in the steering can be caused by wear in the steering shaft universal joints, the steering gear, the tie-rod ends or loose retaining bolts.

16 Steering wheel - removal and installation

Warning: *1995 and later models are equipped with airbags. The airbag is armed and can deploy (inflate) whenever the battery is connected. To prevent accidental deployment (and possible injury), turn the ignition key to LOCK and disconnect the negative battery cable whenever working near airbag components. After the battery is disconnected, wait at least two minutes before beginning work (the system has a back-up capacitor that must fully discharge). For more information see Chapter 12.*

Removal

Refer to illustrations 16.1, 16.2, 16.3a, 16.3b, 16.3c, 16.4, 16.5a and 16.5b

1 Turn the ignition key OFF, then disconnect the cable from the negative terminal of the battery. If the vehicle is equipped with an airbag system, wait at least two minutes before proceeding. Also, if the vehicle is equipped with an airbag, disconnect the electrical connector for the airbag wiring harness below the dash **(see illustration)**.

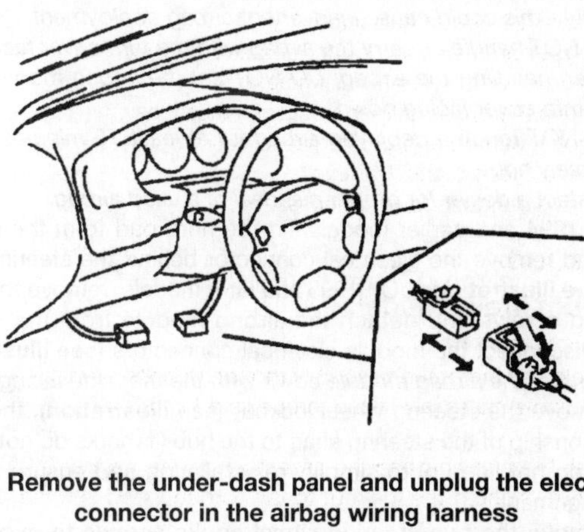

16.1 Remove the under-dash panel and unplug the electrical connector in the airbag wiring harness

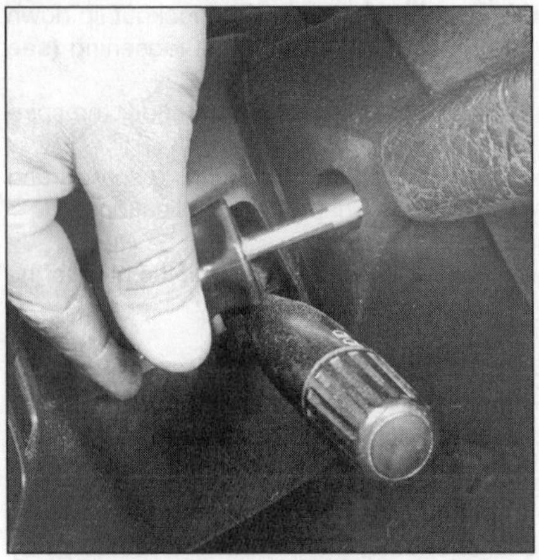
16.2 On 1990 through 1994 models, remove the horn pad retaining screws behind the steering wheel

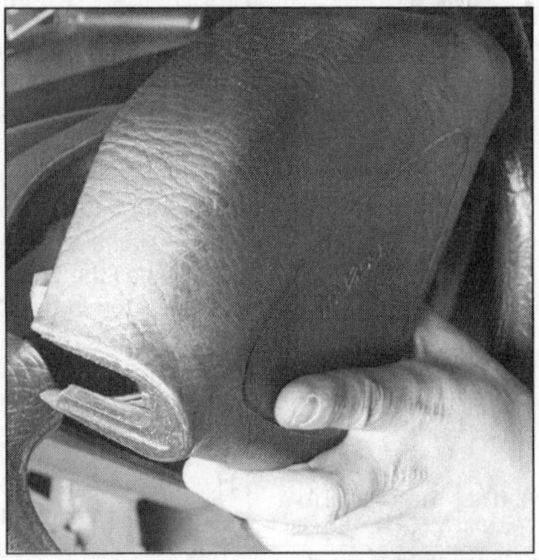
16.3a Lift the horn pad straight out from the steering wheel and . . .

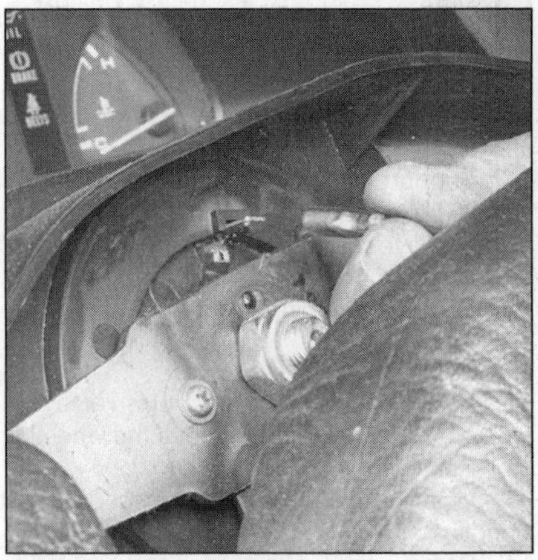
16.3b . . . remove the electrical connector behind the horn pad

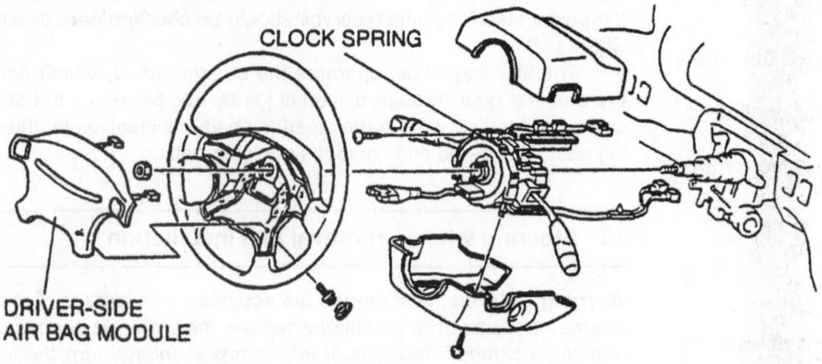

16.3c On 1995 and later models, remove the airbag module screws behind the steering wheel

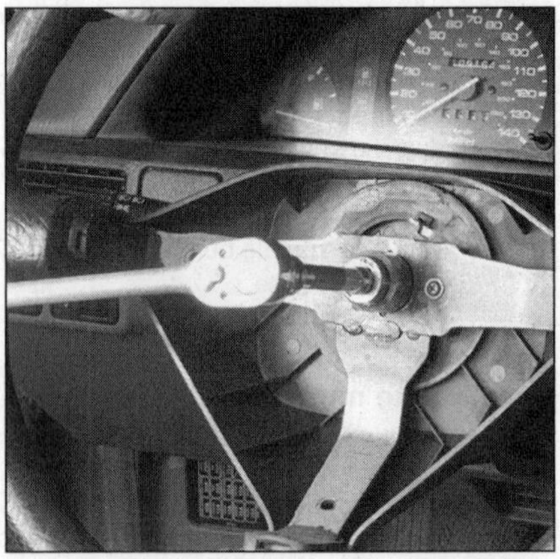
16.4 Remove the steering wheel nut

2 Turn the steering wheel so the wheels are pointing straight ahead, then remove the screws on the backside of the horn pad to the steering wheel **(see illustration)**.

Warning: *On 1995 and later models, follow the airbag servicing instructions prior to proceeding with any steps that may involve the airbag system:*

DO NOT disassemble any airbag component.

DO NOT attempt repair of the airbag system wiring harness.

DO NOT inspect or check the airbag system using an ohmmeter, because this can cause inadvertent deployment of the airbag.

DO NOT disconnect the airbag module (SAS) with the ignition switch ON - this could cause inadvertent airbag deployment.

DO NOT handle or carry the airbag with the trim cover facing you.

When handling the airbag, DO NOT set the airbag module down with the trim cover facing down.

DO NOT touch a deployed airbag for at least 15 minutes - it can be extremely hot.

Contact a dealer for proper disposal of a used airbag.

3 On 1994 and earlier models, lift the horn pad from the steering wheel and remove the electrical connector behind the steering wheel cover **(see illustrations)**. On 1995 and later models, remove the airbag attaching screws and detach the airbag module from the steering wheel. Disconnect the module electrical connectors **(see illustration)**.

Warning: *Set the airbag module down with the trim side facing up.*

4 Remove the steering wheel locknut **(see illustration)**, then mark the relationship of the steering shaft to the hub (if marks do not already exist or do not line up) to simplify reinstallation and ensure steering wheel alignment.

5 Remove the two steering wheel spoke screws to expose the threaded puller holes **(see illustration)** and attach a steering wheel puller. Use the puller to disconnect the steering wheel from the shaft **(see illustration)**.

Installation

6 Make sure that the front wheels are facing straight ahead.

7 To install the wheel, align the mark on the steering wheel hub with the mark on the shaft and slip the wheel onto the shaft. Install the nut and tighten it to the torque listed in this Chapter's Specifications.

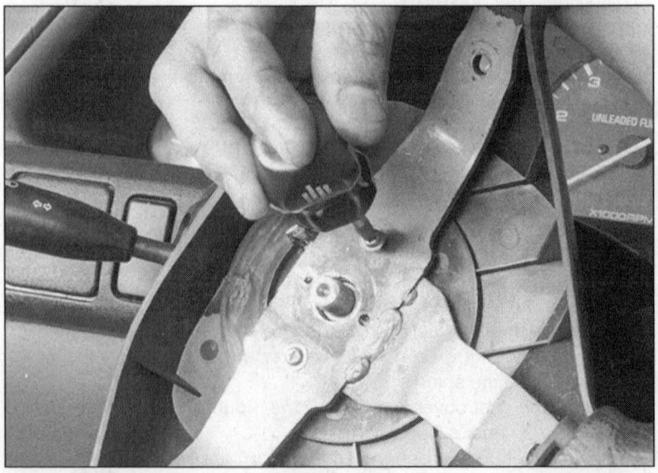
16.5a Remove the two screws on the steering wheel spokes and attach a steering wheel puller

16.5b Use a steering wheel puller to remove the steering wheel

17.2 Remove the cotter pin from the castle nut and loosen - but don't remove - the nut

17.3a Loosen the jam nut . . .

8 On 1995 and later models, plug in the electrical connector for the airbag module and flip down the locking tab.

9 On 1995 and later models, make sure the airbag module electrical connector is positioned correctly and that the wires do not interfere with anything, then install the airbag module and tighten the retaining screws to the torque listed in this Chapter's Specifications.

10 On 1990 through 1994 models, install the horn pad and retaining screws.

11 Connect the negative battery cable. On models with an airbag, reconnect the electrical connector for the airbag wiring harness under the dash.

17 Tie-rod ends - removal and installation

Removal

Refer to illustrations 17.2, 17.3a, 17.3b and 17.4

1 Loosen the wheel lug nuts. Raise the front of the vehicle, support it securely on jackstands, block the rear wheels and set the parking brake. Remove the front wheel.

2 Remove the cotter pin **(see illustration)** and loosen the nut on the tie-rod end stud.

3 Hold the tie rod with a pair of locking pliers or wrench and loosen the jam nut enough to mark the position of the tie-rod end in relation to the threads **(see illustrations)**.

4 Disconnect the tie rod from the steering knuckle arm with a puller **(see illustration)**.

5 Unscrew the tie-rod end from the tie-rod.

Installation

6 Thread the tie-rod end to the marked position on the tie-rod and insert the tie-rod stud into the steering knuckle arm. Tighten the jam nut securely.

7 Install the castle nut on the stud and tighten it to the torque listed in this Chapter's Specifications. Install a new cotter pin. If the hole for the cotter pin does not line up with one of the slots in the nut, turn the nut an additional amount until it slides through easily.

8 Install the wheel and lug nuts. Lower the vehicle and tighten the lug nuts to the torque listed in the Chapter 1 Specifications.

9 Have the alignment checked by a dealer service department or an alignment shop.

18 Steering gear boots - replacement

1 Loosen the lug nuts, raise the vehicle and support it securely on jackstands. Remove the wheel.

2 Remove the tie-rod end and jam nut (see Section 17).

3 Remove the steering gear boot clamps. Slide the boot off.

4 Before installing the new boot, wrap the threads and serrations on the end of the steering rod with a layer of tape so the small end of the new boot is not damaged during installation.

17.3b . . . then mark the position of the tie-rod end in relation to the threads

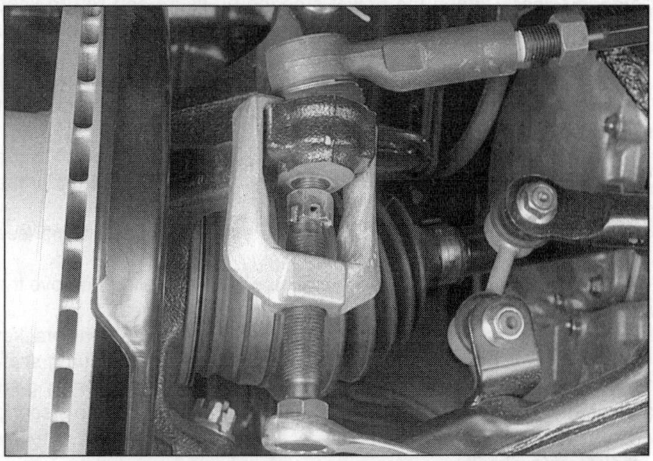

17.4 Disconnect the tie-rod end from the steering knuckle arm with a puller

10

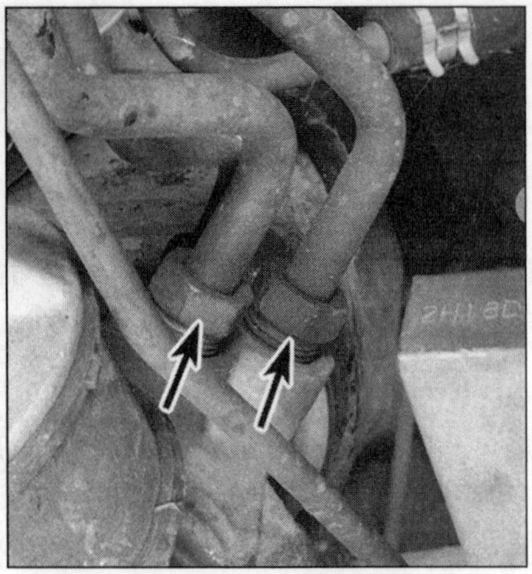

19.2 Disconnect the power steering line fittings (arrows)

19.3 Mark the relationship of the universal joint to the steering gear input shaft and remove the U-joint pinch bolt (arrow)

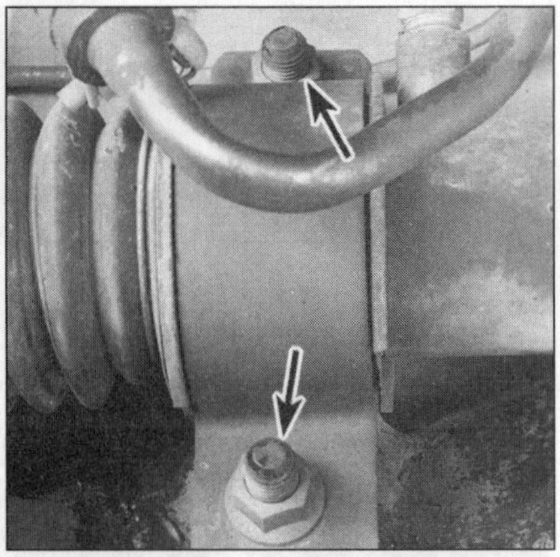

19.7 Remove the steering gear bracket nuts, two on this bracket and two on the other side bracket (not shown in this photo)

5 Place a new inner clamp over the steering gear.
6 Slide the new boot into position on the steering gear until it seats in the groove in the steering rod and install clamps. Tighten the clamps securely.
7 Remove the tape and install the tie-rod end jam nut and tie-rod end (see Section 17).
8 Install the wheel and lug nuts. Lower the vehicle and tighten the lug nuts to the torque listed in the Chapter 1 Specifications.

19 Steering gear - removal and installation

Warning: *1995 and later models are equipped with airbags. Make sure the steering shaft is not turned while the steering gear is removed or you could damage the airbag system. To prevent the shaft from turning, turn the ignition key to the lock position before beginning work or run the seat belt through the steering wheel and clip the seat belt into place. Make sure the ignition switch is OFF.*

Removal

Refer to illustrations 19.2, 19.3 and 19.7

1 Disconnect the cable from the negative terminal of the battery. If the vehicle is equipped with an airbag, wait at least two minutes before proceeding. Loosen the front wheel lug nuts, raise the front of the vehicle and support it securely on jackstands. Apply the parking brake and remove the wheels. Remove the engine undercover splash shield.
2 If equipped with power steering, place a drain pan under the steering gear. Detach the power steering pressure and return lines **(see illustration)** and cap or cover the ends to prevent excessive fluid loss and contamination.
3 Mark the relationship of the steering column universal joint at the steering gear input shaft. Remove the steering column universal joint pinch bolt **(see illustration)**.
4 Remove the steering column cover plates on the firewall in the engine compartment. To remove, mounting nuts are located under the dashboard in side the vehicle.
5 Separate the tie-rod ends from the steering knuckle arms (see Section 17).
6 On manual transmission vehicles with power steering, remove the extension bar/control rod, located under the steering gear.
7 Support the steering gear and remove the steering gear bracket mounting nuts **(see illustration)**. Separate the steering column shaft from the steering gear input shaft and remove the steering gear assembly. **Warning:** *Do NOT turn the steering wheel while the steering gear is removed. If the steering wheel is inadvertently turned, recenter the steering wheel.*
8 Check the steering gear mounting grommets for excessive wear or deterioration, replacing them if necessary.

Installation

9 Raise the steering gear into position and connect the steering gear input shaft and the steering shaft universal joint, aligning the marks.
10 Install the steering gear mounting brackets and nuts and tighten them to the torque listed in this Chapter's Specifications. **Note:** *Torque the upper bracket nuts first, then the lower nuts.*
11 Connect the tie-rod ends to the steering knuckle arms (see Section 17).
12 Install the universal joint pinch bolt and tighten it to the torque listed in this Chapter's Specifications.
13 If equipped with power steering, connect the power steering pressure and return hoses to the steering gear and fill the power steering pump reservoir with the recommended fluid (see Chapter 1).
14 Lower the vehicle and bleed the steering system (see Section 21).

20 Power steering pump - removal and installation

Removal

Refer to illustrations 20.3a, 20.3b and 20.7

1 Disconnect the cable from the negative battery terminal.

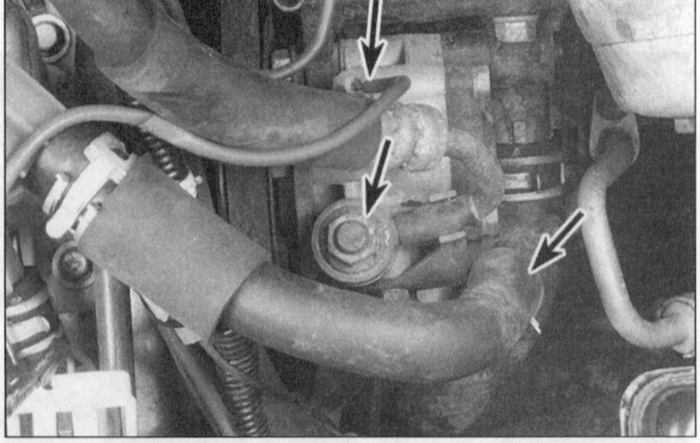

20.3a On 1990 through 1994 models, loosen the fluid return hose clamp (right arrow) and detach the return hose from the power steering pump; remove the pressure line banjo nut (center arrow) and disconnect the pressure line from the pump; remove the pressure switch sensor connector from the pump (left arrow)

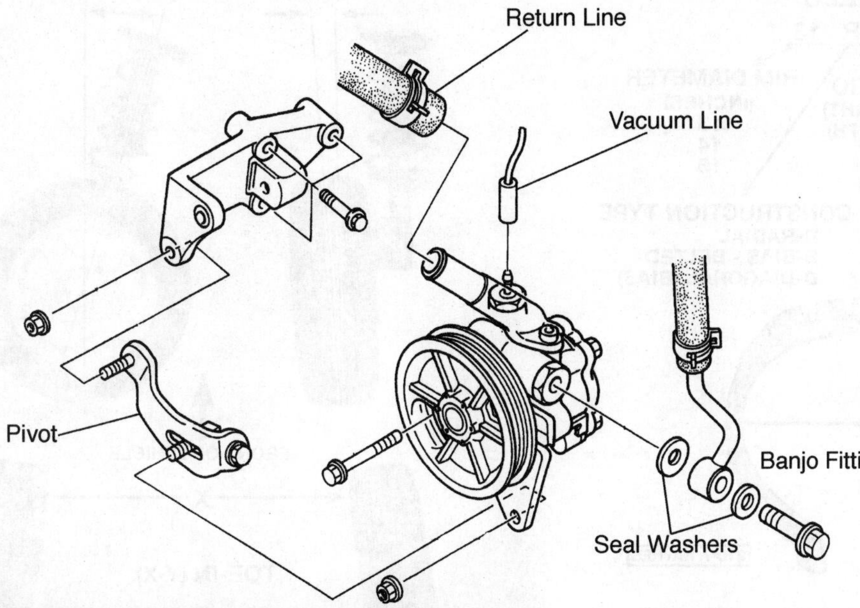

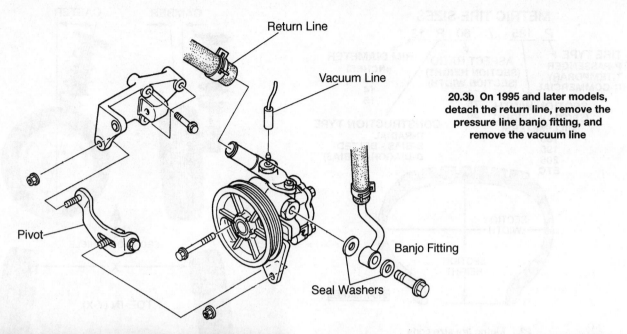

20.3b On 1995 and later models, detach the return line, remove the pressure line banjo fitting, and remove the vacuum line

20.7 Besides the pivot bolt and nut, remove the adjuster bolts and nut (arrows) - 1990 through 1994 shown

2 Using a large syringe or suction gun, suck as much fluid out of the power steering fluid reservoir as possible. Place a drain pan under the vehicle to catch any fluid that spills out when the hoses are disconnected. Cap or cover the hoses to prevent entry of dirt or other contaminants.

3 Loosen the clamp and disconnect the fluid return hose from the pump **(see illustrations)**. Detach the electrical connector from the pressure sensor on the pump, if applicable.

4 Remove the pressure line-to-pump banjo nut **(see illustrations 20.3a and 20.3b)**, then detach the line from the pump.

5 Check the banjo bolt seals and replace if necessary.

6 Raise the front of the vehicle and place it securely on jackstands.

7 Loosen the pivot bolt/nut and adjuster bolt **(see illustration)**, and remove the drivebelt (see Chapter 1).

8 Remove the pivot, adjuster and mounting bolts/nuts, then remove the pump from the vehicle.

9 If access to engine components is required, remove the pump mounting bracket mounting bolts and remove the mounting bracket.

Installation

10 Installation is the reverse of removal. Be sure to tighten the pressure line fitting or banjo bolt to the torque listed in this Chapter's Specifications. Adjust the drivebelt tension following the procedure described in Chapter 1.

11 Top off the fluid level in the reservoir (see Chapter 1) and bleed the system (see Section 21).

21 Power steering system - bleeding

1 Following any operation in which the power steering fluid lines have been disconnected, the power steering system must be bled to remove all air and obtain proper steering performance.

2 Before starting the engine and with the front wheels in the straight ahead position, check the power steering fluid level and, if low, add fluid until it reaches the L (Low) mark on the dipstick.

3 Start the engine and allow it to run at fast idle. Recheck the fluid level and add more new, fresh power steering fluid if necessary to reach the L mark on the dipstick.

4 Bleed the system by turning the wheels from side to side, without hitting the stops. This will work the air out of the system. Continuously check the reservoir and keep the reservoir full of fluid as this is done.

5 When the air is worked out of the system, return the wheels to the straight ahead position and keep the vehicle running for several more minutes before shutting it off, or road test as follows before shutting the engine off.

6 Road test the vehicle to be sure the steering system is functioning normally and is noise-free.

7 Recheck and top off the power steering fluid level to the F (Full) mark on the dipstick while the engine is at normal operating temperature. Add fluid if necessary (see Chapter 1).

10

22 Wheels and tires - general information

Refer to illustration 22.1

All vehicles covered by this manual are equipped with metric-sized fiberglass or steel belted radial tires **(see illustration)**. Use of other sizes or types of tires may affect the ride and handling of the vehicle. Don't mix different types of tires, such as radials and bias belted, on the same vehicle as handling may be seriously affected. It is recommended that tires be replaced in pairs on the same axle, but if

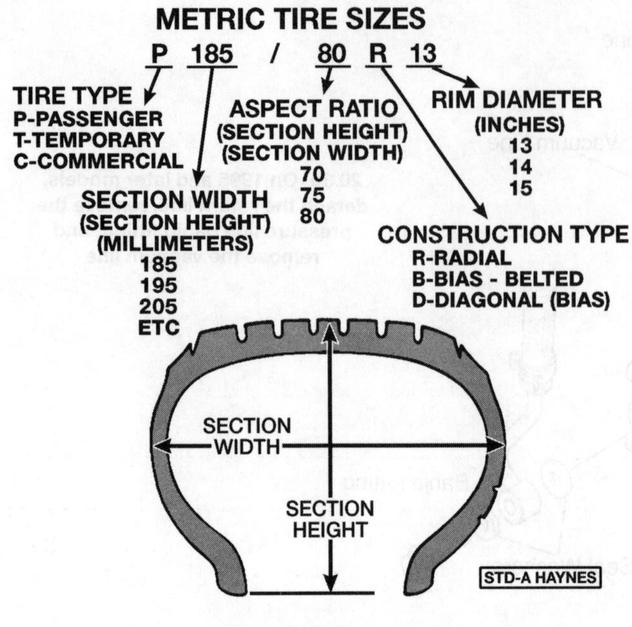

22.1 Metric tire size code

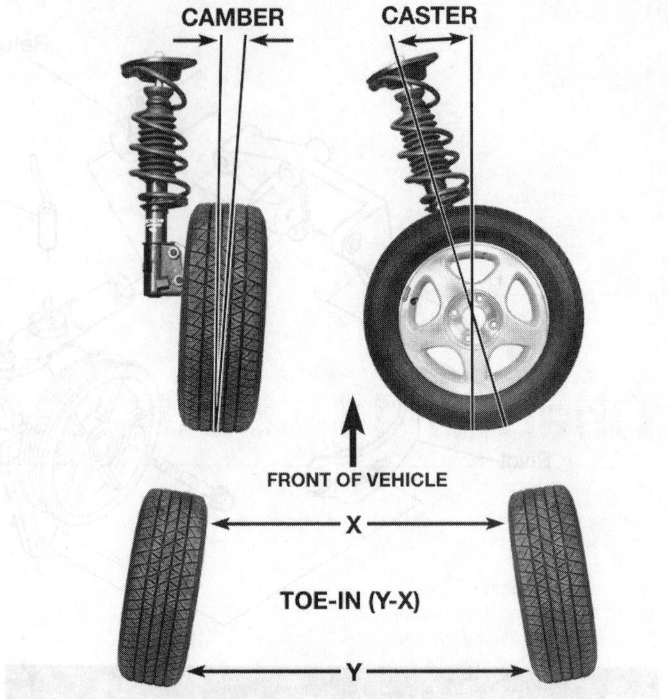

23.1 Camber, caster and toe-in angles

only one tire is being replaced, be sure it's the same size, type, structure and tread design as the other, with the same or better tread wear rating, traction rating, and temperature rating.

Because tire pressure has a substantial effect on handling and wear, the pressure on all tires should be checked at least once a month or before any extended trips (see Chapter 1). Make sure that tires are not worn below the tread depth wear indicators molded into the tread or depth measured is at least the recommended depth in your owner's manual or as recommended by the tire manufacturer.

These models are factory-equipped with either steel or aluminum wheels. If alkaline compounds (road salt or saltwater) get on aluminum wheels, flush both the outside and inside the wheels with water soon. Wheels must be replaced if they are bent, dented, leak air, have elongated bolt holes, are heavily rusted or corroded, have wobble that is noticeable visually (the radial runout is excessive) or if the lug nuts will not stay tight. Wheel repairs that use welding or peening are not recommended. Never use a temporary spare for more than the prescribed driving distance and speed, and do not use the temporary spare wheel with a standard tire.

When installing/demounting tires, make sure the tire shop uses a "non-contact" tire mounting machine if you have aluminum wheels. Tire and wheel balance is important in the overall handling, braking, and performance of the vehicle. Unbalanced wheels can adversely affect handling and ride characteristics as well as tire life. Whenever a tire is installed on a wheel, the tire and wheel should be balanced by a shop with the proper equipment. Make sure the tire shop uses an off-vehicle tire balancer whenever balancing the wheels/tires, or damage to the front transaxle could result.

Rotate tires front to back, and back to front. Do not include "Temporary Use Only" spare tire in the tire rotation.

23 Wheel alignment - general information

Refer to illustration 23.1

A wheel alignment refers to the adjustments made to the wheels so they are in proper angular relationship to the suspension and the ground. Wheels that are out of proper alignment not only affect vehicle control, but also increase tire wear. The front end angles normally measured are camber, caster and toe-in **(see illustration)**. On the front end, toe-in and camber are adjustable. The only adjustment possible on the rear is toe-in. The other angles should be measured to check for bent or worn suspension parts.

Getting the proper wheel alignment is a very exacting process, requiring complicated alignment machines to perform the job properly. Because of this, you should have a shop with a four-wheel alignment machine and technician with the proper training to properly perform these tasks. However, we give the following information describing the basic idea of what is involved with wheel alignment so you can better understand the process and deal intelligently with the shop that does the work.

Toe-in is the turning in of the wheels. The purpose of a toe specification is to ensure stability with controlled parallel rolling of the wheels. In a vehicle with zero toe-in, the distance between the front edges of the wheels will be the same as the distance between the rear edges of the wheels. The actual amount of toe-in is normally only a fraction of an inch. On the front end, toe-in is adjusted by the tie-rod end position on the tie-rod. On the rear end, it is adjusted by an adjuster on the rear suspension lateral link arm. Incorrect toe-in will cause the tires to wear , by making them scrub excessively on the road surface, and will cause the vehicle to be less stable, especially during straight line driving.

Camber is the tilt of the wheels from vertical when viewed from the end of the vehicle. When the wheels tilt out at the top, camber is positive (+). When the wheels tilt in at the top, camber is negative (-). The amount of tilt is measured in degrees from vertical; this measurement is the camber angle. This angle affects the amount of tire tread which contacts the road and compensates for changes in the suspension geometry when the vehicle is cornering or traveling over varying surfaces. It is adjusted on the front end by replacing the lower strut-to-steering knuckle bolt with a special adjusting bolt.

Caster is the tilting of the front steering axis from the vertical. A tilt toward the rear is positive caster and a tilt toward the front is negative caster. Caster is for directional stability by causing the steering to tend to return to center.

Chapter 11 Body

Contents

1 General information

The models covered by this manual feature a "unibody" construction, using a floor pan with front and rear frame side rails which support the body components, front and rear suspension systems and other mechanical components. Certain components are particularly vulnerable to accident damage and can be unbolted and repaired or replaced. Among these parts are the body moldings, bumpers, hood and trunk lids and all glass.

Only general body maintenance practices and body panel repair procedures within the scope of the do-it-yourselfer are included in this Chapter.

2 Body - maintenance

1 The condition of your vehicle's body is very important, because the resale value depends a great deal on it. It's much more difficult to repair a neglected or damaged body than it is to repair mechanical components. The hidden areas of the body, such as the wheel wells, the frame and the engine compartment, are equally important, although they don't require as frequent attention as the rest of the body.

2 Once a year, or every 12,000 miles, it is good to have the underside of the body steam cleaned. All traces of dirt and oil will be removed and the area can then be inspected carefully for rust, damaged brake lines, frayed electrical wires, damaged cables and other problems. The front suspension components should be greased after completion of this job.

3 At the same time, clean the engine and the engine compartment with a steam cleaner or water soluble degreaser.

4 The wheel wells should be given close attention, since undercoating can peel away and stones and dirt thrown up by the tires can cause the paint to chip and flake, allowing rust to set in. If rust is found, clean down to the bare metal and apply an anti-rust paint.

5 The body should be washed about once a week. Wet the vehicle thoroughly to soften the dirt, then wash it down with a soft sponge and plenty of clean soapy water. If the surplus dirt is not washed off very carefully, it can wear down the paint.

6 Spots of tar or asphalt thrown up from the road should be removed with a cloth soaked in solvent.

7 Once every six months, wax the body and chrome trim. If a chrome cleaner is used to remove rust from any of the vehicle's plated parts, remember that the cleaner also removes part of the chrome, so use it sparingly.

3 Vinyl trim - maintenance

Don't clean vinyl trim with detergents, caustic soap or petroleum-based cleaners. Plain soap and water works just fine, with a soft brush to clean dirt that may be ingrained. Wash the vinyl as frequently as the rest of the vehicle.

After cleaning, application of a high quality rubber and vinyl protectant will help prevent oxidation and cracks. The protectant can also be applied to weatherstripping, vacuum lines and rubber hoses, which often fail as a result of chemical degradation, and to the tires.

4 Upholstery and carpets - maintenance

1 Every three months remove the carpets or mats and clean the interior of the vehicle (more frequently if necessary). Vacuum the upholstery and carpets to remove loose dirt and dust.
2 Leather upholstery requires special care. Stains should be removed with warm water and a very mild soap solution. Use a clean, damp cloth to remove the soap, then wipe again with a dry cloth. Never use alcohol, gasoline, nail polish remover or thinner to clean leather upholstery.
3 After cleaning, regularly treat leather upholstery with a leather wax. Never use car wax on leather upholstery.
4 In areas where the interior of the vehicle is subject to bright sunlight, cover leather seats with a sheet if the vehicle is to be left out for any length of time.

5 Body repair - minor damage

See photo sequence

Repair of minor scratches

1 If the scratch is superficial and does not penetrate to the metal of the body, repair is very simple. Lightly rub the scratched area with a fine rubbing compound to remove loose paint and built-up wax. Rinse the area with clean water.
2 Apply touch-up paint to the scratch, using a small brush. Continue to apply thin layers of paint until the surface of the paint in the scratch is level with the surrounding paint. Allow the new paint at least two weeks to harden, then blend it into the surrounding paint by rubbing with a very fine rubbing compound. Finally, apply a coat of wax to the scratch area.
3 If the scratch has penetrated the paint and exposed the metal of the body, causing the metal to rust, a different repair technique is required. Remove all loose rust from the bottom of the scratch with a pocket knife, then apply rust inhibiting paint to prevent the formation of rust in the future. Using a rubber or nylon applicator, coat the scratched area with glaze-type filler. If required, the filler can be mixed with thinner to provide a very thin paste, which is ideal for filling narrow scratches. Before the glaze filler in the scratch hardens, wrap a piece of smooth cotton cloth around the tip of a finger. Dip the cloth in thinner and then quickly wipe it along the surface of the scratch. This will ensure that the surface of the filler is slightly hollow. The scratch can now be painted over as described earlier in this Section.

Repair of dents

4 When repairing dents, the first job is to pull the dent out until the affected area is as close as possible to its original shape. There is no point in trying to restore the original shape completely as the metal in the damaged area will have stretched on impact and cannot be restored to its original contours. It is better to bring the level of the dent up to a point which is about 1/8-inch below the level of the surrounding metal. In cases where the dent is very shallow, it is not worth trying to pull it out at all.
5 If the back side of the dent is accessible, it can be hammered out gently from behind using a soft-face hammer. While doing this, hold a block of wood firmly against the opposite side of the metal to absorb the hammer blows and prevent the metal from being stretched.
6 If the dent is in a section of the body which has double layers, or some other factor makes it inaccessible from behind, a different technique is required. Drill several small holes through the metal inside the damaged area, particularly in the deeper sections. Screw long, self-tapping screws into the holes just enough for them to get a good grip in the metal. Now the dent can be pulled out by pulling on the protruding heads of the screws with locking pliers.
7 The next stage of repair is the removal of paint from the damaged area and from an inch or so of the surrounding metal. This is done with a wire brush or sanding disk in a drill motor, although it can be done just as effectively by hand with sandpaper. To complete the preparation for filling, score the surface of the bare metal with a screwdriver or the tang of a file, or drill small holes in the affected area. This will provide a good grip for the filler material. To complete the repair, see the subsection on filling and painting later in this Section.

Repair of rust holes or gashes

8 Remove all paint from the affected area and from an inch or so of the surrounding metal using a sanding disk or wire brush mounted in a drill motor. If these are not available, a few sheets of sandpaper will do the job just as effectively.
9 With the paint removed, you will be able to determine the severity of the corrosion and decide whether to replace the whole panel, if possible, or repair the affected area. New body panels are not as expensive as most people think and it is often quicker to install a new panel than to repair large areas of rust.
10 Remove all trim pieces from the affected area except those which will act as a guide to the original shape of the damaged body, such as headlight shells, etc. Using metal snips or a hacksaw blade, remove all loose metal and any other metal that is badly affected by rust. Hammer the edges of the hole in to create a slight depression for the filler material.
11 Wire brush the affected area to remove the powdery rust from the surface of the metal. If the back of the rusted area is accessible, treat it with rust inhibiting paint.
12 Before filling is done, block the hole in some way. This can be done with sheet metal riveted or screwed into place, or by stuffing the hole with wire mesh.
13 Once the hole is blocked off, the affected area can be filled and painted. See the following subsection on filling and painting.

Filling and painting

14 Many types of body fillers are available, but generally speaking, body repair kits which contain filler paste and a tube of resin hardener are best for this type of repair work. A wide, flexible plastic or nylon applicator will be necessary for imparting a smooth and contoured finish to the surface of the filler material. Mix up a small amount of filler on a clean piece of wood or cardboard (use the hardener sparingly). Follow the manufacturer's instructions on the package, otherwise the filler will set incorrectly.
15 Using the applicator, apply the filler paste to the prepared area. Draw the applicator across the surface of the filler to achieve the desired contour and to level the filler surface. As soon as a contour that approximates the original one is achieved, stop working the paste. If you continue, the paste will begin to stick to the applicator. Continue to add thin layers of paste at 20-minute intervals until the level of the filler is just above the surrounding metal.
16 Once the filler has hardened, the excess can be removed with a body file. From then on, progressively finer grades of sandpaper should be used, starting with a 180-grit paper and finishing with 600-grit wet-or-dry paper. Always wrap the sandpaper around a flat rubber or wooden block, otherwise the surface of the filler will not be completely flat. During the sanding of the filler surface, the wet-or-dry paper should be periodically rinsed in water. This will ensure that a very smooth finish is produced in the final stage.
17 At this point, the repair area should be surrounded by a ring of bare metal, which in turn should be encircled by the finely feathered edge of good paint. Rinse the repair area with clean water until all of the dust produced by the sanding operation is gone.
18 Spray the entire area with a light coat of primer. This will reveal any imperfections in the surface of the filler. Repair the imperfections with fresh filler paste or glaze filler and once more smooth the surface with sandpaper. Repeat this spray-and-repair procedure until you are satisfied that the surface of the filler and the feathered edge of the paint are perfect. Rinse the area with clean water and allow it to dry completely.
19 The repair area is now ready for painting. Spray painting must be carried out in a warm, dry, windless and dust-free atmosphere. These conditions can be created if you have access to a large indoor work

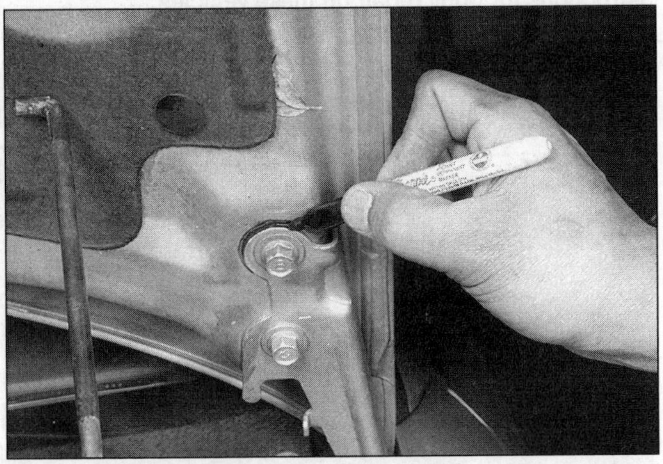

9.1 Before removing the hood, mark around the hinge plate

area, but if you are forced to work in the open, you will have to pick the day very carefully. If you are working indoors, dousing the floor in the work area with water will help settle the dust which would otherwise be in the air. If the repair area is confined to one body panel, mask off the surrounding panels. This will help minimize the effects of a slight mismatch in paint color. Trim pieces such as chrome strips, door handles, etc., will also need to be masked off or removed. Use masking tape and several thickness of newspaper for the masking operations.

20 Before spraying, shake the paint can thoroughly, then spray a test area until the spray painting technique is mastered. Cover the repair area with a thick coat of primer. The thickness should be built up using several thin layers of primer rather than one thick one. Using 600-grit wet-or-dry sandpaper, rub down the surface of the primer until it is very smooth. While doing this, the work area should be thoroughly rinsed with water and the wet-or-dry sandpaper periodically rinsed as well. Allow the primer to dry before spraying additional coats.

21 Spray on the top coat, again building up the thickness by using several thin layers of paint. Begin spraying in the center of the repair area and then, using a circular motion, work out until the whole repair area and about two inches of the surrounding original paint is covered. Remove all masking material 10 to 15 minutes after spraying on the final coat of paint. Allow the new paint at least two weeks to harden, then use a very fine rubbing compound to blend the edges of the new paint into the existing paint. Finally, apply a coat of wax.

6 Body repair - major damage

1 Major damage must be repaired by an auto body shop specifically equipped to perform unibody repairs. These shops have the specialized equipment required to do the job properly.

2 If the damage is extensive, the body must be checked for proper alignment or the vehicle's handling characteristics may be adversely affected and other components may wear at an accelerated rate.

3 Due to the fact that all of the major body components (hood, fenders, etc.) are separate and replaceable units, any seriously damaged components should be replaced rather than repaired. Sometimes the components can be found in a wrecking yard that specializes in used vehicle components, often at considerable savings over the cost of new parts.

7 Hinges and locks - maintenance

Once every 5000 miles, or every four months, the hinges and latch assemblies on the doors, hood and trunk should be given a few drops of light oil or lock lubricant. The door latch strikers should also be lubricated with a thin coat of grease to reduce wear and ensure free movement. Lubricate the door and trunk locks with spray-on graphite lubricant.

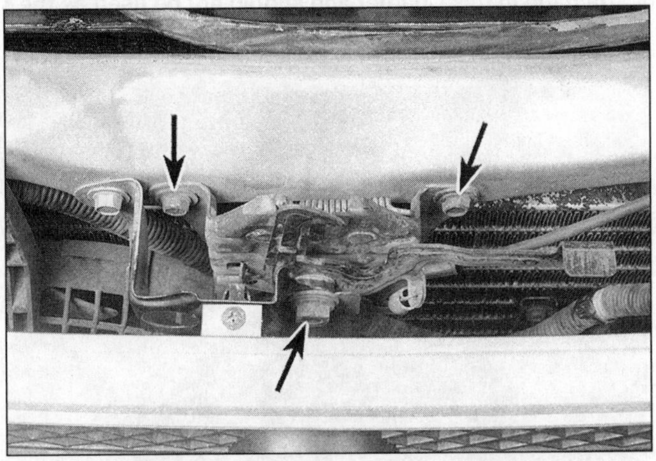

9.10 Loosen the hood latch mounting bolts (arrows and additional bolts below), reposition the latch and retighten bolts, then close the hood to check the fit - repeat the procedure until the hood is flush with the fenders

8 Windshield and fixed glass - replacement

Replacement of the windshield and fixed glass requires the use of special fast-setting adhesive/caulk materials and some specialized tools. It is recommended that these operations be left to a dealer or a shop specializing in glass work.

9 Hood - removal, installation and adjustment

Refer to illustrations 9.1, 9.10 and 9.11

Note: *The hood is heavy and somewhat awkward to remove and install - at least two people should perform this procedure.*

Removal and installation

1 Scribe or felt tip marks around the hinges to ensure proper alignment during reinstallation **(see illustration)**.

2 Use blankets or pads to cover the cowl area of the body and fenders. This will protect the body and paint as the hood is removed.

3 Disconnect the windshield washer tube at the hood.

4 Have an assistant support the hood. Remove the hinge-to-hood bolts.

5 Lift off the hood.

6 Installation is the reverse of removal.

Adjustment

7 Fore-and-aft and side-to-side adjustment of the hood is done by moving the hinge plate slot after loosening the bolts.

8 Scribe or felt tip mark a line around the entire hinge plate so you can judge the amount of movement **(see illustration 9.1)**.

9 Loosen the bolts or nuts and move the hood into correct alignment. Move it only a little at a time. Tighten the hinge bolts and carefully lower the hood to check the position.

10 If necessary after installation, the entire hood latch assembly can be adjusted up-and-down as well as from side-to-side on the radiator support so the hood closes securely, and is flush with the fenders. To make the adjustment, scribe or felt tip mark a line around the hood latch mounting bolts to aid alignment when reinstalling, then loosen the bolts and reposition the latch assembly to align with the striker on the hood, as necessary **(see illustration)**. Following adjustment, retighten the mounting bolts.

These photos illustrate a method of repairing simple dents. They are intended to supplement *Body repair - minor damage* in this Chapter and should not be used as the sole instructions for body repair on these vehicles.

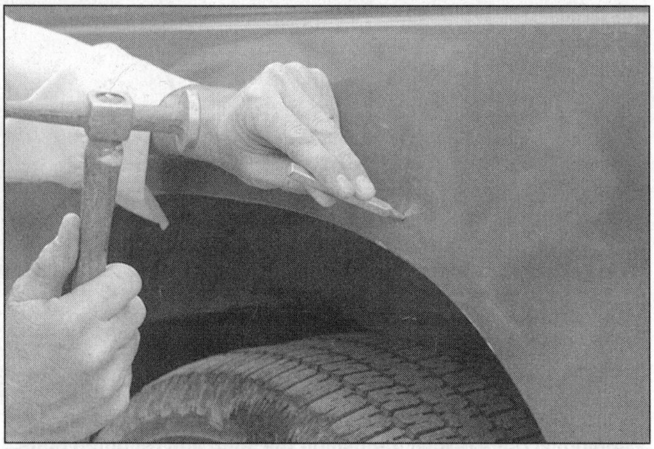

1 If you can't access the backside of the body panel to hammer out the dent, pull it out with a slide-hammer-type dent puller. In the deepest portion of the dent or along the crease line, drill or punch hole(s) at least one inch apart . . .

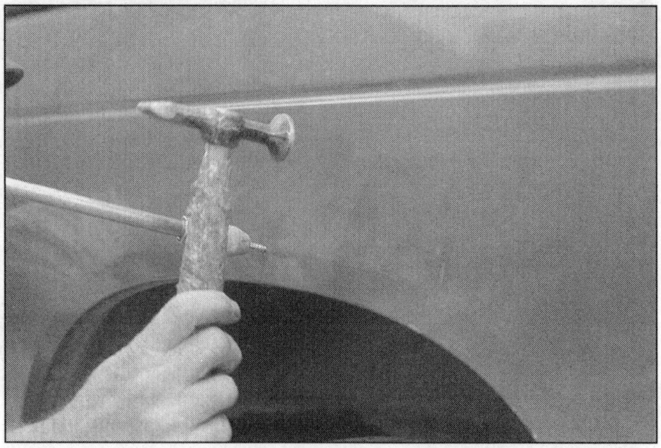

2 . . . then screw the slide-hammer into the hole and operate it. Tap with a hammer near the edge of the dent to help 'pop' the metal back to its original shape. When you're finished, the dent area should be close to its original contour and about 1/8-inch below the surface of the surrounding metal

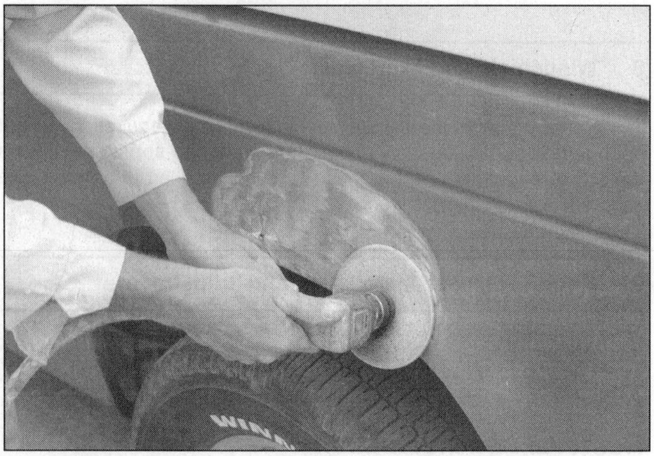

3 Using coarse-grit sandpaper, remove the paint down to the bare metal. Hand sanding works fine, but the disc sander shown here makes the job faster. Use finer (about 320-grit) sandpaper to feather-edge the paint at least one inch around the dent area

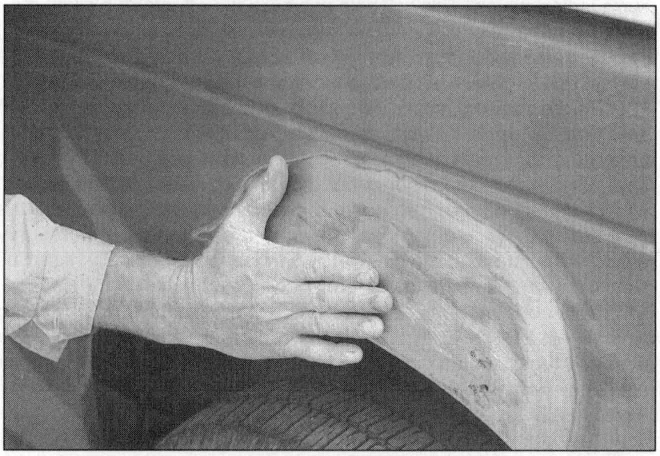

4 When the paint is removed, touch will probably be more helpful than sight for telling if the metal is straight. Hammer down the high spots or raise the low spots as necessary. Clean the repair area with wax/silicone remover

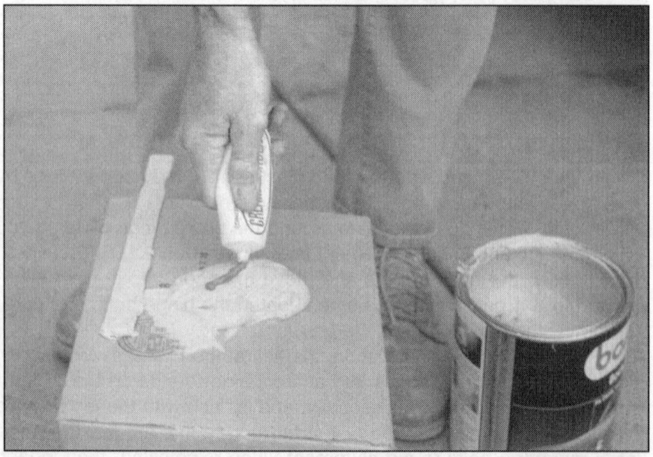

5 Following label instructions, mix up a batch of plastic filler and hardener. The ratio of filler to hardener is critical, and, if you mix it incorrectly, it will either not cure properly or cure too quickly (you won't have time to file and sand it into shape)

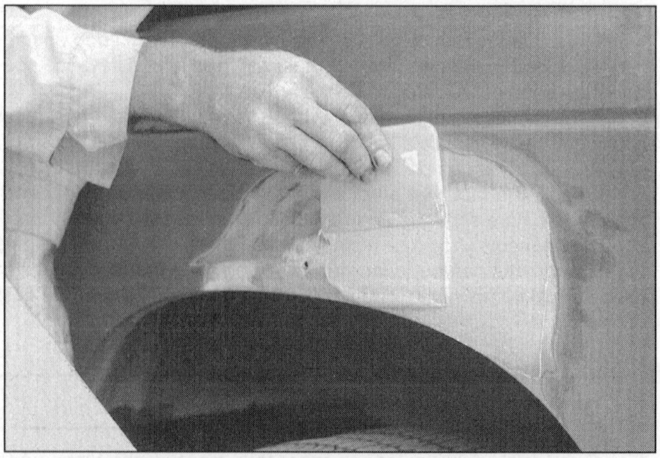

6 Working quickly so the filler doesn't harden, use a plastic applicator to press the body filler firmly into the metal, assuring it bonds completely. Work the filler until it matches the original contour and is slightly above the surrounding metal

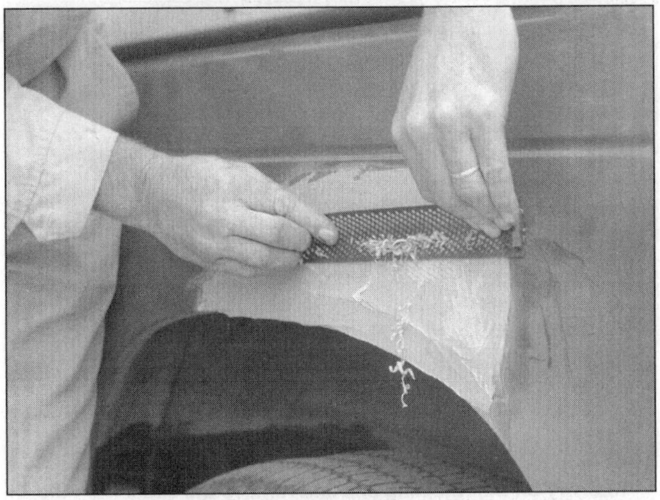

7 Let the filler harden until you can just dent it with your fingernail. Use a body file or Surform tool (shown here) to rough-shape the filler

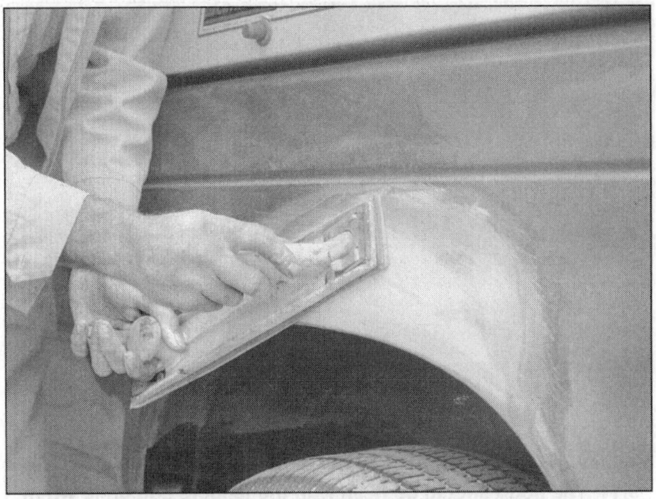

8 Use coarse-grit sandpaper and a sanding board or block to work the filler down until it's smooth and even. Work down to finer grits of sandpaper - always using a board or block - ending up with 360 or 400 grit

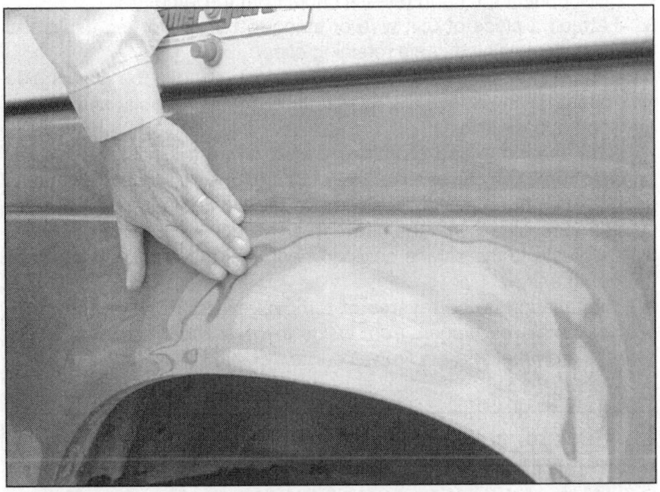

9 You shouldn't be able to feel any ridge at the transition from the filler to the bare metal or from the bare metal to the old paint. As soon as the repair is flat and uniform, remove the dust and mask off the adjacent panels or trim pieces

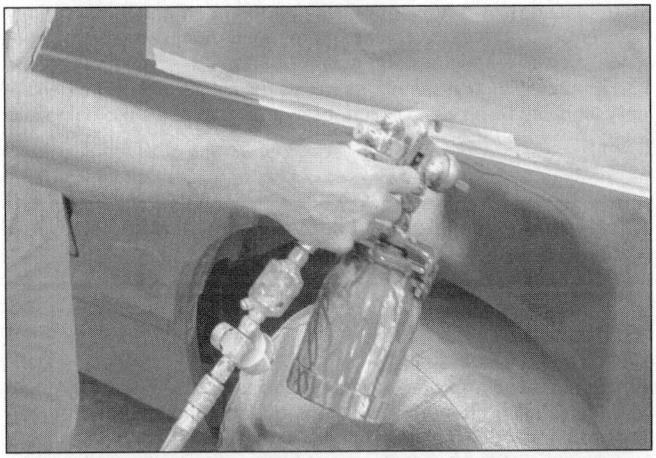

10 Apply several layers of primer to the area. Don't spray the primer on too heavy, so it sags or runs, and make sure each coat is dry before you spray on the next one. A professional-type spray gun is being used here, but aerosol spray primer is available inexpensively from auto parts stores

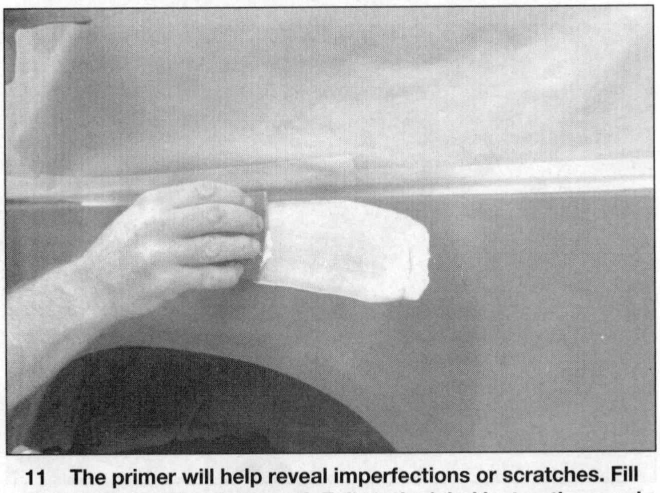

11 The primer will help reveal imperfections or scratches. Fill these with glazing compound. Follow the label instructions and sand it with 360 or 400-grit sandpaper until it's smooth. Repeat the glazing, sanding and respraying until the primer reveals a perfectly smooth surface

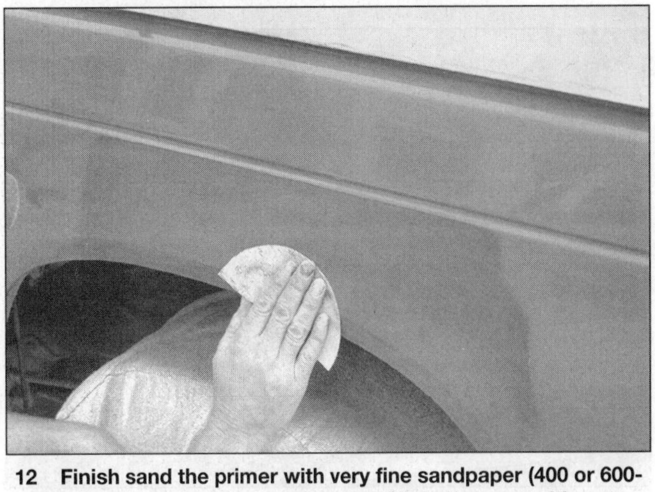

12 Finish sand the primer with very fine sandpaper (400 or 600-grit) to remove the primer overspray. Clean the area with water and allow it to dry. Use a tack rag to remove any dust, then apply the finish coat. Don't attempt to rub out or wax the repair area until the paint has dried completely (at least two weeks)

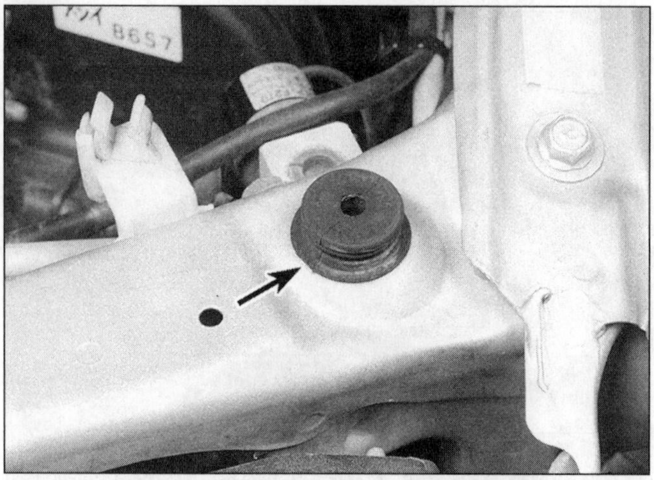

9.11 The hood should be flush with the fenders and grille when the latch is adjusted properly and the bumpers support the hood

11 The hood bumpers on the body and on the hood should support the hood so that the hood is flush with the fenders **(see illustration)** when closed. **Note:** *Adjust the latch so the hood engages securely when closed and the hood bumpers are slightly compressed for proper alignment with the fenders and grille.*

12 The hood latch assembly, as well as the hinges, should be periodically lubricated with white lithium-base grease to prevent binding and wear.

10 Hood release latch and cable - removal and installation

Latch

Refer to illustration 10.2

1 Scribe or felt tip mark a line around the latch to aid alignment when reinstalling, then remove the hood latch mounting bolts **(see illustration 9.10)**. Remove the latch.

2 Disconnect the hood release cable by removing the cable retaining clip near the hood latch and disengaging the cable from the latch assembly **(see illustration)**.

3 Installation is the reverse of removal. **Note:** *Adjust the latch so the hood engages securely when closed and the hood bumpers are slightly compressed* (see Section 9).

10.2 Pry off the retaining clip and remove the cable from the latch assembly

Cable

4 Disconnect the hood release cable from the latch.

5 Attach a piece of thin wire or string to the end of the cable and unfasten all remaining cable retaining clips.

6 Working in the passenger compartment, remove the drivers side kick panel. Then remove the release lever mounting bolts and detach the hood release lever.

7 Pull the cable and grommet rearward into the passenger compartment until you can see the wire or string. Ensure that the new cable has a grommet attached, then remove the old cable from the wire or string and replace it with the new cable.

8 Working in the engine compartment, pull the wire or string back through the firewall.

9 Installation is the reverse of removal. **Note:** *Push on the cable grommet with your fingers from inside the passenger compartment to seat the grommet into the firewall correctly.*

11 Radiator grille - removal and installation

Refer to illustrations 11.1a, 11.1b and 11.1c

1 On 1990 through 1994 models, remove radiator grille by removing the grille screw shown and pulling the grille away from the body **(see illustrations)**, using a small screwdriver if necessary at the grille attachment clips to release the clips. Check the condition of the clips

11.1a For 1990 through 1994 models, remove the grille clip retaining screw . . .

11.1b . . . and pull off the radiator grille. Check the condition of the clips

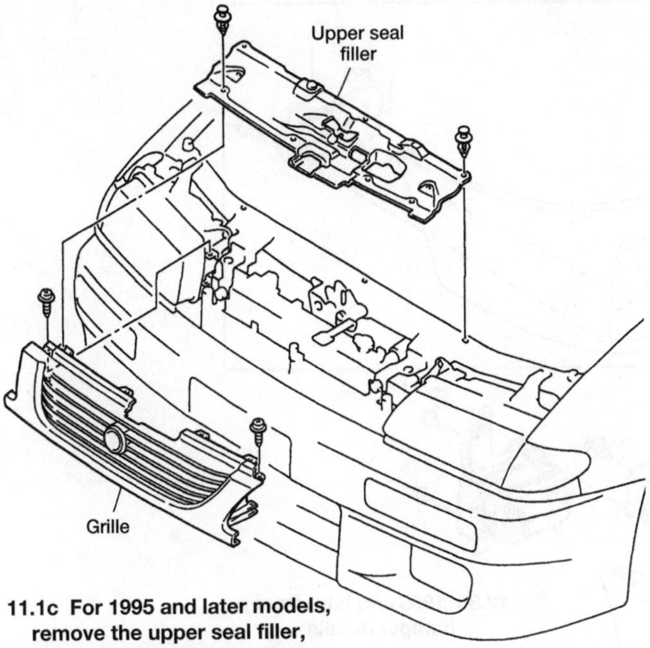

11.1c For 1995 and later models, remove the upper seal filler, remove the two grille retaining screws, and lift off the grille

and replace as necessary. On 1995 and later models, remove the upper seal filler, remove the grille screws shown and lift the grille away from the body **(see illustration)**.

2 On 1990 through 1994 models, remove the screw from both front turn signal/running light (combination light), and remove both combination lights.

3 On 1990 through 1994 models, remove the screws from the lower grill moldings and remove both lower grille moldings.

4 Installation is the reverse of removal. **Note:** *When installing the radiator grille, make sure to install grille retaining clips, as applicable, into the grille, align them with the installation holes in the body, and press the grille securely in place.*

12 Bumpers - removal and installation

Refer to illustrations 12.7a, 12.7b, 12.8a, 12.8b, 12.8c, 12.16a, 12.16b, 12.19, 12.20, 12.22a and 12.22b

Note: *The bumper assembly is heavy and somewhat awkward to remove and install - support the bumper when the bolts are removed - have an assistant help you when performing this procedure.*

12.7a Unscrew the bumper cover screw under the fender lip - 1990 through 1994 model shown

Front bumper

1 Apply the parking brake, raise the vehicle and support it securely on jackstands. Remove the under cover splash shield. Open the hood.

2 Disconnect the cable from the negative battery terminal and disconnect any wiring that would interfere with bumper removal.

3 Remove the screws from both front turn signal/running lights (combination lights) and remove both combination lights.

4 Remove the radiator grille (see Section 11).

5 Remove the headlights (see Chapter 12).

6 Remove the screws from the lower grill moldings and remove both lower grille moldings.

7 Remove the screw(s) attaching the bumper fascia (bumper cover) to the fender at the area of the wheel cutout, and on 1990 through 1994 models, remove the screws retaining the bumper cover at the grille area **(see illustrations)**.

8 On 1990 through 1994 models, working under the bumper, remove the attaching screws at both angle brackets **(see illustration)** and then remove the front bumper reinforcement (main steel beam attached to the body) by removing the bumper reinforcement retention bolts **(see illustration)**. On 1995 and later models, working under the bumper, remove the attaching screws along the bottom of the bumper cover. Then remove the front bumper reinforcement nuts from the body attachment points in the grille area **(see illustration)**. Carefully remove the bumper while disconnecting the front turn signal light connectors, and lower the bumper to the floor or to padded wooden

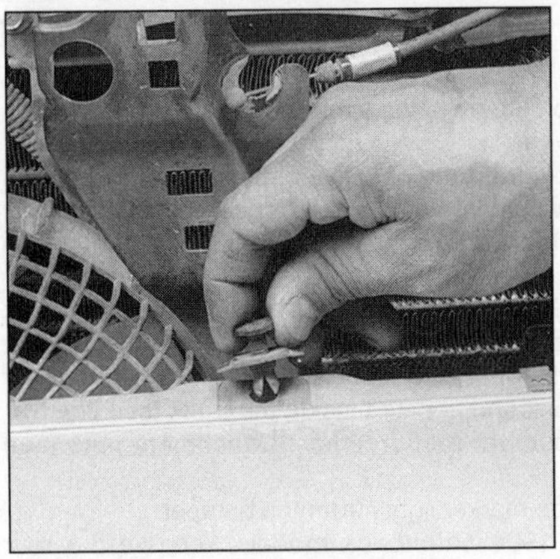

12.7b Unscrew and pull out the bumper cover fasteners at the grille area - 1990 through 1994 model shown

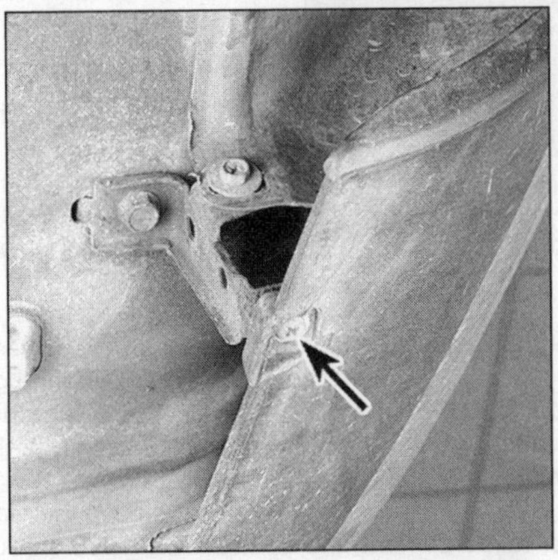

12.8a Remove the bumper angle bracket screws, located near the wheel opening - 1990 through 1994 shown

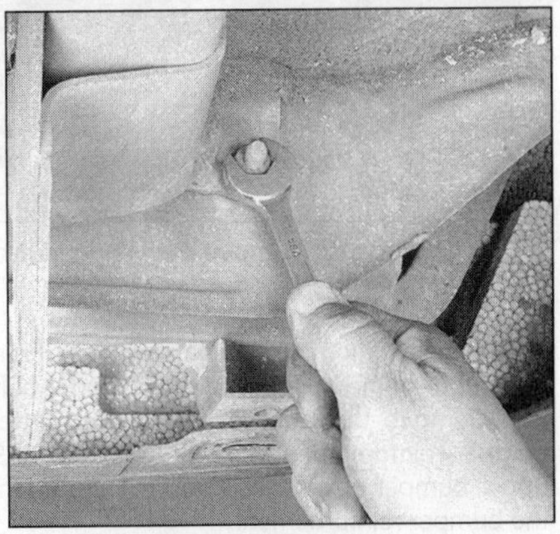

12.8b Under the vehicle, remove the bumper reinforcement bolts, and remove the bumper cover - 1990 through 1994 shown

11

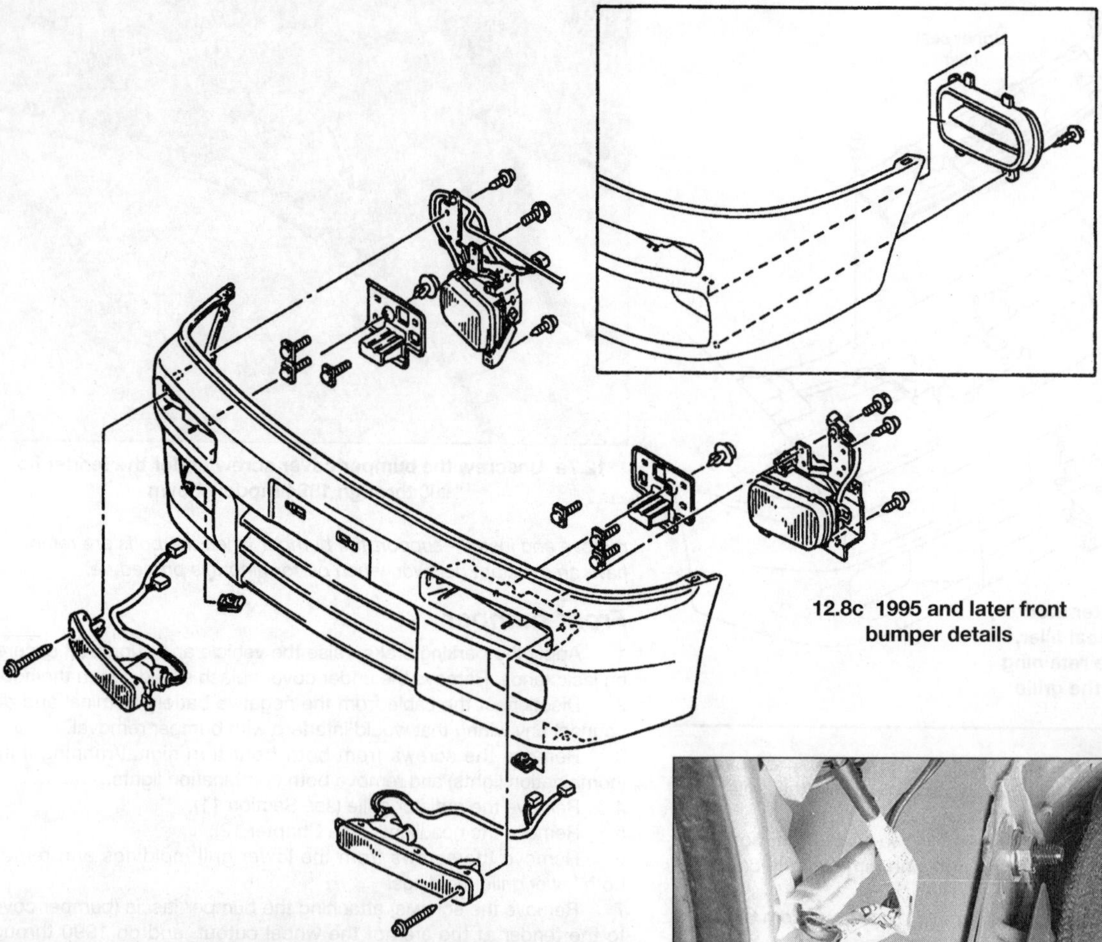

12.8c 1995 and later front bumper details

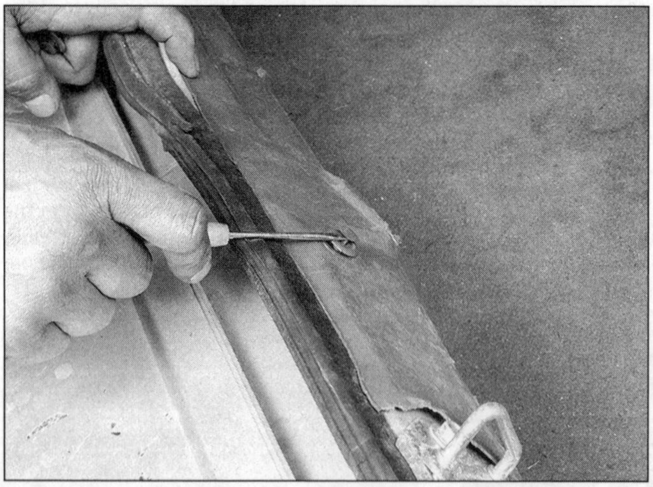

12.16a Remove the inside trunk end trim . . .

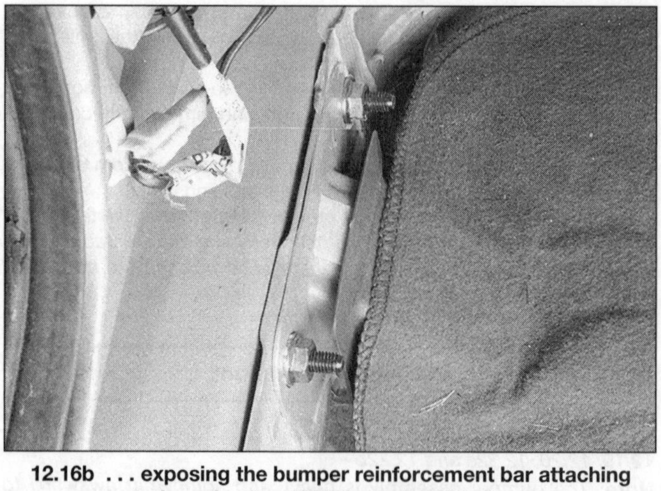

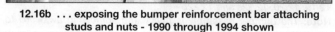

12.16b . . . exposing the bumper reinforcement bar attaching studs and nuts - 1990 through 1994 shown

blocks for additional disassembly below. Front fender removal can be done at this time by removal of the fender bolts.

9 Remove the bumper cover bolts attaching the cover to the bumper reinforcement. On 1990 through 1994 models, push out the upper bumper cover tabs that are inserted into the slots at the top of the bumper reinforcement.

10 Remove the bumper cover from the bumper reinforcement and remove the energy-absorbing foam, located between the cover and reinforcement.

11 Installation is the reverse of the removal procedure.

Rear bumper

12 Apply the parking brake, raise the vehicle and support it securely on jackstands.

13 Disconnect the cable from the negative battery terminal and disconnect any wiring that would interfere with bumper removal.

14 Remove the rear stop/turn signal light (combination lights) (see Chapter 12).

15 On 1990 through 1994 models, inside the trunk, remove the trunk end trim. On 1995 and later models, remove the trunk side trim panels.

16 On 1990 through 1994 Protegé models, remove the two bumper bracket covers at the trunk end, located inside the trunk **(see illustration)** and remove the bumper reinforcement attachment nuts **(see illustration)**.

17 Remove the rear side marker lights from the bumper.

18 On 1990 through 1994 hatchback models, remove the rear license plate light.

19 On 1990 through 1994 models, remove the rear bumper retainer bar, along the top of the bumper assembly. On 1995 and later models,

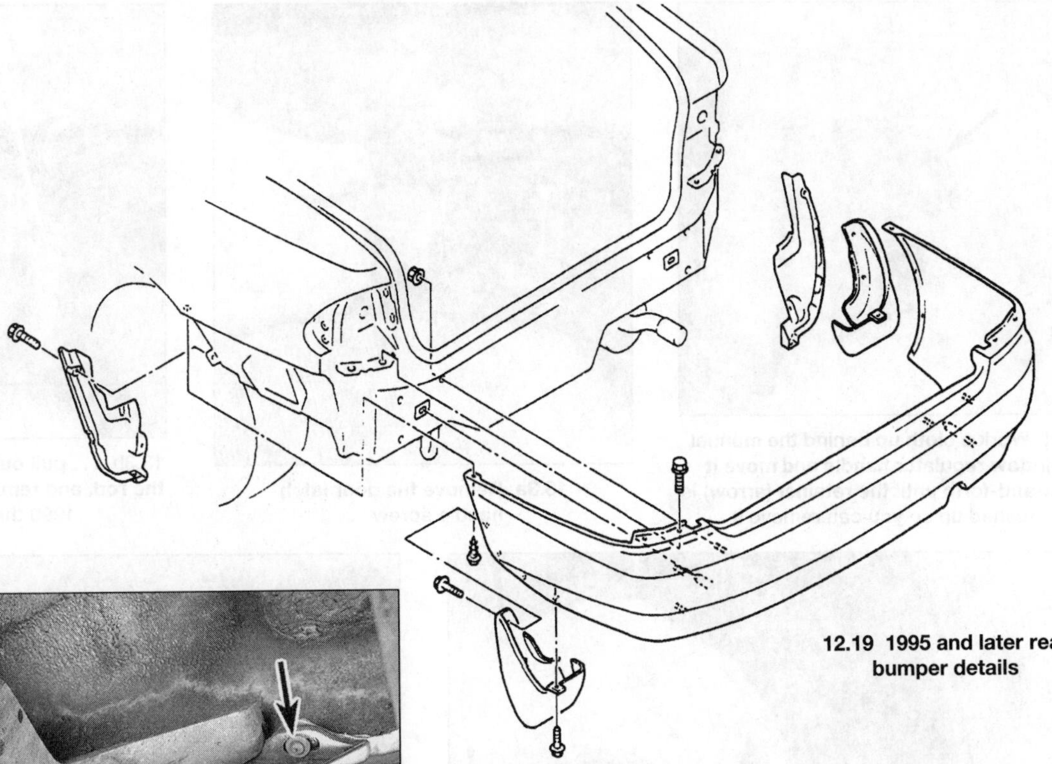

12.19 1995 and later rear bumper details

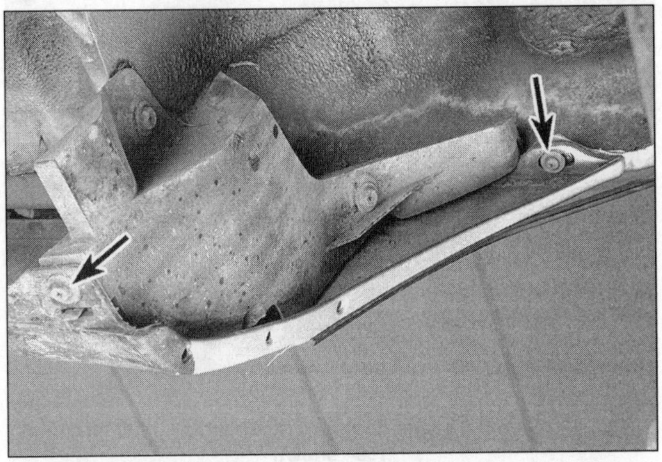

12.20 Remove the bumper cover screws at the wheel openings - 1990 through 1994 shown

remove the rear wheel cutout extensions (flaps and splash shields), remove the bolts under the bumper cover, on the top of the bumper cover, and the nuts inside the trunk **(see illustration)**.

20 On 1990 through 1994 Protegé models, remove the screws attaching the bumper cover to the fender at the area of the wheel cutout **(see illustration)**.

21 On 1990 through 1994 models, working under the bumper, remove the rear bumper reinforcement (main steel beam attached to the body) by removing the bumper reinforcement retention bolts. Carefully lower the bumper part way, supporting the hatchback model bumper while its license plate wiring harness and license plate holder are removed. Carefully lower the bumper fully onto padded wooden blocks for additional disassembly below.

22 On 1990 through 1994 models, remove the bumper cover bolts attaching the cover to the bumper reinforcement **(see illustrations)**. Remove the bumper cover from the bumper reinforcement and the energy-absorbing foam, located between the cover and reinforcement.

23 On 1995 and later models, remove the bumper cover bolts attaching the cover to the bumper reinforcement, and remove the bumper cover from the bumper reinforcement and the energy-absorb-

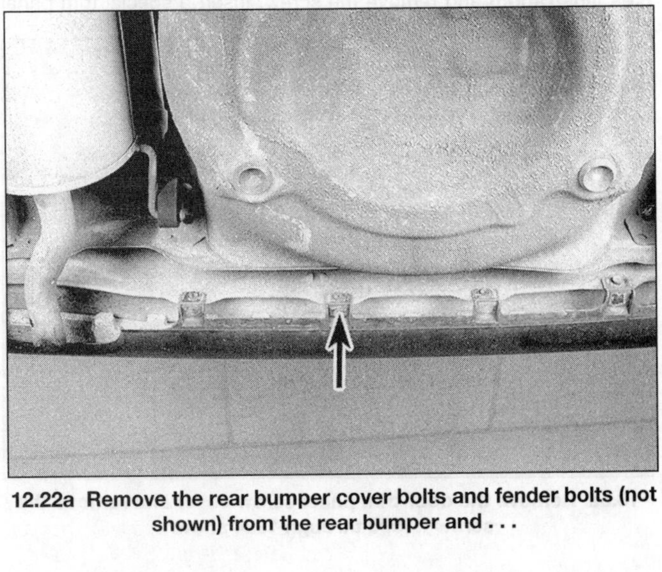

12.22a Remove the rear bumper cover bolts and fender bolts (not shown) from the rear bumper and . . .

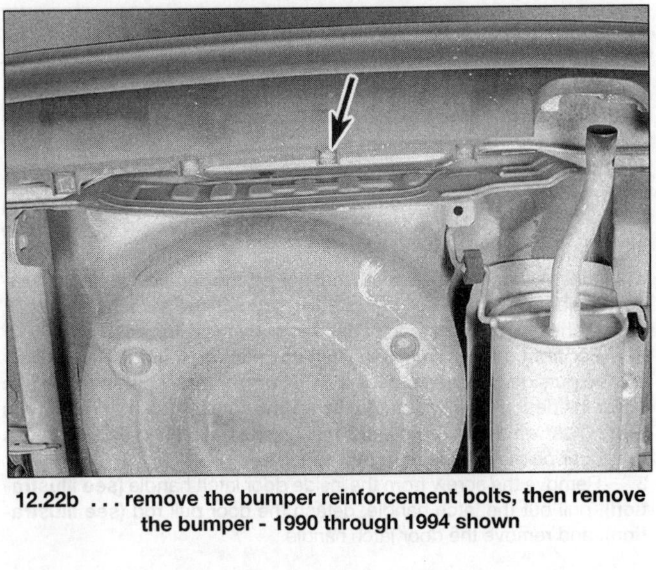

12.22b . . . remove the bumper reinforcement bolts, then remove the bumper - 1990 through 1994 shown

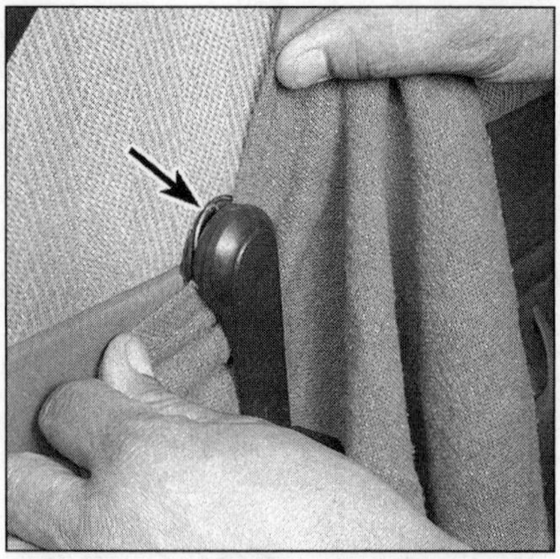

13.1 Work a cloth up behind the manual window regulator handle and move it back-and-forth until the retainer (arrow) is pushed up so you can remove it

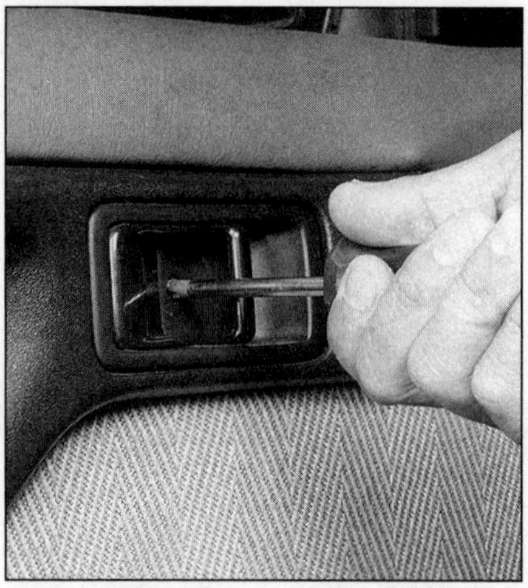

13.3a Remove the door latch handle screw . . .

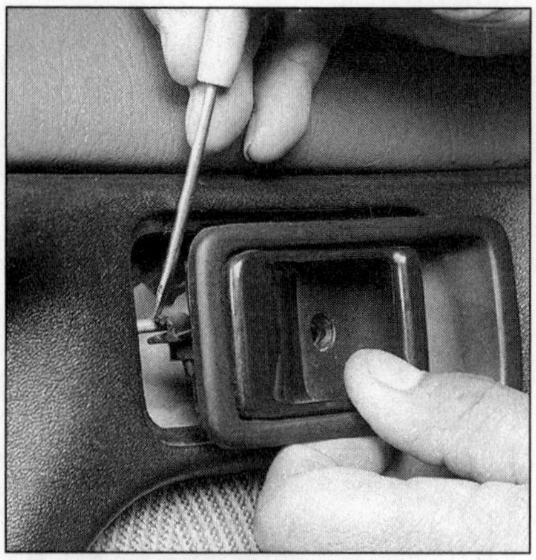

13.3b . . . pull out the latch handle, detach the rod, and remove the door latch handle - 1990 through 1994 shown

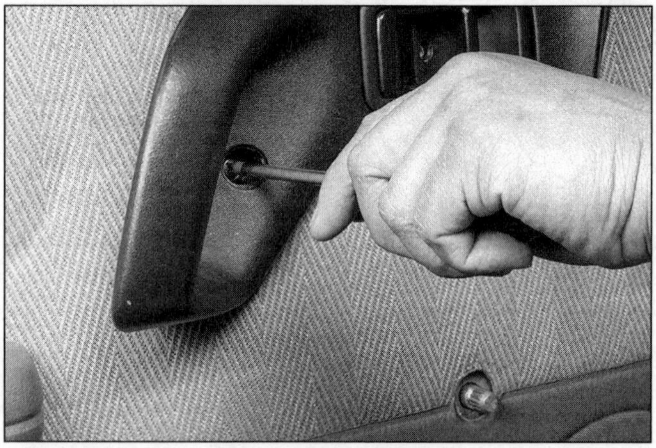

13.4 Remove the screw cap and screw from the door latch cover - 1990 through 1994 shown

13.5 Remove the inside door arm rest/handle - 1990 through 1994 shown

ing foam. Remove the side marker lights and other attached parts as required.

24 On 1990 through 1994 models, remove both rear mud flaps as necessary.

25 Installation is the reverse of the removal procedure.

13 Door trim panel - removal and installation

Refer to illustrations 13.1, 13.3a, 13.3b, 13.4, 13.5, 13.6a, 13.6b and 13.8

Removal

1 On manual window models, remove the window crank by working a cloth back-and-forth behind the handle to dislodge the retainer **(see illustration)**. A special tool is available for this purpose, but it is not essential. With the retainer removed, pull off the handle. On power window models, disconnect the battery, pry out the switch assembly, unplug the electrical connector and remove the switch assembly.

2 For front doors, remove the trim cover inside the door which covers the outside mirror (see Section 26). For rear doors, remove the trim cover inside the door which fills the widow corner area. For rear doors with power windows, remove the pull handle bracket screw, located in the finger pocket on the door trim panel.

3 Remove the screw from the inside door latch handle **(see illustration)**, pull out the latch handle, detach the door pull rod **(see illustration)**, and remove the door latch handle.

4 Remove the screw trim cap and screw from the door latch handle trim panel **(see illustration)**. On 1995 and later front doors, remove the door panel reflector.

5 On 1990 through 1994 models, remove the inside door arm rest/handle **(see illustration)**.

6 Remove the door trim panel screw cover (1990 through 1994) **(see illustration)** and remove the screw. Insert a special trim panel

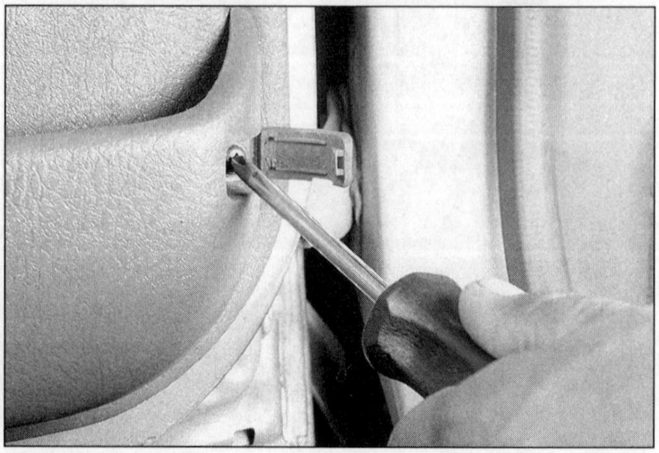

13.6a Remove the door trim panel screw cover and remove the screw - 1990 through 1994 shown

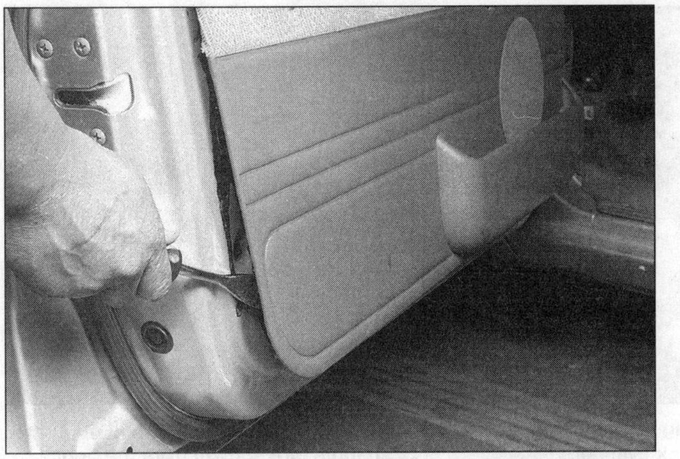

13.6b Use a trim panel removal tool to detach the trim panel retaining clips, then pull the door trim up and out to remove it

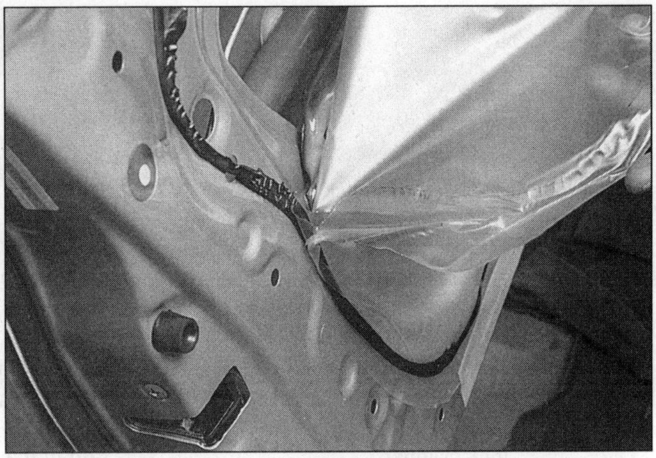

13.8 If the plastic watershield is peeled off carefully, it can be reused

removal tool, a wide putty knife, or a thin screwdriver between the door trim panel and door to disengage the door trim retaining clips. Work around the outer edge until the panel is loose **(see illustration)**.

7 Make sure all of the door trim retaining clips are disengaged. Remove the door trim panel from the vehicle by gently pulling it upwards and out, while disconnecting any electrical connectors.

8 On 1995 and later models, remove the square seal pads between the door trim panel and watershield plastic sheet, or leave it in place if reusing the watershield. For access to inside the door, remove the plastic watershield. Peel back the plastic cover, taking care not to tear it **(see illustration)**.

Installation

9 To install the door trim panel, first press the watershield back into place. If necessary, add more sealant to hold it in place.

10 Prior to installation of the door trim panel, be sure to reinstall any clips which may have come out of the door trim panel during removal.

11 Place the door trim panel in position, making sure that any door panel electrical connectors are connected or routed through the panel as necessary. Press the door trim panel into place until the clips are seated.

12 On 1990 through 1994 models, reinstall and securely tighten the arm rest/handle screws. On 1995 and later front doors, reinstall the reflector on the door trim panel.

13 For front doors, reinstall the outside mirror trim cover, located on the inside of the door. For rear doors with power window, install the pull handle bracket screw, located in the finger pocket on the door trim panel.

14 Reinstall the inside door handle.

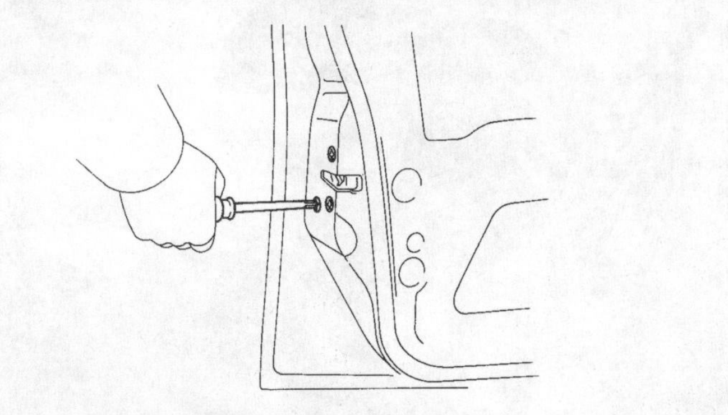

14.3 Remove the latch screws from the end of the door

15 Install the manual window crank or power window switch assembly.

14 Door latch, lock cylinder and handles - removal and installation

1 Remove the door trim panel and the plastic watershield (see Section 13).

Door latch

Refer to illustration 14.3

2 Reach inside the door and disconnect the control links from the latch.

3 Mark the location of the door latch prior to removal. Remove the latch retaining screws from the end of the door **(see illustration)**.

4 Detach the door latch. If equipped with power door locks, remove the door lock solenoid.

5 Installation is the reverse of removal. Align the door latch and tighten the door latch screws securely.

Lock cylinder and outside handle

Refer to illustration 14.6, 14.7, 14.8 and 14.9

6 Through the door inside access hole, remove the outside handle retention bolts/nuts **(see illustration)**. On 1995 and later models, remove the lock cylinder electrical switch retainer and remove the switch.

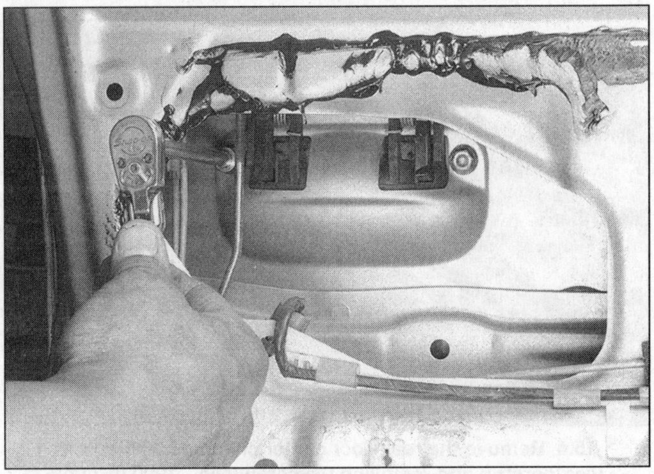

14.6 Remove the outside handle retention bolts/nuts

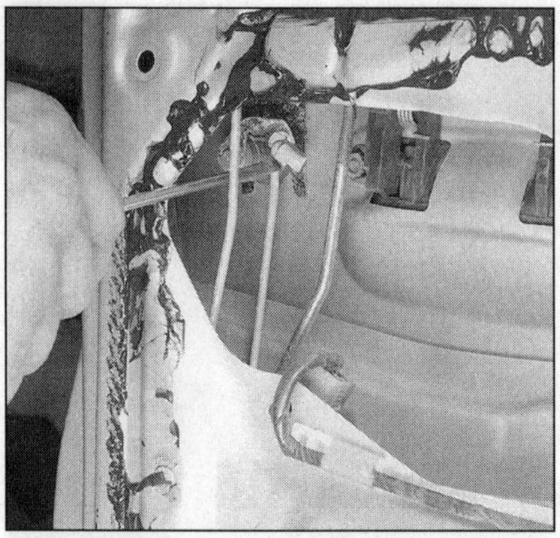

14.7 Remove the control rod from the lock cylinder

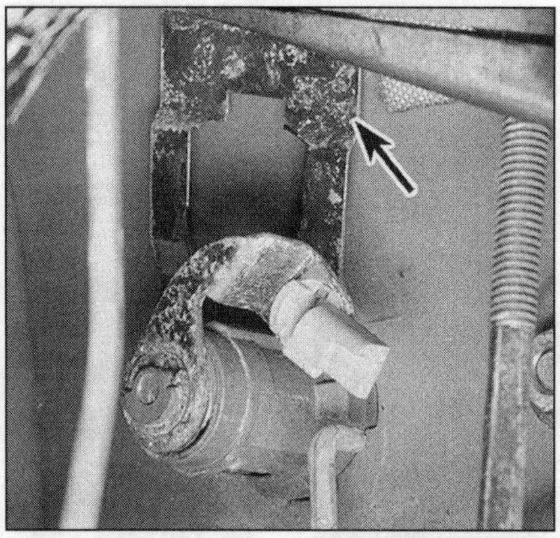

14.8 Pry the retaining clip upwards and off of the lock cylinder

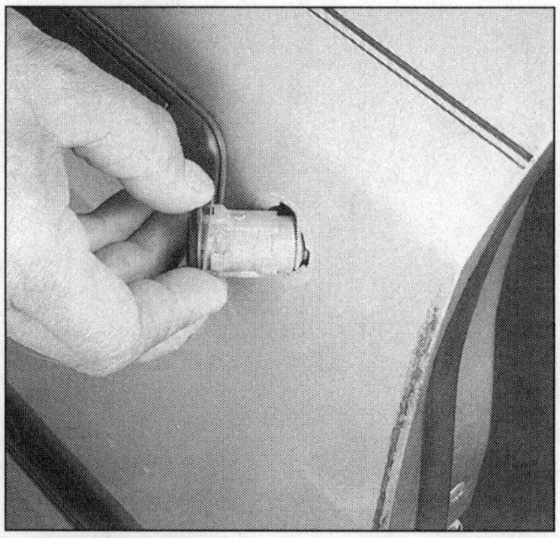

14.9 Pull the lock cylinder and outside handle (not shown) from the door

7 Remove the control rod from the lock cylinder **(see illustration)**.
8 Use a pliers or screwdriver to pry the retaining clip upwards and off of the lock cylinder **(see illustration)**.
9 Pull the outside handle and lock cylinder **(see illustration)** from the door.
10 Installation is the reverse of removal.
11 The door key cylinder electrical switch may be tested if necessary without removal. Disconnect the electrical connector. Check that the electrical continuity between the terminals is 0 ohms (no resistance) when in the unlocked position, and is 1 K-ohms when in the locked position.

Inside handle

12 Refer to Section 13 for removal and installation.

15 Door window glass - removal, installation and adjustment

Refer to illustration 15.4

1 Remove the door trim panel and the plastic watershield (see Section 13).
2 On 1990 through 1994 front windows, open the window to approximately 4 inches from the fully open position. On 1990 through 1994 rear windows, fully open the window. On 1995 and later front windows, fully open the window. On 1995 and later rear windows, raise the glass approximately two inches from fully closed.
3 Disconnect the negative battery cable.
4 On 1990 through 1994 rear door windows, remove the center channel strip by carefully lifting the door weatherstrip on the top of the door, and removing the center channel screw and clip **(see illustration)**. On 1995 and later rear door windows, remove the glass guide channel at the rear of the window.
5 On 1990 through 1994 rear door windows, remove the window regulator from the large opening.
6 Place a rag inside the door panel to help prevent scratching the glass. Remove the glass mounting bolts.
7 Remove the glass by pulling it up and out of the door.
8 On 1990 through 1994 models, remove rear door quarter window glass and carefully pull the weatherstrip free, removing any clips or attachment points - do not pull too hard as this may damage the weatherstrip.
9 Installation is the reverse of removal.
10 Window glass adjustment is by means of slotted adjustment screws. Loosen the adjustment screws, position and hold the glass fully closed in the door frame, and lightly tighten the adjustment screws. Wind the window slowly, checking for smooth travel. Adjust vertically and horizontally to obtain full closure with smooth travel as the window is wound up and down.

16 Window regulator - removal and installation

Refer to illustrations 16.5 and 16.6

1 Remove the door trim panel and watershield (see Section 13).
2 Remove the door glass. For rear doors, remove both the roll-up window and the quarter window (see Section 15). **Note:** *To remove the door glass run channel only, Step 6 below, the glass does not need to be removed.*

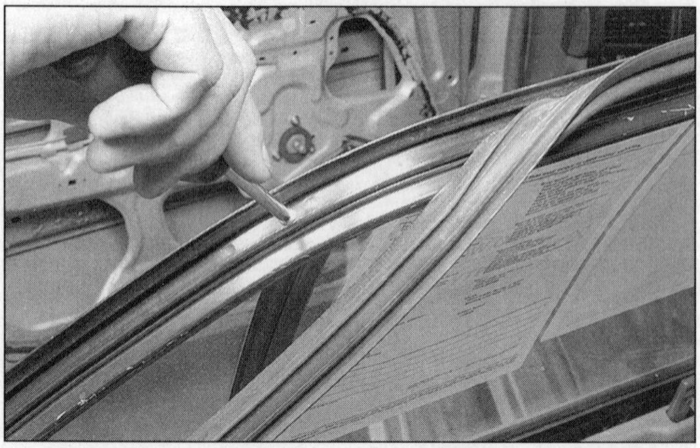

15.4 Remove the rear door center channel by lifting the weatherstrip and removing the screw/clip - 1990 through 1994 shown

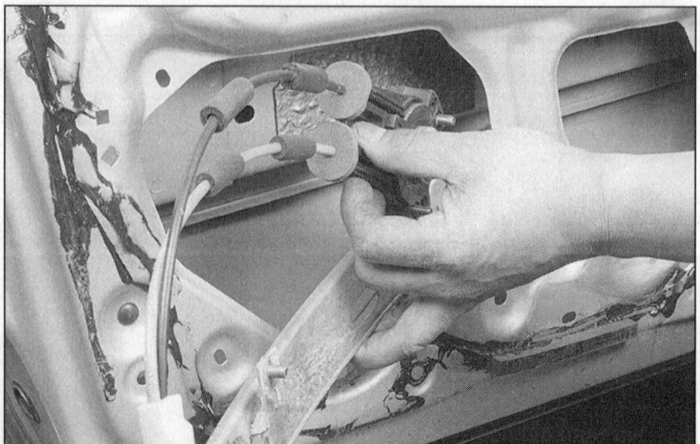

16.5 Unbolt the window regulator assembly and remove from the door - 1990 through 1994 shown

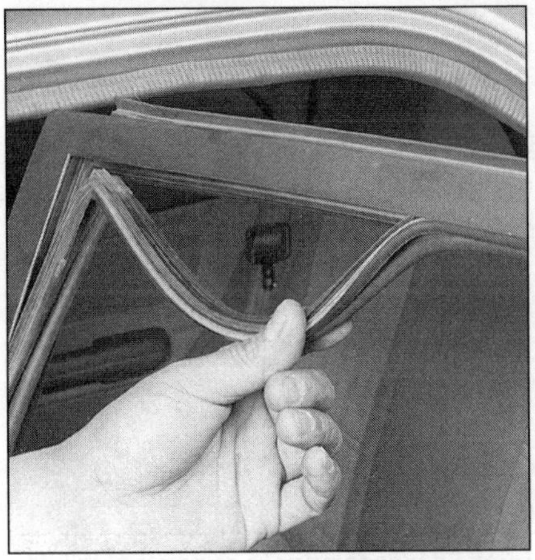

16.6 Remove the door glass run channel as necessary

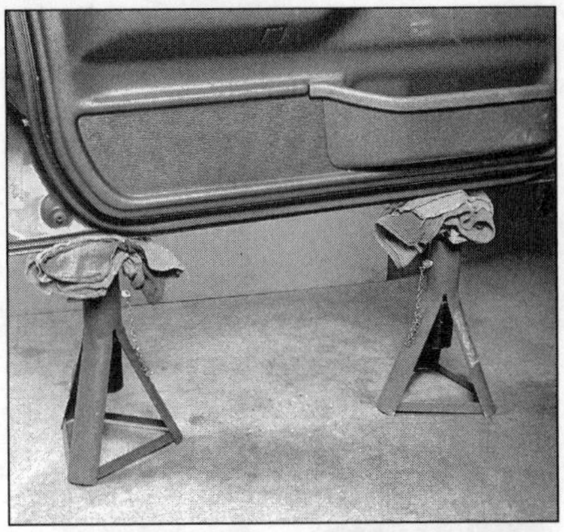

17.3 Use two jackstands padded with rags (to protect the paint) to support the door during the removal and installation procedures

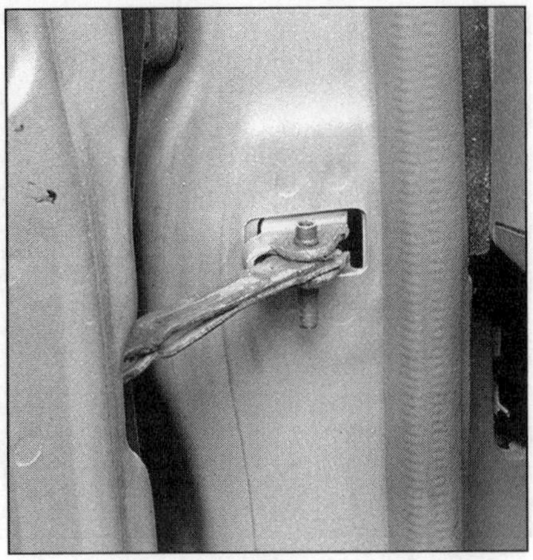

17.4 Remove the bolt and detach the stop strut

3 Mark or measure the location of the manual or power window regulator assembly for reinstallation alignment.
4 For power windows, disconnect the power window electrical connector.
5 Unbolt the window regulator assembly and remove the regulator through the door frame access hole **(see illustration)**.
6 Remove the door glass run channel as necessary **(see illustration)**.
7 Installation is the reverse of removal. During installation, apply multi-purpose grease to the regulator rollers.

17 Door - removal, installation and adjustment

Removal and installation

Refer to illustrations 17.3, 17.4 and 17.5

1 Disconnect the negative cable from the battery.
2 On 1990 through 1994 models, pull back the wiring connector boot at the door hinge area, and disconnect the electrical connector. On 1995 and later models, pull the small pin on the top of the door jamb electrical connector, then unplug the electrical connector.
3 Position a jack or jackstands under the door or have an assistant available to support the door when the hinge bolts are removed **(see illustration)**. **Note:** *If a jack or stand is used, place a rag between it and the door to protect the door paint.*
4 Remove the door stop strut bolt **(see illustration)**.
5 Mark around the door hinges and hinge bolts to aid alignment when reinstalling **(see illustration)**.
6 Remove the hinge-to-door bolts and carefully detach the door.
7 Installation is the reverse of removal. Adjust and securely tighten the door hinge bolts and striker bolts, if removed, as described below.

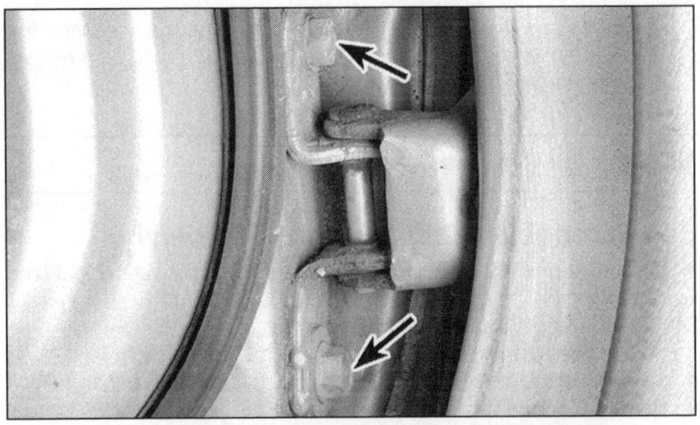

17.5 Mark the door hinge bolt locations (arrows)

Adjustment

Refer to illustrations 17.8a, 17.8b and 17.8c

8 Following installation, locate the alignment marks made during door removal. Make sure the door is aligned properly and adjust it if necessary as follows:

a) Up-and-down and forward-and-backward adjustments are made by loosening the hinge-to-body bolts and moving the door, as necessary. A special offset tool may be required to reach some of the bolts **(see illustration)**.
b) In-and-out and up-and-down adjustments are made by loosening the door side hinge bolts and moving the door, as necessary. A special offset tool may be required to reach some of the bolts **(see illustration)**.
c) The door lock striker can also be adjusted both up-and-down and sideways to provide a positive engagement with the locking

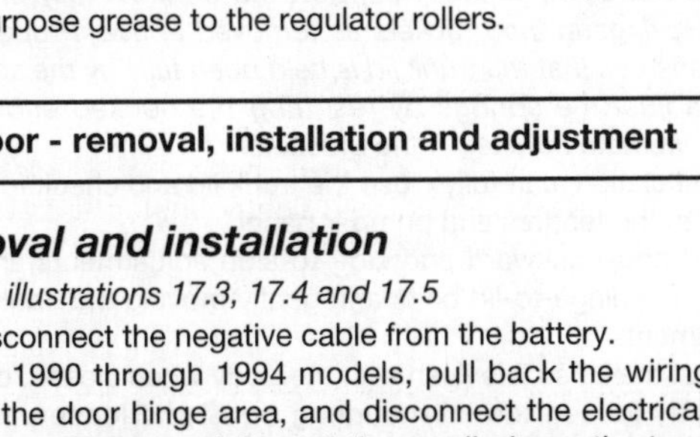

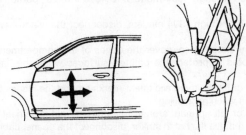

17.8a When adjusting the door up-and-down or forward-and-backward a special wrench such as this one will make the job easier

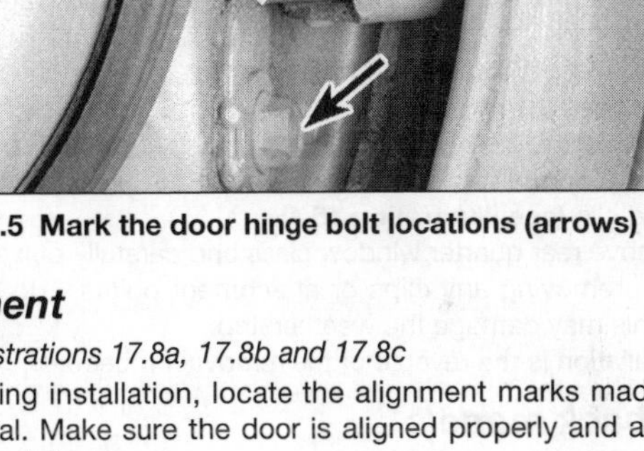

17.8b Adjust the door up-and-down or in-and-out after loosening the hinge to door bolts

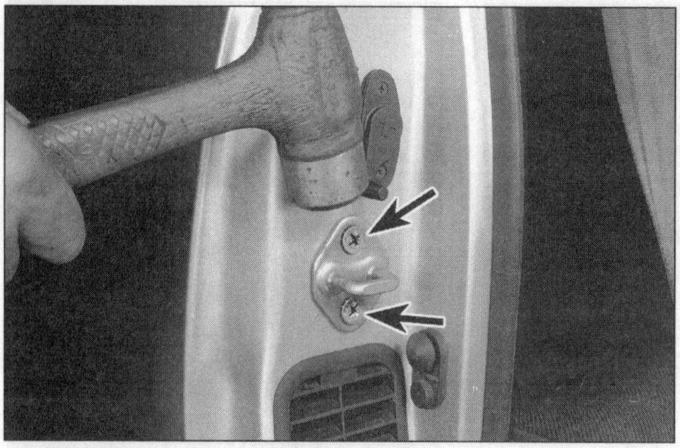

17.8c Adjust the door lock striker by loosening the mounting screws (arrows) and gently tapping the striker in the desired direction

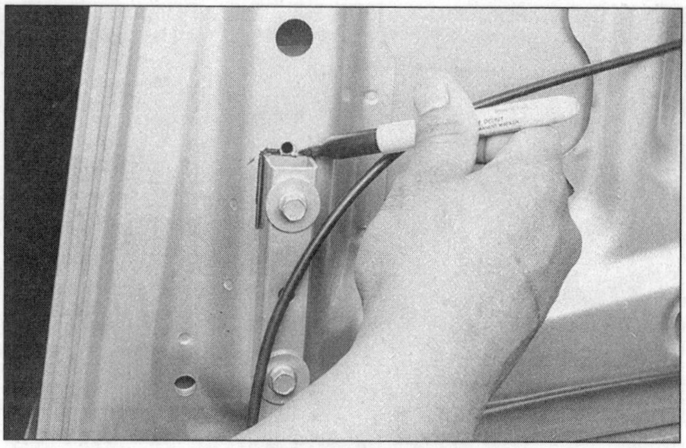

19.6 Mark around the trunk lid hinges prior to removal of the lid

mechanism. This is done by loosening the screws and moving the striker by hand or by lightly tapping with a soft-faced hammer, as necessary **(see illustration).**

18 Rear quarter glass - replacement

Sedan models (1990 through 1994 only)

1 Remove the rear door trim panel and the plastic watershield (see Section 13).
2 Disconnect the negative battery cable.
3 Fully open the roll-up door glass.
4 Remove the center channel strip by carefully lifting the door weatherstrip on the top of the door, and removing the center channel screw and clip **(see illustration 15.4).**
5 Remove rear quarter window glass and carefully pull the weatherstrip free, removing any clips or attachment points - do not pull too hard as this may damage the weatherstrip.
6 Installation is the reverse of the removal procedure.

Hatchback models

7 Remove the upper seatbelt anchor.
8 Remove the inside pillar trim.
9 Remove the quarter window latch.
10 Pull out the quarter window glass.
11 Remove the quarter window hinges and outside molding from the quarter window, as necessary.
12 Installation is the reverse of the removal procedure.

19 Trunk lid - removal, installation and adjustment

Refer to illustration 19.6

Note: *The trunk lid is heavy and somewhat awkward to remove and install - have an assistant available to perform this procedure.*
1 Disconnect the negative battery cable.
2 Remove the lid lock cover inside the trunk lid.
3 Disconnect and remove the trunk opener release cable from the trunk lid.
4 Disconnect the electrical wiring harness from the trunk lid.
5 With the trunk lid open, cover the edges of the trunk compartment with pads or cloths to protect the painted surfaces when the trunk lid is removed.
6 Make alignment marks around the hinge mounting bolts to aid alignment when reinstalling **(see illustration).**
7 While supporting the trunk lid, remove the trunk lid-to-hinge bolts on both hinges and lift off the trunk lid.
8 If the trunk lid springs are to be removed, note the location of the hooked end of each spring at the notches in both the right hand and left hand brackets. Remove the springs from the right hand and left hand brackets using pliers to grip near the hooked end of each spring. **Note:** *The trunk lid springs can be removed with the trunk lid still installed, by opening the trunk lid fully and securely supporting the trunk lid open while removing the springs.*
9 If necessary, remove the trunk lid latch by marking the latch position and removing the bolts, the latch and the lock cylinder.
10 Installation is the reverse of removal. **Note:** *When reinstalling the trunk lid, align the hinge with the marks made during removal. If the springs were removed, securely support the trunk lid fully open and reinstall the springs in the brackets as removed above. Proper spring adjustment ensures that the trunk lid is held open fully by the springs. If necessary, adjust the springs by resetting the hooked ends of the springs into alternate notches in the brackets.*
11 After installation, carefully close the trunk lid and check for proper alignment with the fenders and bumper panel.
12 Forward-and-backward and side-to-side adjustments are made by loosening the hinge-to-lid bolts and gently moving the trunk lid into correct alignment.
13 To adjust the lid so it is flush with the body when closed, open the lid and slightly loosen the lid mounting bolts and loosen the latch striker, tap the striker lightly, close the lid to check alignment, open the lid and securely tighten all bolts. Recheck closing and opening again.

20 Rear hatch - removal, installation and adjustment

Note: *The rear hatch is heavy and somewhat awkward to remove and install - at least two people should perform this procedure.*
1 Disconnect the negative battery cable.
2 On 1990 through 1994 models, remove the hatch wiring harness near the hatch hinge by removing the lower, side and header interior trim panels, the rear seat belt upper anchor, and the rear pillar trim panels.
3 On 1990 through 1994 models, remove the rear portion of the headliner.
4 On 1990 through 1994 models, disconnect the window washer tubing.
5 With the hatch open, cover the edges of the compartment with pads or cloths to protect the painted surfaces when the hatch is removed.
6 Scribe or felt tip mark alignment marks around the hinges to use for alignment when reinstalling.
7 Scribe or felt tip mark around the striker to aid alignment when reinstalling, remove the hatch striker, disconnect the opener cable.
8 Have an assistant support the hatch while detaching the hatch support strut (see Section 21).
9 While an assistant supports the hatch, remove the hatch-to-hinge bolts on both sides and lift the hatch off.

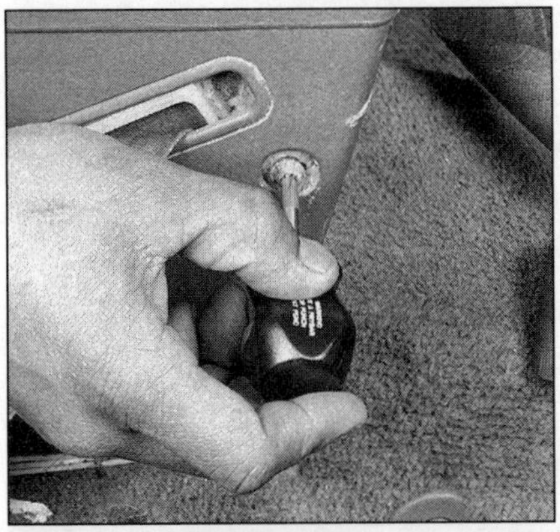

22.2 Remove the rear console screws and remove the rear console - 1990 through 1994 shown

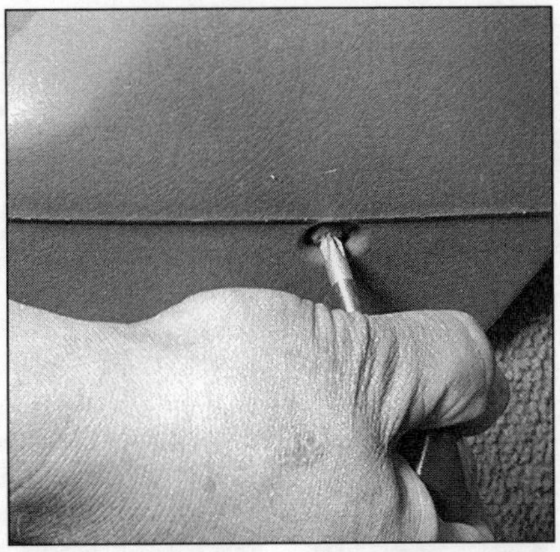

22.3a Remove the front console screws . . .

22.3b . . . the shift knob, and . . .

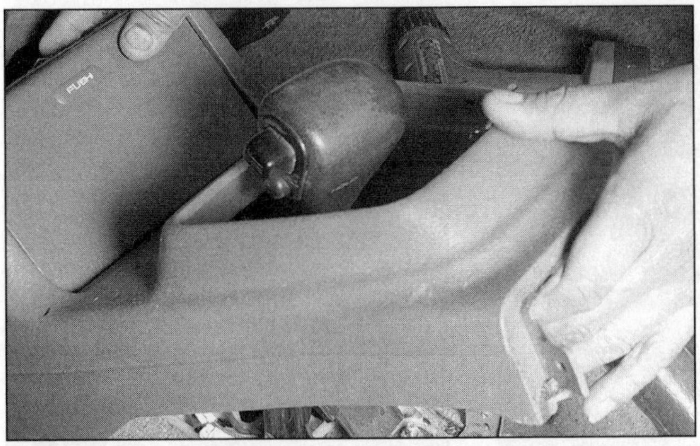

22.3c . . . detach the front console - 1990 through 1994 shown

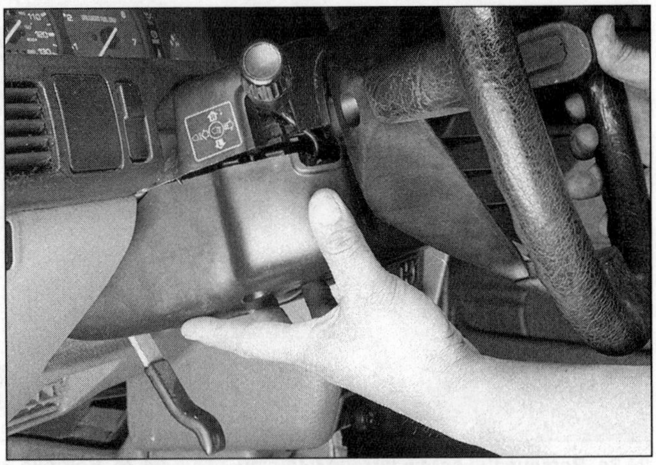

23.2 Remove the steering column lower cover screws and remove the cover. An electrical connector must be removed from the lower cover - 1990 through 1994 shown

10 To remove the opener cable, if necessary, remove the driver's door scuff plate (1990 through 1994) or hatch lever cover (1995 and later), trunk side cover and quarter trim on the driver's side, the opener lever near the front seat, and the rear seat cushion.

11 If necessary, remove the hatch lock by removing the hatch inner trim panel, removing the lock retainer clip, lock cylinder, and lock assembly.

12 Installation is the reverse of removal. **Note:** *When reinstalling the hatch, align the hinges with the scribe marks made during removal.*

13 After installation, carefully close the hatch and check for proper alignment with the hatch opening and the hatch seats tightly against the weatherstrip.

14 Adjustments to the hatch position are made by loosening the hinge to hatch bolts or nuts and gently moving the hatch into correct alignment with the top and bottom sides of the hatch opening.

15 The hatch lock is adjusted by partially loosening the lid hinge bolts and striker bolts, then slowly closing the hatch. Carefully reopen the hatch, tighten the striker and recheck the lock by opening and closing the hatch. Adjust so that the hatch closes fully align with the hatch opening, and seats tightly against weatherstrip.

21 Rear hatch support strut(s) - replacement

Warning: *The support strut is filled with pressurized gas - do not disassemble this component. If faulty, replace it with a new one.*

Note: *The rear hatch is heavy and somewhat awkward to hold securely while replacing the struts - at least two people should perform this procedure.*

1 Open the hatch fully and support it in the open position.

2 Remove the strut bolts and detach the strut from the hatch and the body.

3 Installation is the reverse of the removal procedure.

22 Center console - removal and installation

Refer to illustrations 22.2, 22.3a, 22.3b and 22.3c

1 Disconnect the negative battery cable.

Rear console

2 Remove the rear console screws, and remove the rear console **(see illustration)**.

Front console - at the shift lever

3 Remove the ashtray, remove the shift knob, remove the front console screws, and remove the front console **(see illustrations)**. Disconnect any electrical connectors. **Note:** *On 1990 through 1994 models there are two types of front consoles - a one-piece full front console with integral drawer, and a two-piece small console with a tray slot.*

4 Installation is the reverse of the removal procedure.

23 Steering column covers - removal and installation

Refer to illustrations 23.2 and 23.4

1 Remove the steering column lower cover screws.

2 Remove the steering column lower cover **(see illustration)**,

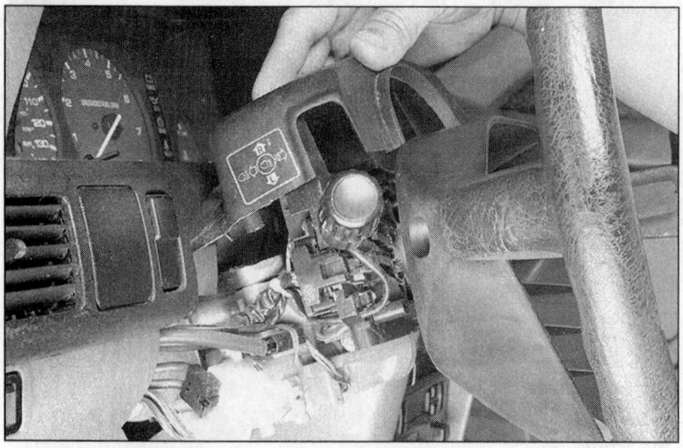

23.4 Remove the steering column upper cover screws and remove the cover - 1990 through 1994 shown

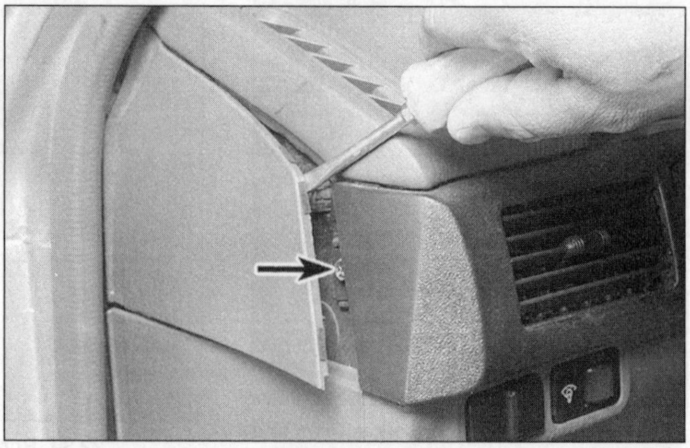

24.2 Remove the side panel and the screw (arrow) retaining the instrument bezel

24.3a Remove the screw (arrow) retaining the instrument cluster bezel

24.3b Remove the instrument cluster bezel screws here and along the bottom of the panel

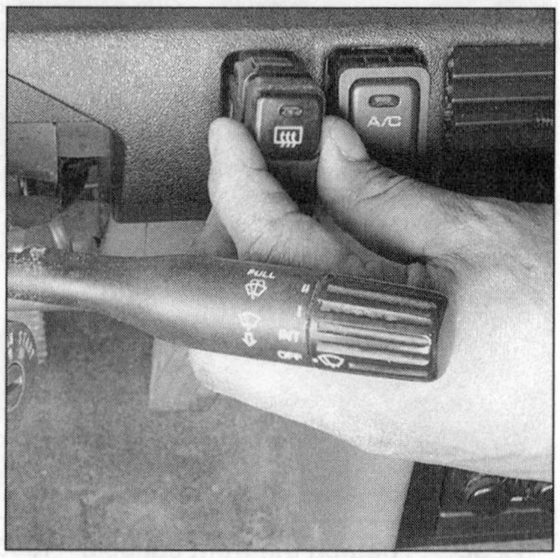

24.4a Pop out any switches on the instrument bezel panel . . .

detaching the electrical connector (1990 through 1994 models).

3 Remove the steering column upper cover screws.

4 Remove the steering column upper cover **(see illustration)**.

5 Installation is the reverse of the removal procedure.

24 Instrument cluster bezel - removal and installation

Refer to illustration 24.2, 24.3a, 24.3b, 24.4a, 24.4b and 24.5

1 Disconnect the cable from the negative battery terminal.

2 On 1990 through 1994 models, remove the side panel and screw retaining the instrument bezel **(see illustration)**.

3 Remove the instrument cluster bezel screws **(see illustrations)**.

4 To remove front-mounted switches, pop out any switches on this panel and disconnect the electrical connectors **(see illustrations)**.

5 Grasp the instrument bezel securely and carefully remove it **(see illustration)**, to detach any pull-out clips, and disconnect any remaining electrical connectors. On 1995 and later models, pull the instrument bezel away to detach the clips from the instrument panel.

6 Installation is the reverse of the removal procedure.

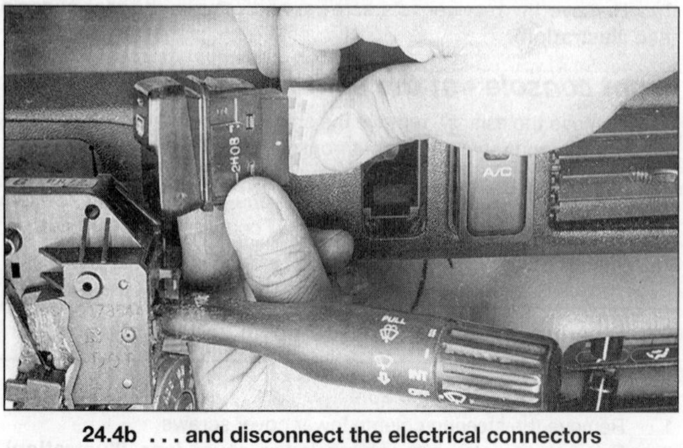

24.4b . . . and disconnect the electrical connectors from this panel

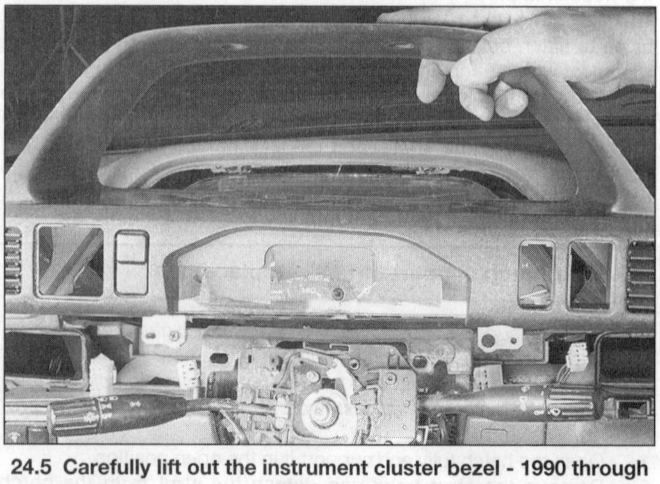

24.5 Carefully lift out the instrument cluster bezel - 1990 through 1994 shown

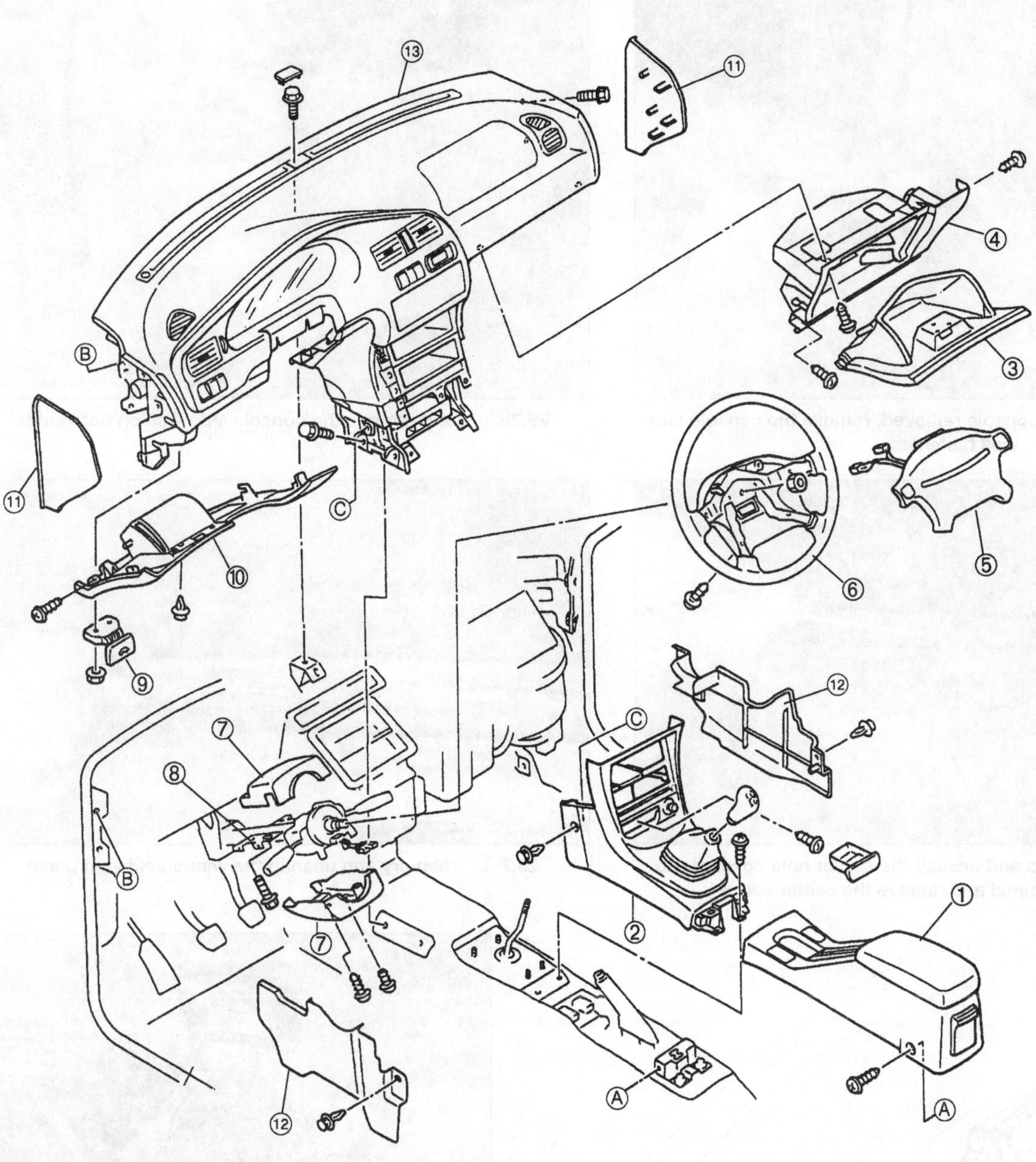

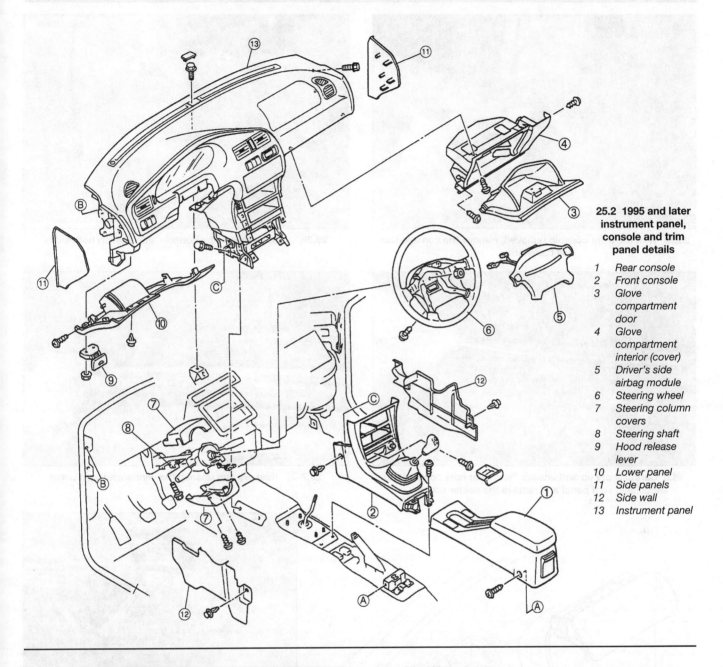

25.2 1995 and later instrument panel, console and trim panel details

1 *Rear console*
2 *Front console*
3 *Glove compartment door*
4 *Glove compartment interior (cover)*
5 *Driver's side airbag module*
6 *Steering wheel*
7 *Steering column covers*
8 *Steering shaft*
9 *Hood release lever*
10 *Lower panel*
11 *Side panels*
12 *Side wall*
13 *Instrument panel*

25 Instrument panel - removal and installation

Refer to illustrations 25.2, 25.3a, 25.3b, 25.6, 25.7, 25.8, 25.10a, 25.10b, 25.10c, 25.12, 25.13a, 25.13b, 25.14, 25.16 and 25.18

Warning: *1995 and later models are equipped with airbags. The airbag is armed and can deploy (inflate) whenever the battery is connected. To prevent accidental deployment (and possible injury), turn the ignition key to LOCK and disconnect the negative battery cable whenever working near airbag components. After the battery is disconnected, wait at least two minutes before beginning work (the system has a back-up capacitor that must fully discharge). For more information see Chapter 12.*

1 Turn the ignition key OFF, then disconnect the cable from the negative terminal of the battery. If the vehicle is equipped with an airbag system, wait at least two minutes before proceeding. **Caution:** *For models equipped with airbags, follow the airbag servicing instructions prior to proceeding with any steps that may involve working around the airbags.*

DO NOT disassemble any airbag component.

DO NOT attempt repair of airbag system wiring harness.

DO NOT inspect or check the airbag system using an ohmmeter, because this can cause inadvertent deployment of the airbag.

DO NOT disconnect the airbag module (SAS) with the ignition switch ON - this could cause inadvertent airbag deployment.

DO NOT handle or carry the airbag with the trim cover facing you when it has been removed and is live (has not been deployed).

When handling the airbag, DO NOT set the airbag module down with the trim cover facing down.

DO NOT touch a deployed airbag for at least 15 minutes - it can be extremely hot.

Contact a dealer for proper disposal of a used airbag.

2 If you're working on a 1995 or later model, refer to the accompanying illustration **(see illustration)** and use the following illustrations in this Section (showing a 1990 through 1994 model) for reference.

3 Remove the rear and front consoles (see Section 22). Remove the

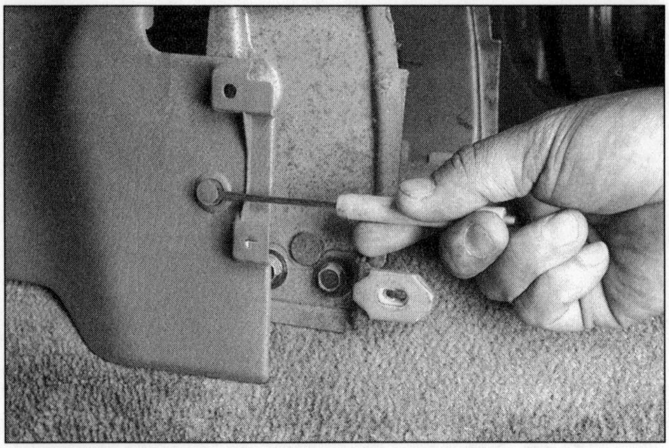

25.3a With the front console removed, remove the console side wall fasteners . . .

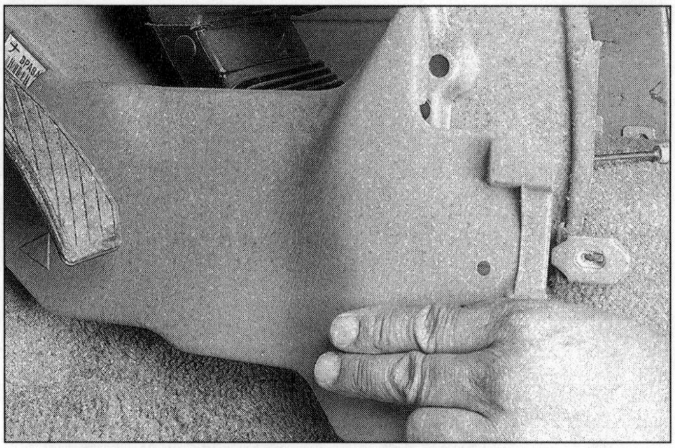

25.3b . . . and remove the console side wall on both sides

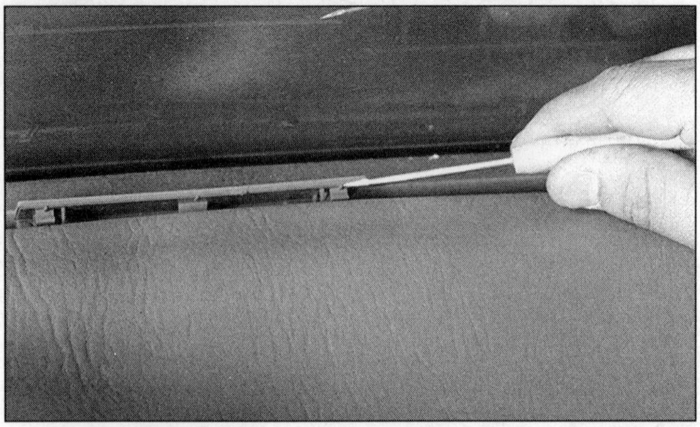

25.6 Carefully pry up and unsnap the center hole cover at the windshield vent panel and remove the center screw . . .

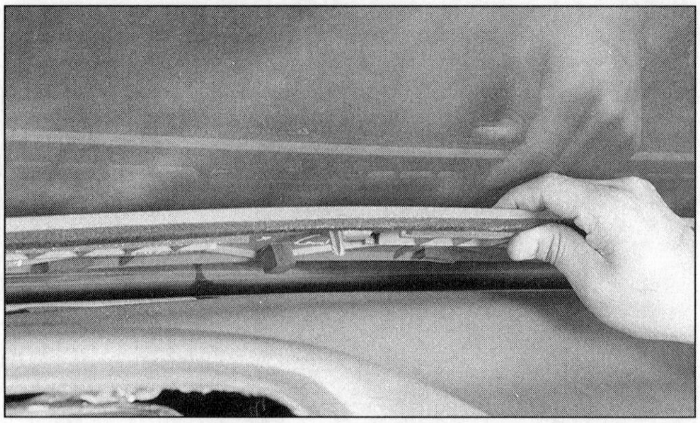

25.7 . . . then pry and unsnap the windshield vent panel

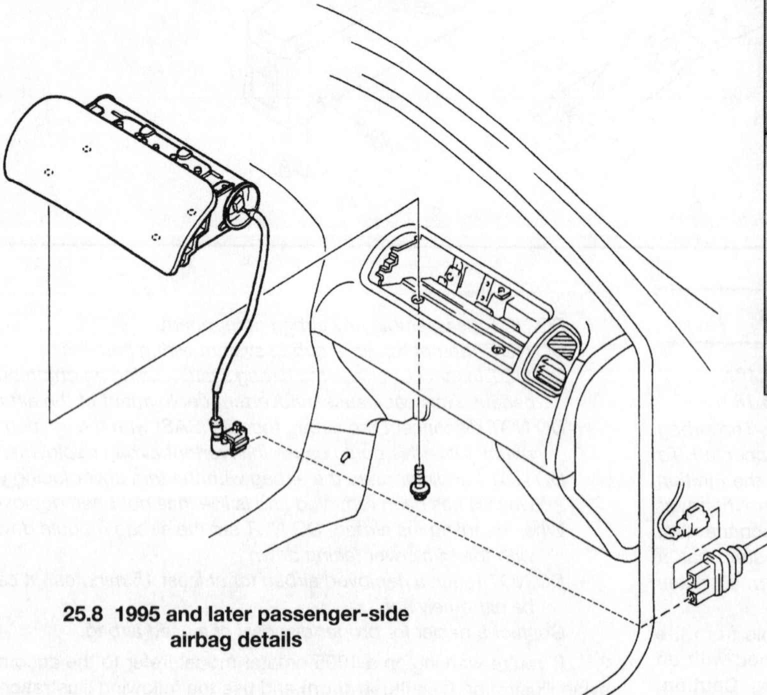

25.8 1995 and later passenger-side airbag details

25.10a Remove the nut behind the hood release knob to detach the knob . . .

25.10b . . . and remove the screws attaching the driver's side underdash panel . . .

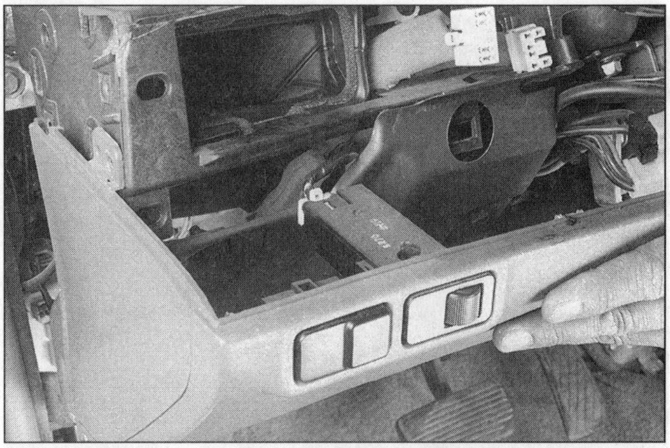

25.10c . . . and remove the underdash panel

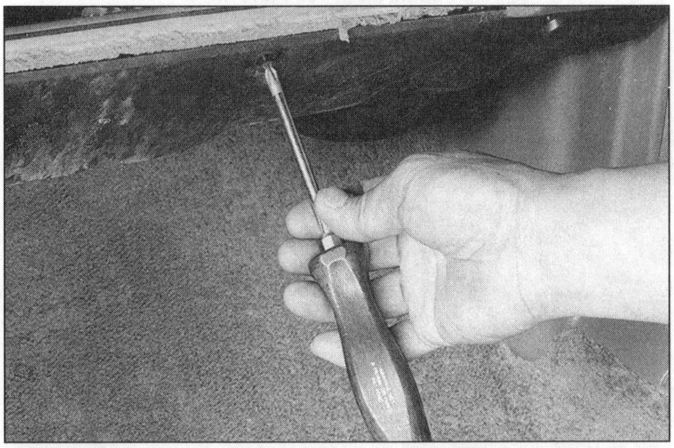

25.12 Remove the underdash panel at the right side of the dash

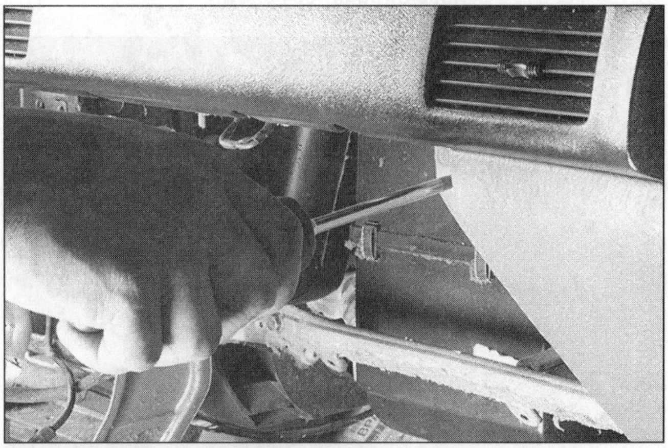

25.13a Remove the right side dash panel screws . . .

two console side walls, visible with the front console removed **(see illustrations)**.

4 On 1990 through 1994 models, remove the ventilation outlet panel on the right side of the dash over the glove box.

5 Remove steering column lower and upper covers (see Section 23).

6 Unsnap the center hole cover on the top of the dashboard at the windshield vent panel **(see illustration)**. Remove the screw at the center of the windshield vent panel.

7 Carefully unsnap the windshield vent panel and remove it from the top of the dashboard **(see illustration)**.

8 On 1995 and later models:

a) Remove the windshield pillar (A-pillar) trim panels by pulling the pillar trim back to disengage the clips and pin, then pull upward to disengage the hook from the body.

b) Remove the glove compartment door by pulling it up on the right side, slide it to the right and remove the door. Then remove the dashboard right side panel at the end of the dashboard, and remove the glove compartment.

c) Remove the passenger side airbag module as follows:

d) Disconnect the airbag electrical connector.

e) Remove the airbag retaining screws from inside the glove compartment area (glove compartment removed).

f) Lift out the passenger side airbag assembly **(see illustration)**.

g) Remove the driver's side airbag module and the steering wheel (see Chapter 10).

h) Detach the steering shaft from the dashboard.

9 Unsnap the dashboard right and left side panels at the ends of the dashboard **(see illustration 24.2)**.

10 Detach the hood release knob from under the dashboard.

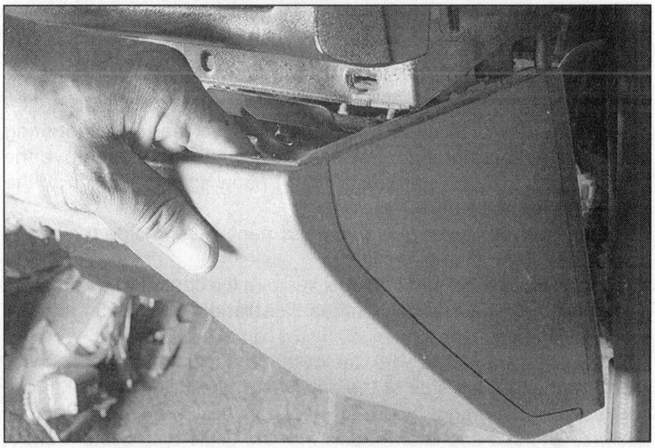

25.13b . . . pull out the dash panel, removing the electrical connector

Remove the lower panel retaining screws from the underdash panel at the driver's side, remove the nut behind the hood release knob and lower the knob, then pull out the underdash panel while disconnecting any electrical connectors **(see illustrations)**.

11 Remove the instrument cluster bezel (see Section 24).

12 On 1990 through 1994 models, remove the glove compartment and remove the underdash panel under the glove box **(see illustration)**.

13 On 1990 through 1994 models, remove the dash panel **(see illustrations)** and electrical connector at the right side of the glove compartment.

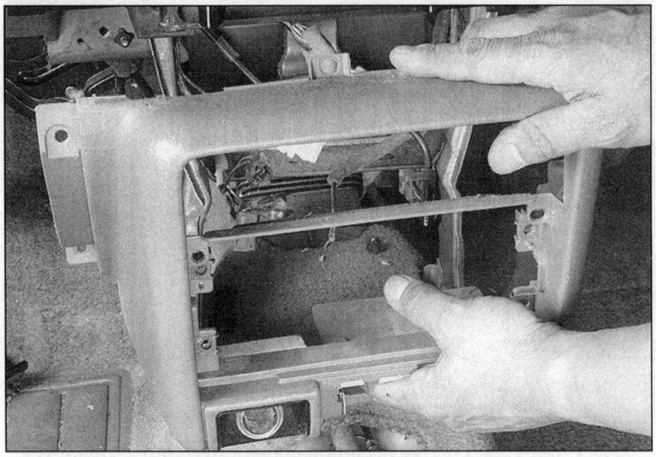

25.14 Remove the center dash panel housing - 1990 through 1994 shown

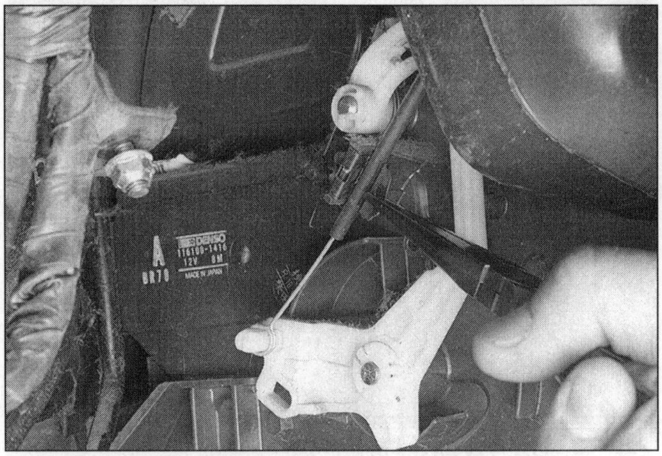

25.16 Detach the heater unit and blower unit control wires - 1990 through 1994 shown

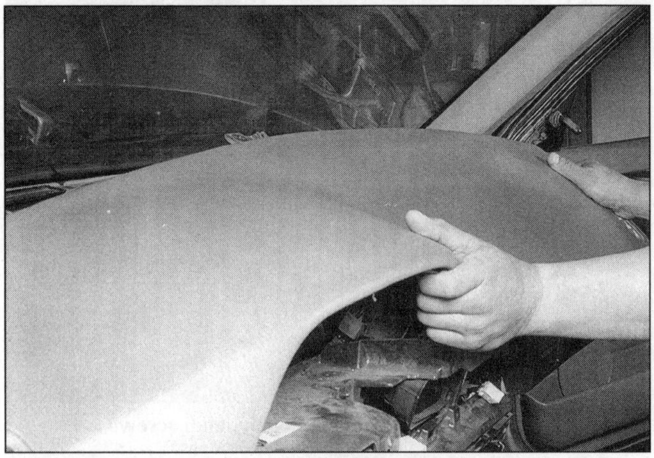

25.18 Remove the instrument panel by tilting and lifting away from the firewall

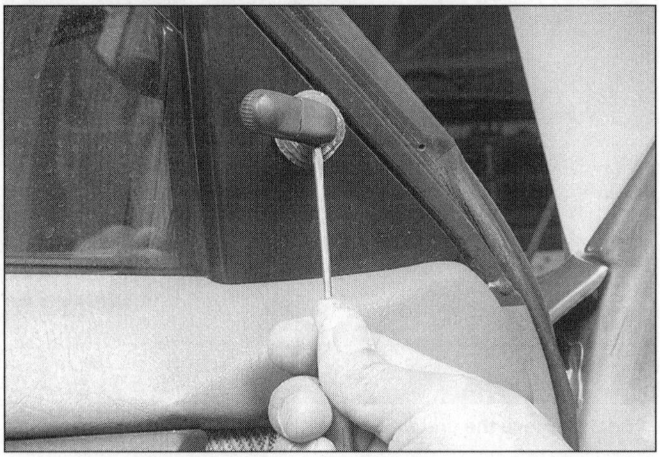

26.1a Pry off the plastic cover panel . . .

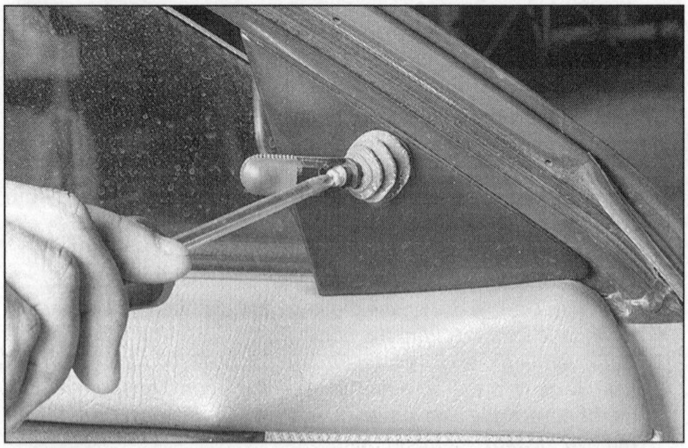

26.1b . . . and remove the handle shaft screw and handle

14 To remove the center dash panel housing the radio and heater controls, remove the radio trim panel, remove the radio mounting screws, the radio antenna, power, and ground cables, remove the heater controls, remove the center dash panel screws and lift off the housing **(see illustration)**.

15 Remove the upper glove compartment cover inside the dashboard.

16 On 1990 through 1994 models, remove the control wires from the heater unit and the blower unit **(see illustration)**. On 1995 and later models with wire-type heater controls, remove the air MIX wire, air INTAKE wire, and MODE wire, the dashboard main electrical connector at the bottom left side of the dashboard, the CPU and PCM connectors, and the orange and blue steering wheel airbag module connectors. On 1995 and later models with the Logic-type heater control unit, remove the PCM connectors, the blower unit connector, the air MIX actuator connector, dashboard main connector, the CPU connector, the orange and blue steering wheel airbag module connectors, and the cabin temperature sensor from the air duct.

17 As necessary, remove the center vertical dashboard frame mount near the floor.

18 Carefully remove the instrument panel **(see illustration)**, while disconnecting the electrical connectors at the left side of the dash, the blower unit, and at the underdash fuse/electrical circuit breaker at the driver's side.

19 Installation is the reverse of removal. When reinstalling the instrument panel and reconnecting the heater controls, see Chapter 3 for control adjustment.

26 Outside mirror - removal and installation

Refer to illustrations 26.1a, 26.1b, 26.2, 26.3 and 26.7

Manual outside mirror

1 Pry off the mirror control handle screw cover, remove the handle shaft screw, remove the handle **(see illustrations)**.

2 Detach the mirror cover inside the door by using a small screw-

26.2 Pry off the mirror panel inside the door

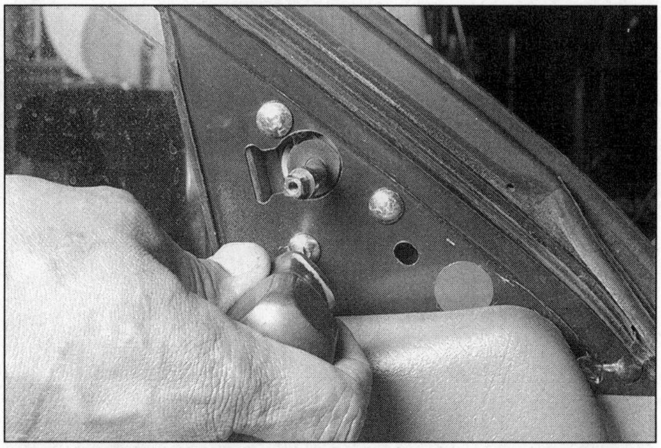

26.3 Remove the mirror retaining screws to remove the mirror

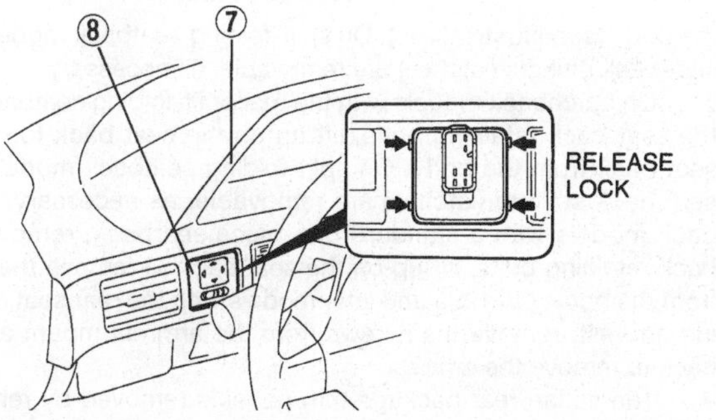

26.7 Detach the power mirror switch from the instrument panel

driver to pry the cover free from the door **(see illustration)**.

3 Remove the mirror retaining screws from inside the door and detach the mirror **(see illustration)**.

Power outside mirror

4 Detach the mirror cover inside the door by using a small screw-driver to pry the cover free from the door **(see illustration 26.2)**.

5 Remove the mirror retaining screws from inside the door and detach the mirror.

6 Unplug the power mirror electrical connector.

7 If necessary to check or repair the power mirror switch, detach the power mirror switch from the instrument panel **(see illustration)**.

8 Installation is the reverse of removal.

Mirror glass replacement

1990 through 1994 manual and power type, 1995 and later manual type

9 Using a hot air blower, heat the mirror.

10 Adjust the mirror so that one edge of the mirror is accessible.

11 While keeping the mirror hot, insert a thin scraper between the mirror glass and the mirror frame, and carefully pry the mirror loose.

12 Remove all remaining adhesive from the back of the mirror glass.

13 Warm the frame with a hot air blower, and gently press the mirror glass in place. Allow to cool before driving.

1995 and later power mirror

14 Push at the top of the mirror glass.

15 Pull the bottom of the mirror glass and remove the mirror from the housing.

16 Install the mirror by hooking the top of the mirror glass onto the frame, then pressing the sides and bottom of the mirror.

27 Seats - removal and installation

Front seats

Refer to illustrations 27.3a and 27.3b

1 Disconnect the seat belt buckle electrical connector near the floor.

2 Remove the seat forward/back travel release handle cover at the side of the seat.

3 Remove the seat rail retaining bolts at the floor, disconnect the

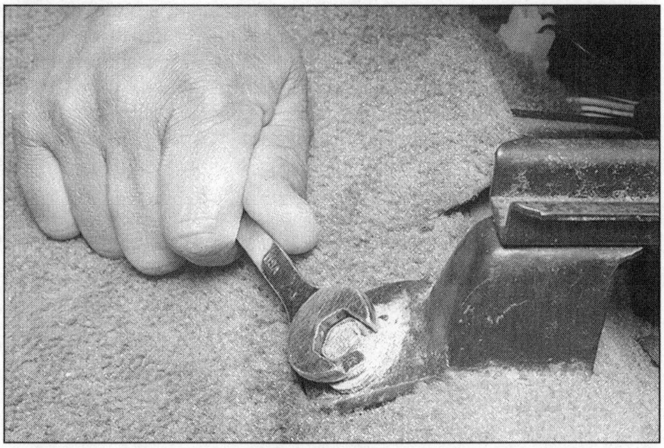

27.3a Detach the seat rail bolt covers, unbolt the front seat rail bolts from the floor . . .

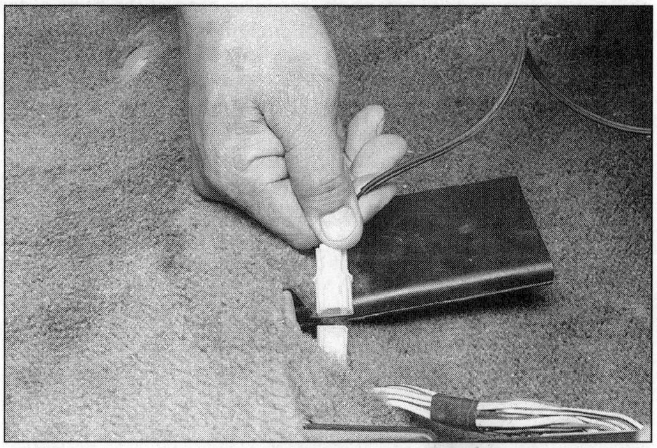

27.3b . . . then detach the electrical connector and remove the seat from the vehicle

11

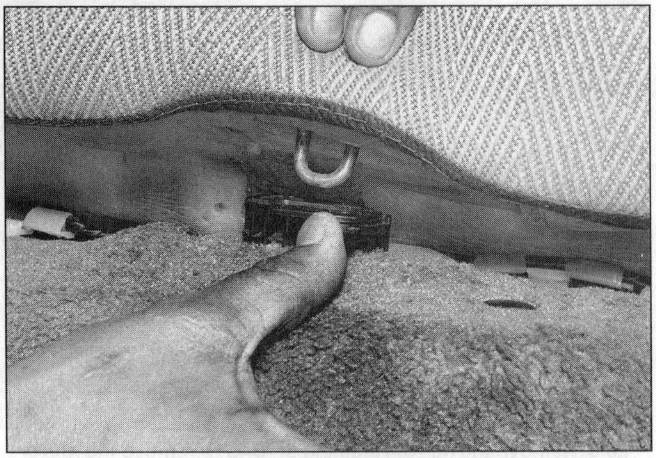

27.5 Press the rear seat cushion retaining clip and lift the rear seat bottom cushion

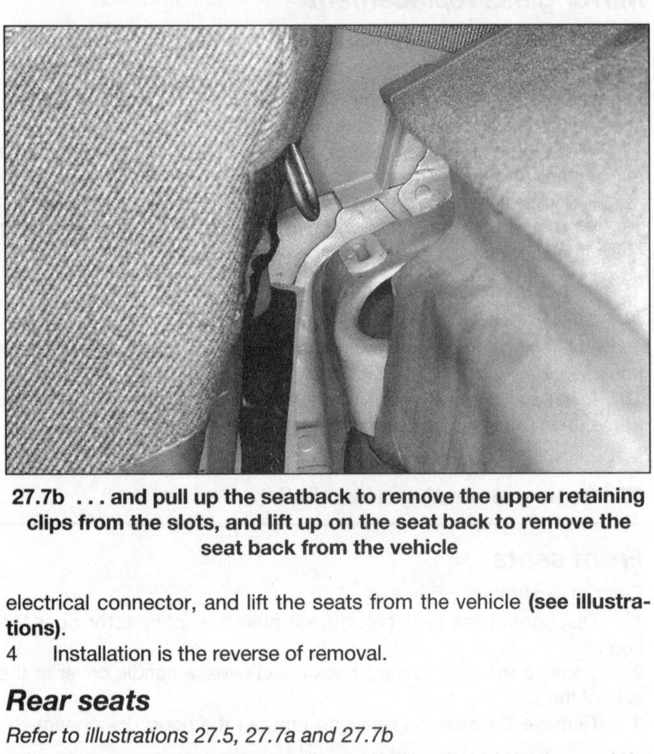

27.7b . . . and pull up the seatback to remove the upper retaining clips from the slots, and lift up on the seat back to remove the seat back from the vehicle

electrical connector, and lift the seats from the vehicle **(see illustrations)**.

4 Installation is the reverse of removal.

Rear seats

Refer to illustrations 27.5, 27.7a and 27.7b

5 On sedan models, detach the retaining clips at the base of the rear seat near the floor **(see illustration)**, lift the front of the cushion up, then pull it out toward the front of the vehicle.

6 On hatchback models, depress the retaining clips at the base of the rear seat cushion **(see illustration 27.5)**, pull the rear seat cushion up and remove it from the vehicle.

7 On sedan models with rear split-folding seatback, remove the side cushion lower nut, unsnap the side cushion from the body, and lift out the side cushions. On sedan models with a standard one-piece seatback and with split-folding seatbacks, remove the seat back retaining bolts, lift up on the seat back to remove the seat back from

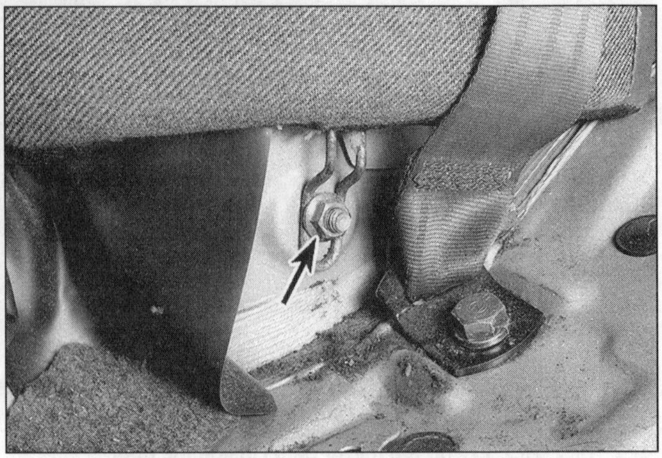

27.7a Remove the rear seatback retaining bolts . . .

the body **(see illustrations)**. On split-folding seatback models, the rear seat back strikers (latches) are removable, as necessary.

8 On hatchback models with the rear split-folding seatback, remove the seat back retaining bolts, lift up on the seat back to remove the seat back from the body. On split-folding seatback models, the rear seat back strikers (latches) are removable, as necessary. On hatchback models with a standard one-piece seatback, remove the seat back retaining bolts, lift up on the seat back to remove the seat back from the body. On 1995 and later models with the rear seat center folding armrest, remove the screws from the armrest mount at the seatback to remove the armrest.

9 The sedan rear package trim panel is removed by removing the rear seatback, removing the high-mounted stoplight, removing the push-pull fasteners and pulling the trim panel forward to disengage the clips on the trim panel from the body.

10 Installation is the reverse of removal. During installation, route the seat belts between the seat bottom and the seatback for accessibility after seat installation.

28 Seat belts - check

1 Check the seat belts, buckles, latch plates and guide loops for any obvious damage or signs of wear.

2 Make sure the seat belt reminder light comes on when the key is turned on.

3 Check that the passive front seat belt drive mechanisms (as applicable) actuate properly during use to travel and latch in place when driver or passenger is seated.

4 The seat belts are designed to lock up during a sudden stop or impact, yet allow free movement during normal driving. The retractors should hold the belt against your chest while driving and rewind the belt when the buckle is unlatched. Check the retractor on each seat belt locks when the belt is quickly pulled. **Note:** *Do not remove the belt retractor covers or disassemble the retractors, as the ELR (Emergency Locking Retractor) has a spring that will unwind and cannot be rewound.*

5 If any of the above checks reveal problems with the seat belt system, disconnect the negative battery cable, and replace the seat belt components and retractor assemblies as necessary.

Chapter 12
Chassis electrical system

Contents

1 General information

The electrical system is a 12-volt, negative ground type. Power for the lights and all electrical accessories is supplied by a lead/acid-type battery which is charged by the alternator.

This Chapter covers repair and service procedures for the various electrical components not associated with the engine. Information on the battery, alternator, distributor and starter motor can be found in Chapter 5.

It should be noted that when portions of the electrical system are serviced, the cable should be disconnected from the negative battery terminal to prevent electrical shorts and/or fires.

Caution: *If the stereo in your vehicle is equipped with an anti-theft system, make sure you have the correct activation code before disconnecting the battery in any of the following procedures.*

2 Electrical troubleshooting - general information

A typical electrical circuit consists of an electrical component, any switches, relays, motors, fuses, fusible links or circuit breakers related to that component and the wiring and electrical connectors that link the component to both the battery and the chassis. To help you pin-

12

3.1a The main fuse block is located in the engine compartment, near the battery

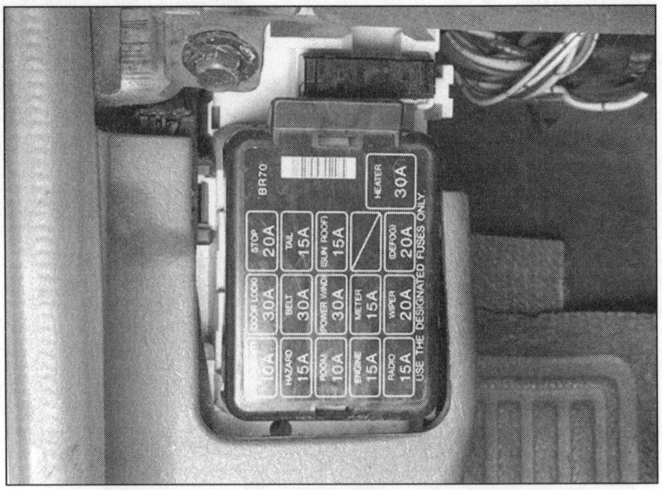

3.1b The interior fuse box is located near the driver's side kick panel

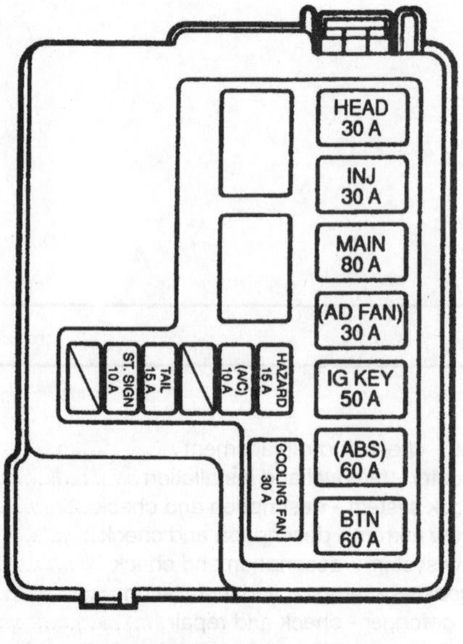

3.1c 1995 and later model main fuse block details

point an electrical circuit problem, wiring diagrams are included at the end of this book.

Before tackling any troublesome electrical circuit, first study the appropriate wiring diagrams to get a complete understanding of what makes up that individual circuit. Trouble spots, for instance, can often be narrowed down by noting if other components related to the circuit are operating properly. If several components or circuits fail at one time, chances are the problem is in a fuse or ground connection, because several circuits are often routed through the same fuse and ground connections.

Electrical problems usually stem from simple causes, such as loose or corroded connections, a blown fuse, a melted fusible link or a bad relay. Visually inspect the condition of all fuses, wires and connections in a problem circuit before troubleshooting it.

If testing instruments are going to be utilized, use the diagrams to plan ahead of time where you will make the necessary connections in order to accurately pinpoint the trouble spot.

The basic tools needed for electrical troubleshooting include a circuit tester or voltmeter (a 12-volt bulb with a set of test leads can also be used), a continuity tester, which includes a bulb, battery and set of test leads, and a jumper wire, preferably with a circuit breaker incorporated, which can be used to bypass electrical components. Before attempting to locate a problem with test instruments, use the wiring diagram(s) to decide where to make the connections.

Voltage checks

Voltage checks should be performed if a circuit is not functioning properly. Connect one lead of a circuit tester to either the negative battery terminal or a known good ground. Connect the other lead to a electrical connector in the circuit being tested, preferably nearest to the battery or fuse. If the bulb of the tester lights, voltage is present, which means that the part of the circuit between the electrical connector and the battery is problem free. Continue checking the rest of the circuit in the same fashion. When you reach a point at which no voltage is present, the problem lies between that point and the last test point with voltage. Most of the time the problem can be traced to a loose connection. **Note:** *Keep in mind that some circuits receive voltage only when the ignition key is in the Accessory or Run position.*

Finding a short

One method of finding shorts in a circuit is to remove the fuse and connect a test light or voltmeter in its place to the fuse terminals. There should be no voltage present in the circuit. Move the wiring harness from side to side while watching the test light. If the bulb goes on, there is a short to ground somewhere in that area, probably where the insulation has rubbed through. The same test can be performed on each component in the circuit, even a switch.

Ground check

Perform a ground test to check whether a component is properly grounded. Disconnect the battery and connect one lead of a self-powered test light, known as a continuity tester, to a known good ground. Connect the other lead to the wire or ground connection being tested. If the bulb goes on, the ground is good. If the bulb does not go on, the ground is not good.

Continuity check

A continuity check is done to determine if there are any breaks in a circuit - if it is passing electricity properly. With the circuit off (no power in the circuit), a self-powered continuity tester can be used to check the circuit. Connect the test leads to both ends of the circuit (or to the "power" end and a good ground), and if the test light comes on the circuit is passing current properly. If the light doesn't come on, there is a break somewhere in the circuit. The same procedure can be used to test a switch, by connecting the continuity tester to the power in and power out sides of the switch. With the switch turned On, the test light should come on.

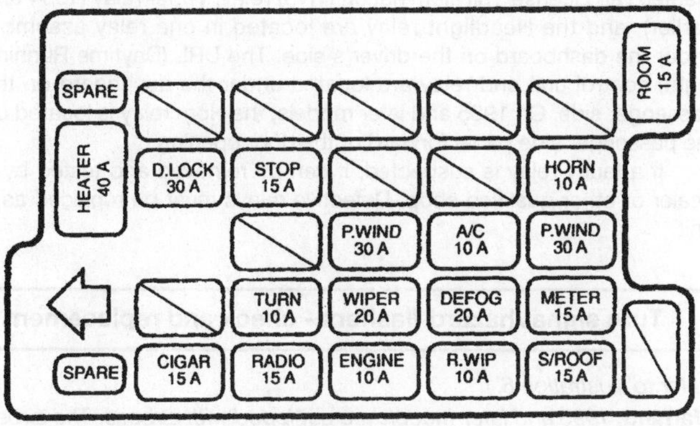

3.1d 1995 and later model interior fuse box details

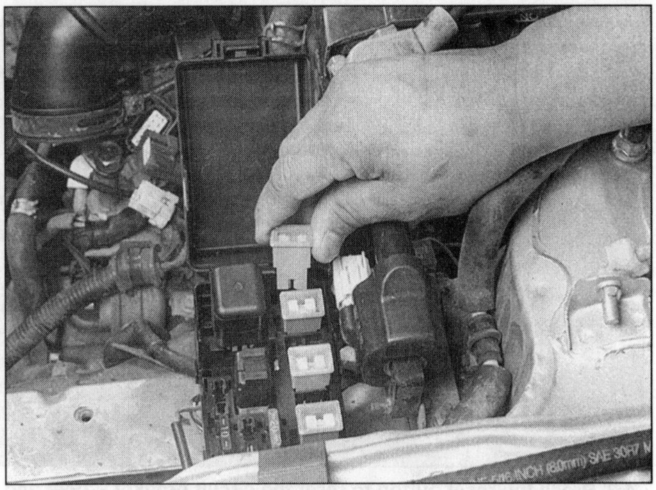

3.3a The main fuses supply circuits with a high current draw

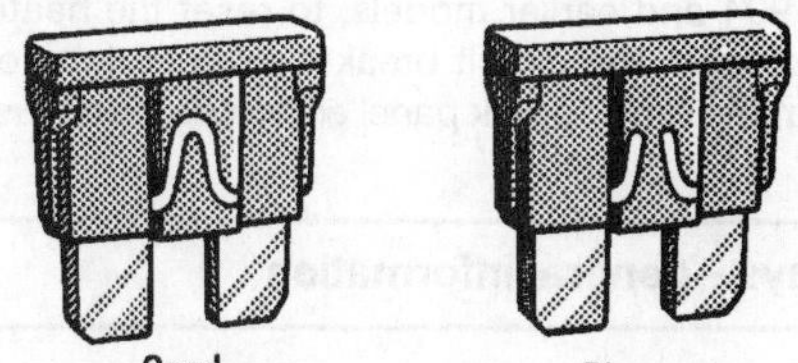

3.3b The fuses are blade type fuses that can be visually checked

Finding an open circuit

When diagnosing for possible open circuits, it is often difficult to locate them by sight because oxidation or terminal misalignment are hidden by the electrical connectors. Merely wiggling an electrical connector on a sensor or in the wiring harness may correct the open circuit condition. Remember this when an open circuit is indicated when troubleshooting a circuit. Intermittent problems may also be caused by oxidized or loose connections.

Electrical troubleshooting is simple if you keep in mind that all electrical circuits are basically electrical current running from the battery, through the wires, switches, relays, fuses and fusible links to each electrical component (light bulb, motor, etc.) and to ground, from which it is passed back to the battery. Any electrical problem is an interruption in the flow of electricity to the electrical component and back to the battery.

3 Fuses - general information

Refer to illustrations 3.1a, 3.1b, 3.1c, 3.1d, 3.3a and 3.3b

1 The electrical circuits of the vehicle are protected by a combination of fuses, circuit breakers and fusible links. The main fuse block is located in the engine compartment on the driver's side, and the interior fuse box is located under the instrument panel on the driver's side of the dashboard **(see illustrations)**.

2 Each of the fuses is designed to protect a specific circuit, and the various circuits are identified on the fuse panel itself. the main fuse block in the engine compartment supplies circuit with high current draws, such as the fuel injection, headlights, cooling fan, air conditioner, etc. The interior fuse box, under the driver's side instrument panel, supplies current to the remainder of the circuits; interior lights, radio, door locks, power windows, instrument panel, wipers, exterior lights, etc.

3 Miniaturized fuses are employed in the main fuse block and the fuse box **(see illustrations)**. These are compact fuses, with blade terminal design. **Note:** *When replacing a fuse, do not attempt to use pliers - always use the fuse puller tool supplied in the fuse box cover for safe removal and replacement, without damaging the fuse itself or neighboring fuses.* If an electrical component fails, always check the fuse first. A blown fuse is easily identified through the clear plastic body. Visually inspect the element for evidence of damage **(see illustration)**, or where possible, perform a continuity check across the fuse terminals with the fuse removed from the fuse block or box. If a continuity check is necessary on the miniaturized (Type A) fuse, the blade terminal tips are exposed in the fuse body.

4 Be sure to replace blown fuses with the correct type. Fuses of different ratings are physically interchangeable, but only fuses of the proper rating should be used. Replacing a fuse with one of a higher or lower value than specified is not recommended. Each electrical circuit needs a specific amount of protection. The amperage value of each fuse is molded into the fuse body.

5 If the replacement fuse immediately fails, this indicates a more serious problem than just a failed or defective fuse. Don't replace it again until the cause of the problem is isolated and corrected. In most cases, this will be a short circuit in the wiring caused by a broken or deteriorated wire, or a failed electrical component.

6 The fuse box under the instrument panel on the driver's side is mounted on the joint box which connects major wiring harnesses and houses the Central Processing Unit (CPU). The CPU controls electrical systems. For access, the kick panel trim must be removed. The CPU is removable for inspection or replacement. A Powertrain Control Module (PCM) is located at the floor behind the center console. The PCM controls engine operation. **Note:** *If the fuse box ROOM fuse is burned out, the dashboard malfunction light will be ON; to replace, turn the ignition switch to LOCK and install the new fuse.*

4 Circuit breakers - general information

Refer to illustration 4.2

1 On some models the circuit breaker resets itself automatically, an electrical overload in a circuit breaker protected system will cause the circuit to fail momentarily, then come back on. If the circuit does not come back on, check it immediately. Note, however, that some circuit breakers must be reset manually. Once the electrical problem is cor-

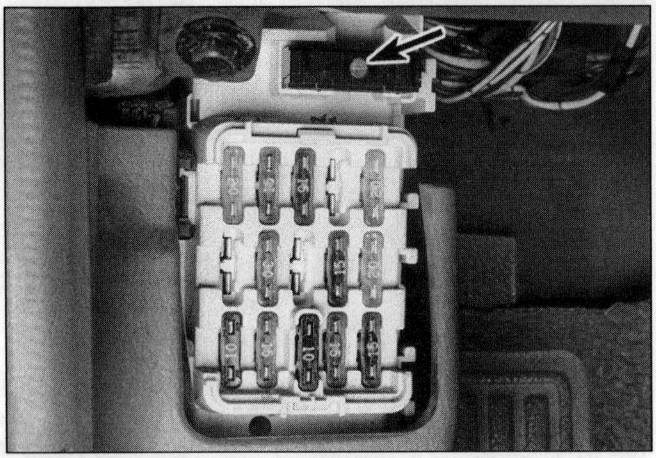

4.2 Press the reset button to reset the circuit breaker - 1994 and earlier models

rected, and the circuit breaker resets, the circuit breaker will resume its normal function.

2 On 1994 and earlier models, to reset the heater manual circuit breaker, press in the circuit breaker reset button, located above the fuse box at the driver's kick panel enclosure **(see illustration)**.

5 Relays - general information

1 Many electrical accessories in the vehicle use relays to transmit the electrical signal to the component. If the relay is defective, that component will not operate properly.

2 The Flasher relay, Door Lock Timer relay, Horn relay, Side Marker/Tail/License/Tail Illumination (TNS) relay, Wiper relay (1994 and earlier), and the Headlight relay are located in one relay assembly under the dashboard on the driver's side. The DRL (Daytime Running Light) control unit and relay are located under the dashboard on the passenger side. On 1995 and later models, the Horn relay is located on the passenger side panel forward of the door opening.

3 If a faulty relay is suspected, it can be removed and tested by a dealer or other qualified shop. Defective relays must be replaced as a unit.

6 Turn signal/hazard flashers - check and replacement

Refer to illustration 6.1

Warning: *1995 and later models are equipped with airbags. The airbag is armed and can deploy (inflate) anytime the battery is connected. To prevent accidental deployment (and possible injury), turn the ignition key to LOCK and disconnect the negative battery cable whenever working near airbag components. After the battery is disconnected, wait at least two minutes before beginning work (the system has a back-up capacitor that must fully discharge). For more information see Section 26.*

1 The turn signal/hazard flasher, a small canister-shaped unit located near the fuse box under the dashboard at the driver's side, flashes the turn signals and the hazard flashers. On 1994 and earlier models, it is mounted on a bracket with the Horn relay, TNS relay, Headlight relay, and Wiper relay. On 1995 and later models, it is located behind the dashboard lower panel under the steering wheel **(see illustration)** and is removed by detaching the dashboard left side panel, the lower panel screws, and the push fastener.

2 When the flasher unit is functioning properly, an audible click can be heard during its operation. If the turn signals fail on one side or the other and the flasher unit does not make its characteristic clicking

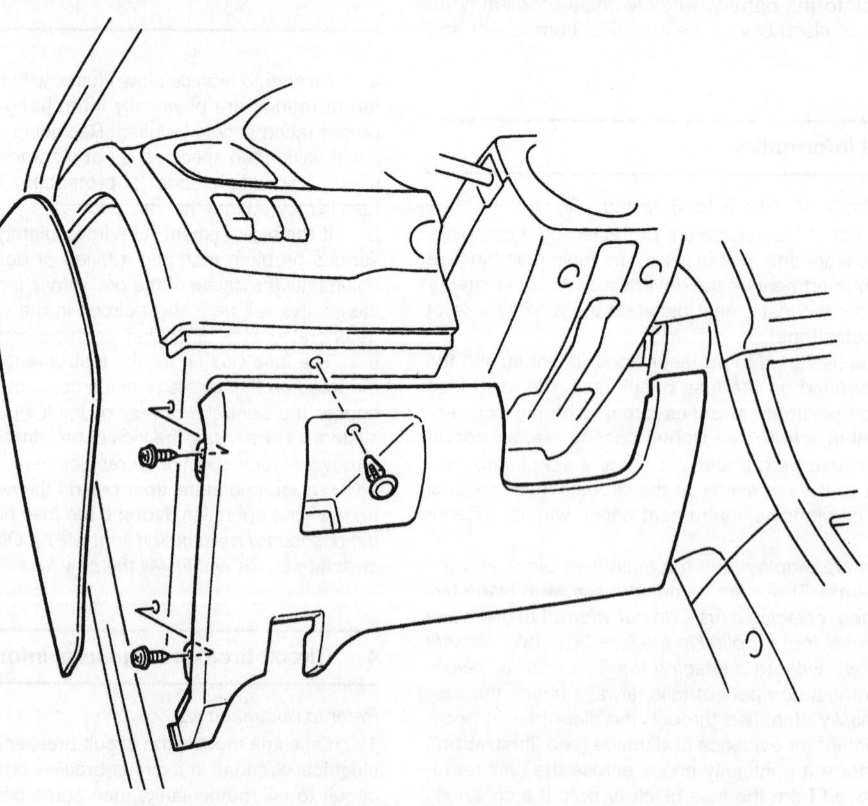

6.1 1995 and later model driver's side lower dash panel removal details

7.5 Remove the combination switch mounting screws - 1994 and earlier model shown

7.6 Slip the combination switch off the steering column and unplug electrical connector(s)

sound, a faulty turn signal bulb is indicated.

3 Flasher relay check: With ignition switch on, operate turn signal switch right and left, checking front and rear turn signals are flashing; actuate Hazard warning switch and check both front and rear signals flash.

4 If both turn signals fail to flash, the problem may be a blown fuse, a faulty flasher unit, a failed bulb, a broken switch or a loose or open electrical connection. If a quick check of the fuse box indicates that the turn signal fuse has blown, check the wiring for a short before installing a new fuse.

5 To replace the flasher, remove the flasher from its mounting bracket, and pull the flasher out of the electrical connector.

6 Also, if a faulty flasher is suspected, it can be removed and tested by a dealer or other qualified shop. Defective flashers must be replaced as a unit. Make sure that the replacement unit is identical to the original. Compare the old one to the new one before installing it.

7 If one side only fails to flash properly, check for burnt out bulbs.

8 Installation is the reverse of removal.

7 Combination switch - removal and installation

Refer to illustrations 7.5, 7.6 and 7.7

Warning: *1995 and later models are equipped with airbags. The airbag is armed and can deploy (inflate) anytime the battery is connected. To prevent accidental deployment (and possible injury), turn the ignition key to LOCK and disconnect the negative battery cable whenever working near airbag components. After the battery is disconnected, wait at least two minutes before beginning work (the system has a back-up capacitor that must fully discharge). For more information see Section 26.*

1 Disconnect the negative battery cable.

2 On 1995 and later models, disable the drivers airbag and remove the airbag assembly (see Chapter 10).

3 Remove the steering wheel (see Chapter 10).

4 Remove the steering column upper and lower covers (see Chapter 11).

5 Remove the combination switch retaining screws **(see illustration)**, clips and latch behind the combination switch.

6 Disconnect the electrical connectors and slide the combination switch off the column. **(see illustration)**. **Warning:** *On models equipped with airbags, handle the combination switch/clockspring assembly very carefully. Damage to the clockspring could cause an airbag system failure resulting in serious personal injury.*

7 Installation is the reverse of removal. On models equipped with airbags, ensure the clockspring is centered properly before installing the combination switch/clockspring assembly onto the steering shaft as follows:

- *a) Position the front wheels pointing straight ahead.*
- *b) Gently rotate the clockspring inner hub clockwise to the end of its stop. Do not force it against the stop.*
- *c) Rotate the clockspring 2-3/4 turns counterclockwise.*
- *d) Align the mark on the inner hub with the mark on the housing* **(see illustration)**.

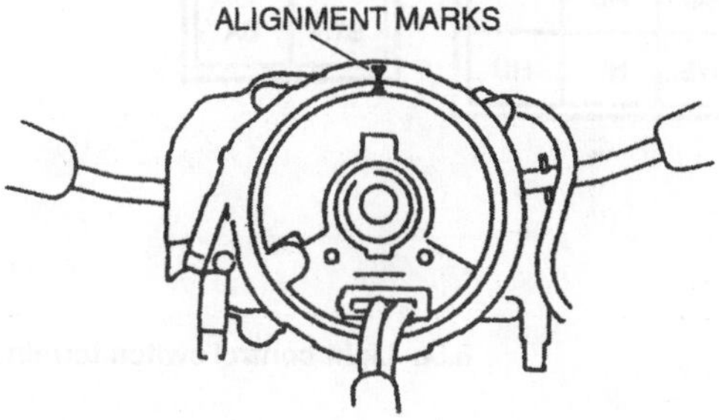

7.7 Airbag clockspring alignment marks

8 Combination switch - check

Refer to illustrations 8.5a, 8.5b, 8.5c, 8.5d and 8.5e

Warning: *1995 and later models are equipped with airbags. The airbag is armed and can deploy (inflate) anytime the battery is connected. To prevent accidental deployment (and possible injury), turn the ignition key to LOCK and disconnect the negative battery cable whenever working near airbag components. After the battery is disconnected, wait at least two minutes before beginning work (the system has a back-up capacitor that must fully discharge). For more information see Section 26.*

Caution: *The combination switch/clockspring assembly on vehicles equipped with airbags can not be disassembled. Replace the complete assembly if any switch fails.*

1 Disconnect the negative cable at the battery.

2 On 1995 and later models, disable the drivers airbag and remove the airbag assembly (see Chapter 10).

3 Remove the steering wheel (see Chapter 10).

4 Remove the steering column upper and lower covers (see Chapter 11).

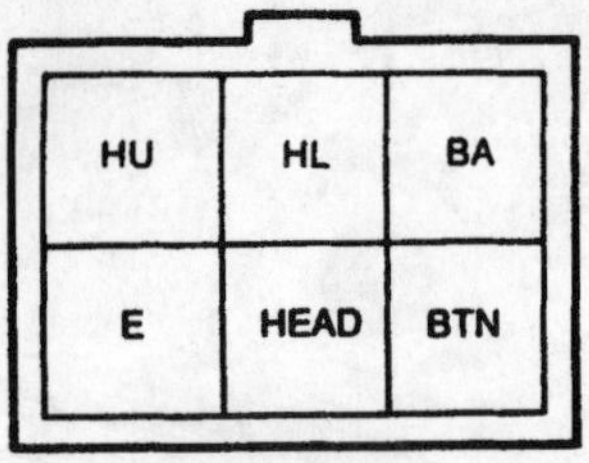

Light switch

Position		BTN	E	HEAD	BA	HU	HL
OFF							
Small		O	O				
Light ON		O	O	O			
	Lo				O		O
	Hi				O	O	
Flash-to-pass			O	O	O	O	

O—O: Continuity

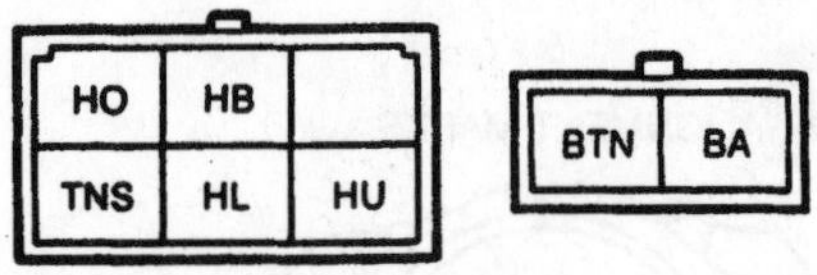

(Canada without cruise control system)
Light switch

Position		BTN	TNS	HB	BA	HU	HL
OFF							
Small		O	O				
Light ON		O	O	O			
	Lo				O		O
	Hi				O	O	
Flash-to-pass		O	O	O	O	O	

8.5a Light control switch terminal guide and continuity table - 1994 and earlier models

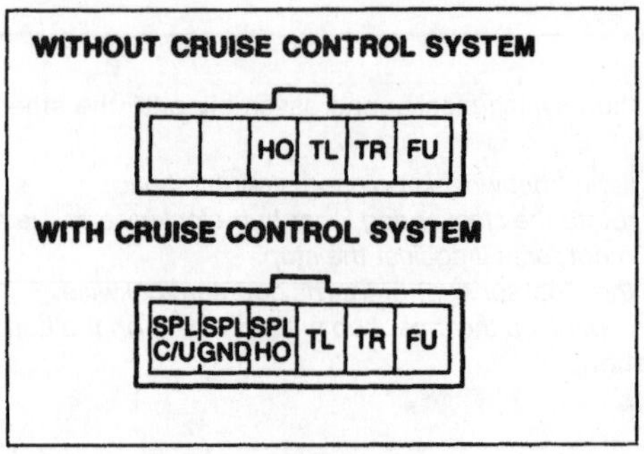

Turn signal switch

Turn	FU	TL	TR
Left	O	O	
OFF			
Right	O		O

O—O: Continuity

Canada

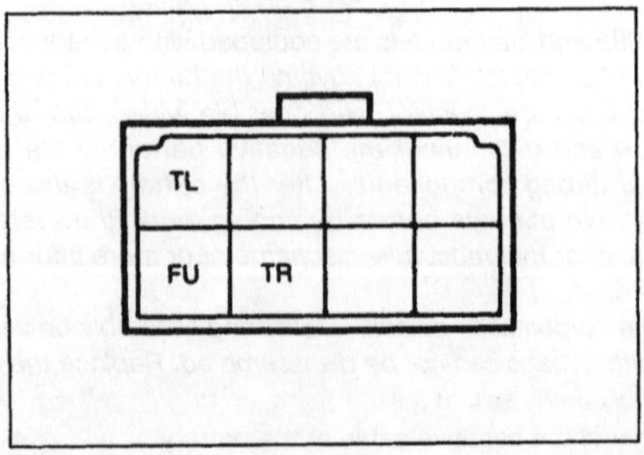

Turn signal switch (Canada without cruise control)

Turn	FU	TL	TR
Left	O	O	
OFF			
Right	O		O

O—O: Continuity

8.5b Turn signal switch terminal guide continuity table - 1994 and earlier models

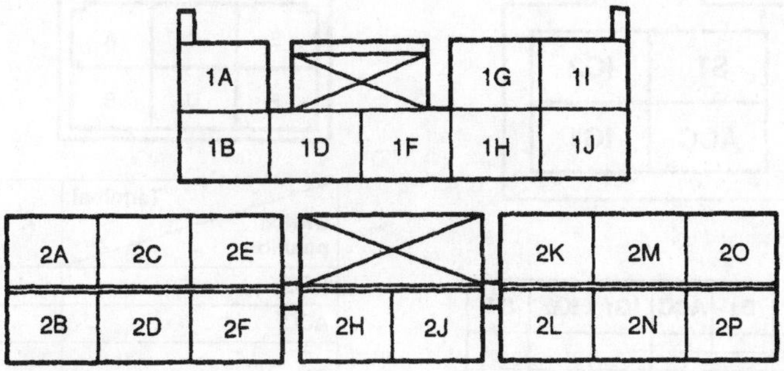

Light	Dimmer	Flash-to-pass	2E	2C	2D	1F	1A	1B	1D
OFF	—	OFF							
		ON						O	O
Parking	—	OFF	O	O					
		ON	O	O				O	O
Headlight	LO	OFF	O	O	O	O	O		
		ON	O	O	O	O	O	O	O
	HI	—	O	O	O	O	—	O	

O—O: Continuity

8.5c Combination switch terminal guide and headlight switch continuity table - 1995 and later models

5 On the combination switch assembly, check for continuity between the indicated terminals using an ohmmeter with the light switch, turn signal switch, and wiper/washer switch in each of the indicated positions **(see illustrations)**.

6 If the continuity between terminals is not as specified in the illustrations, replace the combination switch. Refer to Section 7 for combination switch installation and centering the clockspring, if equipped. See Chapter 10 for steering wheel and airbag installation.

Switch position / Terminal	1I	1H	1G
Left	O	O	
OFF			
Right	O	—	O

O—O: Continuity

8.5d Turn signal switch continuity table - 1995 and later models

9 Ignition switch - check and replacement

Warning: *1995 and later models are equipped with airbags. The airbag is armed and can deploy (inflate) anytime the battery is connected. To prevent accidental deployment (and possible injury), turn the ignition key to LOCK and disconnect the negative battery cable whenever working near airbag components. After the battery is disconnected, wait at least two minutes before beginning work (the system has a back-up capacitor that must fully discharge). For more information see Section 26.*

Switch position		One-touch	2K	2L	2N	2J	2M
Wiper switch	OFF	OFF	O		O		
		ON		O		O	
	LO				O	O	
	HI			O	—	O	
Washer switch	ON					O	O

O—O: Continuity

8.5e Windshield wiper and washer switch continuity table - 1995 and later models

12

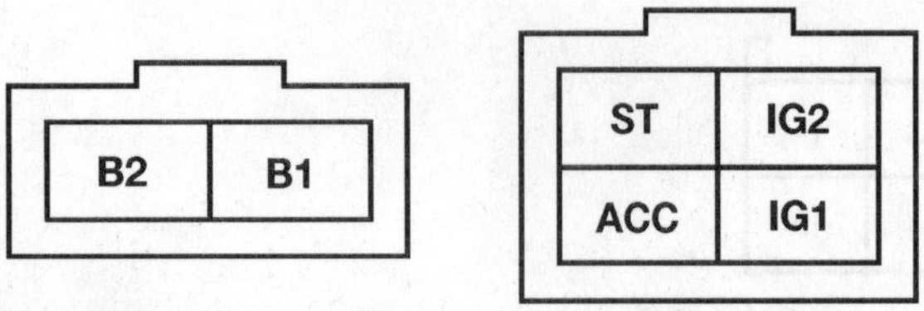

Ignition switch

Position		B1	B2	ACC	IG1	IG2	ST
ACC		O		O			
ON		O		O	O		
			O			O	
ST		O			O		
			O				O
LOCK	TURN						
	RETURN						

9.6a Ignition switch terminal guide and continuity table - 1994 and earlier models

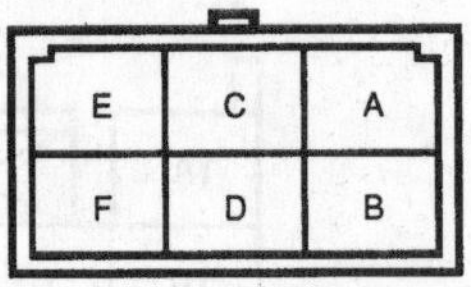

O—O: Continuity

Switch position \ Terminal	A	B	C	D	E	F
LOCK						
ACC			O			O
ON		O	O			O
	O			O		
START		O	O			
				O	O	

9.6b Ignition switch terminal guide and continuity table - 1995 and later models

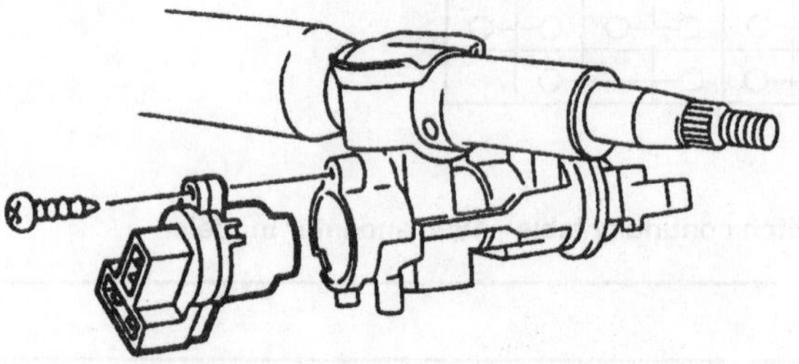

9.8 Ignition switch installation details

1 Disconnect the negative battery cable.
2 On 1995 and later models, disable the drivers airbag.
3 Remove the steering column upper and lower covers (see Chapter 11).
4 Remove the lower dash panel **(see illustration 6.1).**

Check

Refer to illustrations 9.6a and 9.6b

5 Trace the wire from the ignition switch to the electrical connector and unplug the connector.
6 Check for continuity with switch in each indicated position **(see illustrations).**

Replacement

Refer to illustration 9.8

7 Disconnect the electrical connector from the switch.
8 Remove the screw and separate the switch from the steering lock assembly **(see illustration).**
9 Installation is the reverse of removal.

10 Headlight bulb - replacement

Refer to illustrations 10.4a, 10.4b and 10.5

Warning: *Halogen gas-filled bulbs are under pressure and may shatter if the surface is scratched or the bulb is dropped. Wear eye protection and handle the bulbs carefully, grasping only the base whenever possible. Keep bulbs away from children. Allow the bulb to cool before removal. Do not touch the surface of the bulb with your fingers because the oil from your skin could cause it to overheat and fail prematurely. If you do touch the bulb surface, wipe the bulb clean with rubbing alcohol.*

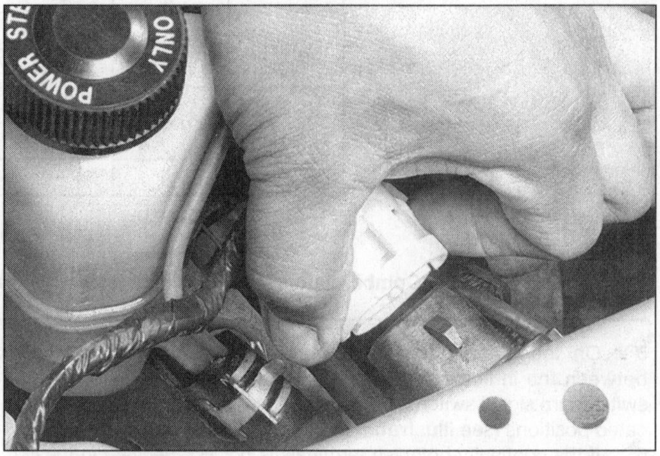

10.4a On 1994 and earlier models, squeeze the tabs and then pull the headlight bulb electrical connector from the headlight bulb

1 Make sure the headlight switch is OFF.
2 Open the hood.
3 Locate the headlight bulb at the rear of the headlight assembly.
4 On 1994 and earlier models, disconnect the electrical connector from the bulb by squeezing the tabs and pulling the electrical connector away from the headlight, then rotate the retainer ring counterclockwise (when viewed from the engine compartment) about one-eighth of a turn **(see illustrations).** On 1995 and later models, disconnect the electrical connector from the bulb and remove the retaining ring.
5 Remove the bulb base **(see illustration).**
6 Make sure the bulb is cool to touch. Grasp the headlight bulb base and carefully pull the bulb out (don't rotate the bulb while removing it). **Note:** *Use the protective cover and carton from the new bulb to promptly dispose of the old bulb.*
7 Install the new headlight bulb with the flat side of the plastic base facing upward, by gently inserting the glass portion of the bulb into the socket. The base of the bulb may need to be rotated slightly clockwise or counterclockwise when inserting it to align the grooves on the bulb base with the tabs in the socket. When the grooves are aligned, push the bulb firmly into the socket.
8 Slide the bulb retaining ring over the plastic base of the bulb. On 1994 and earlier models, lock the retaining ring by rotating it clockwise

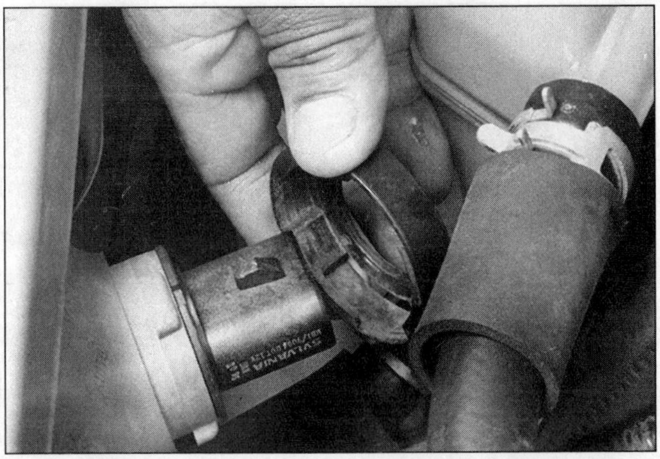

10.4b Rotate the bulb retaining ring counterclockwise about one-eighth of a turn and remove the retaining ring

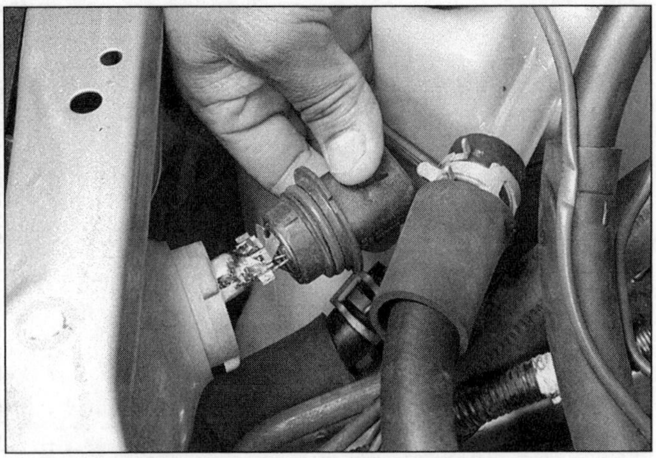

10.5 Pull the headlight bulb assembly straight out of the housing

11.2 Remove the combination light screws and remove the light assembly - 1994 and earlier shown

11.4a Remove the headlight-mounting screws from the front support . . .

(when viewed from the engine compartment). The retaining ring will lock fully when rotated sufficiently and solid resistance is felt.

9 Push the electrical connector into the rear of the bulb base until it snaps and locks into position.

10 Switch on the headlights and check for proper operation. **Note:** *The headlight bulb replacement procedure steps in this Section do not affect headlight aim. However, be sure to check the headlight aim is correct and adjust if necessary per Section 12.*

11 Headlight housing - removal and installation

Refer to illustrations 11.2, 11.4a, 11.4b, 11.5a, 11.5b and 11.6

1 Disconnect the negative battery cable.

2 Remove the front combination light (turn signal/side marker light) retaining screw(s), remove the combination light bulb electrical connector, and pull the combination light assembly off the vehicle **(see illustrations 11.2 and 13.3)**.

3 Remove the headlight bulb electrical connector and remove the headlight bulb (see Section 10). **Warning:** *Halogen gas-filled bulbs are under pressure and may shatter if the surface is scratched or the bulb is dropped. Wear eye protection and handle the bulbs carefully, grasping only the base whenever possible. Keep bulbs away from children. Allow the bulb to cool before removal. Do not touch the surface of the bulb with your fingers because the oil from your skin could cause it to overheat and fail prematurely. If you do touch the bulb surface, wipe the bulb clean with rubbing alcohol.*

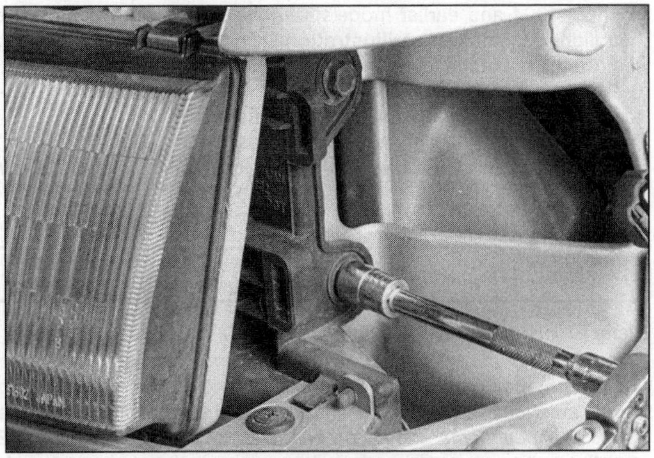

11.4b . . . and the fender

4 Remove the headlight assembly side mounting bolt, accessible with the combination light (turn signal/side marker light) off the vehicle and remove the headlight assembly front mounting bolt, accessible near the grille **(see illustrations)**.

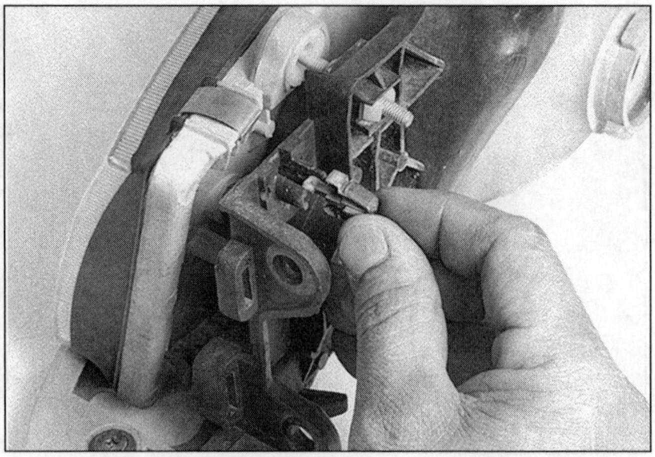

11.5a Remove the headlight clip behind the headlight assembly (unit shown removed from vehicle for clarity) . . .

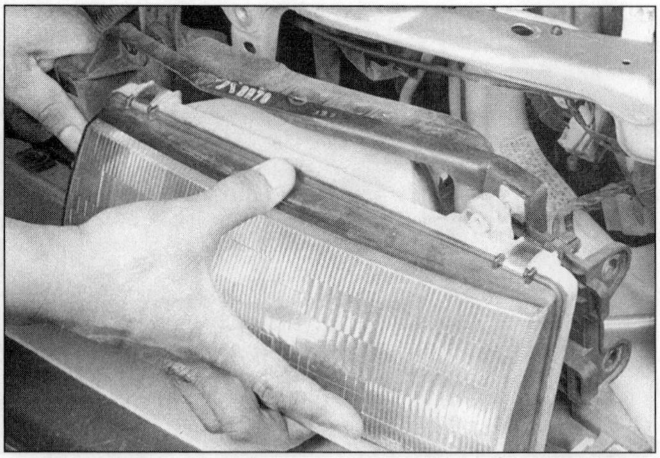

11.5b . . . and remove the headlight assembly

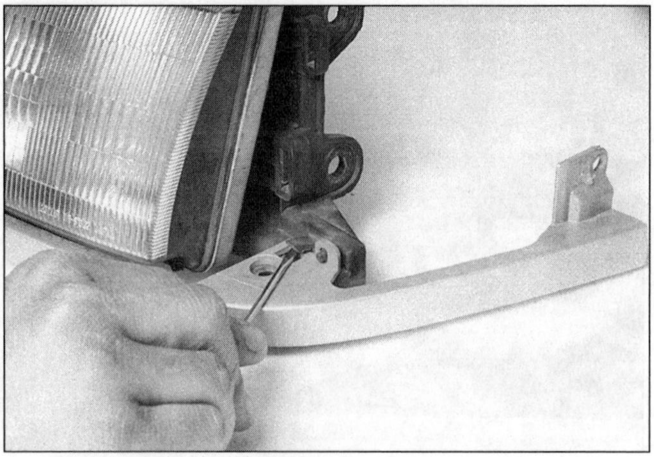

11.6 Remove the lower grille molding screws and remove the molding

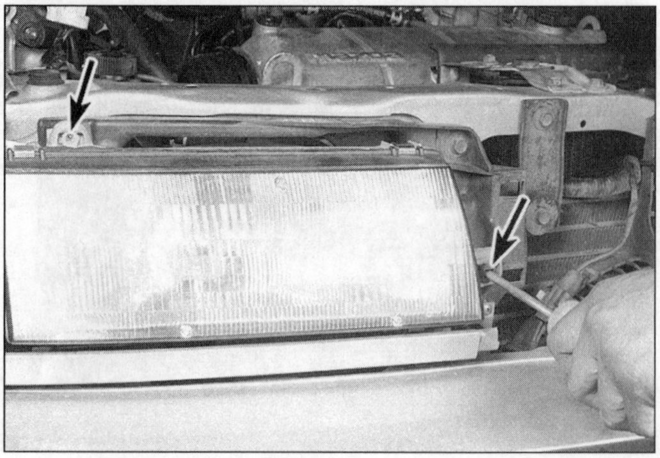

12.1 1994 and earlier headlight adjustment screws (arrows)

5 On 1994 and earlier models, remove the fastener behind the headlight assembly **(see illustration)**. On 1995 and later models, remove the nut at the top of the headlight assembly **(see illustration)**.

6 On 1994 and earlier models, remove the lower grille molding fasteners and the lower grille molding **(see illustration)**.

7 Remove the headlight housing (lens) assembly.

8 Installation is the reverse of removal. Refer to Section 10 for headlight bulb installation.

12 Headlights - adjustment

Refer to illustration 12.1

Note: *It is important that the headlights are aimed correctly. If adjusted incorrectly they could blind the driver of an oncoming vehicle and cause a serious accident or seriously reduce your ability to see the road. The headlights should be checked for proper aim every 12 months and any time a new headlight is installed or front end body work is performed. It should be emphasized that the following procedure is only an interim step which will provide temporary adjustment until the headlights can be adjusted by a properly equipped shop.*

1 1994 and earlier models have two adjustment screws, one to the side controlling left-and-right movement and one above the light for up-and-down movement that are accessible from the front of the headlight housing **(see illustration)**, with the combination light (turn signal/side marker light assembly) removed, and the hood open. 1995 and later models have two adjustment screws, one toward the center of the vehicle controlling left-and-right movement and one closest to the fender for up-and-down movement. They are accessible from the back of the headlight housing with the hood open.

2 There are several methods of adjusting 1994 and earlier headlights. The simplest method requires a blank wall, masking tape and a level floor.

a) *Position masking tape vertically on the wall in reference to the vehicle centerline and the centerlines of both headlights.*

b) *Position a horizontal tape line in reference to the centerline of all the headlights.* **Note:** It may be easier to position the tape on the wall with the vehicle parked only a few inches away.

c) *Adjustment should be made with the vehicle parked 25 feet from the wall, tire air pressure adjusted with the tires cold, sitting level, the gas tank half-full and no unusually heavy load in the vehicle.*

d) *Starting with the low beam adjustment, position the high intensity zone so it is two inches below the horizontal line and two inches to the right of the headlight vertical line. Turn the headlight adjustment screws* ***(see illustration 12.1)*** *until the desired level has been achieved.*

e) *With the high beams on, the high intensity zone should be vertically centered with the exact center just below the horizontal line.* **Note:** It may not be possible to position the headlight aim exactly for both high and low beams. If a compromise must be made, keep in mind that the low beams are the most used and have the greatest effect on driver safety.

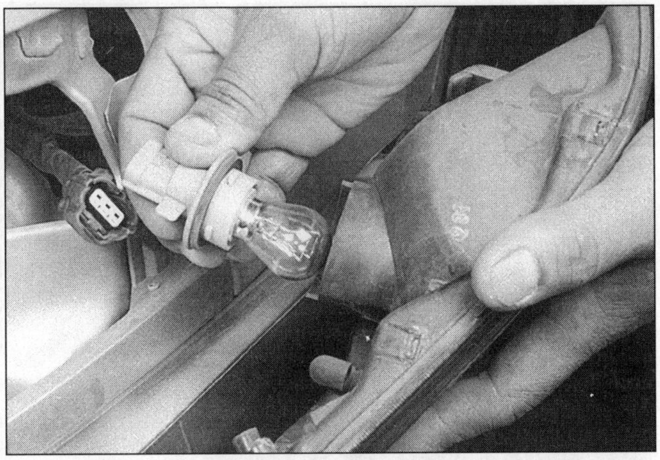

13.3 Unplug the connector and rotate the bulb holders to remove the combination light (turn signal) bulb from the housing

3 To adjust 1995 and later headlights:

a) *With the tire air pressure adjusted to specification and standard size tires mounted on all four wheels, the fuel tank filled, no excess cargo in the vehicle or trunk, position the vehicle on a flat level surface.*

b) *Rock the vehicle by hand several times.*

c) *Adjust the headlights by using a screwdriver at each headlight adjusting points, making sure the horizontal (side-to-side) aiming bubble is within two lines of "0". Then make sure the vertical (up and down) aiming bubble is within two lines of "0".*

4 Have the headlight adjustment checked by a dealer service department at the earliest opportunity.

13 Bulb replacement

Front turn signal, parking and side marker

Refer to illustration 13.3

1 Remove the front light (turn signal/side marker light) retaining screw(s) (see Section 11).

2 Remove the light assembly (see Section 11).

3 On 1994 and earlier models, twist the light bulb holder (socket) counterclockwise and pull it out of the light assembly **(see illustration)**. On 1995 and later models, pull the bulb/socket assembly from its the light assembly socket.

4 On 1994 and earlier models, while holding the combination light bulb holder, rotate the bulb to remove it. Replace the bulb.

5 On 1995 and later models, pull the bulb from its socket and replace the bulb.

6 Installation is the reverse of removal.

Rear brake, turn signal, tail, back-up lights, and side marker

Refer to illustrations 13.8 and 13.10

Sedan

7 Open the trunk lid.

8 Inside the trunk, remove the light housing/ bulb socket holder **(see illustration)**.

9 Twist the combination light bulb being replaced to remove it from its holder (socket).

10 To remove the combination light assembly entirely, open the trunk lid and remove the combination light assembly retaining nut. On 1994 and earlier models, the retaining nut is inside the trunk. On 1995 and later models, the fender-mounted lights are retained by screws exposed when the trunk lid is open. On 1995 and later models, the trunk lid mounted (inboard) combination light is retained by through bolts from inside the trunk lid. Remove the combination light assembly and gasket, while disconnecting the wiring electrical connector **(see illustration)**.

11 On 1994 and earlier models, to remove the sedan rear side marker light, remove the two screws, twist the bulb holder (socket), and pull the bulb to remove it. Press in the new bulb.

12 Installation is the reverse of removal.

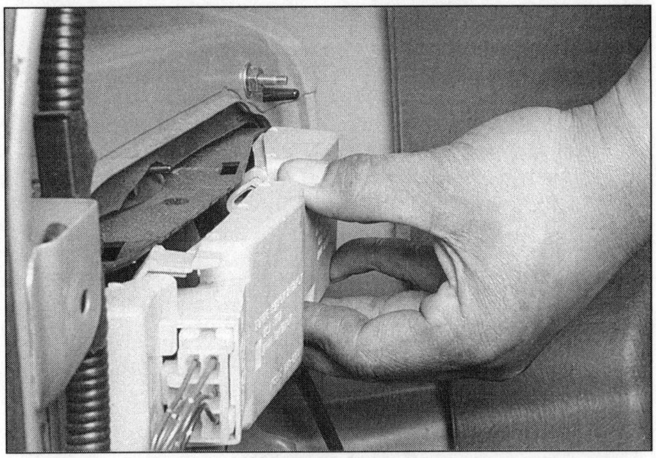

13.8 Remove fasteners to pull out the rear brake light, taillight, turn signal, or backup light

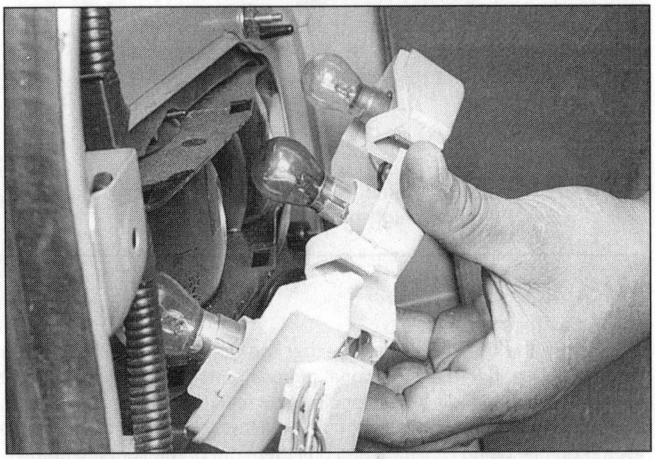

13.9 Remove the taillight bulb holder (socket) to replace the bulbs

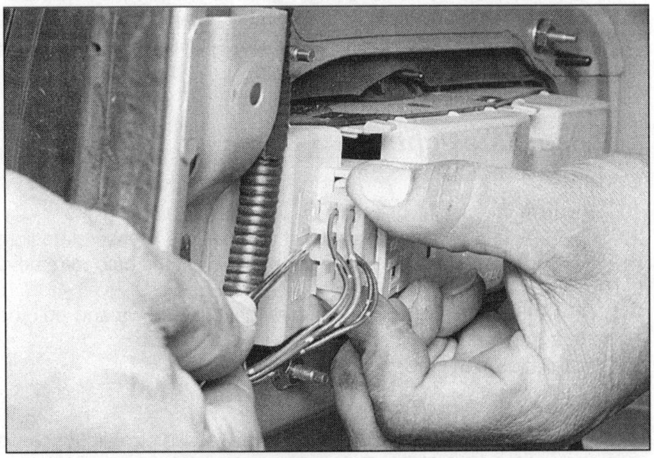

13.10 From inside the trunk, disconnect the combination light assembly wiring harness (sedan models)

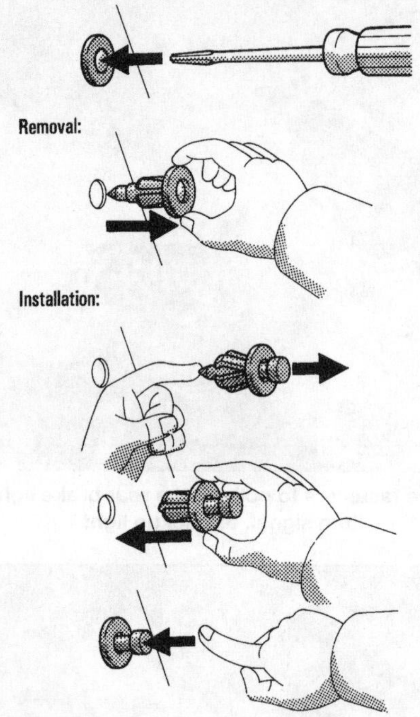

13.25 Push-pull retainer removal and installation details (sedan high-mounted brake light)

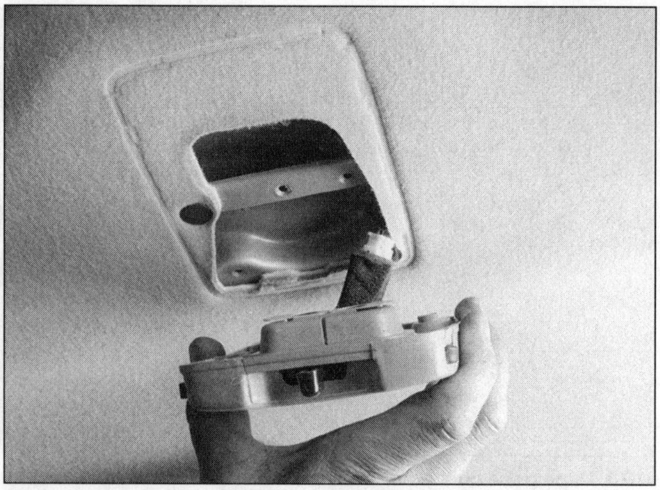

13.34a Remove the screws retaining the overhead light assembly

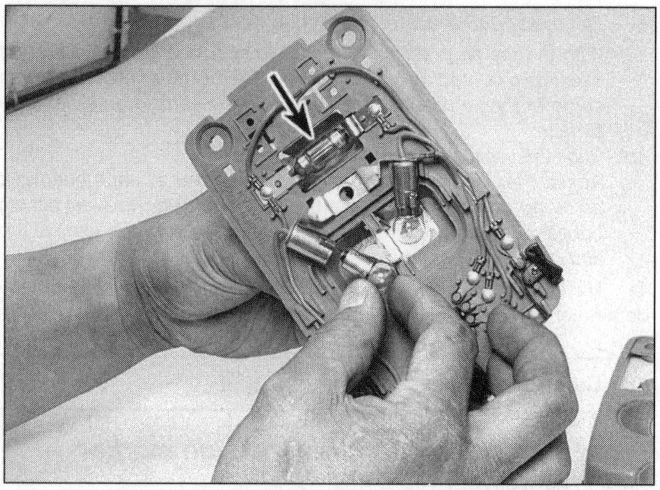

13.34b Remove the overhead map light bulbs

Hatchback

13 Open the rear hatch.

14 Inside the trunk area, open either the brake/taillight/side marker light access panel, the turn signal access panel, or the backup light access panel depending on the bulb to be replaced.

15 Twist the combination light bulb holder (socket) counterclockwise for the bulb(s) being replaced and pull them out of the light assembly.

16 Holding the combination light bulb holder (socket), rotate the bulb being replaced to remove it. Replace the bulb.

17 To remove the combination light assembly, open the rear hatch and remove the combination light assembly retaining nut (inside the trunk). Remove the combination light assembly and gasket, while disconnecting the wiring electrical connector.

18 Installation is the reverse of removal.

License plate light

Sedan

19 Remove the rear license plate for access.

20 On 1994 and earlier models, twist and pull the license plate light holder (socket) out of the slot in the car body. Twist the bulb to remove it. Replace the bulb.

21 On 1995 and later models, remove the lens screws and pull the bulbs out. Replace the bulbs.

22 Installation is the reverse of removal

Hatchback

23 Above the rear license plate, remove the license plate light screws and remove the lens. **Note:** *There are two identical rear license plate lights.*

24 Pull the bulb to remove it. Press in the new bulb.

High-mounted brake light

Refer to illustration 13.25

Sedan

25 On 1994 and earlier models, remove the two high-mounted brake light housing push-pull retaining pins or retaining screws **(see illustration).** Remove the high-mounted brake light housing. Twist and pull the high-mounted brake light holder (socket) and pull it out of the light housing. Twist the bulb to remove it. Replace the bulb.

26 On 1995 and later models, remove the push fasteners to remove the light housing cover.

27 On 1995 and later models, remove the bulb base from the housing. Replace the bulb.

28 Installation is the reverse of removal.

Hatchback

29 On the exterior of the hatch, remove the high-mounted stoplight retaining screws.

30 Rotate the bulb holder (socket) counterclockwise to remove it from the high-mounted brake light assembly.

31 Pull the bulb to remove it. Press in the new bulb.

32 Installation is the reverse of removal.

Interior lights

Refer to illustrations 13.34a and 13.34b

33 For the interior light mounted at the center of the roof, pull the light lens off, and pull the bulb from its holder (socket). Replace the bulb and press the light lens in place.

34 For models with a sunroof, remove the map lights (spot lights) in the overhead panel by removing the rearview mirror, slide back the panel cover, remove the panel, and pull out the map light bulb(s) **(see illustrations)**. Press in the new bulb(s). Installation is the reverse of removal.

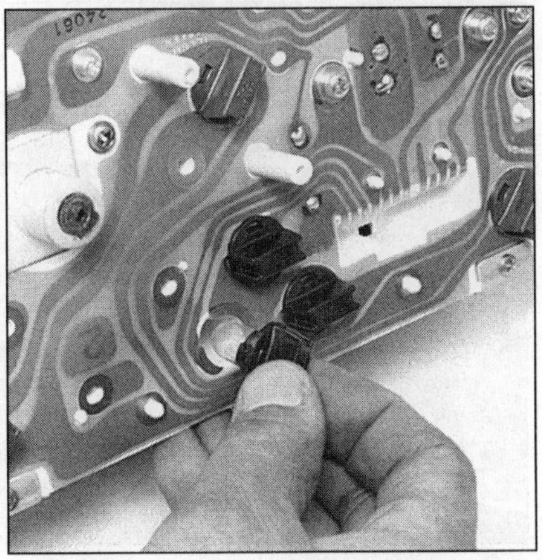

13.36 The instrument cluster light bulbs are removed from the backside of the cluster

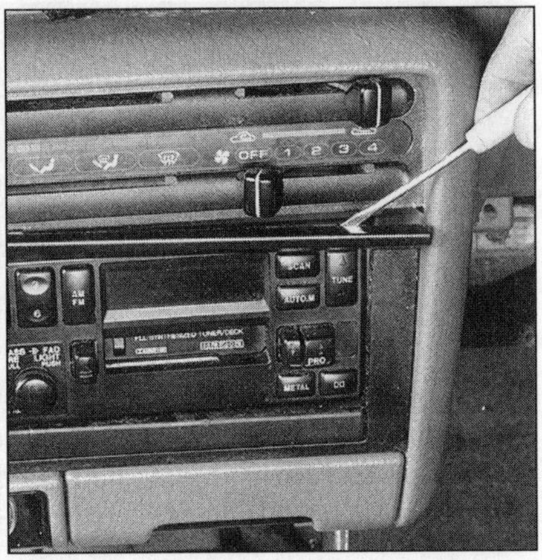

15.2 Carefully pry the trim bezel from around the radio

15.3a Remove the radio retaining screws

35 For models without a sunroof, remove the map lights (spot lights) mounted at the center of the roof by pulling the light lens off, remove the light housing, and twisting the bulb(s) to remove them. Replace the bulb(s). Installation is the reverse of removal.

Instrument cluster illumination

Refer to illustration 13.36

36 To gain access to the instrument cluster illumination light(s), the instrument cluster will have to be removed (see Section 17). The bulb(s) can then be removed and replaced from the rear of the cluster **(see illustration)**.

14 Daytime Running Lights (DRL) - general information

1 The Daytime Running Lights (DRL) system, used on some models, turns the headlights on whenever the engine is started. The only exception is when the engine is on when the parking brake is engaged. Once the parking brake is released, the lights will remain on as long as the ignition switch is on, even if the parking brake is later applied.

2 The DRL system supplies reduced voltage to the headlights so they won't be too bright for daytime use, while prolonging headlight life.

15 Radio and speakers - removal and installation

Warning: *1995 and later models are equipped with airbags. The airbag is armed and can deploy (inflate) anytime the battery is connected. To prevent accidental deployment (and possible injury), turn the ignition key to LOCK and disconnect the negative battery cable whenever working near airbag components. After the battery is disconnected, wait at least two minutes before beginning work (the system has a back-up capacitor that must fully discharge). For more information see Section 26.*

Caution: *If the stereo in your vehicle is equipped with an anti-theft system, make sure you have the correct activation code before disconnecting the battery.*

Radio

Refer to illustrations 15.2, 15.3a and 15.3b

1 Disconnect the negative cable at the battery.

2 Remove the radio trim bezel **(see illustration)**.

3 Remove the radio retaining screws, pull the radio out far enough to unplug the electrical connector and the antenna lead and remove the radio **(see illustrations)**.

4 Installation is the reverse of removal.

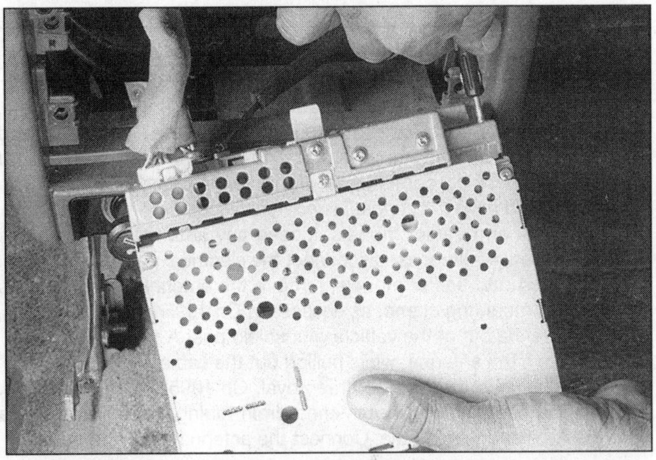

15.3b Pull the radio out of the instrument panel and disconnect the electrical connectors and antenna lead

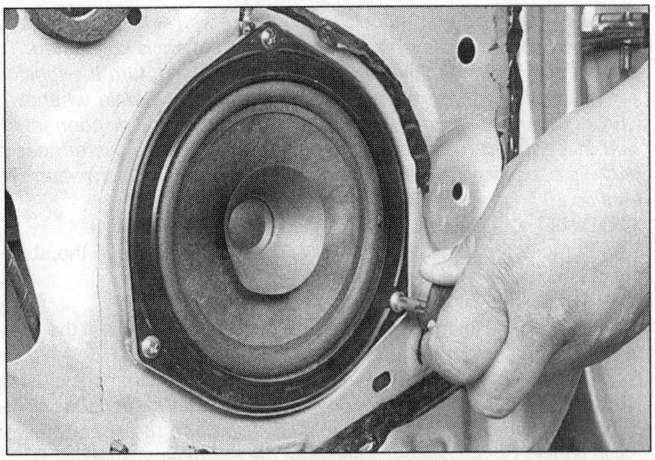

15.6 Remove the speaker electrical connector and the speaker attaching screws to remove the speaker

Speakers

Refer to illustration 15.6

5 Remove the front door trim panel (see Chapter 11).

6 Remove the speaker retaining screws/nuts. Unplug the electrical connector and remove the speaker **(see illustration)**.

7 Installation is the reverse of removal.

12

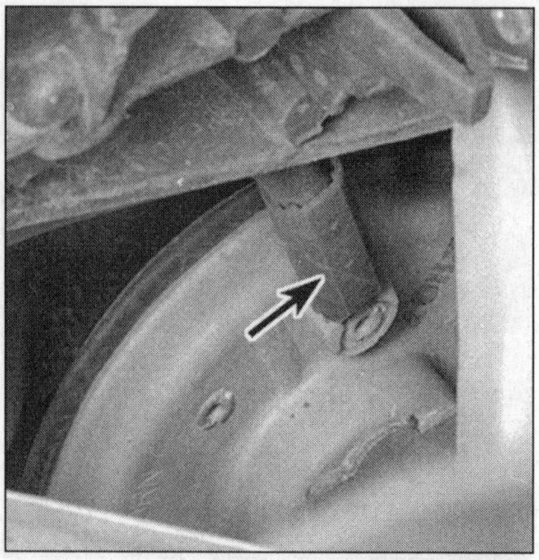

18.4 Disconnect the horn electrical connector (arrow) and remove the horn mounting bolts

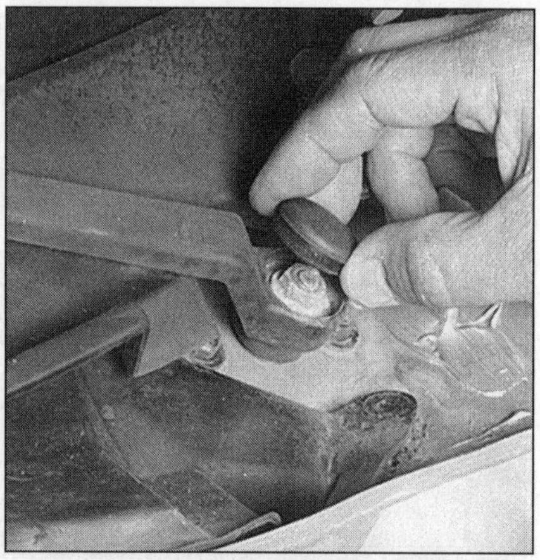
19.6 Remove the wiper arm nut cover for access to the retaining nut

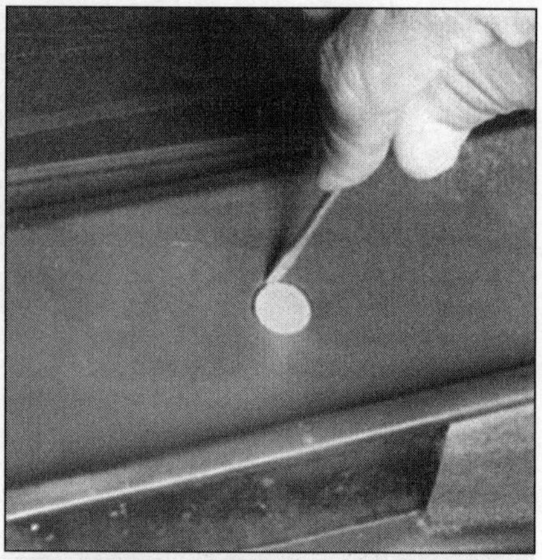
19.7a Remove the cowl grille buttons and screws

16 Antenna - removal and installation

1 Unplug the cable from the radio. On 1995 and later models, Remove the lower dash panel at the driver's side (see Chapter 11) and disconnect the antenna jack. **Note:** *The antenna may be tested if desired, by checking continuity at the antenna cable plug end. The antenna should have full continuity (no resistance).*

2 On 1994 and earlier models, loosen any antenna cable clamps found. For power antennas, disconnect the electrical power connector.

3 On 1994 and earlier models, remove the antenna mount screws or threaded mounting clamp, as necessary. On 1995 and later models, pull the antenna out of the vehicle windshield post A-pillar.

4 Remove the antenna, while pulling out the cable.

5 Installation is the reverse of removal. On 1995 and later models, tape the antenna jack to the antenna drain tubing, pass the antenna into the A-pillar antenna hole. Connect the antenna base and install.

17 Instrument cluster - removal and installation

Warning: *1995 and later models are equipped with airbags. The airbag is armed and can deploy (inflate) anytime the battery is connected. To prevent accidental deployment (and possible injury), turn the ignition key to LOCK and disconnect the negative battery cable whenever working near airbag components. After the battery is disconnected, wait at least two minutes before beginning work (the system has a back-up capacitor that must fully discharge). For more information see Section 26.*

1 Disconnect the cable from the negative battery terminal.

2 Remove the steering wheel (see Chapter 10). Remove the steering column upper and lower covers (see Chapter 11).

3 Remove the instrument cluster bezel (see Chapter 11).

4 Remove the instrument cluster retaining screws and pull the cluster away from the dashboard.

5 Disconnect the speedometer cable from the instrument cluster. **Note:** *Lubrication of a noisy speedometer cable may be done by injecting lithium grease or other suitable lubricant into the speedometer cable housing when disconnected from the instrument cluster.*

6 Unplug the electrical connectors and remove the cluster.

7 Installation is the reverse of removal.

18 Horn - check and replacement

Check

1 Disconnect the electrical connector from the horn under the car.

2 Test the horn by carefully connecting battery voltage to the two horn terminals with jumper wires from the battery.

3 If the horn doesn't sound, replace it. If it does sound, the problem lies in the steering wheel horn switch, horn relay (see Section 5) or the wiring between components.

Replacement

Refer to illustration 18.4

4 Disconnect the electrical connector and remove the bracket bolt **(see illustration)**.

5 Installation is the reverse of removal.

19 Wiper motor - check and replacement

1 The windshield wiper motor is located on the left (driver's) side of the engine compartment. The rear wiper motor (Hatchback model only) is mounted in the rear hatchback door.

Check

Windshield wiper/washer switch

2 Refer to Section 8 for the wiper and washer switch check procedure.

Wiper motor

3 If a motor doesn't work or doesn't park properly and the wiper switch checks okay, the relay or the motor must be replaced.

Replacement

Windshield wiper motor

Refer to illustrations 19.6, 19.7a, 19.7b, 19.8, 19.9, 19.11a and 19.11b

4 Disconnect the cable from the negative battery terminal.

5 Unplug the electrical connector from the wiper motor.

6 Remove the wiper arm plug for access to the wiper arm retaining nut **(see illustration)**. Remove the nut and lift the arm off the shaft.

7 Remove the cowl grille by removing the cowl grille fastener cover buttons and screws and remove the cowl grille **(see illustrations)**.

8 Remove the baffle (cover) over the wiper at the left (driver's) side **(see illustration)**.

9 Remove the wiper motor linkage nut from the wiper motor driveshaft **(see illustration)** and detach the linkage arm.

10 Scribe or mark the wiper motor bracket position before removing the motor from the bracket.

11 Remove the wiper motor bracket retaining bolts, then lower the wiper motor and bracket assembly and remove it from the vehicle **(see illustrations)**.

12 Installation is the reverse of removal.

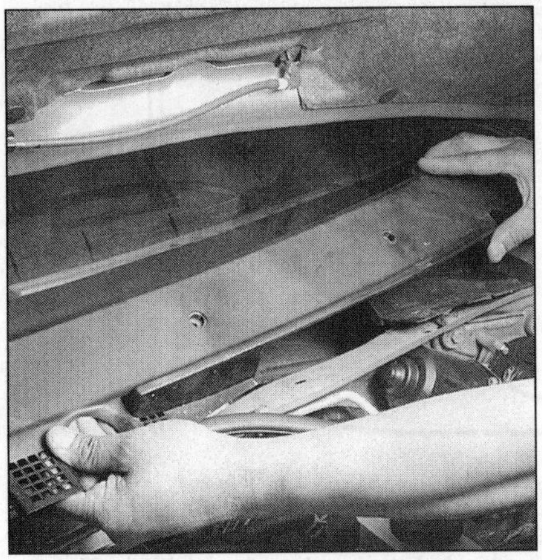

19.7b Lift the cowl grille

19.8 Remove the wiper linkage baffle

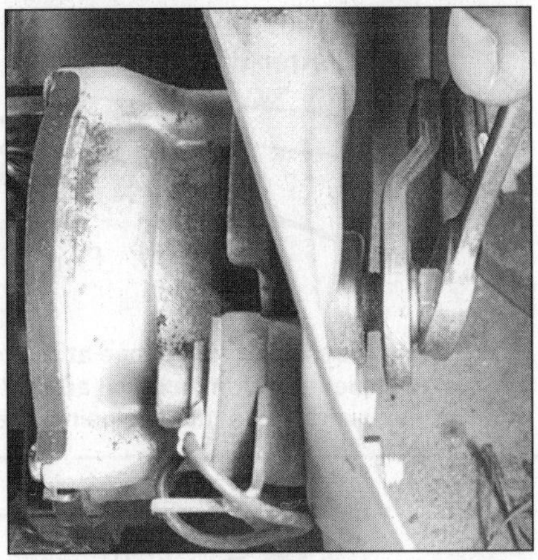

19.9 Remove the wiper motor to linkage nut and detach the linkage arm

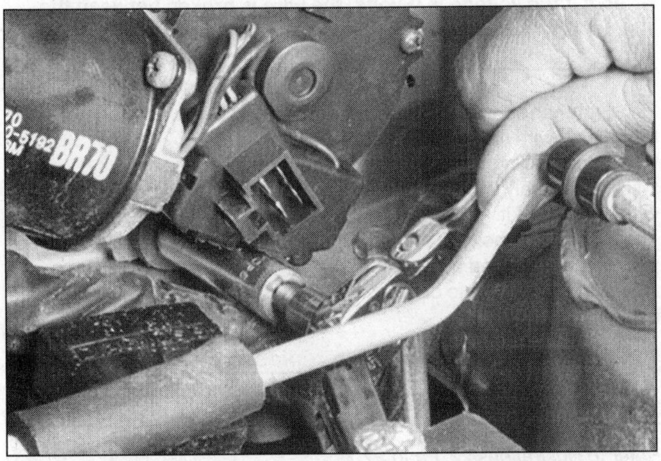

19.11a Unbolt the wiper motor mounting bolts

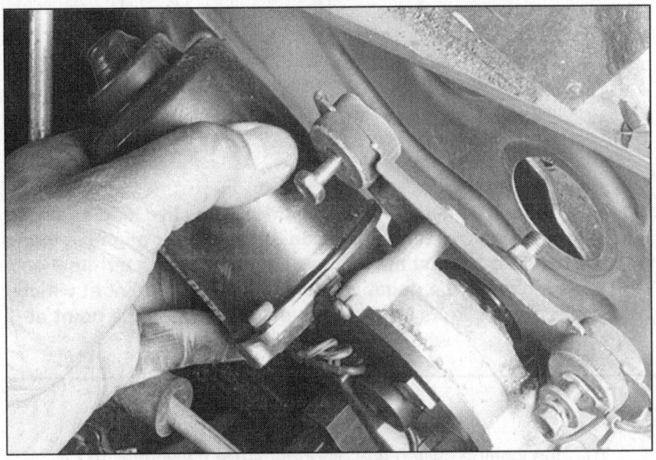

19.11b Remove the wiper motor assembly

Rear wiper motor

13 Remove the wiper arm, then remove the shaft spindle nuts and washers. **Note:** *Clean the wiper arm spindle splines before reinstallation of the wiper arms.*

14 Unplug the electrical connector, detach the wiper linkage, remove the retaining bolts and lower the motor through the rear hatch access hole as an assembly.

15 Installation is the reverse of removal.

20 Rear window defogger switch - check and replacement

Refer to illustration 20.3

Warning: *1995 and later models are equipped with airbags. The airbag is armed and can deploy (inflate) anytime the battery is connected. To prevent accidental deployment (and possible injury), turn the ignition key to LOCK and disconnect the negative battery cable whenever working near airbag components. After the battery is disconnected, wait at least two minutes before beginning work (the system has a back-up capacitor that must fully discharge). For more information see Section 26.*

1 Detach the cable from the negative battery terminal.

2 Remove the instrument cluster bezel (see Section 17) and access the rear defogger switch.

3 Use an ohmmeter to check for continuity at the indicated terminals with the switch in the indicated positions **(see illustration)**.

4 Replace the switch if the continuity is not as specified.

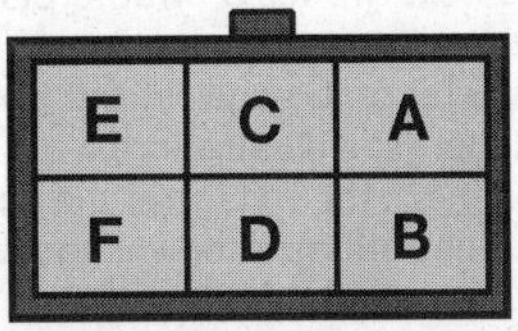

REAR WINDOW DEFROSTER SWITCH

POSITION \ TERMINAL	A	B	C	D	E	F
OFF	●—⊗	—●	●—	—⊗—	—	—●
ON	●—⊗	—●	●—	●—	⊗—	—●

●—●: CONTINUITY

61015-12-20.3 HAYNES

20.3 Rear window defogger switch terminal guide and continuity table

21 Rear window defogger - check and repair

Refer to illustrations 21.6, 21.7 and 21.9

1 The rear window defogger consists of a grid of horizontal heater filament elements baked onto the glass surface.

2 Small breaks in the element can be repaired without removing the rear window.

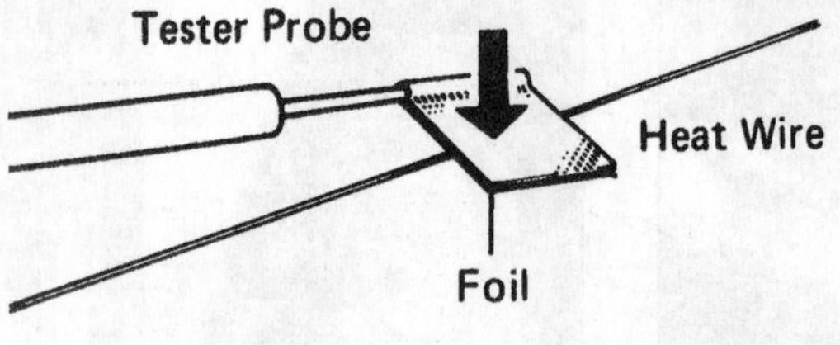

21.6 When measuring the voltage at the rear window defogger grid, wrap a piece of aluminum foil around the negative probe of the voltmeter and press the foil against the wire with your finger

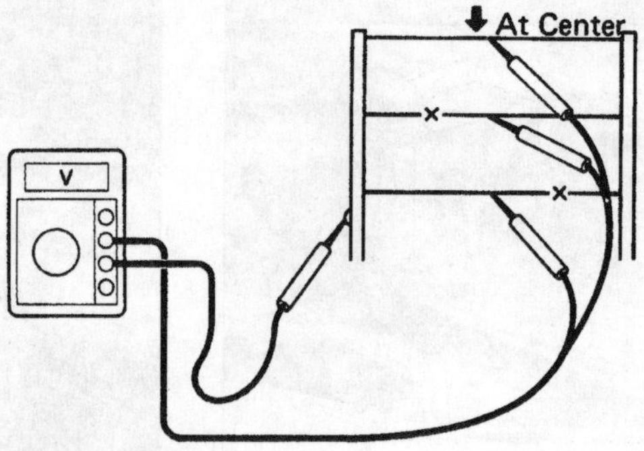

21.7 To determine if a wire has broken, place the voltmeter positive lead against the defogger positive terminal and check the voltage with the negative lead at the *center* of each wire - if the voltage is 5-volts, the wire is unbroken; if the voltage is 10-volts, the wire is broken between the center of the wire and the positive end; if the voltage is 0-volts, the wire is broken between the center of the wire and ground

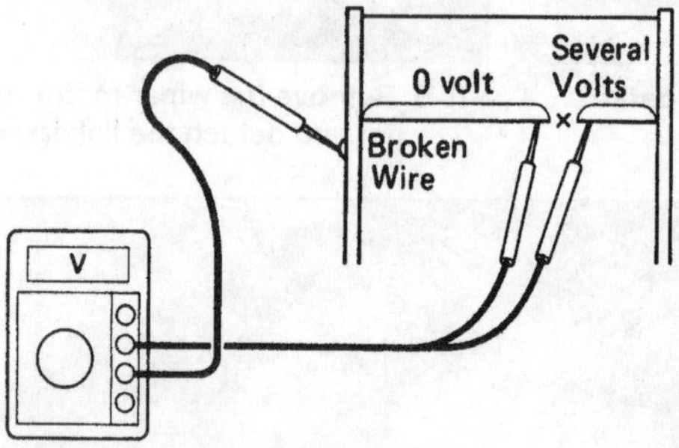

21.9 To find the break, place the voltmeter positive lead against the defogger positive terminal, place the voltmeter negative lead with the foil strip against the heat wire at the positive terminal end and slide it toward the negative terminal end - the point at which the voltmeter deflects from zero to several volts is the point at which the wire is broken

Check

3 Turn the ignition switch and defogger system switches to ON.

4 Determine which side of the window defogger heat grid is negative (connected to ground), and which side is positive (connected to 12 volts).

5 When measuring voltage during the next two tests, wrap a piece of aluminum foil around the tip of each voltmeter probe.

6 Press the foil-covered positive voltmeter probe against the positive side of the defogger grid with your finger **(see illustration)**.

7 Using the voltmeter negative probe, check the voltage at the center of each heater filament element **(see illustration).** If the voltage is 5 volts, the wire is okay (there is no break). If the voltage is high (10 to 12 volts), the wire is broken between the center of the element and the positive end. If the voltage is 0-volts the wire is broken between the center of the element and ground.

8 Connect the negative lead to a good body ground. The reading should stay the same.

9 To find the break, place the voltmeter positive lead against the defogger positive terminal. Place the voltmeter negative lead with the foil strip against the heat wire at the positive terminal end and slide it toward the negative terminal end. The point at which the voltmeter deflects from zero to several volts is the point at which the heater filament element is broken **(see illustration)**. Make note of the location of the area of the heater filament break **Note:** *If the heat element is not broken, the voltmeter will indicate no voltage at the positive end of the heat element but gradually increase to about 12-volts.*

Repair

10 Repair the break in the element using a repair kit specifically recommended for this purpose, such as Dupont paste No. 4817 (or equivalent). Included in this kit is plastic conductive epoxy.

11 Prior to repairing a break, turn off the system and allow it to cool off for a few minutes.

12 Lightly buff the element area with fine steel wool, then clean it thoroughly with rubbing alcohol.

13 Use masking tape to mask off the area being repaired.

14 Thoroughly mix the epoxy, following the instructions provided with the repair kit.

15 Apply the epoxy material to the slit in the masking tape, overlapping the undamaged area about 3/4-inch on either end.

16 Allow the repair to cure for 24 hours before removing the tape and using the system.

22 Cruise control system - description and check

Refer to illustrations 22.1 and 22.7

1 The cruise control system maintains vehicle speed with a cruise control unit (computer), located in the passenger compartment under the dashboard behind the heater blower unit, a speed sensor to signal the cruise control unit, and an actuator located in the engine compartment. The actuator is connected to the throttle linkage by a cable. The cruise control system also consists of the steering wheel cruise control switches, speed sensor in the instrument cluster, brake light switch, clutch switch for vehicles with manual transmissions, and associated wiring **(see illustration)**. Some features of the system requires special testers and diagnostic procedures which are beyond the scope of the home mechanic. Listed below are some general procedures that may be used to locate common problems.

2 Check the cruise control fuse labeled METER (1994 and earlier models) which fuses the instrument panel and STOP fuse (1995 and later models), at the fuse box (see Section 3).

3 Have an assistant operate the brake pedal while you check the operation of the brake lights (voltage from the brake light and clutch switch on vehicles with manual transmission deactivates the cruise control).

4 If the brake lights don't come on or don't shut off, correct the problem and retest the cruise control. Check the clutch switch (Chapter 8).

5 Visually inspect the vacuum hose connected to the actuator, check the control cable between the cruise control actuator and the throttle linkage, and replace as necessary.

6 Check the control cable freeplay as follows: Remove the cable clip and adjust the nut so that the actuator control cable freeplay is approximately 1/32 inch to 3/16 inch when the cable is pressed lightly by your finger.

7 On 1994 and earlier models, a quick test of the remainder of the cruise control system is performed as follows, using a 1.4 Watt test

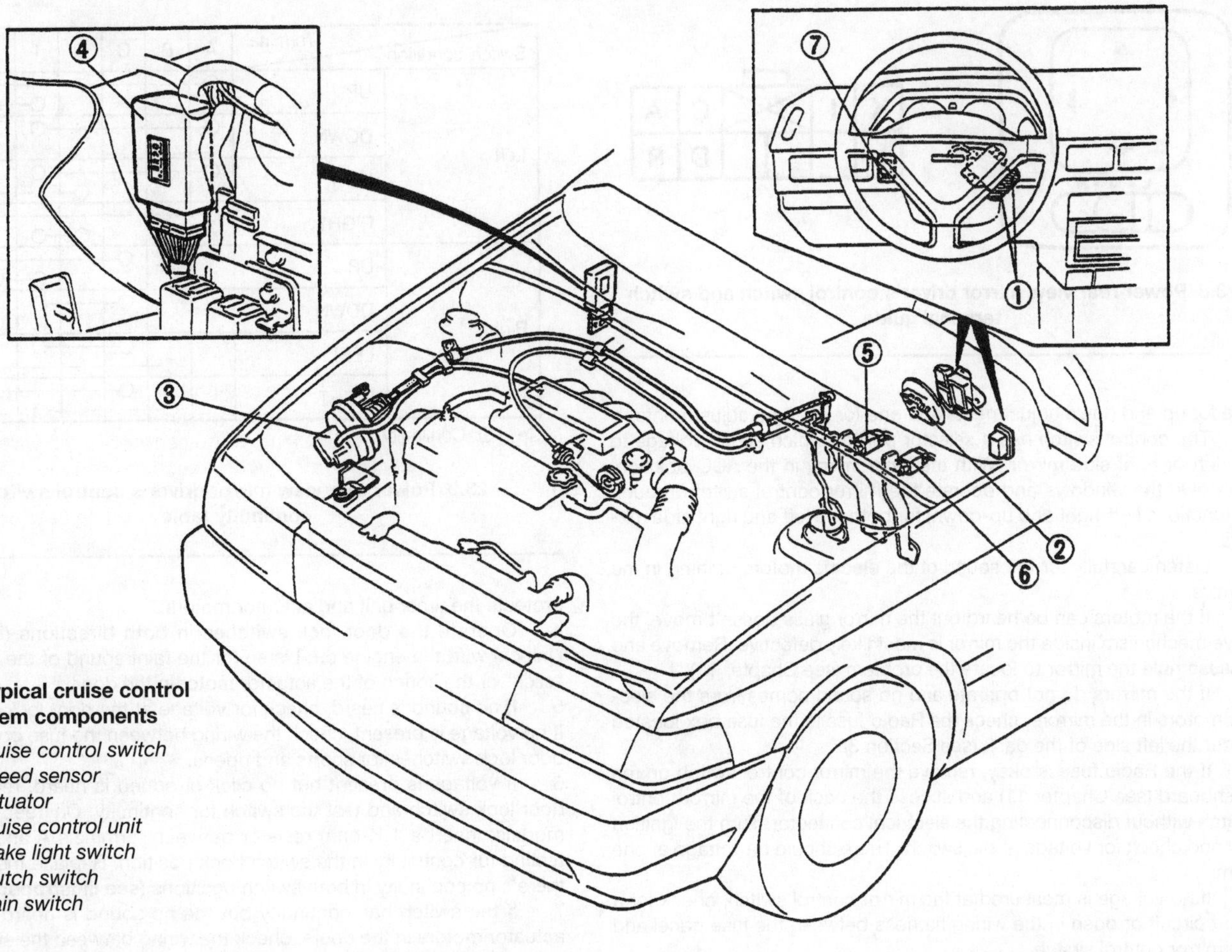

22.1 Typical cruise control system components

1. *Cruise control switch*
2. *Speed sensor*
3. *Actuator*
4. *Cruise control unit*
5. *Brake light switch*
6. *Clutch switch*
7. *Main switch*

light with probes connected between terminals D and F of the cruise control connector **(see illustration)**, located under the dash on the cruise control unit behind the heater blower unit (see Chapter 3 for access). Connect the test light with the cruise control connector still connected to the cruise control unit, and with the Terminal D probe pushed through open Terminal D hole to the electrical connector pin on the control unit.

8 Turn the ignition switch ON, and shift the gear selector lever to D or R on automatic transmission vehicles, or to any gear except neutral on manual transmission vehicles. Check the cruise control Main switch is OFF (Main indicator light is OFF).

9 Press the Resume/Accel switch and the Main switch simultaneously to activate the system test. The Main indicator light will come on. Then operate each switch described below and obtain the two-digit problem code numbers (light flashes; first set of flashes is the first digit of the problem code and then the second set of flashes is the second digit of the problem code). Example: Three flashes, a slight delay, then five flashes, indicates problem Code 35.

10 Pressing Set/Coast switch, problem Code 21 indicates trouble with the cruise control switch.

11 Pressing Resume/Accel switch, problem Code 22 indicates trouble with the cruise control switch.

12 Depressing brake pedal, problem Code 31 indicates trouble with the brake light switch.

13 Turning Ignition switch ON, shift the gear selector lever to P or N on automatic transmission vehicles, or depressing the clutch on manual transmission vehicles, problem Code 35 indicates trouble with the inhibitor switch (see Chapter 6) or clutch switch (see Chapter 8).

14 Test drive the vehicle above 25 MPH, problem Code 37 indicates trouble with the speed sensor or trouble (electrical short or open) in the cruise control system wiring harness.

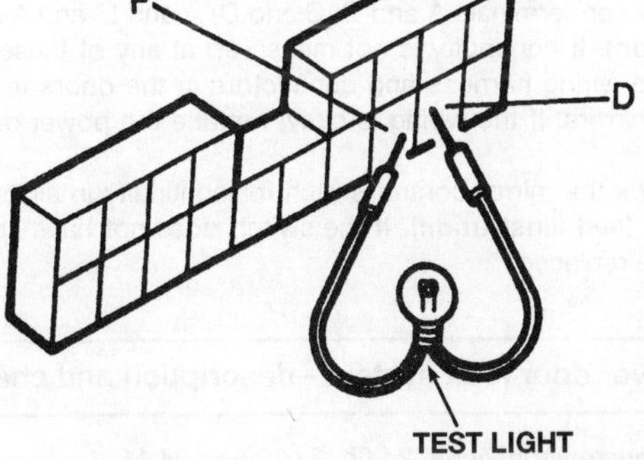

22.7 Cruise control unit (under dash) electrical connector and test light hook up - 1994 and earlier shown

15 Finally, test drive the vehicle to determine if the cruise control is now operating properly. If the problem is not found with the above procedures, immediately take the vehicle to a dealer service department or an automotive electrical specialist for further diagnosis and repair.

23 Power rear view mirrors - description and check

Refer to illustrations 23.8 and 23.9

1 The power rear view mirrors use two motors to move the glass;

12

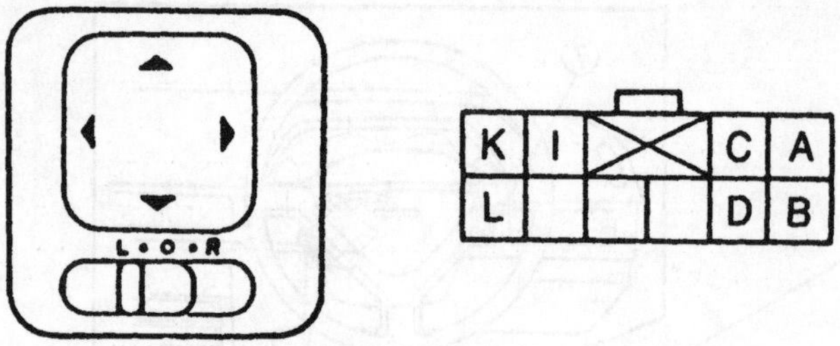

23.8 Power rear view mirror driver's control switch and switch terminal guide

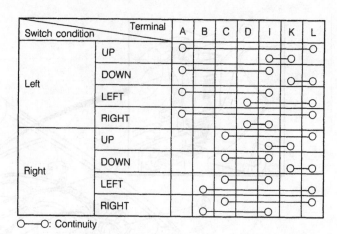

Switch condition		A	B	C	D	I	K	L
Left	UP	O						O
						O	O	
	DOWN	O				O		
							O	O
	LEFT	O				O		
					O			O
	RIGHT	O						O
					O	O		
Right	UP			O				O
						O	O	
	DOWN			O		O		
							O	O
	LEFT			O		O		
			O					O
	RIGHT			O				O
			O			O		

O—O: Continuity

23.9 Power rear view mirror driver's control switch continuity table

one for up and down adjustments and one for left-right adjustments.

2 The control switch has a selector portion which sends voltage to the left or right side mirror. With the ignition key in the ACC position, roll down the windows and operate the mirror control switch through all functions (left-right and up-down) for both the left and right side mirrors.

3 Listen carefully for the sound of the electric motors running in the mirrors.

4 If the motors can be heard but the mirror glass doesn't move, the drive mechanism inside the mirror is most likely defective. Remove and disassemble the mirror to locate the problem (see Chapter 11).

5 If the mirrors do not operate and no sound comes from the electric motors in the mirrors, check the Radio fuse in the fuse box located under the left side of the dash (see Section 3).

6 If the Radio fuse is okay, remove the mirror control switch on the dashboard (see Chapter 11) and access the back of the mirror control switch without disconnecting the electrical connector. Turn the ignition ON and check for voltage at the switch. There should be voltage at one terminal.

7 If no voltage is measured at the mirror control switch, check for a short circuit or open in the wiring harness between the fuse panel and the mirror control switch.

8 If voltage is measured at the mirror control switch, disconnect the mirror control switch electrical connector and check wiring harness electrical connector side to check the power outside mirrors for continuity between terminals A and C, C and D, A and L, and A and B **(see illustration)**. If continuity is not measured at any of these terminals, check the wiring harness and connectors in the doors to the power outside mirrors. If the wiring is okay, replace the power outside mirror(s).

9 Check the mirror control switch for continuity in all its operating positions **(see illustration)**. If the switch does not have continuity, it should be replaced.

24 Power door lock system - description and check

Refer to illustrations 24.6a, 24.6b, 24.10 and 24.11

1 The power door lock system operates the door lock actuators mounted in each door. The system consists of the switches, actuators and associated wiring located in the doors and the relay located under the dash at the driver's side of the vehicle. Diagnosis can usually be limited to simple checks of the wiring connections and actuators for minor faults which can be easily repaired.

2 Power door lock systems are operated by bi-directional actuator motors located in the doors. The lock switches have two operating positions: Lock and Unlock. These switches activate a timer unit which in turn connects voltage to the door lock actuator motors. Depending on which way the timer unit is activated, polarity is reversed, allowing the two sides of the circuit to be used alternately for Lock (down) and Unlock (up).

3 Always check the circuit protection first. The Room fuse provides circuit protection to the power door lock switches. The Door Lock fuse protects the timer unit and actuator motors.

4 Operate the door lock switches in both directions (Lock and Unlock) with the engine off. Listen for the faint sound of the timer unit "click" or the sound of the actuator motor in the door.

5 If no sound is heard, check for voltage at the door lock switches. If no voltage is present, check the wiring between the fuse box and the door lock switches for shorts and opens.

6 If voltage is present but no click or sound is heard, remove the door lock switch and test the switch for continuity. On 1995 and later models, insert a 1 K-ohm resistor between terminals A and B when testing for continuity in the switch Lock position. Replace the switch if there's no continuity in both switch positions **(see illustrations)**.

7 If the switch has continuity but the no sound is heard from the actuator motors in the doors, check the wiring between the switch and the timing unit for continuity. Also check the wiring between the timing unit and the actuator motors for continuity. Repair the wiring if no continuity is measured.

8 If all but one door lock actuator motor operates, remove the trim panel from the affected door (see Chapter 11) and check for voltage at the actuator motor while the door lock switch is operated. One of the connector terminals should have voltage in the Lock position; the other should have voltage in the Unlock position.

9 If the inoperative actuator motor is receiving voltage, but fails to operate, replace the actuator motor.

10 If none of the door lock actuator motors operate, or if they only operate electrically one direction (either up or down only), check the timer unit by using jumpers from the battery **(see illustration)**. The timer unit is located under the driver's left side trim panel in front of the door opening. On 1994 and earlier models, disconnect the timer unit and connect a test wire from the positive battery terminal to the timer unit terminal B, and the timer unit terminal A to ground (negative battery terminal, then connect a jumper wire between timer unit terminals H and D or H and C. The door timer unit should click. If the timer unit does not click, replace the timer unit.

11 On 1995 and later models, do not disconnect the timer unit. Use a voltmeter with the negative test lead to vehicle ground. Backprobe the timer unit terminals and check the following terminals under the indicated conditions **(see illustration)**:

- *a) Terminal A - when actuator is moved to locked position, applied voltage should go from 0-volts to 12-volts then back to 0-volts.*
- *b) Terminal B - when driver's door lock actuator is moved to unlocked position, applied voltage should go from 0-volts to 12-volts then back to 0-volts.*
- *c) Terminal F - when actuator door lock is moved to unlocked position, applied voltage should go from 0-volts to 12-volts then back to 0-volts.*

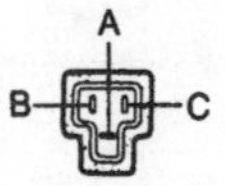

Switch condition \ Terminal	A	B	C
Locked	O	O	
Unlocked	O		O

O—O: Continuity

24.6a Power door lock switch terminal guide and continuity table - 1994 and earlier

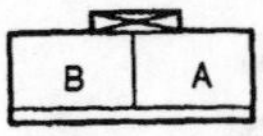

Switch position \ Terminal	A	B
Lock	O	O 1 kΩ ± 5 %
Unlock	O	O

O—O: Continuity

24.6b Power door lock switch terminal guide and continuity table - 1995 and later

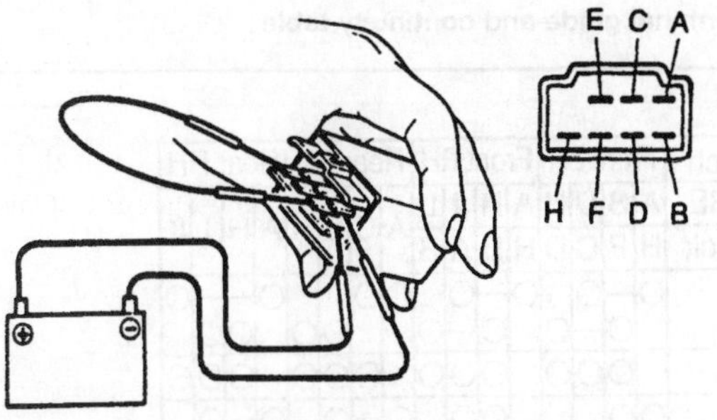

24.10 Door lock timer unit terminal guide and test connections - 1994 and earlier

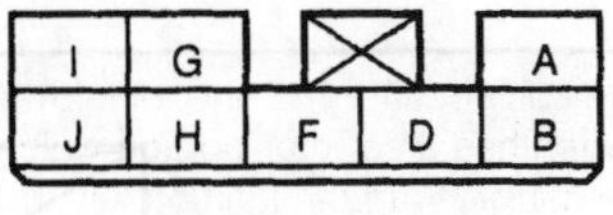

24.11 Door lock timer unit terminal guide - 1995 and later

d) Terminal G - when actuator door lock is moved to unlocked position, applied voltage should go from 12-volts to 0-volts then back to 12-volts.
e) Terminal H - when actuator door lock is moved to locked position, applied voltage should go from 12-volts to 0-volts then back to 12-volts.
f) Terminal I - should measure 12-volts.
g) Terminal J - when connected to ground should have continuity at all times.

Note: *It is common for door lock harness wires to break in the portion of the harness between the body and door (opening and closing the door fatigues and may eventually break the wires).*

25 Power window system - description and check

Refer to illustrations 25.1, 25.7, 25.10a, 25.10b and 25.10c

1 The power window system operates the electric motors mounted in the doors which lower and raise the windows. The system consists of the control switches, the motors (regulators), glass mechanisms and associated wiring **(see illustration)**.

2 Power windows are wired so they can be lowered and raised from the driver's control switch or by subswitches located at the front passenger door, and both rear doors on four-door vehicles. Each window has a separate motor which is reversible. The position of the control switch determines the polarity and therefore the direction of motor operation.

3 Circuit protection is provided by the power window fuse in the fuse box under the dashboard.

4 The power window system will only operate when the ignition switch is ON. In addition, when OFF, the power window safety lockout switch at the driver's control switch disables the switches at the passenger's window also. Always check this switch before troubleshooting a power window problem.

5 These procedures are general in nature. If you cannot locate the problem, take the vehicle to a dealer service department or other qualified repair facility.

6 If the power windows don't work at all, check the power window fuse in the fuse box.

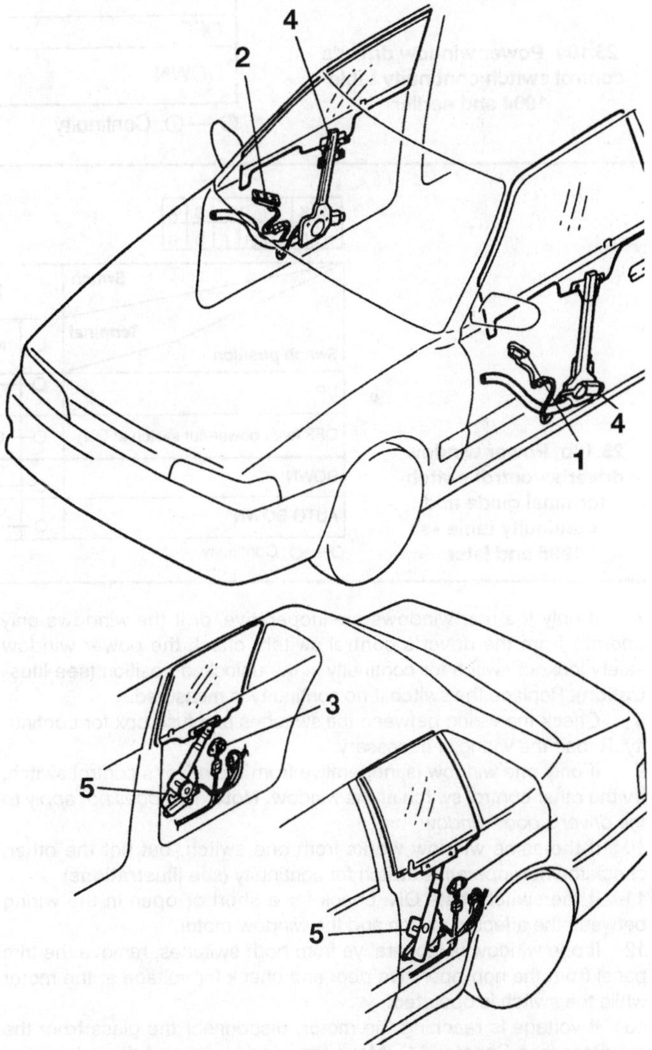

25.1 Typical power window system components

1 Main switch
2 Passenger door switch
3 Rear door switch
4 Front window regulator
5 Rear window regulator

12

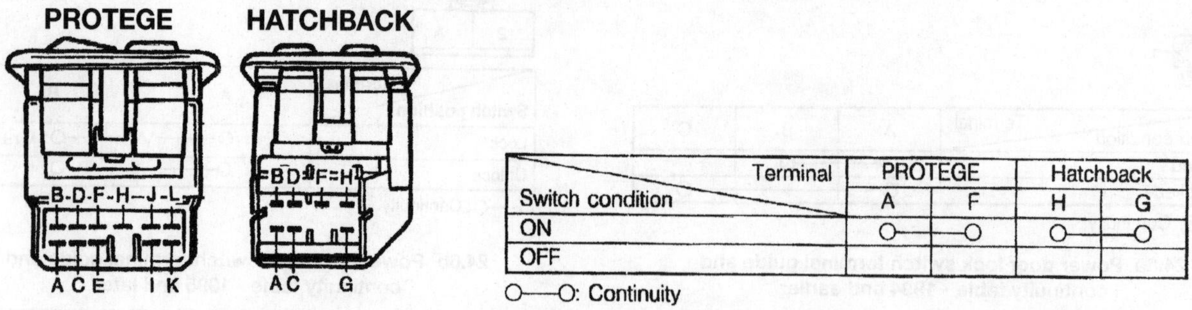

25.7 Power window safety lockout switch terminal guide and continuity table

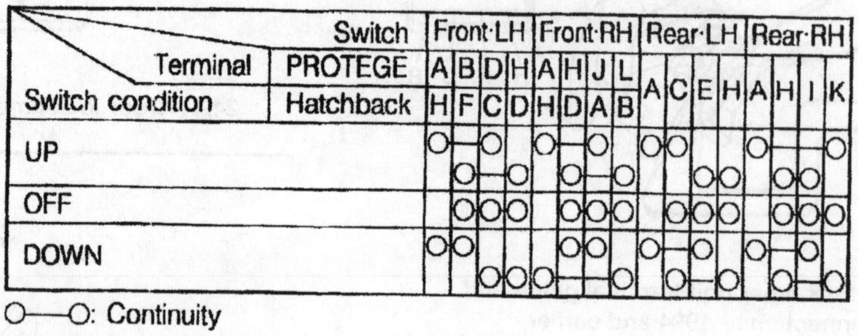

Switch
Terminal
Switch condition
PROTEGE
Hatchback
Front·LH
Front·RH
Rear·LH
Rear·RH
UP
OFF
DOWN
O—O: Continuity

25.10a Power window driver's control switch continuity table - 1994 and earlier

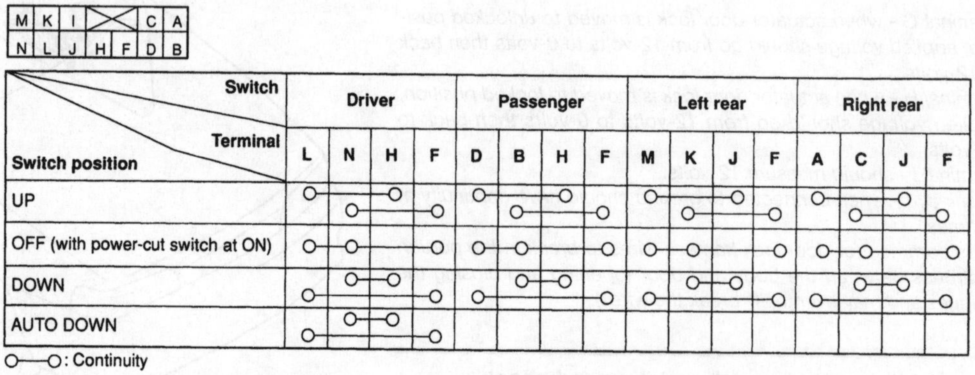

M K I C A
N L J H F D B
Switch
Terminal
Switch position
Driver
Passenger
Left rear
Right rear
UP
OFF (with power-cut switch at ON)
DOWN
AUTO DOWN
O—O: Continuity

25.10b Power window driver's control switch terminal guide and continuity table - 1995 and later

7 If only the rear windows are inoperative, or if the windows only operate from the driver's control switch, check the power window safety lockout switch for continuity in the unlocked position **(see illustration)**. Replace the switch if no continuity is measured.

8 Check the wiring between the switches and fuse box for continuity. Repair the wiring, if necessary.

9 If only one window is inoperative from the driver's control switch, try the other control switch at the window. **Note:** *This does not apply to the driver's door window.*

10 If the same window works from one switch, but not the other, check the non-operative switch for continuity **(see illustrations)**.

11 If the switch tests OK, check for a short or open in the wiring between the affected switch and the window motor.

12 If one window is inoperative from both switches, remove the trim panel from the non-operative door and check for voltage at the motor while the switch is operated.

13 If voltage is reaching the motor, disconnect the glass from the regulator (see Chapter 11). Move the window up and down by hand while checking for binding and damage. Also check for binding and damage to the regulator. If the regulator is not damaged and the window moves up and down smoothly, replace the motor. If binding or damage is found, lubricate and repair or replace parts, as necessary.

14 If voltage is not measured at window motor, check the wiring in the circuit for continuity between the switches and motors. Consult the wiring diagram for the vehicle. Check that each switch applies voltage to the motor when the switch is turned on. If voltage is not applied, replace the window motor.

15 Test all power windows after repair to confirm proper operation.

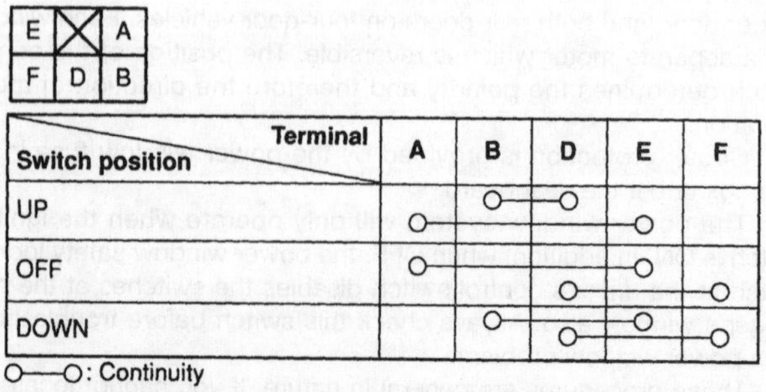

25.10c Power window passenger door control switch terminal guide and continuity table - 1995 and later

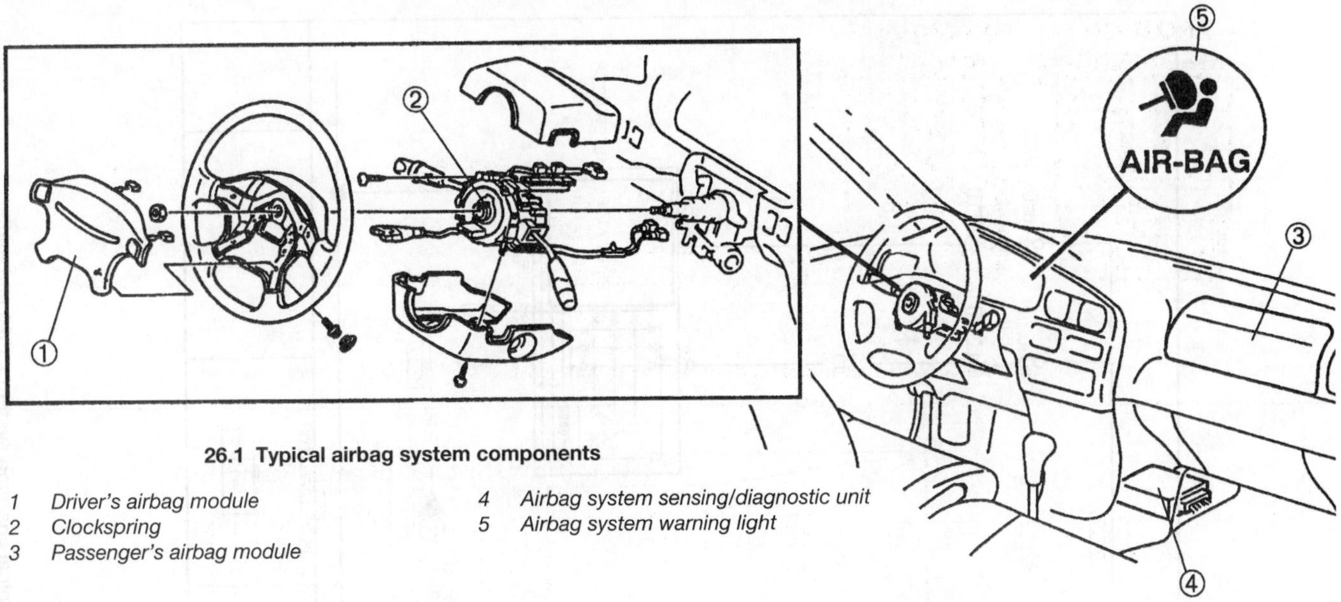

26.1 Typical airbag system components

1 *Driver's airbag module*
2 *Clockspring*
3 *Passenger's airbag module*
4 *Airbag system sensing/diagnostic unit*
5 *Airbag system warning light*

26 Airbag system - general information

Refer to illustration 26.1

The 1995 and later models are equipped with a Supplemental Restraint System (SRS), more commonly known as "airbags." This system is designed to protect the driver and front seat passenger from serious injury in the event of a head-on or frontal collision. It consists of airbag modules in the center of the steering wheel and the passenger side of the instrument panel, and a sensing/diagnostic unit located inside the passenger compartment **(see illustration)**.

Airbag modules

The airbag modules contain a housing incorporating the cushion (airbag) and inflator unit. The inflator assembly is mounted on the back of the housing over a hole through which gas is expelled, inflating the bag almost instantaneously when an electrical signal is sent from the system. The specially wound wire that carries this signal to the driver's module is called a clockspring. The clockspring is a flat, ribbon-like electrically conductive tape which is wound many times so that it can transmit an electrical signal regardless of steering wheel position.

Central airbag sensing/diagnostic unit

The airbag sensing/diagnostic unit contains the safing sensor and an on-board microprocessor which monitors the operation of the system. It checks this system every time the vehicle is started, causing the "AIRBAG" warning light to go on, then off, if the system is operating properly. If there is a fault in the system, the light will go on and stay on and the airbag sensing/diagnostic unit will store fault codes indicating the nature of the fault. If the AIRBAG light goes on and stays on, the vehicle should be taken to your dealer immediately for service.

Servicing components near the airbag system

Nevertheless, there are times when you need to remove the steering wheel, radio or service other components on or near the instrument panel. At these times, you'll be working around components and wiring harnesses for the airbag system. Airbag system wiring is easy to identify; they're all covered by a bright yellow conduit. Do not unplug the connectors for the airbag system wiring, except to disable the system. And do not use electrical test equipment on the airbag system wiring. **ALWAYS DISABLE THE AIRBAG SYSTEM BEFORE WORKING NEAR THE AIRBAG SYSTEM COMPONENTS OR RELATED WIRING.**

Disabling the airbag system

1 Turn the steering wheel to the straight ahead position, place the ignition switch in Lock and remove the key.
2 Disconnect the cable from the negative battery terminal.
3 Wait two minutes for the back-up capacitor to discharge.

Enabling the airbag system

4 Connect the cable to the negative battery terminal.
5 Turn the ignition key to On and verify that the "AIRBAG" warning light comes on for approximately six seconds, then goes off.

27 Wiring diagrams

Refer to illustrations 27.4

Since it is not possible to include all wiring diagrams for every year covered by this manual, the following diagrams are those that are typical and most commonly needed.

Prior to troubleshooting any circuits, check the fuse and circuit breakers to make sure they are in good condition. Make sure the battery is properly charged and has clean, tight cable connections (see Chapter 1).

When checking the wiring system, make sure that all electrical connectors are clean, with no broken or loose pins. When unplugging an electrical connector, do not pull on the wires, only on the connector housings themselves.

Refer to the **accompanying illustration** for wiring diagram color codes.

Color	Code	Color	Code
Blue	L	Orange	O
Black	B	Pink	P
Brown	BR	Red	R
Dark Blue	DL	Purple	PU
Dark Green	DG	Sky Blue	SB
Green	G	Tan	T
Gray	GY	White	W
Light Blue	LB	Yellow	Y
Light Green	LG	Violet	V
Natural	N		

27.4 Wiring diagram wire color code chart

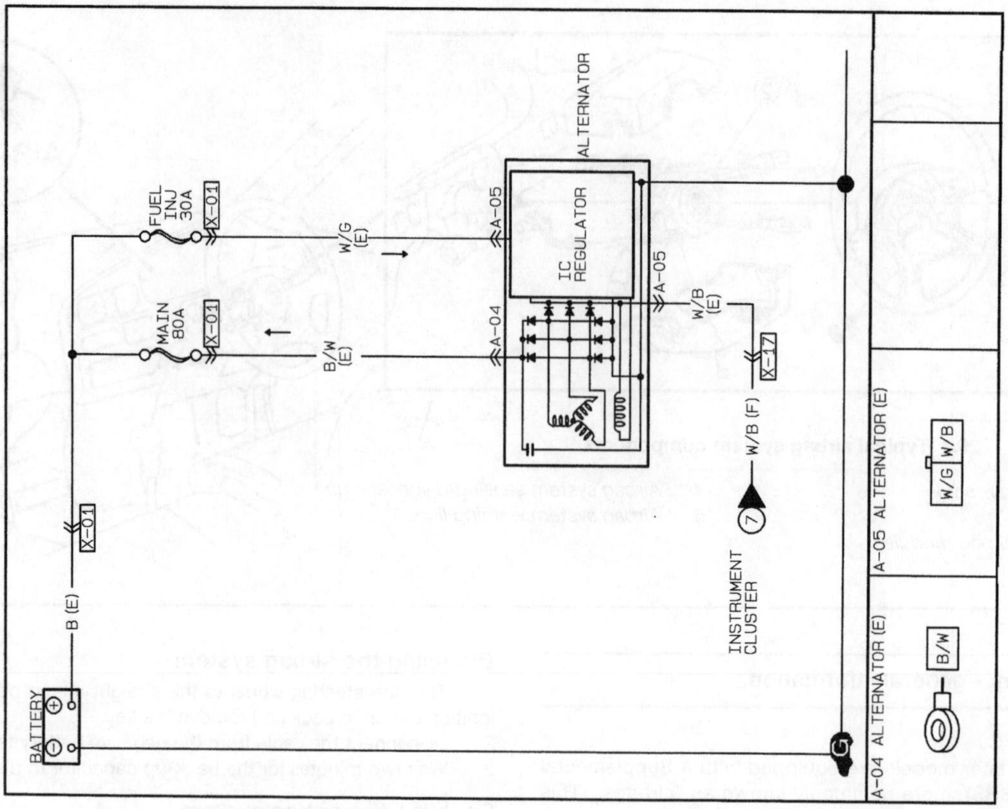

Typical charging system - 1994 and earlier

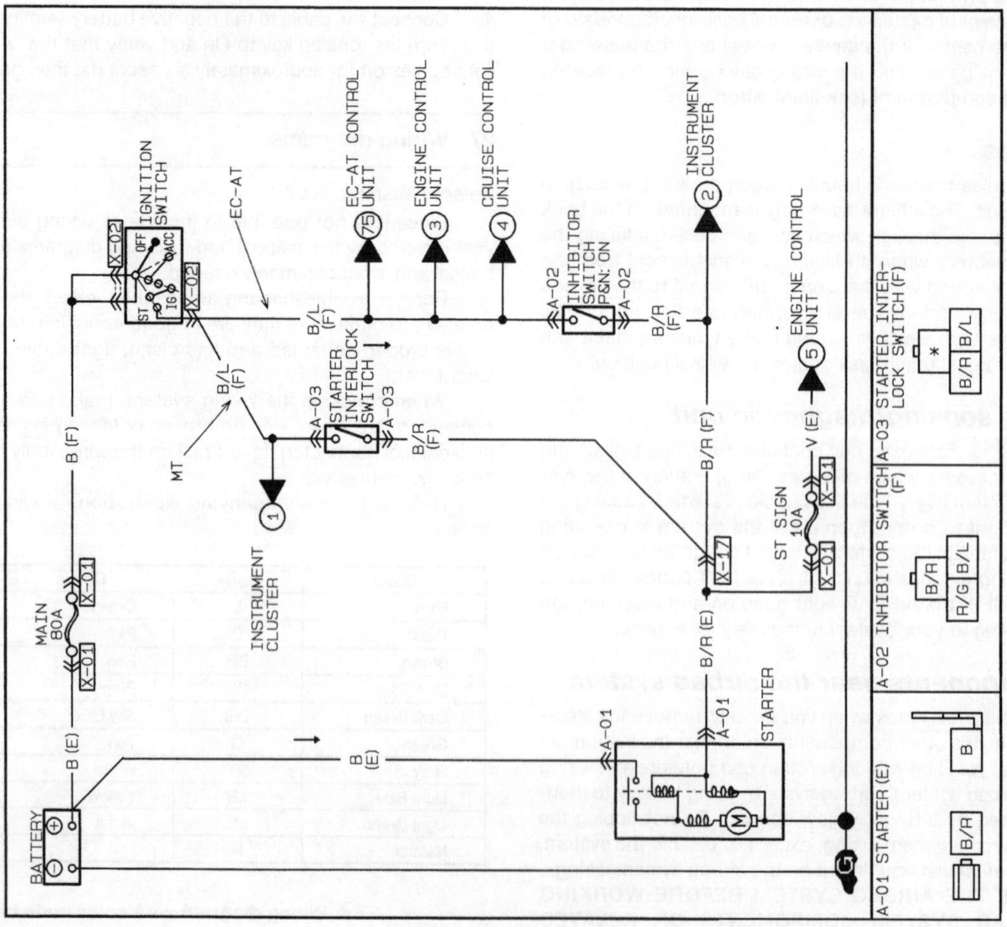

Typical starting system - 1994 and earlier

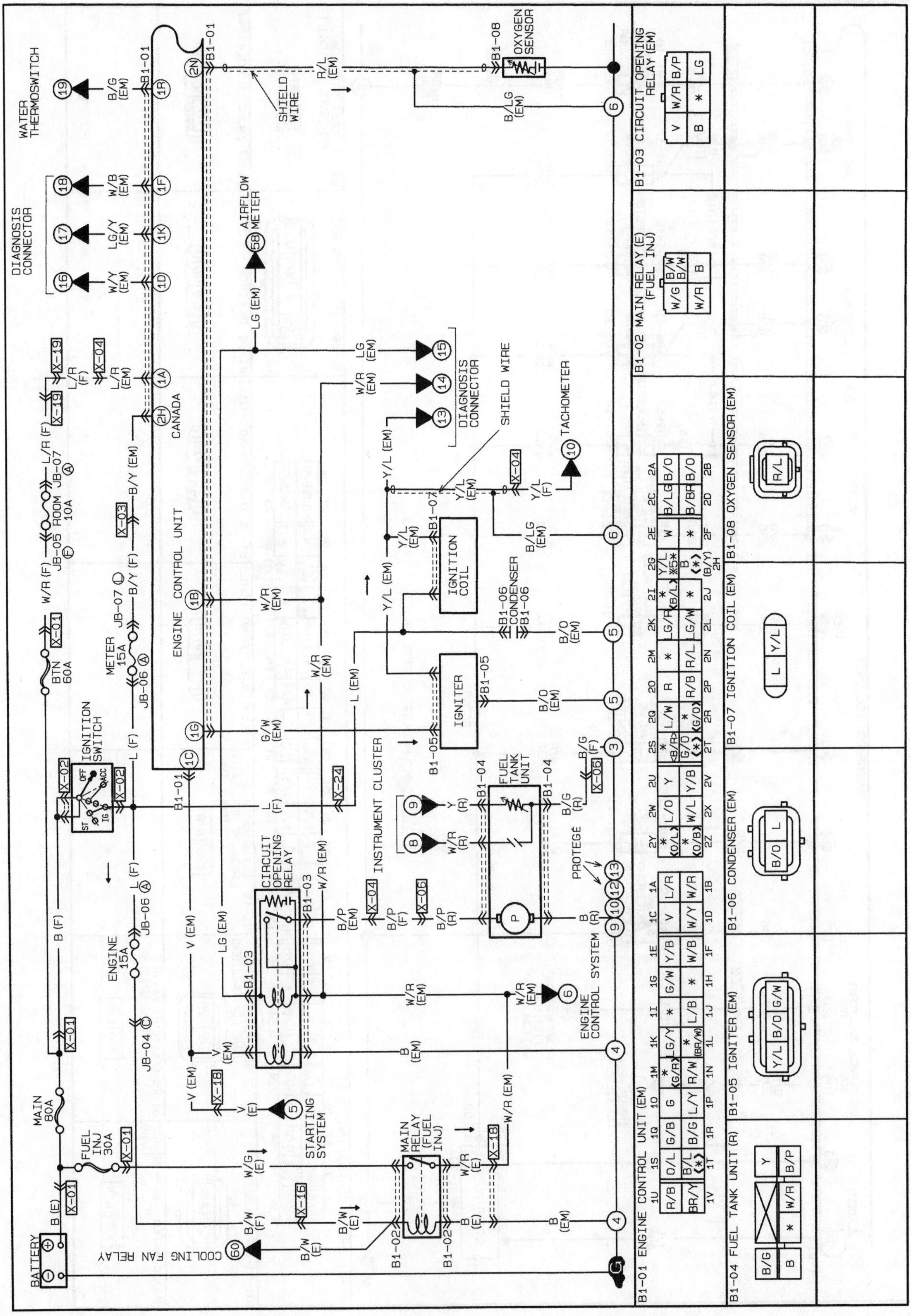

Typical electronic engine control system - 1994 and earlier (1 of 3)

12

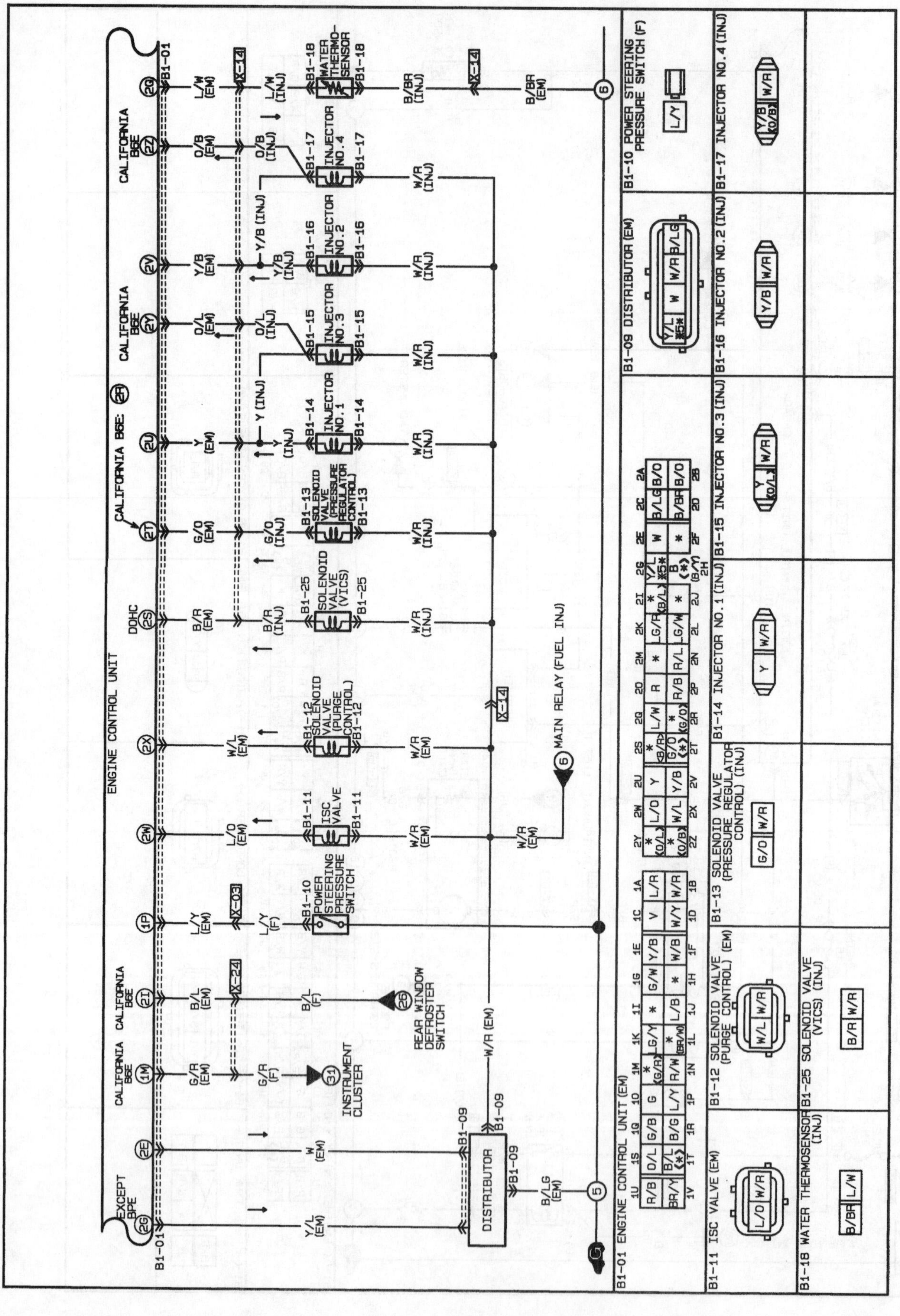

Typical electronic engine control system - 1994 and earlier (2 of 3)

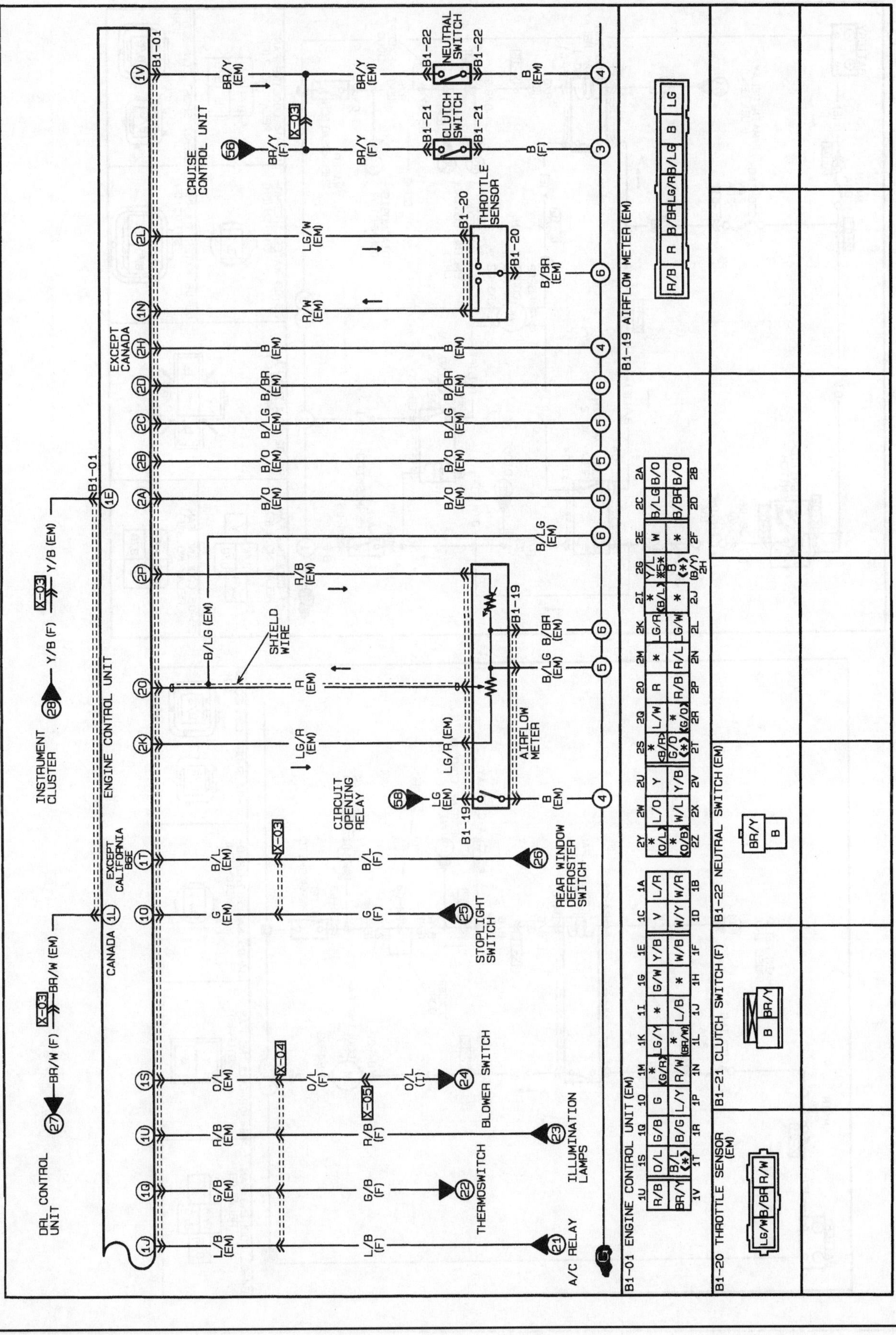

Typical electronic engine control system - 1994 and earlier (3 of 3)

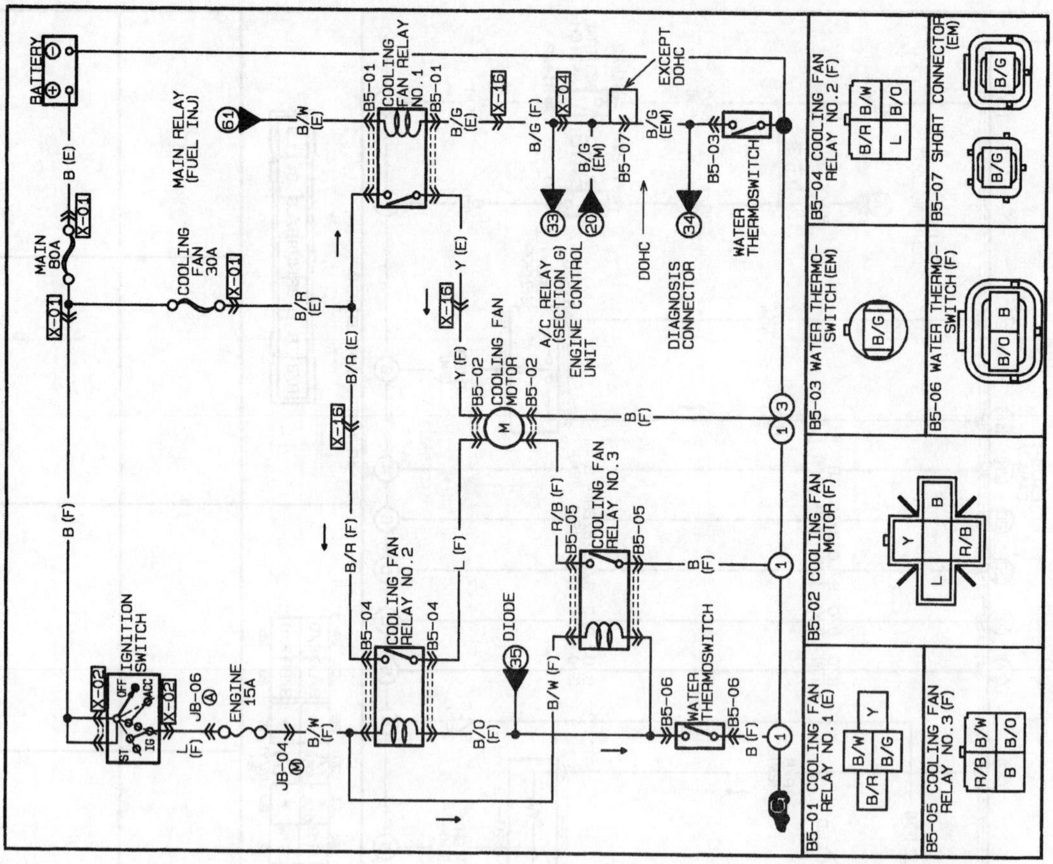

Typical cooling fan system - 1994 and earlier Protegé models

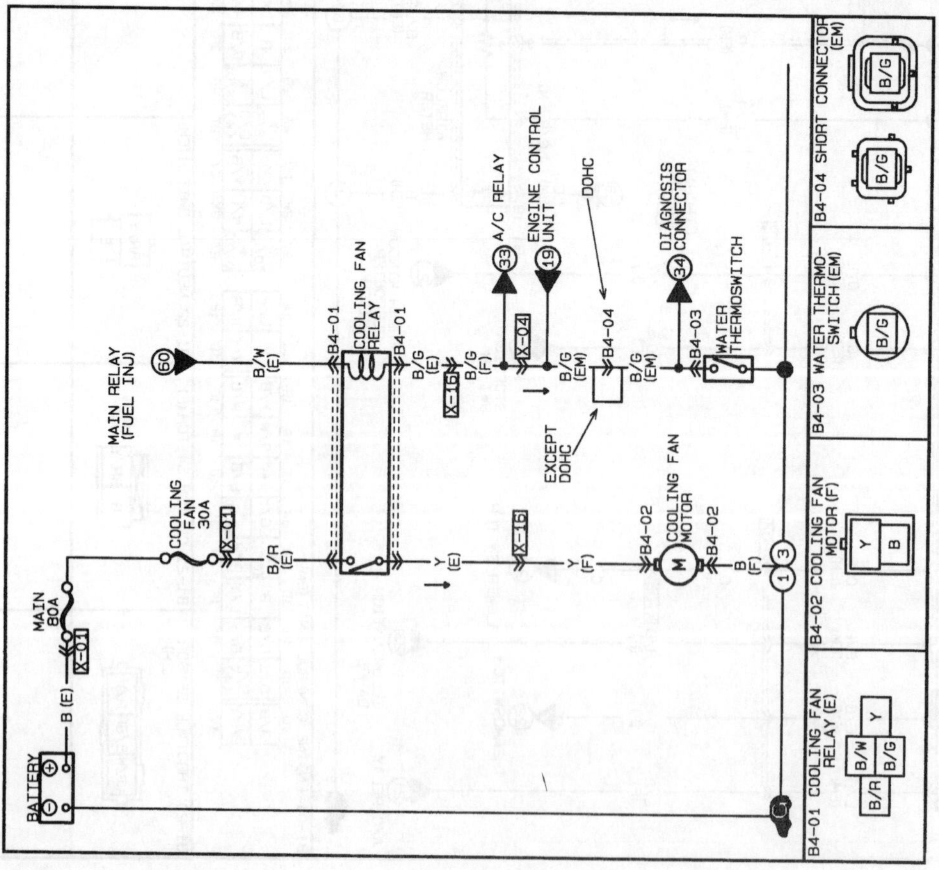

Typical cooling fan system - 1994 and earlier 323 models

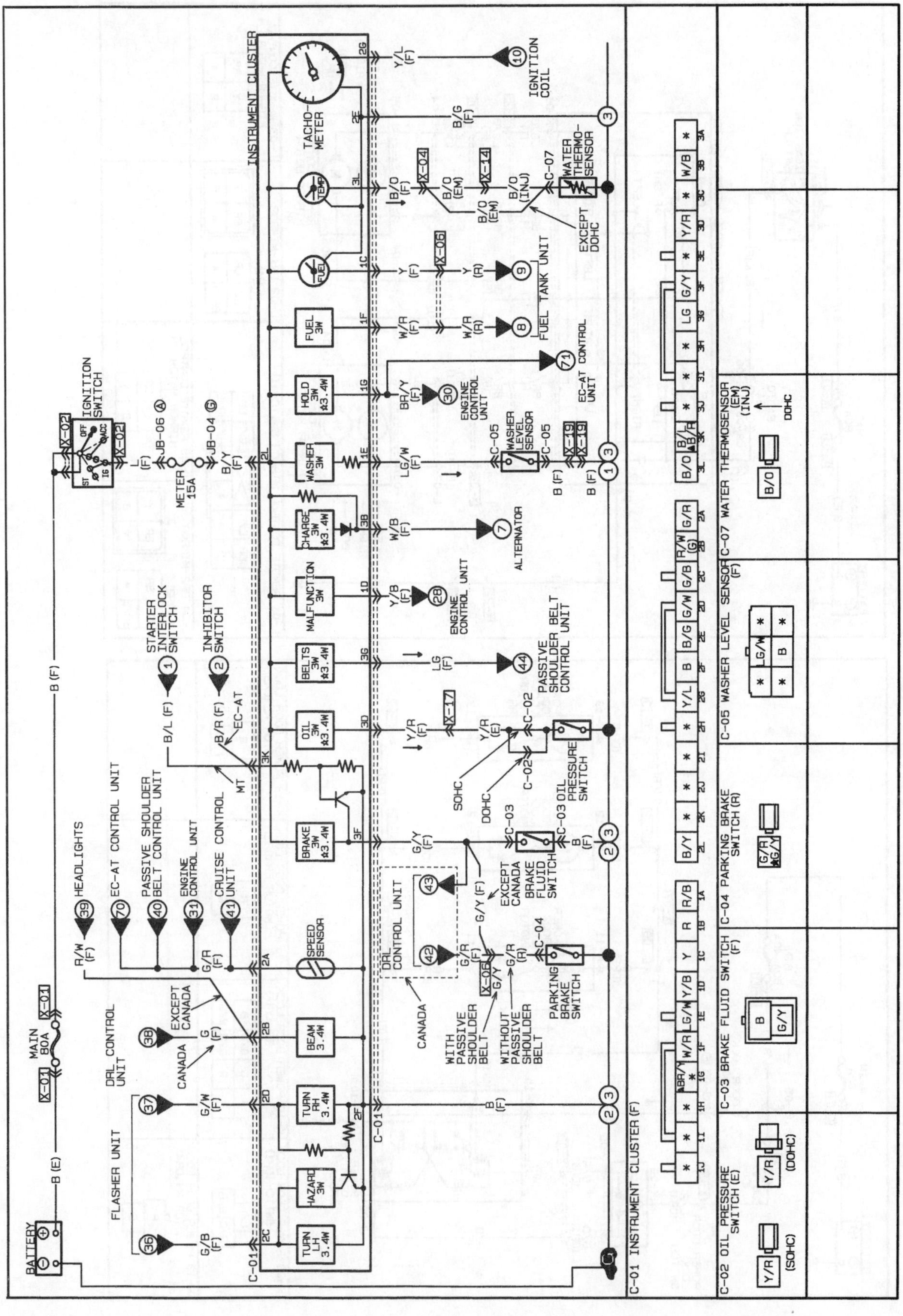

Typical instrument panel - 1994 and earlier

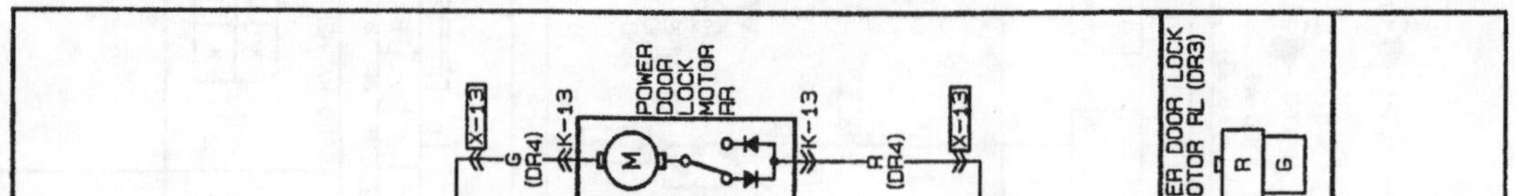

Typical power door lock system - 1994 and earlier

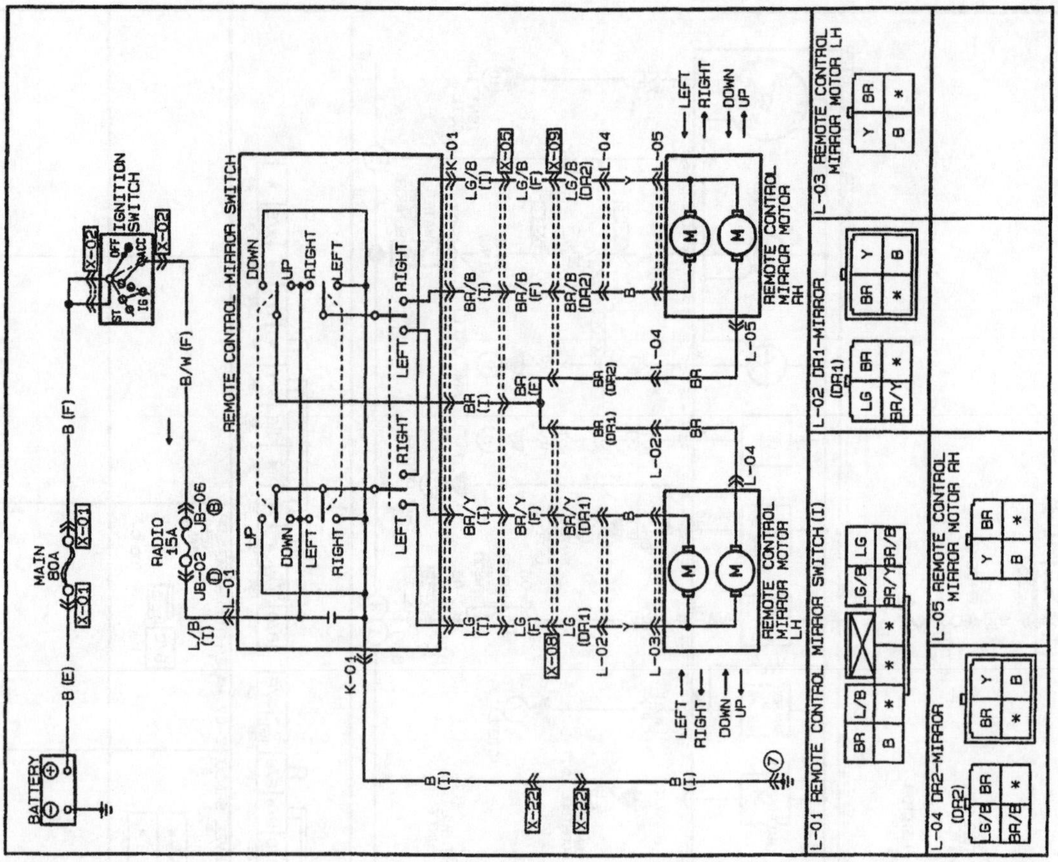

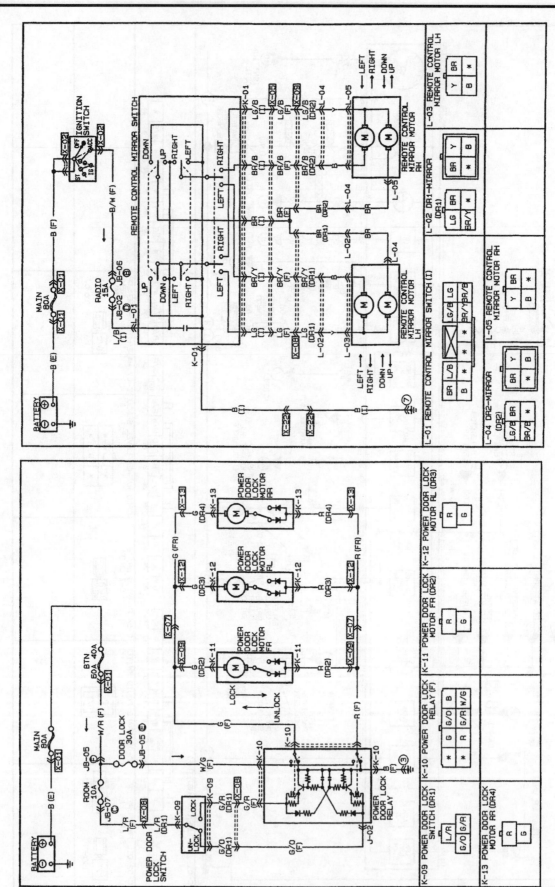

Typical power rearview mirror system - 1994 and earlier

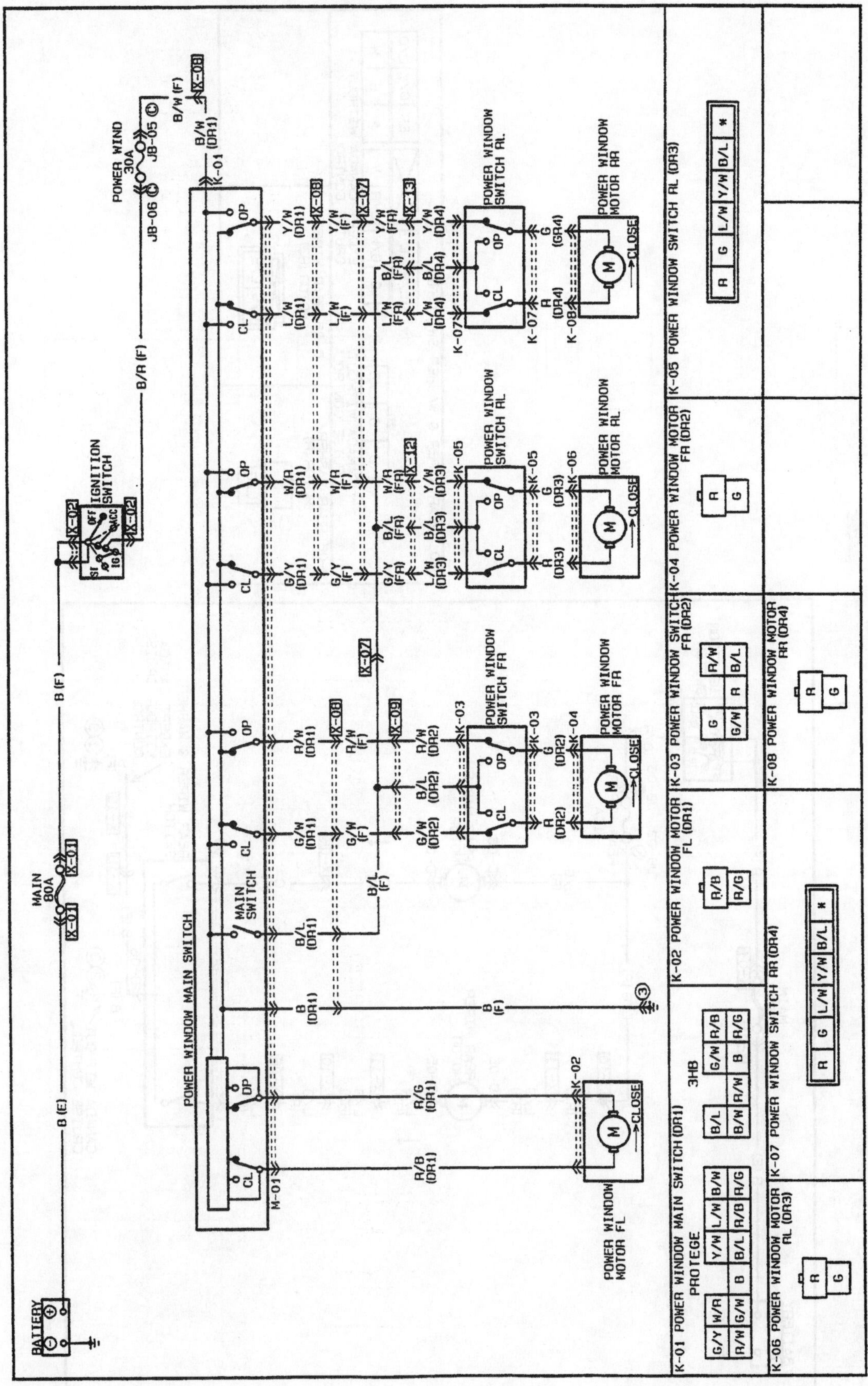

Typical power window system - 1994 and earlier

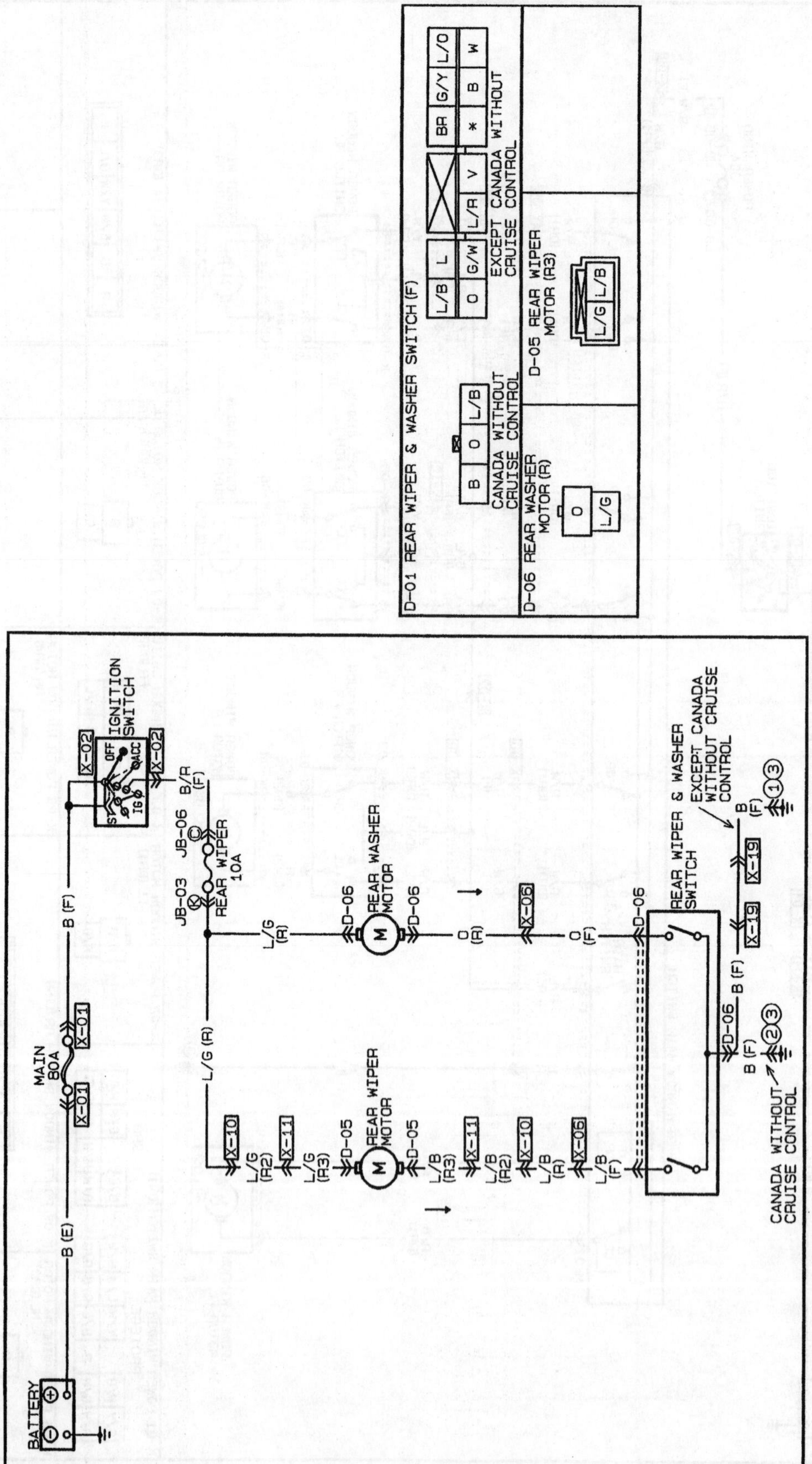

Typical rear wiper and washer system - 1994 and earlier 323 hatchback

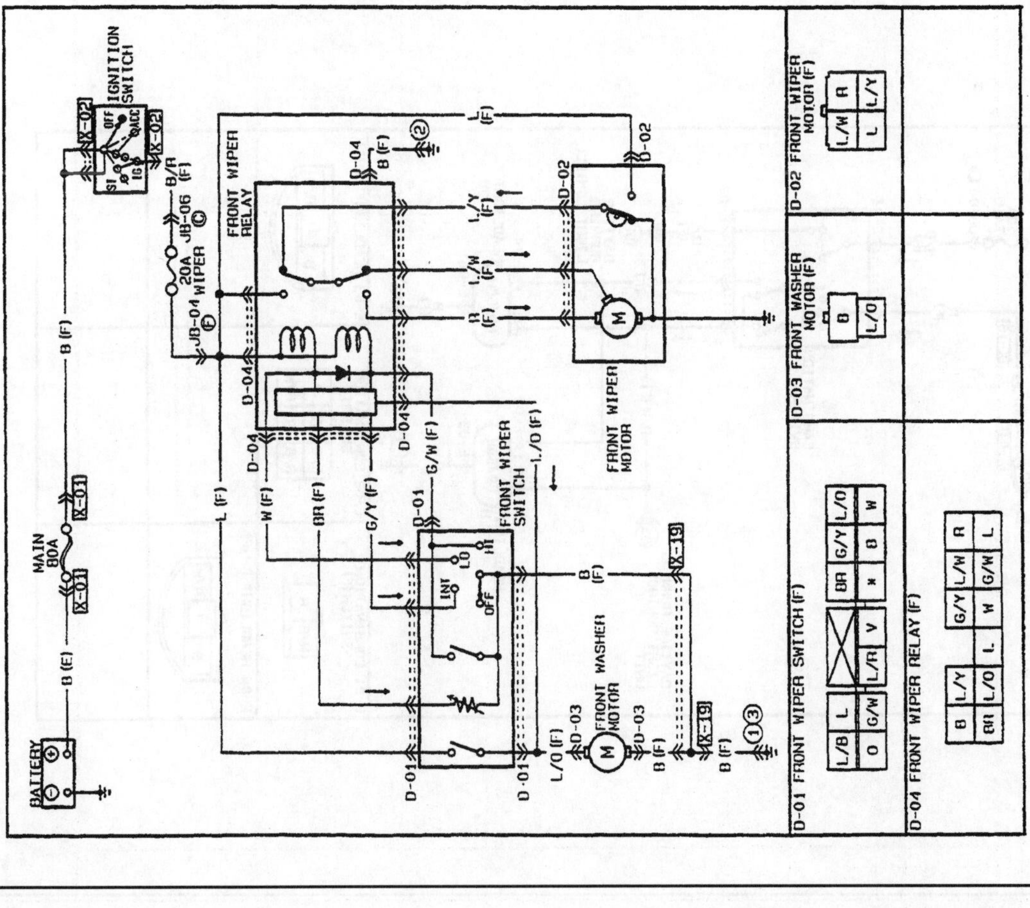

Typical windshield wiper and washer system - 1994 and earlier with cruise control

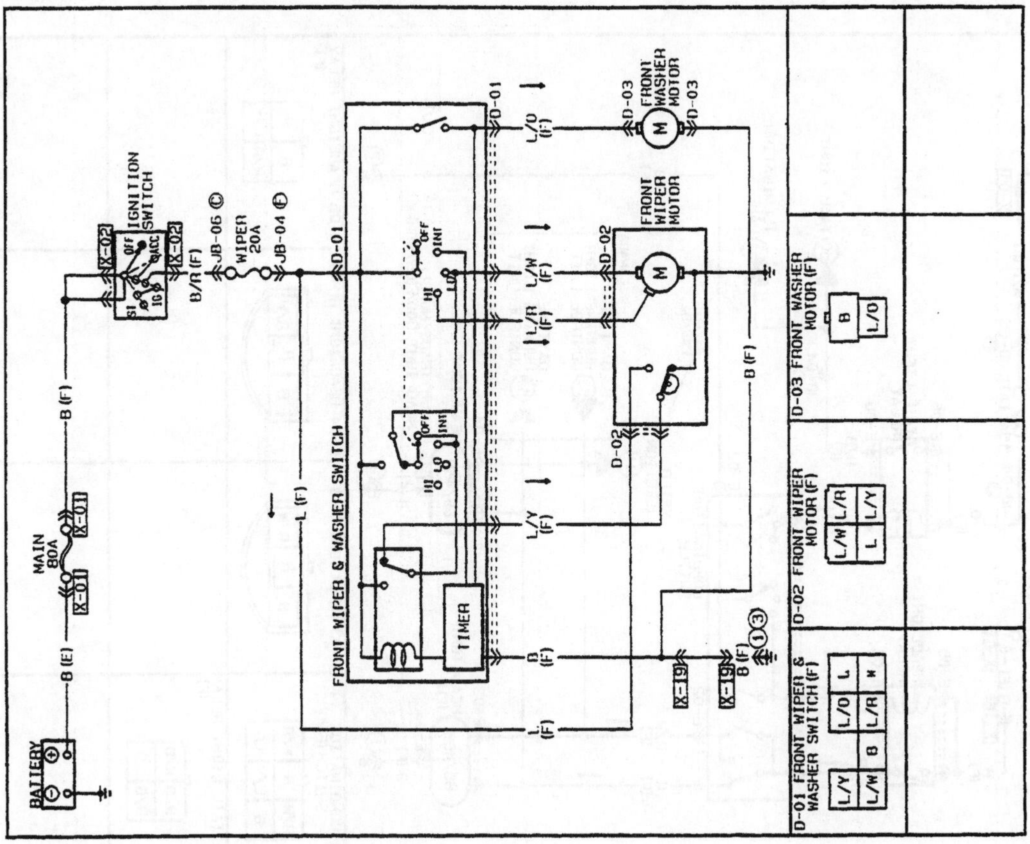

Typical windshield wiper and washer system - 1994 and earlier without cruise control

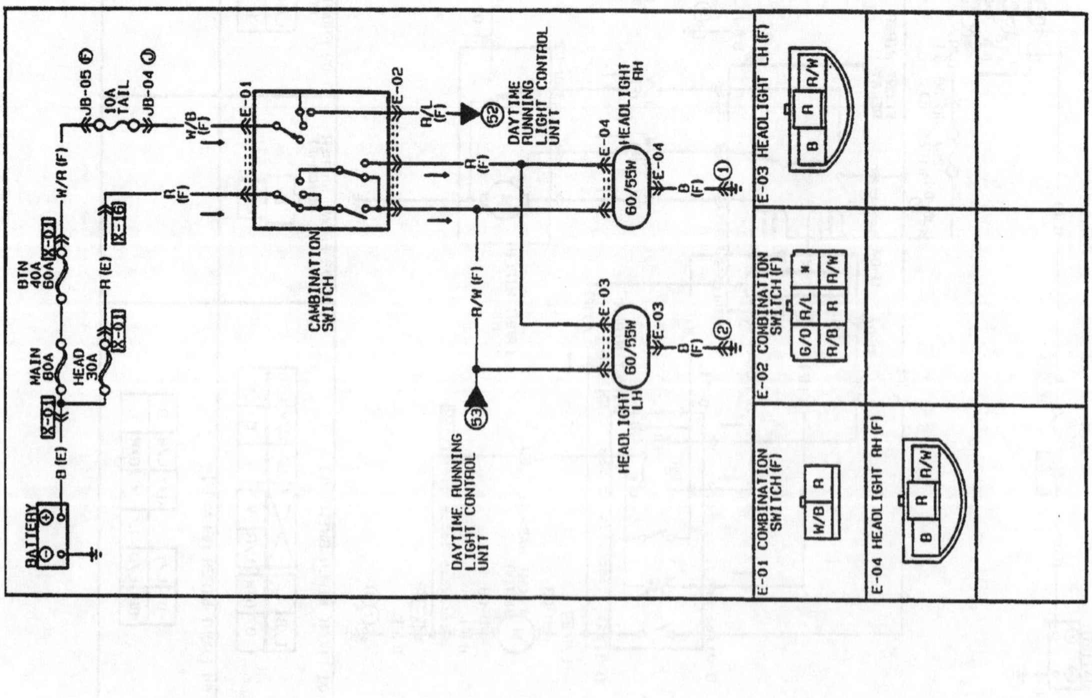

Typical headlight circuit - 1994 and earlier models without cruise control

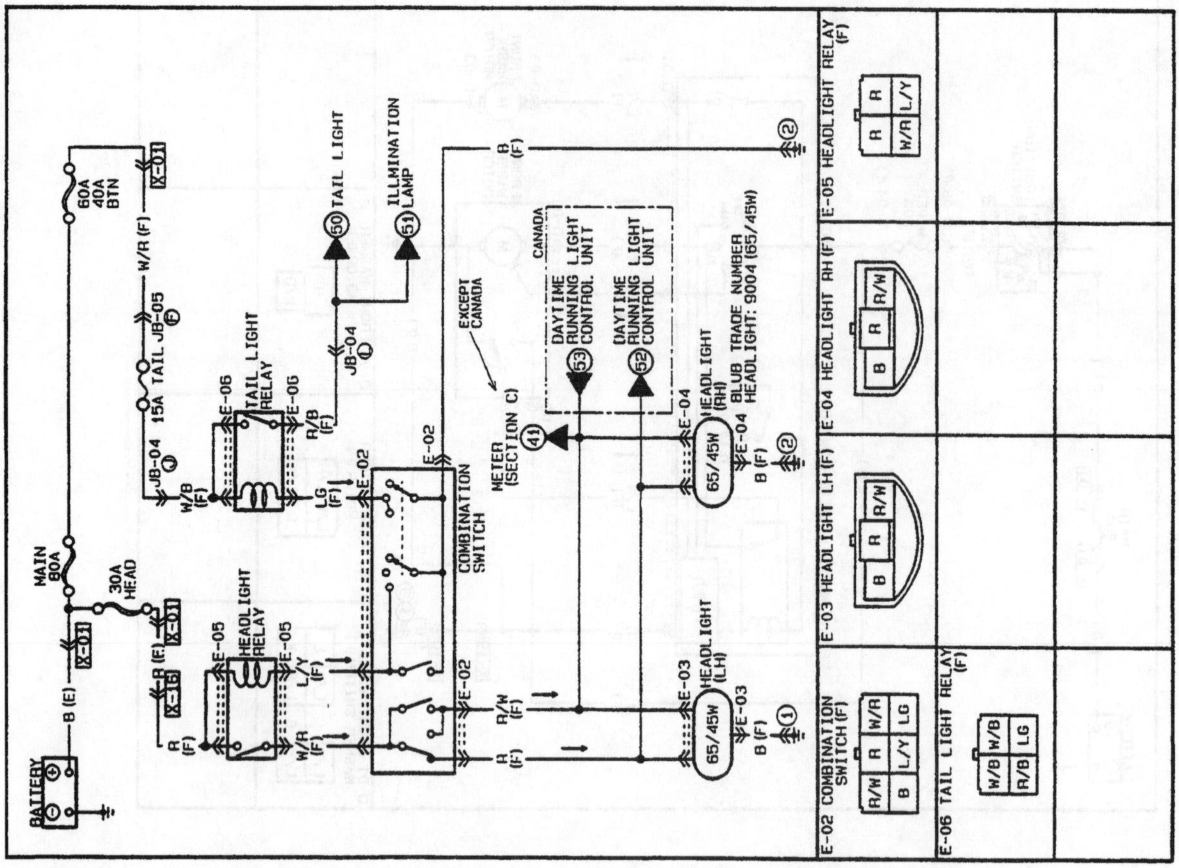

Typical headlight circuit - 1994 and earlier models with cruise control

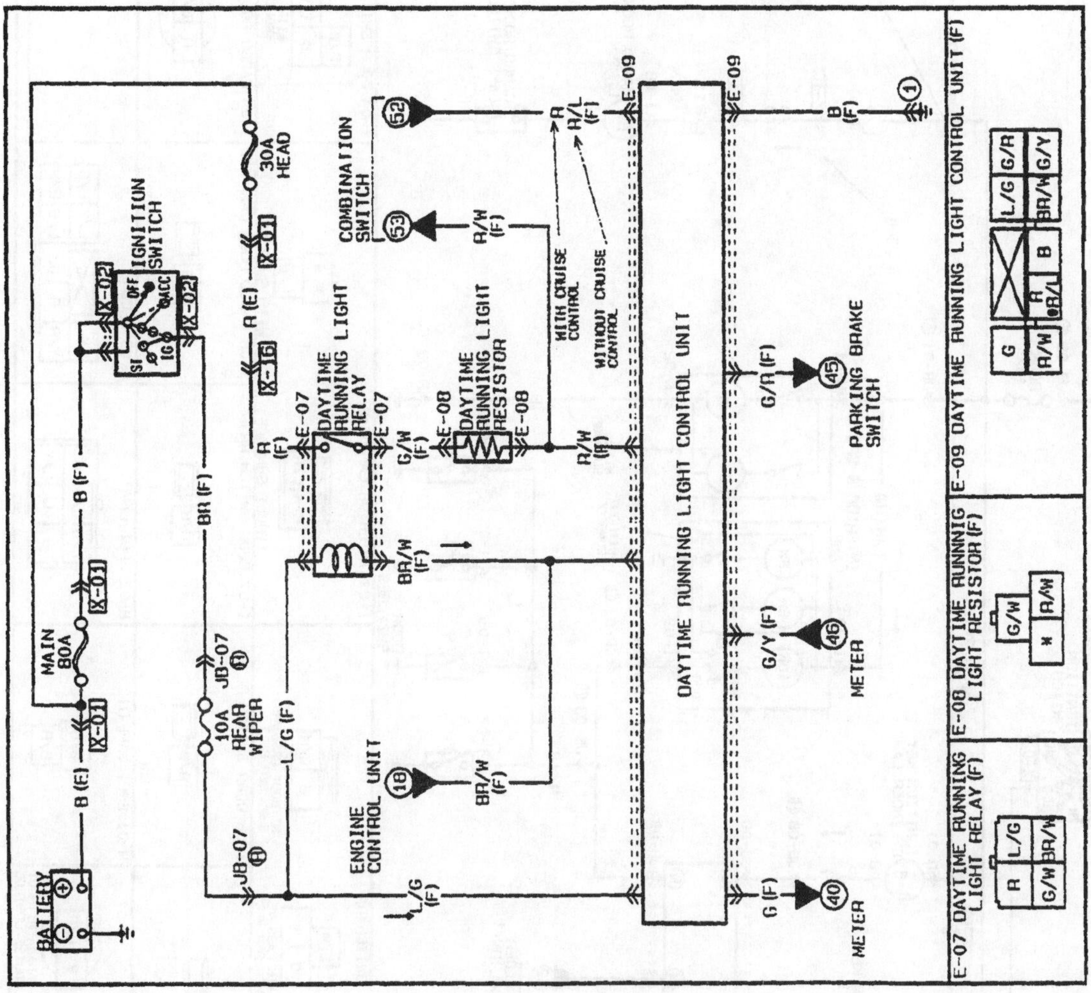

Typical Daytime Running Lights (DRL) system - 1994 and earlier Canadian models

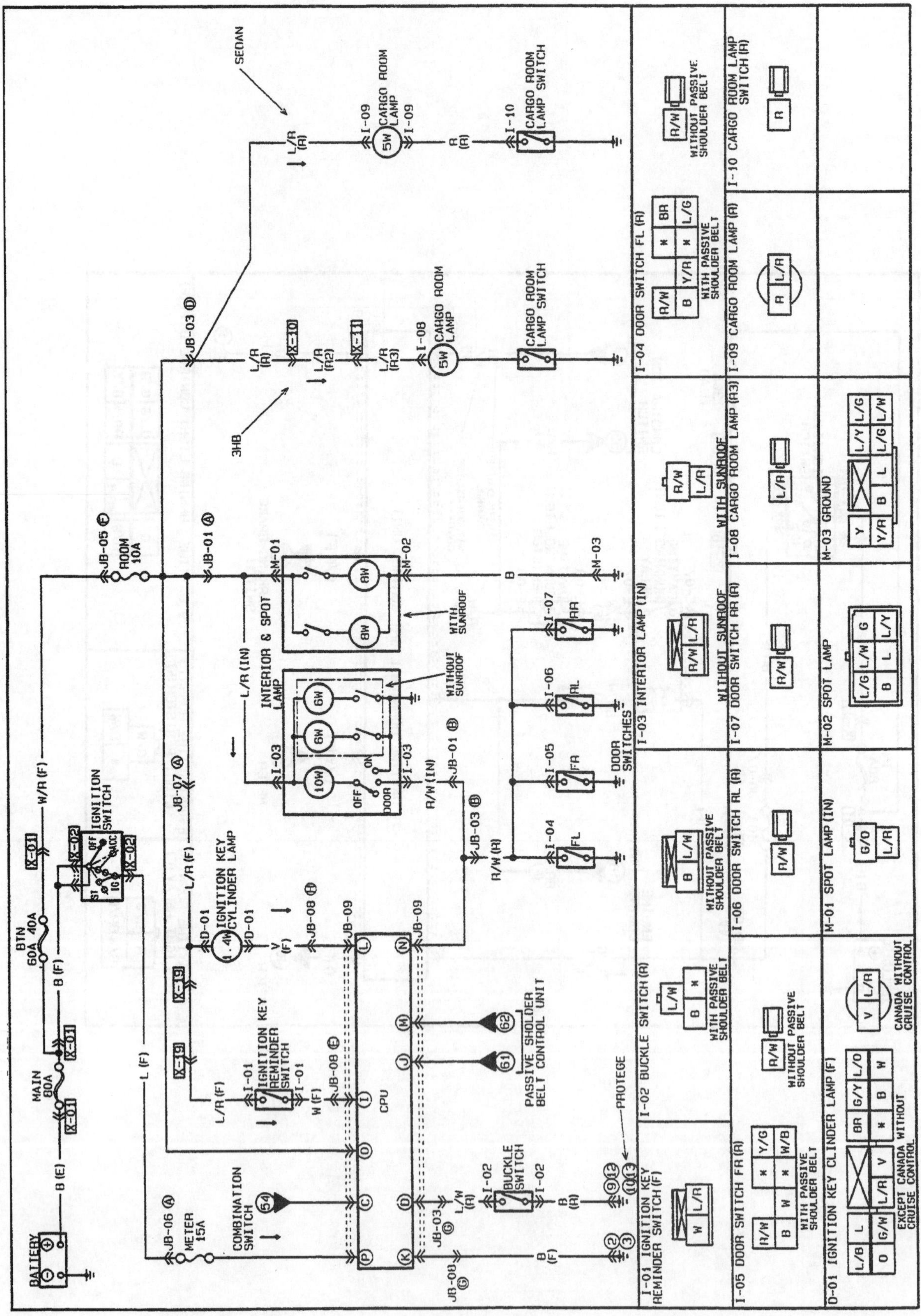

Typical interior lighting system - 1994 and earlier

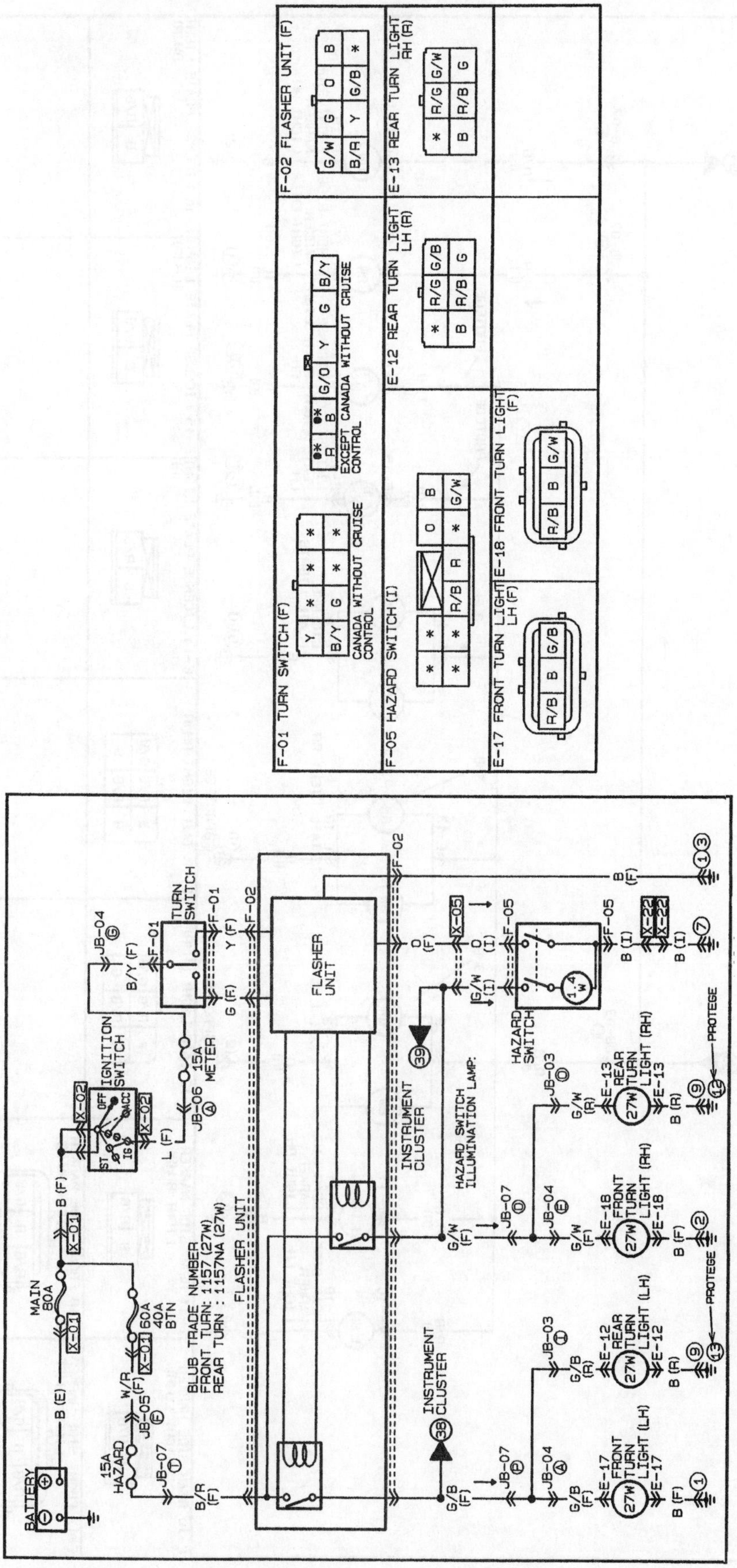

Typical turn signal and hazard flasher system - 1994 and earlier

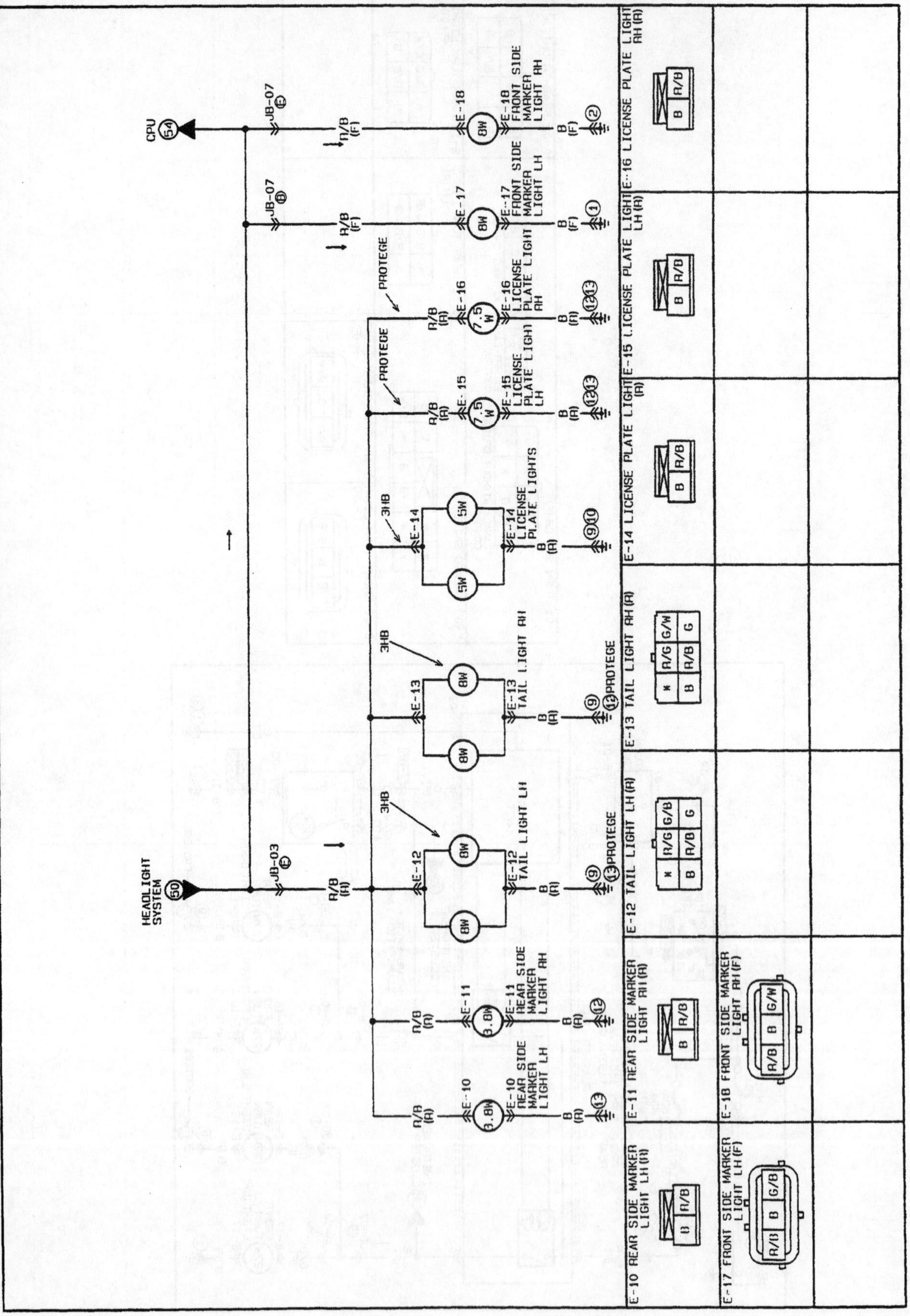

Typical parking light system - 1994 and earlier

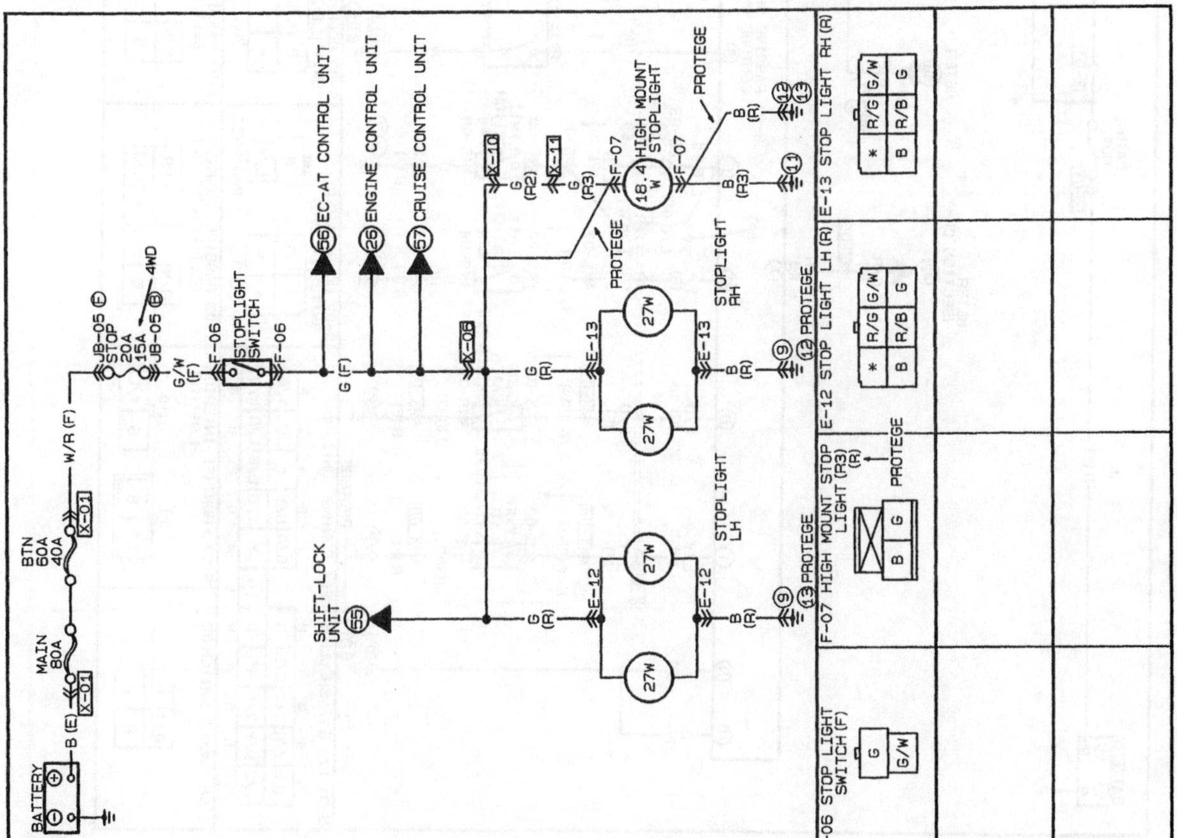

Typical brake light systems - 1994 and earlier

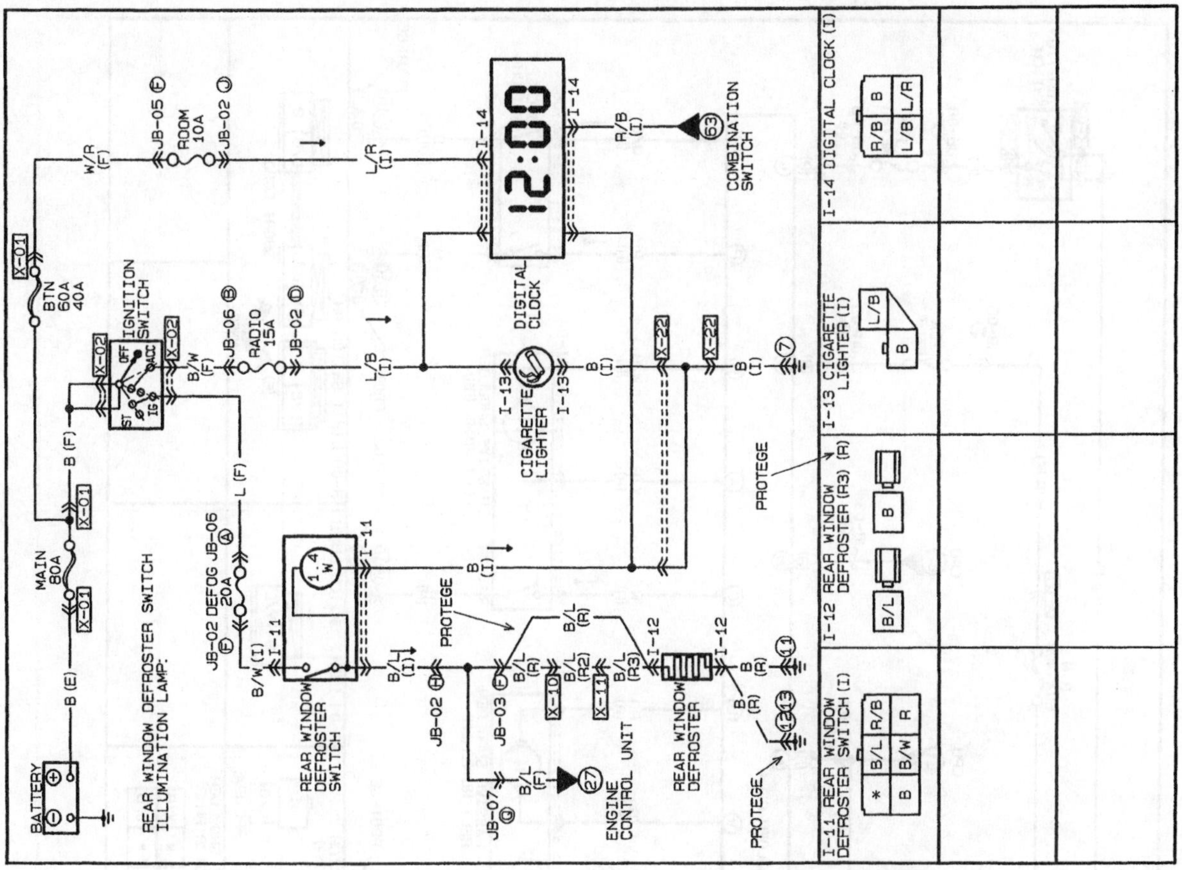

Typical rear window defogger/clock/lighter systems - 1994 and earlier

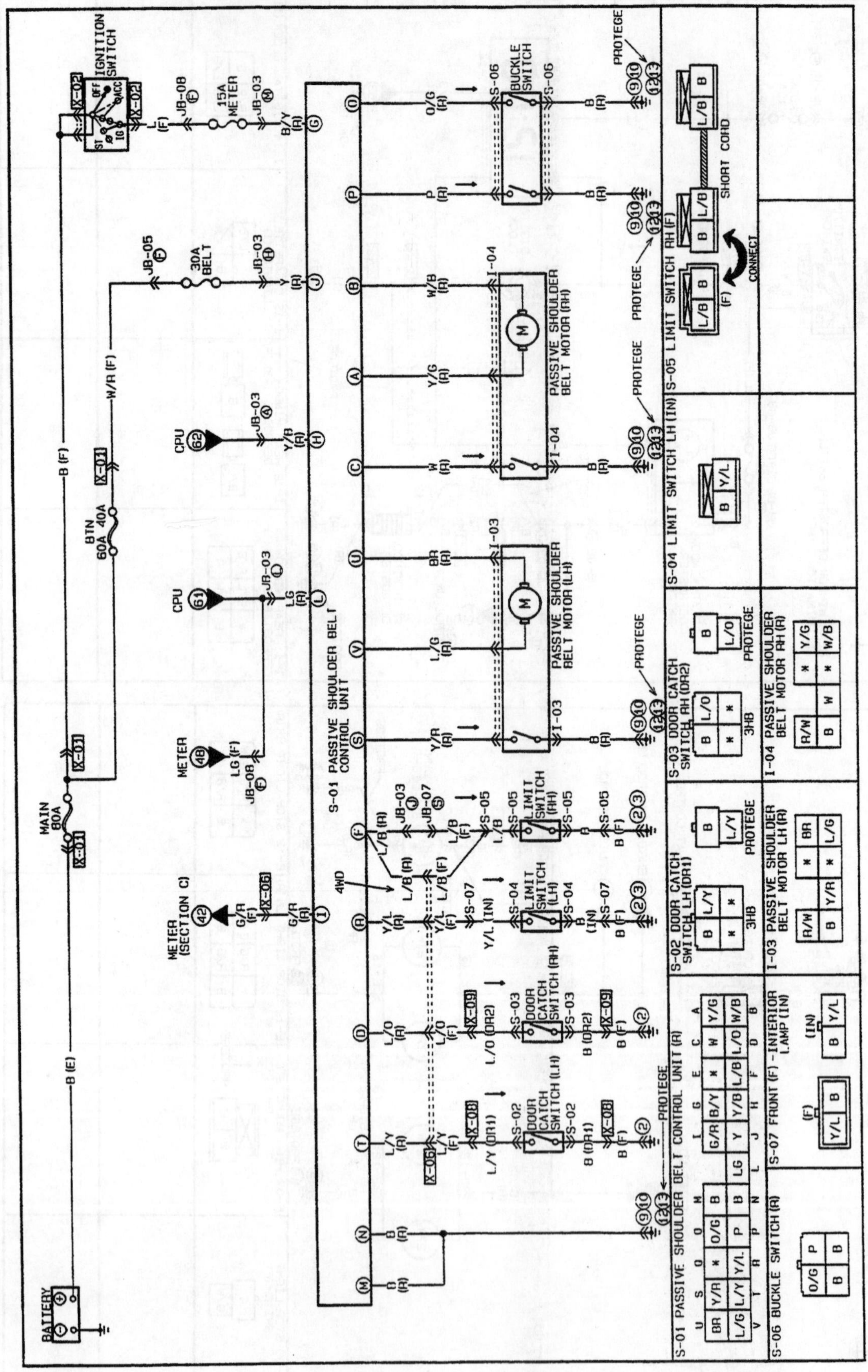

Typical passive shoulder belt system - 1994 and earlier

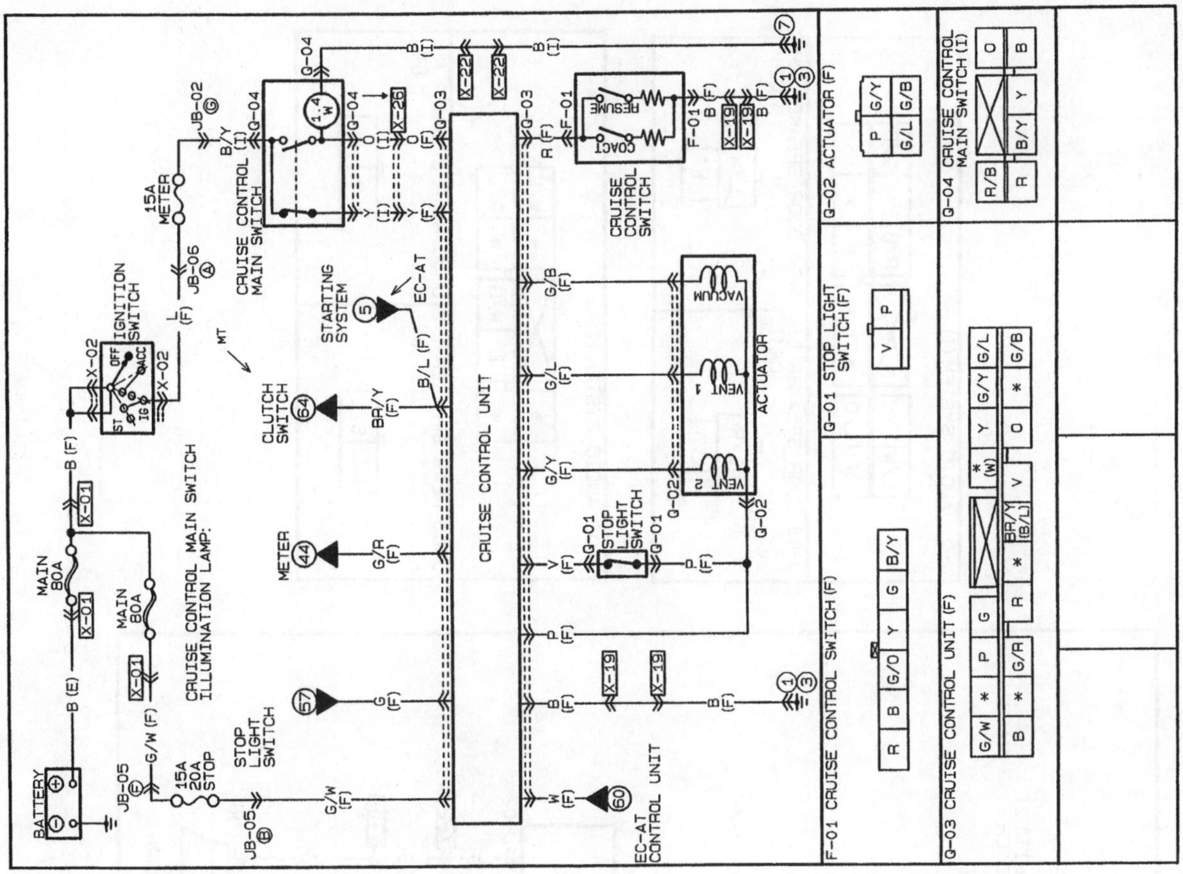

Typical cruise control system - 1994 and earlier

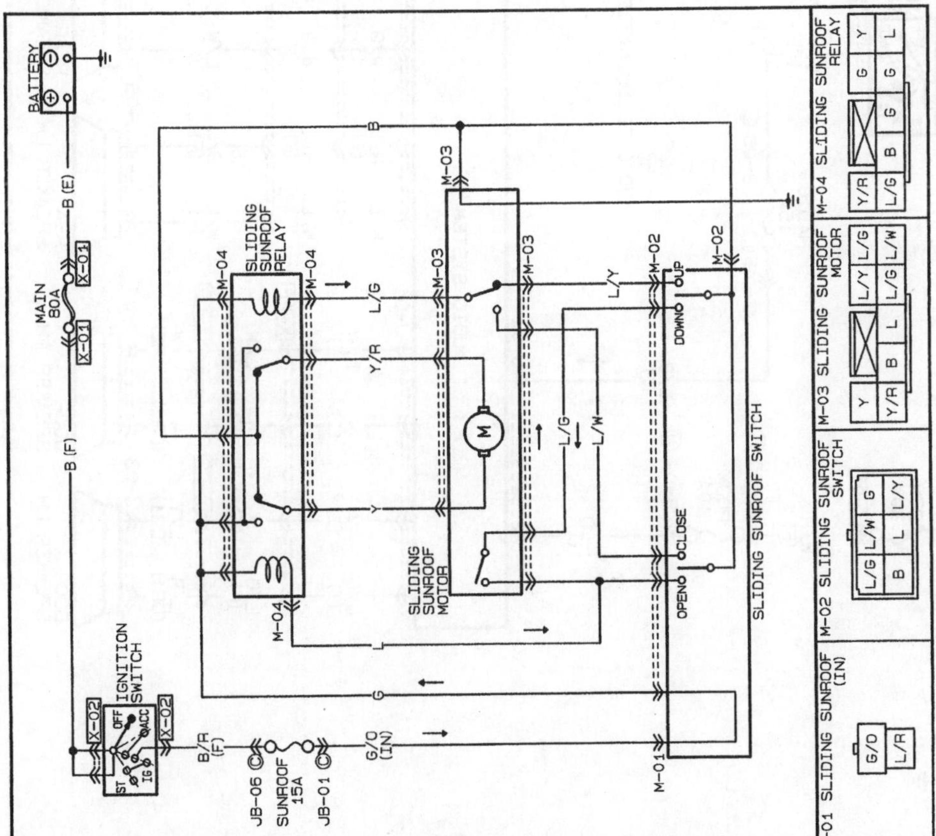

Typical power sunroof system - 1994 and earlier

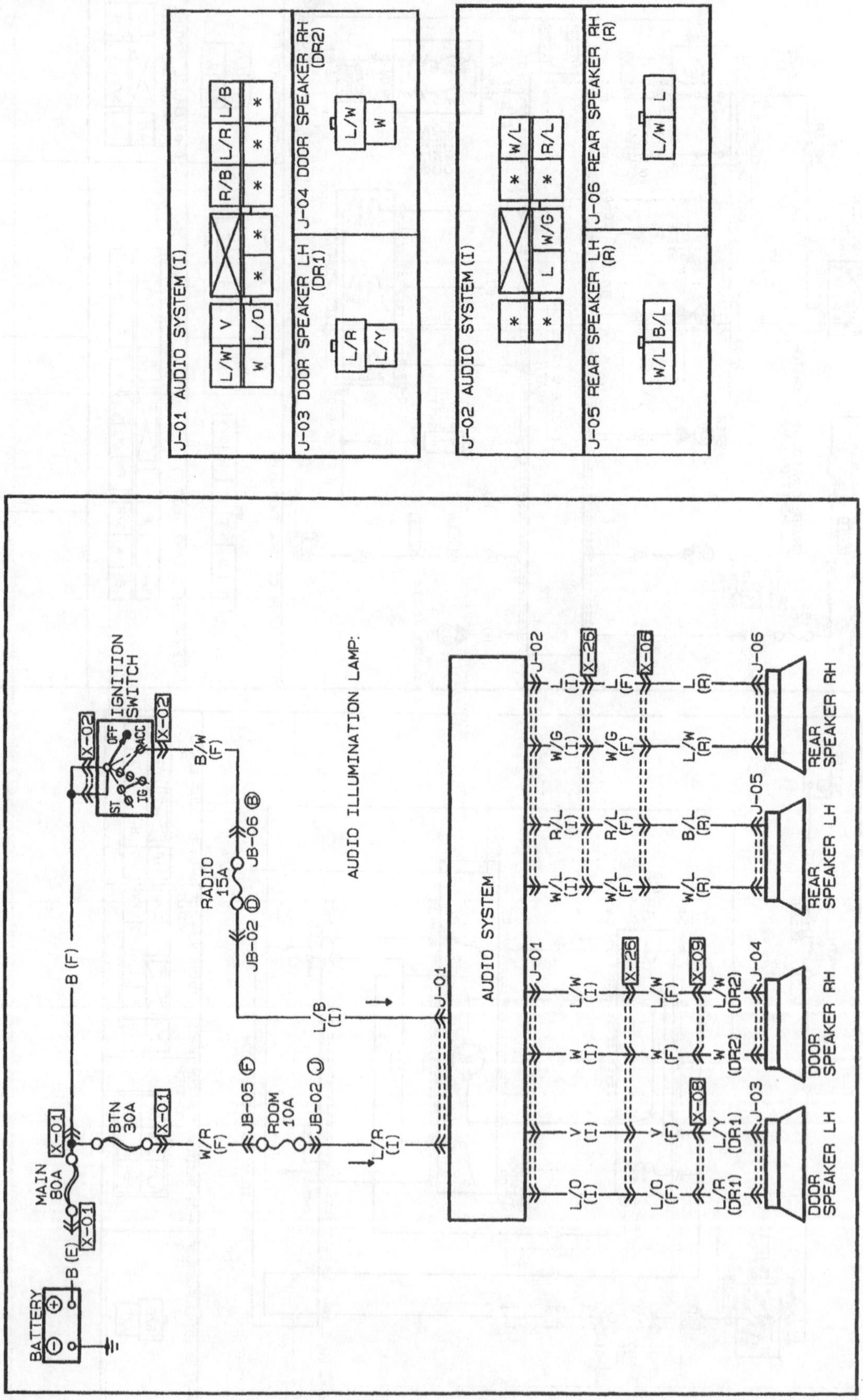

Typical audio system - 1994 and earlier

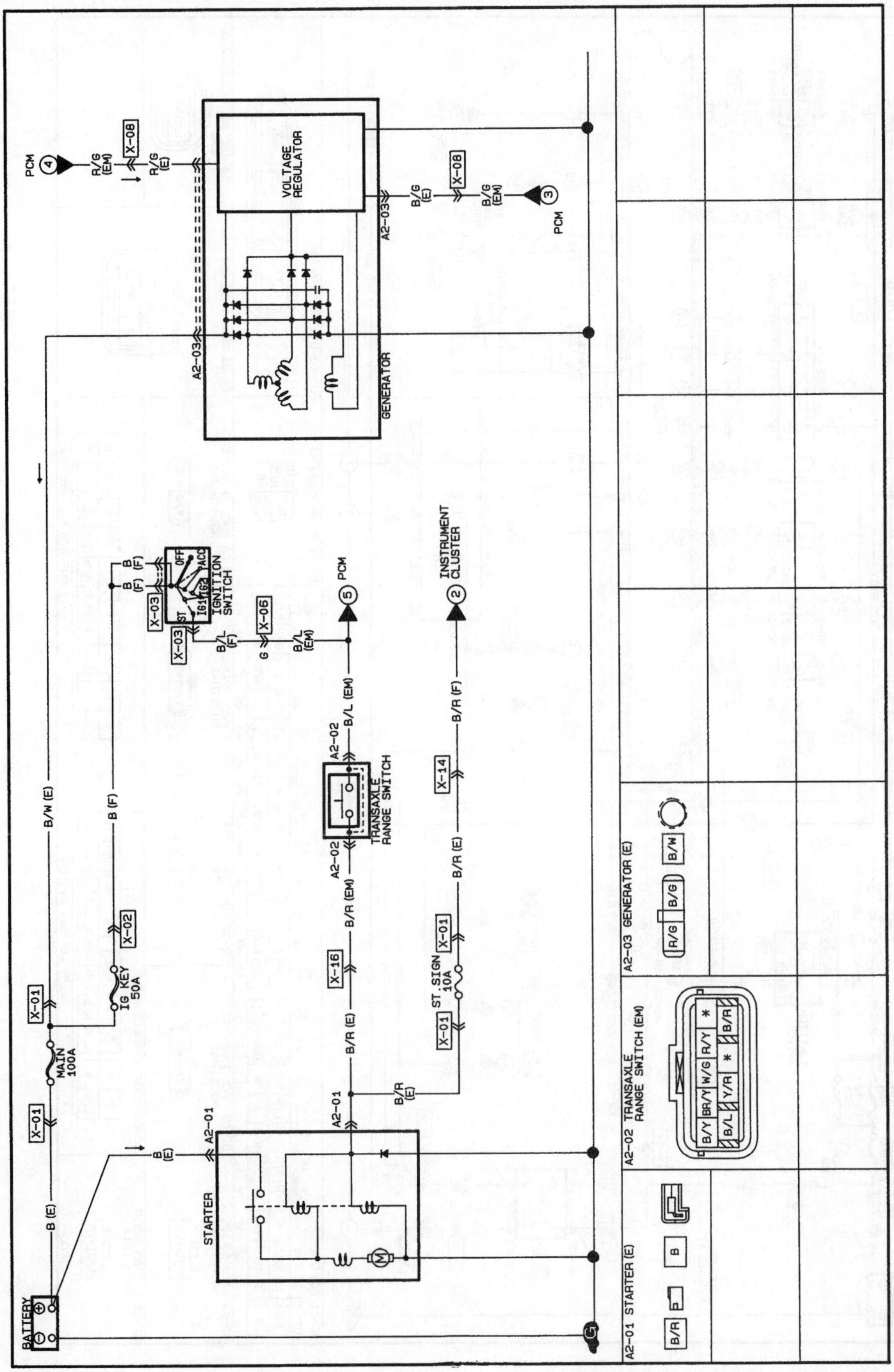

Typical starting and charging systems - 1995 and later

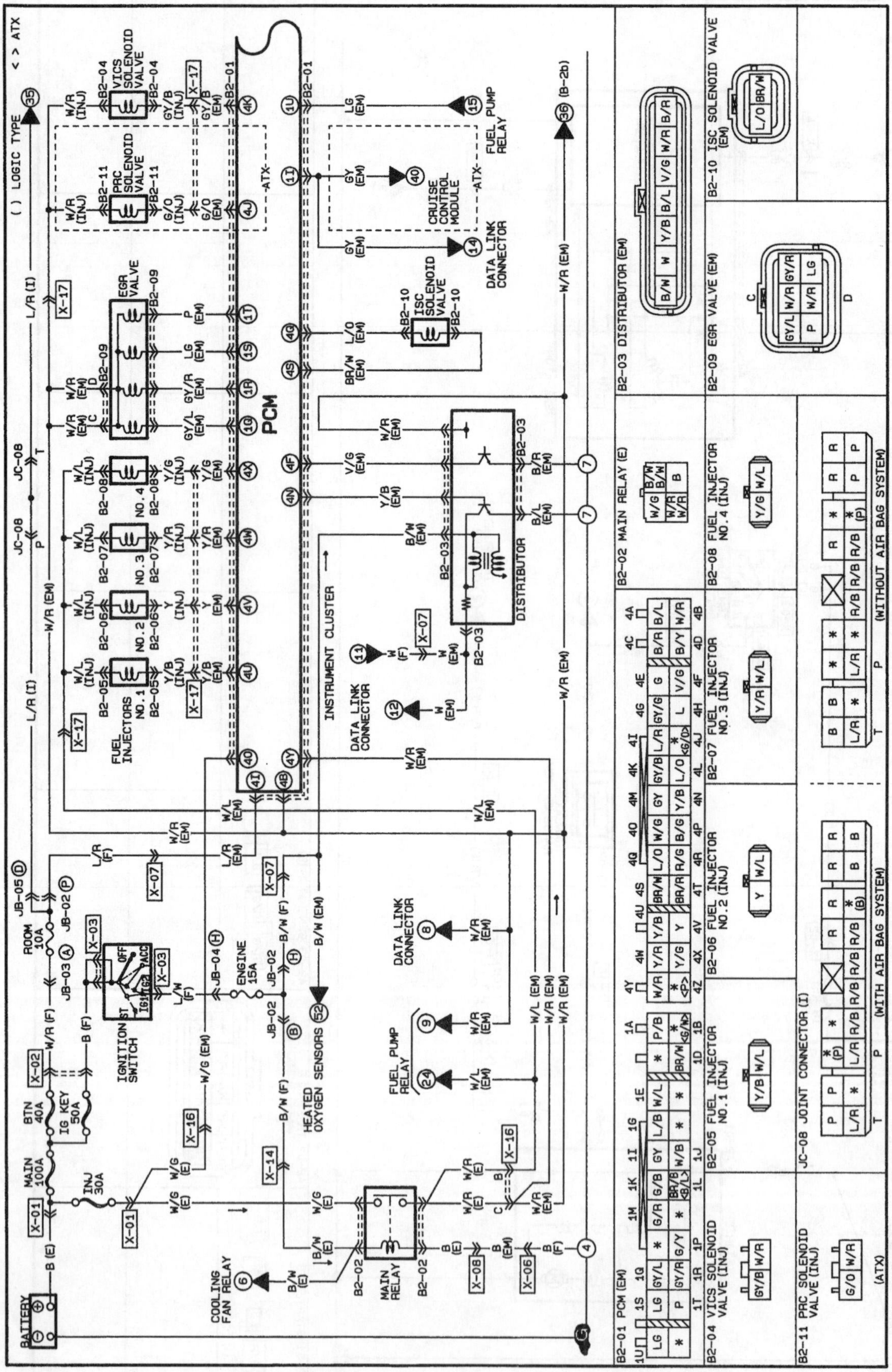

Typical electronic engine control system - 1995 and later (1 of 3)

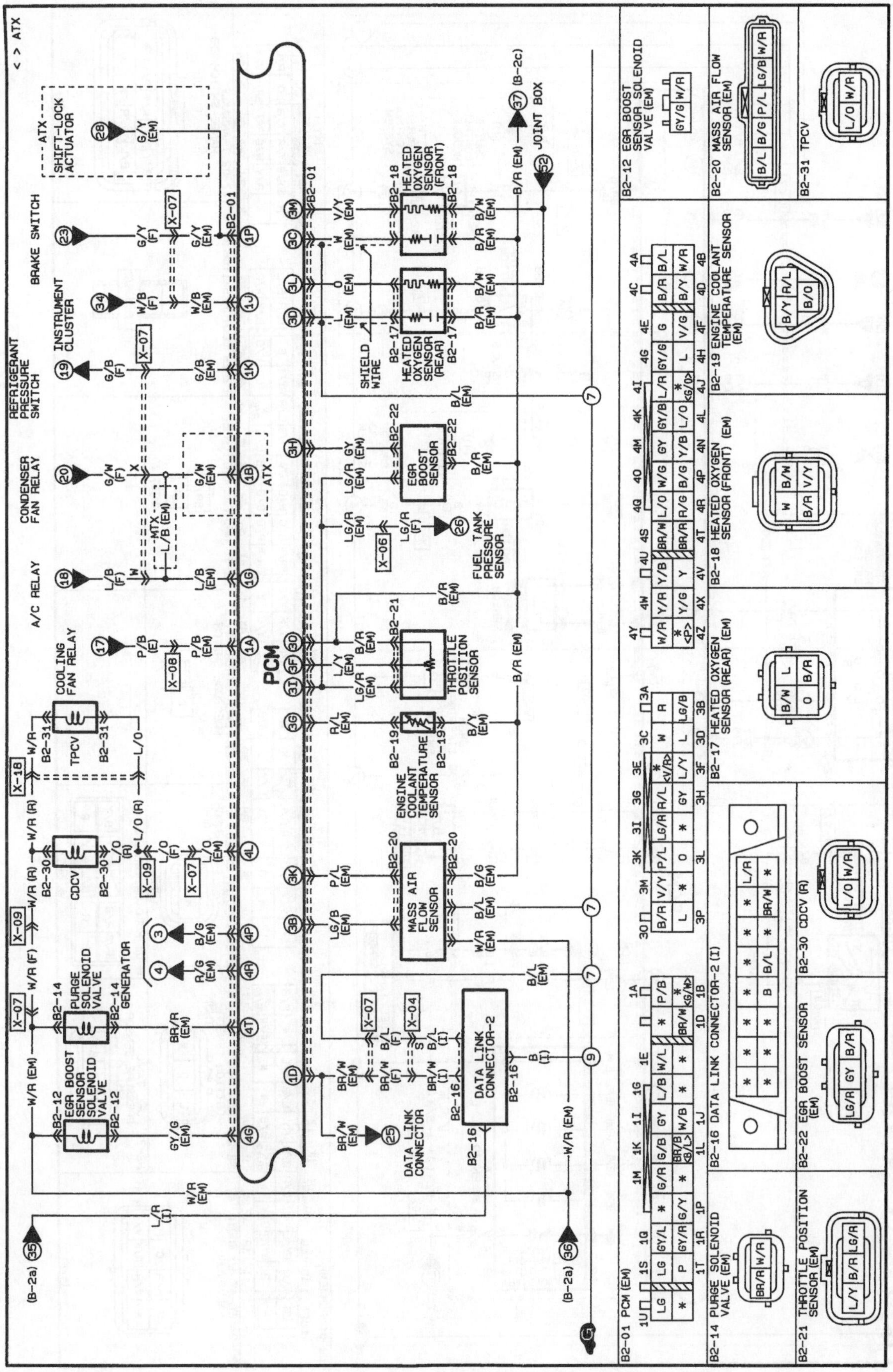

Typical electronic engine control system - 1995 and later (2 of 3)

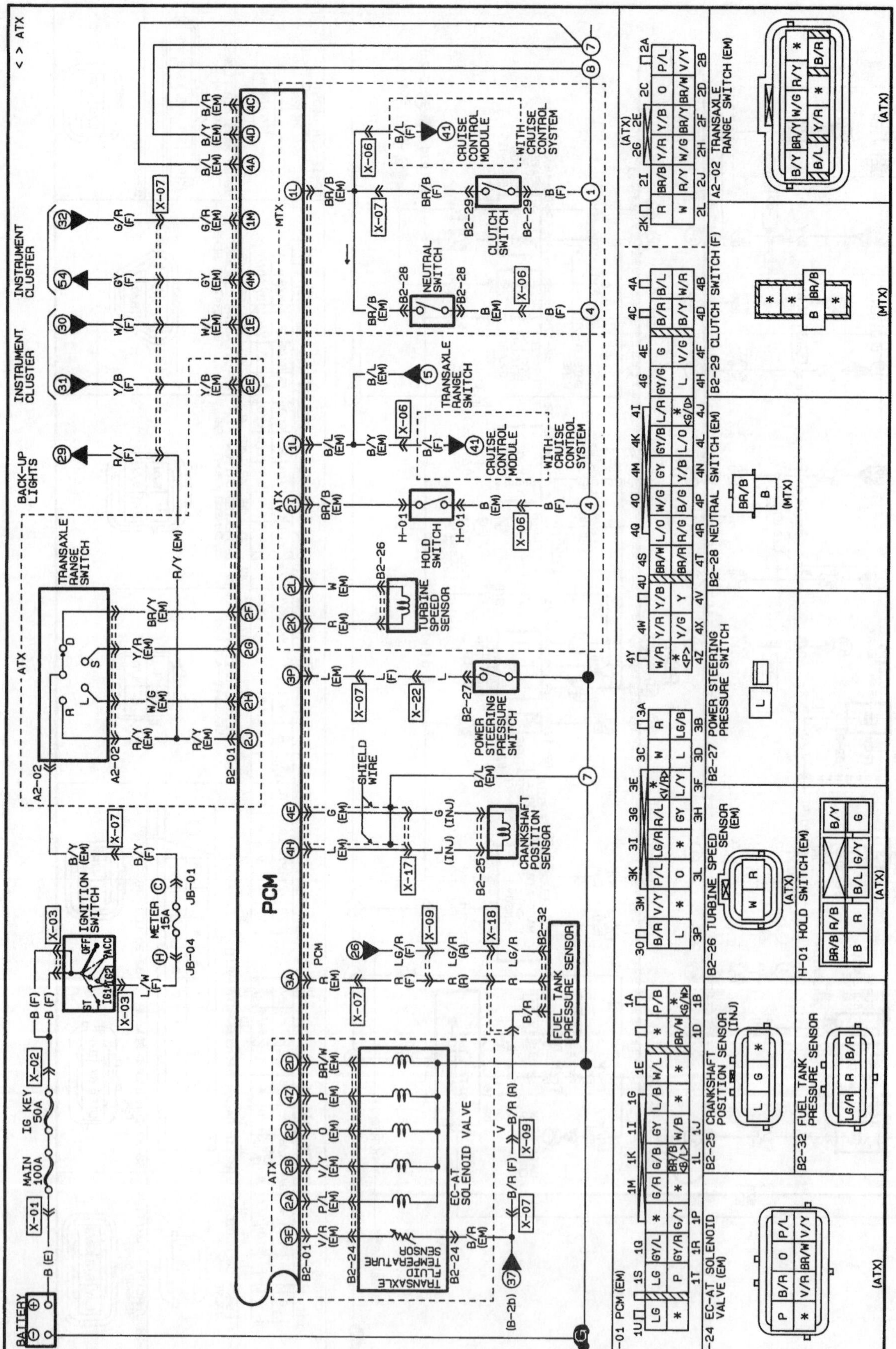

Typical electronic engine control system - 1995 and later (3 of 3)

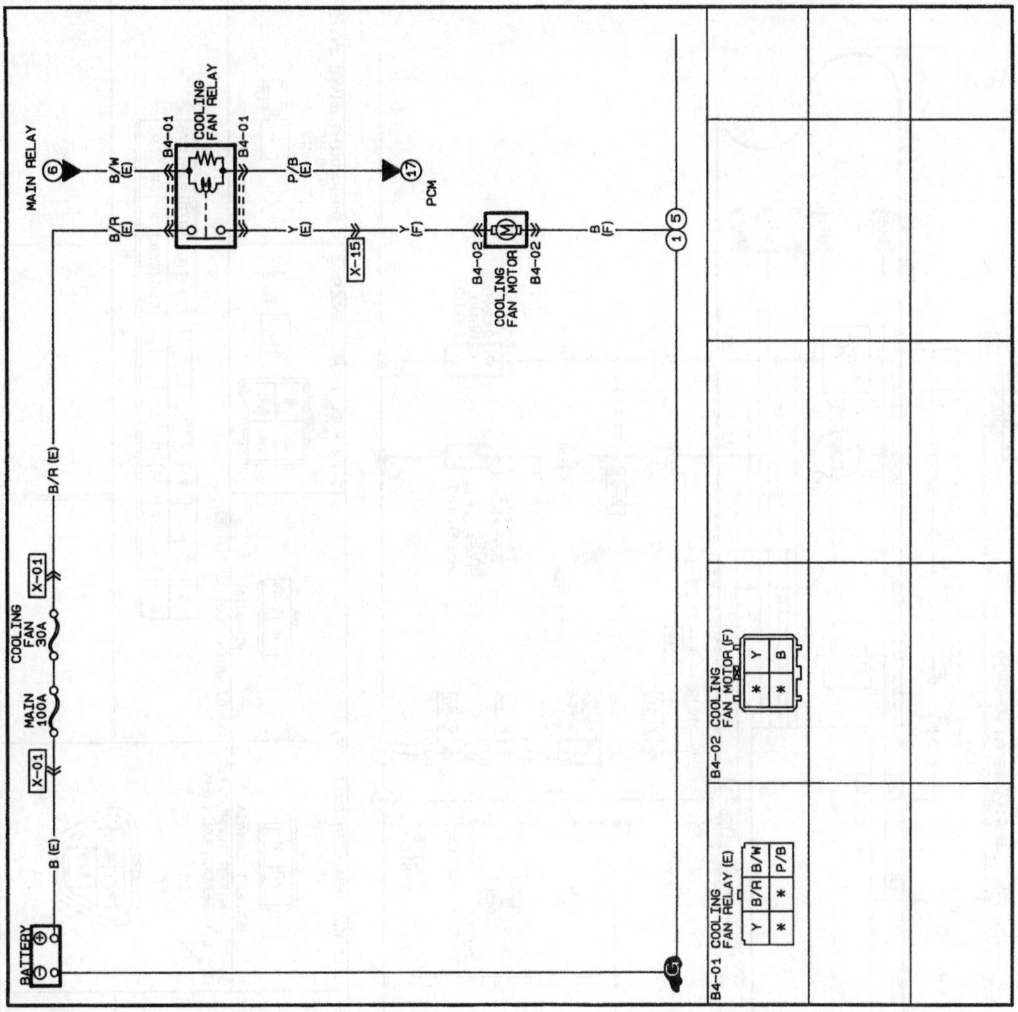

Typical cooling fan system - 1995 and later

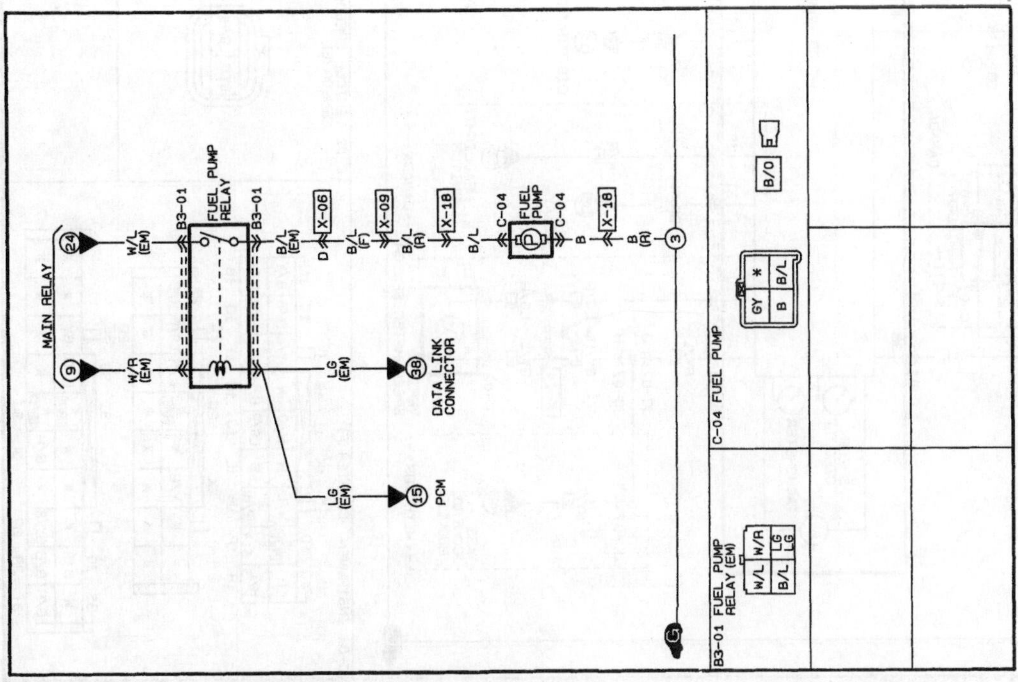

Typical fuel supply system - 1995 and later

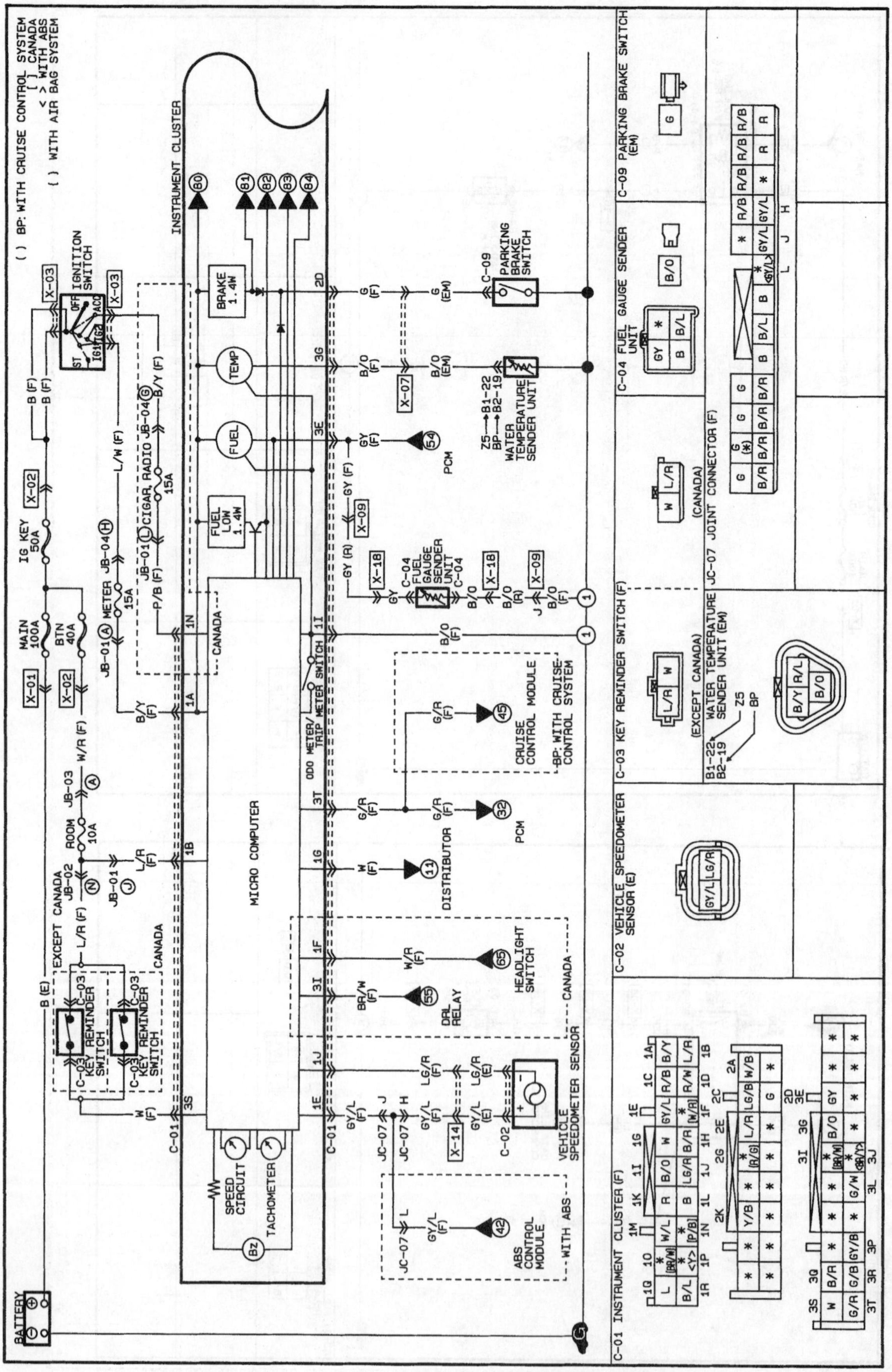

Typical instrument panel - 1995 and later (1 of 3)

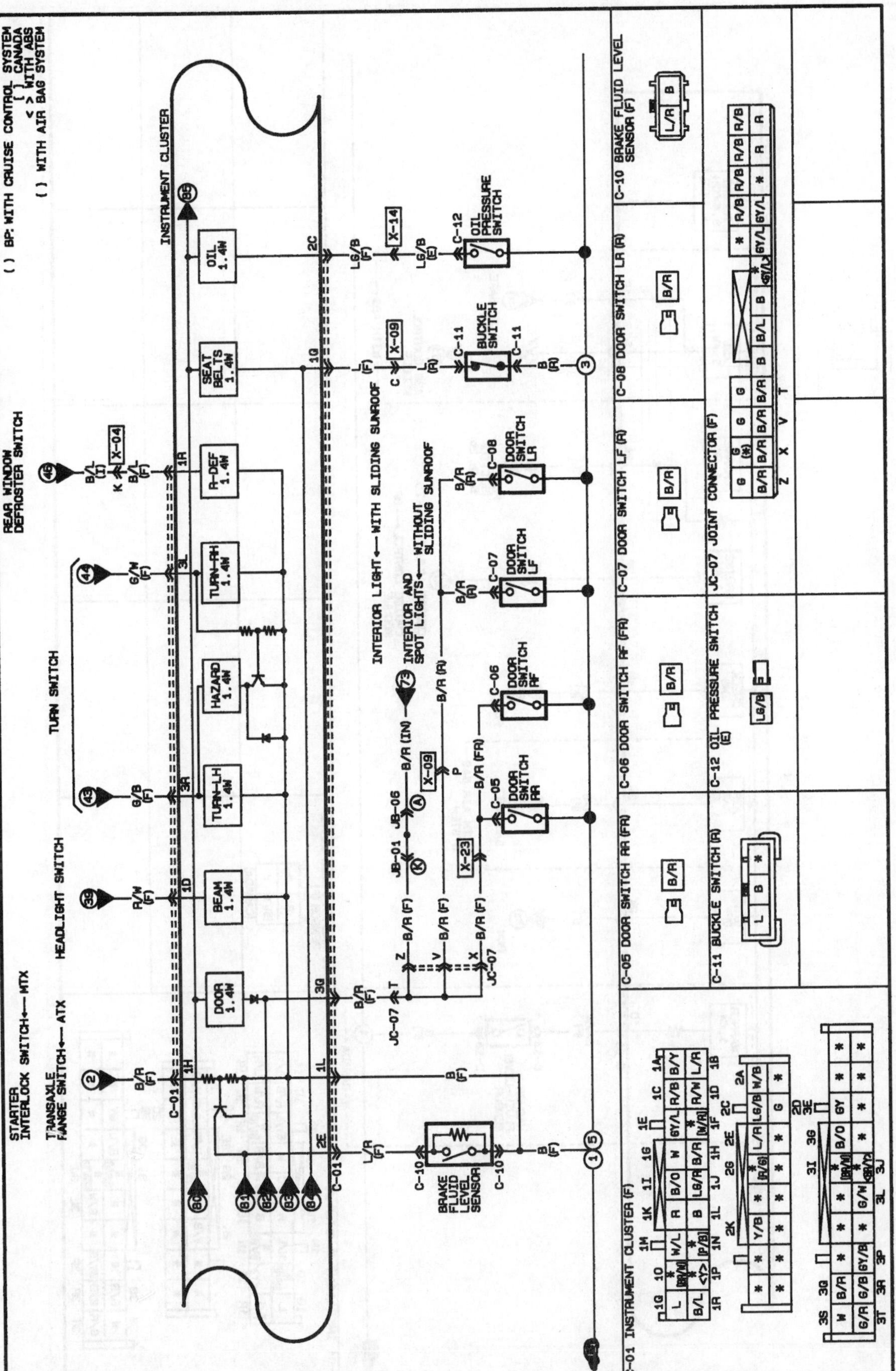

Typical instrument panel - 1995 and later (2 of 3)

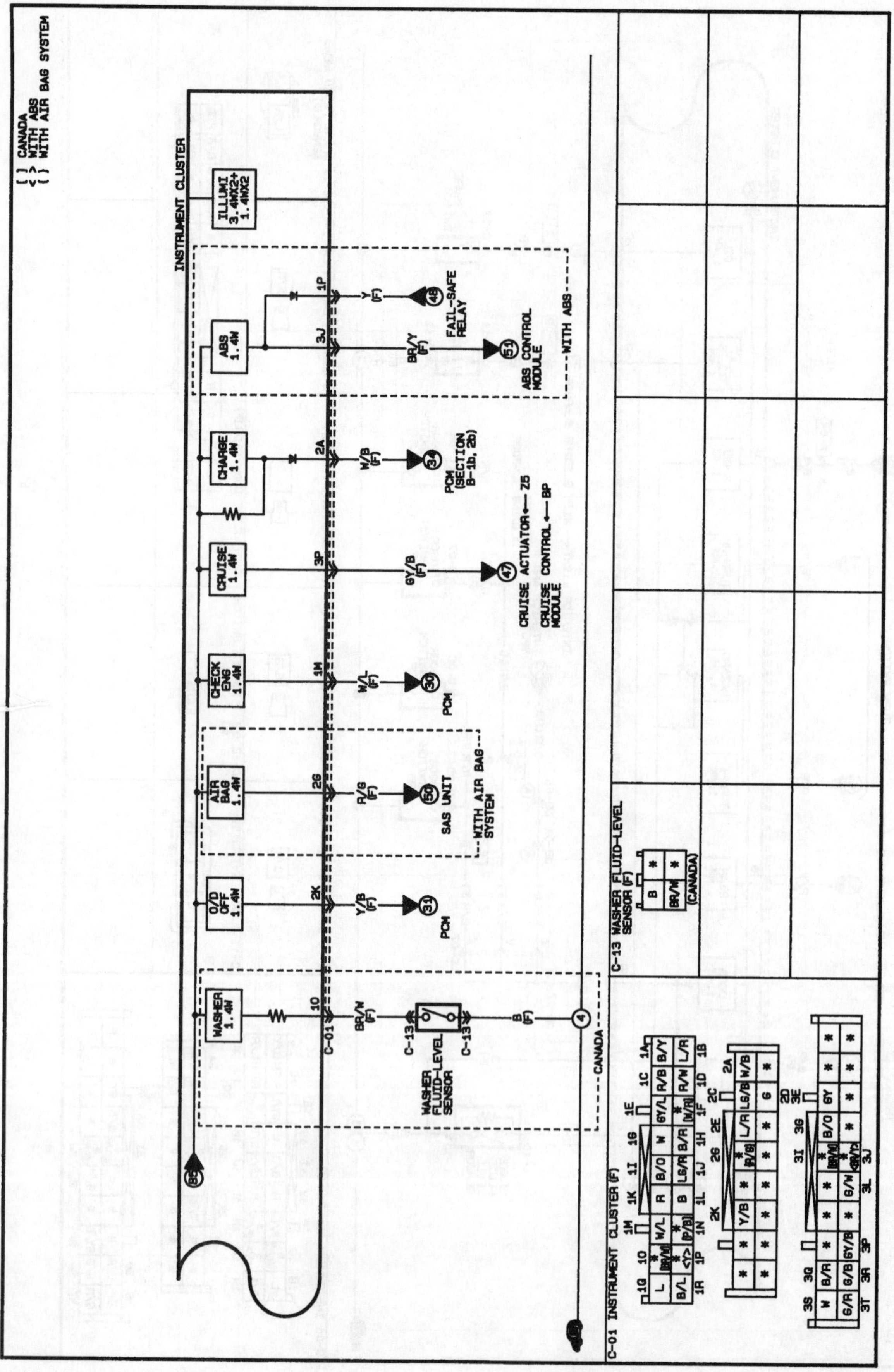

Typical instrument panel - 1995 and later (3 of 3)

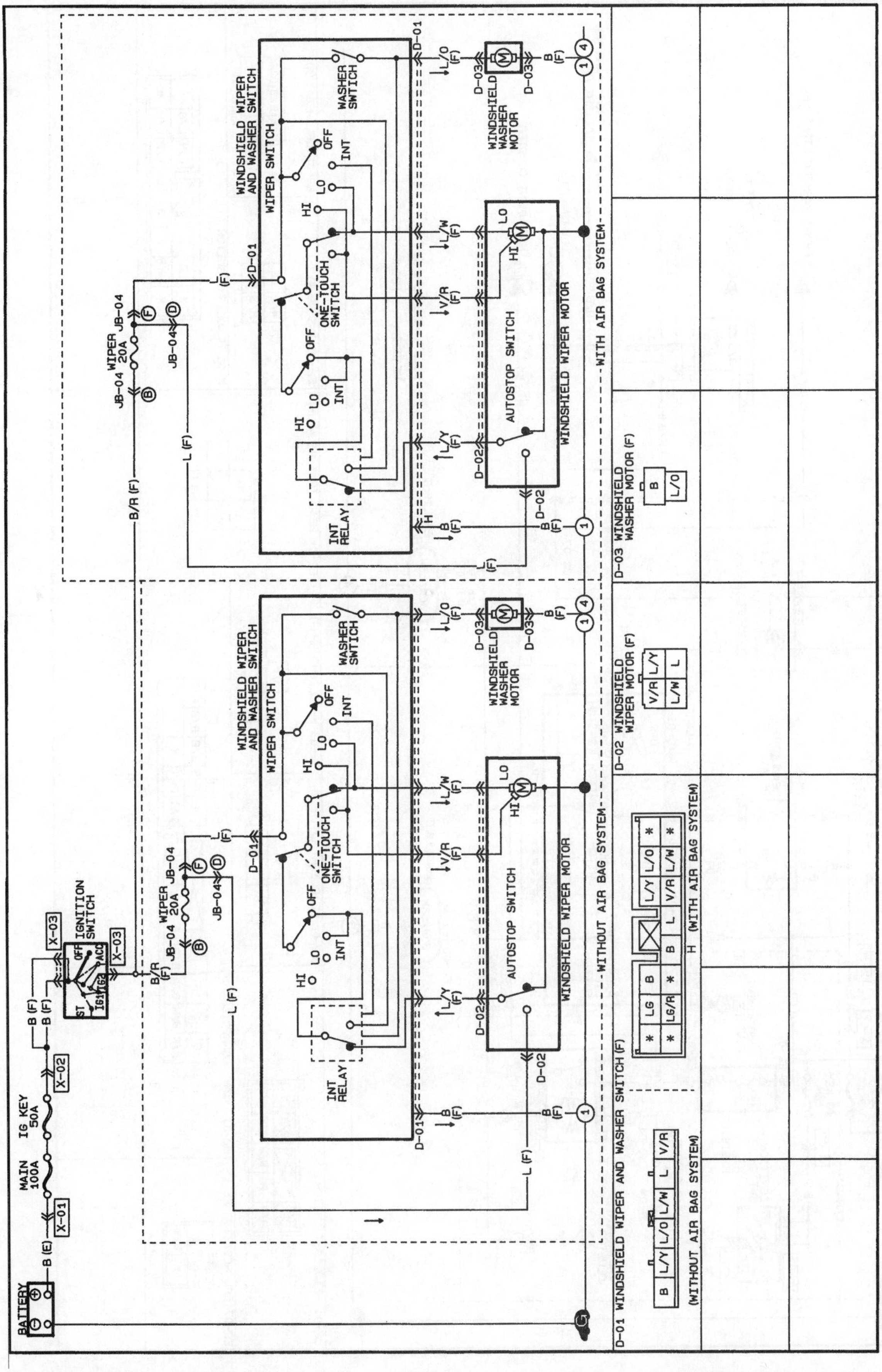

Typical windshield wiper and washer system - 1995 and later

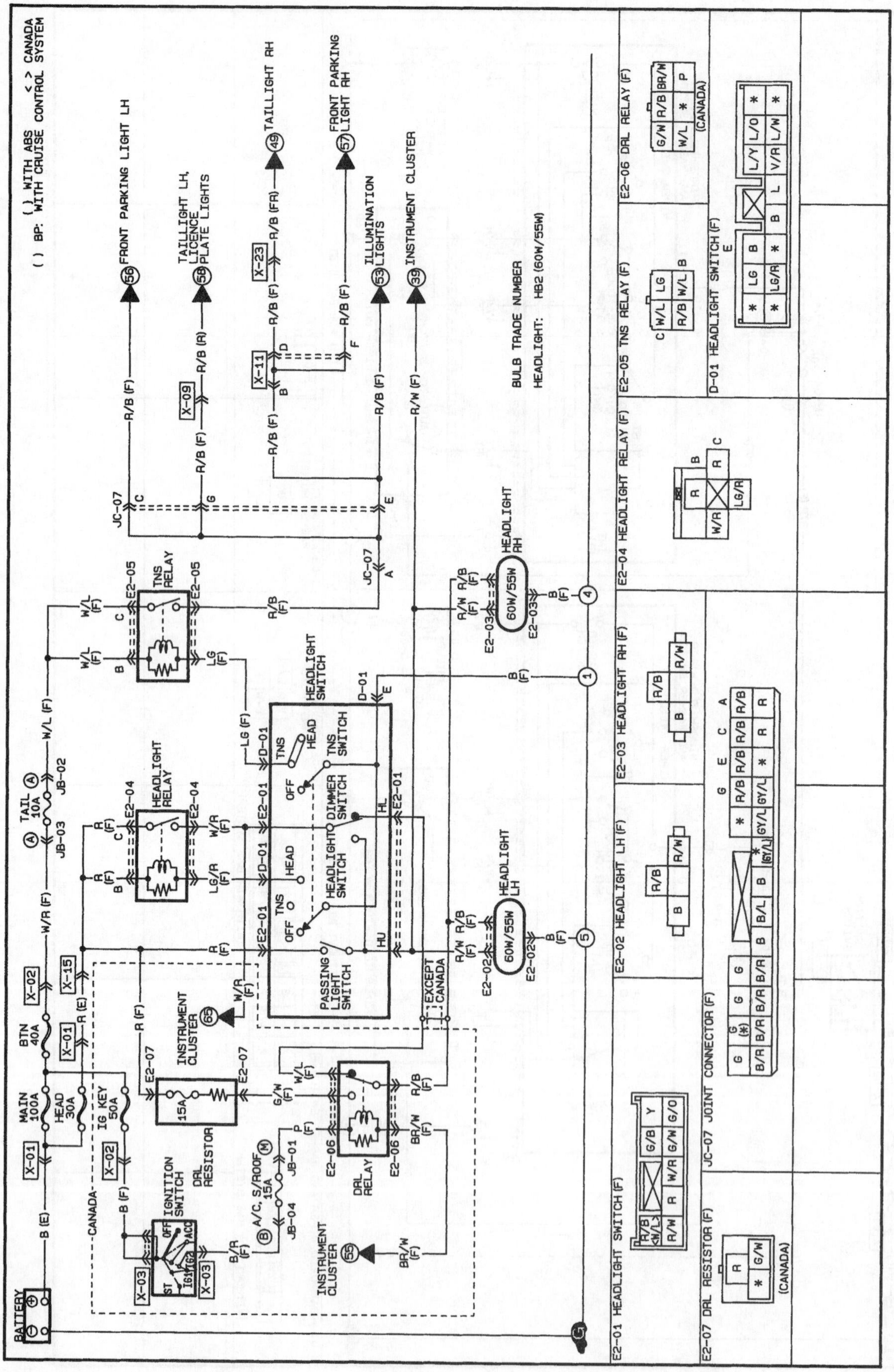

Typical headlight system - 1995 and later

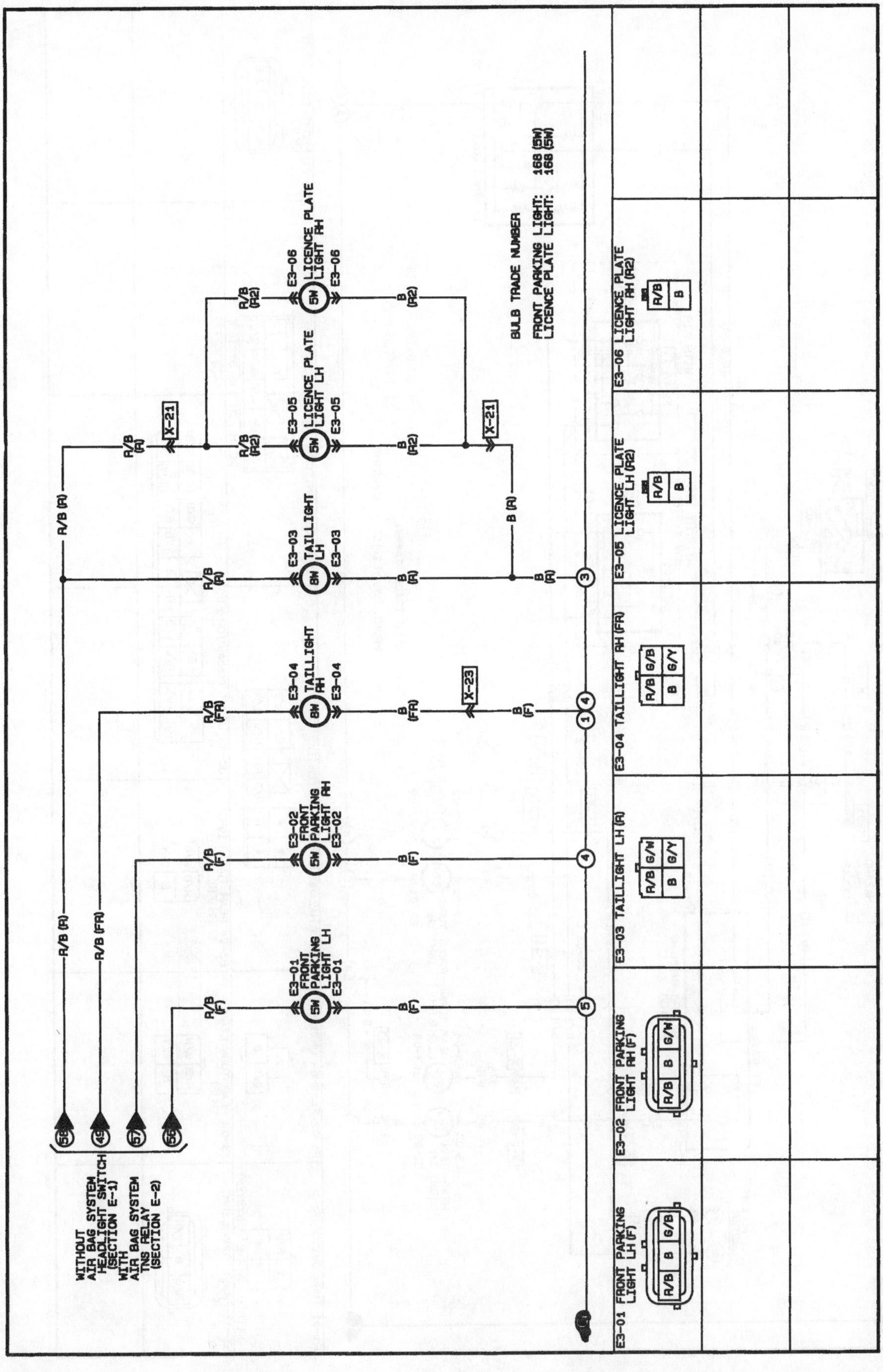

Typical parking light, taillight, license plate light system - 1995 and later

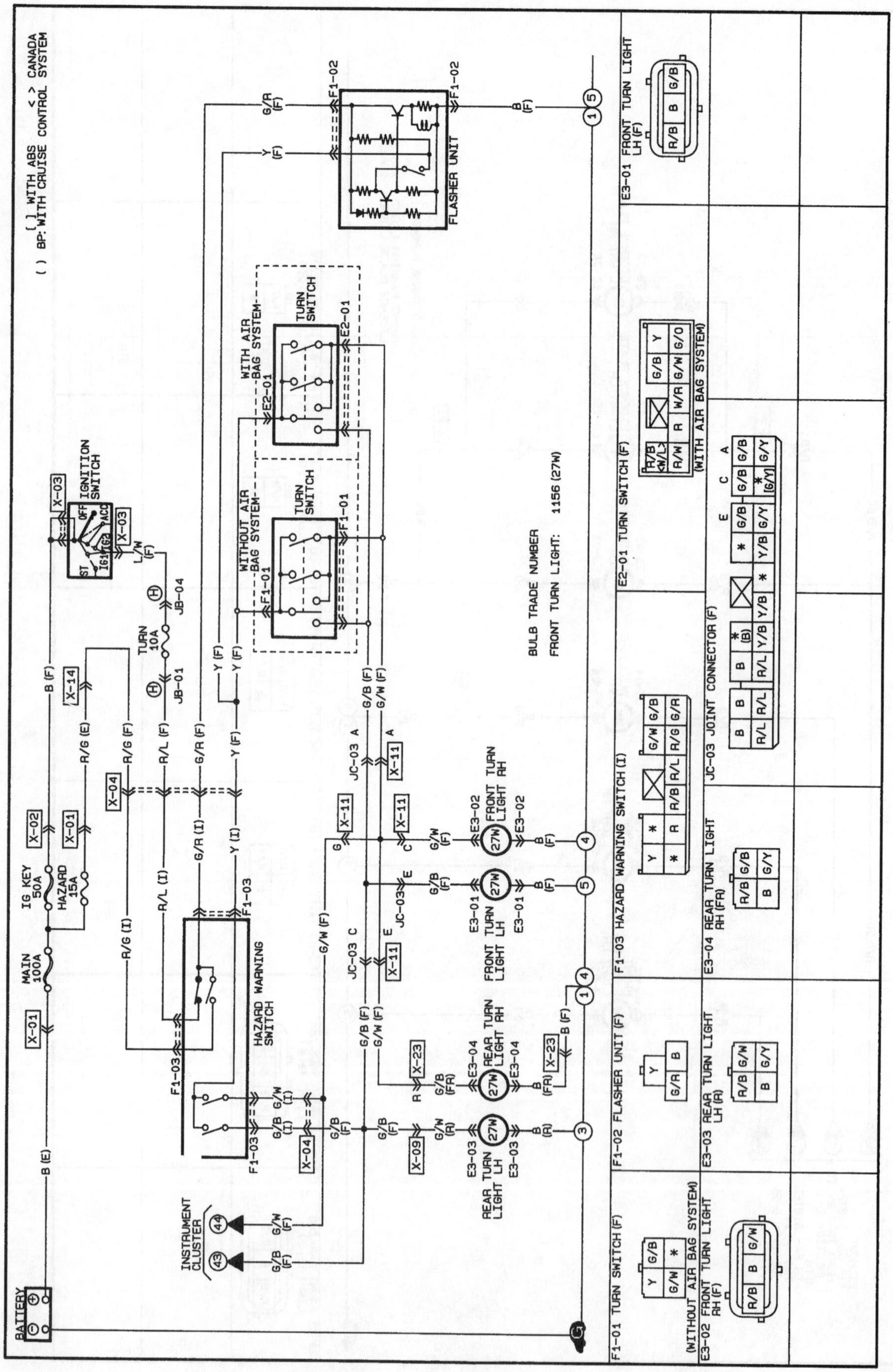

Typical turn signal and hazard warning flasher light system - 1995 and later

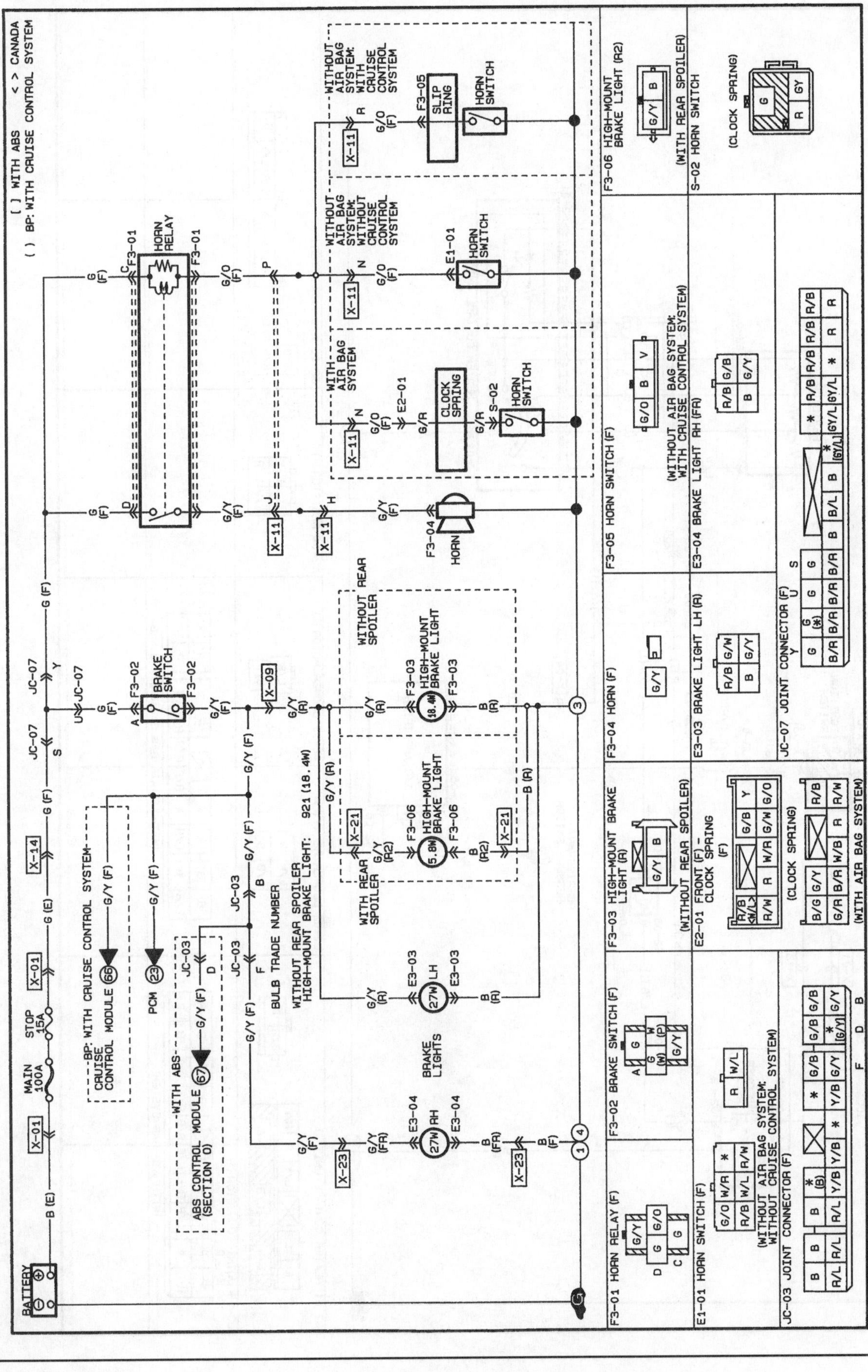

Typical brake light and horn system - 1995 and later

12

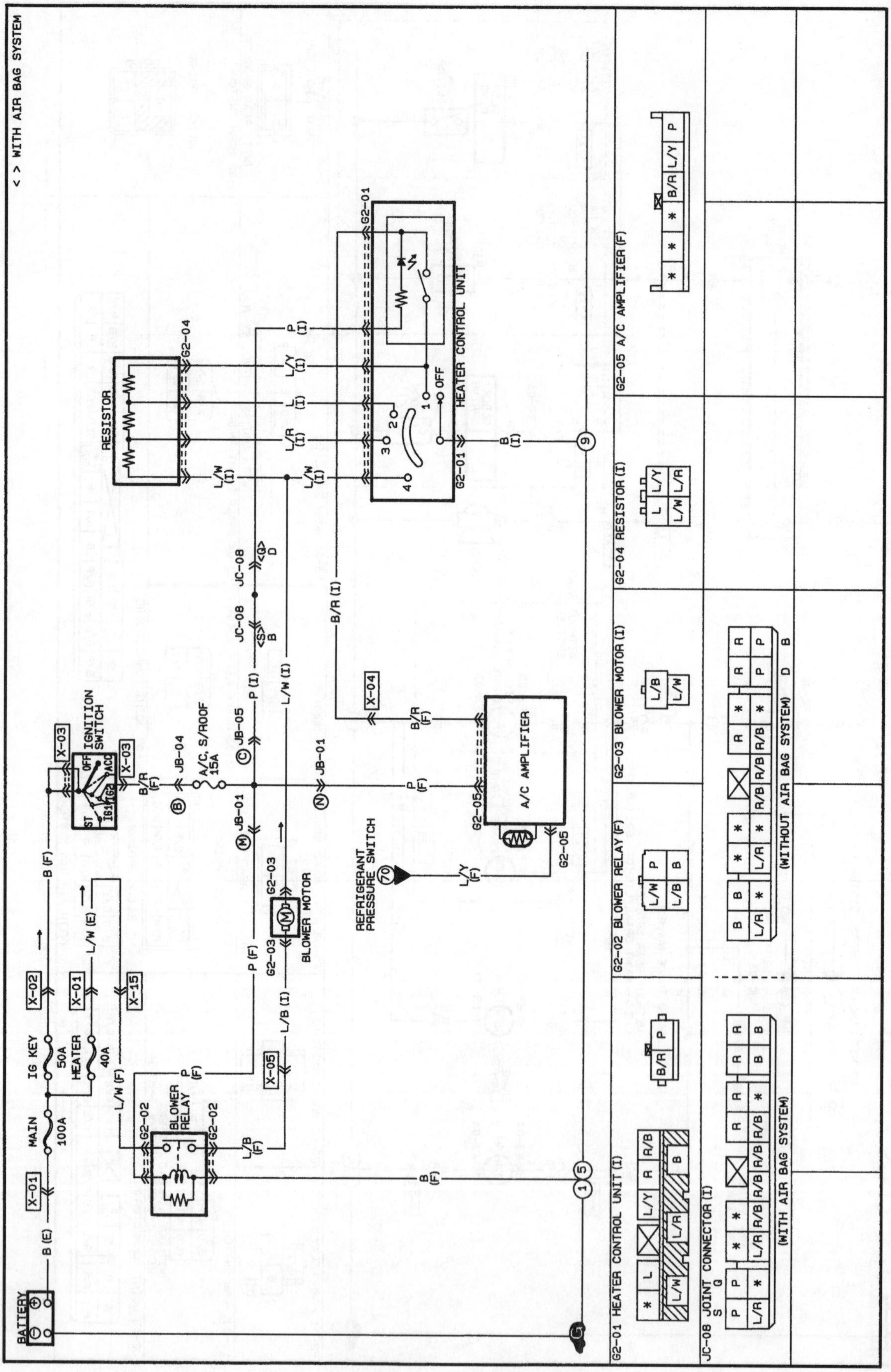

Typical heater and air conditioning control system (non-electronic) - 1995 and later

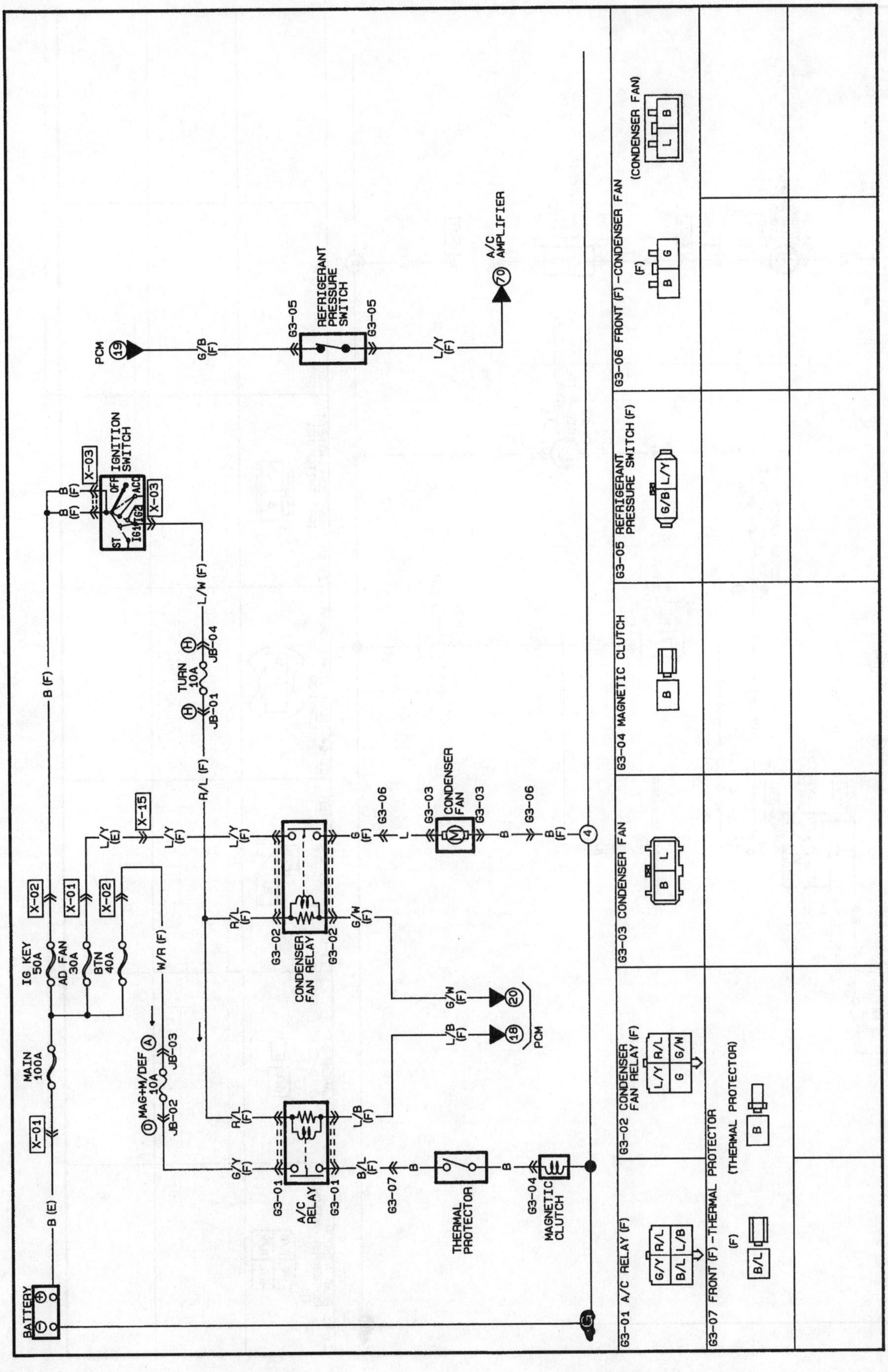

Typical air conditioning compressor and radiator condenser fan system - 1995 and later

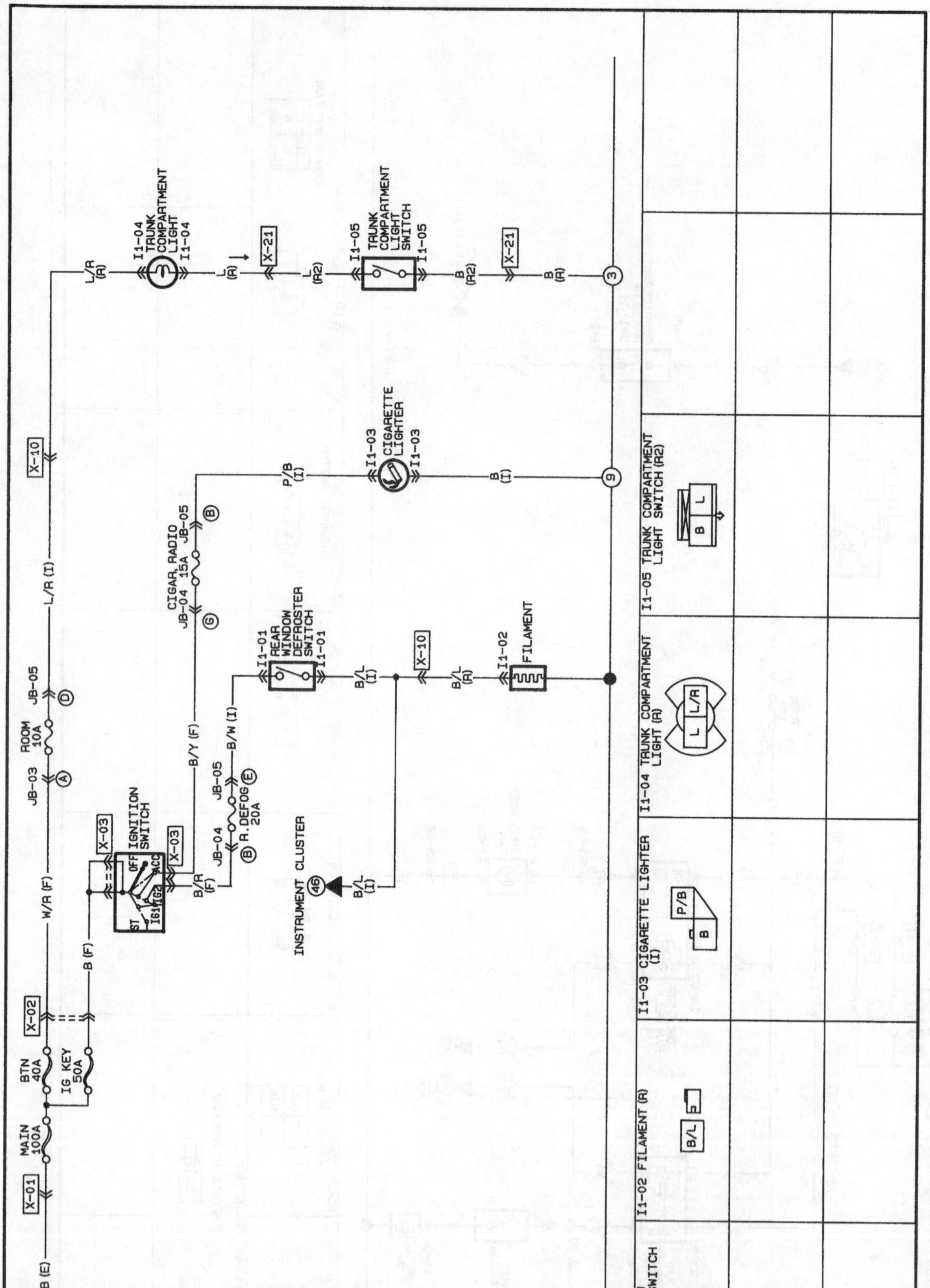

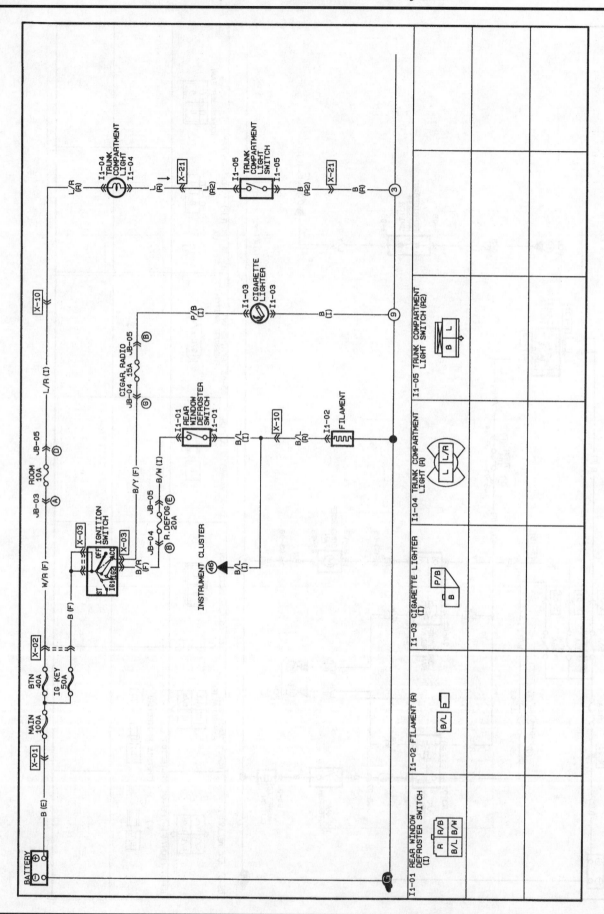

Typical rear window defogger, lighter, trunk light systems - 1995 and later

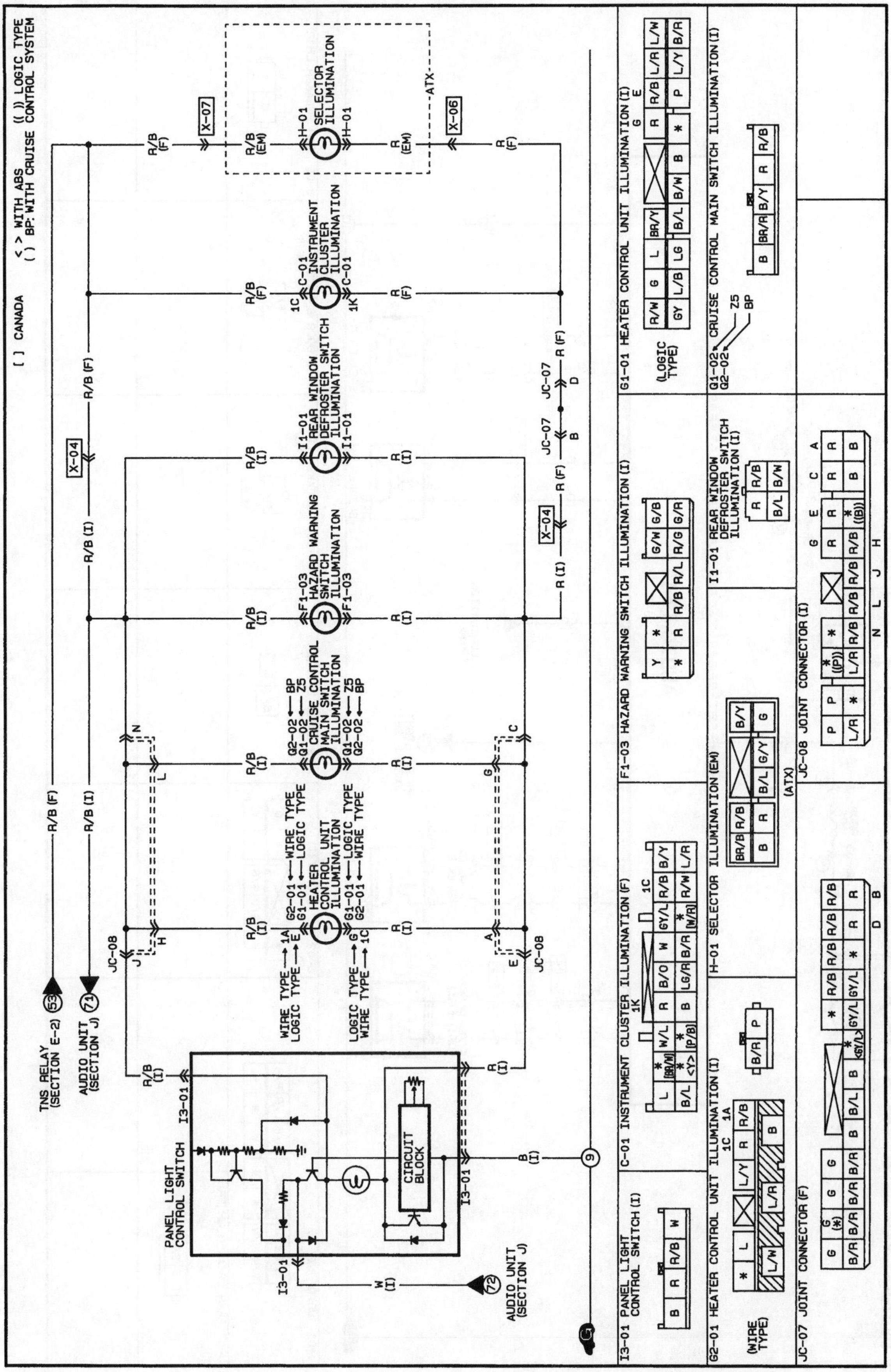

Typical instrument panel illumination lighting system - 1995 and later

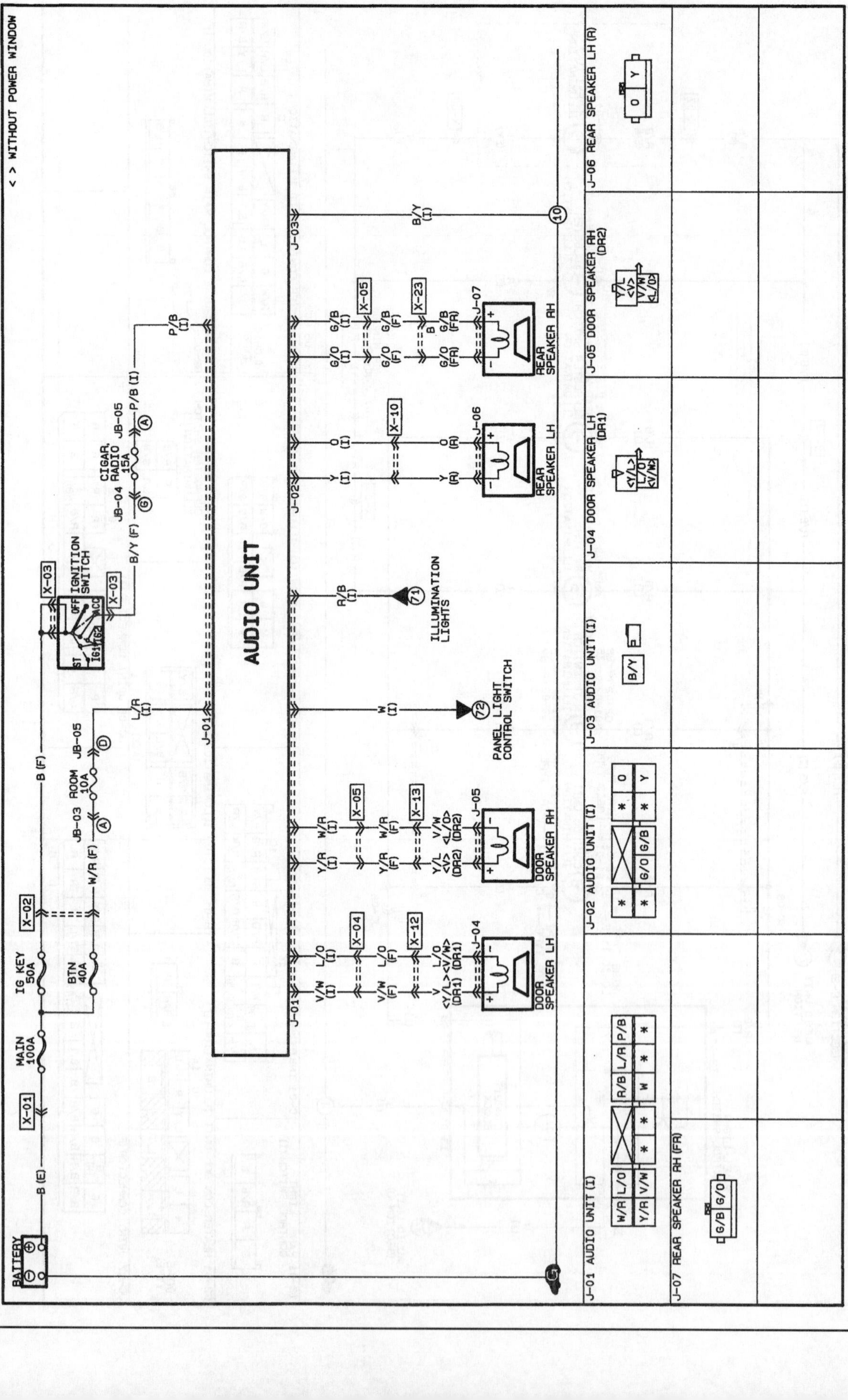

Typical audio system - 1995 and later

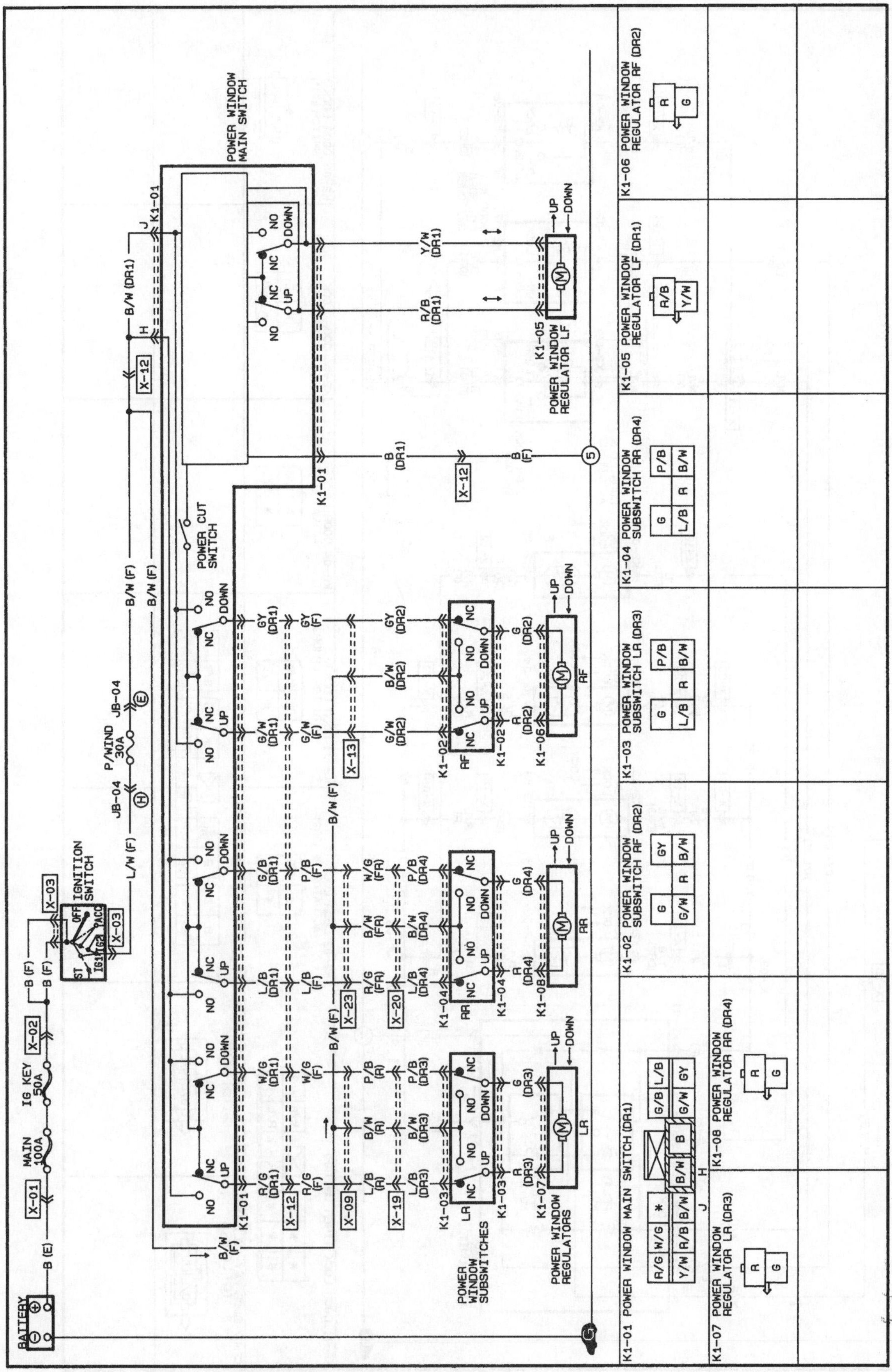

Typical power window system - 1995 and later

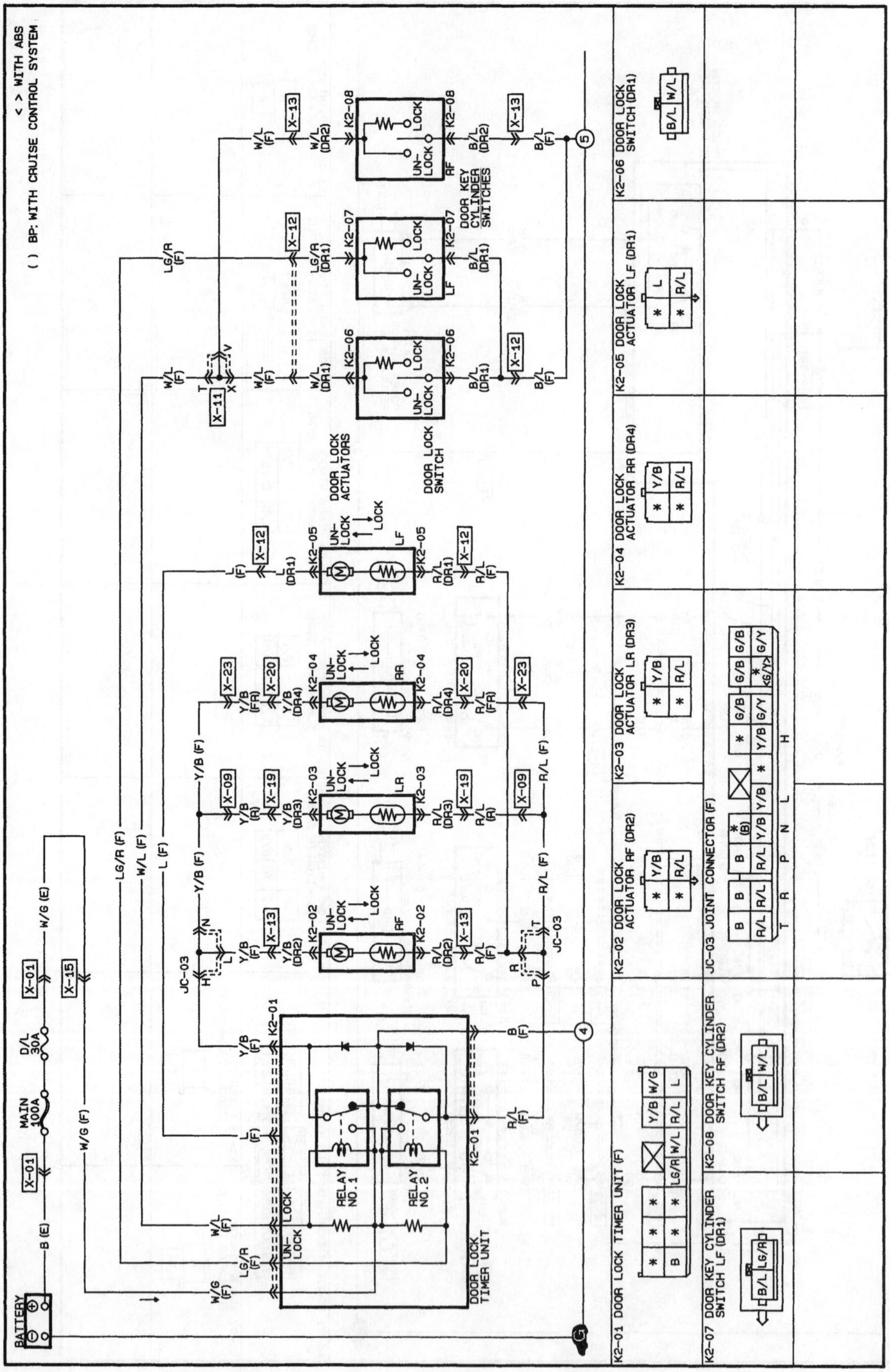

Typical power door lock system - 1995 and later

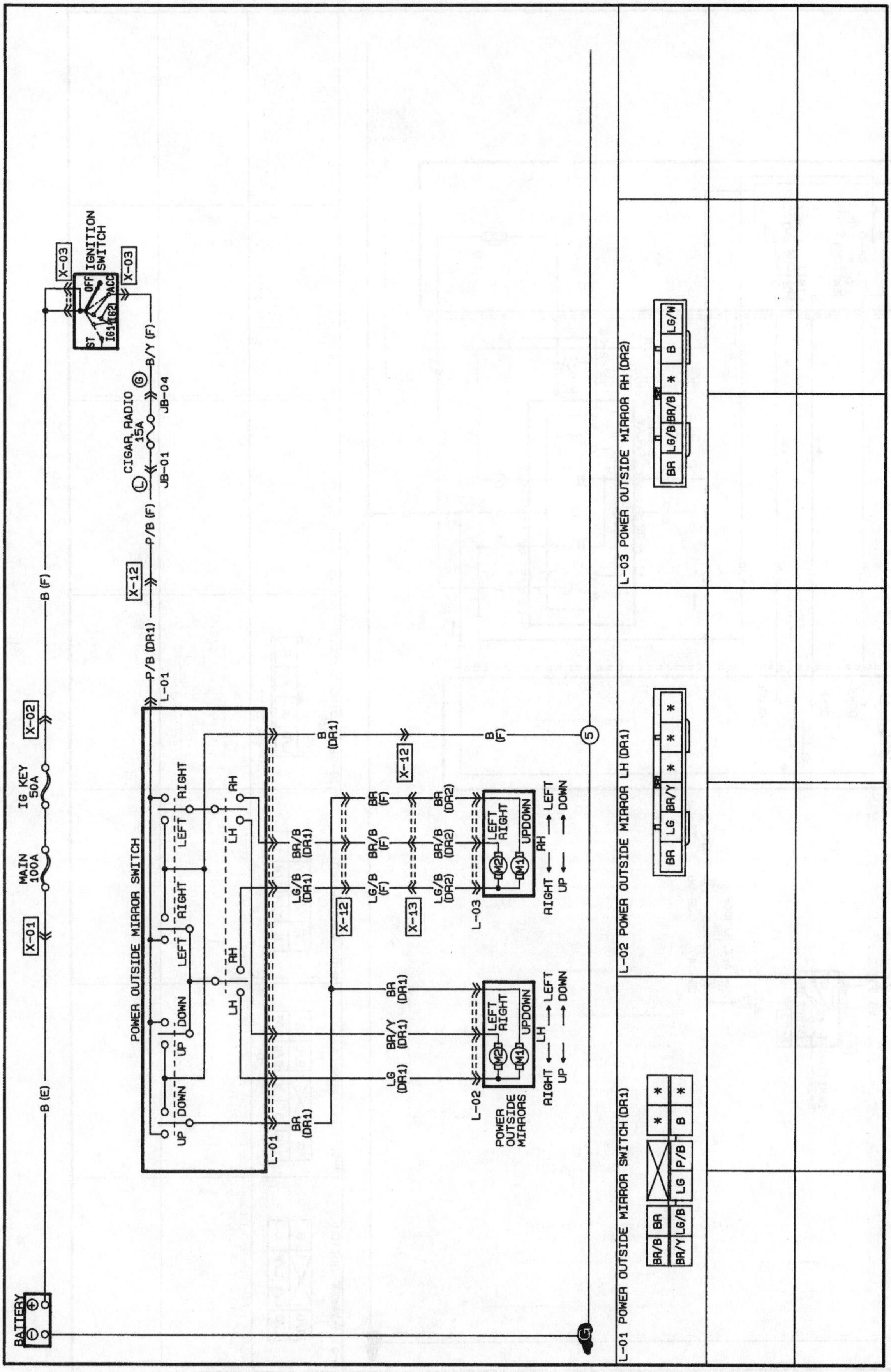

Typical power outside mirror system - 1995 and later

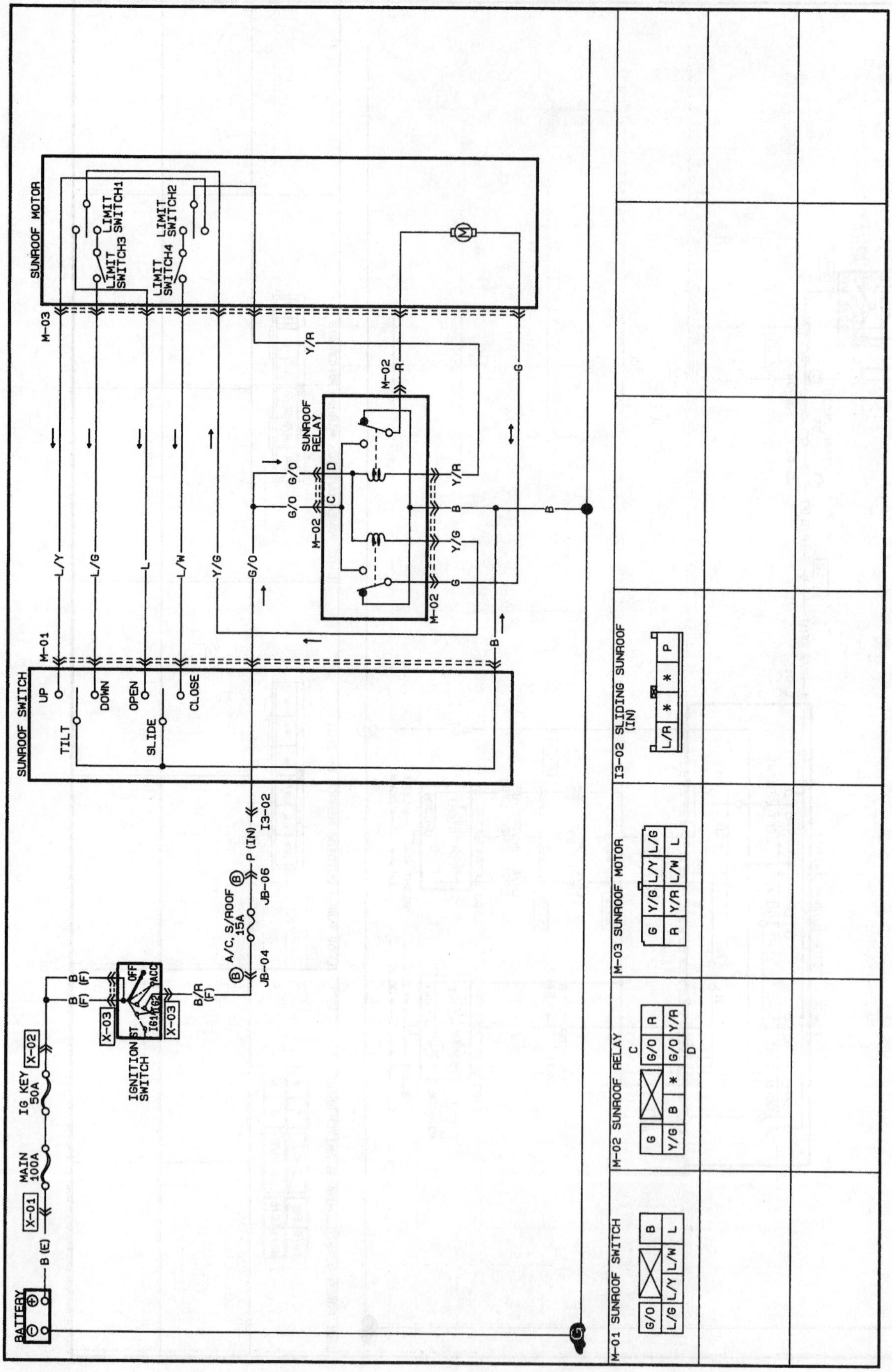

Typical sunroof control system - 1995 and later

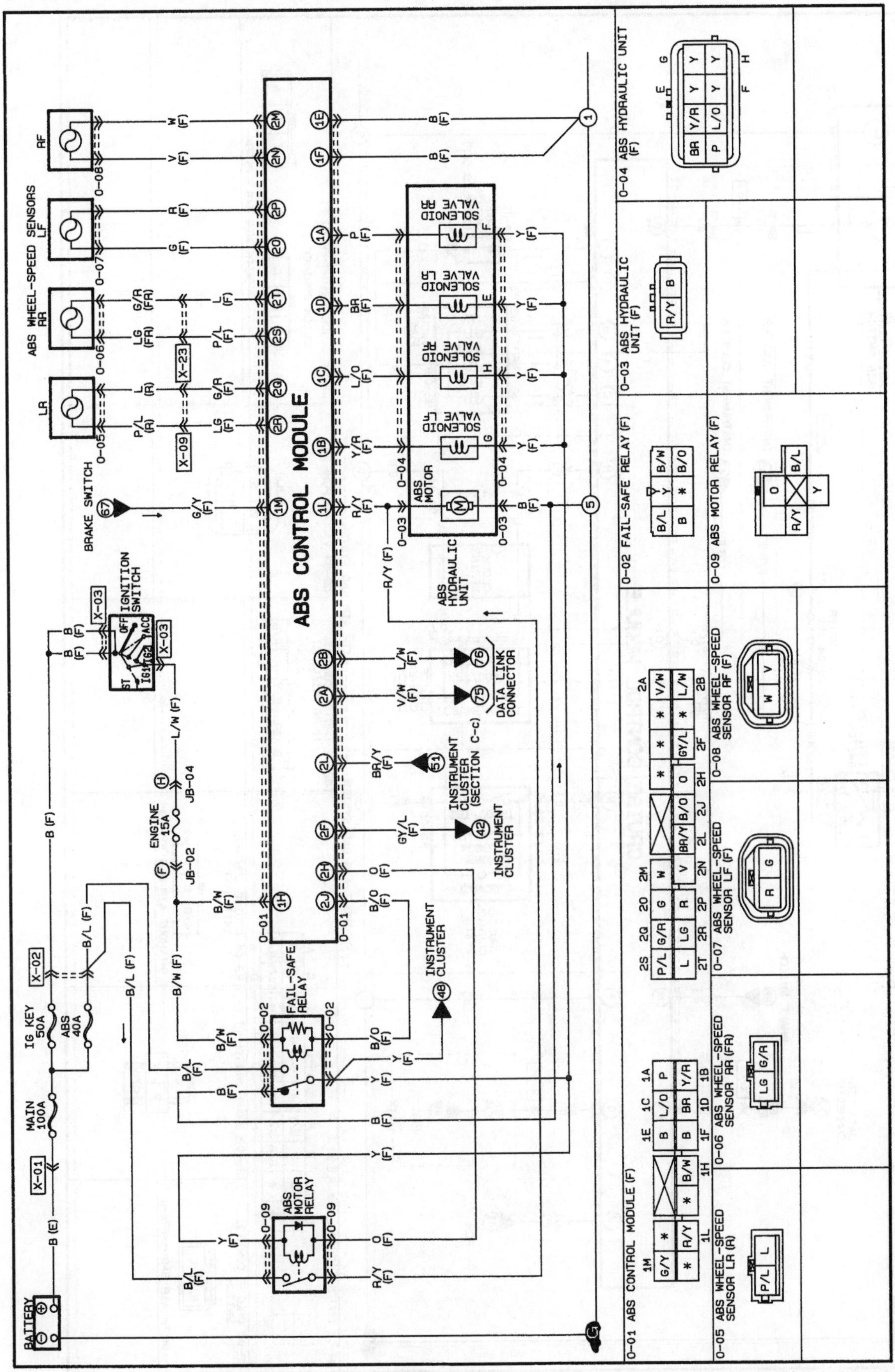

Typical Anti-lock Brake System - 1995 and later

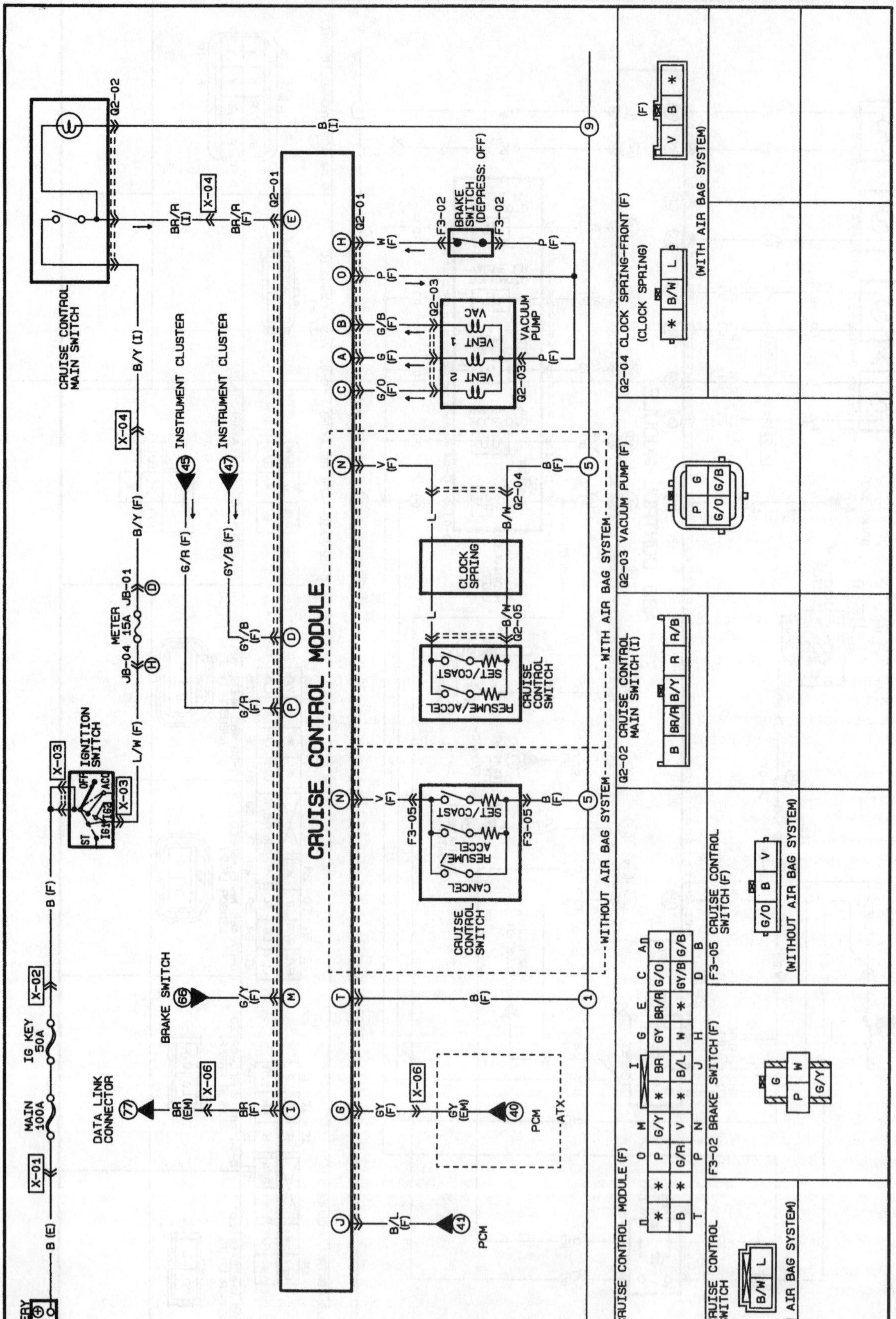

Typical cruise control system - 1995 and later

Index

IND

Haynes Automotive Manuals

NOTE: New manuals are added to this list on a periodic basis. If you do not see a listing for your vehicle, consult your local Haynes dealer for the latest product information.

ACURA
***12020 Integra** '86 thru '89 **& Legend** '86 thru '90

AMC
Jeep CJ - *see JEEP (50020)*
14020 Mid-size models, Concord, Hornet, Gremlin & Spirit '70 thru '83
14025 (Renault) Alliance & Encore '83 thru '87

AUDI
15020 4000 all models '80 thru '87
15025 5000 all models '77 thru '83
15026 5000 all models '84 thru '88

AUSTIN-HEALEY
Sprite - *see MG Midget (66015)*

BMW
***18020 3/5 Series** not including diesel or all-wheel drive models '82 thru '92
***18021 3 Series** except 325iX models '92 thru '97
18025 320i all 4 cyl models '75 thru '83
18035 528i & 530i all models '75 thru '80
18050 1500 thru 2002 except Turbo '59 thru '77

BUICK
Century (front wheel drive) - *see GM (829)*
***19020 Buick, Oldsmobile & Pontiac Full-size (Front wheel drive)** all models '85 thru '98 **Buick** Electra, LeSabre and Park Avenue; **Oldsmobile** Delta 88 Royale, Ninety Eight and Regency; **Pontiac** Bonneville
19025 Buick Oldsmobile & Pontiac Full-size (Rear wheel drive) **Buick** Estate '70 thru '90, Electra'70 thru '84, LeSabre '70 thru '85, Limited '74 thru '79 **Oldsmobile** Custom Cruiser '70 thru '90, Delta 88 '70 thru '85,Ninety-eight '70 thru '84 **Pontiac** Bonneville '70 thru '81, Catalina '70 thru '81, Grandville '70 thru '75, Parisienne '83 thru '86
19030 Mid-size Regal & Century all rear-drive models with V6, V8 and Turbo '74 thru '87
Regal - *see GENERAL MOTORS (38010)*
Riviera - *see GENERAL MOTORS (38030)*
Roadmaster - *see CHEVROLET (24046)*
Skyhawk - *see GENERAL MOTORS (38015)*
Skylark '80 thru '85 - *see GM (38020)*
Skylark '86 on - *see GM (38025)*
Somerset - *see GENERAL MOTORS (38025)*

CADILLAC
***21030 Cadillac Rear Wheel Drive** all gasoline models '70 thru '93
Cimarron - *see GENERAL MOTORS (38015)*
Eldorado - *see GENERAL MOTORS (38030)*
Seville '80 thru '85 - *see GM (38030)*

CHEVROLET
***24010 Astro & GMC Safari Mini-vans** '85 thru '93
24015 Camaro V8 all models '70 thru '81
24016 Camaro all models '82 thru '92
Cavalier - *see GENERAL MOTORS (38015)*
Celebrity - *see GENERAL MOTORS (38005)*
24017 Camaro & Firebird '93 thru '97
24020 Chevelle, Malibu & El Camino '69 thru '87
24024 Chevette & Pontiac T1000 '76 thru '87
Citation - *see GENERAL MOTORS (38020)*
***24032 Corsica/Beretta** all models '87 thru '96
24040 Corvette all V8 models '68 thru '82
***24041 Corvette** all models '84 thru '96
10305 Chevrolet Engine Overhaul Manual
24045 Full-size Sedans Caprice, Impala, Biscayne, Bel Air & Wagons '69 thru '90
24046 Impala SS & Caprice and Buick Roadmaster '91 thru '96
Lumina - *see GENERAL MOTORS (38010)*
24048 Lumina & Monte Carlo '95 thru '98
Lumina APV - *see GM (38035)*
24050 Luv Pick-up all 2WD & 4WD '72 thru '82
***24055 Monte Carlo** all models '70 thru '88
Monte Carlo '95 thru '98 - *see LUMINA (24048)*
24059 Nova all V8 models '69 thru '79
***24060 Nova and Geo Prizm** '85 thru '92
24064 Pick-ups '67 thru '87 - Chevrolet & GMC, all V8 & in-line 6 cyl, 2WD & 4WD '67 thru '87; Suburbans, Blazers & Jimmys '67 thru '91
***24065 Pick-ups '88 thru '98** - Chevrolet & GMC, all full-size pick-ups, '88 thru '98; Blazer & Jimmy '92 thru '94; Suburban '92 thru '98; Tahoe & Yukon '98
24070 S-10 & S-15 Pick-ups '82 thru '93, **Blazer & Jimmy** '83 thru '94,
***24071 S-10 & S-15 Pick-ups** '94 thru '96 **Blazer & Jimmy** '95 thru '96
***24075 Sprint & Geo Metro** '85 thru '94
***24080 Vans - Chevrolet & GMC,** V8 & in-line 6 cylinder models '68 thru '96

CHRYSLER
25015 Chrysler Cirrus, Dodge Stratus, Plymouth Breeze '95 thru '98
25025 Chrysler Concorde, New Yorker & LHS, Dodge Intrepid, **Eagle** Vision, '93 thru '97
10310 Chrysler Engine Overhaul Manual
***25020 Full-size Front-Wheel Drive** '88 thru '93
K-Cars - *see DODGE Aries (30008)*
Laser - *see DODGE Daytona (30030)*
***25030 Chrysler & Plymouth Mid-size** front wheel drive '82 thru '95
Rear-wheel Drive - *see Dodge (30050)*

DATSUN
28005 200SX all models '80 thru '83
28007 B-210 all models '73 thru '78
28009 210 all models '79 thru '82
28012 240Z, 260Z & 280Z Coupe '70 thru '78
28014 280ZX Coupe & 2+2 '79 thru '83
300ZX - *see NISSAN (72010)*
28016 310 all models '78 thru '82
28018 510 & PL521 Pick-up '68 thru '73
28020 510 all models '78 thru '81
28022 620 Series Pick-up all models '73 thru '79
720 Series Pick-up - *see NISSAN (72030)*
28025 810/Maxima all gasoline models, '77 thru '84

DODGE
400 & 600 - *see CHRYSLER (25030)*
***30008 Aries & Plymouth Reliant** '81 thru '89
30010 Caravan & Plymouth Voyager Mini-Vans all models '84 thru '95
***30011 Caravan & Plymouth Voyager Mini-Vans** all models '96 thru '98
30012 Challenger/Plymouth Saporro '78 thru '83
30016 Colt & Plymouth Champ (front wheel drive) all models '78 thru '87
***30020 Dakota Pick-ups** all models '87 thru '96
30025 Dart, Demon, Plymouth Barracuda, Duster & Valiant 6 cyl models '67 thru '76
***30030 Daytona & Chrysler Laser** '84 thru '89
Intrepid - *see CHRYSLER (25025)*
***30034 Neon** all models '95 thru '97
***30035 Omni & Plymouth Horizon** '78 thru '90
***30040 Pick-ups** all full-size models '74 thru '93
***30041 Pick-ups** all full-size models '94 thru '96
***30045 Ram 50/D50 Pick-ups & Raider and Plymouth Arrow Pick-ups** '79 thru '93
30050 Dodge/Plymouth/Chrysler rear wheel drive '71 thru '89
***30055 Shadow & Plymouth Sundance** '87 thru '94
***30060 Spirit & Plymouth Acclaim** '89 thru '95
***30065 Vans - Dodge & Plymouth** '71 thru '96

EAGLE
Talon - *see Mitsubishi Eclipse (68030)*
Vision - *see CHRYSLER (25025)*

FIAT
34010 124 Sport Coupe & Spider '68 thru '78
34025 X1/9 all models '74 thru '80

FORD
10355 Ford Automatic Transmission Overhaul
***36004 Aerostar Mini-vans** all models '86 thru '96
***36006 Contour & Mercury Mystique** '95 thru '98
36008 Courier Pick-up all models '72 thru '82
36012 Crown Victoria & Mercury Grand Marquis '88 thru '96
10320 Ford Engine Overhaul Manual
36016 Escort/Mercury Lynx all models '81 thru '90
***36020 Escort/Mercury Tracer** '91 thru '96
***36024 Explorer & Mazda Navajo** '91 thru '95
36028 Fairmont & Mercury Zephyr '78 thru '83
36030 Festiva & Aspire '88 thru '97
36032 Fiesta all models '77 thru '80
36036 Ford & Mercury Full-size, Ford LTD & Mercury Marquis ('75 thru '82); Ford Custom 500,Country Squire, Crown Victoria & Mercury Colony Park ('75 thru '87); Ford LTD Crown Victoria & Mercury Gran Marquis ('83 thru '87)
36040 Granada & Mercury Monarch '75 thru '80
36044 Ford & Mercury Mid-size, Ford Thunderbird & Mercury Cougar ('75 thru '82); Ford LTD & Mercury Marquis ('83 thru '86); Ford Torino,Gran Torino, Elite, Ranchero pick-up, LTD II, Mercury Montego, Comet, XR-7 & Lincoln Versailles ('75 thru '86)
36048 Mustang V8 all models '64-1/2 thru '73
36049 Mustang II 4 cyl, V6 & V8 models '74 thru '78
36050 Mustang & Mercury Capri all models Mustang, '79 thru '93; Capri, '79 thru '86
***36051 Mustang** all models '94 thru '97
36054 Pick-ups & Bronco '73 thru '79
36058 Pick-ups & Bronco '80 thru '96
36059 Pick-ups, Expedition & Mercury Navigator '97 thru '98
36062 Pinto & Mercury Bobcat '75 thru '80
36066 Probe all models '89 thru '92
36070 Ranger/Bronco II gasoline models '83 thru '92
***36071 Ranger** '93 thru '97 **& Mazda Pick-ups** '94 thru '97
36074 Taurus & Mercury Sable '86 thru '95
***36075 Taurus & Mercury Sable** '96 thru '98
***36078 Tempo & Mercury Topaz** '84 thru '94
36082 Thunderbird/Mercury Cougar '83 thru '88
***36086 Thunderbird/Mercury Cougar** '89 and '97
36090 Vans all V8 Econoline models '69 thru '91
***36094 Vans** full size '92-'95
***36097 Windstar Mini-van** '95-'98

GENERAL MOTORS
***10360 GM Automatic Transmission Overhaul**
***38005 Buick Century, Chevrolet Celebrity, Oldsmobile Cutlass Ciera & Pontiac 6000** all models '82 thru '96
***38010 Buick Regal, Chevrolet Lumina, Oldsmobile Cutlass Supreme & Pontiac Grand Prix** front-wheel drive models '88 thru '95
***38015 Buick Skyhawk, Cadillac Cimarron, Chevrolet Cavalier, Oldsmobile Firenza & Pontiac J-2000 & Sunbird** '82 thru '94
***38016 Chevrolet Cavalier & Pontiac Sunfire** '95 thru '98
38020 Buick Skylark, Chevrolet Citation, Olds Omega, Pontiac Phoenix '80 thru '85
38025 Buick Skylark & Somerset, Oldsmobile Achieva & Calais and Pontiac Grand Am all models '85 thru '95
38030 Cadillac Eldorado '71 thru '85, **Seville** '80 thru '85, **Oldsmobile Toronado** '71 thru '85 **& Buick Riviera** '79 thru '85
***38035 Chevrolet Lumina APV, Olds Silhouette & Pontiac Trans Sport** all models '90 thru '95
General Motors Full-size Rear-wheel Drive - *see BUICK (19025)*

(Continued on other side)

** Listings shown with an asterisk (*) indicate model coverage as of this printing. These titles will be periodically updated to include later model years - consult your Haynes dealer for more information.*

Haynes North America, Inc., 861 Lawrence Drive, Newbury Park, CA 91320-1514 • (805) 498-6703

Haynes Automotive Manuals (continued)

NOTE: New manuals are added to this list on a periodic basis. If you do not see a listing for your vehicle, consult your local Haynes dealer for the latest product information.

GEO

Metro - *see CHEVROLET Sprint (24075)*
Prizm - *'85 thru '92 see CHEVY (24060), '93 thru '96 see TOYOTA Corolla (92036)*
*40030 **Storm** all models '90 thru '93
Tracker - *see SUZUKI Samurai (90010)*

GMC

Safari - *see CHEVROLET ASTRO (24010)*
Vans & Pick-ups - *see CHEVROLET*

HONDA

42010 **Accord CVCC** all models '76 thru '83
42011 **Accord** all models '84 thru '89
42012 **Accord** all models '90 thru '93
42013 **Accord** all models '94 thru '95
42020 **Civic 1200** all models '73 thru '79
42021 **Civic 1300 & 1500 CVCC** '80 thru '83
42022 **Civic 1500 CVCC** all models '75 thru '79
42023 **Civic** all models '84 thru '91
*42024 **Civic & del Sol** '92 thru '95
*42040 **Prelude CVCC** all models '79 thru '89

HYUNDAI

*43015 **Excel** all models '86 thru '94

ISUZU

Hombre - *see CHEVROLET S-10 (24071)*
*47017 **Rodeo** '91 thru '97; **Amigo** '89 thru '94; **Honda Passport** '95 thru '97
*47020 **Trooper & Pick-up**, all gasoline models Pick-up, '81 thru '93; Trooper, '84 thru '91

JAGUAR

*49010 **XJ6** all 6 cyl models '68 thru '86
*49011 **XJ6** all models '88 thru '94
*49015 **XJ12 & XJS** all 12 cyl models '72 thru '85

JEEP

*50010 **Cherokee, Comanche & Wagoneer Limited** all models '84 thru '96
50020 **CJ** all models '49 thru '86
*50025 **Grand Cherokee** all models '93 thru '98
50029 **Grand Wagoneer & Pick-up** '72 thru '91 Grand Wagoneer '84 thru '91, Cherokee & Wagoneer '72 thru '83, Pick-up '72 thru '88
*50030 **Wrangler** all models '87 thru '95

LINCOLN

Navigator - *see FORD Pick-up (36059)*
59010 **Rear Wheel Drive** all models '70 thru '96

MAZDA

61010 **GLC Hatchback (rear wheel drive)** '77 thru '83
61011 **GLC (front wheel drive)** '81 thru '85
*61015 **323 & Protogé** '90 thru '97
*61016 **MX-5 Miata** '90 thru '97
*61020 **MPV** all models '89 thru '94
Navajo - *see Ford Explorer (36024)*
61030 **Pick-ups** '72 thru '93
Pick-ups '94 thru '96 - *see Ford Ranger (36071)*
61035 **RX-7** all models '79 thru '85
*61036 **RX-7** all models '86 thru '91
61040 **626** (rear wheel drive) all models '79 thru '82
*61041 **626/MX-6 (front wheel drive)** '83 thru '91

MERCEDES-BENZ

63012 **123 Series Diesel** '76 thru '85
*63015 **190 Series** four-cyl gas models, '84 thru '88
63020 **230/250/280** 6 cyl sohc models '68 thru '72
63025 **280 123 Series** gasoline models '77 thru '81
63030 **350 & 450** all models '71 thru '80

MERCURY

See FORD Listing.

MG

66010 **MGB** Roadster & GT Coupe '62 thru '80
66015 **MG Midget, Austin Healey Sprite** '58 thru '80

MITSUBISHI

*68020 **Cordia, Tredia, Galant, Precis & Mirage** '83 thru '93
*68030 **Eclipse, Eagle Talon & Ply. Laser** '90 thru '94
*68040 **Pick-up** '83 thru '96 **& Montero** '83 thru '93

NISSAN

72010 **300ZX** all models including Turbo '84 thru '89
*72015 **Altima** all models '93 thru '97
*72020 **Maxima** all models '85 thru '91
*72030 **Pick-ups** '80 thru '96 **Pathfinder** '87 thru '95
72040 **Pulsar** all models '83 thru '86
*72050 **Sentra** all models '82 thru '94
*72051 **Sentra & 200SX** all models '95 thru '98
*72060 **Stanza** all models '82 thru '90

OLDSMOBILE

*73015 **Cutlass** V6 & V8 gas models '74 thru '88
For other OLDSMOBILE titles, see BUICK, CHEVROLET or GENERAL MOTORS listing.

PLYMOUTH

For PLYMOUTH titles, see DODGE listing.

PONTIAC

79008 **Fiero** all models '84 thru '88
79018 **Firebird** V8 models except Turbo '70 thru '81
79019 **Firebird** all models '82 thru '92
For other PONTIAC titles, see BUICK, CHEVROLET or GENERAL MOTORS listing.

PORSCHE

*80020 **911** except Turbo & Carrera 4 '65 thru '89
80025 **914** all 4 cyl models '69 thru '76
80030 **924** all models including Turbo '76 thru '82
*80035 **944** all models including Turbo '83 thru '89

RENAULT

Alliance & Encore - *see AMC (14020)*

SAAB

*84010 **900** all models including Turbo '79 thru '88

SATURN

87010 **Saturn** all models '91 thru '96

SUBARU

89002 **1100, 1300, 1400 & 1600** '71 thru '79
*89003 **1600 & 1800** 2WD & 4WD '80 thru '94

SUZUKI

*90010 **Samurai/Sidekick & Geo Tracker** '86 thru '96

TOYOTA

92005 **Camry** all models '83 thru '91
92006 **Camry** all models '92 thru '96
92015 **Celica Rear Wheel Drive** '71 thru '85
*92020 **Celica Front Wheel Drive** '86 thru '93
92025 **Celica Supra** all models '79 thru '92
92030 **Corolla** all models '75 thru '79
92032 **Corolla** all rear wheel drive models '80 thru '87
92035 **Corolla** all front wheel drive models '84 thru '92
*92036 **Corolla & Geo Prizm** '93 thru '97
92040 **Corolla Tercel** all models '80 thru '82
92045 **Corona** all models '74 thru '82
92050 **Cressida** all models '78 thru '82
92055 **Land Cruiser** FJ40, 43, 45, 55 '68 thru '82
92056 **Land Cruiser** FJ60, 62, 80, FZJ80 '80 thru '96
*92065 **MR2** all models '85 thru '87
92070 **Pick-up** all models '69 thru '78
*92075 **Pick-up** all models '79 thru '95
*92076 **Tacoma** '95 thru '98, **4Runner** '96 thru '98, **& T100** '93 thru '98
*92080 **Previa** all models '91 thru '95
92085 **Tercel** all models '87 thru '94

TRIUMPH

94007 **Spitfire** all models '62 thru '81
94010 **TR7** all models '75 thru '81

VW

96008 **Beetle & Karmann Ghia** '54 thru '79
96012 **Dasher** all gasoline models '74 thru '81
*96016 **Rabbit, Jetta, Scirocco, & Pick-up** gas models '74 thru '91 & Convertible '80 thru '92
96017 **Golf & Jetta** all models '93 thru '97
96020 **Rabbit, Jetta & Pick-up** diesel '77 thru '84
96030 **Transporter 1600** all models '68 thru '79
96035 **Transporter 1700, 1800 & 2000** '72 thru '79
96040 **Type 3 1500 & 1600** all models '63 thru '73
96045 **Vanagon** all air-cooled models '80 thru '83

VOLVO

97010 **120, 130 Series & 1800 Sports** '61 thru '73
97015 **140 Series** all models '66 thru '74
*97020 **240 Series** all models '76 thru '93
97025 **260 Series** all models '75 thru '82
*97040 **740 & 760 Series** all models '82 thru '88

TECHBOOK MANUALS

10205 **Automotive Computer Codes**
10210 **Automotive Emissions Control Manual**
10215 **Fuel Injection Manual, 1978 thru 1985**
10220 **Fuel Injection Manual, 1986 thru 1996**
10225 **Holley Carburetor Manual**
10230 **Rochester Carburetor Manual**
10240 **Weber/Zenith/Stromberg/SU Carburetors**
10305 **Chevrolet Engine Overhaul Manual**
10310 **Chrysler Engine Overhaul Manual**
10320 **Ford Engine Overhaul Manual**
10330 **GM and Ford Diesel Engine Repair Manual**
10340 **Small Engine Repair Manual**
10345 **Suspension, Steering & Driveline Manual**
10355 **Ford Automatic Transmission Overhaul**
10360 **GM Automatic Transmission Overhaul**
10405 **Automotive Body Repair & Painting**
10410 **Automotive Brake Manual**
10415 **Automotive Detaiing Manual**
10420 **Automotive Eelectrical Manual**
10425 **Automotive Heating & Air Conditioning**
10430 **Automotive Reference Manual & Dictionary**
10435 **Automotive Tools Manual**
10440 **Used Car Buying Guide**
10445 **Welding Manual**
10450 **ATV Basics**

SPANISH MANUALS

98903 **Reparación de Carrocería & Pintura**
98905 **Códigos Automotrices de la Computadora**
98910 **Frenos Automotriz**
98915 **Inyección de Combustible 1986 al 1994**
99040 **Chevrolet & GMC Camionetas** '67 al '87 Incluye Suburban, Blazer & Jimmy '67 al '91
99041 **Chevrolet & GMC Camionetas** '88 al '95 Incluye Suburban '92 al '95, Blazer & Jimmy '92 al '94, Tahoe y Yukon '95
99042 **Chevrolet & GMC Camionetas Cerradas** '68 al '95
99055 **Dodge Caravan & Plymouth Voyager** '84 al '95
99075 **Ford Camionetas y Bronco** '80 al '94
99077 **Ford Camionetas Cerradas** '69 al '91
99083 **Ford Modelos de Tamaño Grande** '75 al '87
99088 **Ford Modelos de Tamaño Mediano** '75 al '86
99091 **Ford Taurus & Mercury Sable** '86 al '95
99095 **GM Modelos de Tamaño Grande** '70 al '90
99100 **GM Modelos de Tamaño Mediano** '70 al '88
99110 **Nissan Camionetas** '80 al '96, **Pathfinder** '87 al '95
99118 **Nissan Sentra** '82 al '94
99125 **Toyota Camionetas y 4Runner** '79 al '95

** Listings shown with an asterisk (*) indicate model coverage as of this printing. These titles will be periodically updated to include later model years - consult your Haynes dealer for more information.*

Over 100 Haynes motorcycle manuals also available

Haynes North America, Inc., 861 Lawrence Drive, Newbury Park, CA 91320-1514 • (805) 498-6703